US Trotskyism 1928–1965
Part I: Emergence

Historical Materialism Book Series

The Historical Materialism Book Series is a major publishing initiative of the radical left. The capitalist crisis of the twenty-first century has been met by a resurgence of interest in critical Marxist theory. At the same time, the publishing institutions committed to Marxism have contracted markedly since the high point of the 1970s. The Historical Materialism Book Series is dedicated to addressing this situation by making available important works of Marxist theory. The aim of the series is to publish important theoretical contributions as the basis for vigorous intellectual debate and exchange on the left.

The peer-reviewed series publishes original monographs, translated texts, and reprints of classics across the bounds of academic disciplinary agendas and across the divisions of the left. The series is particularly concerned to encourage the internationalization of Marxist debate and aims to translate significant studies from beyond the English-speaking world.

For a full list of titles in the Historical Materialism Book Series available in paperback from Haymarket Books, visit:
https://www.haymarketbooks.org/series_collections/1-historical-materialism

US Trotskyism 1928–1965
Part I: Emergence

Left Opposition in the United States

Dissident Marxism in the United States, Volume 1

Edited by
Paul Le Blanc
Bryan Palmer
Thomas Bias

Haymarket Books
Chicago, IL

First published in 2017 by Brill Academic Publishers, The Netherlands

Published in paperback in 2019 by
Haymarket Books
P.O. Box 180165
Chicago, IL 60618
773-583-7884
www.haymarketbooks.org

ISBN: 978-1-64259-056-2

Distributed to the trade in the US through Consortium Book Sales and Distribution (www.cbsd.com) and internationally through Ingram Publisher Services International (www.ingramcontent.com).

This book was published with the generous support of Lannan Foundation and Wallace Action Fund.

Cover design by Jamie Kerry and Ragina Johnson.

Printed in the United States.

10 9 8 7 6 5 4 3 2 1

Library of Congress Cataloging-in-Publication data is available.

Contents

Preface to the Documentary Trilogy on US Trotskyism

This book and the next two constitute a documentary trilogy on US Trotskyism, and they are also the second, third and fourth of a currently projected six-volume series on Dissident Marxism in the United States. These are to be made up mostly of primary sources (reflections, reports, analyses, proposals, etc.) produced by US Marxists from the late 1920s through the early 1960s.

The first volume, edited by Tim Davenport and myself, has the title *The 'American Exceptionalism' of Jay Lovestone and His Comrades, 1928–1940*. The present contribution and the next two provide a three-volume presentation of materials – *US Trotskyism, 1928–65*, the first volume subtitled *Emergence: The Left Opposition in the United States*, the second subtitled *Endurance: For the Coming American Revolution*, and the third subtitled *Resurgence: Uneven and Combined Development*. The final volumes projected for the overall series will involve contributions which we are labelling 'independent Marxism' – representing individuals and small groups unaffiliated either with the mainstream Communist Party USA, or with the Socialist Party of America, or with the Lovestone group and the Trotskyist mainstream.

In the history of the world, Karl Marx and Frederick Engels have been among the central figures pushing effectively for a 'democratic breakthrough' that would give people – especially the labouring majority – a decisive say in the decisions affecting their lives, and that would ultimately (it was hoped) create a society of the free and the equal, which at different times they called socialism or communism.[1]

The Marxist tradition exerted, from the late nineteenth century down through the late twentieth century, a powerful influence among those seeking to build working-class movements, struggling for a world better than that divided between powerful minorities and the exploited and oppressed labouring majorities. Within this tradition, however, significant differences arose over how to properly understand and change the world. By the third decade of the twentieth century, an irreconcilable divergence had opened up between a reformist Social-Democratic wing and a revolutionary Communist wing of the Marxist movement.[2]

1 Riazanov 1973; Gabriel 2011; Nimtz 2000; Hudis 2013.

2 For a survey of revolutionary Marxist thought, see Le Blanc 2016.

As time passed, both major currents were overwhelmed internally by a bureaucratisation process that tended to stifle creative and critical-minded thinking and democratic politics. Ultimately, both had become largely discredited by the time the twenty-first century arrived. In the eyes of many, Communism was discredited because it became a repressive and often murderous bureaucratic tyranny which nonetheless proved incapable of surviving, while Social Democracy was discredited because it proved incapable not only of replacing capitalism, but even of maintaining its own modest social reforms in the face of pro-business assaults and austerity programmes.[3]

A challenge for scholars, but also for activists and would-be revolutionaries, is to understand what happened – and also to locate strengths, positive lessons, and durable insights among the failures. In order to do this, it is necessary to engage with some of the best scholarship available, but also to consult primary sources to see what those who actually lived 'back then' had to say. There is a significant body of scholarship dealing with the two major left-wing currents (Social-Democratic and Communist) inside the United States, represented by the Socialist Party of America and the Communist Party USA, as well as some primary source material – much of this is cited in the preface for volume 1 of this series.

There is less material on the 'dissident' currents – those breaking off from and independent of these other two. It is these dissident currents that are the focus of this series. Marxist currents in the United States, both 'mainstream' and dissident, have actually had a significant impact upon labour and social movements that have been of some importance in the shaping of that country's history. This being the case, it strikes some of us as being reasonable and useful to produce such volumes as these, which may be interesting to more people now than they would have been 15 years ago. They may become even more interesting to a greater number of people in the foreseeable future.

While the volume on the Lovestone group contained some illustrations to give a sense of what that particular group and its members looked like, similar illustrations of the US Trotskyists can be found in the just-republished volume by George Breitman, Paul Le Blanc, and Alan Wald, *Trotskyism in the United States: Historical Essays and Reconsiderations* (Chicago: Haymarket Books, 2016). That volume, combined with this one and the next two in 'Dissident Marxism in the United States', provide substantial resources for scholars and – we hope – for activists, but they by no means constitute a definitive account of the story of US Trotskyism.

3 For an outstanding survey, see Eley 2002.

The present volume, then, provides a documentary trilogy of US Trotskyism from the late 1920s to the mid-1960s, with the major introductions that start each volume offering – taken together – an historical and analytical overview. For this overview, I assume full responsibility. My co-editors may agree with much that I say there, but they may have different 'takes' on important questions in which I offer my own.

Of my co-editors for this volume, I have known Andy Pollack since the 1970s (when we were comrades together in the Socialist Workers Party) and Tom Bias since the 1980s (when we were comrades together in the Fourth Internationalist Tendency, a small group mostly composed of people expelled from the Socialist Workers Party)[4] – so the three of us have had the advantage of knowing 'from the inside' something of the political tradition we are helping to present in this book. There is an intimacy that comes from such comradeship, yet it is not always the case that this translates either into full agreement or actual friendship, but I feel fortunate to be able to count these hardworking and dedicated comrades among my friends. Bryan Palmer, an outstanding historian of labour and social movements, I discovered in the early 1990s through writings about one of his mentors, E.P. Thompson.[5] Soon after, along with one of my mentors, Frank Lovell (once the trade union director of the SWP), I actually connected with Bryan, when we found that he wanted to write a biography of US Trotskyism's founder, James P. Cannon. We were determined to assist him as much as we could, and found that, despite differences, we shared much common ground. I have had the good fortune to work with Bryan on two conferences dealing with the history of US Trotskyism, and he too is a close and trusted friend. It has been a great pleasure to collaborate with these three on this project, and I believe our collective effort has resulted in something that will be useful for those who want to understand and, in some cases, to make use of this particular 'dissident Marxist' tradition.

Naturally, although all of the editors share a common sympathy for the US Trotskyist movement, there are different 'takes' one or another of us may have on both minor and major questions, and in our signed introductions none of us presumes to speak for all of us.

Paul Le Blanc

---

4 Information on this can be found in the Encyclopedia of Trotskyism On-Line: https://www.marxists.org/history/etol/document/fit.htm.

5 Palmer 1994.

Acknowledgements

First of all, we must thank the editors of the *Historical Materialism* Book Series – Sebastian Budgen, David Broder, Steve Edwards, Juan Grigera, Marcel van der Linden, and Peter Thomas – as well as the hardworking Danny Hayward and others associated with this incredibly valuable project. The outstanding Brill and Haymarket Books publishing houses are also to be thanked for making this series possible.

Other projects that have been beneficial to our work have been Marxist Internet Archive (https://www.marxists.org) and the Encyclopedia of Trotskyism On-Line (https://www.marxists.org/history/etol), the Tamiment Library housed within the Bobst Library at New York University, the Holt Labor Library, and the Prometheus Research Library.

Each of us, in different ways, is also immensely indebted to those who were part of the history recorded here – whose names are too numerous to record here, but some of which appear in this volume, some of whom we were able to meet and know, and some of whom were very dear friends.

Paul particularly wants to acknowledge support received from La Roche College, which has facilitated some of his work, valuable assistance from Jonah McAllister-Erickson of the University of Pittsburgh's Hillman Library, and the seemingly endless patience, supportiveness, and friendship of Nancy Ferrari.

CHAPTER 1

Introduction: Left Opposition in the United States

Paul Le Blanc

'Left Opposition' refers to what was originally a current in the Russian Communist Party. It was in opposition to the corruption and betrayal of the communist ideal by a bureaucratic dictatorship, and it resisted the elimination of workers' democracy and internationalism from what had been the revolutionary Marxist conception of socialism.

Vladimir Ilyich Lenin had been the long-time leader of the revolutionary Bolshevik current in the Russian socialist movement, and it was this current which led the Russian Revolution of 1917 that gave birth to the Soviet Republic. After designating itself the Russian Communist Party, it helped create the Communist International, meant to facilitate a global transformation from capitalism to socialism. After Lenin's death, however, the Russian Revolution's goal of soviet democracy and the commitment to a liberating revolution worldwide gave way to a bureaucratic dictatorship preaching 'socialism in one country' and advancing cynical policies to enhance its own power and privileges. This change did not take place without a struggle – and the struggle was associated especially with what was called the Left Opposition.

While Leon Trotsky was one of the leaders in opposing bureaucratic degeneration, the oppositional current included a number of prominent revolutionary personalities and thinkers: Eugen Preobrazhensky, Karl Radek, Christian Rakovsky, Lev Kamenev, Gregory Zinoviev, Lenin's widow Nadezhda Krupskaya, and others collaborated in its efforts at various points, seeking to preserve and advance the original, heroic ideals and perspectives associated with the Russian Revolution, the early Soviet regime, and the Communist International.

By the late 1920s, however, powerful forces around the rising dictator Joseph Stalin, consolidating his domination of the Russian Communist Party, were able to smash the oppositionists, and many, including some of the most prominent, abandoned opposition to avoid expulsion from the Communist Party. The fact that Trotsky and a saving remnant of oppositionists held firm had ramifications in the world Communist movement in the late 1920s, including in the United States, giving rise to a small but important international movement.[1]

1 On the general history, see Carr 2004 and Le Blanc 2015a. A primary source for the Left

The Central Figure

To understand this movement, then, one must give attention to the life and ideas of Leon Trotsky. There are a number of useful works that can be consulted to comprehend this brilliant and heroic figure, yet in *Trotsky, A Graphic Biography*, Rick Geary usefully summarises key aspects of the story in the book's first four frames:

> In 1917, Leon Trotsky burst upon the international stage as the brain behind the Russian Revolution. He presided over the complete transformation of his country, not merely a change of government but a total restructuring of society on every level. To many, he was the heroic St. George, slaying the dragon of capitalist repression. To others, he was the ruthless and Satanic purveyor of bloody rebellion, the cold, detached theorist gone mad with power. In truth, he fitted neither of these images. He was a writer, a thinker, a nation-builder – albeit a reluctant one – with deep roots in his Russia's agricultural heartland. Trotsky's dream was for a world free from injustice, inequality, and war, and in this he was absolutely single-minded. To him, the ideas of Karl Marx showed the way, and for one brief moment he set the machinery in motion to achieve that end ... He lived to see his work betrayed and his ideals perverted by those who seized power after him. He would be ejected from the government he helped to establish and hounded into exile and death.[2]

Ejected from the Soviet Union in 1929, Trotsky laboured to build a global revolutionary current that would defend and advance the earlier Bolshevik perspectives. Not at all inclined to name the movement which he led after himself, he preferred to call it 'Bolshevik-Leninist', although a more common tag was 'Left Oppositionist' – but it was the name first given to it by its opponents that really stuck: *Trotskyite* or *Trotskyist*. The term 'Trotskyite' was particularly pejorative, used by those hostile to the movement, having the connotation that those in

Opposition in the Soviet Union from 1923 to 1928 are the three volumes composed mostly of Trotsky's writings in this period: Trotsky 1975, 1980, 1981. Especially on the international movement, see: Alexander 1991; Frank 2010.

2 Geary 2009, pp. 3–4. See also Deutscher 2015; Serge and Sedova 2015; Le Blanc 2015b. A succinct collection of Trotsky's writings in exile can be found in Trotsky 2012.

agreement with Trotsky were in cultish orbit around him. The last three letters made a difference – Trotsky*ist* came to be a term acceptable to many of his co-thinkers.

Defining features of Trotsky's thought included his defence of revolutionary internationalism against Stalin's notion of 'socialism in one country' – understanding that in the global political economy, the fates of the working classes and oppressed peoples of the early Soviet Union were interlinked with those of the 'advanced' capitalist countries and with those in the 'under-developed' colonial and semi-colonial regions.

This tied in with his theory of permanent revolution, which saw struggles against everyday oppression in any country as being intertwined with the struggle for the genuine triumph of democracy, which must be led by the working class in order to be successful, and which would consequently result in the workers coming to power; this would result in continuing transformations in that country in the direction of socialism, but would necessarily also result in the spread of revolution to other countries. Such a successful spread of socialist revolution would be necessary for socialism's triumph in any single country. The failure of revolutions to spread to other countries, he argued, had resulted in the bureaucratic degeneration within the Soviet Republic, of the authoritarianism that accompanied it. Against such developments, he called for the renewal of genuine workers' democracy and revolutionary internationalism.

It was essential for revolutionaries to help build united fronts to advance the struggles of workers and the oppressed within each country for a better life, ultimately for liberation from exploitation, which must culminate in socialist revolution. To advance such goals he insisted on the need to develop a revolutionary party as a genuinely *democratic* collectivity of revolutionaries, guided by Marxist perspectives.

The Collective Project

Those who initiated what came to be known as the Trotskyist movement in the United States were in basic agreement with these ideas associated with Trotsky. Yet they did not see themselves as being in orbit around a particular personality. They were revolutionary socialists who had been engaged in the struggles of US labour, and had been centrally involved in creating what they hoped would be an effective Communist Party that would be capable of leading a transition from capitalist oppression. The pioneers of US Communism were inspired by the 1917 workers and peasants revolution in Russia, led by Lenin, Trotsky, and other outstanding revolutionary Marxists who went on to establish a Communist International in 1919. But many of them were also rooted in deep traditions of American radicalism and labour activism associated, for example, with the Socialist Party of Eugene V. Debs and the Industrial Workers of the World.[3]

It is worth noting that in 1951 the leadership of the Socialist Workers Party, the major force (small as it was) representing Trotskyism in the United States, proposed that the label of 'Trotskyism' be set aside, that instead the party designate itself 'in broad public political agitation as "Socialist" or "Socialist Workers" or "Revolutionary Socialist", alternatively, as the occasion may demand'. Party leader James P. Cannon explained that the label could cause thoughtful workers to view the Socialist Workers Party

> as a sectarian movement, as followers of some individual, and a Russian at that. It is not a suitable characterization for a broad American movement. Our enemies will refer to us as Trotskyists, and we will, of course, not deny it; but we should say: 'We are Trotskyists because Trotsky was a true socialist.' What we are presenting against American capitalism and the labor bureaucracy is the principle of the class struggle of modern socialism … Let our enemies within the movement, that is in the narrow framework of the more political movement, call us Trotskyists. We will not protest. But then we will say we are Trotskyist because he represented genuine socialism and we, like him, are the real Socialists … We have to think of ourselves more and more as representing the Socialist opposition to the American bourgeoisie. I don't think we should do it under the handicap of what appears to the workers as a sectarian or cultist name. That is what the term 'Trotskyist' signifies to them.[4]

For various reasons, however, both in the United States and globally, the name 'Trotskyist' stuck. Perry Anderson commented in 1976: 'One day this other tradition – persecuted, reviled, isolated, divided – will have to be studied in all the diversity of its underground channels and streams. It may surprise future historians with its resources'. A newly republished set of essays by George Breitman, Paul Le Blanc, and Alan Wald, *Trotskyism in the United States: Historical Essays and Reconsiderations*, provides broad outlines of the story of US Trotskyists, and some reflections on the meaning of this phenomenon. This stands as a useful companion to the primary sources provided in the present series.

3 Cannon 1973; Zumoff 2015.

4 Quoted in Breitman, Le Blanc and Wald 2016, p. 51.

Our co-editor Bryan Palmer has also initiated a rich and invaluable exploration of the central founding figure of US Trotskyism, James P. Cannon.[5] More work obviously needs to be done, and it is hoped that what is offered here will help to stimulate such efforts.

American Trotskyists formed the Communist League of America (CLA) in 1928, standing as a beacon of early revolutionary-democratic ideals of early Communism against the corruptions, cynicism, and murderous authoritarianism of Stalinism. In Chapter 2, Bryan Palmer introduces materials giving a sense of the founding years of the CLA, which naturally bear distinctive birthmarks of the struggle against Stalinism. Material in Chapters 7 and 9, introduced by Andrew Pollack, document the ongoing and often difficult efforts to come to terms with this increasingly horrific challenge to revolutionaries – which ultimately resulted in a deep fissure within Trotskyist ranks. Pollack goes much further in Chapter 9, however, in exploring the 1939–40 clashes among the US Trotskyists (with Trotsky himself in the thick of it) around matters having to do with Marxist philosophy and Leninist organisational norms.

Culture Clash

A sense of the dynamics within much of the Trotskyist movement in the late 1930s has been conveyed by Irving Howe, at the time a dedicated young recruit from the Socialist Party's youth group, the Young People's Socialist League, whose majority was won to the about-to-be-formed Socialist Workers Party. The milieu Howe describes was highly intellectualised: 'We took positions on almost everything, for positions testified to the fruitfulness of theory. Theory marked our superiority to "vulgar empiricist" politics, compensated for our helplessness, told us that some day this helplessness would be dialectically transformed into power'.

Adding that 'most of the time … we discussed, debated, and did battle about matters beyond our reach, … as if a correct formulation could create a desired reality', Howe nonetheless emphasises that 'these disputes often concerned issues of genuine importance, with the [Trotskyist] movement groping toward problems that more conventional analysts would confront only decades later. Sometimes these disputes produced vivid writing and speaking in which the talents of leaders, blocked from public outlet, were released through wit and invective'.

5 Anderson 1979, p. 98; Breitman, Le Blanc and Wald 2016; Palmer 2007.

At the same time, he comments that 'the faction fights surely had another purpose we could not then acknowledge: they were charades of struggle, substitute rituals for the battles we could not join in the outer world. ... Not more than two or three hundred people might be present at a discussion meeting, but who did not feel that in pulverizing opponents and smiting dunderheads there was just a touch of Lenin recalled, of Trotsky re-enacted?'[6]

In roughly the same period, Paul Jacobs, another young Trotskyist from New York, experienced a harsh culture clash when he and some younger comrades transferred to Minneapolis, home of a very different species of Trotskyist led by Vincent Raymond Dunne and others who had also led the historic Minneapolis general strike of 1934.[7] 'They really were Bolsheviks, not dilettantes', he recalls, 'and we learned very quickly they were harsh disciplinarians as well'. Recalling 'the more easy-going radical atmosphere of New York' with 'the hours spent schmoozing over coffee in the cafeterias', Jacobs emphasised: 'In Minneapolis, if you were assigned to distribute leaflets at a union meeting, you went – for if you failed to show up without a very good excuse, like maybe dying, you had the prospect of facing Ray Dunne's cold eyes and implacable questions'.

Much of what he was used to in New York was considered 'kid stuff' in Minneapolis. Jacobs elaborates:

> The signs of this toughness were everywhere. When armed guards were needed to protect Trotsky from the expected (and finally successful) attempts of the [loyal-to-Stalin] Communists to assassinate him, the Minneapolis branch supplied the toughest of the volunteers. When Chicago gangsters had attempted to move in on the Minneapolis local of the teamsters, they had literally been thrown down the steps of the union office and told that they would be killed if they returned. ...
>
> The toughness of the leaders was combined with a hard, spare, ascetic quality that became a model for all of us. ...
>
> The very intensity and grimness of the radical movement in Minneapolis left little room for errors or weakness. After only a few weeks in Minneapolis, I understood very well how it was possible for this group of men to successfully run the teamsters' union and why the Minneapolis general strike had been run like a military operation: Ray Dunne and the people around him were very serious revolutionists.[8]

6 Howe 1982, pp. 52–5.

7 Palmer 2013.

8 Jacobs 1965, pp. 52–3.

These two reminiscences suggest that some dynamics coming into play in the factional disputes among the US Trotskyists may have been rooted as much in such cultural divides as in the undoubtedly substantial theoretical differences.

Diversity and Complications

As the 1939–40 factional dispute led to a permanent organisational split, it makes sense here to clarify a decision of the editors. That decision was to focus our efforts on the development of what might be termed the 'mainstream' of US Trotskyism – stretching from the Communist League of America, the Workers Party of the United States, the Appeal Caucus in the Socialist Party of America, and the Socialist Workers Party. To follow dissident factions which split away could have involved a multi-volume work which would have been beyond our abilities. This tilts our account toward the majority current in the Trotskyist movement. Others must do the additional work to trace and elaborate on the story and the ideas of those who fundamentally disagreed and broke away. In some cases, this process has already begun – for example, with the very substantial current led by Max Shachtman that left the SWP in 1940.[9]

Throughout the 1930s, Trotskyists in the United States were certainly engaged with far more than simply anti-Stalinism – this was simply part of their effort to advance the struggles for a better future on the part of workers and all oppressed people. In tandem with efforts to advance revolutionary practice, US Trotskyists naturally sought to develop a deeper understanding of history and theory. Materials in Chapter 5, introduced by Bryan Palmer, provide a vibrant sense of Trotskyist contributions to class struggles in the United States, while

9 Fortunately, Shachtman and his co-thinkers are well served by Peter Drucker's fine biography of the man. Robert J. Alexander's massive study of international Trotskyism has devoted a number of pages to the evolution of Shachtman's organisation. An immense amount of the Shachtman group's theoretical output on Stalinism and the nature of the USSR has been drawn together and sympathetically explicated in two huge volumes edited by Sean Matgama. There is also a good representation of the Shachtman group perspectives on a variety of issues (from the 1940s and 1950s), taken from the pages of its paper *Labor Action*, in the now all-too-rare 1963 collection edited by Hal Draper, *Introduction to Independent Socialism*, and substantial discussion of the Shachtman group's later evolution is provided in Paul Le Blanc and Michael Yates, *A Freedom Budget for All Americans*. See Drucker 1994; Alexander 1991, pp. 793–813, 899–910; Matgamna 1998; Matgamna 2015; Draper 1963; Le Blanc and Yates 2013, pp. 50–1, 57–69, 83–8, 115–26.

materials introduced by Thomas Bias in Chapter 6 indicate some limitations with which Trotskyists wrestled as they engaged with complexities of the anti-racist struggle. Chapter 10, with material introduced by Paul Le Blanc, provides a sense in which these militant activists sought to apply and develop their understanding of history and of Marxist theory.

While far smaller than the Communist Party and the largely reformist Socialist Party, the US ranks of the Trotskyists grew amid the labour radicalisation generated by the Great Depression. By 1935 – after playing an outstanding role in various labour struggles, especially in the Minneapolis general strike – they were able to merge with other radical labour forces to form the Workers Party of the United States. This was soon followed by a decision to enter the Socialist Party in order to link up with that organisation's growing left-wing, although they were soon driven out (along with much of the broader left-wing) by the reformist leadership – and all of these complexities are reflected in materials contained in Chapter 3, introduced by Paul Le Blanc.

The subsequent formation of the Socialist Workers Party, covered in materials introduced by Thomas Bias in Chapter 4, seemed to its members and supporters to be the beginning of an important new phase of revolutionary struggle in the United States. But this development – as is the case with life in general – involved complications. This is reflected in materials introduced by Paul Le Blanc in Chapter 8. On the one hand, there was a proliferation of political disagreements generating political splinter groups that denounced the Trotskyist mainstream for being insufficiently revolutionary, and that were in turn criticised by the Trotskyist mainstream as being 'ultra-left' and 'sectarian'. On the other hand, there was a trend toward de-radicalisation among once-sympathetic intellectuals who sensed that the hoped-for revolutionary triumph would not be realised.

The birth of the SWP took place as part of a coming-together of like-minded groups around the world to establish, with Trotsky, what was called the World Party of Socialist Revolution – the Fourth International. The First International had been established by Marx and others in 1864 but was ripped apart by differences between socialists, anarchists, and trade union reformers in the 1870s; the much more substantial Second International, or Socialist International, arose in 1889 but was largely discredited in 1914 when many of its adherents went along with the imperialist slaughter of the First World War. The Third (Communist) International, now hopelessly infected by Stalinism, was destined to be dissolved by Stalin in 1943, during the Second World War.

In 1938, Trotsky and his adherents anticipated that the traumas of that future global conflict would – as had been the case with the First World War – generate a worldwide radicalisation and revolutionary upsurge. They believed that this would powerfully impact on the three sectors of the world revolution – helping to bring about revolutionary insurgencies against colonialism in the so-called 'underdeveloped' regions, working-class socialist challenges to capitalism in advanced industrial countries, and a militant sweeping aside of Stalinism in the Soviet Union. In such a context, the Trotskyists' revolutionary Marxist programme was destined to prove its relevance to the rising waves of labour militants and revolutionary freedom-fighters.

While aspects of the Trotskyist prophecy came to pass, central aspects of it were borne out – at best – only in partial and fragmented ways. The Second World War was certainly incredibly devastating, and out of that came a global radicalisation and revolutionary upsurge. But although the wave of anti-colonial revolutions began as expected, an unexpected stabilisation in the 'advanced' capitalist countries was achieved, largely due to the immense economic and military power of the United States.

At the same time, the role the Soviet Union played in the victory over fascism and Nazism helped give the Stalin regime a new lease of life and increased its influence in the Communist movement. Communist-led revolutions in China, Vietnam, and Yugoslavia were supplemented by more problematical Communist take-overs in Eastern Europe (in some cases, such as Czechoslovakia, with significant popular support, in other cases such as Poland, with little support, but in all cases with decisive assistance from the Soviet Red Army).

A Cold War confrontation between the capitalist 'Free World' led by the United States and the Communist Bloc led by the Soviet Union dominated world politics for decades, with the ever-present threat of humanity's destruction by the massive numbers of nuclear weapons that both of the great powers were accumulating.

The disappointments and difficulties – and, in some cases, quite unexpected opportunities – brought by the Second World War and postwar developments would generate crises and also new fissures, but there were important new experiences and insights as well. The second and third volumes of this trilogy will be devoted to this period.

Limitations and Strengths

It is worth concluding with an observation on at least some of the elements missing and present in the movement represented in these pages. As Tom Bias emphasises in his chapter on 'The Negro Question', there were – for most of the period under examination – very serious limitations regarding the understanding of the predominantly 'white' membership and leadership of the early

US Trotskyists of the complex dynamics of race. The fact remains that there was an attempt to engage with 'the Negro Question', and over time deepening insights were developed, in part due to the work of C.L.R. James. It is striking that 'the Woman Question' is absent altogether from this volume – because it was more or less absent from discussions, and certainly the press, of the US Trotskyists from 1928 through 1940. Not only were questions of gender absent, but so were discussions of sexuality, nor were there clear signs of environmental sensibilities – all issues that have assumed central importance among radical activists of the late twentieth and early twenty-first centuries. What is present and vibrant are questions of economic justice and labour action, passionate concerns regarding democracy, a significant degree of intellectual integrity, and a stress on organisational seriousness. These too have been of great importance among activists of the late twentieth and early twenty-first centuries.

It is interesting to consider the reflections on such matters of some activists who were associated with the SWP, and then with the political tendency associated with C.L.R. James. Having broken with both, they speak respectfully yet critically of each. At least two of them had been in the SWP from the start, then along with James had been in Max Shachtman's organisation after the 1940 split, then back with the SWP for several years (again with James) from 1947 to 1951 – so their comments reflect significant experience, and they touch on both the limitations and strengths just indicated:

> Cannon was an utterly forthright and courageous man. But Cannon knew almost nothing about blacks or about minorities in this country. He didn't know anything about complexities.
>
> He represented a proletarian quality which we could never have absorbed through, for example, someone like William Z. Foster. Because, although Cannon was a proletarian type, he was the kind of proletarian who could co-exist with a Max Shachtman or an intellectual like James Burnham as long as these intellectuals did not become too flighty. Cannon was not a small or a mean man; he had a basic faith in the proletariat, but he sensed that there was much more to life, to history, to politics and to revolution than just the proletariat. He welcomed intellectuals as long as they did not go off in all directions. C.L.R. James used to say of Cannon that he was not the kind of man who would trample on a minority. He would not line up his majority against you unless you got too far out of line and forced him to do it. Everybody who has a political party has to do that at a certain point. You can't let it be torn apart from whim. He was the kind of chairman who could sit back and not have to interfere with everything going on. He was not an insecure person. …

> Cannon didn't give a damn about the Negro struggle – all he cared about was the class struggle. Not that he was prejudiced; he just took the old socialist position [that racism would be eliminated after the workers' revolution, so black and white workers should simply fight for workers' rights and socialism].
>
> C.L.R. came over [to the United States] in 1938 and while he didn't know what Cannon knew, he knew a lot of things that Cannon didn't know. ... We were able to go beyond the proletarian-ness of Cannon because of C.L.R. James. ...
>
> In many respects Cannon, who was thirty-eight at the time of the split between Stalin and Trotsky and who had been shaped by the experiences of the first World War, remained at the standpoint of the solidarity of the workers. But at the same time he understood his limitations as a proletarian and therefore welcomed intellectuals into the party. ...
>
> [In 1947] Cannon was glad for us to come in [to the SWP again] and permitted us a great deal of freedom, including trusting one of our members to put the paper [*The Militant*] to bed each week. C.L.R. thought we could now give greater breadth and meaning to revolution in the U.S. [and, in fact, James played a central role in reorienting the SWP on the question of race] ... Cannon knew we had ideas and it was understood that we could continue developing them, but we would also do our daily party work in a disciplined way ...
>
> But in 1953 C.L.R. was already becoming a Marxist egocentric, something which, strangely enough, Cannon never became. Cannon never tried to ballyhoo Cannon. ...[10]

One need not accept all of these observations in order to conclude, nonetheless, that they reflect both limitations and strengths of the movement presented in the pages of this book, a movement which certainly merits scholarly examination. As for activists who wish to change the world for the better, it is always a good idea to blend a sense of one's strengths with a sense of one's limitations. By exploring the limitations and strengths of those who went before, it might be possible to overcome some of one's own limitations while enhancing the strengths one brings to the struggle.

---

10 Boggs and Paine 1978, pp. 281–2, 284, 287.

CHAPTER 2

Communist League of America

Bryan Palmer

Revolutionary communism has a long history. But with the Bolshevik achievement of a Soviet state in 1917, revolutionaries and radicals throughout the world looked to the victorious Russians, Lenin and Trotsky preeminent among them, for inspiration. With Lenin's illness in 1923, culminating in his death early in 1924, and Trotsky's inability to thwart Stalin's adroit if ruthless consolidation of power, what would be the consequences in countries like the United States, where communism was anything but well grounded?

Revolutionary communists in the US, who had struggled valiantly throughout the Red Scare of the immediate post-World War I period, breaking out of a clandestine, underground existence to create a legal party that could connect with the mass of American workers, had originally been aided by the Communist International under Lenin. They were guided in all kinds of productive ways. Lenin, Trotsky, Radek, Zinoviev and others encouraged the Americans to adopt strategies and tactics that would facilitate making revolutionary communism a force within the wider labour movement and among other mobilising groups, such as African Americans and immigrants.[1]

This positive, productive, and even-handed contribution of the Communist International to the American revolutionary movement waned over the course of the mid-to-late 1920s. As a former communist turned anti-communist, Benjamin Gitlow, declared in 1940, 'Lenin [had] ruled by virtue of his authority'. Stalin now ruled 'by virtue of his power'. Comintern interventions, often delivered to the American Party by emissaries, backed up by cabled telegrams from Moscow, were increasingly dictatorial and ham-fisted. Gitlow recounted a joke making the rounds among United States communists in the mid-1920s: 'Why is the Communist Party … like the Brooklyn Bridge? Because it is suspended on cables'.[2] Political directives and policy decisions were often mercurial, resulting in disastrous political miscues. The Workers (Communist) Party was balkanised into factional enclaves manoeuvring for favour with Moscow. As James P. Cannon, throughout the 1920s a leading figure within American com-

1 See Cannon 1962; Palmer 2007, esp. 113–65; Draper 1957.

2 Gitlow 1940, pp. 555, 187.

munism and a founder of the Party's most successful united front operation, the International Labor Defense, commented bitterly and earthily to Alexander Bittelman, theoretician of the rival William Z. Foster group, 'Stalin makes shit out of leaders and leaders out of shit'.[3]

Dissident communism in the United States was thus born of failures, frustrations, and factional impasses. The Communist League of America (Opposition), also known as the Left Opposition or CLA, was formally founded in Chicago at a three-day conference, 17–19 May 1929. Conceived as an opposition oriented towards winning back the existing membership of the Communist Party of the United States (CPUSA) to a revolutionary perspective, the CLA could be dated to the Sixth World Congress of the Communist International in the summer of 1928. Cannon and a Canadian comrade, Maurice Spector, read Trotsky's 'The Draft Program of the Comintern: A Criticism of Fundamentals'. The disaffected duo agreed that Trotsky's insights explained how the international revolutionary project had been derailed by a political movement away from the original purposes of revolutionary communism; smuggled the dissident document out of the Soviet Union; and returned to their respective countries committed to defend their critical views and convince others of the validity of their judgement. In the United States, Cannon quickly drew his partner Rose Karsner, and long-time allies in the communist movement, Max Shachtman and Martin Abern, to his cause. All agreed that the sorry state of the American communist movement could be explained by Trotsky's critique.

Cannon and this immediate circle of supporters were soon targeted by the Workers (Communist) Party leadership, led by Jay Lovestone. During a series of lengthy October 1928 Political Committee hearings, attended by over 100 Party members, Cannon, Shachtman, and Abern shocked comrades by tabling their statement in support of Trotsky, 'For the Russian Opposition! Against Opportunism and Bureaucracy in the Worker's Communist Party of America!' [Document 1]. The trio was promptly expelled. Their rallying cry document then appeared in the American Left Opposition's first 15 November issue of a semi-monthly propaganda organ, emblazoned with the title, *The Militant*.

It was not long before other communists throughout the United States were pressured to repudiate Cannon, Shachtman, and Abern. When they refused, or demanded more information, they too were turfed out of the Party. This inevitably drew recruits to the Cannon-led Left Opposition. One such group, headed by Boston's revolutionary birth-control advocate, Dr Antoinette Konikow, formed the Independent Communist League (ICL) and issued a *Bulletin*

3 Bittelman 1963, p. 510.

deploring the 'political trickery and crookedness' associated with the Lovestone Party regime [Document 2]. Cannon, Shachtman, and Abern considered the Konikow statement insufficiently informed by Trotsky's programmatic critique, but in its willingness to break from the bureaucratic methods of Lovestone, the Boston ICL soon made its way into a common cause with the New York-based Left Opposition. In the process, conceptions of what was at stake in the consolidation of dissident communism broadened and deepened, as was the case with other contingents of oppositionists in Chicago, Minneapolis, and elsewhere.

The emerging Left Opposition was given a rough ride by its former comrades. Those selling *The Militant* outside of Communist Party headquarters and gatherings, or speaking publicly about Trotskyist ideas, were subjected to harassment, even beatings. Organised goon squads of Communist Party rank-and-filers descended on forums where Cannon, Konikow, or other Left Oppositionists might be speaking, determined to use physical force to silence left-wing critics. In the pages of the *Daily Worker* the Left Opposition was attacked as 'enemies of the working class', part of an 'internal union of renegades'. These miscreants had 'joined the camp of the plotters of war on the Soviet Union', aligned with 'imperialism, the social democracy, and the counter-revolution'.[4] Shachtman was aghast: 'We looked almost in utter disbelief at what we were seeing and what we were witnessing and what we were participating in. Comrades with whom we had lived and fought both as opponents and colleagues in factional fights for years and years, who had been comrades of ours in every sense of the word – not just politically but personally, were threatening to beat us up or cut us up, just for doing nothing more than selling our *Militant*'.[5]

In these earliest of Left Opposition days, American dissidents had no contact with Trotsky. 'We didn't know whether he was dead or alive', wrote Cannon. But contact with Trotsky was gradually established as the CLA consolidated.[6] After the Opposition's founding conference, Trotsky congratulated his American comrades for building a basis on which the 'bureaucratic centralism' characteristic of the CPUSA could be opposed, writing a letter on the 'Tasks of the American Opposition'. Party leaders in the United States, Trotsky concluded, were prepared to 'put through any zig-zag whatever according to the administrative necessities of the Stalinist staff' [Document 3].

---

4 Wolfe 1928.

5 Shachtman 1963, p. 176; Shachtman 1954, p. 11.

6 Cannon 1944, pp. 74–5.

One of those characteristic zig-zags was the Comintern's turn to the Third Period, an ultra-left Stalinist lurch that handcuffed the Left Opposition somewhat. For one part of the CLA's critique of the Communist International was that it had retreated over the course of the 1920s into parochial defence of the Soviet Union as the homeland of socialism, abandoning the project of building revolutionary possibility around the world. When the Third Period declared the need to confront capitalism with revolutionary mobilisations, proclaiming an end to an era of capitalist stabilisation and class struggle retreat, it seemed as if the Communist International was reasserting its commitment to revolutionary activism. In actuality, the programmatic shift proved an ultra-left recipe for sectarian disaster, abandoning Leninist understandings of the united front as a tactic to develop strategic ways in which Communists could work productively in mass organisations of working-class mobilisation, conditioning new ways for the revolutionary left to influence workers and their allies to take up the politics of root-and-branch opposition to capitalism. As Maurice Spector argued in 'The Cult of the "Third Period"', the consequences were debilitating for the revolutionary project. The Third Period isolated communists in a rhetoric of antagonism. Demands were made that fighting 'red' unions be formed in opposition to the established and compromised mainstream labour organisations. Ugly and counter-productive attack on reformist political bodies as agents of 'social fascism' became mandatory. The result was a Communist Party, USA that was increasingly isolated from the masses of American workers [Document 4].

In calling for a 'United Front on Unemployment' [Document 5], the Left Opposition posited a concrete alternative to the rhetorical absolutism of Third Period sectarianism. This repudiation of ultra-leftism, envisioned and implemented in the unemployed movement that was arguably one of the most significant agitational and organisational initiatives amidst the Great Depression's destructive assault on jobs, promised a politics of intervention in class struggles that would shift the emphasis away from the Comintern's isolating sectarianism. It accented the need to build mobilisations and movements in conjunction with existing bodies of potential resistance, while not abandoning the necessary critique of reformist leaderships.

The Left Opposition had done much to identify what was wrong with the Communist International and what, in the United States, might be done to rectify this situation. But the small forces of dissident Trotskyist communism never numbered more than 200 in these 1928–33 years. The CPUSA was considerably larger; had a significant layer of steeled activists embedded in trade unions and mass organisations; could draw upon the immense resources and prestige of the Communist International; and was, in all manner of ways, far more influential. Isolated and maligned, and struggling to make breakthroughs that never quite managed to materialise, the early CLA soon found itself mired in a factional impasse that pitted two of its founders, James P. Cannon and Max Shachtman, against one another. Factional correspondence [Documents 6 and 7] reveal the depths of the divisions, which related to individual circumstances and styles of work as well as opposed orientations to important questions, many of which unfolded within the international arena. The particular letters reprinted below address differences between the Cannon and Shachtman groups around the advisability of funding Arne Swabeck's travel to Europe to meet with Trotsky and the measures to be taken against a League militant, Bernard Morgenstern, who violated Left Opposition norms in being married before a rabbi. Such matters may seem trivial, but the vehemence of factional reaction – both Swabeck and Morgenstern were members of the Cannon majority – suggests how deeply divided the CLA was in this period.

The fullest account of this factional impasse appears in an excellent compilation of documents put together and analysed by the staff of the Prometheus Research Library. This already published account, reproducing scores of lengthy public and private statements, reveals fault lines separating the Cannon and Shachtman groups, one in which the principled politics of the Left Opposition tended to be compromised by the tendency to personalist combinations and opportunistic adaptations of Shachtman and his principal allies Martin Abern and Albert Glotzer. As this selection of material suggests, Trotsky's intervention in these disputes, which identified lapses of judgement and failures to follow through on basic political assignments in Shachtman's work in the European sections of the Left Opposition, tried to instruct Shachtman about these shortcomings. Within the CLA, Trotsky ultimately played a decisive role in realigning the Cannon majority and the Shachtman minority.[7] Resentments nonetheless still simmered, eventually resurfacing in an irrevocable split between Cannon and Shachtman in 1940.

In the immediate context of the early 1930s, however, Trotsky's intervention advocating an end to the American Left Opposition's factionalism was reinforced by the CLA's emergence as a forceful, if small, force on the stage of class conflict and political mobilisation. Antagonisms lessened as Cannon and Shachtman threw themselves into efforts to ignite an American challenge to

---

7 Prometheus Research Library 2002, which contains, among many other documents, the clearest and fullest statement of the discontents of the Shachtman minority, Martin Abern, Albert Glotzer, and Max Shachtman, 'The Situation in the American Opposition: Prospect and Retrospect', 4 June 1932, pp. 230–81. Drucker 1994 slides over this early factional confrontation in the CLA too easily.

the rise of fascism in Germany. But it would be the Left Opposition's involvement in mass struggles, first in the New York hotel workers' strike and, later, in the dramatic and successful leadership of the Minneapolis teamsters' battles to form an industrial union in 1934 (both conflicts featured in the Labour Struggles section below) that finally ended, for a time, the bitter Cannon and Shachtman fracture of the early 1930s.[8]

By this point the international Left Opposition's original orientation of directing its propaganda to the official Communist parties, with the intention of reclaiming Comintern affiliates to the revolutionary politics of their origins, had borne little in the way of successes. The turn to the Third Period hardened resistance to the Left Opposition and undermined its capacity to effectively challenge the entrenched Soviet bureaucracy. With the growing threat of fascism and world war, moreover, the catastrophic consequences of adhering to a politics of ultra-left, sectarian abstentionism seemed more and more apparent. Joseph Carter's 'Unite To Smash Facism! Forward to Communist Unity and Common Action of All Workingclass Organizations' [Document 8] was an impassioned plea to rally all communist forces before events in Germany proceeded to the point that resistance to fascism was obliterated. But this principled and pragmatic call for unity, voiced by Left Oppositionists from the moment that Hitler's march to power was discernible, originally fell on deaf Comintern ears. By the time the thoroughly Stalinised International finally realised that its Third Period policies had squandered opportunities to build resistance to fascism in a sectarian refusal to make common cause with social-democratic and other reform bodies it was too late, and the half-hearted half-way turn to the united front proposed by the Communist International was too little. The way had been paved for the defeat and decimation not only of the powerful German Communist movement, but also its numerous social-democratic left-wing rivals. Fascism triumphant within Germany sealed the fate of Europe and much of the world, with war now inevitable.

Only when this was painfully obvious did the Communist International react unequivocally. It did so, predictably, not so much by correcting the mistaken policies of the Third Period, but by lurching yet again in an extreme reaction, this time fast-tracking to the right. With the proclamation of the Popular Front, Communist parties around the world were admonished to drop their insistence that only revolutionaries affiliated with the Comintern could lead the class struggle, forming truly revolutionary unions and promoting the politics of class against class. Now, cross-class alliances should be formed, Com-

8 See, for instance, Palmer 2013.

munists must work with all manner of progressive people, and the defence of the Soviet motherland amidst war was the priority against which all actions must be judged. Communists should enter into coalition governments the better to promote these policies and defeat the fascist enemy.

Having struggled for half a decade to convince those affiliated with the Communist International to reclaim their revolutionary heritage, the international Left Opposition under Trotsky's leadership was, by 1933, stalemated in recognition of its meagre accomplishments. With the German debacle and the destruction of the powerful revolutionary German workers' movement, Trotsky had seen enough of Stalinism's politics of defeat. There was also increasing evidence of the Stalinist terror directed against Left Oppositionists, prompting Trotsky to begin to develop his analysis of 'the revolution betrayed'. By September 1933 Trotsky had concluded that the Stalinised Comintern had passed from being a flawed but nevertheless still potentially revolutionary body that it was mandatory for the Left Opposition to direct its work toward, to being a bulwark of counter-revolution that could be bypassed. Stalinism had crossed over into the camp of obstructing rather than advancing revolution. Little more than a corpse of a once healthy revolutionary project, the Communist International as it existed under Stalinism could not be revived. Trotsky thus called for the formation of a new, Fourth International, as well as the establishment of dissident communist parties separate and distinct from existing Stalinist bodies that would take up the cause of a revived International.

The Communist League of America took up this challenge, its National Committee issuing a declaration 'For a New Party and a New International' [Document 9]. In a March 1934 debate at New York's Irving Plaza, Cannon crossed swords with his old inner-Party adversary, Jay Lovestone. The Workers (Communist) Party head who had expelled Cannon in 1928, Lovestone had subsequently himself been expelled as a Right Oppositionist. Yet Lovestone still wanted to reform and unify the Communist International. Cannon was having none of it. 'Too much water had passed over the mill, too many mistakes had been made, too many crimes and betrayals had been committed, too much blood spilled by the Stalinist International', thundered Trotsky's American ally.[9] This perspective, giving the CLA a fresh start, opened the door to increasing and invigorating interventions in the labour movement and to the building of new revolutionary organisations through initiatives undertaken with non-Stalinist revolutionary forces.

9 Cannon 1944, pp. 136–8; 'Big Crowd at Debate: Cannon and Lovestone Discuss Internationals', *The Militant*, 10 March 1934.

1 For the Russian Opposition! Against Opportunism and Bureaucracy in The Workers (Communist) Party[10]

(Excerpts – 15 November 1929)

James P. Cannon, Martin Abern and Max Shachtman

…

2. We have definite views on a series of fundamental questions vitally affecting the whole future of the party and the Comintern …

3. The 'discussion' of these questions conducted up till now has not been a real discussion since many of the documents – in our opinion some of the most important political documents of our time – have been suppressed and concealed from the parties of the Comintern or presented to them in garbled form. The opportunity which has come to us in the recent period to read a number of these documents dealing with some of the most disputed problems of the Comintern in the past five years, together with the rapid confirmation of their correctness by the whole course of events, has shaped our views and convictions. We consider it our revolutionary duty to defend these views before the party.

4. … the arbitrary actions already taken against us (our removal from all positions on October 16) and the plain indications shown in the present hearing of the intention to take further organizational measures and to begin a public campaign against us in the party press make it necessary to state our position without further delay. It must be made clear to the party that the measures are being taken against us solely because of our political views. These views must be presented to the party as they really are.

…

6. We stand on the main line of the document entitled 'The Right Danger in the American Party' (excepting certain erroneous formulations dealing with the world position and role of American imperialism), presented to the Sixth

10 Cannon, Abern, Shachtman 1928.

World Congress of the Comintern by the delegation of the Opposition, in the drafting of which we actively participated. As set forth in this document, we believe that the present leadership of the party, mechanically imposed upon the party by the ECCI against the will of the membership, is a consciously developing right wing whose course and actions are all in the direction of undermining the position of the party in the class struggle. Its activities since the presentation of the document 'The Right Danger in the American Party' to the world congress, have confirmed and not refuted this estimate. The irresponsible adventurism, factional degeneration, and bureaucratic corruption of the Lovestone group leadership are an organic part of its fundamental opportunist character.

7. The latest decision of the secretariat of the ECCI, which undertakes to dismiss a whole series of principled questions raised in our indictment of the party leadership with a formal motion, giving no answer whatsoever to the burning questions of the party in all fields of the class struggle, serves only to strengthen the mechanical stranglehold of the right-wing leadership upon our party. This bureaucratic secretarial method of dealing with disputed principled questions must be emphatically rejected by the party both in form and content, since it has nothing in common with Lenin's teaching regarding the ideological leadership of all Communist parties by the Comintern and the unremitting struggle against opportunism on all fronts.

8. The present attempt of some of the leaders of the Foster-Bittelman group who signed the document on the right danger to abandon that platform, to moderate the struggle against the Lovestone-Pepper right wing, and to effect a political coalescence with them in order to direct their attack against those who remain true to that platform and develop its logical and inevitable international implications, in no way alters the fundamental correctness of the document. It merely demonstrates the political instability of these leaders, which hampers the process of developing an opposition to the present right-wing leadership and line of the party on a principled basis. We have no doubt that the supporters of the Opposition who have regarded the struggle against the right-wing leadership as a principled question will continue to adhere to this position despite the vacillations and maneuvers of a section of the leaders.

9. The problems of the American party are organically bound up with the fundamental questions confronting the Communist Party of the Soviet Union and the Comintern, and cannot be solved separately from them. The left wing of the American party, taking shape in the principled struggle against the right-wing leadership of the party (Lovestone-Pepper group), will go forward only insofar as it recognizes the necessity of a struggle against the right danger on

an international scale and links up its fight in the American party with the Bolshevik fight for the fundamental tenets of Leninism in the Communist Party of the Soviet Union and in the Comintern.

10. The Opposition in the Communist Party of the Soviet Union led by L.D. Trotsky has been fighting for the unity of the Comintern and all its sections on the basis of the victory of Leninism. The correctness of the position taken by the Russian Opposition over a period of five years of struggle has been fully confirmed by events.

a. The struggle led by Trotsky since 1923 for party democracy and against bureaucratism as the pressure of another class upon the party of the proletariat, was absolutely correct then and is even more so now. The adoption of this position by Zinoviev, Kamenev, and others in 1926, and the attempt by Stalin to adopt it now, demonstrates the tremendous pressure of class forces which impel the Communist Party of the Soviet Union to this platform. The struggle for party democracy, against bureaucratism, and for a regime of genuine Leninist self-criticism are burning questions now for every party and for the Comintern as a whole.

b. The necessity for a more relentless struggle against the kulak and the nepman – for an orientation exclusively toward the workers and hired hands, united with the village poor and lower peasantry and in alliance with the middle peasantry – proclaimed by the Opposition, becomes clearer every day. The trend of events and the irresistible pressure of class forces is already driving a deep cleavage in the leadership of the Communist Party of the Soviet Union, and is forcing the Stalin group to struggle against the right wing (Rykov, etc.), with other elements (Bukharin) vacillating between the two.

The platform of the Russian Opposition, prepared for the Fifteenth Congress of the CPSU, indicates the revolutionary policy for the present situation in the Soviet Union. The prediction and warning contained in this platform against the inevitable growth and aggressiveness of a genuine right wing in the party (Rykov, Tomsky, etc.) has been precisely confirmed in the intervening period, particularly in recent months. The activities of this right wing have already necessitated organizational measures in the Moscow Soviet – a proof of the awakening of the proletarian masses of the party to this danger. The 'left' course of the Stalin group in the direction of a struggle against the right dangers, for party democracy and self-criticism, against the bureaucrats, the nepmen, and the kulaks, can become a real left course only insofar as it abandons zigzag movements, adopts the whole platform of the Opposition, and reinstates the tested Bolshevik fighters who have been expelled to their rightful places in the party.

c. The attempts to revise the basic Marxist-Leninist doctrine with the spurious theory of socialism in one country have been rightly resisted by the Opposition led by Trotsky. A number of revisionist and opportunist errors in various fields of Comintern activity and its ideological life in general have proceeded from this false theory. To this, in part at least, can be traced the false line in the Chinese revolution, the debacle of the Anglo-Russian Committee, the alarming and unprecedented growth of bureaucratism in the Comintern, an incorrect attitude and policy in the Soviet Union, etc., etc. This new 'theory' is bound up with an overemphasis on the power and duration of the temporary stabilization of capitalism. Herein lies the true source of pessimism regarding the development of the proletarian world revolution. One of the principal duties of every Communist in every party of the Comintern is to fight along with the Opposition for the teachings of Marx, Engels, and Lenin on this basic question.

d. The Opposition was absolutely correct when it demanded the immediate rupture of the Anglo-Russian Committee and the concentration of all the fire of the Comintern and the British party upon the leaders of the British Trades Union General Council (Purcell, Hicks, and Company) immediately after the betrayal of the general strike. The maintenance of the Anglo-Russian Committee after this event did not serve as a bridge to the British masses but as a partial shield of the traitorous leaders from the fire of the Communists.

e. Rarely before in history has a Marxist-Leninist appraisal and forecast been so completely and swiftly confirmed as in the case of the Opposition theses and proposals (Trotsky, Zinoviev) on the problems and tasks of the Chinese revolution. The line of the ECCI, formulated by Stalin, Bukharin, Martynov, etc., and the rejection of the proposals of the Opposition, which were suppressed and concealed from the parties of the Comintern, have brought catastrophic results and hampered the genuine development of the Communist Party of China and the revolutionary-democratic dictatorship of the workers and peasants. In view of its world-historical importance, a real discussion of the problems of the Chinese revolution, with all the documents being made available, is imperative for all parties of the Comintern. The prohibition of this discussion must be broken down, the truth must be told and the enormous errors exposed down to their roots. Only in this way can the great lessons of the Chinese revolution be learned by the parties of the Comintern.

11. We demand the publication of all the documents of the Russian Opposition, without which the party members do not and cannot know the essential issues of the struggle and cannot form intelligent opinions in regard to them. The

discussion of these issues heretofore has been conducted in an atmosphere of prejudice, misrepresentation, terrorism, outlawing of all thought and inquiry, the substitution of official say-so for the study of documents and facts on disputed questions. All this has been part of a campaign of unparalleled slander against Trotsky – who, after Lenin, was the outstanding leader of the Russian revolution and the Comintern – and was accompanied by the falsification of the history of the revolution itself.

12. We intend, at the coming plenum of the Central Executive Committee, to propose that our party shall take the initiative in demanding the return from exile and the reinstatement into the Communist Party of the Soviet Union with full rights, of Trotsky and the other imprisoned and exiled members of the Russian Opposition. Violence and persecution against counterrevolutionaries is a revolutionary duty; violence and persecution against tried and loyal Bolsheviks is a crime.

13. The consolidation of the Opposition in the American party, which logically and inevitably merges with the path of the Opposition in the Communist Party of the Soviet Union led by Trotsky, has developed in the struggle against the right danger. The pitiful attempt to characterize this Opposition as a 'right' tendency, related to the noncommunist elements such as Lore who have been fighting the party from the right, and anticommunist elements like Salutsky, who have gone completely over to the side of the labor lieutenants of capitalism, does not in the least correspond with political reality and is designed to cover the progressive drift of the party leadership to the right.

On the contrary, the attempts to exclude us from responsible party work, and even from the party itself, along with the proletarian communists who support us, while at the same time the control of the party apparatus and the party leadership in such unions as the needle trades consolidates more firmly in the hands of the opportunists, who fight their communist worker critics with expulsion and physical violence – all this can only accelerate the rapprochement between the right wing and petty-bourgeois elements now outside the party.

14. The Lovestone group leadership, by its opportunist political outlook, its petty-bourgeois origin, its corrupt factionalism, its careerism and adventurism in the class struggle, is the greatest menace to the party. Its mechanical grip on the apparatus of the party grows steadily tighter and chokes out its inner life. Capable, experienced, and trustworthy comrades are one by one removed from responsible posts and replaced by faction agents, incompetents, and upstarts, unknown and inexperienced in any serious work in the class struggle. The party itself, the mass work, and the mass organizations under the influence and direction of the party are thereby undermined.

...

16. By its whole character the Lovestone leadership is the logical American banner-bearer of the demagogic and unscrupulous international campaign against the leaders of the Russian Opposition. The aspirations of certain former leaders of the opposition in the American party to grasp this banner for themselves are pathetically futile. The hopes of the Foster group to escape thereby the factional persecution of the Lovestone group and to secure their organizational positions can succeed only insofar as they surrender their former opposition standpoint. The whole course of the Lovestone group, which has no roots in the labor movement, is toward a monopoly of the party apparatus, and cannot be otherwise.

17. We declare our intention to appeal to the plenum of the Central Executive Committee to reverse the action of the Polcom against us, which is motivated by neither principled foundation nor party interest, and is the result purely of factional considerations and bureaucratic fear of discussion and criticism.

18. The arbitrary decisions made against us cannot in the slightest degree change our position as Communists, since the party we helped to found and build is our party. Reserving the right to express our viewpoint and opinion on these disputed questions, we will continue to adhere to the discipline and decisions of the party as heretofore. Under all circumstances we will continue to live with the party and work for its future. ...

2 What is Wrong with the Communist Party?[11]
(Excerpts, 1928)

Independent Communist League of Boston (Antoinette Konikow et al.)

Certainly the principles of the Communist Party are not wrong. The Dictatorship of the Proletariat, as a transition to Communism, the effective work against capitalism and its conscious and unconscious supporters, the exposé of the Socialist party – these are the strength and glory of the Communist movement.

Then what is wrong? So deeply wrong that it is bound to become dangerous to the movement. What is the reason that so many communists find it impossible to work for communism within the party. The great sore growing larger and deeper in the communist movement is its form of organization carried over from the time of the Russian revolution: namely, the centralized democracy NOW without democracy, the strict discipline NOW without previous discussion, the power acquired by a faction of the Communist Party of the Soviet Russia to demand obedience not only in Soviet Russia, but all over the world.

How Did the Present Leadership of the RCP Attain Such Power?

First, because the Workers of the World look upon them as the direct followers of Lenin, because upon their heads rests yet the halo of the October revolution. All achievements of Soviet Russia for the last ten years are considered to be **their work**. In fact, the workers identified them, just as they do themselves, with the Russian revolution and with Soviet Russia. Whoever is against that faction is accused of being against the October revolution and against Soviet Russia. History made the Russian Communist Party, in the eyes of the workers of the world, the representatives of Soviet Russia, but in reality they represent only a faction in the RCP, which knows how to control its own Party and the Comintern. In the first year of the Soviet government all comrades of the

11 Independent Communist League of Boston [Antoinette Konikow], 1928.

executive committee had their say however deeply they differed. There were no bosses at that time and Lenin attained his influence only through the strength of his arguments and his deep knowledge, certainly not by mechanical control. This has changed since Zinovieff became secretary of the Comintern.

How is the RCP and All Other Communist Parties Controlled by One Faction

He, Zinovieff, was the first to establish boss rule. When he was removed the comrades all over the world gave a sigh of relief, finding out soon that there was only a change of power, Stalin having taken his place. The Russian Communist Party is ruled now by the Stalin-Bucharin faction through the application of the so-called centralized democracy, or rather 'simplified democracy', as a Russian comrade satirically characterized it. …

The same 'simplified democracy' holds good for the organizations of the Comintern and the organizations of all other Communist parties. The ruling factions can perpetuate themselves through perfect control of the party press and all avenues of information. If the majority of any Communist party proves unsuitable to the Comintern, 'simplified democracy' at once begins to work. In other words, the Comintern appoints the comrades satisfactory to themselves.

The Fosterites once had a majority in our party and were simply pushed aside getting the orders practically to give the power over to the minority. The same happened just now in Germany, where the Comintern ordered Comrade Thalman … removed from the majority of the CEC … Thus the Communist parties of the world are always under the full control of the Comintern. There are plenty of factions in different Communist parties bitterly fighting one against the other, but not one of them, however, dares to lift its voice against the Comintern. The Comintern is the infallible judge. To whomsoever it gives its approval, it gives at the same time power to be the leader of the particular party, and its representative in the conference of the International. No opposition against the Comintern ever has a chance to grow within any party, still less to send any delegates to the Comintern.

What supreme mockery was it for the 'Bolshevik' [monthly magazine of the RCP] to glory in the fact, in its August editorial, that the Trotsky opposition did not even have one delegate at the last Congress of the International. The 'Pravda' [daily Communist paper] also points proudly to the fact that all resolutions of the Congress have passed unanimously. The Communist party in Soviet Russia and all over the world is always 'unanimous', because no one dares to have an opinion.

How is This Unanimity in All Communist Parties Brought About?

How is this unanimity brought about? Comrades who dare to differ lose standing and can retain important positions only if they repent and submit. Foster's short stint of independence (refusing during Zinovieff's dictatorship to vote against Trotsky; and fighting against Pepper) was duly punished; from being the leader of the majority he was forced to become a minority leader. He is tolerated now only under conditions of self-effacement. From the other side, a man like Lovestone, whose political trickery and crookedness is admitted by his own supporters, easily keeps his leadership. If he is occasionally caught in trickery or lies, it does not count, for lately maneuvering against comrades of the party is considered quite fashionable.

Lovestone and Losofsky

The latest expose of Lovestone seems to have added to his laurels, I mean the Losofsky statement on the 'American Mix-up' (*Pravda*, No. 176, 31 July). Lovestone and his crowd voted against the decision of the Profintern on the change of the Trade Union policy from 'boring from within' to 'dual unionism'. Imagine his embarrassment when he comes to Moscow and finds that the new policy is supported by Stalin: he realizes that he has not recognized the voice of the master. With his usual impudence he simply denies the fact of his voting against the policy. …

Lovestone's faction is again recognized and supported by the Comintern and it will be so for years. The Fosterites cannot equal his tricks, **and in the struggle for supremacy between factions, trickery and submission to the Comintern are the only things that count.** The orders from the Comintern are to give up factions. It is a standing order for many years. Lovestone swears solemnly that he is through with factions and begs the opposition to stop their disturbance of the party with their faction work. Meanwhile he is secretly making arrangements for the usual faction meetings, and the Fosterites follow his example. Instead of acknowledging frankly the necessity of different opinions in the party and giving all a chance of free criticism and exchange of opinions, which would really do away with factions, the party insists officially that no factionalism exists, but secretly keeps up the struggle of factions just as before.

The Control of Party Members in Soviet Russia

The Comintern and the RCP are becoming so much imbued with maneuvering and diplomacy that they slowly adopt all cheap capitalist political trickery and apply them with vengeance to their own members. In Soviet Russia they decided to kill the Trotsky opposition and acted about it just as the old Czar used to do with revolutionaries. Instead of realizing that an opposition of thousands of members is not a matter of chance, but based on some real foundations, they tried to explain it by mere treachery or personalities, and wanted to annihilate it by persecution and exile. We have heard lately again and again that the Trotsky opposition in Russia is dead and buried. A few months passed and again articles appear in the 'Pravda' that the Trotsky opposition had raised its head and must be killed once again. The most damnable situation is the fact that the same methods are used in Russia, where the building up of Socialism demands the full co-operation of the rank and file and the whole working class. But what has been done? The psychology of submission, called discipline, has been applied so persistently that workers are afraid to express their opinion and are getting used to look with indifference upon acts of mismanagement, corruption, and even plain treason. They have learned by bitter experience that it is dangerous to criticize and expose the grafters and corruptionists who are so near to the leading elements of the party that they get the support of party officials.

…

Revolutionary Methods Must Adapt Themselves to Different Stages of the Work

The Russian Revolution is the first practical application of the Dictatorship of the Proletariat. Naturally it was a hard and difficult task and frictions could not have been avoided. Military communism or war communism, introduced right after the October revolution, was a powerful help at first, but had to be given up to save Soviet Russia. … The strict centralization form of party organization is another sequel of the revolution and is kept up too long. The new conditions demand inner party democracy or the party will not be able to exist. Centralization and strict discipline are necessary in time of war and revolution, but if continued into the period of reconstruction are bound to lead to dissention and opposition.

The Trotsky Opposition

…

Lenin had greatly worried over coming faction fights between Stalin and Trotsky before his death. He had warned comrades in his so-called 'Testament' not against Trotsky, but against Stalin. In fact, he begged the comrades to remove Stalin from the secretaryship of the party, because he feared Stalin would abuse his power. Lenin's 'Testament' was never given to members of the party. His prediction unfortunately only too soon became a reality. For two years all Communist newspapers and magazines were filled with poisonous and misleading statements against Trotsky. No wonder the average comrade became prejudiced against him. The supporters of Trotsky lost their jobs and positions and later were exiled and are now in half starving condition. … Some comrades tell me that no punishment could be severe enough for Trotsky as long as he was a menace to the party. The question is **'was he a menace?'**

Is Trotsky a Menace to the Communist Party?

In reality he pointed out all dangers which threatened Soviet Russia. Had the party accepted his advice Soviet Russian would be stronger and happier today. He pointed out the growing power of the 'Kulak', which would make corn collection in the Soviet Union difficult. He was laughed at. But last spring Soviet Russia to its great consternation found out that it was almost impossible to collect the necessary corn. … [Trotsky] warned the government against the increasing power of Bureaucrats and the suppression of the rank and file. He pointed out the possibilities of graft and counter-revolution. He had not reached his exile in Turkestan when Soviet Russia had its new surprise – the 'Donetz' affair, a disclosure of corruption and graft and counter-revolution of a most shocking nature. The most horrible fact was that the workers and comrades knew about it for years, but could not do anything under the regime of bureaucracy and corruption. … The situation in China also ended in a surprise. Trotsky had warned the comrades against working with the Chinese Bourgeoisie, had demanded many months before the final disaster the withdrawal of the Communists from the Kuomintang and the formation of Soviets. As usual he was laughed at and his advice was followed only too late. The leaders of the RCP are very busy keeping the Communist Party of the world straight and fighting left and right deviations. The real dangers they usually notice only when they get a good blow on the head. …

Stalin Says: 'Communists are Too Independent to be Controlled by Moscow'

The party which glories in being always unanimous, which permits no opposition, is bound to go wrong. Centralization without democracy and discipline without previous discussion can prevail for a while in a proletarian state, but it rests on dangerous premises. First, the majority of the membership does not know the real situation and is kept in ignorance. Second, many members are dissatisfied and disgusted, but fear the loss of position and turn to hypocrisy to stay within the party. Third, crooks support those leaders, because they give them power and economic advantages leading to corruption. What is left for the comrades who see the danger of this factional leadership? Keep up the lie with them, howl with the wolves to strengthen them while thousands are disheartened and thousands are exiled and starved? Comrade Stalin answered the question of American Trade Union Delegates whether it is true that Moscow controls the Communist Party in the United States, with this statement: 'Communists are too independent to be controlled'. Unfortunately, he is wrong again. Only a few comrades seem to object to such control. We are among them. Being expelled from the Communist Party in the United States fortunately does not mean starvation or exile.

3 Tasks of the American Opposition[12]

(Excerpts, 1929)

Leon Trotsky

... The history of the origin of the American Opposition is itself highly characteristic and instructive. After five years of struggle against the Russian Opposition, it required a journey of members of the Central Committee of the American Party ... and even of its Political Bureau, to a Congress in Moscow in order for the first time to find out what so-called 'Trotskyism' is. This single fact is an annihilating indictment against the regime of Party police rule and poisonous falsification. Lovestone and Pepper did not create this regime but they are its staff officers. I convicted Lovestone of a foul ideological falsification (see my book *Europe and America*). Under a fairly normal regime that alone would have been enough to bury a man for a long time, if not for good, or at least to make him confess and repent. But under the present regime, to reinforce their positions, the Lovestones need only stubbornly repeat the falsifications that have been exposed. They do this with utter shamelessness imitating their bosses. The spirit of the Lovestones and Peppers is fundamentally opposed to the spirit of the proletarian revolution. That discipline towards which we strive – and we strive towards an iron discipline – can be founded only upon consciously won convictions which have entered into the flesh and blood.

I haven't had an opportunity of close contact with the other ruling elements of the American Communist Party – except, to be sure, Foster. The latter always seemed to me made of more trustworthy material than Lovestone and Pepper. In Foster's criticisms of the official leadership of the Party there was always much that was true and acute. But as far as I understand him, Foster is an empiricist. He does not want to, or is not able to, carry his thinking through to the end, and make upon the foundation of his criticisms the necessary generalization. For that reason it has never been clear to me in what direction Foster's criticism is pushing him: to the left or the right of the official Centrism. We must remember that besides the Marxist Opposition there exists an opportunist Opposition (Brandler, Thalheimer, Souvarine and others). This same empir-

12 Trotsky 1929.

icism apparently suggests to Foster the whole form of his activity … Foster tries to conceal himself with the defensive coloration of Stalinism in order by this contraband route to move toward the leadership of the American Party. In revolutionary politics the game of hide-and-seek never yet gave serious results. Without a general principled position upon the fundamental questions of the world revolution, and first of all on the question of socialism in a single country, you cannot have permanent and serious revolutionary victories. You can only have bureaucratic successes, such as Stalin has. But these temporary successes are paid for by the defeat of the proletariat and by the falling apart of the Comintern. I do not think that Foster will achieve even those second-class aims which he is pursuing, for the Lovestones and Peppers are much better fitted to carry through a policy of bureaucratic centrism, having no real character, and being ready in 24 hours to put through any zigzag whatever according to the administrative necessities of the Stalinist staff.

The work to be achieved by the American Opposition has international-historic significance, for in the last historic analysis all the problems of our planet will be decided upon American soil. There is much in favor of the idea that, from the standpoint of revolutionary order, Europe and the East stand ahead of the United States. But a course of events is possible in which this order might be broken in favor of the proletariat of the United States. Moreover, even if you assume that America which now shakes the whole world will be shaken last of all, the danger remains that a revolutionary situation in the United States may catch the vanguard of the American proletariat unprepared, as was the case in Germany in 1923, in England in 1926, and in China in 1925 to 1927. We must not for a minute lose sight of the fact that the might of American capitalism rests more and more upon a foundation of world economy with its contradictions and crises, military and revolutionary. This means that a social crisis in the United States may arrive a good deal sooner than many think, and have a feverish development from the beginning. Hence the conclusion: It is necessary to prepare.

As far as I can judge, your official Communist Party inherited no few characteristics from the old Socialist Party. That became clear to me at the time when Pepper succeeded in dragging the American Communist Party into the scandalous adventure with the Party of LaFollette. This low-grade policy of parliamentary opportunism was disguised with 'revolutionary' chatter to the effect that the social revolution will be achieved in the United States not by the proletariat but by the ruined farmers. When Pepper expounded this theory to me upon his return from the United States, I thought that I had to do with a curious case of individual aberration. Only with some effort I realized that this is a whole system, and that the American Communist Party had been dragged into this system. Then it became clear to me that this small Party cannot develop without deep inner crises, which will guarantee it against Pepperism and other evil diseases[,] ... diseases of bureaucratic sterility and revolutionary impotence.

That is why I suspect that the Communist Party has taken over many of the qualities of the Socialist Party, which in spite of its youth struck me with features of decrepitude. For the majority of those socialists – I have in view the governing strata – their socialism is a side-issue, a second-class occupation accommodated to their leisure hours. These gentlemen consecrate six days of the week to their liberal or commercial professions, rounding out their properties not without success, and on the seventh day they consent to occupy themselves with the saving of their souls. In a book of my memoirs I have tried to outline this type of socialistic Babbit. Evidently not a few of these gentlemen have succeeded in disguising themselves as Communists. These are not intellectual opponents, but class enemies. The Opposition must steer its course not on the petty-bourgeois Babbits, but on the proletarian Jimmie Higginses, for whom the idea of Communism, when they are once imbued with it, becomes the content of their whole life and activity. There is nothing more disgusting and dangerous in revolutionary activity than petty-bourgeois dilletantism, conservative, egotistical, self-loving and incapable of sacrifice in the name of a great idea. The advanced workers must firmly adopt one simple but invariable rule: Those leaders or candidates for leadership who are, in peaceful, everyday times, incapable of sacrificing their time, their strength, their means, to the cause of Communism, will oftenest of all in a revolutionary period become direct traitors, or turn up in the camp of those who wait to see on which side the victory lies. If elements of this kind stand at the head of the Party, they will indubitably ruin it when the great test comes. And no better are those brainless bureaucrats who simply hire out to the Comintern as they would to a notary, and obediently adapt themselves to each new boss.

Of course, the Opposition – that is the Bolshevik-Leninist – may have their traveling companions, who, without giving themselves wholly to the revolution, offer this or that service to the cause of Communism. It would of course be wrong not to make use of them. They can make a significant contribution to the work. But traveling companions, even the most honest and serious, ought to make no pretense to leadership. The leaders must be bound in all their daily work with those they lead. Their work must proceed before the eyes of the mass, no matter how small that mass may be at the given moment. I wouldn't give a cent for a leadership which can be summoned by cable from Moscow, or anywhere else, without the masses ever noticing it. Such leadership means bankruptcy guaranteed in advance. We must steer our course on the young proletarian who desires to know and to struggle, and is capable of enthusiasm and self-sacrifice. From such people we must attract and educate the genuine cadres of the Party and the proletariat.

... Those who are afraid of rough work we don't want. The calling of a revolutionary Bolshevik imposes obligations. The first of these obligations is to struggle for the proletarian youth, to clear a road to its most oppressed and neglected strata. They stand first under our banner.

The trade union bureaucrats, like the bureaucrats of false Communism, live in the atmosphere of aristocratic prejudices of the upper strata of the workers. It will be tragedy if the Oppositionists are infected even in the slightest degree with these qualities. We must not only reject and condemn these prejudices; we must burn them out of our consciousness to the last trace; we must find the road to the most deprived, to the darkest strata of the proletariat, beginning with the Negro, whom capitalist society has converted into a Pariah and who must learn to see in us his revolutionary brothers. And this depends wholly upon our energy and devotion to the work.

I see from comrade Cannon's letter that you intend to give the Opposition a more organized form. I can only welcome that news. It wholly follows the line of the views expounded above. In the work which you are doing, well-formed organization is necessary. The absence of clear organizational relations results from an intellectual confusion or leads to it. The cry about a second party and a fourth international is merely ridiculous, and should be the last thing to stop us. We do not identify the Communist International with the Stalinist bureaucracy, that is, with the hierarchy of Peppers in different degrees of demoralization. At the foundation of the International there lies a definite group of ideas and principles, conclusions from the whole struggle of the world proletariat. That group of ideas we, the Opposition, represent. We will defend it against the monstrous mistakes and violations of the 5th and 6th Congresses, and against the usurping apparatus of the Centrists, who upon one flank are wholly going over into the ranks of the Thermidorians. It is too clear to any Marxist that, in spite of the enormous material resources of the Stalinist apparatus, the present governing faction of the Comintern is politically and theoretically already dead. The banner of Marx and Lenin is in the hands of the Opposition. I do not doubt that the American division of the Bolsheviks will occupy a worthy place under that banner.

4 The Cult of the 'Third Period'[13]

(*Excerpts, 1929*)

Maurice Spector

The 'cloud by day and pillar of fire by night' that the Stalin ECCI conjures up to shield its disastrous ultra-left zigzag, is the so-called 'Third Period' invented in the theses of the Comintern Congress last July. Now in every *Daily Worker* contribution to the fraudulent 'enlightenment campaign' this 'Third Period' is invoked with deadly monotony as the latest all-sufficient, all-hallowing fetish before which the credulous party member must make the sign of the cross.

Juggling with 'Periods'

Four years elapsed between the Fifth and Sixth Congresses, during which time the revamped ECCI was the obedient instrument and rubber-stamp of the ruling Right-Center (Rykov-Bucharin-Stalin) bloc. ... [A]t the Sixth Congress ... when Bucharin and Stalin did their juggling with the 'periods'. The official Communist International (Vol. VI No. 9–10) recently smuggled in an editorial admission that 'in 1926–7 ... on the basis of the partial stabilization of capitalism, a revolutionary crisis developed in the far West and East'. This is what the Communist Opposition, of course, said in those years when it was most important to say it. But for transparent reasons the theses of the Sixth Congress (1928) define the interval between the Fifth and Sixth Congresses, inclusive of 1926–7, the 'second period of the post-war capitalism', in a way to suggest that it was not a period of revolutionary possibilities. In the recapitulation of the attributes of this 'second period', its architects conveniently 'forget' to mention the facts of the Chinese Revolution, the British General Strike and the Viennese uprising. It is merely spoken of as a period of 'relative stabilization, defensive struggles of the workers, successful socialist construction in the USSR, growing political influence of the Communist Parties, and inner consolidation of the Comintern'. Nine-tenths of this characterization is falsehood and the remaining tenth needs qualification.

13 Spector 1929.

The method of optimistic lying to maintain the prestige of the leadership and keep up the 'morale' of the home populace is not Marxist but was habitually resorted to by the general staffs in their communiqués during the late world war. The history of the 'second period' was falsified to stifle discussion and prevent the heavy accounting that otherwise Stalin and Bucharin would have had to render. They would have had to explain why they failed to give the correct bolshevik leadership that would have utilized the revolutionary possibilities of this period to develop offensives for the overthrow of the stabilization. They would have had to admit that they displayed no revolutionary initiative but pursued such right-wing and centrist policies that objectively helped to strengthen capitalism, that they staked nearly all on the Kuomintang bourgeoisie, undermined the independence of the Chinese Communist Party, and opposed the propagation of the Soviets. They would have been found guilty of transforming the British Communist Party and the Minority movement into adjuncts of the British General Council, incapable of offering any substantial resistance to the betrayal of the General Strike. Under the shadow of their regime, the Viennese uprising found the Communist Party helpless and bewildered, the Sacco-Vanzetti demonstrations developed really outside the orbit of the Comintern influence, the French Party after heroic proclamations against the American Legion, turned tail and retired for polite demonstration to a Parisian suburb and the Red Day organized by the Czech Party against Fascism was turned into a farce by the passivity of the leadership.

The extension of the political influence of the Communist parties and their inner consolidation during this period are equally myths. The machine man Piatnitski's brochure *Organization of the World Party* establishes for the critical reader that the membership of nearly every communist party declined, as did their trade union influence, press circulation and political activity of the nuclei. The membership of the American Party, it may be recalled, fell from 16,325 in 1925 to 7,277 in 1928. The proceedings of the Sixth Congress will show that every 'monolithic' party was rent by violent factional struggles that resulted in fresh splits in Czecho-Slovakia, the United States, Germany, in addition to those which had already taken place in France, Holland, Belgium, and the Soviet Union. The authors of the 'second' and 'third' periods equally misrepresent the real situation in the Soviet Union, where under their regime the growth of the restorationist elements culminated in a bloodless uprising of the Kulaks creating the grain crisis of 1927–8, and they omit to record the unparalleled development of bureaucracy in party and state apparatus.

A 'New Line' for a 'New Period'

… [T]he rank and file was beginning to get restive. The hammer-blows of the Opposition platform were beginning to sink in especially as the passage of events continued swiftly to vindicate its every important argument and criticism. Repression, deportation, expulsion, slander, and victimization were proving insufficient for the bureaucracy to maintain their grip on office. The grain crisis in Russia, the Chiang Kai-Shek coup in China, the corpse of the Anglo-Russian committee, the consequent weakening of the international position of the Soviet Union …, the exposures of degeneration and corruption in the party and state machines, were too flagrant to dispose of with mere abuse of the Opposition. The growing unrest had to be canalized. The old gag of 'bolshevization' had lost its force. So resort was had first to 'self criticism', which meant anything but criticism, of the leadership, and secondly, a 'new line' for a 'new period'. At the Fifteenth Russian Party Congress (1927) and at the subsequent Ninth Plenum of the ECCI the outlines and the strategy of the 'Third Period' began to emerge. The sophistic Bucharin suddenly discovered that the social-democratic leaders were merging with the state-apparatus and were traitors to the working class and that henceforth only a 'united front from below' was permissible. … Furthermore said Bucharin, the independent role of the communist parties must now be strengthened … with the slogan of 'Class Against Class' for use in forthcoming struggles. Apparently Bucharin-Stalin would have us believe the communist parties knew and practised nothing of their independent role during the active leadership of Lenin before the 'class against class' slogan was launched.

The 'Third Period' with which the 'Right Danger' was tied up, blossomed out into full glory at the Sixth Congress. Bucharin and Stalin, Serrati and Ercoli, Ewert and Thaelmann, Lovestone and Foster equally gave it their blessing. It was a meaningless and platitudinous substitute for the concrete Marxist analysis of the given class relations and world situation upon which communist strategy must base itself. The 'Third Period' is defined as one of capitalist stabilization but of growing contradictions which leads to the danger of fresh wars for the shrinking world market, sharpens the danger of an attack on the Soviet Union, and brings with it a leftward movement of the working class and an intensification of the general crisis of capitalism. This definition adds exactly nothing to the fundamental and elementary communist conception of the epoch of imperialism as one of wars and revolutions and capitalist decline which was as true at the Third Congress in 1922 as at the Sixth in 1928. But because it is so general and vague, the definition of the 'Third Period' unanimously endorsed by the Right and Center at the Congress, has also served as the argument of each of these factions against the other since the struggle in the Right-Center bloc began to assume sharper forms.

The Comintern Rights

The Right Wing in the Soviet Union bases itself socially on the state bureaucracy, and the upper crust of the labor aristocracy, and the new possessing classes. It worked out its real perspectives on the international situation and the stabilization in common with the centrist Stalin party apparatus, in the theory of socialism in one country, which is the revision of the international socialist character of the Russian revolution. It implies the stabilization of capitalism for decades, the attempted retreat to the theoretical positions of the party in 1905 (bourgeois revolution). The rights in the Comintern must formulate their outlook less bluntly than the social democracy which expresses its outright belief in the consolidation of capitalism as a progressive historical factor. The tradition of Marx and Lenin is still strong in the Communist masses, and this compels the Rights to proceed in roundabout ways. …

The ultra-left zigzag is represented by the Russian party bureaucracy which is centrist, that is, it swings between social democracy and communism, between the bourgeoisie and the proletariat. The strength of Stalin is in the party apparatus, which however, is more subject to the pressure of the party masses, with their revolutionary traditions of October. Jointly responsible for the opportunist theories and course of the past six years with the Rights, the fear of the influence of the Opposition among the industrial workers and the awakening of their revolutionary class consciousness, has led the Center to advertise a 'swing to the left', a move which is either shadow-boxing or a swing to the left of the Marxist line. The centrist staffs of the parties of the Comintern, subsidized appointees of Stalin, imitate their master closely or follow out instructions implicitly. The centrists seek to extricate themselves from the fruits of their past collaboration with the Rights unsuccessfully because they cannot follow a true Marxist policy without recognizing the monstrous errors committed in the fight against the Leninist Opposition. Hence the obverse side of Stalin's cooperation with Chiang Kai-Shek is the Canton Putsch.

Ultra-Left Adventurism of Centrists

The centrists interpret their 'Third Period' as an almost immediate revolutionary and war situation. The May Day events in Germany were hailed in extravagant terms as a proof of the rising tide of the revolutionary movement. The terms of the call of the Western European Bureau of the Comintern leave little doubt that the First of August was conceived as some sort of dress rehearsal for the insurrection. The Soviet Union is pictured as in danger of imminent attack. Fascism and social democracy are identified without regard for their specific political functions. The social democratic worker is characterized as the most reactionary element of the working class, and the unorganized worker as the most revolutionary. The leftward movement of the working class is monstrously exaggerated. The slogans of 'united front from below' and 'class against class' are used to liquidate the policy of the united front in general and in the trade union work in particular. All warnings are disregarded. ... The results of this ultra-left adventurism are seen clearly in the United States in the isolation of the party in the fight for Gastonia, in the debacle of the left-wing furriers' strike which it was responsible for, in its failure to exercise any influence on the cloak makers stoppage, in the loss of its base in the needle trades in general, in the playing with the idea of a new socialist trades and labor alliance of dual unions, in its inability to maneuver in connection with the new progressive movement in the trade unions. For the real Left in the Comintern, the Communist Opposition, the basic estimate of the epoch given by Lenin remains valid to day as it was several years ago when it began to fight the theory of national socialism. No real Marxist policy can be pursued until the program of the International is cleared of revisionist undergrowth. We recognize more than ever the force of Lenin's dictum that without revolutionary theory there can be no revolutionary practise. The decline of the capitalist system, however, does not proceed in an unbroken curve. The defeats of the proletariat in 1923 helped the capitalists stabilize the system, and gave the social democracy a new lease of life though on a different basis than before 1914. We cannot disregard the fact that the defeats in China, Great Britain have not strengthened but weakened the proletariat. The contradictions of capitalism are again in the process of maturing and not explosion.

Class against Class

The leftward movement of the workers must not be exaggerated. There is such a movement but it still flows in reformist and parliamentary channels. In Europe it is a movement from the bourgeois parties to the social democracy and on a much smaller scale to the communist parties. In the United States it takes the comparatively primitive form of sporadic struggles in the worst paid industries, in a certain revival of progressivism in the trade unions, in scattered signs of labor party sentiment. Our policies must be adapted accordingly. The united front must be our guide to the winning of the masses, and unity must be our slogan in the trade unions even while we proceed legitimately to the organization of the unorganized. The slogan of 'class against class' as issued by the Comintern looks terribly radical but is in reality a reversion to the Lassallean theory of the single reactionary mass outside the industrial workers. A class movement is not created by the use of so general a slogan but on the basis of the concrete needs and demands of the workers in their developing struggles linked up with the final goals. Not 'class against class' but peace, land and bread was the slogan launched by the bolsheviki even in the directly revolutionary crisis of 1917. The period requires concrete programs of action, flowing not only from the revolutionary estimate of the international situation but expressing the specific characteristic and demands of the situation in each country. The senseless confusion of social democracy and fascism must be abandoned. The former play their main role as agents of the bourgeoisie in the peaceful parliamentary period and the fascisti are their arm in the period of direct civil war, and different tactics must be applied in the approach to each. Millions of workers are still in the fold of the social democracy and their leaders have not yet been 'unmasked' to them. The 'united front from below' cannot be regarded as the exclusive legitimate form of the united front. It cannot be any less permissible now than in the days of Lenin to engage in united fronts from 'above' as well as below. ... It is the Opposition that has been fighting all these years for the independent role of the Communist Party in England, in China, and elsewhere. The idea of Workers and Peasants Parties, and Blocs as a substitute for the party should be expunged from the program and strategy of the Comintern.

5 United Front on Unemployment: An Open Letter to the Communist Party[14]

(*Excerpts, 1931*)

Arne Swabeck

Without any let-up, the economic crisis has been hitting deeper and the ranks of the unemployed workers have increased from day to day, with the beginning of 1931 so far showing the very lowest ebb. Consequently, the economic experts and the financiers, in their New Year 'messages', maintained an extremely cautious tone, in everything except their demands for wage-cuts. From the International Labor Bureau at Geneva comes the announcement that the world's unemployed workers today count 20,000,000, the European share being 11,000,000 – on a whole, a rather moderate estimate.

That there has been a constant decrease of jobs in the United States with an almost exactly corresponding growth of breadlines is evident even to the casual observer. The New York Industrial Commissioner, Frances Perkins, reports factory employment in the state hitting the lowest level on record for December since the establishment of the bureau in June 1914. The December Index for factory employment showed 77.5, a drop of 4.1 from November, which is again the largest decline of any single month since 1920. Steel output during December reached its lowest in six years, production for the month being 38.57 percent of capacity. …

Hoover's Promises

Even to the most gullible, the 'optimistic' promises, made at the famous Hoover conferences more than a year ago, to bolster up the waning confidence in this system for initiating large scale industrial 'emergency' undertakings, alleged to be mounting into billions of dollars to alleviate unemployment, should now have proven themselves incontrovertibly as nought. The railroad magnates

14 Swabeck 1931.

stepped up with the largest single item of alleged expansion but at the end of September 1930 showed a drop of employment on all Class A roads of 261,000 jobs: from 1,747,816 to 1,485,906 or 15 percent. Mr. Wolman of Hoover's Unemployment Commission reports a decrease of the number of workers engaged in public works in June 1930 from the same month of the preceding year. All in all sufficient proof of the fact that capitalism in order to maintain its existence needs an industrial reserve army.

Undoubtedly there have been 'valiant' efforts on the part of the capitalist owners of industry to dispose of the large stocks of 'surplus' products on hand together with a curtailment of production in preparation for a revival. Above all, this is expressed in what is politely called 'efforts to reduce cost of production', in other words, to increase the rapacious speed-up system and further reduce wages. The automobile output, for example, has come down to an estimated total of 3,350,000 for the year compared to the 5,350,000 for 1929. Mr. Wiggin, the president of the Chase National Bank, in his New Year's 'message', added his voice to the many other exploiters demanding a further wage reduction.

Most certainly there have been similar 'valiant' efforts by US capitalism in the ferocious struggle for further re-divisions of the world market. One need only cast a glance at the latest South American 'revolutions' made to order by Wall St., and at the proposed silver loan for the stabilization of China; in other words, attempts at saddling part of the burden of American capitalist restitution upon the shoulders of the workers abroad.

Economic Cycles of Capitalist Production

Despite the efforts of the masters of industry, we have now for more than one year been in the midst of this crisis, an inevitable outcome of the cyclic nature of capitalist production constantly proceeding through its course: depression – 'prosperity' to depression again. That this crisis is more convulsive and more deep-going than preceding ones is a natural outgrowth of the developing process of contradiction between increasingly socialized production and individual capitalist appropriation. It is caused mainly by the general decline of imperialist capitalism especially in Europe and the growing interdependence of the world capitalist economy, making the crisis appear almost simultaneously in every capitalist country, and becoming more acute in all its manifestations. It is caused by the immensely increased expansion of productive capacity due to technical application of science to the machinery of production, growing rationalization and speed-up. It is caused [by] the growing standing army of unemployed cast off from industry even during its 'favorable' period when employment decreased despite the increase in production. It is further caused by the growing intensity of the struggle to reduce the working class standard of living as a whole through what is euphemistically called 'reduction of the cost of doing business'. These are some of the main factors in the present situation.

The contradictions of the savage system of capitalist production and rule have increased enormously, becoming of serious portent for the future. First we must register the fact that henceforth we will have in the rich United States a large standing unemployed army creating a central problem for correct Communist policy.

Present Status of Working Class Movement

At the present moment, the outstanding feature of the situation is still the capitalist offensive, the working class attitude being expressed in a distinctly defensive manner. A ferocious slashing of wages, both directly and indirectly, to a point where many standard trade unions are unable to maintain their officially set scale; a murderous increase of the speed-up system, pitting the employed workers against the unemployed; efforts to saddle the scant charity pittances to the 'most needy cases' entirely upon the backs of the workers; brutal dispersal of unemployment and other working class demonstrations, and mass arrests of the Communist vanguard.

Is there as yet an actual working class resistance to this offensive? Unquestionably, there is a growing widespread mass discontent which has not yet assumed concrete forms: the illusions of the capitalist charity crumbs as a solution still prevail; the working class political ideology has not yet reached beyond the boundaries of the capitalist parties but still swings within the sphere of transferring allegiance from the Republicans to the Democrats – here and there growing support to reformism; 1930 shows fewer strikes on record than any year during the past decade despite the drastic wage cuts; there is not yet a mass response to the fight for the unemployed led by the Communist vanguard. In fact, we must record a decided drop in such response once manifested, largely, however, due to the blundering tactics of the Communist Party leadership. In sum and substance the situation presents itself to us at this moment as a downward curve of the working class movement.

From Wrong Estimates Flow Wrong Conclusions

At the very inception of this crisis the bottom fell out entirely from the party leadership's estimate of the general trend and from the tactical policies it pursued, resulting in a constant narrowing down of the movement and preventing the rich potentialities from materializing. Its cry of widespread workers' radicalization, workers' offensive struggle already culminating in a revolutionary upsurge came to nought, shattered upon the rock of realities and further negated by its own inclination toward opportunist distortions of the slogans for immediate demands.

We witnessed in the early part of the struggle the attempts to set up a national organization of unemployed councils, ready made by mere administrative orders from above and within the artificial limitations of the TUUL. It remained confined to the party and circles immediately sympathetic to it, unable to develop roots in the life of the masses. There can, of course, be no other result from this sort of short cut maneuver, which attempts to skip over a whole stage of diligent preparation essential for an actual mass foundation upon which to set the workers into motion and from which alone can spring genuine organization. Correct tactics during the period of the low ebb become the preparations for the flood tide – the rise of the movement. But just as surely, the hitting of a too high key from a note of an entirely fictitious revolutionary upsurge produces a relapse, a setback. In serious matters of revolutionary politics from this relapse flows the inevitable consequence – downward sliding. This became expressed in the opportunist tendency of the party leadership to concentrate almost exclusively on the slogan of relief, embodied in a spurious 'unemployment relief bill'. Further, in a collection of signatures for the bill, also to be presented to congress, turning the workers' attention in that direction and to that extent away from the powerful dynamics of mass struggle.

Playing into the Hands of Reformism

Is it surprising that the party leadership found itself in a position unable to make any other distinction from social, liberal and ordinary bourgeois reformers, also framing 'relief bills', except the vulgar opportunism of the amount of dollars and cents demanded for each worker per week? Next the leadership even reduced its original demand for $25.00 weekly benefit per worker to $15.00, putting it exactly on a par with a similar 'bill' for $15.00 per week now proposed by a newly organized New York committee representing civic, social welfare groups and conservative trade union leaders. Such a policy will in no way serve as preparation for the next stage, for the coming upturn in the movement for active resistance to the capitalist offensive. It cannot mobilize the workers under the Communist banner but on the contrary helps to put new life into an otherwise rather feeble social reformism.

In the revolutionary movement there is no escape from the inevitable logic of erroneous policies. A general strategy which runs counter to the basic curve of the specific period leads to a continuous decimating of the forces available. In this respect matters stand not any better with the hunger marches of unemployed now initiated by the party leadership. The very slogan itself, hunger march, is wrong, as it leads, even under the best of circumstances, to a separation of the unemployed, from the employed. With the objective of marching to reinforce the demand for the fifteen bucks weekly relief, however, just as glibly promised by the civic reformers and pursuing methods which deliberately make the small Communist vanguard an easy target for police dispersion, we must not be surprised at the working masses remaining passive bystanders. Thus there are very good reasons why, despite the splendid prerequisites for the beginning of a real proletarian movement, this negative result is all that the balance sheet can show to date.

The next immediate future will undoubtedly bring a further rise of prerequisites of a class movement of the American workers. The low ebb will be followed by an upward curve of workers reassembling their forces, entering into active resistance and gradually assuming the offensive. With this in view the problem of the Communist movement of correct revolutionary policy becomes a seriously pressing matter.

What Must be Done?

Facing a coming crucial period of an upward turn, our mass activities must be of such a nature as to effectively prepare for its success, give the correct direction for the working class struggle and establish Communist leadership. This means, first of all, a correct evaluation of the present defensive character of the movement; secondly, it means a correct program for today and in anticipation of the next steps, when fighting for immediate demands, a sharpening of the general line of demarcation from reformism. Concretely the following points must be emphasized:

1. It is absolutely necessary to make clear the general object and limitations of immediate partial demands and not to arithmetically add new demands for every ill of the present situation appearing as solutions

in themselves, such ends only in reformism pure and simple. Partial demands for partial objectives are advanced by the Communists essentially for the purpose of setting the workers into motion against their class enemy and in such a way that the struggle will lead ever more toward the revolutionary goal. In this unemployment situation, with its slashing capitalist offensive, particularly the demands which unite the unemployed with the employed and prepare for a working class offensive. We must make clear that partial demands are never advanced by Communists in the reformist sense of being in themselves a solution, we must say definitely: 'There is no solution to the unemployment problem under capitalism'.

2. Based upon the above considerations the demand for the six-hour day without any reduction in pay must become the central immediate demand. It should be clear that this demand has the widest base of appeal and tends the most directly to set into motion and embrace unitedly both the unemployed and employed workers. As a direct slogan of action it can become a very effective means of preparation for the working class offensive in the next stage.
3. Other demands to be linked up with this most outstanding one should be formulated not from the view of having as many as possible, seemingly covering every need, but from the view of becoming definite rallying points. For example:
    a. Immediate unemployment relief from the bosses and their government;
    b. Extension of large-scale credits to the Soviet Union. The last mentioned demand has a particularly direct bearing on the world aspect of unemployment and furnishes a means of cementing the natural interests between the Soviet Union and the world proletariat.
    c. The forms, methods and tactics applied in the agitation struggle for the unemployed are of as equally vital importance and can become correct only when thoroughly inspired by serious efforts toward a broad united front basis. The hunger marches must be made demonstrations in which all workers can participate and further fight jointly for their common interests under the proper broad slogans. It is necessary to effect a reorganization of the unemployed councils genuinely on a united front foundation. Especially should serious efforts be made to include the existing trades unions and working class organizations even to the extent of such whose leadership, in an effort to offset possible rank and file revolts, pretends to be championing the needs of the unemployed. Efforts toward a

correct Leninist united front policy includes in particular the direct approach to the rank and file through the workshops, the breadlines, the union meetings but also the formal approach to the organizations officially.

d. Above all it is necessary for Communists to draw the complete revolutionary implications of the unemployment struggle. To tie up the agitation for the immediate needs in an indissoluble bond with the struggle for the socialist revolution and in such a manner that each step for the realization of the former becomes progressively a step toward this final goal, is an inescapable duty of the Communist movement.

6 'The Red Army Sings the International Sometimes When It is Not Absolutely Necessary'[15]

(*Excerpts, 1933*)

James P. Cannon to Vincent Ray Dunne

I received your letter of December 26 in which you enclosed the big half of your rather heavy installment on the expenses of the international delegate.[16] Thanks to the prompt and resolute motion at Minneapolis and a similar one here in New York we can say now that Arne's [Swabeck] departure is assured, and that it will not be delayed. The boycott of the Shachtman Clique on this project up to day has been complete – not one of them has contributed a cent. But in spite of this our delegate will be on the boat in the very near future. You see, it does look as though some of the boys are getting mad and are not only taking off their coats but also their shirts. That's a bad sign for the people who started the trouble. Your letter, with the enclosure, made a stirring impression here. We know well enough that the money you are digging up is like so much

15 Cannon 1933a.

16 Up to 1933 the Communist League of America's contact with Trotsky and the International Left Opposition in Europe had been monopolized by Shachtman and his group. Trotsky was disappointed in Shachtman's performance in 1930, when Trotsky, his movements restricted, had instructed Shachtman to promote his views at an April 1930 conference where it was hoped that the German and French sections of the International Left Opposition would consolidate an organizational presence. This failed to happen, and Trotsky indicted Shachtman for the failure, disappointed that his American comrade could not transcend cliquism, promote the programmatic positions of the Left Opposition, and follow through on political assignments. In May 1932 Trotsky wrote publicly to the League referring to 'the false and damaging positions of Comrade Shachtman on all the international questions, almost without exception'. [Trotsky to CLA, 19 May 1932, in Breitman and Lovell (eds.) 1973, p. 98]. It was in the aftermath of this development, and in the context of worsening League factionalism, that the Cannon majority proposed sending Arne Swabeck to Europe to engage in discussions with Trotsky, and for Cannon to take over Swabeck's position as National Secretary. The Shachtman group opposed Swabeck going to Europe with especial vehemence [Eds.].

skin peeled off your own frame. It makes a fellow feel like doing a little better than his best with this kind of support.

The confirmation of our judgment in the question of the international delegate, and of the complete falsity of the attempt first to defeat it and then to sabotage it, has come with a suddenness that is rather terrific. We have just received a circular from the International Secretariat to the effect that the *Copenhagen delegation* (i.e. the Old Man and those who were there with him) had proposed a *Preliminary International Conference* for the purpose of preparing for the formal International Conference which is scheduled. The Secretariat, with the European sections assenting, unanimously agreed to the proposal, the Preliminary Conference is called AND WE ARE CALLED ON TO SEND OUR DELEGATE RIGHT AWAY! ... In other words, the decision of the NC on the whole matter *anticipated* just what was done or attempted to be done at Copenhagen and our action paralleled the action taken abroad. ... Those who represented our proposal for a preliminary conference as some kind of a bureaucratic outrage against the membership will now have to explain why the whole international organization has acted on the same lines *as a matter of course.* Well, those Minneapolis Shachtmans and those New York Cowls will learn in good time that it is not sufficient for a faction to be noisy and venomous; it is necessary once in a while to be right.

In view of the crisis in the organization, and of the necessity now for everyone to put everything he has into the scale, I have decided to return to full-time work for the League when Arne leaves. As soon as I get through some preliminary work in the office I intend to take to the road again, and you can expect to see me in Minneapolis before the winter is over. It isn't exactly a 'propitious' time for a man to take a chance – or rather, to compel his family to take a chance – on economic survival as a professional worker for the League. *The Militant* is on the rocks, we are in the worst financial straits we have been for a long time, the work is disorganized by the worst kind of an internal fight, and most of our members are out of work and unable to contribute. But in spite of that, or rather just because of that, I have come to the conclusion, after careful deliberation, that it has to be done in order to accelerate the solution of the crisis and point the League toward its really great tasks and opportunities. I mean the decision seriously and will not turn back. All that I ask is that those who also mean things seriously go along with me and do their part in their own way.

The last time I gave up private employment and went to work for the movement was in the Spring of 1919 at the height of the post-war anti-Red hysteria. The period of professional work for the movement commenced then lasted for ten straight years and a few months over. Let us hope that the present enlistment will not be shorter.

You will probably be hearing about the Morgenstern case, if you have not heard already. Morgenstern's statement and the statement of the NC will be sent out shortly. The night Morgie got out of prison his family induced him to go through a marriage ceremony with a Rabbi officiating at the home of his Father. Morgie was present at the last meeting of the NC and presented a statement on the matter. He said he had done it in a moment of sentimental weakness to gratify his parents who had never had much joy out of him; that he recognized the seriousness of the mistake; that he did not intend in the slightest way any reconciliation with bourgeois ideology and religious superstitions; that he considered the act as a contradiction to everything he had done since he joined the movement at the age of 17; that he recognized that he had compromised his position as a leading comrade and wanted to resign from the NC in order not to compromise it; and that he was willing to accept any decision the NC would make in his case and that he wanted a chance to make good the mistake by his future work in the ranks.

Strangely enough, this manly and straightforward statement did not please Shachtman and Abern. They appeared to be not in the least interested in helping a comrade with a really splendid record in the movement to make good an error. They want to kill Morgenstern and, through him, to strike at others – so one must judge their statements that, in spite of his record and his statement that meets every reasonable demand the NC could make, he should be expelled from the League. In any case they demanded that he be suspended for one year. This we refused, and they say our refusal is prompted by 'factional protection' which 'will be so much the worse for us'. The decision of the NC is a statement condemning the action of Morgenstern and explaining the principle reasons therefor; an acceptance of his resignation as an alternate member of the NC; and a declaration that Morgenstern's past record and his present stand entitle him to the opportunity to make good the error as a member of the League. We will have to pay for this decision, for the case of a comrade being married by a Rabbi is a case made to order for demagogy. On such an issue they will muster the votes of those people whose chief recommendation is that they were not married by a Rabbi and were married instead by a police magistrate.

... we do not intend to make any concessions to such a lynching spirit in this case, or in any other case. The height of a faction fight is just as good a time as any to teach the new members by example that leaders worthy of the name must not only be politically-minded, but must also be honest and not afraid of demagogy.

One might ask why the derelictions of Morgenstern, which are purely individual and isolated, can be grabbed up so eagerly as an 'issue', and why people who maintained an unruffled indifference to such overshadowing questions as the international resolution can work up such a lather about it. The explanation, of course, lies in the inescapable logic of a faction that is not grounded on principle. Having no principle political differences, or not daring to bring them forward and defend them, they must resort to all kinds of personal issues. Hence the campaigns against Cannon, against [Sam] Gordon, against Swabeck, etc., with all kinds of accusations that are true or false, mostly false, but in any case personal and not fundamentally political. They grabbed the Morgenstern-Rabbi issue because they *need* such an issue and need it badly. What they need on top of that is a good case of 'white chauvinism'[17] around which they can conduct a campaign and demand a mass trial of the culprit provided of course that he does not belong to their clique.

At the last meeting S and A presented a motion for a national conference for 1 May. They think, on the basis of the vote against the co-optations,[18] and

17 Cannon was referring to the show trials conducted by the American Stalinists around charges of 'white chauvinism', the preeminent example of which was the Harlem Yokinen trial detailed in the Communist Party pamphlet *Race Hatred on Trial* (1931). No doubt racism existed among Communist Party members, and among Left Opposition members. Cannon's position, however, was that such racism was best challenged, combatted, and eradicated in 'a calm atmosphere; an atmosphere free from demagogy, hypocrisy and incitement; an atmosphere created by teachers of the proletariat, not by terrorizers'. See Cannon 1931 [Eds.].

18 Co-optation refers to attempts by both factions in the League, the Cannon majority and the Shachtman minority, to maintain or secure a majority position on the New York resident National Committee by co-opting comrades on to the NC who would vote with the specific faction in question. Shachtman initiated the tactic in 1931, as international issues became particularly factionally intense and Shachtman proposed to absent himself from the NC to travel in Europe, reporting for *The Militant* on developments in Spain and working with emerging Left Opposition groups, especially one in England. To offset his absence from New York and NC votes, Shachtman proposed that Morris Lewit, editor of the League's Jewish publication, *Unser Kamp*, and a dedicated Shachtman faction supporter who had, in 1930, used his wages as a skilled plumber to finance a Shachtman European tour to touch base with Trotsky, be co-opted on to the NC. Cannon successfully opposed the move. Then, as factional line-ups hardened in the months leading up to the June 1932 CLA National Committee Plenum, Cannon overplayed his authority by proposing a blatant factional co-optation of three of his trusted allies to the NC: Louis Basky, Sam Gordon, and George Clarke. Because such co-optations were highly irregular, taking place outside of the appropriate deliberations of a National Conference, Cannon proposed submitting the enlargement of the NC to a national referendum of the CLA membership. The move backfired, and Shachtman, Abern, and others effectively mobilized opposition, resulting in a vote of 59 in favor of Cannon's co-optations, 65 against, and 10 abstaining. Complicating the issue was that one of Cannon's candidates for co-optation, Gordon, did

the resolutions against the sending of an international delegate, that they can count on a majority. Their usual superficiality is playing them another trick here. They will find that quite a few comrades who voted against the co-optations for one reason or another do not mean by that to turn the League over to Shachtman and Abern to play with. ... We are for the conference, as before, and so decided, but we specified that the date be set only after the conference documents are ready, so that there will be adequate time for the discussion both here and in other sections. That will probably require at least three months after the adoption of the documents. Therefore the conference will hardly be possible by May 1st – probably a month or two later. The July 4th week looks most feasible. This will also give time for the return of the international delegate. Wouldn't it be absurd for an organization that prides itself on internationalism first of all and above all to rush through a conference, after all that has happened since the Plenum, without waiting for the report of its international delegate and without giving the other sections a chance to express their opinions?

I don't think we will have any cause to regret our action in sending an international delegate at this time nor our selection of the person. Among all those who have been pushing and crowding forward on international missions of various kinds, both before our expulsion from the party and since, there is hardly one that has a better claim to the honor than Swabeck. A founder of the party, a prominent worker for Communism from the inception of the movement in America, an outstanding militant in the trade union movement – how many who sit in the international conference, outside the Russian delegation, will be able to show a longer or better record? Not many, if any and I venture to say that the international comrades will get a far more serious impression of our League though him than they have had before.

... They talk about Swabeck as though Swabecks grew on bushes for any fool with a stick to knock down. Shachtman is the inspirer of this thoroughly rotten tendency. It was he who set in motion the theory about the 'degeneration' of the 'old guard' and blinded the young comrades to the importance of past records and present performance on the part of those who had passed the 'age limit'. Well, we can be sure this diseased sentiment will not have any lasting influence. And when we overcome it let us make sure that we have set up some barriers against its reappearance.

---

not meet the League's constitutional requirements for NC membership, which stipulated a minimum of four years in the communist movement and two years in the CLA. The vote against Cannon's proposed co-optations in 1932 is what is referred to above [Eds.].

... The red army sings the Internationale sometimes when it is not absolutely necessary, or so it seemed to me when I was visiting the army camps. It keeps up the spirit. The spirit which must animate the vanguard now is the spirit of unrelenting struggle to raise the League out of the crisis and set it on the road to the fulfillment of its great historic mission.

7 'The Knife is at Their Throat'[19]

(Excerpts, 1933)

Max Shachtman to Maurice Spector

... 1. The decision of the branch on the Swabeck *luxuereise* did not come too soon, but it is highly satisfactory. Be assured that I understand the position you're in with regard to the score of new comrades who can but too easily be disheartened by being plunged into what is at first blush a rather obscure internal dispute. New York, Boston, Chicago, Youngstown, and Toronto – the distinct majority of the membership – have now registered their protests against this plan; but it appears that Cannon and Swabeck intend to go through with it at all costs – and one of the costs may quite likely be the weekly *Militant*. The latter is, as you will have gathered, hanging by a thread now and the somewhat dubious office management which has brought about the crisis is being veiled behind the age-old charge of factional sabotage on our parts. The sabotage presumably consists in my devoting seven months now to full-time work without one single penny of wages; Lewit's and Bleeker's full-time work on *Unser Kampf* for a year now without having drawn a *sou*; and the fact that our friends in the New York branch are not only the heaviest, but virtually the sole important financial contributors in the organization. If my skin were not so impervious to the venom of Cannon, I would feel more outraged at the insolence of the man who makes the charges against us, but who never distinguished himself by his sacrifice for the movement, as we recall ....

2. The Morgenstern case came up at the last Committee meeting, where I finally made the motion for his suspension from the League for a year, emphasizing that were there a normal situation I would have moved for his expulsion, even as he had himself expelled two comrades from the Philadelphia Young Communist League years ago for no greater a crime against Communism – marriage by a religious ceremony. Cannon presented a lengthy resolution. It must be read to the very bottom before you realize that M. is not being praised for his act, but ... condemned. No action is taken against him beyond the harmless 'censure'. His 'voluntary' resignation from the Committee (continued member-

19 Shachtman 1933.

ship would have been too much, don't you think?!) was accepted. The scandal is made worse by the fact that throughout the trial it seemed that not Morgenstern, but Shachtman, had to be investigated and punished! At the end, Cannon launched into a declamation for the benefit of the gallery assembled outside the door. When he reached the exclamation: 'You shall not lynch our comrade Morgenstern!' (Yes, literally!), I said: 'Save your campaign speeches for the proper occasion, Cannon. You're in the National Committee now!' I could almost hear the applause from outside the door. This clear-cut case of Tammany protection for 'one of the boys', accompanied by a stink-bomb offensive against those who demanded simple Communist procedure in his case, will not serve to increase Cannon's prestige, or that of his 'revolutionary kernel', Morgenstern included.

3. Our most important problem now is the National Conference. … we presented a demand at the last meeting for a conference on May 1. It was voted down in favor of Cannon's motion 'endorsing the idea' of a conference on St. Nimmerlein's Tag, which means absolutely nothing. The post-plenum discussion results were a grievous disappointment to Cannon and he realizes his weak position. The muttered threats of a split in the event that the 'Communist group' (I must enlighten you: Cannon means himself) is in the minority, continue to be peddled in the corridors. We took action on the Conference only after thoroughly sober reflection, be sure. Morris [Lewit] and Sylvia [Bleeker] brought back a careful report from the various branches, and the demand is universal – without a single exception. You will err to think that Cannon made any progress in the land with his campaign about 'Landauism' etc. To the contrary, it proved a boomerang, and the decisive results on the co-optations (you are correct about his having blundered seriously on this score) will indicate that I am right. Take St. Louis, for instance. They voted against the co-optations. Then Goldberg, under a misapprehension about a whispered report about what Chicago was going to do, prevailed upon the local comrades to vote *for* the co-optations. He explained craftily to Morris that it was done in order to give Cannon a false impression about his strength; this would impel him to call a conference in the expectation of 'winning'; St. Louis would appear on the scene with a delegate vowed to trounce the Cannon faction! If you stop laughing long enough at this naïve Machiavellianism, you will see that the aims, at any rate, of the St. Louis comrades are laudable. Chicago, now, on its own initiative, has unanimously adopted a resolution (which we proposed to the Committee to endorse, but which it did not) calling for a Conference on May 1, and John [Edwards] and Al [Glotzer] are staunchly for it. So is Cowl; so are our two comrades who built the Davenport branch; so is Boston; so is Angelo, who supports us; so are the great bulk of the New York comrades.

Will the Conference be another June Plenum? I more than doubt it. If I had any idea that would repeat the wretched events of the Plenum, I would continue to oppose the idea. I have held off with my agreement to a Conference for two reasons, neither of which holds water any longer: 1) the Plenum atmosphere created by Cannon, which has now completely worn off; not even Cannon seeks any longer to do much exploiting of my 1931 visit to Europe and the complications surround it. And how could he, and what results would he obtain? It *is* a bit tedious to have dinned into your ears the worn echoes of a dispute that originated a year or a year and a half ago, and the comrades don't pay much attention to it. It will appear at a Conference only as a sadly decomposed wraith. 2) my uncertainty about a staff with which to replace the present 'leading kernel' – a most important question, for what political indictment of the present leadership can be presented without following it with inevitable organizational proposals and alternatives? Here too the situation has improved considerably. I believe that Marty [Abern] is now prepared to take the place in the work which properly belongs to him; all the comrades have commented on the fact that his activities have increased considerably, and during the branch elections there was a spontaneous demand from the New York membership that he take the post of organizer instead of Oehler, who has proved to be not only factional but incompetent. We resisted the demand not so much on Marty's account but because of our desire to cooperate as much as possible, and not to leave ourselves open to the demagogic charge of 'removals'. As for a new National Committee, there is timber aplenty in our group, and of an infinitely superior quality to the saplings and petrified redwood proposed in the late referendum. There are not only Marty, Al, Edwards, you and I, but also Lewit and Jack Weber, a comrade I am desirous of proposing for the next Committee. He has not been in the League for the period required by the Constitution, that is true; but his case in no way resembles Gordon's. Weber is not only a highly intelligent, well-informed, well-poised scholar, but a man of considerable experience in the movement. Engineer by profession, he has been in the movement for two decades at least, to my knowledge. He taught in the Rand School in his old S.P. days; entered the Communist movement at the very outset; joined the opposition some while ago. Interestingly enough, Cannon sent him into our group! That is, after his first visits with Cannon at the time he joined the League, he sized up the man with uncanny accuracy. He stands high in the eyes of the New York comrades and his articles (even if they are drawn out) on Japan have aroused considerable interest concerning himself. If I draw so long a portrait, it is only to acquaint you more intimately with a well-balanced and reliable comrade whom you find it a pleasure to meet and for whom you will feel no need to apologize if he joins you on a National Committee.

... The self-satisfied office-chair squatting which form the beginning and end of Swabeck's horizon, and Cannon's for that matter, is compelling the League to stagnate in its own tiny pool. We propose to draw up a resolution, separate from the general theses on which formal agreement is so easy to reach, dealing with the 'Internal Situation and the Next Tasks of the League', or words to that effect. It will be an arraignment of the whole inner-course and the methods of the leadership of the Cannon group. This is not a 'political question' in the grammar-school definition of the terms adhered to by Oehler; but it is nevertheless of the highest significance for the League at the present time. Cannon has established a regime in the League – I am not throwing around the word loosely – which is *mutatis mutandis* on a par with Landau's. Perorations on principle for the purpose of executing unprincipled games; the arbitrary suppression of minority views (failure to issue an internal bulletin during the discussion; suppression of our lengthy pre-Plenum statement; refusal to send out our concluding word on the post-Plenum discussion; bureaucratic prohibition against attending 'Weisbord's meetings'; failure to provide Saul and Carter with an opportunity to defend their views in the discussion on a national scale, etc., etc.); the artificial exacerbation of disputes and the manufacture of 'differences' where they do not exist ('our fundamental differences on policy with the Boston branch' – a new song from the Cannon repertory); the paralyzing of the New York branch with factional intrigue and disruption, simply because it burns no incense at Cannon's shrine, and the impeding of the work in Toronto for the same good reason – all this and much more from the voluminous catalogue created by Cannon in the last year alone, will constitute an arraignment against which he will have to draw to the very bottom of the wells of cunning for a reply. At the same time, we intend to present in the same pre-Conference statement a positive criticism of the stagnation of the League and our proposals that the League strike out boldly on a course which will enable it to quit its present circle existence and slough off the elements who thrive on such an existence (Cannon, by the way, exemplified them), gaining by that new recruits who will more than make up for the dubious losses.

The internal situation has reached the stage where to desist from a Conference will only render the difficulties more acute. It is either or! We must accept the inevitability of a Cannon incubus in the leadership, plus a sniping criticism here and there, now and then; or else we must challenge it openly. I am determined on the latter. Remember this: if we emerged from the Plenum to our present position despite the handicaps which you refer to with such painful accuracy, it is a sign not of our weakness, but of our strength.

Now that Cannon, despite his previous boasts that he would agree to a conference the minute the minority demanded it, has voted down our proposal, we intend to exercise our constitutional right to demand it from the membership directly. The statutes provide that it can be convoked by the Executive Committee or membership of branches representing the majority of the League. This can and should be done – but done promptly, else our objective will not be obtained. Chicago is already recorded unanimously. Boston will vote this week on it. New York will undoubtedly carry our motion tomorrow night. So will St. Louis, Cleveland, Youngstown and Davenport. If Toronto throws its vote into the balance, the knife is at their throat. …

8 Unite to Smash Fascism! Forward to Communist Unity and Common Action of All Working-Class Organizations[20]

(*Excerpts, 1933*)

Joseph Carter

The Communist International's silence has been broken. For over three and a half years the Left Opposition led by Comrade Trotsky has been hammered, persistently and loudly, for a Marxian program against the growing danger of Fascism in Germany. We made this the center of all our agitation and propaganda. The tactic of the united front of the Communist Party, Social Democratic party, and the trade unions was urged as the unifying method which would wield the working masses against the enemy which threatens all.

The Left Opposition's proposals were called 'counter-revolutionary'. Our struggle against the false theory of 'social fascism' and the 'united front from below' has won for us the epithet of 'Left social Fascist'. But epithets solve nothing. Life itself has vindicated the analyses of the Bolshevik-Leninists.

Hitler has come to power. The working-class organizations are being destroyed. Communist and Socialist workers are being murdered. It must be said openly that the treacherous policies of the Stalinist leaders of the Communist movement combined with the criminal tactics of the Social Democracy are responsible for this situation.

As early as January of last year Comrade Trotsky wrote: 'The about-face of the Stalinists is inevitable'. … 'The correctness of our position will become apparent in action with each passing day. When the ceiling overhead bursts into flame, the most stubborn bureaucrats must need forget about prestige. Even genuine privy councilors, in such situations, jump out of windows in their underwear. The pedagogy of facts will come to the assistance of our criticism' (*What Next?* Pages 182–184).

Valuable time has been lost. The theory of the Stalinists, originated by the big chief himself, that Fascism and Social Democracy are 'twin brothers', the latter being social Fascists, that is Fascists who use Socialist phrases, made it

20 Carter 1933.

impossible for the Communists to utilize the differences between the two. The elementary fact that Fascism means the destruction of all organizations based on the working class, including Social Democracy, was overlooked. Instead, at a time when Fascism was growing and as late as the Twelfth Plenum of the Executive Committee of the Communist International (Sept. 1932) and later, the view was expounded that Social Democracy must be smashed **first**, before the **immediate** Fascist danger could be crushed.

In 1929 William Pieck, one of the leaders of the German Communist Party wrote: 'Social Democracy has become an integral part of the State apparatus and is growing more and more ripe **to play the chief part should a Fascist form of government be established'**. … A few months later, Thaelmann proclaimed … 'it is very difficult to maintain the line of separation between the development of a social Fascist dictatorship, when it has reached the stage, as in Germany, of a social democratic government using the most reactionary weapons of violence and the methods of Fascist dictatorship'. …

How could a united front of the Communist and Social Democratic parties be proposed under such conditions? It was impossible.

The 'united front from below under revolutionary leadership' was offered to the Social Democratic workers, who for a time were called 'social Fascists'! It is obvious that if the socialist workers were ready to follow Communist leadership they would not be members of the Social Democratic party!

Still more. Manuilsky proclaimed at the XI Plenum of the Communist International (1931) that: 'Fascism in Germany, in the Hitler form, may be on the downgrade, and in fact, is already on the downgrade as a result of the activity of our party'. … The danger, we were told, was that 'the bourgeois dictatorship in Germany is taking Fascist forms under … Social Democracy'. The Fascist danger was seen everywhere except where it really existed. …

Several months later [in March 1933] … a dispatch to the *New York Times* … [reported] that the Comintern had proposed to the Socialist and Labor International a united front of the two organizations, internationally and on a national scale, against German Fascism. … The Stalinists in North America could not believe that a change could be made so soon!

But lo and behold the next day's issue of the *Freiheit* and the March 18 number of the *Daily Worker* reprint the entire manifesto of the Communist International [calling for a new united front]. … These people who have lost all revolutionary self-respect and independence know on which side their bread is buttered. Years of servility to Stalinist bureaucracy had corrupted them. Servility is their paramount 'virtue'. …

The manifesto itself attempts to cover up the previous policies of the Communist International. It is made to appear as though this is only the latest of a series of such proposals. But what has become of the theories that 'national and social Fascism are being fused', that the Social Democracy must be destroyed **first** ....

So-called United Front Proposals

Two proposals of the German Communist Party to the Social Democracy are cited as instances of offers of the united front. Even if this were so, it would be in complete violation with all the theories and practices of Stalinism.

In both cases they were in the form of ultimatums. On July 20, 1932, when Von Papen took power, the party issued a general strike call and urged the Social Democratic Party and the trade unions to join in. **The central bodies were not approached.** It was a continuation of the 'united front from below under revolutionary leadership'. The Socialist workers did not respond. The strike call was answered only by the more revolutionary masses. It failed.

When Hitler seized power another general strike call was issued – with no previous preparation through united front action with the Social Democratic party and the trade unions on the basis of a concrete minimum program as the Left Opposition had proposed. Even if the central committees of these organizations had been approached – as the manifesto claims despite contrary reports at the time in the party press – it was in an ultimatist manner, either you accept the general strike on January 31st or ... The Socialist workers would not be won for such a policy. The proof: the strike was a miserable failure.

Proposals of Manifesto

In its practical proposals the manifesto merely repeats sections of the program of the Left Opposition: 'Carry out definite actions against the attacks of Fascism and reaction on the political, trade union, co-operative and other organizations of the workers ...'. We read further [however, that] 'the Communist International considers it possible to recommend the Communist parties during the time of common fight against capital and Fascism ... **refrain from making attacks on Social Democratic organizations ...**'.

What is meant by 'refrain from making attacks on Social-Democratic organization?' Surely it cannot mean physical attacks ... In reality it means a 'non-aggression pact!' No criticism while in action, no recollection of the crimes of the Social Democracy! ...

What it signifies is temporary fusion, organic unity rather than united front between the Communist and Socialist organizations. The present leaders of the Communist International are not alien to such practices. During the Chinese revolution, the British General Strike, in the anti-war struggle, such was and is [their] policy.

The Communists, while maintaining a discipline of action in the united front, retain their political identity not merely in words but in deeds. The struggle for the defeat of Fascism is a step to winning the workers for a Soviet Germany. In this struggle the programs of social democracy and Communism are counterposed. The worker will be able to choose between the two. To refrain from attacking the Socialist organizations in this sense is false and treacherous. The statement in the manifesto and all it implies, on this score, must be fought by all revolutionary workers.

The Left Opposition welcomes the turn of the Communist International in its proposal for a united front with the Socialist organizations. But the turn is not sufficient.

An honest and complete condemnation of the false theories of the CI is essential. Party democracy must be restored. The Communist International must be regenerated. The Left Opposition and all honest expelled Communists must be reinstated into the Communist parties to insure the process. The press of the Communist International must be thrown open for thorough discussions of the problems confronting the movement, particularly Germany.

The Soviet Union is in Danger!

Above all, the party of the Soviet Union must be regenerated. … At a time when the material resources of the Soviet Union, and particularly its Red Army, should be mobilized in case of Fascist onslaught and be ready to reply to a call of the German proletariat, the workers' dictatorship is being threatened by serious and immediate internal dangers. The fortress of the world revolution, the Soviet Union, is in danger.

The Left Opposition raises with a thousand fold emphasis the demand for the return of comrade Trotsky and the Russian Bolshevik-Leninists to their rightful place at the head of the Russian party and the Soviet Union. The Communist workers must take up this demand in their party and the YCL units, at membership meetings, in the press.

For Communist Unity

The revolutionary youth in and around the Young Communist League must reject the cynical, light-minded, wise guy, attitude towards the German events. In the United States we must put pressure on the leaders of the official Communist movement for a genuine turn, for the regeneration of the Communist International.

...

The working-class and student youth must be mobilized into a powerful united front movement of Communist, Socialist, and non-party workers against German Fascism and the capitalist offensive. Above all it is necessary to sound the alarm in the ranks of the organized Communist and Left-wing movements. There is little time left. Events are moving with giant speed. *Tomorrow* may be too late. Act now!

9 For A New Party and a New International[21]

(*Excerpts, 1933*)

National Committee, Communist League of America

After the ignominious collapse of both Social Democracy and the Communist International in Germany, and the subsequent inability of both these organizations to draw any lessons from this historical catastrophe, it is impossible any longer to conceal the fact that a revolutionary organization of the proletariat capable of leading it to victory does not exist. It must be created anew. …

From this time onward the Communist League of America ceases to regard itself as a faction of the official Stalinist party, which has become a direct brake on the development of the workers' movement, and invites the cooperation of all revolutionary workers, regardless of their present affiliation or non-affiliation, in common efforts leading to the construction of a genuine communist party in America.

Taking the necessity to create a new party as the point of departure, the Communist League proposes a frank and comradely discussion with other individual groups and organizations, aiming toward the same goal, and submits for their consideration the following points:

American Perspectives

Under the terrific pressure of the crisis years, the conditions have been rapidly maturing for the class awakening of the American workers and for an enormous acceleration of the class struggle. In the next period, the social contradictions will explode in a series of gigantic class battles, in the course of which the workers can assimilate the revolutionary lessons in an abridged form and rapidly leap forward on the path toward revolutionary action. To assist and guide this process, a new party, wresting the banner of communism from the sabotaging bureaucratic clique of Stalinism, must be created. …

21 Communist League of America, National Committee 1933.

Fundamental Principles

… [T]he new party can come into existence, take shape, and grow up to the requirements of its historic task, only if it stands on a firm programmatic foundation and tolerates no conciliation toward reformist and centrist currents. For this program no new revelation is needed. The revolutionary teachings of Marx and Engels … are the fundamental principled guide to the new party.

The first four Congresses of the Comintern, conducted under the leadership of Lenin and Trotsky, have concretized these teachings and applied them, in a series of unsurpassed theses and resolutions, to the basic problems of our epoch. The ten-year struggle of the International Left Opposition (Bolshevik-Leninist), during which the guiding ideas of the first four Congresses of the Comintern were carried forward and counterposed on each and every important question of the living movement to the degenerating course of Stalinism, have been summarized in the eleven points adopted by the International Preconference of the Left Opposition. …

For Revolutionary Internationalism – Against the Theory of Socialism in One Country

The theoretical source of the degeneration and final downfall of the Communist International and its national sections, including the American, was the rejection of the Marxist principle of revolutionary internationalism and its substitution by the theory of socialism in one country. The Communist movement, which has been destroyed by this reactionary nationalist theory, cannot arise again without a clear and categorical rejection of it.

Defense of the Soviet Union

The ten-year regime of Stalinism has strangled the party and the workers' organizations in the Soviet Union and has facilitated enormously the danger of a counterrevolutionary capitalist overthrow. The Stalinist regime has undermined the foundation of the Soviet state and is leading it toward destruction. The social content of the October revolution, however, is still alive and, by its property character, which is a decisive criterion, the Soviet Union remains, even with the monstrous bureaucratic distortion, a workers' state.

The defense of the Soviet Union, encircled by a world of class enemies and systematically weakened from within by the Stalinist regime, is the unconditional duty of the international proletariat. The formation of new parties and a new International does not contradict this task but is necessitated by it. The *reform* of the Soviet workers' state in the USSR and its defense against capitalist intervention and *counterrevolution*, now depend upon the formation of strong revolutionary organizations in the capitalist countries, which will be capable of putting up a revolutionary resistance at home to capitalistic military ventures, and of exerting pressure on the internal regime in the USSR and influence the Soviet proletariat. …

But it is precisely in the task of defending the Soviet Union at the moment of danger that the present Stalinist parties are most completely impotent. … The internal reform and regeneration of the Soviet state and its defense against world imperialism, is the joint task of the new parties in the capitalist countries and the Soviet Union.

The United Front

From its inception, and also in the process of its formation, which may be more or less prolonged, the new party will naturally take part in the living movement of the working class and employ therein the tactic of the united front. This tactic, which presupposes temporary agreements with reformist organizations for specific actions, requires a categorical rejection of the theory of 'social fascism' and the 'united front from below only'. On the one hand, the new party should conduct negotiations and make temporary agreements with the official representatives of reformist organizations when they take a step forward under the pressure of the masses – a tactic which the Stalinists have rejected 'in principle'. And on the other hand, it will reject any proposals for a 'non aggression pact' excluding criticism – which the Stalinists have accepted.

Trade Union Policy

The new party will find its road to the masses and gain influence over their movement only on the condition that it follows a Marxist policy on the trade union question, that is, the most important question of the American movement. Such a policy requires a penetration of the workers' mass organizations as they exist in reality, regardless of the form, and at the same time an irreconcilable struggle against the capitalist agents within them. The Stalinist dogma of 'red' paper unions and the opportunistic policy of 'adaptation' to the reactionary leadership in the trade union movement are equally pernicious.

Against the Right-Wing Apologists of Stalinism

The new party cannot represent a mechanical combination of 'opposition' groups, but will be obliged to take a precise attitude toward each of them with respect to its platform and, especially, with respect to the *general direction* of its development. The Brandlerist clique (Lovestone, Wolfe, and Company) … remains in fundamental unity with Stalinism on all the principled questions and shamefully justifies and apologizes for its systematic errors and crimes. The irreconcilable struggle of the new party against Stalinism presupposes and requires an equally unrelenting hostility to the right-wing camp followers of Stalinism.

Party Democracy

The new party must establish within its ranks a regime of democratic centralism, which permits freedom of discussion and criticism on the one hand and unity of action on the other. The free election of officials from top to bottom, the control of the officials by the rank and file, and the right of every member to express his opinions in an atmosphere free from baiting and threats of expulsion, must be combined with a clearly defined principled foundation for party membership and a disciplined unity of the entire organization in action before the outside world.

Forces for the New Party

The Communist League, as it is at present constituted, does not consider itself a party and has no intention of anticipating the real establishment of the new party by proclaiming itself as such. The task now is to recognize firmly that our role as a faction striving to reform the party of official Stalinism is exhausted, to strike out on a completely independent path, and to prepare, in cooperation with other groups and organizations moving in the same direction, for the formation of a new party.

In the course of its struggle to reform the official party, as a faction of it, the Left Opposition worked out a program, consolidated a cadre of principled militants, and formed the skeleton of a national organization. These accomplishments can be regarded now as part of the capital of the new movement – not all that is necessary for the formation of the party, but contributions to it.

What is needed now is the coming together of the various groups of revolutionary workers who have broken, or who are in the process of breaking, with reformism and centrism, as well as those dispersed individual revolutionists who have been repelled by the Stalinist bureaucracy and remain without affiliation. It is self-evident that the working out of a common program, and the eventual concentration of these forces in a single party, must be preceded by an exchange of opinion and discussion and, very probably, will involve a transition period of cooperation before the final fusion. ...

Submitting the foregoing points for discussion, we on our part are ready to give attentive and comradely considerations to any different proposals and to bring them to the attention of our members and supporters by publication in the *Militant*, together with our comments on them, ... open[ing] for discussion the question of a new party and a new International.

CHAPTER 3

Building Revolutionary Forces

Paul Le Blanc

The question of how to build up a revolutionary party was discussed often by James P. Cannon, and it is worth considering his remarks, given that they offer insights into how, over the years, the US Trotskyists were inclined to approach the matter:

> The revolutionary labor movement doesn't develop along a straight line or a smooth path. It grows through a continuous process of internal struggle. Both splits and unifications are methods of developing the revolutionary party. Each, under given circumstances, can be either progressive or reactionary in its consequences. The general popular sentiment for unification all the time has no more political value than for a continual process of splitting which you see taking place interminably in the purist sectarian groups. ... Splits are sometimes absolutely necessary for the clarification of programmatic ideas and for the selection of forces in order to make a new start on a clear basis. On the other hand, in given circumstances, unifications of two or more groups which approach programmatic agreement are absolutely indispensible for the regroupment and consolidation of the forces of the workers' vanguard.[1]

In contrast to this, Trotskyists have often been tagged by critics as being – almost by definition – hopeless sectarians determined to take over, split, or wreck those they perceive as opponents. Accounts of Trotskyists joining together in the 1930s first with the American Workers Party (AWP) of A.J. Muste and later with the Socialist Party of America (SP) led by Norman Thomas are prime examples of this inherent destructiveness, according to biographers of Muste and Thomas.

Leilah Danielson's in many ways valuable biography of A.J. Muste – offering a quotation from Cannon – asserts that the quote fragment she offers 'suggests' that Cannon and his comrades viewed 'Muste and former AWP members with contempt, used deception to push their agenda, and were consumed by theor-

1 Cannon 1972, p. 189.

etical discussions that fostered factionalism and precluded effective organizing and party growth' – implying that, in fact, Muste was pathetically naïve to think that 'he would be able to control and reform the Trotskyists'. Norman Thomas's biographer W.A. Swanberg – asserting that 'the Trotskyites ... contributed little to [the SP] but factionalism about Russia and Spain' – writes that 'the Trotskyites had been contaminating the Party for only fourteen months when the Socialists, with Thomas's blessing, expelled them by vote in August 1937'.[2]

Looking first at Muste and the AWP, we can see – in comments that Muste's biographer chooses to ignore – that Cannon and his comrades felt something other than contempt. Cannon wrote:

> The AWP was not a homogeneous organization. Its progressive character was determined by two factors: (1) through its energetic activities in the mass movement, in the trade unions, and in the unemployed field, it had attracted some rank and file militant workers who were in dead earnest about fighting capitalism; (2) the general direction in which the American Workers Party was moving at the time was clearly to the left, toward a revolutionary position. ...
>
> The outstanding personality in the American Workers Party was A.J. Muste, a remarkable man who was always extremely interesting to me and for whom I always had the most friendly feelings. He was an able and energetic man, obviously sincere and devoted to the cause, to his work ....[3]

Danielson prefers a different quote, in which Cannon speaks about preventing 'the Stalinists from swallowing up' the Muste group, and refers to removing 'a

2 Danielson 2014, p. 192; Swanberg 1976, p. 218. Sadly, Danielson misquotes more than once (for example p. 403): 'Paul Le Blanc disputes the notion that there was "a sectarian impulse within the tradition of American Trotskyism" (Breitman, Le Blanc and Wald, *Trotskyism in the United States*, xi), but my research has suggested otherwise'. In fact, the passage from which Danielson wrenches the quote fragment involves a somewhat different point. Another historian had pointed to a particular quote by a US Trotskyist as 'a dramatic illustration of a sectarian impulse within the tradition of American Trotskyism', and Le Blanc disagreed with that interpretation of the quote – although, deeper in the text than the four-page introduction to which Danielson seems to have restricted her attention, Le Blanc touches on more than one sectarian impulse cropping up among US Trotskyists (such impulses being common among many political tendencies). Danielson's account, in contrast, seems to indicate that Trotskyists are sectarian simply *because they are Trotskyists*.

3 Cannon 1972, pp. 170–1; he feels strongly enough about these points to make them again on page 177.

centrist obstacle' by 'effecting a unity with the proletarian activists and the serious people, isolating the frauds and fakers, and discarding the unassimilable elements'.[4]

Some writers give considerable stress to some prominent AWP figures who rejected the merger, such as J.B.S. Hardman (who Cannon saw as 'unassimilable' and a 'faker' because he was unwilling to jeopardise his major staff position with the Amalgamated Clothing Workers), and some around Louis Budenz and Arnold Johnson, who preferred to join the Communist Party (into which they certainly had hoped to lead the entire Muste group). But a significant number of AWP stalwarts chose to remain in the unified organisation, including Hilde Ageloff, Morris Chertov, Anne Chester, Ted Grant, Ernest Rice McKinney, Sam Pollack, Ruth Querio, Regina Shoemaker, Ted Selander, Art Preis, James Burnham, and others. These were representative of the 'proletarian activists and serious people' that Cannon wanted to unite with, including, as we have seen, Muste himself.

As indicated in material presented here, Muste himself saw the merger in very positive terms. At the same time, as noted by Musteite Anne Chester, 'we of the AWP ... carried with us a great suspicion of Cannon based on the fear that he and his comrades would make internationalists of us'.[5] Yet we can see in the article presented here Muste's own strong reconciliation of the AWP's national focus and the Trotskyists' revolutionary internationalism. In Cannon's letter to another Musteite, Ruth Querio in Allentown, Pennsylvania, we can also see Cannon's down-to-earth engagement with the former AWP comrades there as they were going through the difficult transition (made more complex by several comrades on the scene preparing to bolt to the Communist Party).

There were, indeed, sharp debates – as indicated in the contribution by Max Shachtman in this section – which centred on the question of whether the unified organisation, the Workers Party of the United States (WPUS), should take advantage of a new opening and merge into the Socialist Party of America. This has been referred to as 'the French Turn' – because it was first initiated by Trotskyists in France (at Trotsky's urging) – designed to increase Trotskyist forces by entering larger Social-Democratic and Socialist parties, notoriously reformist but beginning to radicalise under the impact of the Great Depression. Muste aligned his former AWP comrades in a bloc, which included a faction headed by Hugo Oehler (having a reputation for sectarianism) and others, to oppose this entry tactic. Anne Chester recalled:

4 Cannon 1972, p. 177; Danielson 2014, p. 192.

5 Anne Chester, in Evans 1976, p. 109.

> We had great faith in Muste and continued to look to him for leadership in the united organization. Six months later an internal struggle developed between Oehler and Muste on one side, and Cannon and Shachtman on the other over the question of entry into the Socialist Party. As in all struggles of deepgoing political differences, rumors and slanders ran rampant, aimed especially at Cannon. I wanted to hear Cannon's answer to the charges, but they remained unanswered. Jim patiently waited for the political differences to develop until they became clear to the entire membership, brushing aside all such secondary matters as slanders, so that the decisions would be made on the issues that counted – the political issues.[6]

The nature of the discussion was a revelation to many of the newcomers. 'This Bolshevik method of a free, democratic, organized factional struggle to settle serious differences over program and policy was brand new to us', recalled yet another AWP veteran, Ted Grant. 'In the ... AWP, when a difference arose, all sides were given equal time to present their views, with A.J. (as we always called Muste) in the chair. He would speak last, skilfully reconciling the different viewpoints into an "all-inclusive" motion which was generally accepted. His prestige and influence were so great that almost everyone would defer to him'. But in the convention debate, 'Jim's critical analysis was a revelation to us'. Grant elaborated that 'he fairly but mercilessly dissected the political position of each group in our [oppositional] bloc. We noticed at once that Jim didn't stoop to petty debater's points or misrepresent an opponent's position. He stated each position fully and fairly and answered them squarely in such a way as to obtain the maximum educational value for the membership'. During a break in the conference, Cannon ambled over to the table where a number of Musteites were sitting, to chat, joke, and put them at their ease. 'We felt an immediate kinship with him and we communicated easily'.[7] But what was decisive was the political content of the debate. Morris Chertov explained:

> He discussed dialectical thinking, which perceived real class forces in motion and development, as opposed to the rigidity of the sectarians' thought, which was guided by abstract and sterile formulas. A failure on our part to see past the discredited Socialist Party label to the hundreds of revolutionary workers being drawn to the ranks of the SP would cut us

6 Ibid.

7 Grant, in Evans 1976, pp. 95, 96, 97.

> off from these workers. These potential recruits to revolutionary socialism would fall prey to reformist or Stalinist leadership and instead of strengthening the revolutionary forces in America would be used against us by our enemies.[8]

Grant notes that by the time of the 1936 WPUS national convention, 'the decision to enter the SP was approved by an overwhelming majority including a number of Muste's leading supporters'. Muste's position seemed 'obdurate' and 'narrow', Chertov recalls, and he 'lost many of his followers, like myself, who had developed a sense of personal loyalty to him'. Anne Chester noted: 'In the process of this tremendously educational battle, Muste proved himself incapable of revolutionary political thinking, and our attitude, which previously had been that of children looking up to our papa, began to change'. The shift was dramatic. A group of former AWP members approached Muste during a lull, 'telling him we were convinced he was dead wrong', recounts Chertov. 'Then we moved over to where Cannon was sitting, and told him that we had broken from Muste, and were now supporting him'.[9]

The final issue of the *New Militant* ran a front-page editorial, provided in this volume, but indicating with crystal clarity that the Trotskyists were joining the Socialist Party 'as we are, with our ideas and traditions'. Stating that 'the Socialist workers are now in a state of evolution toward a consistent Marxist conception of their tasks', the editorial adds that 'not the least of the forms that dialectics takes is the conflict, the give and take, of ideas about theory, strategy and tactics'. It goes on to explain that 'differences must be threshed out by free discussion among the membership, and not decided by bureaucratic decrees of self-constituted Popes. A party without democracy is not a party'. The editorial concludes: 'The best and, indeed, the only guarantee for a normal solution of disputed questions is the fullest democracy in educational work and discussion, coupled with an attitude of responsibility and discipline'.

At the same time, it presents a more glowing picture of the Socialist Party that the Trotskyists were entering than was accurate. Twenty years after the fact, historian David Shannon noted that, with a membership that had dropped – after the departure of the Old Guard to form the Social-Democratic Federation – from 19,000 to about 12,000, 'the Socialist Party was dying before its invasion by the followers of Trotsky', and Cannon himself believed 'the party was not viable. It was already in the stage of violent ferment and disintegration

8 Chertov, in Evans 1976, p. 103.

9 Grant, Chertov, and Chester, in Evans 1976, pp. 97, 104, 109.

in 1936 at the time of our entry', especially given the dominance of caucuses led by relatively egotistical individuals who were either prepared to gravitate into the orbit of Franklin D. Roosevelt's New Deal, or were in the process of being absorbed by trade union bureaucracies, or were politically fuzzy. The Clarity and Militant caucuses were incapable of living up to their names. What was crucial to the Trotskyists, however, was connecting with the 'worker activists and rebellious youth' who definitely were members of the SP.[10]

The initial approach of Cannon and his comrades once inside the SP, however, was not that of a fighting faction. They were inclined to initiate discussions and activities to oppose the horrific repression in the Soviet Union, the so-called Moscow Trials, as well as a defence campaign for Leon Trotsky. They were also sharply critical of the Stalinist-initiated People's Front, which they argued was a class-collaborationist betrayal, particularly clear as it was playing out in the Spanish Civil War, but which also involved a rapprochement with liberal capitalism in the United States (support for Franklin D. Roosevelt). Yet the Trotskyists for the most part sought to integrate themselves into the new organisation before making waves. According to Cannon, the Trotskyists joining the SP sought first to be 'integrated into the party, plunge into practical work and thus to establish a certain moral authority with the rank and file of the party; establish friendly personal relationships especially with those elements of the party who are activists and therefore potentially of some use' in the class struggle. Life would soon bring political issues to the fore. 'We didn't have to force discussion or to initiate the faction struggle artificially', he commented. 'We could well afford to let the political issues unfold under the impact of world events. And we didn't have long to wait'.[11]

By the end of 1936, a majority of the membership of the Young People's Socialist League (YPSL) had become 'pure and simple Trotskyites', according to Thomas, six months after the Trotskyist entry took place, and in order to stop this development, he argued there 'is little time to lose', fearing – in the words of one of his biographers – that 'if he waited until the next regular national convention in 1938, the mushrooming radical faction would not only capture most of the party machinery, but quite probably would wrest party leadership from him'. An emergency convention was therefore organised in March 1937 to smash the red menace. Aspects of the 'Crisis in the Party' are detailed in the article by that name, reproduced in this section. By September, the Trotskyists had been purged, and in the opinion of another of his biographers, the result was not simply due to the loss of hundreds of

10 Shannon 1967, p. 254; Cannon 1972, pp. 236, 237, 239.

11 Cannon 1972, p. 239.

members 'but the debilitating effects of the many wasted months of internal party struggle when the Party might have been active as an organized force in aiding the drive for industrial unionism sparked by John L. Lewis, the Congress of Industrial Organizations (CIO) and the militant sit-down strikes'.[12] The same comment has been made regarding the Trotskyists – that applying the 'French Turn' diverted them from the great working-class battles of the 1930s.

In fact, Socialist Party members were in the thick of the first major sit-down strike in Flint, Michigan in 1936–7, and some of them were also in the process of being won to Trotskyism. 'After seven years' membership in the Socialist Party, striving for the true path to socialism ... the facts have shown us that the Socialist Party had not and can not provide the leadership necessary', declared Kermit and Genora Johnson, key militants in the Flint sit-down strike. 'We are leaving the Socialist Party and joining the Socialist Workers Party to build the vanguard of the coming revolution unhampered by reformist maneuvers, petty intriguers, opportunists and careerists'.[13] W.A. Swanberg summarises aspects of the impact for the Socialist Party:

> The Trotskyites, who had entered about 300 strong, took more than 1,000 with them when they left, including part of the Socialist youth organization, which Thomas had treasured as the Party's future. With their departure the California Party became virtually extinct, as was the one in Minnesota, and Illinois, Ohio, and Massachusetts were among those badly hurt.[14]

In contrast, the Trotskyists found themselves, after their mass expulsion from the Socialist Party, in a condition of greater strength and soaring morale. 'We accumulated invaluable political experience, and we more than doubled our forces as a result of the entry and one year's work in the Socialist Party'. Especially significant was the substantial base the Trotskyists had been able to establish in the maritime and auto industries. Cannon concluded that – as the dust settled – he and others were struck by

> the revelation that while we had been concentrating on this inner political work inside the Socialist Party, we had been at the same time developing, practically without any direction from our central leadership, our

12 Johnpoll 1970, p. 181; Steward 1974, p. 154; Fleischman 1969, p. 181.

13 Jackson 2008, p. 48. Also see Dollinger and Dollinger 2000.

14 Swanberg 1976, p. 218.

> trade union work on a scale we had never approximated before and had at least begun the proletarianization of the party. We had won over to our side the majority of the Socialist youth and the majority of those Socialist workers really interested in the principles of Socialism and the Socialist revolution.[15]

15 Cannon 1972, pp. 239, 251–2. On the expanded base in the auto industry, in addition to Dollinger, see Devinatz 2005, pp. 53–82. On Trotskyists in maritime, see: Lang 1943; Kerry 1980.

1 The Workers Party is Founded[16]

(December 1934)

A.J. Muste

The Workers Party of the US did not emerge suddenly from nowhere. It was born of the merger of the Communist League of America and the American Workers Party, itself the outgrowth of the Conference for Progressive Labor Action. Each organization took pride in its past. It did not disown that past in coming into the merger. Rather did each organization by its participation in the merger bear witness to its appreciation of the history of the other.

Before launching on the main theme of this article, two observations on the significance of the merger may be made. In the first place, a number have asked the question, Why is it that precisely the group which has been most concerned about theory, and on the other hand, the group which has been most 'activist' have got together? Without entering now into a discussion as to the exactness of the description here employed, it may be pointed out that at one point in the evolution of the movement, the elaboration of theory may be the prime need, and at another the application of theory in action. However, there cannot be, and never is, a divorce between sound theory and sound practice. A group which devotes itself to the discussion of theory in the Marxian sense does not do it for the sake of agreeable mental exercise, as an alternative perhaps to working crossword puzzles. It is concerned with theory because it needs to know how to act and will not act on a merely opportunistic basis. Elaboration of theory leads, therefore, to practical work in the labor scene. On the other hand, a group which seeks to act in a responsible and not an adventurist spirit in the revolutionary movement, which is concerned about ultimate and not merely about immediate aims, may indeed scorn Talmudic theologizing and debates which lead simply to more debates; but it cannot be indifferent to theory. It can render a service which the trade union bureaucrats, for example, cannot render, not merely because its members may individually be more honest or self-sacrificing, but chiefly because it has a clear conception of the economic

16 Muste 1935.

and political system, the role of the working class, etc., and therefore can thread its way through the complex maze of events. That is to say, it must fall back on theory. If it does not find theoretical questions answered by any existing political party it must hammer out theory for itself and build a new party. Thus the fusion of the CLA and the AWP was not accidental. Moreover, the fusion will bear fruit which neither group by itself could have produced.

Another question which has been raised is, Why is it that the most 'internationalist' and the most 'nationalist' group got together? The first comment on that question is naturally that one cannot believe everything he reads in the papers, especially in the *Daily Worker*. Seriously, the point of the revolutionary internationalism of the CLA has been that it is a fatal error to make the laying of the foundations of the socialist economy in the Soviet Union and the so-called 'defense of the Soviet Union' the almost exclusive concern of the revolutionary movement; that the defense of the Soviet Union itself today depends upon the growth and victory of revolutionary parties in capitalist countries and that energy must be concentrated on that task. When the AWP has insisted that the revolutionary movement must be built in the United States it has done this, not with any notion that a revolutionary movement could be national in character, but precisely because it was so deeply concerned that the working class of the United States should do its part in the world revolutionary movement. It inveighed sometimes against sentimentality and romanticism about labor internationalism because it was so deeply concerned about building the international revolutionary movement realistically and so avoiding a repetition of the tragic debacle which overtook the movement in 1914 with the outbreak of the war and again in 1932 under the onslaught of Fascism in Germany and elsewhere. Again, therefore, the merger is the correct and natural outcome of the history of the two groups.

The merger also signifies that we are not slaves to the past. Our faces are set to the future. We go to meet the test of action.

Objective conditions vary in different countries; the working class is at different stages in its evolution. Consequently the crucial issue before the revolutionary party is not the same in different countries or at different periods. The trade union issue is the master issue in the United States today. By the manner in which it meets that issue the Workers party will justify or stultify itself in the initial period of its existence.

Reactionary employer interests and the 'liberal' Roosevelt administration are well aware of the fact that it is over the right of workers to organize and bargain collectively, in the organizing campaigns and strike struggles of the past two years, that capitalism and the working class are locking horns today in the US. By might and main, by direct and brutal or indirect and subtle means, they seek to prevent organization, to build company unions, to postpone the issue over Section 7a of NRA to prevent strikes, to break them, and where unions are formed to confuse the membership and corrupt the leaders so that the unions may not become or remain genuine instruments of struggle.

Without in most cases thinking the problem through, with wrong or incomplete theory perhaps, if they have any at all, the masses of the workers also sense the significance of the conflict. And this includes not a few white-collar, professional and technical workers, who until recently hardly thought of themselves as 'workers' at all. They are fighting for bread and butter of course. What else should starving men and women fight for? But they sense the need for power in order to get bread; they know that power comes from organization; they fight magnificently and starve in order to get recognition of their union. In the room in which Okey Odell, the Ohio union strike leader, lay recovering from his wounds last August, surrounded by armed union members determined to fight it out with any vigilantes who might try to seize him again, a special guard stood before the federal union charter these union workers had received from the AF of L pledged to die before they would permit it to be taken away!

In certain more sophisticated quarters of the labor movement, there are those who do not see what is plain to the capitalists and politicians on the one hand and the working masses on the other. The avowed social democrats and the unavowed ones, including some of those who regard themselves as devotees of the 'American approach', think of course that the class struggle is fought primarily and mainly at the polls. One of them recently remarked that Upton Sinclair in his EPIC campaign for governor of California had carried the class struggle in that state to the highest point it had ever reached, and did not even mention the marine workers' strike that raged up and down the Pacific coast last summer, and the general strike in the San Francisco area! No, not Upton on his soap-box but Tom Mooney in jail is still the symbol of the class struggle in California.

At the other extreme are doctrinaires and Leftists to whom the unions, especially those in the AF of L, are company unions, Fascist unions, 'bulwarks of capitalism', etc. Until recently at least the CP held to this estimate and proceeded to do its utmost to divide the working class by building its own sectarian, paper 'industrial' unions: Others holding this estimate stand in holy aloofness from the present struggles of the workers and their ill-advised attempts to organize, perhaps condescending to lift up their voices to preach the one true doctrine to deaf ears. Those with syndicalist leanings may participate actively and courageously in strike struggles, but they will have nothing to do with the unions which conduct or grow out of these strikes. Some day, they feel blissfully certain, objective conditions will compel the workers to rise spontaneously, to turn their backs suddenly upon the past and its misguided struggles, and to put over the revolution.

To reject these attitudes does not mean that we accept the present leadership of the AF of L, its structure, its policies, its attitude toward employers and government. For the Marxist that is even more impossible than it was at an earlier period. The unions cannot in the period of capitalist decline fulfill the functions, achieve the gains for the workers, that were possible when capitalism was still able to give substantial concessions at least to large sections of the population. The class-collaboration philosophy becomes more dangerous as the capitalist crisis deepens, will prove fatal if it prevails as that crisis reaches its climax.

The struggle of the unions against the employing class and the government is genuine and has a progressive character, therefore, only in the degree that within the unions the struggle against the bureaucracy and its policies goes on. This intra-union struggle can be effectively waged by the rank and file, the progressive and Left elements, only if they are organized. Who shall lead and inspire in this struggle and the organization for it, if not the politically developed, the theoretically trained workers? In other words, the revolutionary party? Correctly, therefore, the Workers Party of the US places in the forefront of its Program of Action for the next six months the organization of the Left-progressive wing in the unions.

Neither the Socialist Party as a whole nor any section of it worth mentioning has a clear conception of the crucial nature of this task. In effect, therefore, they all strengthen the hands of the trade union bureaucrats and, so far as they have influence, commit the movement to a non-militant and reformist attitude. The Right wing has of course always served the union officialdom in exchange for votes and jobs as 'labor lawyers', etc. At the Detroit convention they fought bitterly against even a mild censure of the AF of L leaders. Today they are openly seeking an alliance with the unions under their present leadership in a Labor party – to the Right of where the SP has supposedly stood.

Meanwhile the adolescent and unrealistic character of the leadership of the various shades of 'Militants' is clearly illustrated by the fact that they engage in most violent shadow-boxing with the Right wing over the 'united front' with the CP (or that poor relation of the CP, Lovestone, of whom the RPC is in turn a poor relation) and over what they are going to do, or think they are going to do, when war or the revolution comes – but back down before the Right wing on the trade union issue, the test of the revolutionary realist today. The Militants do not concentrate on building the Left-progressive wing in the unions. They concentrate on getting posts in the unions which, in the absence of a Left-progressive wing under the leadership of revolutionary forces, can only result in the Militants becoming assimilated to the trade union bureaucracy, as has happened often enough in previous years. It is inconceivable that the workers, the miners, e.g. or the steel workers, who know the union situation from the inside and whose very livelihood in many instances depends literally upon the outcome of the struggle against the union bureaucracy, can long follow such leadership, can postpone joining the Workers party and thus assisting most effectively in building the Left wing in the unions.

The unions are instruments of struggle, agencies of collective bargaining, etc. within the capitalist system. By themselves, they are not revolutionary instruments. In fact, left to themselves they become 'pure and simple', degenerate into rackets, fail even as collective bargaining agencies. What transformations, revolutionary changes, new formations, may occur in the economic organizations, and the economic struggle, as on the one hand the economic crisis deepens and on the other hand the revolutionary party gains the confidence and leadership of the masses, is subject matter for analysis in future issues of this magazine. Even among those who may differ on these matters, there can be agreement – there must be if disaster is not to overcome the American working class – that today: in the US the main sector of the class struggle is the movement of workers of all categories into unions, the fight for recognition of the right to organize, the strike struggles, the fights against the trade union bureaucrats. In the shops, mines, stores, offices; in union halls; on the picket lines; on the streets of Toledo, Minneapolis, Milwaukee, San Francisco, the steel and textile and automobile and mining towns, that struggle rages and will rage in the months ahead. Build the unions; organize the workers; develop their militancy: broaden, deepen, intensify, politicalize the day-to-day struggles; fight the bureaucrats; build the Left-progressive wing – this is the program of revolutionists today, the program of the Workers Party.

The so-called Communist Party has clearly demonstrated how such a program should NOT be carried out. Abandoning the conception of party democracy and workers democracy completely, the CP has espoused a mystical, absolutist, utterly un-Marxian conception of a party which can do no wrong, which stands outside and above the working class. (From this to an absolute ruler over the party itself is only a step). This leads to a fatal lack of faith in, actual contempt for, the working class. It finds expression in the theory of social-Fascism (working-class organizations that do not accept our domination are Fascist); in united-front-from-below maneuvers (these stupid asses will not see through our clever scheme to crush them); in using strong-arm methods to break up the meetings of other labor groups; in 'capturing' unions and other mass organizations by political trickery or main force; in manipulating union machinery so as to put party members in office; in calling strikes and telling the workers what the strike is about after they get out on the sidewalk. At this very moment we are seeing another ludicrous and yet tragic illustration of what this attitude leads to. Members of independent building trades unions fostered by the CP are in open revolt against the party which, after years of building separate sectarian, often paper, unions all along the line, has suddenly realized the futility of that course and now proceeds quite as mechanically and dictatorially to try to liquidate every independent union it can lay its hands on, regardless of the circumstances which gave it birth, its mass base or the will of the membership!

The Workers Party will not utter its own doom in advance by using such methods in its trade union work. It will rely upon the correctness of its analysis and program, the persuasiveness of its propaganda, above all upon the activity, devotion and militancy of its members in the unions to win the confidence first of the progressives and then of the broad masses in the unions.

No fact stands out more clearly from a survey of the present scene than the need of a revolutionary party with a sound trade union program. The masses are in motion. They continue to press into the unions. One strike struggle follows upon the heels of the other. Yet for lack of effective organization of the Left-progressive wing, itself the result of the disastrous policies of the CP and SP, many strikes are prevented, no strike has gained results proportionate to the spirit displayed by the workers, the issue of unionization in the traditional anti-union strongholds in the basic industries is still unresolved, the old AF of L machine continues in the saddle. The fact that the workers continue to organize in the AF of L does not mean that they have a naive confidence in the present leadership. On the contrary, textile, steel, automobile, marine workers, to mention but a few instances, know that this leadership cannot be trusted. They are ready to welcome a new leadership which will display vigor and a sense of reality. Wherever the idea of building an organization of Left-progressives has been broached, it has met with an instant response. In fact, the movement is already under way independently in many sections of the country.

No organization except the Workers Party is in a position to take advantage of the opportunity and to give leadership to the movement. The CP is in this field hopelessly discredited and at sea. The SP, apart from all other considerations, is so torn with conflict and confusion that it cannot devote attention to this crying need of the workers. In Toledo and Minneapolis the forces that by merging have constituted the Workers party have already demonstrated their ability and gained the attention of the masses.

Thus with confidence and determination we address ourselves to the task of building the Left-progressive wing in the unions – building the Workers Party of the US – building the new, the Fourth, International!

2 Letter to Ruth Querio[17]

(17 January 1936)

James P. Cannon

Dear Comrade Querio:

I received your letter and was glad indeed to hear from you. I fully appreciate the extraordinary difficulties which confront the comrades in the Allentown situation, and have the warmest admiration for those who persist in the struggle to develop the branch into a revolutionary organization, worthy of the name. Nobody is born a Bolshevik. It takes time and great effort and travail to weld a group of people of different personalities and temperaments into a homogeneous organization. When, as is the case in Allentown, one has to begin with a membership which, as a whole, is comparatively new to the political movement, the difficulties are only magnified. That is what we always have to keep in mind about the Allentown situation. It excludes a quick solution of the difficulties; similarly, it makes it impossible for the Political Committee to solve the problem by means of single decisions or disciplinary measures. Time and education and experience are all necessary factors.

On the other hand, it is very obvious to us that we are making headway. The fact that you have succeeded in organizing 20-odd comrades into a grouping which really attempts to face the political issues, and to carry out the party line, and that this group grows in political understanding and self-confidence as the struggle develops – this is a positive gain. You must not underestimate it. Whatever happens, we are now assured of a serious political nucleus in Allentown. In the end it is bound to prevail. For political ideas and a political line are far more powerful than all the intrigues and tricks and prejudices of a transitory majority. If our group there really assimilates the ideas and methods of Bolshevism, we need have no fear for the future.

We are now going through a period of the richest political experience, and we are all learning from it. Perhaps we, ourselves, were not free from mistakes in the Allentown situation. It seems to me that some very good comrades, who have the making of Bolsheviks, have taken a position against us in Allentown. We must hope that their antagonism is temporary and we must aim to win

17 Cannon 1992.

them over. Above all, we have to convince them by our personal attitude that we do not pursue personal aims and that we are not animated, in any way, by sentiments of personal antagonism or personal revenge. On the contrary, we have to make it clear, we have to convince those comrades who have good faith, that we want to advance a political line which is necessary for the building of the party and the mass movement, and that we want to unite every possible comrade on the basis of that line. We must look ahead; we have a long work before us. It will do us no good to lose our heads and cry for immediate and final solution of the situation, which is still maturing. We must persist and persevere and take consolation in the fact that we are gaining, and will continue to gain as long as we act like Bolshevik politicians and not like chickens with their heads cut off. Danton said that audacity was the first merit of revolutionists. He might have added that patience comes next in order. Please don't think that I am simply lecturing you. I am really directing this just as much at myself, because impatience is my own fault, also.

We are going to have a party convention on February 28th. It will be a historic affair, a turning point in the development of our movement. We want to keep our movement united, if it is possible. The trend of the national party sentiment is on our side. That will make its influence felt in Allentown and will help you. We do not want any explosions or splits before the convention, if we can avoid them. We will have the majority and that will impose upon us the duty of conciliating the minority. Once the political line is established by the convention – and we must not make any compromises when it comes to a question of principled lines – then we must try to keep the movement united on the basis of that line. Above all, we must not let personal antagonisms reach the point where they provoke artificial splits.

In this next period, as I have suggested to comrade Gordon, much attention should be devoted to the caucus group which we have organized around our political platform. You should have frequent meetings, devoted to a discussion of political problems, so that the group will become further strengthened and consolidated, on a political basis. That is the most profitable work that can be done now, and it is also the best way to insure your eventual victory in the branch and in the mass movement. I hope to come to Allentown, at least once, before the convention for a branch discussion meeting and also for a discussion meeting with the group. I also hope that the most active comrades will begin to plan far in advance to attend the party convention which will be open to all party members.

With Bolshevik greetings and personal regards,
J.P. Cannon

3 Marxist Politics or Unprincipled Combinationism?[18]

(*Excerpts, February 1936*)

Max Shachtman

Introduction

The national tour of all the important party branches which I completed several weeks ago brought me face to face with a number of questions and problems which arose in the course of discussion with numerous comrades. These discussions firmly convinced me of the urgent necessity of putting before the entire membership of the party and the Spartacus Youth League a detailed record of what has happened in the year of the party's existence. The ignorance of the party situation which the Oehler and the Abern-Weber groups have vied with each other to preserve in the party's ranks, and the systematic confusion and direct falsifications which they have, each in its own way, disseminated from coast to coast, demand that such a record be set down in writing for the information of the membership. The present document, however, pursues no mere informational ends; it is not intended to substitute for a history, properly speaking, of our movement. It does aim to extract from the record of the party's history some of the essential and highly illuminating political lessons which our present situation dictates must be drawn if we are to progress along revolutionary lines.

To draw together what seems to be loose ends; to place men and things in their proper place so that an otherwise incomprehensible jumble begins to take on the appearance of a coherent and significant picture; to draw up a balance sheet of ideas, proposals, events, progress, retreats, at every stage of the development of the movement; to compare what was predicted with what finally took place, what was adopted with what results it yielded, what was proposed with what the situation showed was required; to trace a complicated situation back to its causes; to test and check men and groups and ideas on the touchstone of practice – these are elementary obligations of every

18 Shachtman 1936.

revolutionist. But these obligations cannot be properly discharged without a simple working knowledge of the facts. Lies, rumor and gossip are as misleading a factor in casting up a political balance sheet as forged checks would be in casting up a bank balance. And what a mass of political forged checks are afloat in our party! One has only to go through the country and discuss our political problems with an average group of comrades to be overwhelmed by the realization that a prerequisite for the further progress of our movement is the clear establishment of those facts of party history which are necessary for that balance sheet, that accounting, that report of stewardship which the membership has the right and duty to demand of the leaders at the coming national convention.

'A revolutionary organization', wrote Trotsky on February 17, 1931, in his comments on the crisis in the German Left Opposition, 'selects and educates men not for corridor intrigues but for great battles. This puts very severe obligations upon the cadres, above all on the "leaders" or those who lay claim to the role of leaders. The moments of crisis in every organization, however painful they may be, have this positive significance, that they reveal the true political physiognomy of men: what is hidden in the soul of each of them, in the name of what he is fighting, if he is capable of resistance, etc.'.

Our party is at present in a crisis. It can emerge from it healthier and stronger than ever only if the nature and cause of the crisis is understood. The politically primitive mind, shallow or entirely empty, or the philistine dilettante who dabbles in revolutionary politics on Monday and retires with a discouraged sigh on Tuesday, can see only the fact that 'the leaders are squabbling again'. Truax, for example, a former member of our National Committee, who represents the first type referred to, resigns from the party because, he writes, there is 'too much factionalism' in it. In the big political disputes agitating the party, all he can see is 'factionalism'.

This document is not addressed to dilettantes, dabblers and blatherskites. It is meant for the serious revolutionists in the party, both 'advanced' and 'backward'. It is meant above all to address the militant, knowledge-hungry youth of our movement. In a sense it is dedicated to them. In the strictest meaning of the word, they are the hope of tomorrow. The devastation of the Stalinist and social-democratic parties has virtually wiped out the bulk of the war and postwar generation. Just as the communist movement was built, between 1914 and 1919, primarily on the young generation, so the movement for the Fourth International must draw most of its troops from the young generation of today, those not yet corrupted by the virus of political decay.

But precisely because of that, the youth must be trained in the spirit of revolutionary Marxism, of principled politics. Through its bloodstream must run a powerful resistance to the poison of clique politics, of subjectivism, of personal combinationism, of intrigue, of gossip. It must learn to cut through all superficialities and reach down to the essence of every problem. It must learn to think politically, to be guided exclusively by political considerations, to argue out problems with themselves and with others on the basis of principles and to act always from motives of principle. And in order to think and act correctly, the youth (the adults as well!) must always have the facts before them; and if they do not have them, they must demand them.

This document, therefore, pursues a purely political aim. If the reader grows impatient at this or that point with the multitude of details, he will have to bear in mind that we desire to present all the facts that have a bearing on those questions in dispute which have engendered our present party crisis. We are loath to leave anyone a reasonable basis for arguing that we have neglected to reply to one or another point or to throw light on one or another dark corner. We are experiencing, in our opinion, a crisis of growth. We are experiencing what Zinoviev once pithily described as the 'birth pangs of a communist party'. In the field of obstetrics as well as in the field of politics, these birth pangs can be moderated, and finally eliminated entirely, not by an amateurish approach, not by a futile wringing of hands and whining and whimpering, not by prayer, but by increasing our fund of knowledge.

In the present case, this document aims to contrast two main lines of thought and action: the line of revolutionary Marxian politics – principled politics, which make possible a consistent, firm and progressive course; and on the other side, personal combinationism, cliquism and unprincipled politics, which can produce only an inconsistent, weak-kneed and essentially reactionary course. The first is the line for which our group has fought, first in the Communist League of America and for the past year in the Workers Party of the US. The second is the contribution made by the Abern-Weber group.

The contrast can be made only by presenting the two lines, by describing them, by recording what each of them looked like in theory and practice at each stage of our development, by checking them with the results they yielded. In order that the contrast may be scrupulously exact, we have preferred to present not merely our opinions, but indisputable factual material: minutes, convention records, theses, resolutions, motions, statements, letters, etc. Without them, no objective judgment of the party situation is possible. The work of our coming convention, which has the task of making just such a judgment, will, we hope, be facilitated by this compilation.

Max Shachtman
New York, January 20, 1936

Two Lines in the Fusion

The Workers Party has its roots in the two groups that came together to found it in December 1934, the Communist League of America and the American Workers Party. If we deal, at least at the outset, primarily with the former, it is not out of narrow patriotism for the organization to which many of us once belonged, but for these reasons: firstly, because an account of what occurred within the CLA, especially in the last year of its existence, is indispensable to an understanding and illustration of the political course of our group; and secondly, because the internal struggle of the same period in the CLA is, in any case, reproduced on a more extensive scale in the WP today.

The CLA was built up in the course of a protracted struggle for the principles of revolutionary Marxism. Occurring as it did in the face not only of the most violent opposition of the powerfully organized Stalinist apparatus, but of a series of discouraging defeats of the proletariat on a world scale, and in a period of social and political reaction, this struggle necessarily limited the scope of the League's expansion and influence. Understanding the nature of this struggle, the leadership of the League set itself firmly against any illusions of an early 'mass influence'. The main work of the League was conceived to be of a propagandistic nature: the presentation and development of the ideas of the International Left Opposition, and the formation of a solid cadre of revolutionists capable of defending these ideas.

In this respect the CLA was far from unique in the history of the movement. It was merely passing through the first of what may, roughly speaking, be called the three stages of the evolution of the revolutionary organization: a propaganda group which concentrates on hardening the initial cadres on the basis of clearly defined principles; then a more active group in the process of transition to a mass movement, which concentrates on presenting its formerly elaborated principles to the masses in the form of agitational, day-to-day slogans, but which is not yet strong enough to step very far beyond the boundaries of literary and oral agitation; finally, the larger movement, which not only calls itself a party but which can discharge the responsibilities incumbent upon an organization claiming to defend the daily as well as the historical interests of the proletariat, which can actually set masses into motion – in other words, a party of action.

The objectively unwarranted attempt by numerous wiseacres who refused to understand this process of evolution, and who pursued 'the masses' without 'wasting time' on forging the instrument – cadres – without which systematic revolutionary work in the class struggle is inconceivable, always ended either in opportunism or adventurism. The chief protagonists of such attempts in this country, Weisbord and Field, ended up, as is known, without 'mass work' and without cadres. These furious critics of our 'sectarianism' finished with the most miserable and sterile of all sects.

The position of the CLA was complicated, moreover, by its position as a faction of the Third International, operating outside of it. Like its propagandistic position in general, this was not a matter of choice, but a condition dictated by a series of objective circumstances, primary among which was the fact that the Comintern had not yet exhausted its possibilities as a revolutionary Marxian organization, and that it was impossible to establish, a priori, whether or not it could be brought back to the road of proletarian internationalism by a combination of our work and the pressure of events themselves.

With the accession to power of the Hitlerites, and the unanimous endorsement by the Comintern sections of the treacherous capitulation of the Stalinists in Germany, the International Left Opposition voted to cut loose from the Third International. The slogan was issued: Build the Fourth International! Build new communist parties in every country! This decision could not but have profound effects on every section of the Left Opposition movement, and, in turn, upon the revolutionary movement in general.

In every country, at least in the important ones, the sections of the ILO (International Left Opposition) were confronted with the imperative need of making a decisive turn. The role of a faction of the Third International had to be given up, and the road taken towards an independent movement for new parties and a new International. A tremendous historical task by its very nature, it could neither be decreed nor accomplished overnight. Everywhere, the ILO entered a transitional stage, between a propagandist group (a faction) and an independent mass organization (a party). This stage was represented by the interval between *proclaiming the need* of a new International and new parties and their actual establishment. It was not enough to proclaim the need of the new party, nor even to recognize the gap referred to. The essence of the problem was: how, in each country, to bridge this gap in the briefest possible time allowed by the concrete conditions prevailing in the land and the relationship of forces in the working class and revolutionary movements.

That is to say, the general acknowledgment of the need of the new party related essentially to the reasons for its formation; it was not yet sufficient as the instrument for forming it. The instrument was (and is) the strategy and tactics that must be applied in each specific country in order to arrive in the swiftest and solidest manner at the goal.

In arriving at the strategy and tactics to be employed in the United States for attaining our goal, we were fortunate in having at our command the rich treasure trove of experience of the revolutionary movement for decades back. We invented no new method, because none was needed. We did not have to wonder and fumble, because we were provided by Marxism (i.e. by the distillation of living experience) with the key to our problem. But in no case is this key already completely grooved for every situation. Revolutionary politicians – like locksmiths – must take the broad, blank key which is already generally outlined by Marxism and adjust it to the grooves of the concrete situation; otherwise the door to the problem will not yield to our efforts.

In addition to wanting to build something, one must know how. And in the case of building the revolutionary party, alas! there is no simple, universal, rigid formula. The First International, for example, was unevenly developed and heterogeneously composed. The *Communist Manifesto* was written as the program of the (non-existent) International Communist Party, but it was compelled to set down different tactical approaches to the problem of creating this party in the various countries: to revolutionary democrats, militant nationalists, trade unionists, social reformists, etc. The Third International, which marked the second attempt to form the International Communist Party, came into being after the Russian Revolution, which gave it incalculable advantages over its predecessor. Yet even its task was no easy one, and its development was far from uniform. It is sufficient to mention the fact that from October–November 1914, when the need for the Third International was first proclaimed, until the formal founding of the International in March 1919, four and a half years elapsed. And even then, at the First Congress, the International was little more than a name and an idea outside of Russia.

The parties themselves were built differently in different countries. In Spain with the revolutionary syndicalists and the young socialists. In Germany by a fusion of the tiny Communist Party with the large left wing of the Independent Social Democratic Party. In England by a merger of four communist groups (plus one socialist temperance society). In France and the United States by winning the majority of the official Socialist Party. In Italy by breaking off a minority of the official Socialist Party, and then by fusing this minority with a subsequent communist majority of the same SP. In Norway by the direct affiliation to the CI of the federated Labor party. In Czechoslovakia by the affiliation en bloc of the official social democracy. In China by the direct transformation of a propagandist group of students and intellectuals into a proletarian communist party.

In a word, there was and could be no universal formula, applicable everywhere and under all conditions. More accurately, if there was a universal formula, it was this: the small propagandist groups of communists must convert themselves into mass communist parties by winning to their side the militant workers who are moving, however uncertainly and hesitantly at first, in the same general direction.

In the work of building the American section of the Fourth International, the leadership of the CLA derived its 'national' line from the international line. Six years of intensive assimilation of the ideas of proletarian internationalism as set forth in the programmatic material and defended in the struggles of the ILO (now the ICL [International Communist League]) had prepared the CLA to act automatically in that spirit. The international line was dictated to us by a *universal turn* from propaganda groups or sects to the mass movement, to the masses, towards the formation of independent parties *internationally*. In this sense, the turn of the ICL was basically an *international turn*. (Only because it has entered into our current jargon shall we speak henceforth of a 'French turn' too; in essence it is really a misnomer, for the tactic employed by the French Bolshevik-Leninists was merely an application, in the field of concrete French political realities, of the international turn from propagandist faction to independent party).

Because conditions differ in each country, because the relationship of forces is different, the tactical line that must be applied to reach the goal of the new International and new parties must also, of necessity, differ. At this point, one can establish the difference between the sectarian idealist and the active, Marxian materialist. The former proceeds from an idea, rigidly conceived and unadjustable to concrete material realities. Wherever the latter fail to conform to his preconceived idea, he turns his back contemptuously and angrily upon them and enters a world of fantasy which corresponds to his idea. That is why sectarianism means isolation, unreality. The Marxian materialist not only derives his ideas from the material and concrete reality, but bases his activities upon it, and, taking things as they actually are, plunges into the living world in order to shape it into 'what it should be'. If the Marxian philosopher must not only interpret the world, but also change it, it is necessary, in order to accomplish the latter, to approach it first as it is in reality, and not as if it was already 'what it should be', as if it was already changed.

That is why the Marxists in every section of the ICL applied the international turn concretely, i.e. in different ways in each country, differing in accordance with the realities of the organized social and political life of the working class, and yet were able to endorse each other's tactics without, by that fact, revealing any difference in principle or strategy. In France, the tactic used to carry out the international turn carried the Bolshevik-Leninists into a section of the Second International. In England, it made them a faction of a centrist party affiliated with none of the Internationals. In Holland, it carried them to a fusion with a leftward-moving centrist organization – the OSP [Independent

Socialist Party] – for the purpose of forming an independent revolutionary Marxian party of the Fourth International. In Australia, it carried them to their self-transformation into an independent party – as it did in Chile and elsewhere. In other countries, the international turn did not (nor, given the concrete conditions, could it as yet) change the organizational position of the section of the ICL. Widely though the tactics differed in each country, the CLA leadership and membership were able to support them all, with understanding and enthusiasm, because there was no conflict in the various tactics pursued so far as intelligent Marxists were concerned.

In carrying out this international turn from a faction to an independent party, the ICL underwent an acute crisis.* This crisis has more than a purely 'historical' significance, because at bottom the problems involved are identical with those which underlie the present situation in the Workers Party.

At every turn in world politics, especially when it is an abrupt turn, the revolutionary movement experiences a crisis of greater or lesser acuteness. It may be characterized as the crisis engendered by the need of adaptation to the new situation or the new requirements. In this period, two currents tend to crystallize in the movement. One, represented by the conservative, sectarian element, clings to the yesterday, which the new situation has rendered obsolete. The other, the progressive element, brings over into the tomorrow only that part of yesterday which fits the new situation. In a small propaganda group, a sect (be it in the best or the worst sense of the term), the crisis seems to assume particularly acute forms. The group is rigidly trained, and this is its great positive side because it steels a firm cadre. But inevitably some, instead of becoming steeled – that is, firm but flexible – become petrified and are unable to bend to the requirements of the new situation. Therein lay the essence of the crisis of the ICL, which produced rifts in a number of its sections.

---

* Not the ICL alone, to be sure. The debacle in Germany left no section of the labor movement unscathed. If it necessitated the turn of the ICL which thereupon produced a crisis in its ranks, it should not be forgotten that it also produced the complete upsetting of the 'Third Period' philosophy in the Third International and the still far-from-ended convulsions in the Second International. The CPLA, for example, also felt its effects, for what happened in Germany and subsequently precipitated the movement for a new party in the ranks of this semi-trade union, semi-political organization and led to the formation of the American Workers Party in Pittsburgh in December 1933, an event of signal progressive importance. In the CPLA (1933–4) the effects of the world crisis in the labor movement manifested themselves in an almost exclusively progressive and healthy manner.

Politics and the class struggle are hard taskmasters. They command and we must jump. Else we remain marking time, on one spot, and the living movement leaves us behind. The group, instead of contributing its trained cadres to the living movement, becomes a reactionary obstacle to proletarian progress. On the whole, it may be said that the years of training the cadres prepared the CLA for the 'jump' from a faction to a party. But it would be blindness to deny that, in another sense, the past of the CLA – its isolation from healthful contact with the mass movement – was a heavy heritage. Its leadership was composed not of 'group people' but of 'party people', founders and builders of the Communist Party in this country and even of the revolutionary movement before it. They did not 'choose' the group existence; it was forced upon them. They could not arbitrarily or artificially break out of the circle existence whenever they wanted to (as Weisbord and Field tried to do with such fatal results). They had to wait for the proper moment and the propitious situation. The international turn of the ICL was the indication that the moment and the situation had arrived.

But it cannot be underscored sufficiently: the whole history of the labor movement reveals an iron law operating in the evolution of such groups. Under certain conditions, they – and they alone – play a consistently progressive role. Under other conditions, they may be converted into their opposite and play a reactionary role. Under the new conditions of the struggle, the CLA leadership (Cannon, Shachtman, Swabeck), in harmony with the decisive elements of the ICL, declared: If we do not break out of our sectarian, propagandistic existence, we are doomed! This formula we repeated and repeated until it became part of the living consciousness of the bulk of the CLA membership and thus prepared them for the big step forward that had to be taken.

This indisputable formula encountered, however, not a little resistance. We who had stood firmly by the principles and organization of our movement for years, resisting successfully every effort to dilute them in an opportunistic sense, undisturbed by the superficial critics of our intransigent and stubborn adherence to fundamental principle (which they erroneously labelled 'sectarianism'), were suddenly, but not unexpectedly, confronted by comrades who had gotten a rush of organizational patriotism to the head – at the wrong time, in the wrong place, and in the wrong way. What? We are doomed, you say? 'Cannon and Shachtman have no faith in the CLA' – 'The CLA is not just a "nucleus" of the new party' – 'The CLA is not a swamp or a sect' – 'They are preparing to liquidate us into some centrist morass or other' – and more of the same.

Yet, our formula remained indisputable. A propaganda group which, when the situation demands a turn to the masses, does not make this turn, and make it resolutely and decisively, is doomed to hopeless sectarianism …

The Workers Party up to the June Plenum

The building of an effective political party, especially a revolutionary Marxian party, is hardly the simplest thing in the world, and unfortunately there are no cut-and-dried universal formulae which can be applied to every situation at every time. What we have to go by are the general experiences of the revolutionary movement; what we can always guide ourselves by is the good rule: base yourselves always on the tested and unassailable principles of Marxism, and after making a political analysis of each concrete situation, act politically; avoid rigid formalism, subjective considerations, personal combinations, old prejudices; allow for the aid which time and corroborating events will always bring to your political line. But above all, have a political line, based upon a political analysis of the situation or problem which is before you concretely.

With these general rules for building the party, we have been able to see more than a day ahead and to be prepared in advance accordingly. That too is why our organizational methods, so violently criticized by all our inner-party opponents, were not the product of caprice, of accident, of episodic contingency, but, on the contrary, the logical, thought-out product of a consistent political line.

The Weberites and Oehlerites in the CLA first broke their pick, in one sense, on abstract and formalistic comparisons in making their political analysis of the AWP. The CLA was a revolutionary Marxian group, they declared (and they were right), and the AWP was a typically centrist group (and they were wrong because that characterization was inadequate and consequently false). …

The fused party represented a unity of two different streams. It was only at its inception. It is ridiculous to imagine that the unity is all accomplished by the mere fact of a unity convention. Its real unification and solidification can be effected only in the course of joint work and joint elaboration of policy, the prerequisite for which is the breaking down of old organizational barriers and mutual political and psychological suspicions, the establishment of mutual confidence, and above all the establishment of an atmosphere which makes possible effective joint work and joint elaboration of policy. The unity which we worked so hard and carefully to establish can easily be disrupted, especially if anything is done to heighten the feeling, on one side, that the other is composed of windbags, hairsplitters and spittoon philosophers, and on the other side, that the first is composed of hard-boiled centrists and opportunists. Instead of sharpening and crystallizing prematurely and unnecessarily any divergent tendencies that may exist, it is imperative (*especially in view of the fact that both organizations had just gone through a solid year of internal discussion prior to the fusion!*) to plunge the party into concrete day-to-day work, to create a normal atmosphere instead of a superheated one, to make possible the assimilation of all assimilable elements and not to declare, a priori, that this, that or the other comrade is unassimilable and must have an 'ideological campaign' launched against him.

The main core of the party leadership is sound, and it is essential to facilitate the collaboration of its ranks, precisely in order that it may be able, *unitedly*, to deal with inimical and unabsorbable elements, and deal with them in such a way and at such a time as will not create the suspicion in anyone's mind that the leadership is out to chop off heads, or – to put it more plainly – that the ex-CLAers are out to 'Bolshevize' the party overnight by lopping off – whether for good reasons or not – one AWP man after another. The party is not only very young, but in many sections very immature. It is stupid to approach every one of its internal problems as if it were a solid, long-established, 'old-Bolshevik' party and to act accordingly. It is like a political baby, in many respects, and it must be nursed along through all the disorders of infant growth. Essentially, that is the way to cement the fusion under the concrete conditions obtaining at the time. The Oehler line, sectarian and factional, is the way to disrupt the fusion ...

The Origin of the Weber Group

The origin of the Weber group, like its political position in general, is shrouded in that obscurity and mystification which are characteristic of cliques that operate in the dark, shamefacedly, without banner unfurled, without candidness, without principled platform. ...

The CLA was essentially a propaganda group which, for a whole series of historical circumstances chiefly beyond its control, had to suffer all the maladies of a circle, a sect. All its progressive features combined – and they were many – were not strong enough to eliminate entirely these maladies, brought on basically by its enforced isolation from the health-giving flow of the broad class struggle. Just as it would be philistinism to ignore the great contributions to the revolutionary movement which even this small propaganda group was able to make and did make, so it would be gross sentimentalism and misplaced patriotism to ignore the negative aspects of its existence. Among these negative aspects are tendencies to routine conservatism; to personal frictions which become exaggerated beyond all proportion to their real importance; to yielding to isolation and becoming ingrown and contented with things as they are; to bitterness with your isolation becoming transformed into finding fault with this or that comrade, this or that group for objective difficulties basically beyond anyone's control; to a dozen and one other of the evils attendant upon the life of a propaganda group.

In the course of the early years of the CLA (1932–3), these negative aspects of the League's life were manifested in an increasingly violent struggle in the leadership and the ranks which divided them into two groups, the Cannon and Shachtman factions. It would lead us too far afield to go into the details of this internal struggle. Nor is it necessary, if only because of the facts that it has long ago been outlived and effectively liquidated and that it had no basis in political or principled differences. It appeared to revolve around accusations of organizational abuses on the one side and similar delinquencies on the other, for both sides repeatedly stressed the absence of serious political differences as the basis of the fight. What is necessary is that a political explanation be given of ***why*** the fight took place, what was its nature, and how it was and why it had to be settled. The Weber group today lives essentially on poisoned reminiscences of that obsolete struggle; it still circulates the faction accusations of Shachtman against Cannon and vice versa as the material with which it 'educates' its supporters. It tears situations and arguments right out of their context and in a thoroughly absurd – not to say criminal – manner applies them to present-day situations which have no kinship with those of the past. …

The fight to get the party to come out in favor of a left wing in the SP and to do something about it was initiated by us; at best we got perfunctory aid in June from the Weberites; at worst, i.e. as a rule, they joined in the cheap Oehlerite clamor about our 'liquidationism'. The fight for a realistic, Marxian unity policy in the unemployed field was initiated by us and sabotaged by the Musteites; the Weberites either played possum on the whole issue or else – as is now the case – they sign their names to the shameful avowals of indiscipline and defiance of the party made by the Musteites, to the policy which plays into the hands of the reformists and Stalinists. The fight against Stalinist influences in our party, manifested so crudely in Allentown, was initiated and carried through by us, for a long time together with Muste; when his factional interests caused him to make a 180-degree turn on the Allentown situation, he found the Weberites on hand to help him shield the microbe-bearers of Stalinism.

Now, when we have initiated a new step forward for the forces of the Fourth International in this country, when we propose entry into the SP and YPSL, the Weberites again come forward with their sterile, negative position, in the same dead spirit and with the same arguments – reeking of sectarian timidity (to say nothing of the same factional distortions) – they advanced a year and a half ago against fusion with the AWP. …

A Final Note: The Muste Group

From every point of view, the Muste group represents a far more significant quantity and quality in the labor and revolutionary movements than do the Weberites. This is not so because Muste knows more than, or even as much as, Weber does about the theory of the permanent revolution, but because he represented to a considerable degree an authentic *movement* of class-conscious militants who have evolved from general labor education, trade union progressivism and activism in the class struggle to the ranks of the Bolshevik political movement. Each one of us has evolved in his own way to the point; important is the fact that, despite halts on the road and even excursions into bypaths, the Muste group did not remain standing still but moved to a left-wing position with greater or lesser consistency. Its evolution is, I think, a unique one in modern world labor history, if only because of the fact that it developed to the point that it did principally on the basis of the lessons drawn from empirical experience (in the best sense of the term) in the class struggle, and not so much on the basis of Marxian theory and perspective more or less developed in advance. Precisely therein, however, lies an essential weakness ...

In qualifying the AWP and its leadership (more than a year ago) as centrist, we not only did not designate them thus for the purpose of 'abuse' (the very concept is absurd in this connection) but, quite the contrary, as an indication of their *progressive* character. Just as the centrism of Stalin is reactionary, for it marks a departure to the right of the Marxian position of the Russian Communist Party of yesterday, so the centrism of the AWP was progressive, for it marked a departure to the left of the position of its precursor, the CPLA. That is why we only smiled patiently at those pseudo-intransigents in our own ranks at that time who appealed to us (presumably 'old Bolsheviks') to be on our guard against fusing with 'people who will never become communists' (Glotzer), just as we had to shrug our shoulders impatiently at the same pseudo-intransigents who made a bloc with 'people who will never become communists' against ... us.

Our course with regard to the Musteites was at all times grounded on a clear line, worked out with a long-time perspective, of the closest and most loyal collaboration for the purpose of jointly advancing the movement for the Fourth International, of steering it carefully through its first difficult period, of protecting it from its numerous foes both outside and inside the party. From the point of view of straightforward progress, the first six months of the existence of the party were undoubtedly its most fruitful ones. That was made possible by the loyal collaboration of the Musteites with the Marxian core of the CLA. Our standpoint was, throughout the whole first period (we expressed it more than once), that while we were anxious to facilitate the utmost cooperation with the Weberites, and even with the Oehlerites, the *main* basis for the progressive development of the party consisted in the collaboration between the elements grouped around Muste and those grouped around us, not the *whole* basis, but the *main* basis. It was on the foundation of this joint, intimate work that the Muste group, in that period, made a consistently progressive contribution to the advancement of our movement.

The sharp, totally uncalled-for rupture of this collaboration which was effected on Muste's initiative at and after the June Plenum indicates above all – and we are perfectly ready to acknowledge the fact – that we had overestimated the speed and the quality of Muste's development from an uncertain centrist position on political questions to the more sure-footed and consistent position of Marxism. Muste, brought face to face with the need of drawing another, and more significant, logical conclusion from the whole course he had been pursuing in common with us, drew up short, balked, stood stock still, then moved backward, and, because we were pressing for another step forward, the breach necessarily occurred. …

Or take the situation in Allentown. Muste now seeks to present matters as if we had, somehow, invented a 'situation' in Allentown for the purpose of hounding 'honest workers', or that whatever trivialities may have been involved there, our 'arbitrary' decisions kept making them worse. Yet the Allentown problem is as old as our party, and has always revolved around one central point: the inability or unwillingness of some of the local comrades to resist the infiltration of Stalinist ideas into our movement, their lack of understanding of how dangerous to the working class Stalinism is, their lack of understanding of how to combat it, and the fact that at times they become the direct bearers of Stalinism in our ranks.

As early as 13 January 1935, the PC heard a report from its representative, Oehler, as to the situation in Allentown, and established the need of 'assisting the comrades in clarification on the question of united-front activities with the CP and the Unemployed Councils and particularly against the CP labor party agitation'. Time and again, the PC concerned itself with the Allentown situation, and always with the same problem: how to combat Stalinism, or more accurately, how to get Reich and Hallett to stiffen a bit against Stalinist encroachments. Up to October 28, when the PC sent out a statement on Allentown to all party branches, and even as late as November 11, the problem continued to occupy us all. And what is more, without a single exception, the PC was always unanimous in its decisions. We made no proposal that Muste ever rejected as 'arbitrary', or for any other reasons; Muste never made any proposals that we rejected on any grounds.

Now, however, confronted with the fact that his faction strength is melting away from him, Muste sacrifices the interests of the party for the presumed interests of holding together his Allentown caucus and rushes to the defense of the same Reich from whom the PC found itself compelled, time and time again, to dissociate itself. He covers up, shields, condones the most defiant violations of elementary communist discipline. Instead of helping the Allentown comrades advance towards a revolutionary Marxian education, he coddles them, tickles them, tells them what fine, upright, sturdy proletarians they are and that, being honest workers, they have a right to make grave errors and to strike stiff blows at the party, especially when they have caucus leaders who will shield them not merely from disciplinary measures, but from any efforts to correct their wrong line, dispel their suspicions and prejudices, and help in their education as revolutionary Marxists. Muste doesn't educate his followers; he flatters them. And workers, however honest they are, require not flattery from their leaders, but a correct and straightforward line of policy. And centrist vacillation, doubling on your own tracks, constant self-repudiation, are hardly a satisfactory substitute for a consistent revolutionary line.

Conclusion

Those who find in what has been written here only an account of a faction fight, of sectarian-circle strife, of a tempest in a teapot, will only cause the author to doubt the efficacy with which he brought forward his central point. Yet we believe that it is sufficiently clear for most if not all our militants, above all our youth, to discern and understand. Precisely because we want to uproot the last remnants of what has become the reactionary features of sectarian-circle existence, precisely because we want to crush the spirit and methods of intrigue, precisely because we want to redouble the preparations for embarking on the broader field of the class struggle, do we stress so much the main point of this document. Dozens of the details in the document are, in themselves, unimportant. They are adduced here for two reasons: to put an end to some of the corridor versions of events, and to illuminate or illustrate a far more important point.

We have before us a truly breath-taking job: the building of a powerful Bolshevik party in the citadel of world reaction. But this party will never be built – or if it is built, it will never stand up in a crisis – unless it has as its spinal column a steel cadre: hard, tough, firm, flexible, tempered. The two are inseparable: a cadre without a party is a skeleton without flesh or muscle; a party without a cadre is a mass of gelatine that anybody's finger can go through. And how else will the Bolshevik cadre be tempered unless, on every occasion, it has hammered into it more and more of the wisdom we have tried to learn from the great teachers: a deep respect for principle and a hatred for cliquism and intrigue, an equally deep regard for objective judgment of problems and a suspicious intolerance of subjective and personal considerations, a political approach to all political problems and a political solution for them. Now more than ever before are these indispensable, for the revolutionists function today amid a veritable sea of corruption and decay of the old movements, the poisonous fumes of which cannot but be felt in our own ranks unless we constantly counteract them.

Slowly, but surely, the basic elements of the Marxian cadre are being assembled; it has not been a work of days or even months, and it is yet far from completed. In the decisive leadership of the party today are represented not merely the best traditions and forces of the American communist movement, and the revolutionary movement before it, but also the strongest concentration of forces of those, old and new, who have entered the movement of the Bolshevik-Leninists in this country in the last seven years. The fact that the ranks of our group comprise elements from the old Cannon faction, the Shachtman faction, the Carter group (even such 'splinter' groups as the old Field faction, the Garrett-Glee faction, etc.), plus such elements from the old AWP as Selander, Ramuglia and West (of the NC), the Toledo militants, half the Allentown militants, most of the NY activists – all these indicate that you have here no personal combination, no chance clique that the first real wind will disperse, but the concentration of determined Marxian forces on the basis of a *consistent, principled, political line*. The scattering of the Muste group to the four corners of the political globe is a warning sign of the inefficaciousness of a vacillating line as an integrating force. The melting away of the Weber group is a sign that a clique can hold together only when it operates in the dark, that combinationism, however clever it may appear for a time, has a disintegrating effect.

Unless all indications are false, our party is preparing in its overwhelming and decisive majority to take an audacious step forward. Audacious, and at the same time hazardous. Taking this step will not diminish our problems, but multiply them, with this advantage, to be sure, that we shall have a far larger arena in which to solve them. This step would prove our complete undoing, however, and no problem would be solved, if we did not proceed, tomorrow as today and yesterday, like the revolutionary Marxian internationalists we aim to remain. If we do, we shall make great progress, and if we fail we shall be hurled back for years. If the stress we have repeatedly laid on those main lines that have divided our party's ranks for the last year, and the CLA before it, serves to clarify our problems in the minds of comrades who have not always understood them fully, then this document will have accomplished its purpose of being an additional guarantee that the bigger problems we shall face tomorrow will prove easier of solution.

4 Workers Party Calls All Revolutionary Workers to Join the Socialist Party[19]

(1936)

The New Militant

The Cleveland convention of the Socialist Party finally smashed the Old Guard domination, and the Old Guard withdrew. By rejecting the Old Guard, the convention ratified the slogan of an inclusive, democratic party, open to all who stood for the goal of socialism and who are willing to work loyally within the framework of the party.

From these two significant developments we draw two conclusions:

1. By breaking with the Old Guard and by opening its doors to revolutionary workers, the Socialist Party becomes the best rallying ground for the revolutionary forces in building the party of the American proletarian revolution.
2. Taking the militant Socialists at their word, the revolutionary workers outside the Socialist Party should immediately join it.

Acting on these conclusions, the National Committee of the Workers Party exercising the authority expressly given to it by the party convention, has formally dissolved the organization and all its members are joining the Socialist Party. The Spartacus Youth League has taken similar action to join the Young People's Socialist League.

These conclusions and the actions proceeding from them, are the result of a careful and concrete analysis of the course of development of the Socialist Party during the last two years.

19 Editorial, *New Militant*, 1936.

Turning Point at Detroit

The Detroit convention of the Socialist Party in 1934 marked a decisive turning point in the history of the movement. The Declaration of Principles then adopted, despite the ambiguity and confusion of its formulations, made a sharp break with the classical reformism of the postwar Social Democracy, and gave evidence of a determination not to repeat the terrible mistakes and crimes of the parties which had led the Austrian and German masses to the yoke of Fascism. The Waldmans, Pankens and Oneals rightly characterized the document as a break with 'democratic Socialism', i.e. the cowardly and treacherous Social-Democratic reformism of the war and postwar years.[20]

Though the leftward tendency of the Socialist Party has not achieved programmatic clarity and, in some respects, retrogressive steps were taken at Cleveland, nevertheless the general trend of the party, as measured by the activities of its membership and the increasing violence of its collisions with the extreme right wing of the party, is undoubtedly progressive. This is to be seen, for example, in the fruitful work of the Socialist militants among the unemployed – a field completely neglected in the past; in the tendency to coordinate the work of Socialists in the trade unions, despite the resistance of party reactionaries allied with the trade union bureaucracy; in the firm stand of the Left Wing in breaking the hidebound reactionary opposition to the United Front; and in the steadily increasing interest of the party membership in the fundamental questions of the revolutionary program, above all in the consistent development within the Socialist Party on the question of the struggle against war.

The Question of War

War is the most crucial issue of this epoch. On this question the Social Democracy foundered and collapsed in 1914. On this question both the international Social Democracy and the degenerate Third International reveal their ideological bankruptcy and their readiness to betray the working class to the imperialists. It is this question that divides the proletariat of today into the two camps: those who will and those who will not fight against imperialist war.

20 Reference is made here to Louis Waldman, Jacob Panken, and James Oneal – leaders of the Socialist Party's 'Old Guard', hostile to militant and revolutionary currents. [Eds.].

Alone of all the important parties of the Second International, the Socialist Party of America took a firm and courageous stand against capitalist government 'sanctions'. Alone of all these parties, the American party repudiated the fictitious distinction between 'peaceful' and 'aggressive' capitalist nations. In spite of the terrible barrage of Stalinist pressure, the Socialist Party has continued to develop more clearly and decisively toward a genuinely revolutionary conception of the nature of the proletarian struggle against war. In this field the Cleveland convention made its most important theoretical contribution, adopting a detailed resolution which goes further in the direction of a Leninist position against war than any Socialist party has ever done.

Naturally it remains to be seen to what extent this developing position on war has been and will be assimilated by the party membership. Undoubtedly, this position will not become fully integrated into the actions of the Socialist Party without a systematic educational campaign. Such an educational campaign will scarcely be complete unless it involves all the basic questions which are inextricably involved in the war question – the international nature of the class struggle, the road to power, the nature of the workers' state, etc. – questions on which clarity in the Socialist ranks lags considerably behind the development of the war issue.

The Break with the Old Guard

Indeed, the most basic and far-reaching gains made by the Socialist Party do not yet lie in the realm of theoretical clarification. The revolutionary potentialities in the Socialist Party have been best expressed by its break with the ossified Old Guard. We have often pointed out what, in our opinion, has constituted the main weakness of the fight against the Old Guard; it was permitted to look like a purely organizational fight between groups contending for power, while the basic programmatic issues underlying that struggle were not clarified. Fighting for corrupt and reactionary principles, the Old Guard, nevertheless, has formulated the issues more clearly than its opponents. But fortunately for the future of the working class movement, the break was irrevocably made at Cleveland and the Socialist workers are free to develop their destiny without the deadening influence of the Old Guard.

And what a noxious, poisonous influence the Old Guard was! What a debilitating influence the Waldmans and Pankens exerted on a generation of Socialist workers! In ideological solidarity with the Scheidemanns and Noskes who slaughtered the German revolutionists and delivered the European working class back into the hands of capitalism; repudiating every vestige of Marxism which remained imbedded in the Social Democracy even in its opportunist years preceding the war; either part of or allied with the class-collaborationist trade union bureaucrats – not to speak of all the outright racketeering among the Old Guard! – and even now railing Dubinsky and Hillman into the Roosevelt camp; comfortable, aging Philistines, stern and implacable only against revolutionists and militants – for a decade and a half these traitors poured their poison into the minds and hearts of Socialist workers. The socialist worker, seeking a way out from capitalism, could find guidance, in all those years, only in the venal and corrupt *Jewish Forward* or its English version, the *New Leader*. The worker or student seeking to learn something of scientific socialism was delivered into the hands of the Algernon Lees of the Rand School! Groups of workers engaged in struggle against repressive administration in their unions, if they were naïve enough to bring their problems to the Julius Gerbers, were betrayed to the bureaucrats not only by being restrained from struggle, but also by the direct process of stool-pigeoning. The Old Guard gave aid to not a single one of the important struggles for democratic rights on behalf of political prisoners! They did not lift a finger to aid the organization of the millions of unemployed. Under their regime the Socialist Party had all the vices of the European Social Democracy without even the advantage of being the party of the masses.[21]

Degeneration of the Communist Party

Now the Socialist workers are freed of this horrible, parasitic excrescence. At first thought, indeed, it appears incredible that thousands of militant workers and youth could have joined the Socialist movement while the Old Guard ruled the party. They joined, of course, in spite of the Old Guard. The main influx has come since 1928. That influx was only possible because of the degeneration of the Communist Party.

---

21 Philip Scheidemann and Gustav Noske were prominent in the right wing of the German Social Democratic Party that oversaw the murderous repression of the 1919 Spartakist uprising, in which revolutionaries Rosa Luxemburg and Karl Liebknecht (among the many others) killed. David Dubinsky and Sidney Hillman were leaders of the International Ladies Garment Workers Union and the Amalgamated Clothing Workers of America – both having ties with the Socialist Party 'Old Guard', with which Algernon Lee (director of the Socialist Party's Rand School) and Socialist Party functionary Julius Gerber were also identified. [Eds.].

The revolutionary workers have been joining the Socialist Party since 1928 because the relative autonomy of state and local organizations made it possible for them to function in it, even though under fearful handicaps. In the Communist Party they could not function at all. It is no mere coincidence that the Socialist Party has grown precisely in the years since the Communist Party, yoked to the 'national Socialism' of Stalin, ceased in actual fact to be a party. It is no accident that the growth of the Socialist Party began in the same year that we, then the Left Opposition, were expelled from the Communist Party. The CP became nothing more than a rigid apparatus-clique; even the memory of party democracy disappeared; scoundrels and nonentities were appointed by Stalin and consecrated overnight as 'beloved leaders'; party policies were infinitely closer to those of the Old Guard than to those of militant Socialism. From this repellent caricature of a revolutionary organization, an organization neither revolutionary nor a party, thousands of revolutionary workers recoiled. From the first they chafed at the Philistine passivity imposed by the Old Guard, and now they have smashed through the Old Guard.

It is extraordinary, indeed, to contemplate the dialectics of this swift development. The Socialist Party is left an empty shell by the surge of revolutionists to the Communist Party in 1919. But the Communist Party becomes a stifling apparatus. Workers recoil and enter the Socialist Party and give it new life. But in the process they have also transformed the party and driven out the Old Guard [Social] Democrats who controlled it. Thus the drive of the proletariat to revolutionary organization asserts itself in spite of all obstacles.

Party Democracy

That drive is, of course, not completed. It is just beginning and will not end this side of the American proletarian revolution. The Socialist workers are now in a state of evolution toward a consistent Marxist conception of their tasks. Not the least of the forms that dialectics takes is the conflict, the give and take, of ideas about theory, strategy and tactics. Only that which is dead – like the prison regime of the Old Guard and the caricature of monolithism which is the Communist Party – provides no arena for ideological differentiation. The mature revolutionist seasoned in the front lines of the class struggle, conscious of the manifold practical problems of the party and the significance of the day to day drudgery, knows very well what a powerful aid to these tasks is the clarifying word, the sharp arrow pointing out the road ahead. Theory and practice go hand in hand in a healthy revolutionary movement. Naturally, there are differences that arise at every crucial turning of the road.

These differences must be threshed out by free discussion among the membership, and not decided by bureaucratic decrees of self-constituted Popes. A party without democracy is not a party. The best and, indeed, the only guarantee for a normal solution of disputed questions is the fullest democracy in educational work and discussion, coupled with an attitude of responsibility and discipline. There is only one cure for the terrible blight of mental stultification which Stalinism and Old Guardism have brought into the labor movement: we must recapture, and make a living part of the heritage of the revolutionary movement, the Marxist principle that the free discussion of ideas is the only method whereby the proletarian vanguard can collectively hammer out the correct program that it needs if it is to work out the salvation of the human race.

We are confident that in such an atmosphere of democracy and discipline, the Socialist Party will grow as never before. Already, with the ousting of the Old Guard in New York and the simultaneous influx of revolutionary elements the party has taken a swift leap forward in membership and activity. The party is still in relation to the American working class, in its practical impact upon it, primarily a propaganda organization. But it is today the party that can, given the correct developments within it, become the party of the masses. We revolutionary Internationalists who are called 'Trotskyites' begin our work in the Socialist Party with the fullest confidence in the outlook for the future.

We are not afraid of isolation. There are times when the revolutionists, if they are to remain true to their principles, have no other alternative. For more than seven years we endured repression and slander, contumely and physical assault, in an isolated struggle for principle. We survived. We are proud of our struggle. We retract nothing and repent nothing. We are not afraid of isolation when circumstances impose it. But no less courage is required to turn away from isolation and move toward the mass party when conditions open the way for such a step. It would be sectarian folly to reject the opportunity to participate in a broader movement, bringing to it all our heritage and all our ideas, which have been confirmed by every development in the international working class movement.

Joining the Socialist Party as we are, with our ideas and traditions, we urge all revolutionary workers to do likewise and to add their energies to the efforts of the many thousands of socialist workers in a common struggle to build a powerful party of revolutionary Socialism.

5 The Crisis in the Party[22]

(March 1937)

Socialist Appeal

During the past month it has become clear to every alert party member that our party is in the midst of a serious crisis. It would be a mistake, however, to imagine that the existence of more or less organized 'factions' or 'groups' is the mark of the crisis. On the contrary, groups and factions are entirely normal and healthy in the life of an active and democratic political organization. It is through such groups, functioning within the disciplined framework of the party as a whole, that differing ideas and methods are presented for discussion and decision to the party membership. Though internal groups may and should disappear temporarily from time to time, on the rare occasions when there is no important divergence on political issues among the membership – indeed, a group which is not built on a specific political platform is of necessity an unprincipled organizational clique – nevertheless the long continued absence of groups is a sure proof not of united vigor, but of sterility and political death. This is precisely the meaning of the complete absence of internal groupings in the parties of the Communist International. They are absent in the CI because critical thought is prohibited. Differences of opinion are settled not by democratic discussion, but by expulsion – or, in the Soviet Union itself, by the still more direct methods of the GPU.

The existence of groups in our party, then, is not what indicates the crisis. What shows that there is a crisis is, rather, the fact that certain groups and individuals in the party call for the *splitting* of the party, call for the *expulsion*, not merely for the *political defeat*, of the group or groups to which they are opposed.

22 Editorial, *Socialist Appeal* 1937. The *Socialist Appeal* was a modest periodical within the Socialist Party of America. It was initiated by left-wing lawyer Albert Goldman, who had joined the CLA after being expelled from the Communist Party in 1933, then on his own decided to join the Socialist Party of America. After the CLA dissolved and joined the SP, he reconnected with his old comrades, and the *Socialist Appeal* became an organ of the Trotskyists within the SP. After their expulsion, the Socialist Appeal became the name of their newspaper, though in 1941 the name *The Militant* was re-adopted. [Eds.].

It is essential that the party membership understand the exact political nature of the crisis, so that it may act on the basis of such understanding, and not through either ignorance or prejudice.

The present crisis, as the *Appeal* has already made clear, is not something altogether new and unexpected. It is, in reality, simply one stage further in the process of development which began nearly four years ago, and which has twice before reached the level of crises: once in connection with the 'Declaration of Principles'; again at the Cleveland Convention. The actions taken at Cleveland, the split with the main forces of the Old Guard, in New York, Pennsylvania and Connecticut, though representing a progressive answer to the immediate issue then so sharply posed, were yet insufficient to solve the fundamental problem. For this reason, the subsequent sharpening of new conflicts, the breaking out of a new crisis could not have been avoided, no matter what efforts were made at postponement. The calling of the Special Convention precipitated the new crisis at the new stage of the development of the party as a whole. This result necessarily followed from the calling of the Special Convention precisely because the fundamental problem is not yet solved. And until it is solved, in one of the only two possible ways, new crises, in varying degrees of intensity, will periodically arise.

What, then, is the fundamental problem? The *Appeal* has repeatedly stated it; it is neither complex nor mysterious. It is simply this: will the party continue forward on the road through which it will become the revolutionary party of the American working class? Or will it slip back into reformism and disintegration? Since 1933 this has been the basic problem underlying every other issue in the party, and every organizational struggle; and it will continue to dominate the party until it is finally settled, one way or the other. For it is not yet settled. Even the split with the main forces of the Old Guard did not settle it, as the present situation in the party makes sufficiently obvious.

Since Cleveland the problem has, in some measure at least, been fitted into a new setting. This is due to the extraordinary rapidity of social and political changes, both nationally and internationally. To mention but a few of the more important: The new imperialist war has moved appreciably nearer, and throughout the world all political policies are dominated by preparations for the war. The social conflict in Spain reached the climax of open civil war. The General Strike in France showed that the French proletariat is on the eve of decisive struggles. The Soviet bureaucracy, seeing the approach of the war, finds it necessary to advance its new policy with multiplied speed and ruthlessness, as shown above all by the Moscow Trials. In this country the CIO movement and the wave of strikes show in their own way the deep repercussions of the growing international clash of forces. All of these great events, directly or indirectly, consciously or unconsciously, leave their impress on our party, and help to determine the present program and relationships of groups and individuals.

For a considerable time following the adoption of the new People's Front orientation by the Communist International, the chief object of the Communist party in this country with reference to the Socialist party was to obliterate the memories of the 'Third Period' and of the Madison Square Garden episode. The violent abuse of the Third Period changed to kindliness. Social-fascists became the best of comrades. The united front and then the People's Front became the order of the day. But an unfortunate conflict arose, and Browder was placed in the most perplexing dilemma faced by any of the little leaders of the Third International. The new line of the CI with respect to the parties of the Second International was predicated on the assumption that these parties were reformist, social-democratic, in policy; and indeed flowed from the fact that the CI itself had taken over a reformist policy. But in this country the Stalinists discovered that the Socialist party was rapidly leaving reformism and social democracy behind; so determinedly, in fact, that in the Spring of 1936 it split with the spearhead of reformism and recruited into its own ranks the revolutionists from the former Workers' party. Here was a formidable obstacle indeed: The plan of the CP to enlist the masses of the democratic countries for the coming war dictated joining with the reformist parties of the Second International in anti-revolutionary Popular Fronts which would simultaneously make ready a mass recruiting base for the war and wipe out any independent revolutionary political organization. But the Socialist party of the US, though still formally a member of the Second International, was proving a recalcitrant mistress. Instead of leaping happily into the arms of her Peoples Front lover, she was turning in the opposite direction, toward direct struggle against capitalism – even, unfortunately for Browder, against democratic capitalism – and against the approaching war. She carried through her divorce action against Waldman, and then – horror of horrors – instead of knocking at Browder's door on 13th Street, she was discovered consorting with 'the vanguard of the bourgeoisie, the counter-revolutionary assassins', in short, the Trotskyites.

Stalinists 'Help' Us

The blows fell on Browder. And to cap them off, the Socialist party insisted, insisted against the very best and most sympathetic advice of the Ninth Convention of the Communist party, on conducting an independent working-class campaign in the 1936 Elections. This was too much. And from then on the Stalinists have carried on against the erring Socialist friends a campaign whose intensity and viciousness is unparalleled in the history of the labor movement in this country – all, of course, as the recent 'Appeal to Socialists', published by the Stalinists, points out, in the most friendly spirit 'of comradely assistance', all of course 'to help you in the task of saving and building your party'.

Consider the election campaign. What did the Stalinists say to us? They said that we were the tools of the Landon-Liberty League-Hearst combination. They said quite flatly that Norman Thomas was the stooge of Hearst and Landon. They said that we were destroying working-class unity and directly aiding fascism and reaction because we pointed out that Roosevelt also was an agent of the bourgeoisie. The main fire of their attack, identical with the attack of the Social-Democratic Federation (because proceeding from an identical political line), during the entire campaign was directed against us. Every vote they gave to Roosevelt, master-strategist of American imperialism, was a blow against reaction (Browder boasted about it in his post-election report); every vote they took away from us was a victory for progress.

It has been the same with every issue which has arisen during the months since Cleveland. When we point out that the issue in Spain is socialism vs. capitalism, that the workers of Spain cannot win in the end by confining their struggle to the preservation of capitalist democracy, then we are, say the Stalinists, allies of Franco. When Norman Thomas and Devere Allen join a Committee to defend the right of asylum and of a fair hearing, so fatefully threatened by the Moscow Trials and the lynch campaign against Trotsky, they have become tools of assassins. When the *Call* calls for no support of the US government in any war, Browder, in his Madison Square Garden speech, carefully suggests that it is preparing to sell out the United States to Japan. When our comrades call for a class-struggle policy in the Workers' Alliance and an end with behind-the-back deals with supervisors and purely parliamentary slogans, they have become disrupters of the unity of the unemployed. When our party demands as an international perspective a break with the class collaborationism of the People's Front and an advance along the road of revolutionary struggle for socialism, we have gone over into the fascist camp and have joined the enemies of the Soviet Union. And in recent weeks, in California, Newark, New York City, Boston, our comrades distributing leaflets and literature, are set upon physically by Stalinist hoodlums.

Stalinist Cure for SP

But the efforts of the Stalinists are not by any means confined to mere pedagogy. They propose to do more than to teach us little lessons in Marxism-Stalinism. Browder is a practical man as well as the teacher of the American proletariat. He intervenes more directly and with more specific proposals. During recent months especially the mimeograph machine and printing presses of the Stalinists have devoted a flattering amount of attention to material specifically designed for Socialist party members. Scarcely a meeting goes by that we don't have placed in our hands a lengthy document explaining just what is wrong with us and just what we should do to cure it (as Amter gracefully puts it: 'You are the patients. You must also be the doctor. We Communists can only assist you'). The trouble with the Socialist party, as summed up by the Stalinist diagnosticians, is: You have swallowed the Trotskyist poison. The prescribed cure is simply: You must vomit forth this poison. A leaflet recently distributed by the Chicago YCL to 'All Sincere Young Socialists', puts it in capital letters: 'THE RIDDING OF YOUR RANKS OF THIS POISON IS TASK NO. 1 FOR SINCERE YOUNG SOCIALISTS!'

There is nothing accidental in the appearance of these documents. Already last June, at the Ninth Convention of the CP, the Socialist party was told 'if you swallow poison, be sure to have a glass of emetic on hand and drink it quickly'. The approach of the Special Convention poses the question more sharply. As already commented on in the *Appeal*, Browder posed the central task of the coming months in his 4 December report to the Central Committee. It is advisable to quote again from this report the lines which have given the leading directive for Stalinist activity since that time: 'The Socialists must understand that nothing of a constructive nature can come out of the Socialist party except on the basis of struggle against the counter-revolutionary Trotskyite poison. The Socialist party must rid itself of its poisonous influence ...'. Then, more concretely: 'The only way to rid the Socialist party of Trotskyite influence is by concentrating the struggle for the expulsion of the Trotskyites against their most apparently harmful manifestations. The Socialist party has called a special convention for the next March, as you know. We must consult with the best elements in the Socialist party about their problems in the most helpful way ... They must prepare for the March convention of the Socialist party to get results, to win the Socialist party for the united front and make a clean break with counter-revolutionary Trotskyites'.

Here, then, announced openly by the chief spokesman of the Communist party, is the proposal of the Stalinists for the solution of the present crisis in our party. It is summed up in the central slogan: Expel the Trotskyites!

As the Convention draws nearer, the activity of the Stalinists redoubles. One of its latest, and most extraordinary, manifestations is a 16-page brochure, handsomely printed, entitled 'Appeal to Socialists', and obligingly distributed to all Socialist party members free of charge. Every party member should, we urge, take advantage of this generosity; it is a document to read and to ponder.

'Through this bulletin', the 'Appeal to Socialists' begins in a thoroughly comradely fashion, 'we wish to participate in your pre-convention discussion'. The Stalinist conclusion will not come as a surprise. If the Socialist party is to be saved, 'it can only be done by the convention definitely deciding to break with all Trotskyite and semi-Trotskyite policies, and the complete elimination of the Trotskyites from the Socialist party'.

To understand fully the exact meaning of the Stalinist attack, it is necessary to answer carefully two questions: (1) Just what are the 'Trotskyite and semi-Trotskyite policies' with which the party is asked to break? (2) Just who are the 'Trotskyites' whom the Stalinists want to have 'eliminated'?

(1) The Stalinist literature makes absolutely clear what they mean by the Trotskyism which, like a cancer, is eating out the vitals of the Socialist party. Trotskyist poison, says Browder in his report, leads the Socialist party to come 'out in principle against the Peoples Front in America and advocated its liquidation in France and Spain'. Further, Trotskyist sectarianism leads to 'an unprincipled split with its local organizations, which had somewhat of a mass base in Connecticut and Pennsylvania; it split with the New York Old Guard which had trade union connections'. In addition, 'Trotskyism' calls 'on the Spanish people to abandon their present democratic struggle supposedly for an immediate socialist revolution' (from the Chicago YCL pamphlet). And Trotskyism calls for no support of any war undertaken by any capitalist government.

The list could be easily multiplied. But the general point is clear: 'Trotskyism' means anything, anything whatever, which opposes the present People's Front line of the Comintern, any criticism of the People's Front anywhere, any opposition to Stalinist social-patriotism in favor of the revolutionary struggle against war, any belief that the issue of our epoch is that between socialism and fascism and not between democracy and fascism; in short, 'Trotskyism' means any advocacy of the ideas and methods of revolutionary Marxism, as opposed to Stalinist class collaborationism and betrayal; it means any sign of refusal to accept ideological dictation from the CI, any breath of criticism against the Soviet bureaucracy.

This conclusion is of great significance. Some comrades delude themselves with the notion that the attack of the Stalinists is directed merely against the died-in-the-wool 'Fourth Internationalists', against those who base their political position on the complete theory of the 'permanent revolution', the complete analysis of the Soviet Union which is associated with this theory, etc. Let them not be deceived. It may be that the Stalinists look upon the Fourth Internationalists in the Socialist party as the chief immediate danger and the most unrelenting advocates of revolutionary as opposed to Stalinist ideas. But their attack is directed against *every* idea and policy which is incompatible with the present line of the CI, and will continue until every such idea and policy is beaten down – unless, of course, that attack meanwhile is met and defeated.

(2) We are led to a similar conclusion in answer to the question: Who, in the eyes of the Stalinists, are the 'Trotskyites'? Does this mean the Socialist party members who were once members of the former Workers party? Once again, do not be deceived. Let us consult the 'Appeal to Socialists': 'Under the influence of these fascist agents within the working class' the Socialist party 'discovered that the line of the Seventh World Congress, the policy of the People's Front in the struggle against reaction and fascism was "opportunistic"'. In this respect, then, the entire party is apparently Trotskyite. (It should be kept in mind that this 'discovery' was made by the Socialist party some while before the entrance of the Workers' party members). Let us go on: 'The real danger of the Trotskyites to the Socialist party is seen by the extent to which they have corrupted some of the elements of the former "Left". They have practically captured the *Socialist Call*. They maneuvered and succeeded with those persons who are close to their views ... to take over the *Socialist Call* and removed the former editor, Levenstein, who was not satisfactory to the Trotskyites'. Now comes a real revelation: 'The present staff in the national office is, like the *Call* following a policy very close to the Trotskyites ...'. One entire article is entitled, 'The *Socialist Call*'s Trotskyite line'. And Norman Thomas's Trotskyite leanings have been a hundred times assailed in the Stalinist press.

Against whom is the Stalinist attack directed? The Stalinists themselves give the answer: against everyone, anyone, who does not accept the Stalinist ideology; that is, against every revolutionary Socialist, every genuine left-winger, every near left-winger, in the Socialist party. And the attack will not rest until every revolutionist, every left-winger, is whipped into line – unless, once more, we stand up like revolutionists and like men, and smash the attack head on.

What is the aim of the Stalinist attack on the party? The whole content of their campaign, as well as the nature of the international line of the CI, give the answer. The aim is to destroy the Socialist party as an independent political force; to make the Socialist party simply an instrument of Stalinism. And, after all, what other aim could the Stalinists have? To succeed in accomplishing this aim is, in point of fact, a life-and-death matter for Stalinism. The Stalinist preparations for the war cannot be carried through if a strong revolutionary current blocks the social-patriotic path. The war is not far off. Therefore the

Stalinists *must* use every device to break up any revolutionary or potentially revolutionary organization in this or any other country before the war begins.

We 'exaggerate the danger of the Communist party'? The *Appeal* has often been thus criticized. Let the critics consider the fate of the Spanish Socialist Youth. Two years ago they were a powerful organization, moving rapidly in a revolutionary direction, the main hope of the Spanish working class. The Stalinist campaign swung into action. With the help of demagogic – and most friendly – 'unity' slogans, they put across a merger between the Socialist and Stalinist youth into an 'independent revolutionary youth organization'. Today this organization is an affiliate of the Third International, part and parcel of the Stalinist world machine, committed to the most extreme Popular Frontism, its internal political life strangled, and now in the forefront of those in Spain who are hounding the revolutionists who call for a revolutionary struggle against Franco. In Catalonia the Socialist and Communist parties united, and the subsequent history is identical. Politics, alas, is not a nursery game. There is only one way to make peace with Stalinism: and that is by becoming a Stalinist – though even that, as the Trials show, is often not enough.

The Stalinists propose, as their solution for the party crisis, that the Convention 'expel the Trotskyites'. Suppose it were true – as we have seen it is not – that they meant merely, expel the former Workers party members. What then? Would the Stalinists then be 'satisfied'? They themselves make it plain that they would not be.

Then would come the turn of the *Call* Board, with its policies 'taken from Trotskyism'; then of the National Office, with its 'strong Trotskyite influence'; then of all the 'semi-Trotskyites' that the 'Appeal to Socialists' refers to; then of every party member who does not capitulate politically. And each successive amputation would make the next only the easier; the expulsion of the 'extreme Trotskyists' would knock away the solid support of the Left Wing, would leave the remaining left-wingers a hundred times more helpless.

The political mechanics of the process are unquestionable: The expulsion of any section of the Left Wing will *guarantee* the disintegration of the party as an independent political force. The direction of the development of the past four years would be immediately reversed. The party would head back with lightning speed into reformism and class collaborationism, and collapse with a thud into the arms of the Peoples Front.

The Paul Porter Pamphlet

It is not our intention in this article to analyze at length the attack of the Old Guard reformists on the party. The *Appeal* has done this before. And, besides, the Old Guard campaign is identical in political content with the campaign of the Stalinists, from the vicious gibes at the 'Thom-Trotskyist' Socialist party, to the central slogan of 'Expel the Trotskyists'.

The task now is to study the influence of these attacks against the party from the outside on various groups and individuals within the party. Nor is it necessary to speculate whether any given group or individual is to be numbered among those 'best elements of the Socialist party' with whom Browder, in his report, promised to 'discuss … about their problems'. That there are direct agents of the Stalinists in our ranks is more than probable but that is a minor matter. What is more important is to trace the influence of the Stalinist *ideas* and proposals.

Naturally these ideas and proposals find their most receptive audience in those members whose traditional positions have been farthest toward reformism; indeed, the Stalinists have in large measure merely gone back to the ideas which were once the special property of traditional reformists and near-reformists. Thus it is not at all surprising to find one of the closest parallels to the Stalinist attack emerging from the Wisconsin organization. Paul Porter's recent pamphlet, 'Which Way for the Socialist Party?', published for party discussion by the State Executive Board of Wisconsin, with an introduction by the State Secretary, deserves the careful attention of every party member.

It does not require a microscope to discover the character of the general political content of this document. An entire section is headed, 'The Need for an International Peoples Front'. We discover that in this country a farmer-labor party will be 'a Peoples Front in effect, if not in name'. We learn that the war danger now arises from 'the war plans of the fascist nations'. The duty of the Socialist party is to 'ward off' the war danger. In doing so, however, workers' sanctions are a minor weapon (in fact, exclusive insistence on them is 'in our opinion, a new outcropping of syndicalism'); chiefly we must put 'pressure on the government', with such aims as: 'Vigorous opposition to the maintenance of armaments *greater than needed for coast defense*' (our emphasis); 'Removal from the War, Navy, and State Departments, and from the armed forces, of all pro-fascists …; Nationalization of munitions industries'. Our peace policy 'should support the peace policy of the Soviet Union; and it should demand that the American government cooperate … with the government of the Soviet Union and with those People's Front governments that may be established, in their efforts to prevent war through collective security'. We discover that the criticisms of the People's Front in Spain and in France do 'not stand up'. Even the criticisms of Blum's 'neutrality policy' in connection with the Spanish Civil War is pretty much unjustified. 'The major difficulty with the People's Front policy, in the present period, is that it has not been applied extensively enough'. 'Not the disruption of the People's Fronts, but their extension into an International People's Front strong enough to overawe (!!) the Fascist International, is the urgent need today. In the US it is the duty of Socialists to push *our government* in that direction' (our emphasis).

Even Browder must be a little breathless if he has read these last proposals.

We have seen enough to draw an irrefutable conclusion: The Porter pamphlet expresses the political line of the Communist International.

Let us go on. What will the Socialist party do about this Farmer Labor party which is to be an American expression of the People's Front? 'The building of such a party is our foremost responsibility'. And when it comes? If a federated party, our party will of course affiliate. But – observe – 'there are, however, a number of serious objections that may be raised against the federated structure'. An individual membership basis seems on the whole best – after all, it is 'a question of tactics, not of principle'. And, of course: 'Whatever the structural relationship of the Socialist party to the farmer-labor party, Socialists must continue to function as a disciplined group. Liquidation of our party is unthinkable'. So does Porter piously conclude, after just having laid the basis for the liquidation of the Socialist party into the Farmer Labor party, and the transformation of socialist activity into that of an educational league within the Farmer Labor party.

Thus, similarly, with the Socialist leagues in the unions.

'There is today a widespread demand in the Socialist party for leagues of Socialists in all unions. The purpose is a sound one (we are all men of good will, in Comrade Porter's eyes): to coordinate the efforts of Socialists so that they may more effectively advance our cause. The tactic is, in most instances, of doubtful character for it may become self-defeating ... As against the formation of a Socialist league is the more diplomatic and fruitful policy of mobilizing all Progressives around a program that will be of clear and unmistakable benefit to the union'.

On the basis of his political views, how, then, does Porter analyze the internal situation in the party, and what solution does he propose? Unfortunately for the purposes of dramatic effect, there is no surprise coming. The trouble with the party is the 'isolationist trend ... that is thoroughly harmful ...'. 'The comrades in this group ... in practice ... are anti-internationalist and anti-Socialist'. 'The spearhead of this tendency is the Trotskyist group, but their view has spread to others. Apparently, the majority group of the *Socialist Call* Editorial Board has fallen under their influence. At least, the article in the issue of Jan. 16, 1937, entitled "Party Perspectives, No. 3 – The Fight Against War" illustrates this tendency at its worst'. 'Foremost among those who are isolating the party from the labor movement are the Trotskyists …' (for did not the mass workers in Wisconsin elect 10 candidates to the legislature – though somehow losing two-thirds of the party membership in the process – while the sectarian 'Trotskyists' across the State line, in Minnesota, merely built up one of the most powerful and militant trade union movements in American history – somehow quadrupling the party membership meanwhile, in the months since Cleveland?) Incidentally, it should be noted that 'Still another group tending toward isolation is one illustrated by Norman Thomas'.

What then to do? Porter is not, of course, in a position to raise the cry for expulsion and split in quite the direct language of the 'Appeal to Socialists'. Nevertheless, he makes clear that this is the real meaning of his chief concrete proposal. The main danger to the party, he has shown, comes from the sectarian Trotskyists. 'Their dominant concern is one of bitter hostility to the Soviet Union' (the glib manner in which hostility to Stalinism is translated into hostility to the Soviet Union should be noted). 'The history of the Trotskyists affords little evidence that they can aid the Socialist party or the cause of Socialism'. 'True, there are some now associated, in varying degree, with the Trotskyists who may be able to reverse their trend and constructively assist in the tasks we outlined in the previous section; but this they can do only by abandoning the precepts of Trotskyism'. 'If they (the sectarian Trotskyists) cannot accommodate themselves to the needs of the time, then they must be required to part company with us'.

This is plain enough talking. The price of remaining in the party, if Porter has his way, is to be: acceptance of his Peoples Front program. And he has already made up his mind that the greater part of the 'sectarians' will not get under the line: does he not point out that only *some*, now *associated with* the 'Trotskyists' have a chance of 'reversing their trend'. But bluntly: Expel the Trotskyists; split the party. And expel them why? Because of their ideas; because their ideas are incompatible with Porter's plans for the liquidation of the party as an independent revolutionary force. It is always amusing to notice how 'democratic' in practice are all the brave Right-Wing defenders of Democracy.

And Porter searches around for a formula under which to expel the Left. He has not worked out anything entirely satisfactory, but he offers one approach: 'Almost none of them (the Trotskyists) were members of our party a year ago. They were members of another party, the Workers party, and entered our ranks surreptitiously during the confusion caused by the Old Guard split. We say *surreptitiously*, for no request for admission was ever submitted to a national convention ... nor even to the NEC. Those locals which admitted them had no authority to do so ...'. It thus turns out that the Trotskyists are not really members of the party at all; and all the Convention has to do to solve the problem is to recognize this. Have we heard this idea expressed before? Let us turn back to the 'Appeal to Socialists'. We read: 'When the Trotskyites entered the Socialist party it was without the consent or understanding of the members themselves'. Amter's entire article in 'Appeal to Socialists' should be read alongside of Section 3, Chapter I, sub-section 4, of Porter's pamphlet.

The Massachusetts Liquidators

Porter's pamphlet is not an isolated phenomenon. We do not intend, however, to list all of its parallels in other sections of the party. There have been such documents as those issued by the 'Socialist Action Committee' in Indiana, centering as usual on the slogan of 'Expel the Trotskyists'. This Committee turned out to be composed of Communist party members and sympathizers. Recently in Connecticut, a 'Committee of Correspondence' – the name so appropriately taken over from the days of '76 – has blossomed forth to save the party. Its first communication is pure Stalinism, open and undisguised. And its concrete proposal is, of course, 'expel the sectarians'.

But a word or two is needed on the Massachusetts group headed by Alfred Baker Lewis, Bertram Wellman, and Albert Sprague Coolidge. The political position of this group was established in a signed statement appearing in the January issue of the Massachusetts 'State Organizer'. The solution for the Socialist party is to be found in working 'for a broad Farmer-Labor party'. 'To do this we need surrender none of our socialist principles, none of our socialist activities; we need only to follow sound tactics and established propaganda means in carrying them on. If we can, let us affiliate as a party. *If we cannot, let us work within the movement individually and maintain our organization now as we are, later as a Socialist League within the broader party which we shall help grow about us*'. What does this mean? It means nothing more nor less than: *liquidation of the party*. An independent party organizes and leads the masses as an independent force, sustaining all the complex functions that are involved in being a political party. The Massachusetts group proposes to transform the party into a purely educational association which will be part of a 'Farmer Labor party'. Gomberg, in New York, who holds this same position, drops all hypocrisy, and in party meetings openly and unambiguously declares for the liquidation of the party.

Shortly after this document appeared, Hal Siegal made a hurry-up trip from Altman headquarters to Massachusetts. Subsequent to his visit, a special issue of the 'State Organizer' was put out, containing a much longer statement by the Lewis-Wellman-Coolidge group. The work of a finer hand was now in evidence. The formulas were altered. 'Liquidation' was declared to be, in the Porter manner, unthinkable – though naturally the political position which involves liquidation necessarily, was retained. The main fire of the new statement was concentrated – against the 'sectarians'. The anti-Socialist character of the group associated with the *Appeal* was brought out in paragraph after paragraph. What is wrong with the party? The sectarians, the Trotskyists. How to solve the party problems? There was no need to state it explicitly, for the 'solution' follows from the whole logic of the statement: the solution of the Stalinists – the expulsion of the Left.

Observe the logic, for it is not without importance: The danger to the party comes from the sectarians; the perspective for the party is to liquidate it into a Farmer Labor movement; to realize this perspective, the party must expel the sectarians. And Porter and Lewis are consistent. To accomplish their aim – which is in cold fact, stripped of verbiage, the aim of the Stalinists: namely, the destruction of the party as an independent political force – they must expel the 'sectarians', precisely because these same 'sectarians' refuse to accept this aim, of liquidation, and thus constitute an insurmountable obstacle to it.

The Altman Group

How significant, how very significant it is to find that in all the documents of the Stalinists, including the major opus, 'Appeal to Socialists', in the Porter pamphlet, in the statements of the Massachusetts liquidators, there is not one single word of criticism of the Altman group. Not one word. The sectarians, the Trotskyists, the semi-Trotskyists, the majority of the *Call* Board, Zam and Tyler, the staff in the National Office, Norman Thomas, all are chided with one or another degree of severity ('more in sorrow than in anger', as Porter remarks). But not one word of annoyance against Altman.

No one will be so naive as to imagine that this is accidental. The truth is: *the Right Wing of the party, in its present stage of development, made up of a heterogeneous brew ranging from religious pacifist to Fabians to Populists to outright Stalinists, has taken form back of the Altman group*. The Altman leadership constitutes the front line of the Right Wing.

That this should be so is required by circumstances. The party membership would not conceivably swallow open pacifism and liquidationism and Stalinism. Therefore the pacifists and liquidationists and Stalinists cannot be in the forefront of the Right Wing. The Right Wing must manufacture for itself a 'left front'; and the Altman leadership is admirably suited to the purpose.

Are not the Altmanites 'good left wingers'? Of course they are: just read their literature and hear them speak – they continually emphasize it. Are they not 'against the People's Front'? Certainly they say so, time after time. Are they not 'against the liquidation of the party'? No one repudiates 'liquidationism' more indignantly. Are they not for a 'left wing position on war'? Who could dream otherwise, in the face of their protestations?

Or so, at any rate, the Altman group appears *to the bulk of its own active membership*, as well as to a number of other party members who have not yet fully clarified to themselves the party situation.

But let us pause a while. Are we quite sure just what the Altman position is? Somehow, it has never been written down concretely. Somehow, the Altman group has never had time to commit itself in writing. *The Altman group is branded with the outstanding mark of an unprincipled clique*: the group was formed *first*, and its platform and program are to be formulated – *afterwards*. When? When, if at all, it becomes clear just what organizational combination will prove most advantageous, at which time the program can be adapted accordingly. In the statement sent out 10 February 1937, calling for the national organization of the group, we read: 'A program embodying our basic theoretical stand as well as our position on the immediate issues facing the party is now under preparation and will be published shortly'.

'Against the People's Front'? No doubt. But somehow, under the Altman administration in Local New York, members are brought up on charges for criticizing Blum or Caballero; somehow Murray Baron, outstanding Altmanite, calls those who criticize the People's Front in Spain 'strike breakers'; somehow Local New York finds itself entangled with the North American Committee to aid Spanish Democracy; somehow Comrade Spector is brought up on charges by an Altmanite for defending publicly the position on the persecution of the POUM adopted by the National Action Committee and published in the *Call*. 'Against liquidation'? Of course. But somehow Murray Gross, a signer of the statement, advocates Socialists joining the American Labor party as individuals in spite of the decision of the ALP that anyone joining it must renounce membership in any other party. Somehow Gomberg, an open liquidationist, votes with the Altman group. Somehow Lash, working in the heart of the Altman group, proposes a 'reorganization' of the YPSL which would destroy all its independent political life. 'For a left wing position on war'? Naturally. But Local New York, last June, found itself marching in a Peace Parade of the American League against War and Fascism, and even now has a representative on some kind of committee negotiating or 'coordinating' with the League. And party members publicly advocating pacifism, collective security and the rest of it are somehow never found guilty of those 'violations of discipline' to which the sectarians seem so addicted.

Still, a clear political position on the key problems confronting the movement is no doubt an abstract and minor matter – hair-splitting, as Porter and Lewis call it – when the party is in a state of crisis. Perhaps we do Altman an injustice. Perhaps his group *has* a position on 'the crucial question'. And, in truth – if by the crucial question we mean the internal question – it has. Nor is it alone in its position: it shares its point of view with Lewis, with Porter, and with the Stalinists. Let us investigate briefly:

What is the main danger to the party? The 10 Feb. statement answers: 'the unfortunate trend within the party toward sectarianism and isolation. The undersigned definitely feel that there has been a drift toward sectarianism within the party and this drift must be arrested *by immediate action*' (our emphasis). 'We cannot allow the outlook of the *Socialist Appeal* to set the tone of the party'. Who are the sectarians? Merely the former members of the Workers party? By no means: the Altman conclusions coincide with the conclusions of the 'Appeal to Socialists': 'The Zam-Tyler group … very much like the reactionary Old Guard, … fear the idea of a Labor party for they fear contact with the masses. Such contacts would destroy their pretty illusion of the "revolutionary upsurge" of the workers. Rather than face reality, they hide their heads in the sand and continue to speak in theoretical pronouncements but doing nothing to apply these in their daily life …'. The 'entire outlook' of the Zam-Tyler group 'tends toward DeLeonism and monolithism …'. 'The Zam-Tyler slate' in the city elections 'was supported by the ultra-sectarian caucus of the members of the former Workers party'.

Who are the friends of Altman in the party? 'Another aspect of this same division is in our attitude toward other elements within the party, particularly Wisconsin. We consider these sections of the party loyal Socialists, and although we differ with them on many questions, are willing to make sacrifices to secure harmony within the party'.

What 'sacrifices' are you prepared to make? Porter laid down the terms of the sacrifice clearly enough: the sacrifice of revolutionary principle; and, first and foremost, the sacrifice of – the Left Wing. Let us go further in the Altman statement: 'The acid test today is the question of cooperation with the power caucus within the party formed by members of the former Workers party. We consider this group to base itself upon reactionary sectarianism and feel its ideology and general perspective to be injurious to the best welfare of the party. This group has made scant headway since its formation … primarily because it has stamped itself within the party as a Communist opposition rather than as a Socialist group ... We have no intention of helping the party to become an anti-Communist, anti-Soviet league ... Therefore, we have declared that a condition of unity (with the Zam-Tyler group) must be a refusal to make political deals with this power caucus ...'. A basic plank in the proposed 5-point program for 'left wing unity' is: '2. United group without the Trotskyites' (our emphasis).

But does the Altman leadership draw the final conclusion of the 'Appeal to Socialists' – namely, on the basis of its analysis of the party situation, expulsion of the 'Trotskyites'? At first glance, apparently not. Point 4 of the 'unity program' reads: 'A general statement be sponsored by joint committee stressing need for unity in party. We affirm our belief in the free expression within the Socialist party of every point of view *within the limits of Socialist thought*' (our emphasis). Altman makes no bones about exclusion of the Trotskyists being a necessary condition for a united *group*. But what does that mean with reference to the party as a whole? This Point 4 gives the answer. Does the position of the 'ultra-sectarians' come within the confines of 'socialist thought'. The statement proves that, in Altman's eyes, it does *not*. The ultra-sectarians are 'anti-Soviet' and function as a '*Communist opposition rather than as a Socialist group*'. Murray Baron, in his speech to the first open meeting of the Clarity group, made it quite plain: the Trotskyists now in our party, he declared, are '*outside agitators*' – this is the exact phrase. The only possible conclusion is, therefore: expel them.

This, then, is the political anatomy of the Altman group laid bare. Because of the wholly bureaucratic manner in which the leadership of the group functions, because of its lack of an openly declared program, because of its demagogic hypocrisy, it is true that the bulk of the membership of the group does not understand the true meaning of its policy, and would repudiate it if it were understood. Let the membership call its leaders to account, and drag them into the light. Eyes should be opened at least a few steps before the edge of the cliff.

The Clarity Group

The *Appeal* has already defined the general character of the political position of the Clarity group (i.e. the Zam-Tyler group). We do not propose here to review in detail its history and record. In the present concrete situation in the party, the Clarity group is the major section of the *Center*. It is on record against expulsions or splits, as well as against liquidation; while at the same time it refuses unity of the Left Wing as proposed by the Appeal Association. Its policy is dictated by its ambiguous and equivocal position, trying to play both ends against each other. It is compelled to reject the thesis of the Right Wing that 'the main danger is from the sectarian left' and likewise to reject the thesis of the Left that the main danger is from the splitters and liquidators of the Right. It tries to uphold the formula that 'the danger is both from the Right and from the Left', that the struggle must be carried on along two fronts. Its spokesman declare publicly that they are prepared to make temporary blocs either with the Right or with the Left: that is, either with those who are trying to split the party in the interests of Popular Frontism or with those who are determined that the party shall continue forward along the revolutionary road. One of their spokesman (Trager) expresses his wish for a general bloc with the Appeal Association – in a speech to the Appeal Institute; another (Zam) rejects the idea of a *general* bloc in favor of the 'either-or' formula; while in New York a number of the Clarity leaders are in almost constant negotiation with the Altman leadership (having even gone so far as to fight for a joint Convention Delegate slate with Altman, until at the last moment the attempt was abandoned).

Such are the vicissitudes of a centrist policy. Curious and lamentable results follow. A large part of the membership of the Clarity group is comprised of genuine and militant left-wingers who are in essential agreement with every important aspect of the Appeal platform and program. But they are discovering that to maintain their ambiguous position they must constantly grant programmatic concessions. The People's Front position of the *group*, for example, omits any reference whatever to Spain – that is to say, any reference to the People's Front where it is decisive. But in the YPSL in New York, the members of the Clarity group support the same resolutions on the People's Front and Spain which were adopted by the Appeal Institute! That is: the Clarity group has two quite different positions on the People's Front and Spain – one for the YPSLs and one for the party. They are compelled to pose as a 'unity group' fighting against threats of split from the Right and threats of split from the Left: though they can advance no shred of evidence to demonstrate that the Left in any way, either explicitly or implicitly, stands for split or expulsion. They are forced to say that there is a Right danger of liquidationism and a Left danger of sectarianism. But when pinned down to define where the 'danger of sectarianism' is to be found, they can give no answer: Zam was asked this question at the Appeal Institute in Chicago; he could hardly have declared that the Institute represented a 'sectarian' danger, with its members before him – three-fourths of them prominent activists in the trade union and unemployed movements; and finally he said that sectarians could be discovered – in Colorado and Camden, NJ.

What is the effect of the Clarity position in the party crisis? In spite of the fact that it is against a split, in spite of the fact that the bulk of its followers are genuine left-wingers or anxious to become so, the failure of the Clarity group to unite firmly with the revolutionary Left Wing necessarily weakens the struggle against the splitters and liquidators, necessarily aids Altman. How could it be otherwise? By having a group separate from the Appeal group, Zam-Tyler tend to confirm the contention of Altman and the Stalinists that the 'Trotskyites' are hopeless sectarians, with whom no one can get along. By continuing conciliatory moves toward Altman and negotiations with him, Zam-Tyler make it easier for him to marshal his forces, and harder for the left to fight back *politically*. By watering down their program, Zam-Tyler weaken the resistance to the ideas of the Right Wing and of Stalinism. By calling for a simultaneous struggle against both Left and Right, Zam-Tyler disperse left-wing energies which should now be wholly concentrating on the job of saving the party for revolutionary socialism by defeating the campaign of the Right. And in the long run their policy condemns their own group to utter disintegration. If the Right succeeds in its plans to expel the left, what then would be the fate of the Clarity group? If it remained in the Party it could do so only as the helpless captive of the Right, bound hand and foot. If the Right Wing fails – as the Left is determined it shall fail – the Clarity group will only find that the vacillating policy of its leadership has let its own right flank slip over into the camp of Altman, while its left-wingers join in the united struggle of the Left.

The Perspective of the *Appeal*

The point of view of the *Appeal* has always been clear and unambiguous. We stand for the completion of the development of the Socialist party into the revolutionary Socialist party of the American working class, the party of militant class struggle and vigorous mass action, basing itself upon the full program of Marxism. As the most efficient and rapid instrument for achieving this goal, we have proposed and continue to propose unity of all left wing forces in the party on the foundation of the Marxist answer to the key questions now confronting the party: the People's Front, Spain, the trade union question and mass work, disciplined party activity, inner-party democracy, the internal crisis in the party. We have sought, and continue to seek, that unity through a fusing of the Clarity group, the supporters of the *Appeal*, and hitherto unconnected left-wingers. Up to the present the Clarity group has rejected such unity. The pressing needs of the party, however, as well as the rapid deepening of the international crisis and the approach of the new war, do not permit us meanwhile to sit passively by. The Appeal Institute held in Chicago marked an immense step forward in the forging of a united revolutionary left wing, rallying together around the Appeal program and perspective a substantial percentage of the most militant and active party members, and forecasting complete and firm left-wing unity for the near future.

Right now the problem of the Convention faces us, and faces us with the threat of expulsions and splits issuing from the Right Wing. To defeat this threat, we propose the only course of action that is most effective in defeating splitters and liquidators: we propose an uncompromising political struggle against them. Splitters cannot be bought off by kind words and conciliation; such an approach only makes them more bold and ruthless. They must be defeated *politically* before the eyes of the party membership. The Left Wing does not propose to conquer them by expulsions and splits. Far from it. The Left Wing has no need to solve political problems by bureaucratic and organizational measures. It is sufficiently confident of its ideas and policies to rest its case upon the democratic decision of the membership.

A united Left Wing is the best and surest means for defeating the splitters and liquidators. If this is impossible in these next weeks, we propose and insist on full and loyal collaboration among all of those forces who are against a split and for a revolutionary party. **No** collaboration, **no** bloc, on **any** issues, with the splitters. Such collaboration, however temporary and minor, can only aid the Right Wing, can only injure the interests of the Left and of the future of the party. Specifically: the members of the Clarity group must prevent their group from entering into a bloc with the Altman group on any question whatever; collaboration with Altman is collaboration with Lewis and with Porter, and thus in the last analysis concession to the campaign of the Stalinists.

This is not the occasion for a detailed statement of Convention proposals. From a firm political line and a clear perspective these follow as practical and concrete applications. How fully the Convention will be in a position to *solve* the fundamental issue is not yet, by the nature of the case, clear. This much, however, the Convention can accomplish, and through this can guarantee the advance of the party: an orientation of the party toward mass work, above all work in the trade unions; provisions for compulsory disciplined leagues in the mass organizations; full participation of all groups in the party in the responsible direction of party work, in accordance with their relative strength, and comparative abilities and talents; solid guarantees of inner-party democracy.

There is not much time. To all those active party members who are resolved in their hearts that our party shall become the revolutionary leader of the working class, that it shall smash through the barriers of class collaboration, and defeat the plans of Stalinism for the harnessing of the workers to the war machine of imperialism, we say:

Forward with us!
For a revolutionary party of mass struggle, rooted in the unions!
Against the splitters and liquidators; against class collaboration and Popular Frontism!
For a united, disciplined, democratic party!
For the workers' revolution! For international socialism!

CHAPTER 4

Founding the Socialist Workers Party

Thomas Bias

As the year 1937 drew to a close and 136 workers and activists gathered in Chicago to launch a new revolutionary socialist party, the world situation seemed in many ways more fraught with crises than the crisis-ridden times of the early twenty-first century.

For most of eight years, one US worker in four could not find a job. Farmers devastated by drought were fleeing the Midwest to pick fruit in California or to do whatever jobs they could get. Across the Atlantic, fascism was destroying what semblance of freedom remained – including independent trade unions and parties of the working class – and actually beginning the process of attempting to wipe out whole peoples, Jews and Roma (gypsies) in particular. In Spain, partisans of a People's Front – a coalition of the Communist Party with anarchists and social-democratic and liberal capitalist parties – were engaged in civil war with a home-grown fascist movement aided by Italy and Germany, and they were getting the worst of it. The German Third Reich ('empire' in German) was beginning the process of swallowing up whole countries to its east. And across the Pacific the fascists' ally, the Empire of Japan, was engaged in a conquest of China, which would soon be extended to French Indochina, the US-controlled Philippines, Burma, Thailand, and the Dutch East Indies, today known as Indonesia.

The period seemed apocalyptic. The late 1930s, and the first half of the 1940s remains unmatched for sheer death and destruction. As the Chicago convention opened, its delegates knew that war was coming, and they knew that it would be more catastrophic than the Great War of 1914–18. Their perspective was that revolution would follow the Second World War and that, unlike after the First, revolution would not fail in every country but one. On the immediate agenda was the formation of a new world party of socialist revolution, a fourth attempt to build such a party since the launching of the International Working-Men's Association in 1864. The challenges facing the new party were great, but so was its confidence. James P. Cannon, who became the party's first National Secretary, wrote in 'The New Party Is Founded' (included in this volume):

> With a firm theoretical position and a decisive orientation to mass work, the new party of the Fourth International has every right to face the future

> with confidence. This confidence is also fortified by the objective political situation and by the present state of affairs in the radical labor movement. All signs point to a mighty acceleration of the class struggle as the country slides into another devastating crisis and the inevitable war draws ever nearer to the point of explosion.

The Chicago delegates represented a political organisation of roughly 1,500 members, who had been unceremoniously expelled from the American Socialist Party earlier in the year. The pretext for their expulsion had been their refusal to support the Republican candidate, Fiorello LaGuardia, in his campaign for re-election as Mayor of New York City. Their real 'crime' was their revolutionary perspective, in contrast to the Socialist Party leaders' programme of reform of capitalism while leaving the class of bankers and businessmen – the 'one percent', as the Wall Street occupiers of 2011 would come to call them – firmly in power as before.

Those 1,500 revolutionary socialists had come from different origins. One group had come out of the Communist Party when the conflict in the Third – or Communist – International led to the expulsion of Trotsky and his supporters from Communist Parties all over the world. They saw themselves as having chosen the revolutionary leader Leon Trotsky over Joseph Stalin, the leader of the privileged bureaucracy in the Soviet Union. After the victory of Hitler in Germany in 1933 – brought about in large measure because of the divisive policies of the Communist Party and the anti-revolutionary policies of the Social Democratic Party – Trotsky called on his supporters to abandon their attempts to reform the Communist parties and Communist International. Instead, they must build new revolutionary parties in their own countries and work toward the formation of a new – Fourth – International on a world scale. In the United States, Trotsky's supporters, organised in the Communist League of America, turned their attention to activity in the working class and to other formations that were doing similar work. They united with the American Workers Party in 1935 to form the Workers Party of the United States.

At the same time, hundreds of revolutionary-minded young people were finding their way into the Socialist Party and its Young People's Socialist League (YPSL). They did not like what they saw in the much larger American Communist Party, and horrific news from the Soviet Union led them to the conclusion that Stalin and the parties under his leadership did not represent the way forward for the working class.

At the urging of Trotsky, then in exile in Norway, the Workers Party of the United States dissolved itself, and its roughly 700 members joined the Socialist Party in 1936. They campaigned for its presidential candidate Norman Thomas.

The left-wing Socialists published a newspaper called the *Socialist Appeal*; as a consequence, they were often called the 'Appeal Faction'.

The Appeal Faction was actively involved in the Teamsters Union's over-the-road organising campaign, in the maritime unions on both coasts and the Great Lakes, and in other labour struggles of the newly formed Congress of Industrial Organizations (CIO). It also brought to Americans' attention the horrific Moscow Trials, which condemned to death most of the remaining leaders of the Russian Revolution of 1917, including Gregory Zinoviev, Lev Kamenev, Karl Radek, Nikolai Bukharin, and – tragically (given the 1941 onslaught of Hitler's legions into the Soviet heartland) – many of the Red Army's most dedicated and capable senior officers. The Appeal Faction organised a commission of inquiry, headed by the philosopher and educator John Dewey, which examined the evidence and concluded that the Moscow Trials were frame-ups and that its prime defendant-in-absentia, Leon Trotsky, was innocent of the charges lodged against him.

It was out of this experience that the Chicago delegates formed a new party from people who had come from the Workers Party and from the Socialist Party – they called their new party the Socialist Workers Party. They agreed to a fundamental programme, agreement with which was the primary basis for membership in the new SWP, a Declaration of Principles, included in this chapter. They agreed to a party Constitution to define the organisational structure and the requirements of membership. Also included in this chapter is a brief article by party leaders Cannon and Max Shachtman explaining the need for democracy in decision-making and disciplined unity in action once the decisions are made, an article entitled, 'The Internal Situation and the Character of the Party'.

As awful as world conditions were at the opening of 1938, the new Socialist Workers Party rose to the challenges with confidence and optimism. A party of 1,500 people was understood to be a tiny organisation which needed massive growth to have any influence. But as one of the delegates to that convention, George Breitman, later recalled: 'I am sure most of the delegates shared my conviction that we had participated in something truly significant: the launching – at last! – of the party that would lead the American workers in their coming socialist revolution'. Breitman went on to comment, from the vantage-point of 1978, that 'the whole process has proved to be slower and more complicated than it seemed to me in Chicago forty years ago'.[1]

1 Breitman 1982, pp. 17–18.

Breitman's historical sense is worth reflecting on. One aspect of the historical process he emphasised was the shaping of the leadership layer of the US Trotskyists out of the rich traditions of the American Left:

> One of the greatest strengths of the SWP cadre lay in its continuity with the struggles from the start of the century – the IWW and revolutionary syndicalism, Debs's fighting election campaigns, opposition to U.S. entry into World War I, efforts to absorb the meaning of the Russian revolution and Leninism, the development of a left wing of the SP, the birth of the new CP and its early attempts to adapt to American realities.[2]

Breitman emphasised that the initial leaders and cadres of US Trotskyism 'had not merely read or heard about these events; they grew up in them and were shaped by them'. He added: 'Their experience provided the basic political capital of their movement and explains its ability to avoid many of the costly mistakes beginners are prone to make'. The three central leaders of US Trotskyism in 1938, as in 1928, were James P. Cannon, Max Shachtman, and Martin Abern, but here too Breitman insists on viewing the matter historically. 'In 1929 they did not have more than 100 followers, but in 1938 they claimed fifteen times that number, and the leadership was broader and included a new generation of rebels against capitalism. Cannon, Shachtman, and Abern themselves were different in 1938 – they had grown and matured'. In the earlier period, Breitman comments, 'they still had too great a tendency to shoot from the hip', while a decade later he perceived in their political practice a greater 'maturity, sense of realism, patience'.[3]

Not only had the Trotskyist membership dramatically increased in quantity, but it had been tempered and enriched by a variety of experiences. These included participation in the militant unemployed movement of the Great Depression, as well as momentous strikes in Minneapolis, Toledo, Flint, and elsewhere, and other struggles as well – including most recently within the Socialist Party. 'The SP leaders saved the party from "Trotskyism", but in the process they virtually destroyed it by expelling the best and most active members',

2 Breitman 1982, pp. 18–19. The IWW refers to the Industrial Workers of the World, widely seen as the foremost example of revolutionary syndicalism in the United States from 1905 into the 1920s. Reference to Debs's election campaigns relates to the mass Socialist Party of America, led by Eugene V. Debs, a dynamic candidate for President from 1900 to 1920. Information on these and related matters can be found in: Kornbluh 1998; Ginger 2007; Draper 1957; Cannon 1962; Palmer 2007.

3 Breitman 1982, pp. 19, 29.

according to Breitman. 'We emerged with more than twice the numbers we had on joining and won a decisive majority of the YPSL, too. Morale was high, because our self-confidence had also grown as we met the various challenges posed to us by the SP environment and acquired new know-how from its earlier access to the mass movements of the time'.[4]

Breitman also emphasised some serious limitations of the new SWP – in relation to consciousness and composition, as well as programme and activism – with regard to African Americans and other racial minorities, and also women. Something approximating what he deemed an adequate approach did not crystallise until the 1960s (although some advances in the black liberation struggle could be found during World War II). Noting the deepened perceptions in later years regarding the 'centrality of the Black struggle' to the struggle for socialism, and 'the combined character of the struggles for women's liberation and workers' power', he reflected:

> In most areas the SWP in 1938 was far ahead of both American society and the American radical movement, but in others it was not. The fact that we have made considerable progress in some of these areas since 1938 is not a cause for complacency but it is evidence that the party we launched then must have had foundations solid enough to enable us to correct shortcomings. No party is perfect, all parties make errors; the question is whether they can recognize their errors and correct them.[5]

Well before the end of the twentieth century, the organisation described by Breitman had – for all practical purposes – passed out of existence. The challenges facing humanity are no less great two decades into the twenty-first century, than had been the case in 1938. But the confidence and optimism of a new party, as described in Breitman's comments, are missing at the time of this writing. A party of 1,500 people in 1938 America was understood to be a tiny organisation which needed massive growth to have any influence. Eight decades later, a socialist group of 1,500 is considered quite large – even though it may seem to have less impact on its environment than was the case with Breitman's organisation.

What happened? What can be done about it? How can a revolutionary leadership, with confidence, optimism, and – mostly importantly – intelligent strategy and tactics and dedicated fighting cadres, be assembled in today's

4 Bretiman 1982, p. 23.

5 Breitman 1982, p. 33.

political context? For those sharing George Breitman's revolutionary socialist sensibilities, the future of the working class, indeed of human society, depends on the answers that arise from the ongoing discussions, and an understanding of the discussions and debates of past generations can only aid today's revolutionists in coming to answers that can advance the struggle to its final victory.

1 The New Party is Founded[6]

(*1938*)

James P. Cannon

All the experience of the class struggle on a world scale, and especially the experience of the past twenty years, teaches one lesson above all others, a lesson summed up in a single proposition: The most important problem of the working class is the problem of the party. Success or failure in this domain spells the difference between victory or defeat every time. The struggle for the party, the unceasing effort to construct the new political organization of the vanguard on the ruins of the old one, concentrates within itself the most vital and progressive elements of the class struggle as a whole. From this point of view every concrete step in the direction of a reconstructed party has outstanding importance. The convention of the left-wing branches of the disintegrated Socialist Party at Chicago over the New Year's weekend, which resulted in the formal launching of a new organization, the Socialist Workers Party, section of the Fourth International, thus claims first attention from the revolutionary internationalists throughout the world. For them – and their judgment is better than any other because they foresee and prepare the future – it marks a new milestone on the historic road of workers' liberation.

The reconstruction of the revolutionary labor movement in the form of a political party is not a simple process. In the midst of unprecedented difficulties, complications and contradictions the work goes ahead, like all social movements, in *zigzag* fashion. The new movement takes shape through a series of splits and fusions which must appear like a Chinese puzzle to the superficial observer. But how could it be otherwise? The frightful disintegration of the old movements, on a background of worldwide social upheaval, disoriented and scattered the revolutionary militants in all directions. They could not find their way together, and draw the same basic conclusions, in a day. The new movement is fraught with catastrophic reverses, forward leaps and deadening periods of seeming stagnation. But for all that it is a movement, with an invin-

6 Cannon 1938.

cible historic motor force, and it moves along. The Chicago convention, which brought all the preceding work of the Fourth Internationalists in the US to a fruitful culmination, is a forceful reminder of this fact.

The Chicago convention itself was a striking illustration of this contradictory process of fusion and split – and a step forward. It crossed the last *t* and dotted the last *i* on the split of the moribund Socialist Party. At the same time, it recorded the complete fusion of the left-wing socialists with the former members of the Workers Party, just as the Workers Party earlier came into existence through a fusion of the Communist Left Opposition and revolutionary militants of independent origin. The invincible program of the Fourth International is the magnet which attracts to itself all the vital revolutionary elements from all camps. It is the basis, and the only basis, on which the dispersed militants can come together and forge the new movement.

This was demonstrated once again at the Chicago convention when the resolution for the Fourth International was carried without a single dissenting vote. The two currents, former Workers Party and 'native' socialists, which were about equally represented, showed complete unity on this decisive question. The 76 regular and 36 fraternal delegates from 35 cities in 17 states, who constituted the convention, came to this unanimous decision after due consideration of the question and ample pre-convention discussion. Although the great bulk of time and discussion at the convention were devoted to American affairs, and properly so, the great matters of principle embodied in the international question inspired and guided everything.

This significant victory of the Fourth International in America cannot be without far-reaching influence on the international arena. The brief period of struggle as a faction within the Socialist Party comes to a definite end, and the American section of the Fourth International takes the field again as an independent party, with forces more than doubled, without any losses or splits, and with a firmer unity than ever before. Principled politics in this case also has proved to be the best and most effective kind of practical politics.

Those too-clever politicians of the centrist school have sought to avoid clear-cut answers to the international question in the hope of keeping divergent forces together. They have nothing to show for it but disintegration and splits, and the creeping paralysis of blind-alley pessimism in their ranks. The 'Trotskyists', on the other hand, have held their own ranks firm, and have united with other serious revolutionary forces in an expanding movement inspired by enthusiasm and confidence in its future. That is, first of all, because they put the main question of internationalism squarely. Experience showed that the left-wing socialists who mean business, and they are the only ones worth counting, preferred this kind of politics.

When our plenum-conference last July decided to take up the impudent challenge of the gag-law bureaucrats of the SP and fight the issue out without compromise, some comrades questioned the wisdom of this strategy, fearing disintegration in our ranks. The convention removed all ground for argument on this score. In the five-months campaign from July to New Year's we not only held our own, but gained. Numerous branches not affiliated to the organized left wing in July, were represented by delegates at the convention. Denver; Salt Lake City; Kansas City, Joplin and St. Louis in Missouri; Rochester; Quakertown, Sellerville and a third branch in Pennsylvania – these were among the new branches enlisted under the banner of the new party at the convention. As for the remnants of the Socialist Party, it did not claim the attention of the convention in any way. Nobody felt the necessity for discussion on this dead issue of the past. All attention was directed to the future – to the problem of penetrating the mass movement of the workers and the struggle against Stalinism.

The outstanding point on the agenda, and the one allotted the most time in the discussion, was the trade union question. And even this discussion was pretty much limited to the narrower question of practical work and tactics in the trade unions and the exchange of experience in this field. The principles and strategy of Bolshevism in regard to the trade unions were regarded as clearly established and taken for granted.

The predominance of the trade union question in its practical and tactical aspects corresponded to the most pressing needs of the hour, and to the composition and temper of the convention. The slogan 'to the masses' dominated the convention from beginning to end. The conception of the Fourth Internationalists as primarily a circle of isolated theorists and hairsplitters, a conception industriously circulated by the centrists who maneuver all the time with non-existent 'mass movements' in a vacuum, could find little to sustain it at Chicago. The great bulk of the delegates consisted of practical and qualified trade unionists who have done serious Bolshevik work in the labor movement and have modest results to show for it.

The discussion and reports from the various districts clearly showed that we already have a good foundation of trade union activity to build upon. Our positions and influence in various unions – such as they are – have not been gained by appointment or sufferance from the top, but by systematic work from below, in the ranks. That is all to the good. What is ours is ours; nobody gave it to us and nobody can take it away.

It must be admitted that the preoccupation of our national movement with problems of theoretical education carried with it a certain neglect and even a minimizing of trade union work. A serious weakness and a danger which should not be concealed. The Chicago convention was one continuous warning and demand to correct this fault and to do it by drastic measures. But if systematic national organization and direction of our trade union work have been lacking, our comrades in various localities and unions, guided by a sure instinct and a firm grasp of their theory, have gone to work in the unions with a will and have achieved good results. In some cases the fruits of their work stand out conspicuously. The convention heard matter-of-fact reports from all sections of the country. In sum total this work and its results, considering the size of our movement and its freedom from 'big' pretensions, impressed the convention as fairly imposing.

This discussion, and the concrete program which issued from it, gave the convention its tone and its buoyant spirit of proletarian optimism. Revolutionary activists in the class struggle, in general, have no time for skeptical speculation and pessimistic brooding. Our proletarian convention reflected no trace of these diseases, so fashionable now on the intellectual fringes of the movement. The trade union discussion was a striking revelation that the revolutionary health of a party, and of its individual members, requires intimate contact with the living mass movement, with its struggle and action, its hopes and aspirations.

The whole course of our convention was turned in this direction. It was decided to 'trade unionize' the party, to devote 90 percent of the party work to this field, to coordinate and direct this work on a national scale, and to establish the necessary apparatus to facilitate this design.

Our trade union work in the days ahead is concerned, of course, not as an end in itself – that is mere opportunism – but as a practical means to a revolutionary end. In order to aim seriously at the struggle for power a party must be entrenched in the sources of power – the workers' mass movement and especially the trade unions. Our convention could devote itself so extensively to the practical side of this question only thanks to the fact that the theoretical ground had been cleared and firm positions on the important principle questions consciously worked out.

The party arrived at these positions by the method of party democracy. Six months of intensive discussion preceded the convention. Three months of more or less informal discussion on the Spanish, Russian and international questions after the July plenum, were followed by another three-month period of formal discussion. This discussion was organized by the National Committee. Internal discussion bulletins were published, membership meetings were held, etc. All points of view were fairly presented. The bulk of the space in the bulletins and approximately equal time in the membership meetings were given over to minorities which turned out in the end to be tiny minorities.

In a live and free party, where members do their own thinking and that is the only kind of a party worth a fig – everybody does not come to the same conclusion at the same moment. Common acceptance of basic principles does not insure uniform answers to the concrete questions of the day. The party position can be worked out only in a process of collective thought and exchange of opinion. That is possible only in a free, that is, a democratic party.

The method of party democracy entails certain 'overhead charges'. It takes time and energy. It often interferes with other work. On occasions it taxes patience. But it works. It educates the party and safeguards its unity. And in the long run the overhead expenses of the democratic method are the cheapest. The quick and easy solutions of bureaucratic violence usually claim drawn-out installment payments in the form of discontent in the ranks, impaired morale and devastating splits.

Discussions among the Bolsheviks, sometimes taking the form of factional struggle, are carried on in dead earnest, corresponding to the seriousness of the questions and of the people involved. A philistine reading one of our pre-convention discussion bulletins, or listening by chance at a membership meeting, might well imagine our party to be a mad-house of dissension, recrimination, revolts against the leadership and, in general, 'fights among themselves'. But, to get a clear picture, one must judge the democratic process at the end, not in the middle. True, Bolsheviks are in earnest and they readily dispense with polite amenities. They put questions sharply, because as a rule, they feel them deeply. And nobody ever thinks of sparing the sensibilities of leaders; they are assumed to be pupils of Engels who warned his opponents that he had a tough hide.

But it is precisely through this free democratic process, and not otherwise, that a genuine party arrives at conclusions which represent its own consciously won convictions. The discussion is not aimless and endless. It leads straight to a convention and a conclusion – in our case a conclusion so close to unanimous, that its authority is unshakeable. Then the discussion can and must come to an end. The emphasis in party life shifts from democracy to centralism. The party goes to work on the basis of the convention decisions.

The resolutions submitted to the convention by the National Committee on all the important questions, formulating the standpoint which has been advocated in our press, were all accepted by the convention without significant amendments. Much preconvention discussion had been devoted to the Russian question, as a result of the unspeakable Moscow Trials and the subsequent blood purges. Some comrades challenged the designation of the Soviet Union as a workers' state, although frightfully degenerated, which can yet be restored to health by a political revolution without a social overturn. This minority opinion, however, found little echo in the ranks.

The resolution of the National Committee, which calls for the unconditional defense of the Soviet Union against imperialist attack – a position which necessarily presupposes an uncompromising struggle against the Stalinist bureaucracy in war or peace – was adopted by a vote of 66 against 3 for one minority position and 2 for another. This virtual unanimity is the best assurance for the future theoretical stability of the party. A false position on the question of the Russian revolution, now as always since 1917, spells fatal consequences for any political organization. The revolutionary Marxists have always said they would be at their posts and be the best fighters for the Soviet Union in the hour of danger. As this crucial hour draws near the American soldiers of the Fourth International have renewed this declaration and pledge.

With a firm theoretical position and a decisive orientation to mass work the new party of the Fourth International has every right to face the future with confidence. This confidence is also fortified by the objective political situation and by the present state of affairs in the radical labor movement. All signs point to a mighty acceleration of the class struggle as the country slides into another devastating crisis and the inevitable war draws ever nearer to the point of explosion. Meanwhile the situation among the radical labor groupings and tendencies is clearing up. Stalinism is self-disclosed as the movement of jingo-traitors. The Socialist Party of Altman, Thomas & Co. – having expelled its vitalizing left wing – presents only the pathetically futile spectacle of an opportunist sect, lacking the merit of consistent principle on the one side or of mass support on the other. The Lovestoneites, the one-time unacknowledged attorneys of Stalinism are now merely the attorneys and finger-men of pseudo-progressive labor bureaucrats in a couple of important unions. The various groups and cliques which challenged the *bona fide* movement of the Fourth International and attempted to fight it from the 'left' have all, without exception, fallen into pitiful disintegration and demoralization.

The Socialist Workers Party, unfurling the banner of the Fourth International from the hour of its birth, has no rival in the field. It is the only revolutionary party, the heir of the rich traditions of the past and the herald of the future.

2 Declaration of Principles[7]

(1938)

Part I

The Decline of Capitalism

Capitalist society, based upon the private ownership of the means of production and exchange and upon the free exploitation of labor by the bourgeoisie, came into being through the revolutionary struggle of the bourgeoisie, supported by the workers and peasants, against the feudal lords and their retainers. In its initial periods, capitalism was a mighty progressive force, shattering the outmoded social and political forms of feudal society, vastly expanding the productive mechanism, and encouraging on an unprecedented scale the development of science and technique. The achievements of capitalism have brought mankind, for the first time in history, to the point where the material conditions are present which would enable all men to be supplied with the means for a full and ample life. Food, clothing, shelter, and the marvelous products of modern invention, could be provided for such abundance as to remove forever hunger, material want, and insecurity; and thereby form the foundation for a new and magnificent age of social and cultural development.

Now, however, the social and political forms of capitalism, effective once in the struggle against feudalism, themselves constitute an insurmountable obstacle to the utilization of further advance of the productive forces. The capitalist property relations, the subordination of production to profit instead of the fulfillment of human needs, the artificial restrictions imposed by national boundaries and national politics, not merely block the development of production, but actively sabotage it. Capitalism has entered the stage of its decline on a world scale. The successive cyclical crises of capitalist economy extend their scope and depth; and the intervening boom periods are unable to shake off the devastating effects of the preceding crisis. Capitalism is unable even to make use of the latest inventions and scientific products. The declining rate of profit pushes the bourgeoisie to desperation, to the attempt to place the entire burden upon the masses, and to efforts at adventurist solutions in foreign wars.

7 Socialist Workers Party 1938.

Wide-scale unemployment becomes a permanent feature. The relative standard of living of the masses is progressively lowered, and is grotesquely out of line with what is made possible by the productive mechanism. The fear of insecurity is common to all except the most privileged. War is an ever-present threat when not an actuality, and the weight of the armament programs adds to the oppression of the masses. And in its insane and frantic attempt to preserve the rotted system which supports its power and privilege, the bourgeoisie and its agents systematically destroy every social and human value, imposing upon men a moral regime of lies and viciousness and maddened terror.

Wars and Revolutions

The period of the decline of capitalism is marked by an almost constant series of wars and revolutions. The imperialist powers, confronted by the inadequacy of their internal markets and the decline of the rate of profit, are compelled to seek new outlets for surplus capital and new possibilities for capital accumulation, as well as cheaper raw materials and profitable markets for the goods which their own populations cannot purchase. The peace of exhaustion following the war of 1914–18 lasts only long enough to permit sufficient preparation for the new war. In a world divided up and farmed out among the great powers, the mutual struggle for capital outlets, raw materials, and markets, becomes ever more intense.

The nations are plunged into economic, tariff, and exchange struggles, and armament competition, finally issuing in the armed struggle of worldwide imperialist war. At the same time, the masses, driven to desperation by the lash of the crisis, by the weight of exploitation, tyranny, and war, fight back in widespread wars for liberation on the part of the colonial peoples and in the revolutionary struggle of the working class for its emancipation.

Fascism

In the period of capitalist decline, the bourgeoisie is able to maintain a sufficient measure of profits and its own position of social privilege only by constantly reducing the general living standards of the dispossessed majority, by imposing upon it unemployment, insecurity, curtailed social services, and periodically resorting to war. The resistance generated among the masses by this course completes the material preconditions of revolutionary crises, and poses the question of the overthrow of the capitalist order as the sole solution. When such crises near climax, and the working class, because of the lack of a strong revolutionary party, fails to act decisively for the revolutionary solution, it suffers internal demoralization and loses the confidence of the middle-class masses ruined by the crisis. Under the domination of finance capital, a fascist movement is then able to succeed in mobilizing the desperate middle-class elements and even certain demoralized sections of the working class on a wholly reactionary basis. Capitalist rule is reconsolidated through the victory of fascism, and capitalist society is temporarily 'saved' by the destruction of the workers' organizations, wholesale terror and violence against working-class militants, and the suppression of all forms of independent class expression.

Under the totalitarian regime of fascism democratic rights are done away with, and the institutions of democracy are either abandoned or made inoperative. The trade unions, political parties, and all other independent organizations of workers and farmers, and even many independent bourgeois organizations, are smashed or compelled to become a passive part of the state machinery. The right to strike is abrogated. Terror is exercised not only against revolutionists, but against any workers engaged in a militant struggle for their own defense. Divisions are sown among the people by appeals to the basest racial prejudices and nationalistic passions. Science, art, and education are perverted to the degenerate service of the totalitarian state. Through its iron control fascism is able to drive down the standard of living of the masses and thrust upon them the costs of the crisis, and at the same time to head unchecked toward the wars made inevitable by the depth of the internal social crises. Thus, in the period of its decline, capitalism allies itself with everything that is archaic and destructive and reactionary, and threatens to drive whole nations, perhaps mankind itself, back into barbarism and savagery.

The Position of the United States

In spite of its magnificent natural resources and its unparalleled industrial plant, the United States is in no way exempt from the influences of the world decline of the capitalist order. On the contrary, as has been proved by the war of 1914–18 and by the economic crisis of 1929, and is being further proved in the rapid approach of the new world war and the new economic crisis, the United States is inseparably interlocked into the system of world imperialism. With the war of 1914–18, the United States rose to the position of the leading imperialist power at the very time when capitalism everywhere had entered its decline and conflicts between the great powers were therefore intensified. American imperialism cannot expand further, or even maintain its existing world position, without cutting deeply into the share of world power now in the hands of the other imperialist nations, as well as into the living standards of the masses in the United States itself, in Latin America, South America, Europe, and Asia, whom it exploits directly or from whom it exacts tribute. The economy and politics of the United States are inextricably connected with crises, wars, and revolutions in all parts of the world. The phenomena of capitalist decline –

economic crises unprecedented in their depth, mass unemployment, inability to utilize inventions and technological improvements, insecurity, violations of democratic rights, the ever present threat of war – are all present, many to an exaggerated degree, in the United States. Nor can the United States, under capitalism, escape the more dire extremes of the new war and fascism. In the very nature of the power of United States imperialism lie the irrepressible conflicts that herald its collapse.

The Only Road

For capitalism there is no way out, no alternative to the perspective of crises of cumulative intensity, growing unemployment and impoverishment, insecurity, political tyranny, fascism, war, and chaos, ending in collapse of the social order and a relapse into barbarism. And there is only one alternative to capitalism. That alternative is to do away with capitalism itself, to wipe out its central and insurmountable conflict by taking the ownership and control of the natural resources, the productive plant, and means of exchange, out of the hands of private individuals and corporations, and placing that ownership and control in the hands of society itself, to be used for the fulfillment of human needs and not for profit. The only alternative, the only possible solution, is to build a socialist society. Thus, and only thus, can men achieve plenty, security, peace, and freedom.

The Role of the Working Class

In the struggle against capitalism and for socialism, the central role, following both from its key position in the process of production and likewise from the coherence and discipline imposed upon it by the methods of production, must be filled by the working class, in particular by the industrial working class. The working class will, however, require the support of other sections of society who are also exploited and oppressed. Large sections of the middle classes, the debt-ridden small farmers, the Negroes as a persecuted race, colonial and semi-colonial peoples fighting against imperialist exploitation, these must be won by the working class as its allies. Only through the social revolution and socialism can all of the oppressed and exploited, and indeed all of mankind, find deliverance from insecurity, want, and tyranny.

The Capitalist State

In any society, the real power is held by those who own and control the means whereby that society lives, the instruments of production, distribution, and communication. In capitalist society, such ownership and control is held and exercised by the big bourgeoisie, by the bankers and industrialists. Through its hold on the major natural resources, the factories, mines, banks, railroads, ships, airplanes, telegraph, radio, and press, the big bourgeoisie effectively dominates capitalist society, runs society in such a manner as to secure and maintain its own interest and privilege, and upholds the system of the exploitation of the great majority. The state or government, far from representing the general interests of society as a whole, is in the last analysis simply the political instrument through which the owning class exercises and maintains its power, enforces the property relations which guarantee its privileges, and suppresses the working class. In these essential functions all of the organs and institutions of the state power cooperate – the bureaucracy, the courts, police, prisons, and the armed forces. The particular political forms of capitalist society (monarchy, democracy, military dictatorship, fascism) in no way affect the basic social dictatorship of the controlling minority, and are only the different means through which that dictatorship expresses itself. The belief that in such a country as the United States we live in a free, democratic society, in which fundamental economic change can be effected by persuasion, by education, by legal and purely parliamentary methods, is an illusion. In the United States, as in all capitalist nations, we live, in actuality, under a capitalist dictatorship, and the possibilities for purely legal and constitutional change are therefore limited to those which fall within the framework of capitalist property and social relations, which later are severely curtailed by the circumstances of the decline of capitalism and in the long run, if the capitalist dictatorship continues, involve fascism for the United States as elsewhere. Genuine freedom can be realized only in a society based upon the economic and social equality of all individuals composing it, and such equality can be achieved only when the basic means of production, distribution, and communication are owned and controlled, not by any special class or group, but by society as a whole.

The Conquest of Power

Since the capitalist state is the political instrument of capitalist dictatorship, and since the workers can carry out socialization only through the conquest and maintenance of political power, the workers must, as the necessary political phase of the change of ownership and control of the productive mechanism, take control of state power through the overthrow of the capitalist state and the transfer of sovereignty from it to their own workers' state – the dictatorship of the proletariat.

Opportunities for the workers to take power have come and will come in the course of the disintegration of material life and of culture under capitalist dictatorship. The masses find themselves faced with growing hunger, impoverishment, curtailment of social services, and the threat or actuality of fascism and war. When the profound social discontent generated by the crisis of capitalism extends to a decisive majority of the working class and of the productive sections of the population generally, and when these have been won to the perspective of revolutionary change, the workers will be in a position to take power and to put an end to the destructive course of capitalist dictatorship.

The fundamental instruments of the workers' struggle for power cannot be the existing institutions of the governmental apparatus, since these represent basically the interests only of the capitalist minority. They must, on the contrary, be class organs, arising out of the class struggle, forged in the course of united actions of the workers and their allies, and representing genuinely and democratically the interests of the great majority, of the workers and their allies. Such organs the Russian workers found in the *soviets* or councils of the workers, soldiers, and peasants. The exact form which the workers' councils, or soviets, will take in any given nation cannot of course be predicted in advance, since this will depend in part upon the special experiences and traditions of the class struggle within the given nation – in the United States, for example, the councils could conceivably be a development from general strike committees. Nevertheless, it can be certain in advance that it will be through these councils, alone democratically representing the interests of the workers and of the great majority, that the workers will overthrow the capitalist class, and through a transfer of sovereignty from the existing governmental apparatus to the councils, will take state power. The workers will destroy the whole machinery of the capitalist state in order to render it incapable of counterrevolutionary activity and because it cannot serve as the instrumentality for establishing the new social order. Its place will be taken by a workers' state, based upon the workers' councils.

The Workers' State

The workers' state is a temporary political instrument making possible the transition to the classless socialist society. Its task is to defend the workers' revolution against its enemies, both within and without, and to lay the foundations for socialism and the final elimination of all classes and class rule. Like every other state, therefore, the workers' state is, under one aspect, a dictatorship. Unlike every other state in history, however, it is a dictatorship exercised by the great majority against the counterrevolutionary minority. And, equally unlike every other state, its aim is not the perpetuation of its rule, but on the contrary, through the provision of material plenty for all and through education, to abolish the remains of class division in society and thus to eliminate the necessity for state coercion, that is, to do away with itself, with any form of state whatever. In an industrially advanced nation, the workers' state will be able from the outset to assure and continually extend far more genuine and substantial democratic rights to the masses than ever accorded to them under capitalism. Through the councils, the masses will exercise free and democratic control over all the policies of the workers' state, not merely in political questions but in the vital plans for socialist construction, will freely elect all officials and maintain the permanent right of recall. Salaries of officials will have the level of a skilled worker as their maximum. Through factory and other types of industrial and agricultural committees, the workers will participate in the fullest possible degree in social and economic administration. The workers' state will not have a professional army, but will depend on a mass workers' militia, in which distinctions other than those required for technical efficiency will be abolished and democratic control over officers will be exercised by the ranks. While the workers' state will necessarily reserve to itself the indispensable right to take all requisite measures to deal with violence and armed attacks against the revolutionary regime, it will at the same time assure adequate civil rights to opposition individuals, groups, and political parties, and will guarantee the opportunity for the expression of opposition through the allotment of press, radio, and assembly facilities in accordance with the real strength among the people of the opposition groups or parties.

The most important of the socioeconomic measures to be taken by the workers' state in its initial period is the expropriation and socialization, without compensation, of all monopolies in industry and land; all mines, factories, and shipping; all public utilities, railroads, airplane systems, and other organized means of communication; all banks, credit agencies, gold stores; and all other supplies and services that the revolutionary government finds it necessary to take over in order to lay the foundations of a socialist society. This socialization of the means of production and exchange will injure only the small handful of financiers, landlords, and industrialists whose private control of the resources of the country is the source of hunger, unemployment, and insecurity for the bulk of the people. The policy of socialization pursued by the workers' state will make possible the guarantee to every willing worker of a well-paid job, security against unemployment, insurance against industrial risks, old age, and sickness; and will further provide adequate educational, recreational, and cultural opportunities for the entire population. There will be no need for the workers' state to impose arbitrary, premature, and oppressive measures upon small individual proprietors, craftsmen, and small-scale farmers. The example of the social and personal advantages of the socialist organization of production, and assistance from the workers' government, can be trusted to lead them to voluntary collectivization. Socialism will release the productive forces to serve the needs of men, and will enable production to be planned rationally in terms of actual social requirements. It will allow the utilization of every technical improvement. The leisure and educational opportunities which will accompany these material advantages, together with the removal of the dead weight of the perverted capitalist culture, will offer every individual possibilities for the fullest creative development.

The Socialist Society

With the provision of material abundance through planned socialist production, and the great educational and cultural advances thereby made possible, the socially useless and parasitic classes, as well as the remnants of capitalist ideology, will be eliminated. The entire population will be transformed into a community of free producers owning and controlling the total productive wealth and resources of society, and freely and consciously working out their own destiny. The need for coercion and repression of socially alien classes will disappear with the disappearance of these classes, and together with them, of all classes. With it will vanish the need for a state machinery – even for the workers' state. The state as an institution for the domination, repression, and coercion of men will be replaced by a purely technical administration for the handling of the general business of society. The noblest objective of the human race – communism, the classless socialist society – inaugurating a new era for all of mankind, will be realized.

The working class can build a complete socialist society only on the basis of a world division of labor and resources, and world cooperation. The revolutionary party in this country does not aim merely to lead the working class of the United States in revolution, but to unite with the workers of all other countries in the international revolution and the establishment of world socialism. Modern forces of production have compelled capitalism itself to transcend national boundaries, and the conflict between the world economy of capitalism and the outlived, constricting national political boundaries is a major source of the disastrous evils which confront the modern world. Capitalist imperialism cannot, however, achieve a harmonious society. World socialism is the only solution for the conflicts and disorders of the modern world, as well as for the major conflicts within a single nation. A socialist society will rationally and scientifically utilize the natural resources and productive machinery of the earth in the interests of the people of the earth, and will solve the conflict between the efficient development of productive forces and the artificial restrictions of national boundaries. It will grant the rights of free cultural self-determination to all nations. In these ways, world socialism will remove the causes of international wars, which under capitalism now seriously threaten to send mankind back into barbarism or complete destruction.

Part II

The Revolutionary Party

The working class, under capitalism and in the initial stages of the socialist revolution, is neither economically nor socially, nor ideologically homogeneous. It is united in terms of fundamental historical class interest, and by the urgent needs of the daily class struggle. However, it still remains divided by different income levels and working conditions, by religion, nationality, culture, sex, age. Through the perverting influence of capitalist oppression and propaganda, it is further divided by conflicting ideologies, and weakened by the low cultural and educational level of many of its members. There are, moreover, the divisions between various sections of the working class and its potential allies in the revolutionary struggle. For these reasons, the working class cannot, as a whole or spontaneously, directly plan and guide its own struggle for power. For this, a directing staff, a conscious vanguard, arising out of the ranks of the proletariat and based upon it, participating actively in the day-by-day struggles of the workers and in all progressive struggles, and planning clear-sightedly the broader strategy of the longer-term struggle for state power and socialism, is indispensable. The staff and vanguard constitutes the revolutionary party.

The entire experience of our epoch demonstrates irrefutably that without the leadership of the revolutionary party the lasting victory of the workers is impossible. Without an adequate, firm, and strong revolutionary party, the magnificent heroism, militancy, and self-sacrifice of the workers lead and can only lead to sporadic and unconnected battles for partial aims which achieve no lasting conquests and prepare the ground for defeats.

The revolutionary party must be forged in active struggle. Its leadership cannot be imposed from above. It can be won only by demonstrating in action the correctness of its program and the superiority of its tactics. The support of the party cannot rest upon demagogy – the universal instrument of all other political parties. It cannot be imposed on the masses by force and against their will, but must be based upon free acceptance by the decisive sections of the masses. The membership of the revolutionary party comprises the most advanced, determined, and devoted militants in the struggle for socialism, voluntarily united on the basis of tested principles and welded together in rigorous discipline.

The program of the revolutionary party rests upon the great principles of revolutionary Marxism expounded by Marx, Engels, Lenin, and Trotsky, and representing the summation of experience of the working class in its struggle for power. These principles have been verified in particular in the experiences of the last world war and by the victory of the Russian proletarian revolution.

They have been concretized in the basic documents of the first four congresses of the Communist International and the fundamental programmatic documents put forward by the movement for the Fourth International in the past fourteen years. The SWP stands upon the main line of principle developed in these documents.

The organizational structure of the revolutionary party, enabling the party to carry through its historic tasks, rests upon the principle of democratic centralism. This means the fullest inner-party democracy combined with centralized direction and rigid discipline in action. Inner-party democracy guarantees full and free discussion of all party problems, and freedom of criticism both of policies and of the leadership. The leadership, up to and including the highest bodies, is freely and democratically elected by the membership, and subject to its control and removal. The administration of the party is centralized, with lower units subordinate to the higher units. In public and in action, all members are required to carry out the discipline of the party.

Capitalist economy and politics are today worldwide in their basis and scope. The great crises of the modern world – economic crisis, war, revolution – are international in character. The struggle against capitalism and the solution of the problems of the modern world in a world socialist society are likewise international. Consequently, the revolutionary party, if it is to be able to lead this struggle, must itself be an international party, planning its course in terms of an international strategy applied tactically in terms of the local conditions and circumstances of any given nation, and organized in national sections adhering to a single unified national center.

The working class can conduct partial defensive actions and even achieve certain offensive gains on the basis of the united front and a nonrevolutionary perspective. It can take and maintain power, however, only when a decisive majority has been won to the concrete program of the revolution, and this is possible only through the firm and active leadership of the revolutionary party. Similarly, the leadership of the revolutionary party is required to secure the defense of the workers' state and to carry out the organization of socialist economy. The role of the revolutionary party as the leader of the class continues until all forms of class organization, including both the state and all political parties, have disappeared, giving way to the classless socialist society.

The Second International

The Second International (now known as the Labor and Socialist International), answering at one time the needs of one stage in the development of the working class, performed a great progressive function in the mass organization of workers and in the spread of the ideas of socialism. During the period of relative prosperity and stability of capitalism at the beginning of this century, however, and with the rise of imperialism, which fostered the growth and dominance of a labor aristocracy and a conservative trade union and party bureaucracy associated with it, the Second International and all of its major constituent parties were corrupted, and degenerated into patriotic props of bourgeois democracy. The leadership abandoned the road of revolutionary class struggle for power in favor of class collaboration and purely reformist activities aiming at partial demands sought within the framework of capitalism. It accepted, in principle and in practice, the policy of participation in bourgeois coalition governments: that is, of service as political executives for the bourgeoisie.

The extent of the degeneration was fully revealed in 1914, when the parties of the Second International in Europe went over in a body to full-blown social patriotism, and within each country became the recruiting agents within the working class for the imperialist war. Following the war, these parties and the International became the chief bulwark of capitalism against the rising tide of proletarian revolution; in Germany, the leading party of this International drowned the revolution in blood, and handed the power back to the German bourgeoisie. The intervening period has only confirmed the lessons of those years. From instruments of reforms, especially for the labor aristocracy, they were converted, after the war, into agencies for wiping out the previously conquered social reforms of labor, whose existence was no longer tolerable by a declining capitalist order. Everywhere, the Second International and its parties have functioned as a brake set against the workers' revolution, and have proved not merely their inability to lead the workers to victory, but – as in Italy, Germany, and Austria – their certainty of condemning the workers to defeat and finally to fascism. At the present time, the most important remaining parties of the Second International (Great Britain, France) have already proclaimed their social patriotism in the coming war, have voted for the imperialist armament budgets, and are making ready once again to lead the masses to slaughter for the cause of 'democratic' imperialism, and in Spain the party of the Second International, administering the bourgeois government of the People's Front, is making impossible the success of the military struggle against the fascists by subordinating the working class to the bourgeoisie and at the same time liquidating the revolutionary conquests of the workers within the Loyalist territory. Organizationally, the Second International functions merely as a bureaucratic secretariat, and the apparatus of all the major parties is firmly in the hands of hidebound reformist bureaucracies.

Experience thus proves that the Second International is an International of defeat and betrayal and is totally bankrupt as an actual or potential leader of the revolutionary movement. Its reform is excluded on both political and organizational grounds. The development of the revolutionary party in the present era requires the complete and absolute break, both organizationally and politically, with the Second International.

The Third International

The Third, or Communist, International, was projected by Lenin immediately following the betrayal of the Second International to the war, and founded in the fire of the October insurrection in Russia. In its early years, under the guidance of the leaders of the mightiest triumph of the working class, the Third International was the flaming inspiration of the oppressed masses of the entire world. The workers' state in Russia was successfully defended against its enemies, its power consolidated, and the foundations of a socialist economy established; mighty battles were fought everywhere by the working class on the international arena; the programmatic documents of the early years of the International summed up the great and permanently valid principles of revolutionary Marxism, and applied those principles to the conditions of our time.

But the failure of the revolution in the advanced nations and the physical and moral exhaustion of the masses as the result of the imperialist war and the revolutionary struggles enabled the Stalinist clique to gain control of the Soviet state apparatus, the Communist Party of the Soviet Union, and subsequently the Communist International and all of its sections. With Stalin and his adherents in control, and proceeding from the reactionary and anti-Marxist policies of attempting to build a pretended socialism within the national confines of the Soviet Union alone, in independence of the international revolutionary struggle, and of suppressing Soviet, workers', and party democracy in the interests of bureaucratic control and privilege, the history of the Third International and its sections became one of decline, degeneration, and decay.

The entire Third International has become a mere appendage of the Stalinist bureaucratic machine, utilized as an instrument to serve the interests of the bureaucracy, and against the interests of the working class both of the Soviet Union and of the entire world. The events of the past four years – the collapse of the German Communist Party at the advent of Hitler, the proceedings of the Seventh Congress of the Communist International, the adoption of the policy of the People's Front, the new constitution of the Soviet Union, the policies currently pursued within Spain and China, and above all the unprecedented series of trials, executions, and purges beginning within the Soviet Union but now being extended by the GPU throughout the world – these events make clear the extent and profundity of the degeneration of the Third International. The Third International is now being used to enlist the masses within the 'democratic' imperialist countries to support one of the imperialist coalitions in the approaching world war, and to smash all opposition to the new war. The Third International stands within the international working class as the chief bulwark of capitalism and the chief obstacle to the socialist revolution.

The organization of the Third International and its sections is rigidly monolithic in character. No slightest semblance of party democracy remains. The control of bureaucratic absolutism extends from top to bottom. Its regime is compounded of lies, frame-ups, treachery, and terrorism.

No hope whatever of the reform of the Third International or its sections remains. In policy and organization, in ideas and practices, it is hopelessly and utterly bankrupt. The development of the revolutionary party, the continued defense of the remaining conquests of the Russian revolution, the struggle for proletarian power, are inseparable from an uncompromising break with and intransigent struggle against the Third International.

Centrist Parties and Groupings

From time to time within nearly every country in the modern world, parties or political groupings develop in terms of a program which seeks an intermediary position between revolutionary Marxism (representing the unequivocal historical interests of the working class) and reformism (representing in the last analysis the interests of the bourgeoisie operating within the working class). Prominent examples of such parties include the British Independent Labour Party, the Germany Socialist Workers Party (SAP), the Spanish Workers Party of Marxist Unification (POUM), the Brandler-Lovestone groups – and many of them have during recent years been affiliated to the so-called London Bureau. These centrist parties and groupings, which attempted to straddle between the two major class forces in modern society, are by their very nature sterile and incapable of leading an effective and successful struggle for the socialist revolution. Though progressive as a stage in the evolution from reformism to revolutionary Marxism, centrism, stopping short of transformation into revolutionary Marxism, functions in practice to disorient the workers, acts as a cover for reformism both of the Social Democratic and Stalinist varieties, and blocks the revolutionary struggle for workers' power. Revolutionary Marxism, therefore, cannot tolerate any conciliation with centrism.

The New International

War, fascism, the economic crises of capitalism, are international phenomena. The conflict between the restrictions which national boundaries place upon the development of the productive forces and the international character of economy is a world problem. Socialism by its very nature is an international social order. So too, if the workers' movement and the workers' revolution are to succeed, must they be international, and directed in terms of an international strategy. Because of the unequal development of the countries of the world, and since state power is national under capitalism, its conquest must begin in some given nation or nations. But the seizure of power in one country can endure and can go forward toward socialism only by the extension of the revolution to the entire world, and by the building of socialism as a world system. The SWP therefore rejects the utopian and anti-Marxian theory of 'socialism in one country'.

The revolutionary party must thus be an international party, with sections in every country. Its strategy must be worked out in terms of an international perspective, with national tactics adapted to the specific peculiarities and conditions within each nation, but all flowing from the international strategy.

The recognition of the hopeless bankruptcy of the existing Internationals of the working class, of the Second and Third Internationals, and of the impossibilities of their reform, is consequently inseparable from the recognition of the imperative need for building the new, Fourth International, based upon the uncompromising principles of revolutionary Marxism. The rebuilding of the revolutionary party in the United States is an integral part of the rebuilding of the revolutionary party internationally, of the formation of the Fourth International.

The revolutionary party in the United States collaborates in the fullest measure with all groups, organizations, and parties in all other countries standing on the same fundamental program as our own, and cooperates with them in the elaboration of a complete world program. The SWP, therefore, is affiliated with the Bureau for the Fourth International as its section in the United States.

Parties in the United States

1 The Socialist Party

Following the split of the world's working-class political movement by the social-patriotic betrayal of the Second International and the subsequent organization of the Communist International, the Socialist Party of the United States entered a long period of stagnation. Politically it stood at the right wing of the parties of the Second International, but, unlike the European parties, it had little mass influence. Its policies were class collaborationist and thoroughly reformist in character. Its perspective was based upon the achievement of petty reforms within the framework of capitalist society, and its activities were confined largely to trivial parliamentary contests chiefly within the sphere of municipal politics. Within the trade unions, so far as it functioned at all, it acted only as a prop for the reactionary old-line bureaucrats. Internationally, it restored and maintained its affiliation to the Second International, that is, to the organization which engineered the social-patriotic betrayal to the war and which smashed the socialist revolution in the West European countries.

Following the victory of Hitler in Germany, a progressive ferment set in among the membership, the active section of which was resolved to learn from and profit by the lessons of the German defeats. This ferment took form as an organizational struggle of the Militant faction against the stranglehold of the Old Guard, representing reformism in its most crass and reactionary expression. The struggle reached a head at the Cleveland convention in 1936, as a result of which the main sections of the Old Guard split away from the Socialist Party to form the Social Democratic Federation, through which their policies continue in operation.

Both before and after the Cleveland convention, there was an influx into the Socialist Party of unaffiliated revolutionists, and of an entire revolutionary group, the former Workers Party. The revolutionists already within the party fused with these incoming revolutionists, joining in the common struggle for an uncompromising revolutionary policy and a genuinely revolutionary party. The spectacle of the rapid advance of the revolutionary current, however, dismayed and alarmed the centrists and right-wingers who were still in control of the apparatus of the Socialist Party. Resolved to prevent at all costs the transformation of the party into a clear-cut revolutionary organization, they called the Chicago convention in March 1937, in an attempt to cut off the revolutionary current. Failing in this attempt because of the resistance of the membership, they took bureaucratic measures in the summer of 1937 to split the party. In flagrant violation of the convention decisions and the will of the membership, they utilized their control of the national apparatus to put an end to party democracy and then to expel the revolutionary wing. The decisive political motivation for the expulsion of the revolutionists was the determination of the old-line leadership to swing the party sharply to the right, exemplified by the treacherous decision to support the capitalist candidate for mayor of the New York People's Front, extending from the Lovestoneites and Stalinists to the Republican Party.

The entire active militant membership rallied to the revolutionary wing, and stood with unbroken ranks, firm in the resolve to carry forward the great task of rebuilding the revolutionary party in this country. The centrists and right-wingers have retained only the formal shell of the Socialist Party, a hopeless, miserable, impotent clique, already falling apart in a dozen different directions and sinking in its bulk to sterile passivity. That Socialist Party is now only a dead husk. It offers no hope; it has no policy, no perspective. There is no hope for it any longer on the American political scene. The comparatively small number of individual militants remaining within it can function in the revolutionary movement of the working class only by breaking immediately and finally with the Altman-Thomas-Tyler Socialist party, and with everything for which it stands.

2 The Communist Party

The Communist Party of the United States is a faithful replica of the sections of the Communist International everywhere. Its main function is to prepare the mass support of the United States government in the coming imperialist war; it has already announced publicly its support of that war and its intention of acting as the lynch gang to take care of all those who oppose the war. In compliance with the policy of the People's Front, it supports capitalist candidates and capitalist parties in elections, and utilizes its full influence to direct the workers away from independent proletarian action. It acts as the propagandist for the Moscow trials and has already begun the introduction of the system of the Moscow trials into this country, a step which will lead to ever-increasing attempts at the frame-up, terrorization, even assassination of working-class militants.

Within the labor movement, the Communist Party of the United States plays a reactionary role. Indeed, its policy in practice is not less reactionary than that of the old-line trade union bureaucrats with whom it is allied. The primary concern of the Communist Party is not with the immediate needs of the workers and their unions; it seeks only to manipulate the unions in accordance with the requirements of the People's Front in preparing the social-patriotic betrayal to the war. The Stalinists within the unions are ready to make any deal whatever with either bureaucrats or bosses, to engineer any type of sell-out, and in general devote their energies to the crushing of every sign of progressive and militant opposition. In their use of gangsterism, lies, frame-ups, and bureaucratism, the Stalinists in the unions are distinguished from the older-style reactionary bureaucrats only by the greater skill, thoroughness, and ruthlessness of the Stalinists in applying their anti-working-class and counterrevolutionary methods.

Far from offering any hope whatever in the task of building the revolutionary party, the Communist Party of the United States is a counterrevolutionary agency, the chief obstacle within the working class to building the revolutionary party. It is true that there are at present, either within the Communist Party or its various collateral organizations, many individuals with militant and even revolutionary sentiments who, though dissatisfied with the party and its policy, do not yet realize the full implications of the policy and are not yet ready to break sharply with Stalinism. These elements will inevitably come into sharp conflict with the treacherous policies and leadership of the Communist Party. The revolutionary party will be a rallying banner for all those who break with Stalinism. But this can be accomplished only through the unremitting, constant, and uncompromising struggle against Stalinism itself in all its forms and on every field.

3 Labor and Farmer-Labor Parties

There is at present in this country, as on other occasions in the past, a movement toward the formation of various sorts of labor and farmer-labor parties. In a few states and localities such parties are already in existence, and functioning as political organizations.

Mass labor and farmer-labor parties are all defined in political character as *reformist*. As such, the programs and activities are directed to securing reforms within the framework of capitalist society, and against the revolutionary overthrow of capitalism. The solution of the historical problems of the working class – the defeat of fascism, the abolition of war, the gaining of material security – none of them can be secured without the revolutionary overthrow of capitalism. In the present era the continuance of capitalism makes war, fascism, impoverishment for the masses, inevitable. It therefore follows – as is also demonstrated conclusively by the experience of the labor movement – that these reformist parties act in practice and in crises as bulwarks of capitalism and enemies of the socialist revolution. Their false program and perspective disorient the masses, turning them aside from revolutionary class struggle, and permit the forces of reaction to consolidate without effective opposition.

The history of the present labor party movement in the country reinforces these conclusions. The American Labor Party in New York was specifically founded by the trade union bureaucrats to gather votes for Roosevelt from those workers whom the Democratic Party could no longer dupe or attract, and who would not therefore have voted for a presidential candidate on an old-party ticket. Similarly, in 1937, it brought nearly a half a million labor votes to the capitalist candidate LaGuardia. So, in the rest of the country, the labor party movement is used by the bureaucrats to bolster up and refurbish capitalist politics, to provide a new coating to make capitalist politics palatable to the masses. There is every indication that the present labor party developments, however far they may be extended, will continue the efforts to make deals and bargains with the two existing capitalist parties, perhaps even to fuse with one or another section of these parties, and will strive to maneuver to a position of holding the 'balance of power' between them by playing off one against the other. Far from constituting independent class politics, the present labor party development is, from the point of view of the bureaucrats and the bourgeoisie, the method for preventing the growth of independent class politics.

For such reasons, the revolutionary party cannot for a moment compromise with the program of the labor and farmer-labor parties. It must consistently and vigorously put forward its own full revolutionary program as the *only* solution to the problems of the workers and of the masses generally, and must strive at all times to recruit directly into its own ranks. Nor can the revolutionary party properly take the initiative in advocating the formation of labor or farmer-labor parties.

Nevertheless, the labor party movement, from the point of view of the workers themselves, does reveal a progressive development in general towards class consciousness. In spite of the channels into which it is led by the bureaucrats, it shows in the masses a growing realization of the true character of capitalist politics as summed up in the Republican and Democratic parties and a striving for independent political action. To stand aside completely from such a development where it comprises the bulk of the militant and advanced sections of the workers would be hopelessly sectarian for the revolutionists. Where the labor party develops as a genuine mass movement separate from the capitalist parties, the revolutionists must remain in the midst of the workers who are passing through that experience precisely in order to make certain that the workers will draw the lessons from that experience which are required in order to go on from it to revolutionary class politics. Uncompromising, programmatic independence on the part of the revolutionary party is an indispensable precondition for any activity in which revolutionists may engage, especially through their trade unions, in broad and significant labor party movements. Whenever the revolutionists find themselves in a labor party, they will stand at each stage for those concrete policies and actions which sum up a progressive and class perspective, for complete breaks with the capitalist parties and no support of candidates on capitalist tickets, for direct mass actions and avoidance of limitation to parliamentary activities, for full internal democracy, for support and defense of concrete working-class rights against their invasion from any source, including invasions from candidates of the labor party itself, etc.

The SWP

In the light of the considerations set forth in this Declaration of Principles, and basing itself upon the great principles herein outlined, the convention of revolutionary socialists held in Chicago from December 31, 1937 to January 3, 1938, establishes the SWP as an independent organization. We call upon all revolutionary militants to join with us to build the SWP into the mass revolutionary party which will lead the working class of the United States to power, and which, together with the revolutionists of all countries united in the Fourth International, will achieve the victory of the international revolution and of world socialism.

Part III

The Aim of the SWP

The main specific task of the SWP is the mobilization of the American masses for struggle against American capitalism, and for its overthrow. To this end the party will seek to win the support of the industrial and agricultural workers by its activity within their mass organizations, and to establish an alliance between the workers and farmers and other sections of the middle class ready and able to join labor in a struggle against the big capitalist class. The SWP will support and seek to give leadership to all progressive struggles, whether for immediate or more far-reaching demands, to strikes, organization campaigns, demonstrations, mass actions for relief and jobs and social insurance, mass fights against lynching, evictions, foreclosures, violations of civil rights, and against every type of reaction. While relying primarily on mass actions, propaganda, and agitation as the means for furthering its revolutionary aim, the party will also participate in electoral campaigns, though at all times contending against the fatal illusion that the masses can accomplish their emancipation through the ballot box. Election campaigns will serve primarily as a means for revolutionary propaganda, and candidates who are elected will utilize their offices first of all to expose the sham of capitalist democracy and to promote the mass movement of the workers. The party will endeavor constantly to educate the militant workers in the principles of revolutionary Marxism. Everywhere, by direct participation, it will seek to demonstrate in action the applicability of its principles and tactics and the competence of its leadership.

The Trade Unions

The trade unions are the elementary and basic organs of working-class defense against capitalist aggression, and of all trade unions, the most important are those of the workers in the large shops, mills, factories, and mines of the basic industries. The primary field of party work is trade union activity.

In trade union policy, the party stands for the methods of militant class struggle, the organization of the unorganized, industrial unionism, in all fields where this is feasible, and broad inner-union democracy. The party fights against policies of class collaborationism, against bureaucratism, gangsterism, and racketeering, and against reliance on the government and governmental agencies. The party, while in no degree relaxing its support of the unions and their struggles, fights also against those forces within the unions which carry out these reactionary policies, against the trade union bureaucracy and against all other reactionary tendencies in the unions – in particular against Stalinism. The party stands for the closest cooperation between the trade unions and the unemployed for their common interest, and opposes any discrimination against the unemployed workers.

The party stands for trade union unity, since a divided trade union movement weakens the defensive strength of the workers against reaction, and facilitates the coming of fascism. The party does not, however, make a fetish of 'unity at all costs'. While against the policy of building paper 'red unions', as advocated by the Stalinists in the so-called third period, and in favor of working within the genuine existing unions, which are for the most part reformist in policy and leadership, the party recognizes that special circumstances may have brought about the development of genuine unions outside the chief central trade union body or bodies, and in such cases it supports these independent trade unions while working for their reintegration into the mainstream of the labor movement, and where the existing central body or bodies refuse to organize a given field, the party favors its organization in any case on a temporarily independent basis.

In keeping with its stand for trade union unity, the party favors the unity of the AFL and the CIO on the foundation of progressive trade union policy. In the division of the labor movement into AFL and CIO, the party recognizes the historically more progressive character of the CIO movement in its policies of industrial unionism and organization of the unorganized. Nevertheless, the CIO does not have an exclusive claim to support, both because of its own reactionary features – its extreme violations of trade union democracy and its class collaborationism – and more especially because the AFL remains a genuine mass organization of a section of the American working class. Consequently, in the case of concrete disputes between the two and in questions of conflicting fields of operation for party members, there is no universal formula in favor of either organization; each such issue must be settled on its own merits in the light of the specific circumstances involved.

The party supports and builds the trade unions. It is not content, however, to work in them at the level of mere and 'pure' trade unionism. It seeks to build within the unions a broad progressive wing based on progressive trade union policies. And at all times it aims to raise the level of class consciousness of the trade union members, and to politicalize their thoughts and activities to the fullest possible degree.

The Middle Classes

Though the leadership in the revolutionary struggle for socialism can be held only by the working class, the working class cannot succeed in its struggle without winning to its side broad sections of the middle classes, of the farmers, professional workers, small shopkeepers, etc. The middle classes in modern society, occupying a social position which causes them to vacillate between the two basic decisive classes – bourgeoisie and proletariat – have no independent social perspective or program for society as a whole, and thus in crucial situations tend always in their bulk to throw their weight to one or the other of the two decisive classes. It would therefore be fatal from a revolutionary point of view for the working class to attempt to win the middle classes by abandoning its program (the program of revolutionary socialism) and accepting as substitute some specious 'middle-class program' (as is done in the case of the tactic of the 'People's Front'). On the same grounds, the SWP rejects the conception of a 'two-class party' (farmer-labor party, etc.), which is an attempt to put two different classes on the same plane by organizing them into a single party with a single program. Preserving its own program intact, the working class must win the middle classes, especially their lower, more impoverished, and more discontented strata, by first demonstrating to them the power and strength of the working class in action, and second, by supporting those specific demands and struggles of the middle classes which are directed implicitly against capitalism and whose full achievement requires the sharpest struggle against capitalism itself: demands for mortgage relief, tax relief in the 'lower brackets', better conditions of farm tenancy, improved conditions for the lower-paid professional workers and technicians, etc.

In agriculture, the revolutionary working-class party bases itself primarily upon the agricultural proletariat, whose interests it defends at all times, even when need be, against the middle-class farmers. The living conditions of the great mass of farm tenants, sharecroppers, and smaller independent farmers are in this country at almost a subhuman level, in many instances indeed well below that of the industrial workers. In recent years also, many of the professional workers have been feeling the full weight of capitalist decline both in the lowering of their own living standards, and likewise in the growing disparity between the tasks they are trained to accomplish and the inability of capitalism to provide any way to make use of their training. These sections of the population are beginning to organize in defense of their immediate interests. Support of their progressive demands and struggles, linking of those struggles with the struggles of the proletariat, and a bold and vigorous policy on the part of the revolutionary party will save them from fascism – to which they will otherwise turn – and win them to the socialist revolution.

Negroes and Other Oppressed Racial Groups

The Negroes compose the most exploited and persecuted section of the population of this country. Racial differences and antagonisms, moreover, are exploited by the capitalist dictatorship to drive down the standard of living of all workers and to keep them from uniting against their oppressors. The SWP will seek to break down the vicious chauvinistic 'superiority' prejudices with which the bourgeoisie systematically poisons the minds of the white workers. It will aim to convince the white workers on the one hand, and the workers of the Negro and other oppressed racial groups (such as the Japanese, Mexicans, and Filipinos) on the other, that their interests are the same. Workers, regardless of race, must be united in economic and political organizations for a common struggle. The SWP stands for the complete equality of the Negroes and all other races, and will fight against every form of race discrimination – economic, political social, against wage differentials, lynching, Jim Crowism, the barring of Negroes and other racial groups from the trade unions, discrimination against them where they are in unions, and all other forms of racial and national chauvinism. At the same time it points out that the Negro masses cannot achieve deliverance by reliance upon Negro capitalists or middle-class Negroes or upon so-called Negro capitalism. Only by the complete abolition of capitalism will the Negroes gain freedom from discrimination, exploitation, and tyranny.

The Unemployed

The enormous and largely permanent army of the unemployed during the period of the rapid decline of capitalism is a vast depository of every kind of social discontent. In a position where the conduct of their lives has lost social meaning, the unemployed will join with the movement that convincingly fights for their demands and opens to them the prospect of a new and integral place in the social order. Unless the working-class movement, by giving support to their struggles and by vigorous presentation of the revolutionary way out of the crisis, draws in the unemployed, they will be a prey to chauvinistic and military propaganda, to false social nostrums, and to fascist demagogy. The SWP will resist all efforts to erect barriers between the employed and unemployed, will constantly stress the community of interest between them, and will show in action how the fight of employed and unemployed against their common oppressor can be united. It supports and helps organize the struggles of the unemployed masses for relief, for jobs, against evictions, for social insurance, etc. It stands for the unity of the employed and unemployed, by the organization of the latter into a movement directly associated with the trade unions.

The Youth

Throughout its existence, the capitalist system has been marked by the extreme and shameful exploitation of children and youth. Today, in the decline of capitalism, it is unable even to offer jobs at starvation wages to millions of the youth, but holds out for them a life of frustration and sterility, and the destruction and degradation of fascism and war. It is particularly from the ranks of the youth, with their physical vitality, their courage, and their moral idealism, that the SWP can and must expect to recruit the best militants in the struggle for socialism. The party will champion and the progressive interests, aims, and demands of the youth, and will carry out as an urgent and most important task the building of a broad youth organization, based upon the principles of revolutionary Marxism, which will embrace young workers, farmers, and students. The party, however, rejects the conception that the youth constitute a special or independent 'class' in modern society, with special historical interests and program. A youth movement which will be of aid in the struggle for socialism must be an integral part of the revolutionary workers' movement, and must base itself upon the perspective of their program.

The Struggle against Imperialist War

Since war is inevitably bred by capitalist society, the only genuine struggle against war is precisely the struggle against the social system which breeds it, the struggle against capitalism and for socialism. Only through the elimination of the causes for war will war itself be done away with. Through socialism alone can mankind establish the foundations for enduring peace.

The SWP is against every imperialist war and opposes all wars fought by any and all imperialist states, whether fascist or democratic, since such wars can only be reactionary in character and counter to the interests of the masses and of the revolution. In the imperialist United States, the SWP fights against war preparations and militarization, but at the same time always makes clear that war cannot be permanently prevented unless the imperialist government of the United States is overthrown and its place taken by a workers' state, that lasting peace is possible only under socialism.

Pacifism attempts to divorce the struggle against war from the prosecution of the class struggle against capitalism. In practice, therefore, pacifism is entirely futile and powerless against war itself, and still further, spreads illusions about the nature of war which divert the masses from the genuine struggle against it and play into the hands of imperialism. The SWP, consequently, exposes the futility and illusions of pacifism. In the United States, pacifism is particularly dangerous because its ideas are so widespread and influential, and because it is in a sense the 'official' imperialist doctrine – indeed, the ideological preparation for the next imperialist war bases itself largely on the notion that from the point of view of the United States it will be a 'war for peace'.

If, in spite of the efforts of the revolutionists and the militant workers, the US government enters a new war, the SWP will not under any circumstances support that war but will on the contrary fight against it. The SWP will advocate the continuance of the class struggle during the war regardless of the consequences for the outcome of the American military struggle, and will try to prepare the masses to utilize the war crisis for the overthrow of US capitalism and the victory of socialism.

The SWP opposes and will continue at all times to oppose every form of social patriotism, all advocacy of 'national union' or 'suspension of the class struggle' during wartime, and will make clear to the workers that no war conducted by the capitalist government of the United States can be to their interest, or be any other than a war for imperialist profit and plunder.

The policy of the SWP with respect to imperialist war holds good under all conditions: it applies if the war is conducted between the fascist imperialisms and the 'democratic' imperialisms in the same manner as if the war takes place between coalitions including both fascist and 'democratic' imperialisms on each side. It applies also if the United States is in military alliance with the Soviet Union. In the latter case, the SWP would unreservedly support the Soviet Union against imperialism, but would expose the treacherous imperialist aims of the United States in the alliance, would call for the overthrow of US capitalism and its replacement by a revolutionary workers' government, which alone could carry forward the war in the interests of labor, of the revolutionary defense of the Soviet Union, and of the world socialist revolution. The practical steps which our party will take in the course of its opposition to such a war will be decided in light of the consideration of the need of facilitating the utmost aid to the Soviet Union's armed forces against an imperialist power in conformity with our position of defense of the Soviet Union from imperialist assault.

Colonial Peoples

The struggle against imperialist war is inseparable from the struggle against imperialism in general, and therefore, from support of the wars of enslaved peoples against their imperialist oppressors, of colonies against the nations which keep them in servitude, of nationalities, races, and minorities which suffer from the yoke of oppressors, of workers' states against capitalist states. The SWP is not neutral or indifferent in such wars, but actively supports the oppressed against the oppressors.

United States imperialism, exploiting the masses within its national boundaries, at the same time and to an even greater degree, exploits the peoples of Latin and Central America, Cuba, Puerto Rico, Hawaii, Liberia, the Philippines. These people are thus the potential allies of the American workers in the struggle against US imperialism, and neither they nor the American workers can expect to win freedom except in joint combat against the common enemy. The SWP supports every progressive struggle of these peoples. It stands for the immediate and unhampered right of self-determination for them, free from military, political, or economic intervention or pressure by the US government. It stands for the immediate and unconditional independence of all the territories, colonies, and dependencies of the US and for the withdrawal of all troops from them. It is opposed to any attempt by American imperialism, open or masked, to infringe upon the right of self-determination of any nation or people.

The revolutions in the colonies, semicolonies, and spheres of influence of United States imperialism are integrally and reciprocally related to the revolutionary struggle against that imperialism at home. A successful revolution in the United States would be decisive for the emancipation of the toiling masses throughout Latin America; while, on the other hand, a revolution beginning in one of the Latin American countries, or in one of the colonies or semicolonies of the US, could spread throughout the continent and powerfully accelerate the development of the class struggle and the revolution within the United States. The SWP regards it, therefore, as a central task to aid and support the revolutionary movement in these nations and colonies, and to establish the closest relations with the revolutionists and revolutionary organizations within them.

The Defense of the Soviet Union

The Russian revolution, the greatest event in the history of mankind, is the guide and inspiration of the workers of the entire world. All the years of imperialist assault and sabotage, of the misrule, treachery, and finally usurpation of Stalinism, have not yet succeeded in destroying the foundations of the workers' state, nor did they prevent the Soviet Union, the product of that revolution, from demonstrating the immense superiority of the socialist organization of society over even the most developed forms of capitalism, and have not succeeded in wiping out the great social conquests of the revolution. The economy and social relations established by the revolution still remain, against the blows of Stalinism, providing the foundation, once the Soviet Union is cleansed of the poison of Stalinism, for victorious resumption of the march toward socialism. It is, consequently, the elementary and imperative duty of all workers, and especially of the revolutionary party, to defend the Soviet Union unconditionally against any and every imperialist nation. The defense of the Soviet Union cannot, of course, rest primarily upon the League of Nations or attempted alliances with capitalist nations, but is essentially based upon and inseparable from unrelenting struggle against the counterrevolutionary policies of Stalinism, which now imminently threaten to complete the betrayal and liquidation of the Russian revolution, and inseparable equally from the extension of the workers' revolution to other nations, which, in the last analysis, is the only effective defense of the Russian revolution.

Coalition Governments

When a working-class party enters a coalition government of the bourgeois regime, it thereby accepts responsibility for the administration of the bourgeois state and functions thus as an agent of the class enemy. Such an action is incompatible with revolutionary class struggle, which is directed toward the overthrow of the bourgeois state and the triumph of a workers' regime. The SWP will under no circumstances whatever enter or give political support to any bourgeois government.

Democracy and Fascism

The SWP stands unequivocally for the fullest and most complete democracy, possible only by the victorious achievement of socialism. Indeed, this is presupposed in the very ideal of socialism, or the fullest and most meaningful democracy is realized only with the realization of socialism. Nevertheless, it is not democracy in the abstract or mere democratic forms devoid of content to which the SWP gives allegiance. The SWP defends and aims to extend the concrete democratic rights of the masses, for these alone are of actual value and significance.

Capitalist democracy, though permitting a certain number of these concrete democratic rights, is in the last analysis a mask for the dictatorship of the bourgeoisie. At no time does it or can it permit the wide or genuine exercise of democratic rights by the masses. Under capitalist democracy, the working class must fight to extend to the maximum all democratic rights, which capitalism, especially in the period of decline, seeks to curtail. The defense of democratic rights, the defense of genuine democracy, demands in the end the social revolution, since only through the revolution will democracy for the masses be achieved. The defense of the fraud of capitalist 'democracy' – which is the rule of capitalist exploitation – only guarantees in the end the crushing by fascism of even those limited democratic rights and institutions which capitalism is 'normally' compelled to tolerate.

In the decline of capitalism, the growing internal conflicts of capitalism in nation after nation make it necessary for the bourgeoisie, if it is to maintain its social dictatorship and class domination, to abolish or reduce to a shell the capitalist democratic form of government and go over to fascism. Fascism does away with all of the democratic rights of the masses. But fascism also, since it is the outgrowth and product of capitalism in decline, can be defeated finally only through the socialist revolution. The effective struggle against fascism cannot, therefore, be divorced from the struggle against capitalism itself and for socialism.

Democratic rights are necessary for the masses at all times in order for them to organize, and to facilitate political education and propaganda in the ideas of socialism. The SWP therefore stands at all times for the defense and extension of the democratic rights of the masses, and advocates the broadest possible united fronts for such defense.

Though insisting upon the fundamental identity in social character between all forms of capitalist dictatorship, the SWP recognizes the rise of the conflict between capitalist 'democracy' and fascism, which sometimes assumes the sharpest forms, even those of civil war. While at all times pointing out that only the socialist revolution can in the end defeat fascism, and advocating the continuance of the class struggle for socialism under all circumstances, the SWP will, as a stage in the struggle for socialism, utilize every conflict between 'democratic' capitalism and fascism to smash the latter and to advance the interests of the independent class movement of the workers in their irreconcilable struggle against capitalist rule itself under any form. Such policies as the purely electoral joint support of Hindenburg against Hitler in Germany, or of Van Zeeland against Degrelle in Belgium, are not a means of struggle against fascism, but of destroying the class independence of the workers, thus facilitating the advance of fascism, and are consequently contrary to the principles of the SWP. Support of one of the imperialist coalitions in the coming war on the alleged grounds that the given coalition was 'democratic' and arrayed against fascism, far from being an active defense against fascism, would be social-patriotic treachery, and altogether contradictory to revolutionary principles, and to the interests of the working class. However, support of the military struggle against Franco in the Spanish civil war has been not merely consistent with revolutionary principle but the sole possible policy for revolutionists with respect to the Spanish civil war and the only road of development toward the Spanish workers' revolution. The attitude toward analogous civil wars in other countries, including the United States, which involved an armed internal war between a fascist camp and a bourgeois-democratic camp, would be the same: all technical and military support in the joint struggle against fascism as an inseparable part of the preparation for the socialist revolution.

The People's Front

The policy and tactics of the 'People's Front' are merely the classic policy and tactics of class collaboration and coalitionism renamed and reapplied in the circumstances of the present time. The People's Front combats the program of Marxism and the class struggle for socialism: that is, it attempts to crush the independence of the working class, subordinating it ideologically, politically, and organizationally to the bourgeoisie. The People's Front, formulated and advocated in its most vicious form by Stalinism, proposes national unity and class peace on the basis of a program for the alleged defense of bourgeois democracy. The aim of the People's Front is to prepare for mass support to the coming imperialist war in the 'democratic' nations. The result of the People's Front, as already proved conclusively by experience in both France and Spain, can only be the thrusting back of the revolution, the weakening and disorientation of the workers, betrayal to the war, and in the end the victory of fascism. The SWP therefore rejects and combats People's Frontism.

The United Front

The working class must be united if it is to achieve victory. The most decisive unity will be gained when the majority of the working class unites on the basis of the ideas of revolutionary Marxism. Meanwhile, in spite of organizational and political differences, the workers must achieve united action in order to defend their rights and advance their interests. If they do not, wage and relief cuts, increasing abrogation of political and civil liberties, and finally, war and fascism, are assured.

United action in the interests of the workers cannot be gained through the People's Front, which is in actuality the abandonment of the workers' struggle, nor from the pseudo-united front 'only from below', once advocated by the Stalinists, nor from unity based on paralyzing 'non-aggression pacts'. The SWP stands for and advocates broad, honest, carefully defined united fronts of organizations on specific issues facing the workers, in which each organization, loyally adhering to the united front, retains its political and organizational independence, and its right to criticism either for failure to carry out the united front agreement or on questions of program and principle. Such united front actions develop the mass power of the workers, show the workers the need and value of unity, expose the weakness or treachery of reactionary and reformist leaders, and give the revolutionary party the opportunity to prove in action the correctness of its principles and tactics. United front actions are thus indispensable preparations for the revolutionary unity which, in the revolutionary crisis, will enable the workers to take power.

3 The Internal Situation and the Character of the Party[8]

(*1938*)

James P. Cannon and Max Shachtman

The Socialist Workers Party is a revolutionary Marxian party, based on a definite program, whose aim is the organization of the working class in the struggle for power and the transformation of the existing social order. All of its activities, its methods, and its internal regime are subordinated to this aim and are designed to serve it.

Only a self-acting and critical-minded membership is capable of forging and consolidating such a party and of solving its problems by collective thought, discussion, and experience.

From this follows the need for assuring the widest party democracy in the ranks of the organization.

The struggle for power organized and led by the revolutionary party is the most ruthless and irreconcilable struggle in all history. A loosely knit, heterogeneous, undisciplined, untrained organization is utterly incapable of accomplishing such world-historical tasks as the proletariat and the revolutionary party are confronted with in the present era. This is all the more emphatically true in the light of the singularly difficult position of our party and the extraordinary persecution to which it is subjected. From this follows the party's unconditional demand upon all its members for complete discipline in all the public activities and actions of the organization.

Leadership and centralized direction are indispensable prerequisites for any sustained and disciplined action, especially in the party that sets itself the aim of leading the collective efforts of the proletariat in its struggle against capitalism. Without a strong and firm central committee, having the power to act promptly and effectively in the name of the party and to supervise, coordinate, and direct all of its activities without exception, the very idea of a revolutionary party is a meaningless jest.

8 Cannon and Shachtman 1938.

It is from these considerations, based upon the whole of the experience of working-class struggle throughout the world in the last century, that we derive the Leninist principle of organization, namely, democratic centralism. The same experience has demonstrated that there are no absolute guarantees for the preservation of the principle of democratic centralism, and no rigid formula that can be set down in advance, *a priori*, for the application of it under any and all circumstances. Proceeding from certain fundamental conceptions, the problem of applying the principle of democratic centralism differently under different conditions and stages of development of the struggle can be solved only in relation to the concrete situation, in the course of the tests and experience through which the movement passes, and on the basis of the most fruitful and healthy interrelationship of the leading bodies of the party and its rank and file.

The leadership of the party must be under the control of the membership; its policies must always be open to criticism, discussion, and rectification by the rank and file within properly established forms and limits, and the leading bodies themselves subject to formal recall or alteration. The membership of the party has the right to demand and expect the greatest responsibility from the leaders, precisely because of the position they occupy in the movement. The selection of comrades to the positions of leadership means the conferring of an extraordinary responsibility. The warrant for this position must be proved, not once but continuously by the leadership itself.

It is under obligation to set the highest example of responsibility, devotion, sacrifice, and complete identification with the party itself and its daily life and action. It must display the ability to defend its policies before the membership of the party, and to defend the line of the party and the party as a whole before the working class in general. Sustained party activity, not broken or disrupted by abrupt and disorienting changes, presupposes not only a continuity of tradition and a systematic development of party policy, but also the continuity of leadership. It is an important sign of a serious and firmly constituted party, of a party really engaged in productive work in the class struggle, that it throws up, out of its ranks, cadres of more or less able leading comrades, tested for their qualities of endurance and trustworthiness, and that it thus ensures a certain stability and continuity of leadership by such a cadre.

Continuity of leadership does not, however, signify the automatic self-perpetuation of leadership. Constant renewal of its ranks by means of additions and, when necessary, replacements, is the only assurance the party has that its leadership will not succumb to the effects of dry-rot, that it will not be burdened with dead wood, that it will avoid the corrosion of conservatism and dilettantism, that it will not be the object of conflict between the older elements and the younger, that the old and basic cadre will be refreshed by new blood, that the leadership as a whole will not become purely bureaucratic 'committee men' with a life that is remote from the real life of the party and the activities of the rank and file. Like leadership, membership itself in the party implies certain definite rights.

Party membership confers the fullest freedom of discussion, debate, and criticism inside the ranks of the party, limited only by such decisions and provisions as are made by the party itself or by bodies to which it assigns this function. Affiliation to the party confers upon each member the right of being democratically represented at all policy-making assemblies of the party (from branch to national and international convention), and the right of the final and decisive vote in determining the program, policies, and leadership of the party.

With party rights, the membership has also certain definite obligations. The theoretical and political character of the party is determined by its program, which forms the lines delimiting the revolutionary party from all other parties, groups, and tendencies in the working class. The first obligation of party membership is loyal acceptance of the program of the party and regular affiliation to one of the basic units of the party. The party requires of every member the acceptance of its discipline and the carrying on of his activity in accordance with the program of the party, with the decisions adopted by its conventions and with the policies formulated and directed by the party leadership. Party membership implies the obligation of 100 percent loyalty to the organization, the rejection of all agents of other, hostile groups in its ranks, and intolerance of divided loyalties in general. Membership in the party necessitates a minimum of activity in the organization, as established by the proper unit, and under the direction of the party; it necessitates the fulfillment of all of the tasks which the party assigns to each member. Party membership implies the obligation upon every member to contribute materially to the support of the organization in accordance with his means.

From the foregoing it follows that the party seeks to include in its ranks all the revolutionary, class-conscious, and militant workers who stand on its program and are active in building the movement in a disciplined manner. The revolutionary Marxian party rejects not only the arbitrariness and bureaucratism of the CP, but also the spurious and deceptive 'all-inclusiveness' of the Thomas-Tyler-Hoan party, which is a sham and a fraud. Experience has proved conclusively that this 'all-inclusiveness' paralyzes the party in general and the revolutionary left wing in particular, suppressing and bureaucratically hounding the latter while giving free rein to the right wing to commit the greatest crimes in the name of socialism and the party. The SWP seeks to be inclusive only in this sense: that it accepts into its ranks those who accept its program and rejects from membership those who reject its program.

The rights of each individual member, as set forth above, do not imply that the membership as a whole, namely, the party itself, does not possess rights of its own. The party as a whole has the right to demand that its work not be disrupted and disorganized, and has the right to take all the measures which it finds necessary to assure its regular and normal functioning. The rights of any individual member are distinctly secondary to the rights of the party membership as a whole. Party democracy means not only the most scrupulous protection of the rights of a given minority, but also the protection of the rule of the majority. The party is therefore entitled to organize the discussion and to determine its forms and limits.

All inner-party discussion must be organized from the point of view that the party is not a discussion club which debates interminably on any and all questions at any and all times, without arriving at a binding decision that enables the organization to act, but from the point of view that we are a disciplined party of revolutionary action. The party in general not only has the right, therefore, to organize the discussion in accordance with the requirements of the situation, but the lower units of the party must be given the right, in the interests of the struggle against the disruption and disorganization of the party's work, to call irresponsible elements to order and, if need be, to eject them from the ranks.

The decisions of the national party convention are binding on all party members without exception, and they conclude the discussion on all those disputed questions upon which a decision has been taken. Any party member violating the decisions of the convention, or attempting to revive discussion in regard to them without formal authorization of the party, puts himself thereby in opposition to the party and forfeits his right to membership. All party organizations are authorized and instructed to take any measures necessary to enforce this rule.

4 Constitution of the Socialist Workers Party[9] (*1938*)

Article I. Name

The name of the organization shall be the Socialist Workers Party (hereinafter referred to as 'the party').

Article II. Purpose

The purpose of the party is set forth in its Declaration of Principles: its purpose shall be to educate and organize the working class for the abolition of capitalism and the establishment of a workers' government to achieve socialism.

Article III. International Affiliation

The party is affiliated to the International Bureau for the Fourth International. Its National Committee is empowered, subject to approval of the International Bureau, to enter into fraternal relations with groups and parties in other countries not affiliated to the bureau with the aim of drawing them closer to or into the movement for the Fourth International.

Article IV. Membership

Section 1. Every person who accepts the Declaration of Principles of the party and agrees to submit to its discipline and engage actively in its work shall be eligible to membership.

Section 2. Applicants for membership shall sign an application card reading as follows: 'I hereby apply for membership in the Socialist Workers Party. I

9 Socialist Workers Party 1938.

accept the Declaration of Principles and Constitution and agree to abide by the discipline of the party and to engage actively in its work'.

Section 3. Every member must belong to a duly constituted branch of the party in the territory where he resides, or at his place of work, if such a branch exists. In territories where no branch exists, applicants shall be admitted as members-at-large.

Section 4. All applicants for membership shall be endorsed and recommended by two persons who have been members for not less than three months. Action by the party branch on applications for membership takes place to the absence of the applicant.

Section 5. An official membership card shall be issued to each member.

Section 6. A member desiring to leave one locality for another must apply to his branch for permission and receive a transfer card, which is to be deposited with the branch of the locality to which the member moves. If no branch exists in the new locality, the member shall remain a member-at-large.

Section 7. The National Committee is empowered to accept groups or organizations of individuals, eligible under Section 1 of this article, as members *en bloc*, and to assign them to the proper branches.

Article v. Units of Organization

Section 1. The basic unit of the party shall be the branch, formed on a territorial or occupational basis. A branch shall consist of not less than 5 nor more than 50 members. When a branch achieves a membership of 50, it shall be subdivided into two branches. Exceptions can be made only by permission of the National Committee.

Section 2. Wherever two branches exist in the same locality, a local executive committee shall be formed by elections at a joint membership meeting. Where three or more branches exist in the same locality, a local executive committee shall be elected at a city convention.

Section 3. In such cases as may be decided by the National Committee, state or district executive committees, elected by state or district membership meetings or by local or district conventions, shall be formed.

Article VI. Administration

Section 1. The highest governing body of the party is the national convention. Its decisions shall be binding upon the entire membership.

Section 2. Between national conventions, the authority of the convention, subject to the decisions of the convention itself, is vested in the National Committee elected by the convention.

Section 3. The National Committee shall be comprised as follows:

Par. 1. There shall be 24 members, elected by the national convention, plus one member selected by the NEC of the YPSL.

Par. 2. The national convention shall also elect 10 alternates, to fill vacancies in the National Committee in the order decided upon by the convention.

Par. 3. Members of the National Committee may be dropped from the committee and/or from the party only by vote of the national convention. Members of the National Committee may, however, for cause be suspended from membership and be barred from all rights as members, pending final decision of the party convention, by vote of two-thirds of the membership of the National Committee.

Section 4. The National Committee directs all the work of the party, decides all questions of policy in accord with the decisions of the convention, appoints subordinate officers and subcommittees, including the Political Committee, and, in general, constitutes between conventions the functioning authority of the party.

Section 5. The local governing body of the party shall be the local executive committee, or where only one branch exists, the branch executive committee. Where state or district executive committees shall be constituted, the National Committee shall decide their relation to the local and branch executive committees.

Section 6. The branch executive committee shall be elected by the membership of the branch, and is subordinate to the branch membership. Its duties are to direct the activities of the branch, and to act with full powers for the branch between branch meetings. This section applies likewise to local executive committees.

Article VII. Young People's Socialist League

Section 1. The Young People's Socialist League is the youth organization of the party for work among the young workers, young farmers, and students.

Section 2. The YPSL is guided in its activities by the Declaration of Principles of the party, party politics and decisions.

Section 3. The YPSL is politically subordinate to the party but enjoys autonomy to decide its own organization problems, and to elect to its own officers and committees.

Section 4. Members of the YPSL over the age of twenty-one, who have been members of the YPSL for six months, must apply for membership in the party.

Section 5. In all corresponding organs of the party and the YPSL, there shall be an exchange of representatives, each enjoying full rights (voice and vote).

Article VIII. Initiation Fees and Dues

Section 1. Each applicant for membership (other than charter members) shall pay an initiation fee of fifty cents, which shall be receipted for by an initiation stamp furnished by the national office. The entire initiation fee shall be aid to the national office.

Section 2. Each member shall pay a monthly dues of fifty cents, which shall be receipted for by dues stamps furnished by the national office through the branch treasurer (or local or district treasurer), and affixed to the membership card of each member. In addition, all members are expected to make regular voluntary contributions according to their means.

Section 3. Unemployed members or housewives not otherwise employed shall pay ten cents per month, which is receipted for by a special stamp issued by the national office.

Section 4. Where branches are joined in local or district committees, one half of all regular dues payments (twenty-five cents) shall go to the national office; three-tenths (fifteen cents) shall go to the local or district committee; the remainder (ten cents) shall go to the branch. Where local or district committees do not exist thirty-five cents of each fifty cents dues shall go to the national office. Dues of members-at-large and unemployed members shall go in full to the national office.

Section 5. Members of the youth organization who are simultaneously party members shall pay party dues of ten cents per month, the entire amount going to the national office.

Section 6. A special international assessment of ten cents per member per month shall be paid by all members and receipted by a special stamp; to be sent to the International Bureau for the Fourth International.

Section 7. Members who are three months in arrears in payment of dues shall cease to be members in good standing and shall be so notified by the branch executive committee. Members six months in arrears shall be stricken from the rolls of the party.

Article IX. Discipline

Section 1. All decisions of the governing bodies of the party are binding upon the members and subordinate bodies of the party.

Section 2. Any member or organ violating the decisions of a higher organ of the party shall be subject to disciplinary actions up to expulsion by the body having jurisdiction.

Section 3. Charges against any member shall be made in writing and the accused member shall be furnished with a copy in advance of the trial. Charges shall be filed and heard in the branch to which the member belongs. Where the member is also a member of any higher body charges may be filed either in the branch or in any higher body of which he is a member. Charges filed before the branch shall be considered by the branch executive committee (or a subcommittee elected by it) at a meeting to which the accused member is summoned. The branch executive committee shall submit a recommendation to be acted upon by the membership of the branch. Charges considered by higher bodies of the party shall, however, be acted upon by said bodies.

Section 4. Action by any unit or organ in disciplinary cases deemed improper by a higher unit may be changed by direct intervention of a higher body.

Section 5. Any member subjected to disciplinary action has the right to appeal to the next higher body, up to and including the national convention. Pending action on appeal, the decision of the party body having jurisdiction remains in full force and effect.

Article X. Qualifications for Elections

Section 1. Except in the case of newly organized branches, members of local and branch executive committees must have been members of the party for at least three months, and members of the district committee must have been members of the party for at least six months.

Section 2. Members of the National Committee must be members of the party for at least one year.

Article XI. National Conventions

Section 1. The national convention of the party shall be held once a year. The NC may by two-thirds vote postpone the national convention for not more than six months, provided that a notice of such postponement be given not later than one month before the time for the convention call. Such action may be nullified on the demand of the branches representing at least one-third of the membership.

Section 2. The call for the convention, together with an agenda and the proposals of the National Committee shall be issued at least sixty days before the date of the convention for discussion in the local organizations and the official publications. An internal bulletin shall be issued during the convention discussion period.

Section 3. Representation at the convention shall be proportionally based upon the dues-paying membership in good standing at the time of the convention call. Branches organized after the convention call shall have fraternal representation.

Article XII. Amendments

Amendments shall be made to this constitution by majority vote of the national convention.

Article XIII. Press

All organs of the party are subject to and under the direction of the party and National Executive Committee.

CHAPTER 5

Labour Struggles

Bryan Palmer

The Communist League of America's capacity to build revolutionary organisations through fusions, entries, and founding the Fourth International-affiliated Socialist Workers Party was premised on a 1933–4 breakthrough. Stymied by its inability to win over masses of Communist Party members in the 1929–33 years, the Left Opposition descended into a debilitating and often highly personalised factionalism pitting the League's two leading figures, James P. Cannon and Max Shachtman, against one another. Many factors contributed to what all in the small CLA recognised as a deteriorating situation. These were the 'real dog days of the Left Opposition', wrote Cannon retrospectively.[1] The heady days of optimism that had united Cannon, Shachtman, Rose Karsner, and Martin Abern in the beginnings of American communism's dissident movement early in 1929 gave way to despair by the end of the year, the disaffection extending into the early 1930s. Cannon, for one, withdrew into what appeared to many, including close comrades such as Arne Swabek, to be a defeatist posture of 'stalling and delaying', abdicating administrative responsibilities and leaving the League in a leaderless lurch.[2] The CLA's New York branch was a hothouse of factional tension, and the American Left Opposition appeared to be splitting apart at the seams.

One factor contributing to this worsening situation was the isolation of the League. For the early years of the Great Depression, the American Left Opposition was limited in what it could accomplish among the masses of workers. Its numbers were miniscule compared to those involved in the Communist Party or drawn to its periphery. Class struggle before 1933–4 was at a low ebb, the working class reeling from the destructive impact of economic collapse. The Communist Party's Third Period advocacy of 'Red-led' dual unions further meant that many revolutionaries and militants opted out of the American Federation of Labor mainstream labour organisations.[3] Trade union conservatism

1 Cannon 1944, pp. 90–1.

2 Swabeck to Cannon, 5 December 1929, Box 3, File 2; Swabeck to Cannon, 8 April 1930, Box 3, File 3, James P. Cannon Papers, State Historical Society of Wisconsin, Madison, Wisconsin; Prometheus Research Library 2002, p. 509.

3 Devinatz 2007.

thus predominated in the depths of the economic crisis. Where new initiatives were launched, as in the unemployed movement, identifiable Trotskyists found it exceedingly difficult in the period before 1934–5 to break the monolithic hold over bodies like the Unemployed Councils that were controlled by the CPUSA.[4]

For the Communist League of America, trade union questions were of central importance, 'a life and death question for the American communist movement'.[5] *The Militant* bristled with reports of class struggles, and the CLA championed the necessity, in contrast with the approach of the Communist Party, of working within AFL unions, where the masses of organised workers still found themselves in the early 1930s.[6] Dissident miners' movements, such as the Progressive Miners of America (PMA), formed in September 1932, were an especial focus of the CLA, which had a weak presence in the Illinois-based opposition to the bureaucratic machine of John L. Lewis's United Mine Workers of America. But for the most part, the American Left Opposition was on the sidelines of class struggle in the years 1928–32.

This changed in 1933–4. After five years of the Great Depression, workers were fighting their way out of the doldrums of defeat and despair. Louis Adamic reported in 1934 that the United States was on the verge of a massive class upheaval, predicting that the country would find itself rocked by 'thousands of bitter disputes between capital and labour and between radical or revolutionary and conservative (in many cases racketeering) labour unions'. He warned of an 'avalanche of rank-and-file strikes with full union recognition as their chief objective'. These battles prefigured the industrial union movement of the later 1930s, the Congress of Industrial Organizations, or CIO. 1934, with a general strike wave that galvanised the American South and its textile mills, San Francisco's docks, mid-western trucking in Minneapolis, and Toledo's auto parts industry, was the year that signalled the revival of class struggle in the United States.[7] The *New Republic* chronicled a growing working-class proclivity to use the strike in the summer of 1934, declaring that for many labouring people the establishment of their rights was a matter of 'now or never'. Belief spread that workers had to 'hang together [or] … hang separately'. For its part, *Business Week* denounced 'Government by Strike', insisting that general strikes 'cannot win', and that they amounted to nothing less than 'insurrection … in one word, revolution'.[8]

---

4 On the unemployed movement, see Leab 1967; Rosenzweig 1975; Rosenzweig 1976.

5 Cannon 1931.

6 Cannon 1944, pp. 142–3; Cannon 1933a; Cannon 1933b.

7 Adamic 1934, esp. pp. vii, ix, 456–7; Preis 1964; Brecher 1974.

8 Quoted in Palmer 2013, p. 24.

The Communist League of America was revived by this upturn in the class struggle. In March 1933, New York's cafeteria workers struck. Over the course of the following months, the struggle escalated to include dozens of the metropolitan centre's leading hotels and restaurants. At the height of the battle, 30,000 strikers led by the Hotel and Restaurant Workers branch of the Amalgamated Food Workers were walking picket lines, marching down Park Avenue protesting against Franklin D. Roosevelt's labour policies, and packing Madison Square Gardens to offer thunderous applause to agitators urging the waiters and cooks on to victory. One of those speakers was Cannon, whose rousing speech from the Gardens was broadcast throughout the city: 'Extend the hotel strike to all food workers. Our motto is class solidarity. Our goal is: those who do not work shall not eat!'[9]

Joining Cannon on the Madison Square Gardens podium were radical journalist Heywood Broun; Lovestoneite labour lieutenant, Benjamin Gitlow; Wobbly poet Arturo Giovannitti; the radical pacifist, the Reverend A.J. Muste; and the leading strike organiser, B.J. Field. Something of a united front of the left, the strike unfolded with Field, a member of the CLA, as its undoubted inspiration and recognised spokesman. The Left Opposition thus figured prominently in the hotel workers' revolt. But Field proved an undisciplined League member, never managing to assimilate to the Left Opposition's programmatic orientation or its culture of political work. Once elevated to the status, however fleeting, of leader of a mass strike, he grew arrogant and dismissive of his Left Opposition affiliation and the CLA support that had helped him to rise within the ranks of the hotel and restaurant workers. Eventually expelled from the League, Field pushed the strike to defeat, compromising virtually everything that had been gained in months of militant struggle [Document 1].

That the Left Opposition was willing to expel a strike leader who had grown metaphorically too big for his class conflict britches showed some naysayers on the left that the nascent Trotskyist movement was serious. That seriousness was then borne out in what was undoubtedly the American Left Opposition's finest class struggle hour, a series of decisive victories in the Minneapolis teamster drive to industrial unionism in 1934. As Cannon argued in 'Minneapolis and Its Meaning', the CLA's trade union policy was vindicated in these often violent teamster confrontations with recalcitrant employers, intransigent police, and manoeuvring, often 'progressive', politicians. The method of Minneapolis included the necessity of transforming mainstream AFL unions into fighting entities, doing so in ways that promoted militant class struggle unionism. This

9 '10,000 Fill Mass Rally: Madison Square Gardens Jammed With Strikers', *The Militant*, 31 January 1934.

meant refusing to rely on the agencies of the state to settle disputes; utilising the power of labour to organise strikes aggressively, but never losing sight of the necessity of settling conflicts advantageously so as best to consolidate gains for the working class. 'Minneapolis' was, in 1934, a rallying cry for combative workers across the United States, as well as a concrete demonstration that revolutionaries could indeed lead workers to trade union victories [Document 2].

Class struggles such as the New York hotel workers' strike and the Minneapolis teamsters strikes, in conjunction with the 1933 realisation that new parties of revolutionaries had to be formed outside of the existing Stalinist organisations affiliated with the Communist International, brought the American Left Opposition into closer working relations with other socialists and potentially revolutionary groups. One such body was the American Workers Party (AWP), established in December 1933 by militants working in the Conference for Progressive Labor Action. Led by A.J. Muste, the AWP aimed to Americanise Marxism, and it pioneered the non-Communist Party mobilisation of the unemployed in the early 1930s, spearheading the formation of Unemployed Leagues. In Akron, Ohio, League activists played a pivotal role in supporting the Auto-Lite strike for United Automobile Workers of America recognition in the auto parts industry, a violent, epic conflict that was proceeding in the spring and summer of 1934, at the same time that the struggles in Minneapolis were unfolding. As we have seen above, these events culminated in the fusion of the AWP and the CLA.

The newspaper of the new Workers Party, *New Militant*, championed a course for labour distinct from that of the oscillating Communist Party, which was shifting gears from the sectarian ultra-leftism of the Third Period into the class collaboration of the Popular Front. A.J. Muste's 'Labor Marshalls Forces for Banner May Day', struck just this kind of agitational chord, promoting May Day activities in 1935. One year later, Swabeck's 'Roosevelt Steals Labor Party Thunder' warned workers of the dangers of succumbing to the illusory promises of the New Deal, which dangled carrots of enticement in front of labour's collective nose, the better to dampen militancy and deflect independent working-class political action into support for the Democratic Party [Documents 3 and 4]. Following the Workers Party's entry into the Socialist Party, Cannon and other original CLA figures continued to promote the necessity of going 'Deeper into the Unions' [Document 5]. This message would be a common theme running through Cannon's writing for *Labor Action*, a San Francisco Socialist Party weekly that bore the stamp of 'a Trotskyist agitational paper'.[10]

10 Cannon 1944, pp. 244–5. For Cannon's *Labor Action* journalism, see Cannon 1958, pp. 97–124.

The flurry of fusions, entries, and party formations that characterised dissident Trotskyist communism in the 1934–8 years, complicated further by necessary attention given to international developments – among them the rise of fascism and the outbreak of the Spanish Civil War – inevitably lessened somewhat the role that the American Left Opposition could play in the trade unions. Fusions and entries were not universally endorsed by all of the original CLA corps. Valued trade union organisers occasionally broke from their original League affiliation, further weakening the Left Opposition's capacity to intervene directly in the class struggle. One such dissident was the talented trade union organiser, Hugo Oehler. Oehler opposed the entry of the Workers Party into the Socialist Party, arguing that it would lead revolutionaries down the road of reformism; along with long-time Cannon collaborator Tom Stamm and Chicago retail workers' organiser and future anti-Vietnam war author Sidney Lens, Oehler formed the Revolutionary Workers League in 1935. He had worked as a Communist Party activist in the southern mill towns and Colorado mining territory in the late 1920s and early 1930s, and then, upon his public affiliation with the Communist League of America, agitated among Illinois miners, roused the New York hotel and restaurant workers, and traveled to Minneapolis in 1934 to work with the unemployed in the Trotskyist-led Minneapolis Central Council of Workers.

Forging an active presence in the trade unions, however important to the American Left Opposition, thus proved an uphill battle in the late 1930s. By the time of the formation of the Socialist Workers Party in 1938, the central development within the American labour movement was the rise of industrial unionism and the formation of the John L. Lewis-led CIO. Auto was a pivotal mass production sector. Trotskyists such as Bert Cochran were active in militant caucuses in United Automobile Workers (UAW) locals in Detroit, Cleveland, and elsewhere, first as entryist members of the Socialist Party and then, following their expulsion from the SP and the founding of the SWP, as overt Left Oppositionists. They challenged the bureaucratic trajectory of the nascent CIO. Communist Party activists proved a critically important current in unions like the UAW, and Cochran would later describe their machinations as a 'Borgian conspiracy'. Cochran and the SWP struggled to negotiate the complicated factional alignments within the Auto Worker, aligning with other dissident socialists in constantly running a gauntlet sided on the Popular Front left by the Communist Party and on the right by more traditional trade union officialdoms, which were also split into more or less social democratic camps. Cochran helped draft a 20-point programme in April 1938 that, for a time, was taken up for his own purposes by the mercurial UAW President Homer Martin. But on the whole, whatever their presence in the new industrial unions, Trotskyists were outflanked by their Communist Party adversaries.[11]

B.J. Widick's 'Labor Unity – A New Stage' reveals how the American Left Opposition addressed the historic significance of the rise of industrial unionism, and the trajectory towards ending various schisms in the House of Labor. At the same time, Widick and his comrades in the Socialist Workers Party, as weak as was their position of influence in the trade unions and their industrial wing in the CIO, often stood alone in raising critical assessments of how the revolutionary potential of mass production unionism was being undermined by its ostensible left wing, the Stalinised Communist Party. Other developments also threatened workers' organisations and well-being. At the close of the 1930s, employers had gathered strength in opposition to the industrial union drive and the Roosevelt New Deal state was ramping up demands for 'labour unity' in preparation for war. Bureaucratic ossification, the suffocation of union democracy, and the dampening down of militancy all threatened to pacify the workers' revolt, bringing to an end sit-down strikes, wildcats, and impressive mass production union drives in auto, steel, electrical, and various resource sectors of the economy. Fascism was gaining ground, with vigilante terror increasingly directed against the labour movement and the reactionary gospel of the Reverend Gerald L.K. Smith gaining ground throughout the United States. In strongholds of proletarian militancy, such as Akron and Minneapolis, where the heritage of workers' struggles led by non-Stalinist revolutionary leftists lived on, defence guards were formed to safeguard the unions from fascist attack.

Where the old Communist League of America founders played a decisive role in the trade union movement was, of course, among the teamsters of Minneapolis. Early advocates of the League, Carl Skoglund and Vincent Ray Dunne, charted a successful industrial union drive among the Minneapolis truckers, recruiting to their Trotskyist cause a young militant, Farrell Dobbs. Dobbs, catapulted into the leadership of the teamsters' upheaval and always schooled in trade union strategy and tactics by Skoglund and Dunne, built on the Minneapolis victory to orchestrate a massive eleven-state union drive that, by 1938, brought 250,000 drivers and affiliated workers into the International Brotherhood of Teamsters (IBT). Future IBT head, and a figure associated with the

11 Caucus formation, left-right division, and relations of various tendencies with the established, bureaucratic leadership of the UAW were indeed byzantine. See Cochran 1977, pp. 127–55, 368; Prickett 1968; Keeran 1980, pp. 186–204; Dollinger and Dollinger 2000, pp. 36–52.

ugliest of trade union gangsterism, Jimmy Hoffa, acknowledged Dobbs's brilliance and lasting contribution to United States trade unionism. Hoffa wanted nothing to do with Dobbs's 'political philosophy' or 'economic ideology', but insisted nonetheless that the Left Oppositionist had 'a vision that was enormously beneficial to the labour movement', stressing that it was Dobbs who was the 'master architect of the Teamsters' over-the-road operation'. The Dobbs, Skoglund, Dunne leadership was in large part responsible for the explosive growth of the national IBT from 1934 to 1939, with workers organised in the trucking sector expanding from 75,000 to over 400,000.[12]

Revolutionaries who accomplished this, however, had to be vanquished, and Dobbs's teamster tetralogy – *Teamster Rebellion* (1972), *Teamster Power* (1973), *Teamster Politics* (1975) and *Teamster Bureaucracy* (1977) – provides an exhilarating account of the militant victories of a Left Opposition-led working-class mobilisation followed by a chilling account of subsequent repression. In the end, the Socialist Workers Party members and militant IBT activists who built trade unionism in Minneapolis and the American mid-west into a powerful agency of working-class advance, were subjected to IBT-head Dan Tobin's red-baiting and escalating attacks; vicious physical assault by Hoffa-led union thugs; the Minnesota Federation of Labor barring Trotskyists from AFL unions; the political machinations of state agencies, including the Minnesota Department of Labor, which in effect decertified unions led by the Trotskyists; and trumped-up legal charges that saw Tobin, Roosevelt's State Department, the Attorney-General, and the Federal Bureau of Investigation collude in railroading 18 SWP members and IBT militants (29 had been indicted) to jail. This final blow, delivered one day after the Japanese bombed Pearl Harbor, was orchestrated in the climate of wartime, the conviction of the SWPers and others on charges of seditious conspiracy being something of a foregone conclusion.[13]

To preserve the gains of the class struggle, then, was anything but easy. American Trotskyists knew that union struggles for collective bargaining rights were, in and of themselves, never enough. A political struggle for working-class independence always had to be waged. As Trotsky himself stressed in discussions with members of the Socialist Workers Party in 1940, including Dobbs, what could be gained in times of favourable circumstances could easily be lost. It was necessary to utilise victories like those achieved in Minneapolis to develop class struggle policies that nurtured the class consciousness of the mass of workers. It was the ultimate aim of dissident communists to cultivate resol-

12 For a summary of the many issues addressed in this paragraph see Palmer 2013, pp. 223–48.

13 Palmer 2013, pp. 237–48.

ute understandings that class interests must animate labour's actions, and that wage earners could never rely on a trade union leadership compromised in its capacities to stand against both capital and the state. As Trotsky declared unequivocally in 'The Death Agony of Capitalism and the Tasks of the Fourth International' (1938), 'The historical crisis of mankind is reduced to the crisis of revolutionary leadership'. Militant trade unions, even a labour party, were necessary in the escalating class struggles of a decaying global capitalist order. But they were no substitute for the creation and development of a revolutionary party, which alone could insure that mass workers' organisations did not gravitate towards 'compromise with the bourgeois-democratic regime'.[14]

14 Trotsky 1998, pp. 35, 40.

1 The End of The New York Hotel Strike[15] (*1934*)

The Militant

Left Wing Fights to Rebuild Amalgamated Union

The general strike of the New York hotel workers was finally called off by action of a membership meeting last week on the recommendation of the general strike committee. According to the terms laid down by the Regional Labor Board all strike breakers are to be discharged and all strikers reinstated within two weeks. Strikers not reinstated within that time are to be given preference in future hiring. Since no provision was made for the recognition of shop committees or shop delegates in the supervision of the return to work, the workers were left without any real check on the employers in preventing discrimination. As could only be expected under the circumstances the bosses are discriminating right and left and are making a concerted drive to break up the union.

Discrimination against Strike Militants

A so-called 'citizens committee' of five on which the union has only one representative, is obviously without power to protect the workers against discrimination even if it should be so disposed. And when it is considered that this committee was appointed by the notorious Judge Panken, fresh from his exploits in breaking the taxi strike, the idea of it functioning in any way as an aid to the strikers has to be dismissed altogether.

There is no doubt that the hotel bosses aim to interpret the settlement as a basis for the establishment of the infamous 'merit system' in hiring and firing workers and that a blacklist of the leading militants among the strikers will be attempted.

---

15 *Militant* 1934c.

Despite the militant struggle of the workers, and the stirring example of solidarity, courage, and sacrifice it called forth from the ranks, the result has to be recorded as a defeat. A reorganization of the union and preparation for new struggles confront the hotel workers as a necessity in their aim to establish union conditions and recognition in the industry.

NRA and the Strike Leadership

The Regional Board played a highly effective part in defeating the aims of the strike; and its designs in this respect, clear to every class conscious militant, were supplemented perfectly by the conservative, belly-crawling policy of the officials of the union – Field, Costas, and Kaldis. These unworthy leaders, posing originally as progressives and even as Left wing militants, showed themselves up in action as no better than ordinary routine trade union bureaucrats, fearful of the 'public opinion' of the bourgeois world and utterly indifferent to the public opinion of their own rank and file, especially of its militant and class conscious section. Basing themselves on the most backward and reactionary elements in the union, these careerists intrigued and conspired against the strike militants, disorganized and disrupted the strike machinery, sabotaged the functioning of the most important committees and demoralized the ranks of the strikers by their general incompetence, bureaucratic methods and conservatism.

The 'Food Workers Industrial Union' (Stalinists), which was almost completely isolated at the beginning of the strike, could only thrive on this policy and practice of the leadership and add to the general demoralization. Working from the start to break up the Amalgamated and gain some advantage for their own '18th Street union' – the disruption of a strike in process is small matter to them – the Stalinists were able to exploit the gross mistakes of the leadership in order to add to the general demoralization.

The Left Wing Organizes

It was not until the Left wing, following the line of *The Militant*, made a sharp break with the officials and began to organize the fight against them, that the advances of the Stalinist wrecking crew were checked and a genuinely constructive movement for the preservation of the Amalgamated began to take shape. The election of Hugo Oehler as Chairman of the Strike Committee in a session called over the heads of Field & Co., and the rallying of the best fighters in the union around the picket committee – the center of class struggle policy in the strike under the chairmanship of James Gordon – were two outstanding signs of the rapid gains of the bona-fide Left wing that is fighting for the Amalgamated union and its future.

Rebuild the Amalgamated

The Left wing brought forward a program for saving the strike by concentrating on relief, picketing and a class struggle policy to the end. Frustrated in this aim by the whole course of the official leadership, the Left wing is now fighting to reform the ranks of the union, to rebuild the organization, fight the blacklist and keep up the relief to support its victims, and cleanse the union of its careerist leadership. The motion of James Gordon, at the first meeting of the Executive Board of the Union after the ending of the strike, to reject the report of Field and to declare no confidence in the leadership, was carried by a vote of 14 to 2. In this the strength of the revolt against the Field administration is indicated.

The task of the Left wing is now to lead the revolt to the very end without any compromise and to steer it into constructive channels for the rebuilding of the Amalgamated Food Workers, the defeat of the Stalinist disrupters and the preparation of the coming struggles to unionize the hotel industry under the banner of the Amalgamated.

2 Minneapolis and Its Meaning[16]

(*1934*)

James P. Cannon

Standing by itself, the magnificent strike of the Minneapolis truck drivers would merit recognition as an extraordinary event in modem American labor history. Its connection with the second wave of labor struggles to sweep the country since the inception of the NRA, however, and its indubitable place as the high point of the present strike wave, invest the Minneapolis demonstration with an exceptional importance. Therefore it has come by right to be the subject of serious and attentive study and of heated discussion. This discussion, despite all the partisan prejudice and misrepresentation injected into it, is bound on the whole to have a profitable result. The best approach to the trade union question, the key question of revolutionary politics in the United States, is through the study and discussion of concrete examples.

The second strike wave under the NRA raises higher than the first and marks a big forward stride of the American working class. The enormous potentialities of future developments are clearly written in this advance. The native militancy of the workers, so impressively demonstrated on every strike front in recent months, needs only to be fused with an authentic leadership which brings organization, consciousness, and the spirit of determined struggle into the movement. Minneapolis was an example of such a fusion. That is what lifted the drivers' strike out above the general run. Therein lies its great significance – as an anticipation, if only on a comparatively small, local scale, of future developments in the labor movement of the country. The determining role of policy and leadership was disclosed with singular emphasis in the Minneapolis battle.

The main features of the present strike wave, on the background of which the Minneapolis example must be considered, are easily distinguishable. Now, as in the labor upsurge of last year, the attitude of the workers toward the NRA occupies a central place. But the attitude is somewhat different than it was before. The messianic faith in the Roosevelt administration which characterized the strike movement of a year ago and which, to a certain extent, provided

16 Cannon 1934.

the initial impulse for the movement, has largely disappeared and given place to skeptical distrust. It is hardly correct, however, to say, as some revolutionary wishful thinkers are saying, that the current strikes are consciously directed against the NRA. There is little or no evidence to support such a bald assertion.

It is more in keeping with reality to say that the striking workers now depend primarily on their own organization and fighting capacity and expect little or nothing from the source to which, a short year ago, they looked for everything. Nevertheless they are not yet ready even to ignore the NRA, to say nothing of fighting against it directly. What has actually taken place has been a heavy shift in emphasis from faith in the NRA to reliance on their own strength.

In these great struggles the American workers, in all parts of the country, are displaying the unrestrained militancy of a class that is just beginning to awaken. This is a new generation of a class that has not been defeated. On the contrary, it is only now beginning to find itself and to feel its strength. And in these first, tentative conflicts the proletarian giant gives a glorious promise for the future. The present generation remains true to the tradition of American labor; it is boldly aggressive and violent from the start. The American worker is no Quaker. Further developments of the class struggle will bring plenty of fighting in the USA.

It is also a distinct feature of the second strike wave, and those who want to understand and adjust themselves to the general trend of the movement should mark it well, that the organization drives and the strikes, barring incidental exceptions, are conducted within the framework of the AFL unions. The exceptions are important and should not be disregarded. At any rate, the movement begins there. Only those who foresaw this trend and synchronized their activities with it have been able to play a part in the recent strikes and to influence them from within.

The central aim and aspiration of the workers, that is, of the newly organized workers who are pressing the fight on every front, is to establish their organizations firmly. The first and foremost demand in every struggle is: recognition of the union. With unerring instinct the workers seek first of all the protection of an organization.

William S. Brown, president of the Minneapolis union, expressed the sentiment of all the strikers in every industry in his statement: 'The union felt that wage agreements are not much protection to a union man unless first there is definite assurance that the union man will be protected in his job'. The strike wave sweeping the country in the second year of the NRA is in its very essence a struggle for the right of organization. The outcome of every strike is to be estimated primarily by its success or failure in enforcing the recognition of the union.

And from this point of view the results in general are not so rosy. The workers manifested a mighty impulse for organization, and in many cases they fought heroically. But they have yet to attain their first objective. The auto settlement, which established the recognition of the company union rather than the unions of the workers, weighs heavily on the whole labor situation. The workers everywhere have to pay for the precedent set in this industry of such great strategic importance. From all appearances the steelworkers are going to be caught in the same runaround. The New York hotel strike failed to establish the union. The New York taxi drivers got no union recognition, or anything else. Not a single of the 'red' unions affiliated to the Trade Union Unity League has succeeded in gaining recognition. Even the great battle of Toledo appears to have been concluded without the attainment of this primary demand.

The American workers are on the march. They are organizing by the hundreds of thousands. They are fighting to establish their new unions firmly and compel the bosses to recognize them. But in the overwhelming majority of cases they have yet to win this fundamental demand.

In the light of this general situation the results of the Minneapolis strike stand out preeminent and unique. Judged in comparison with the struggles of the other newly formed unions – and that is the only sensible criterion – the Minneapolis settlement, itself a compromise, has to be recorded as a victory of the first order. In gaining recognition of the union, and in proceeding to enforce it the day following the settlement, General Drivers Union No. 574 has set a pace for all the new unions in the country. The outcome was not accidental either. Policy, method, leadership – these were the determining factors at Minneapolis which the aspiring workers everywhere ought to study and follow.

The medium of organization in Minneapolis was a craft union of the AFL, and one of the most conservative of the AFL Internationals at that. This course was deliberately chosen by the organizers of the fight in conformity with the general trend of the movement, although they are by no means worshippers of the AFL. Despite the obvious limitations of this antiquated form of organization it proved to be sufficient for the occasion thanks to a liberal construction of the jurisdictional limits of the union. Affiliation with the AFL afforded other compensating advantages. The new union was thereby placed in direct contact with the general labor movement and was enabled to draw on it for support. This was a decisive element in the outcome. The organized labor movement, and with it practically the entire working class of Minneapolis, was lined up behind the strike. Out of a union with the most conservative tradition and obsolete structure came the most militant and successful strike.

The stormy militancy of the strike, which electrified the whole labor movement, is too well known to need recounting here. The results also are known, among them the not unimportant detail that the serious casualties were suffered by the other side. True enough, the striking workers nearly everywhere have fought with great courage. But here also the Minneapolis strike was marked by certain different and distinct aspects which are of fundamental importance. In other places, as a rule, the strike militancy surged from below and was checked and restrained by the leaders. In Minneapolis it was organized and directed by the leaders. In most of the other strikes the leaders blunted the edge of the fight where they could not head it off altogether, as in the case of the auto workers – and preached reliance on the NRA, on General Johnson, or the president. In Minneapolis the leaders taught the workers to fight for their rights and fought with them.

This conception of the leadership, that the establishment of the union was to be attained only by struggle, shaped the course of action not only during the ten-day strike but in every step that led to it. That explains why the strike was prepared and organized so thoroughly. Minneapolis never before saw such a well-organized strike, and it is doubtful if its like, from the standpoint of organization, has often been seen anywhere on this continent.

Having no illusions about the reasonableness of the bosses or the beneficence of the NRA, and sowing none in the ranks, the leadership calculated the whole campaign on the certainty of a strike and made everything ready for it. When the hour struck the union was ready, down to the last detail of organization. 'If the preparations made by their union for handling it are any indication', wrote the *Minneapolis Tribune* on the eve of the conflict, 'the strike of the truck drivers in Minneapolis is going to be a far-reaching affair ... Even before the official start of the strike at 11:30 p.m. Tuesday the "General Headquarters" organization set up at 1900 Chicago Avenue was operating with all the precision of a military organization'.

This spirit of determined struggle was combined at the same time with a realistic appraisal of the relation of forces and the limited objectives of the fight. Without this all the preparations and all the militancy of the strikers might well have been wasted and brought the reaction of a crushing defeat. The strike was understood to be a preliminary, partial struggle, with the objective of establishing the union and compelling the bosses to recognize it. When they got that, they stopped and called it a day.

The strong union that has emerged from the strike will be able to fight again and to protect its membership in the meantime. The accomplishment is modest enough. But if we want to play an effective part in the labor movement, we must not allow ourselves to forget that the American working class is just beginning to move on the path of the class struggle and, in its great majority, stands yet before the first task of establishing stable unions. Those who understand the task of the day and accomplish it prepare the future. The others merely chatter.

As in every strike of any consequence, the workers involved in the Minneapolis struggle also had an opportunity to see the government at work and to learn some practical lessons as to its real function. The police force of the city, under the direction of the Republican mayor, supplemented by a horde of 'special deputies', were lined up solidly on the side of the bosses.

The police and deputies did their best to protect the strikebreakers and keep some trucks moving, although their best was not good enough. The mobilization of the militia by the Farmer-Labor governor was a threat against the strikers, even if the militiamen were not put on the street. The strikers will remember that threat. In a sense it can be said that the political education of a large section of the strikers began with this experience. It is sheer lunacy, however to imagine that it was completed and that the strikers, practically all of whom voted yesterday for Roosevelt and Olson, could have been led into a prolonged strike for purely political aims after the primary demand for the recognition of the union had been won.

Yet this is the premise upon which all the Stalinist criticism of the strike leadership is based. Governor Olson, declared Bill Dunne in the *Daily Worker*, was the 'main enemy'. And having convinced himself on this point, he continued: 'The exposure and defeat of Olson should have been the central political objective of the Minneapolis struggle'. Nor did he stop even there. Wound up and going strong by this time, and lacking the friendly advice of a Harpo Marx who would explain the wisdom of keeping the mouth shut when the head is not clear, he decided to go to the limit, so he added: 'This [exposure and defeat of Olson] was the basic necessity for winning the economic demands for the Drivers Union and the rest of the working class'.

There it is, Mr. Ripley, whether you believe it or not. This is the thesis, the 'political line', laid down for the Minneapolis truck drivers in the *Daily Worker*. For the sake of this thesis, it is contended that negotiations for the settlement of the strike should have been rejected unless the state troopers were demobilized, and a general strike should have been proclaimed 'over the heads of the Central Labor Council and state federation of labor officials'. Dunne only neglected to add: over the heads of the workers also, including the truck drivers.

For the workers of Minneapolis, including the striking drivers, didn't understand the situation in this light at all, and leaders who proceeded on such an assumption would have found themselves without followers. The workers of Minneapolis, like the striking workers all over the country, understand the 'central objective' to be the recognition of the union. The leaders were in full harmony with them on this question; they stuck to this objective; and when it was attained, they did not attempt to parade the workers through a general strike for the sake of exercise or for 'the defeat of Governor Olson'. For one reason, it was not the right thing to do. And, for another reason, they couldn't have done it if they had tried.

The arguments of Bill Dunne regarding the Minneapolis 'betrayal' could have a logical meaning only to one who construed the situation as revolutionary and aimed at an insurrection. We, of course, are for the revolution. But not today, not in a single city. There is a certain unconscious tribute to the 'Trotskyists' – and not an inappropriate one – in the fact that so much was demanded of them in Minneapolis. But Bill Dunne, who is more at home with proverbs than with politics, should recall the one which says, 'every vegetable has its season'. It was the season for an armed battle in Germany in the early part of 1933. In America in 1934, it is the season for organizing the workers, leading them in strikes, and compelling the bosses to recognize their unions. The mistake of all the Stalinists, Bill Dunne among them, in misjudging the weather in Germany in 1933 was a tragedy. In America in 1934 it is a farce.

The strike wave of last year was only a prelude to the surging movement we witness today. And just as the present movement goes deeper and strikes harder than the first, so does it prepare the way for a third movement which will surpass it in scope, aggressiveness, and militancy. Frustrated in their aspirations for organization by misplaced faith in the Roosevelt administration, and by the black treachery of the official labor bureaucracy, the workers will take the road of struggle again with firmer determination and clearer aims. And they will seek for better leaders. Then the new left wing of the labor movement can have its day. The revolutionary militants can bound forward in mighty leaps and come to the head of large sections of the movement if they know how to grasp their opportunities and understand their tasks. For this they must be politically organized and work together as a disciplined body; they must forge the new party of the Fourth International without delay. They must get inside the developing movement, regardless of its initial form, stay inside, and shape its course from within.

They must demonstrate a capacity for organization as well as agitation, for responsibility as well as for militancy. They must convince the workers of their ability not only to organize and lead strikes aggressively, but also to settle them advantageously at the right time and consolidate the gains. In a word, the modern militants of the labor movement have the task of gaining the confidence of the workers in their ability to lead the movement all the year round and to advance the interests of the workers all the time.

On this condition the new left wing of the trade unions can take shape and grow with rapid strides. And the left wing, in turn, will be the foundation of the new party, the genuine communist party. On a local scale, in a small sector of the labor movement, the Minneapolis comrades have set an example which shows the way. The International Communists have every right to be proud of this example and hold it up as a model to study and follow.

3 Labor Marshalls Forces for Banner May Day[17] (*1935*)

A.J. Muste

All reports about May Day preparations indicate that more American workers and more trade unions will participate in demonstrations this year than ever before. These workers are more militant, more free from illusions, more in the mood for new adventures than at any previous period. For the Workers Party of the US observing its first May Day this is the most significant feature of this year's celebration. Its meaning must be clearly understood. It must be utilized to the fullest extent in all speeches and discussions on May Day, as well as in all our work in the ensuing months.

Half a century ago American workers, engaged in desperate and dramatic struggles for the eight-hour day, made the First of May a labor holiday. The idea was taken up a few years later by workers in other countries and presumably May Day became the International Labor Day. Of the associations which gather round May Day – anti-militarism, class solidarity, labor internationalism, revolutionary aims of the working-class – we need not speak here.

Before the Crisis

May Day ceased, however, to be observed generally by the American workers. For a time, in certain of the larger cities, foreign-speaking groups demonstrated in considerable numbers; but even they became in large measure apathetic during the hectic boom period from 1924 on. In the main during this period American workers shunned May Day. They believed the propaganda of the boss press and of their own reactionary trade union leaders that May Day was for 'foreigners', 'ungrateful reds', etc. who did not appreciate the fact that the American working class was something unique and led a charmed life of perpetual prosperity under a special brand of capitalism, USA model.

The crisis has put a period to all that. It is clear that there is nothing unique about American capitalism, clear certainly that it leads no charmed life. As a

17 Muste 1935.

part of world-capitalism it is in decline, and in its decline brings untold suffering on the masses who in this land of boundless resources and an unsurpassed productive machinery have in five brief years seen their standard of living cut in half.

Rising magnificently at the first opportunity, the American workers have since the spring of 1933 made great advances in organization and fought a series of important battles. In the course of those struggles one illusion after another has been ruthlessly dissipated.

The New Deal has not brought back prosperity. The doubt as to whether capitalism can be reformed is eating deep into the minds of the workers.

Short Cut Proves a Trap

The NRA proved not to be a magic gate to union organization. The conviction that it is useless to look to the Roosevelt administration or to any capitalist government, to give genuine support to fighting unions gains ground.

Trade union leaders, committed to 'cooperation' with the bosses and the bosses' government, sell out strikes, are seen to be 'cooperating' indeed – to keep the boss on top and the workers under – and that lesson sinks in.

In the presence of such harsh realities bunk loses its hold. The bunk of the militarists and super-patriots. The bunk of the red-baiters. The Hearst campaign has fallen flat among the workers. The AF of L bureaucracy got nowhere with its latest attempt to oust radicals from the unions. In fact they themselves have to try now to put on a 'radical' cover. They collaborate with Socialists, hoping that that will convince the workers that they are 'as progressive as anybody'. On occasion AF of L demagogues collaborate, at least in effect, with Communists, as did Coleman Claherty in Akron recently when he was selling out the strike!

Radical Thought Gaining

The workers in ever increasing numbers are becoming interested in radical solutions for their problem. They will march this May Day proudly side by side with the Workers Party, with other parties and groups, with which they used to think it disgraceful and 'un-American' to associate! Brushing away from their eyes the webs spun by the bosses' propaganda, they are making May Day their own again!

Thus May Day emphasizes once more the correctness and the critical importance of the decisions of the founding convention of the Party on the mass organizations and mass work. We must get into the unions and the unemployed organizations. We must become intimately bound up with them and with their struggles. Never has there been such an opportunity to draw close to the masses, masses that are in motion, masses bent upon struggle. To neglect this opportunity is treason of the blackest sort.

The Wrong Way

For revolutionists to draw near to the masses does not mean, however, to come down to their level of political development, to cater to their prejudices, to take a place at the tail-end of the procession. The Communist Party having treated the workers like robots for years may now treat them like children to be humored and given a stick of candy. Neither attitude grows out of true respect for the worker, and the second will no more win the American worker in the end than did the first, which has had to be ignominiously abandoned. The CP having for years branded AF of L bureaucrats as social-fascists may now embrace them as 'comrades in arms'. Neither attitude was based on a realistic analysis and neither is a service to the working class.

The confidence won by responsible revolutionists because they fight side by side with the masses in their struggles, because they labor harder than any others to build the unions and the unemployed leagues, that confidence so hardly won is precious. It must not be prostituted by giving any countenance to the Utopian notions of a Long, a Coughlin, an Upton Sinclair, or whoever it may be, with the idea that there is something 'American' about this tactic, that having thus 'gone along' with the workers, with big masses, we have a 'movement', we are no longer 'isolated from the masses', and presently we shall slip over a revolutionary program on this 'movement'. Having a yearning for being lost in a crowd is a very human failing. So is the desire to win a following quickly. But it is not a distinguishing mark of a revolutionist. Such 'movements' as we have mentioned do not overthrow capitalism. If they do not turn Fascist, they end in a swamp or in a blind alley. Even a very superficial reading of American history makes that clear.

Against False Shibboleths

The responsible Marxian party will use the confidence that it wins from the masses to expose illusions, fallacies and falsehoods. On this May Day in the

United States it will agitate against every form and manifestation of racial prejudice; against every illusory idea as to how the workers will win power and build a new world; against all half-baked panaceas; against nationalism and for internationalism.

The American workers have certain peculiar conditions to face and only at our peril do we ignore that fact. But the American worker is not now, any more than he was in the Coolidge-Hoover era, some peculiar species of animal. He is a worker under capitalism. His interest is one with that of the workers of all lands. This May Day 1935 gives us an unprecedented and priceless opportunity to tie in his struggles with the worldwide struggles of the working class, to teach the lesson of Revolutionary Internationalism. It is well that the Workers Party of the US is in existence to seize that opportunity.

For a Workers' World

Marching side by side with our brothers, sisters, comrades, in the unions and the unemployed organizations, we raise the banner of the Workers Party and the Fourth International. We sound forth again the historic battle-cry of the international revolutionary movement. Workers of the world, unite! You have nothing to lose but your chains! You have a world to gain! Given such a program and such a spirit the workers can be confident that –

> The earth shall rise on new foundations;
> We have been naught, we shall be all!

4 Roosevelt Steals Labor Party Thunder[18]

(1936, excerpts)

Arne Swabeck

Labor Chiefs Use New Deal as Safety-Valve

During the last few weeks the plea for Roosevelt's re-election has gained new converts and new adherents with amazing speed from the trade union movement. It is taking on the character of a clean sweep. But the manner in which the plea is presented, and in view of the present objective conditions, it is not at all surprising that the labor party question fades into the background with the same ease that this sweep gains in momentum. Or, perhaps it would be more correct to say that the labor perambulator is being hooked onto the Roosevelt bandwagon.

This stampede started last January when John L. Lewis whooped through the United Mine Workers convention a unanimous resolution for Roosevelt's re-election. Following the lead Labor's Non-Partisan League came into being. It was sponsored by the Lewis-Hillman forces. The American Federation of Hosiery Workers convention and the Amalgamated Clothing Workers General Executive Board next fell into line. Two international union presidents, David Dubinsky and Emil Rieve, quickly deserted the Socialist Party for their new and real allegiance. Wm. Green, on the opening day of the AF of L Executive Council second quarterly meeting, advocated the President's re-election. And two days before this the delegates to the United Automobile Workers convention voted without a dissenting voice to support the Roosevelt candidacy.

Raw Deal for Auto Workers

Nobody will suspect that the auto workers harbored feelings of special gratitude to Roosevelt. They cannot possibly have forgotten his infamous automobile agreement which was foisted upon them during the spring of 1934. ... [It]

18 Swabeck 1936.

postponed the organization of the autonomous international union so much desired by the organized automobile workers.

... The decision of the auto workers convention simply means that it follows the lead of the Committee for Industrial Organization. This is of double significance when viewed in relation to the labor party question. It must be remembered that on the whole the unions of the CIO and its supporting unions, like the auto workers, represents the section of organized labor which is travelling in a progressive direction. This is indisputable. It is also the section of organized labor that has shown the greatest vitality and growth, and particularly so when a comparison is made with a number of unions, distinctly craft in make-up and in spirit, which have remained stagnant for some time, or actually lost ground.

No Serious Labor Party Swing

... There is not a serious movement on foot, nor are there any serious forces available for a national labor party, or farmer-labor party, or third party in 1936. Those who still attempt to create the impression that there are, like the Stalinists do, are simply up to their old pernicious game of deception. An editorial in the 7 May *Daily Worker* finally acknowledges that, **'A Farmer-Labor Presidential ticket in 1936 is now out of the question'**, but it maintains that the prospects are as good as ever for a farmer-labor party this year. ...

Superficially it may seem that the fervent desires nurtured by the Stalinists were to be realized through the conference call sent out by the Minnesota Farmer-Labor Party. However, the appearance in this case is also deceptive. The conference call is issued to individuals, not to organizations. Obviously these individuals are expected to do nothing more than to explore the possibilities of a labor party. But what they are to explore becomes further clear in the announcement that a farmer-labor presidential ticket is not to be considered at this conference. In other words, the sponsors of the conference consider the presidential ticket to be a matter settled by the Roosevelt endorsements. Nothing further remains to be explored but how to swing the labor party sentiment successfully into the re-election campaign.

Local Bodies Powerless

A labor party sentiment has been recorded in a number of local unions. Much of it is motivated on progressive grounds. To an extent it arises out of disappointment with promised New Deal measures which were not realized; to an extent also out of disappointment with 'New Deal blessings'. Above all it arises out of fears of reaction and an instinctive but unclear fear of Fascism. But in view of the general lack of understanding of what the requirements of a party of the workers must be, it is particularly these fears that help to drive the organized workers into marching formation in the Roosevelt camp.

It would be ridiculous to expect that local unions should take the initiative in organizing a national labor party apart from or in opposition to their parent bodies. It would be worse than ridiculous to assume that such a party can be brought about without the organizations of the industrial bloc and its leaders as well. However much the Stalinists may put forward the appearance and attempt to invest it with the qualities of something real, however much they may attempt to convene labor party gatherings made up of singing societies and hiking clubs, to be addressed by liberal celebrities, these efforts will not carry any social weight. …

FD's Eye on 1936

The stampede for Roosevelt has been cleverly manipulated by the deliberate and carefully planned policies emanating from the White House and the 'progressive' labor leaders. Roosevelt and his 'brain trusters' – whatever is left of them … – have for some time had their eyes on the November elections. Special emphasis has been laid in all the promissory notes upon the labor legislative program, the alleged social security measures, the tax program to soak the rich, the need of curbing Wall Street and the need of preventing the invasion of the people's rights by the courts. Roosevelt declares himself to be against war and Fascist tyrannies and for a 'people's government'. By these ingenious campaign devices, the Rooseveltians aimed, and rather successfully, to forestall the emergence of a labor party, or a third party, in 1936.

The adept pupils of these demagogic cunning devices, who are holding high posts in the progressive union bloc, follow up the campaign in the same high key. They are for aggressive unionization, industrial unionism, and against reaction. John L. Lewis started the ball rolling at the UMW convention with a mighty attack on the Liberty League. An easy target. These leaders are now all against war and Fascist tyrannies and they also have broad views on the people's front. It is therefore not at all unnatural that they should direct the genuine fears of reaction and the fears of war and Fascism into the safe channels in support of Roosevelt's re-election. …

No Labor Party Wanted Now

Of course, the truth is that these 'progressive' leaders, in harmony with Roosevelt, do not want a labor party, or a third party and certainly not before their own preparations are well done; not before they are sure they can keep it within the proper reformist bounds. Even then they can be expected to yield only to pressure. Their aim can then be expected to aim to utilize such a development to counterpose the growth of a revolutionary movement. As solid converts to the New Deal, they aim to lay out the line of march with Roosevelt today and perpetuate his program tomorrow – if need be, by means of a third party.

Today they attempt to make a distinction between Roosevelt and the Democratic Party. How can any real distinction be possible? Roosevelt is the standard-bearer of his party – one of the two capitalist parties. From this party he receives his mandate and this carries with it the duty to serve finance capital. Need there be any doubt that this is the responsibility to which he will remain loyal even more decisively and unequivocally after his reelection.

The trade union support of Roosevelt could not be unexpected. It is destined to go down as one of the great illusions of 1936. It has become possible primarily due to the lack of revolutionary education of the working class. After 1936 new disillusionments are sure to begin. Will a third party carrying on the New Deal tradition and program then prove a solution? Most decisively not! And it is well to remember that this is the only kind of a labor party that can reasonably be expected. Hence there remains one main conclusion to draw. Today and tomorrow the struggle for Socialism must go on.

5 Deeper into the Unions[19]
(*1936*)

James P. Cannon

Not the least of the reasons for the renewed vitality and, firm, healthy growth of the socialist movement in California, is the newly developed activity of many of its members in trade unions and the increased attention the party as a whole is devoting to this field.

The turn toward trade-union work means the turn toward new life for the Socialist Party in the West. It means reconstructing the organization on a proletarian foundation. And that is what is needed first of all, if we are to be a real force in the class struggle and not a mere club of well-meaning people which never offends anybody, and which nobody ever thinks of taking seriously.

It takes a fighting organization to make a revolution, and the place to build it is inside, not outside, the broad labor movement. That means, primarily, the trade unions. We still have a long way to go to complete this necessary transformation of the party. What has been done so far – and it is all to the good – is, after all, merely dabbling. We will not really get down to business until we devote nine-tenths of our time and attention to trade-union work.

The trade unions are the elementary and basic organizations of the workers and the main medium through which the socialist idea can penetrate the masses and thus become a real force. The masses do not come to the party; the party must go to the masses. The militant activist who carries the banner into the mass organization and takes his place on the firing line in their struggle is the true representative of resurgent socialism.

And it is not enough by any means to have a few 'specialists' attending to this function while the others occupy the cheering section in the grandstand. Nothing is more absurd and futile than such a party. Auxiliary organizations can and should be formed to enlist the support of sympathizers and fellow-travelers. But the party of the proletariat, to my notion, should be conceived as an organization of activists with the bulk of its members – everyone eligible, in fact – rooted in the trade unions and other mass organizations of the workers.

19 Cannon 1936.

At this point we always come to the old moth-eaten and utterly ridiculous contrast of theory and practice. There is neither sense nor profit in such a debate, for the theory of Marxism, as Engels explained many times, is a guide to action. Let muddleheads argue which comes first and which is more important. As an all-around nuisance and futilitarian the misnamed 'Marxist' who mulls over theory in a vacuum is tied by the vulgar activist who is 'all motion and no direction'. Effective revolutionists unite theory with practice in all their activity.

Engels fought on the barricades in his youth. Marx, the formulator of the theory of the proletariat, devoted an enormous amount of time to the practical work of organization in the First International, and he remained a revolutionary war horse till the day of his death, sniffing the battle from afar. Lenin was a thinker and a doer. And Trotsky, the greatest revolutionary man of action the world has ever seen, elucidated problems of theory on a military train in the heat of civil war.

The purposeful activism of the educated socialists must be directed primarily into the trade unions precisely because they are the immediate connecting link with a broader circle of workers and therefore the most fruitful field of activity. When the socialist idea is carried into the workers' mass organizations by the militant activists and takes root there, a profound influence is exerted upon these organizations. They become more aware of their class interest and their historic mission, and grow in militancy and solidarity and effectiveness in their struggle against the exploiters.

At the same time, the party gains strength from the live mass contact, finds a constant corrective for tactical errors under the impact of the class struggle and steadily draws new proletarian recruits into its ranks. In the trade-union struggle the party tests and corrects itself in action. It hardens and grows up to the level of its historic task as the workers' vanguard in the coming revolution.

The trail-blazing work of the socialist activists in the California unions has opened a path for the party as a whole. There can be no doubt that the near future holds great successes for the party if it follows that path.

6 Labor Unity – A New Stage[20]
(*1938*)

B.J. Widick

John L. Lewis recently offered to resign as chairman of the Committee for Industrial Organization provided that William Green as president of the American Federation of Labor would do likewise. 'It then may be possible', declared Lewis, 'for the remaining leaders of the Federation of Labor and the remaining leaders of the CIO to conclude a peace pact, in which event the contribution made by Mr. Green and myself would be of some value'. That was a gesture the importance of which lies not in the fact that if carried into action Green would become merely another unemployed member of the musicians' union while Lewis still retained power in the CIO, but that it symbolizes the tremendous and basic changes in the labor movement during the past year under the impact of the social crisis.

Perhaps even more striking was the attitude which Daniel J. Tobin, president of the teamsters union, largest and most powerful AF of L affiliate, took at the AF of L convention this year. One may well ask, what is really happening in the labor movement that a 66-year-old fellow-traveler of the AF of L executive council looms as the leader of a progressive revolt within the AF of L against the reactionary policies advocated by that board, on the question of labor unity? And above all, one asks, will there be unity? On what basis and to whose advantage? These are the problems that concern the militant and revolutionary workers. In their answer lies the future of the American labor movement.

It was no secret that the huge lay-offs in mass production industries cut deeply into the dues-paying membership of the CIO, while the AF of L appeared to be prospering, relatively speaking. The membership figures released at the AF of L convention were imposing enough: over 3,600,000 dues-paying and 1,400,000 unemployed members. A total membership of 5,000,000 compared to a very generous estimate of 4,000,000 dues and non-dues paying CIO unionists. The bitter struggles within the CIO such as appeared in the autoworkers union and elsewhere promised a stormy future. Newspapers were filled with

20 Widick 1938.

talk of disintegration of the CIO. The action of the International Ladies Garment Workers Union, 400,000 strong, in refusing to participate in the formation of CIO councils tended to give credence to those pessimistic views of the CIO's future. Would the CIO unions be forced to make peace, one by one, with the AF of L executive council? Yet precisely at the moment when things looked dark for the CIO, the edifice of the AF of L cracked wide-open at the convention, showing that the perennial domination of the aristocracy of labor over the industrial proletariat was doomed. In the past two years the AF of L itself had been forced as a defensive measure to organize many plants on an industrial basis.

In marked contrast to previous depressions, no wave of wage cuts have swept across the industrial scene this last year – a remarkable tribute to the power the proletariat has found in organizing industrially under the banner of the CIO. The AF of L registered 800,000 new members in this same critical year. But most outstanding was the signing of a pact covering 250,000 drivers with substantial wage increases. This was the achievement of the teamsters union, under the progressive influence of the Minneapolis labor movement. Superficially, the gains of the teamsters union, tended to reaffirm the hegemony of the AF of L in the entire labor movement. Actually it was a victory for the movement of industrial workers, and this was strikingly brought out at the AF of L convention. While the collapse in building activity seriously crippled the building trades department of the AF of L, heart of the die-hard craft-unionists, the gains of the teamsters effected a significant shift in the very social base of the AF of L.

It is reflected in the fact that the teamsters have taken control of the Central Labor unions from the building trades unions in such key centers as Akron, Cleveland, Minneapolis, San Francisco, Seattle, among others. By the very nature of their work, the truck drivers serve as a powerful buffer force between CIO and AF of L unions. When 350,000 truck drivers say they will not fight the CIO but fight for labor unity, the 'die-hard' clique in the AF of L becomes a general staff without an effective army. Months ago, an official CIO-AF of L coordinating committee representing the Industrial Union Council and the Central Trades and Labor Assembly was set up in Akron, Ohio, without unfavorable action from top AF of L leaders, although that was feared.

Further evidence of the change within the structure of the AF of L, and the effect of the social crisis, is the defeat of Mathew Woll, John P. Frey, and the other bureaucrats of the executive council when their demand that the convention endorse an attack on the New Deal (from the reactionary viewpoint) was rejected. That expressed in distorted form the desires of the rank and file AF of L for a solution to their problems along more progressive lines. The 'socialism' of the New Deal over which Woll shuddered was exactly the only aspect which attracts the workers, even though they are dangerously deceived.

One year ago we pointed out that the cost of civil war between the CIO and the AF of L would soon work towards the direction of unity. The suicidal strife between Dave Beck, Seattle teamsters union czar, and Harry Bridges, Stalinist director of the West Coast CIO was then at the height of its fury. The losses in wages, the arrests and imprisonment of leaders on both sides, the passage of strike-breaking and union-smashing legislation, coupled with the blows of the social crisis, forced a change in that disastrous policy. Beck recently urged an 'economic united front with the CIO despite political differences'. When Akron, Ohio, cops broke a mass picket line in May at the Goodyear plants, sending hundreds of CIO workers to hospitals for treatment against tear-gassing and clubbing, labor mobilized under a United Labor Defense Committee composed of all AF of L and CIO unions in that area. 'We'll be next if the cops get away with it', the AF of L unionists realized. The committee has been placed on a permanent basis now. Similar stories of united action can be repeated in many cities. Fear of wage cuts, fear of growing reaction, and the obvious need for labor solidarity in these critical times have intensified the sentiment for unity in the rank and file of the AF of L and the CIO. This burning desire has forced its way into the highest ranks of the labor bureaucrats.

The independent railroad brotherhoods of nearly 2,000,000 members face the most serious challenge of many years in their negotiations with management. Already a strike vote has been taken by 1,000,000 members against acceptance of a proposed 15% wage cut. Only the united strength of the entire labor movement can give the railroad workers effective support against government or management treachery. It is of the utmost concern to the AF of L and the CIO to prevent a wage cut in this basic industry so that the example might not become a contagious one to the employers. This situation impels the brotherhoods towards desiring and becoming a part of the united labor movement.

The hegemony of the industrial workers in the American labor movement and the vital needs of this decisive force are bringing a rapid shift in the direction of unity. There are no longer any fundamental reasons that justify the separation of the AF of L and the CIO. This is evident to the rank and file workers in both sections. The leaderships are on the spot. Perhaps unity will take the form, in terms of leadership, of a Dan Tobin-John L. Lewis-George M. Harrison combination. For over a year we have heard reports in high CIO circles that Tobin would be Lewis's candidate for president of a united labor movement. David Dubinsky, president of the ILGWU, is very anxious to emerge as the great 'compromiser' in the labor movement. But these considerations are secondary.

It is the content and not the form of labor unity that is decisive. The question no longer is pro-CIO or pro-AF of L. Industrial unionism is a fact.

Roosevelt and Labor Unity

The message of President Roosevelt to the AF of L convention urging unity of the labor movement was hailed in many sections of the labor movement as a powerful factor in bringing about peace. It is undeniable that Roosevelt wants labor unity. The questions that must be answered, however, is what kind of unity? This summer a Roosevelt-appointed commission went abroad to study the British Labor Disputes Act, and the Swedish arbitration system. Why? Surely the 'Brain Trust twins', Corcoran and Cohen, know the provisions of those laws. The *New York Times* carried a complete analysis of them. What was desired by Roosevelt was publicity for the idea of arbitration, for the idea of 'peaceful settlement' of the disputes between unions and management. Roosevelt is looking for a legislative method of taking away the right of labor to strike. And this idea is carefully being built up.

Simultaneously with this maneuver, another Roosevelt commission went into action. It was the Maritime Commission whose aims are (1) to build up a powerful merchant marine through huge subsidies, (2) to smash maritime unions. Both are essential points in Roosevelt's war plans. Maritime labor is to be crushed by taking away the union's vital right of control of hiring halls, and by the creation of 'training schools for seamen', i.e. for strike-breakers. Government fink halls instead of union halls. The progressive role of the Sailors Union of the Pacific lies precisely in its intransigent fight against this government strikebreaking. The war crisis in Europe caused Roosevelt to accelerate his activities to curb any independent and militant tendencies in the labor movement. Hence his message to the AF of L convention. Less than six months ago he refused to make such a statement, according to a revelation of Dan Tracy, president of the AF of L electrical workers union. But the war crisis forced Roosevelt to discard his usual caution in avoiding stepping on anyone's toes.

Outright passage of a Hill-Shepard Bill or a similar measure which would break the back of the labor movement in war time has proven too difficult at this stage. A more gradual build-up is necessary from Roosevelt's point of view. Commissions to deal with 'specific' problems. That is the way. Perhaps we shall even see a commission on labor unity. And even more important, the controversy over the Wagner Labor Disputes Act offers another wedge for the Roosevelt administration to foist union-controlling legislation on the labor movement.

The AF of L executive council was voted power by the convention to seek amendments to the Wagner Act. Its criticism of the Act was primarily reactionary. It helped the CIO, i.e. the industrial proletariat, in its organizing campaigns, the council declared. The Act, or rather the interpretation of it by the National Labor Relations Board, hurt a few AF of L unions. It made a few unjust decisions. Of any real criticism, that the Act and the NLRB didn't help labor enough, we heard not a word from the AF of L. So a campaign to modify it has begun. It so happens that this is precisely the program of the US Chamber of Commerce. Here lies Roosevelt's opportunity. Pretending to succumb to the pressure of the AF of L and of the Chamber of Commerce, he will announce or permit modification of the Wagner Act – and slip in provisions similar to those contained in the British Disputes Act. And another chain in binding labor during war will have been forged! The fight against altering the Wagner Act carried on mainly by the CIO unions is therefore a progressive one and it must be supported. Roosevelt views labor unity as a step vital to 'national unity' in war time. Counterposed to this is our concept of labor unity against 'national unity' in labor's struggle to block another world imperialist slaughter.

The recent war crisis also served to expose clearly the role which the union bureaucracy will play more openly in the future. William Green, speaking on Czechoslovakia sounded like an editorial from the *Daily Worker*. He has already publicly announced support of Roosevelt's war plans. John L. Lewis in Mexico City did his part to try to swing Latin American workers behind the aims and needs of American imperialism. The never-ending poison of nationalism which the Stalinists feed their members and the labor movement is a guarantee that no matter what opponent America has in the next war, the patriotism of the CP is assured. Its special role in wartime will be the hounding of all progressives and revolutionists. Against this entire scheme of chaining the American labor movement to Roosevelt's war machine stands an ever increasing section of the unions. The strong anti-imperialist war resolutions passed by the Minneapolis AF of L and the Lynn, Mass., CIO unions is a sign of this development. The fight against the Hill-Shepard or May Bill by the entire labor movement is another indication. Real support for the original Ludlow war referendum bill also came only from the labor movement; the SWOC and the United Automobile Workers of America are two of the major unions which endorsed the war referendum proposal.

Future of the CIO

The key to a thorough understanding of the CIO lies in recognizing that it is primarily a social movement reflecting the needs, desires and aspirations of the conscious and decisive section of the industrial proletariat. It expresses itself on the economic front through industrial unions. Its political arm is Labor's Non-Partisan League. It represents a historical break with the traditions of conservatism in the AF of L. And it is inevitable that, under the limitations of purely economic struggles in an epoch of social crisis, the workers will turn more strongly in the direction of political action. Labor's Non-Partisan League of today must necessarily become the basis of a serious Labor Party development of tomorrow unless war or a not impossible temporary upswing in industrial and business activity postpones it. The vital importance of the CIO movement to the progressive and revolutionary workers rests in understanding this conception.

The convention of the CIO called for November marks a milestone in its history. Here the conflicts, contradictions, present and future of the CIO will be decided one way or another. It faces three major problems requiring urgent solution. Every recent development within the CIO indicates that it will stand ready to negotiate its differences with the AF of L and unite. The rubber workers convention and the New Jersey CIO conventions took clear and progressive positions on this question recently. So have many other CIO unions. The presence of delegates from the International Ladies Garment Workers Union, 400,000 strong, at the CIO convention would virtually guarantee a proper policy on labor unity. Indirectly, the ILGWU exerts great pressure. Its refusal to accept the Lewis leadership unqualifiedly, and its withdrawal from CIO council building moves helped curb the CIO zealots. Now, a tactical change in policy for a drive within the CIO would be a great impetus for labor unity, as was Tobin's action at the AF of L convention. Which course the ILGWU adopts, remains to be seen. Its executive board is meeting a few days prior to the date of the CIO convention.

Two events in the CIO served to bring out its most serious weakness and internal menace, i.e. the Stalinists. It took the acute crisis in the autoworkers union and the division in the West Coast CIO to warn the entire labor movement of the disastrous consequences of the Stalinist 'rule or ruin' policy. Serving only the interests of the Soviet bureaucracy, the Stalinists opened up a reckless campaign to smash Homer Martin, president of the autoworker unions, mainly because he opposed their war-mongering 'collective security' program. Harry Bridges, Stalinist West Coast CIO director, alienated the AF of L movement by his raiding, he split the Maritime Federation of the Pacific in an effort to obtain dictatorial control over the maritime workers, and drove the SUP back into the

AF of L by his 'rule or ruin' tactics. All this was done with the objective of chaining the militant maritime workers to Roosevelt's war plans. And on the East Coast, the National Maritime Union, Stalinist-dominated, accepts the government fink halls for the same reason. In every union, and many CIO unions are controlled by them, the Stalinists frame-up militants, engage in an orgy of red-baiting against progressives, trample on union democracy, and ignore the most elementary union tasks necessary to preserve the unions.

Within the CIO itself the reply to those ruinous policies was not long in forthcoming. The Los Angeles Progressive Trade Union conference, dealt Bridges and the Stalinists a heavy blow when they proclaimed publicly their opposition to that reactionary clique. They issued a 60-page booklet giving a detailed account of the Stalinist wrecking activities in the West Coast CIO. They demanded that Lewis remove Bridges from his appointed post!

The six-point program of the Los Angeles progressives offers a real weapon in fighting the Stalinist union wreckers and their bureaucratic allies.

1. Labor solidarity in the struggle for better conditions of employed and unemployed alike. We offer aid to any union, AF of L, CIO or railroad brotherhood which is engaged in such a struggle.
2. Organize the unorganized.
3. Industrial unionism in the industries for which it is suited. No raids on existing organizations.
4. An actual democracy in the trade union movement.
5. Struggle against anti-labor legislation and government interference whether through use of courts, the National Guard, the police or otherwise. For the enforcement and extension of workers' rights.
6. For independent political action to supplement the trade union struggle. Around this program of action the CIO can have a progressive future.

Insofar as this program finds expression at the CIO convention will the convention have a progressive character. Against this platform will be rallied the Stalinists and other reactionaries in the CIO.

For supporting the Stalinists in the autoworkers union, and for appointing Bridges as West Coast Director, John L. Lewis bears responsibility to the CIO membership. The temporary successes of the Stalinists in the CIO are largely due to Lewis's assent to their 'rule or ruin' policy. Yet the defeat of the Stalinists rests not merely in a change of policy on Lewis' part. Quite the contrary. Only where the CIO rank and file unites behind the Los Angeles program will a really serious struggle against the Stalinists be possible. The Lovestonite theory of 'using' one bureaucracy to fight another revealed itself bankrupt in the auto union crisis. Martin, in the autoworkers union, answered the Stalinist attack with an essentially progressive program, unfortunately applied in a bureaucratic fashion. It was this weakness that played directly into the hands of the Stalinists, and along with the intervention of John L. Lewis, won for them, at least temporarily. The subsequent dismissal of militant organizers known as oppositionists to the Stalinist wreckers casts an ominous shadow on the future course of the union.

The third question before the coming CIO convention is the future course of Labor's Non-Partisan League. The CIO leadership apparently has learned nothing from the bitter experiences suffered by the policy of supporting Democratic or Republican 'friends of labor'. Martin L. Davey was elected governor of Ohio with CIO support. He used the National Guard to break the 'Little Steel' strike. Now the CIO is supporting Charles Sawyer, in Ohio. He is a millionaire corporation lawyer, described two years ago by the CIO leaders as a 'reactionary capitalist'. In Pennsylvania, the LNPL again endorses Governor Earle for re-election after a public break in the primaries. In New Jersey, the Hague machine controls the Democratic party and holds a strong influence over the Republicans, and the CIO workers won't swallow either. Yet the CIO leaders quietly ignored the mandate of a special state-wide convention last winter to set up a Labor Party. This was done by a simple device. The executive committee elected at the Labor Party convention later reconstituted itself as the executive committee for Labor's Non-Partisan League. Now it refuses to run independent candidates when this is the only course left outside of boycotting the elections or supporting the Hague machine.

Labor against Fascism

Incipient American fascism found its leading vocal expression in 'I am the Law' Frank Hague, mayor of Jersey City, and member of the national committee of the Democratic Party. His ruthless crushing of CIO organizing drives, his expulsions of 'outside agitators' from the city through vigilante force, his redbaiting, and above all, his tremendous political power make him a serious challenge to the labor movement. It is a sad commentary on the state of the AF of L movement in New Jersey that many prominent AF of L leaders endorse Hague. One central union council even passed a resolution to that effect. Hague is out to protect the sweatshops of his area from unionism. He has fought the efforts of the CIO to organize those exploited workers by thuggery and by clever demagogy. The CIO record against him is deplorable. Stalinist stooges, weak-kneed 'liberal' congressmen, fake Stalinist 'civil liberties' committees, Sir Galahads of the Norman Thomas stripe, have tilted with the effect of a Don Quixote against the Hague menace. Surrounded by Stalinists, W.J. Carney, militant New Jersey CIO director, has found himself swamped by the resolution-passers while the courageous SWOC workers at the Crucible steel lodge in Jersey City find themselves alone in a successful fight for unionism against Hague. In the fact that the steel workers district council of New Jersey adopted a militant program of action for organizing in Hague's domain – the best way to fight him – lies the hope of smashing Hagueism. It should hardly be necessary to add that the Stalinists spend most of their time fighting the steel workers' policies.

Elsewhere in America a similar acceleration in the growth of vigilante movements directed primarily against the union movement was witnessed this past year. The terror against the CIO in New Orleans; the vigilante attack on the CIO workers in Westwood, California; the kidnapping and beating of union organizers everywhere; these are cumulative manifestations of the growth of reaction. Rev. Gerald L.K. Smith again finds audiences for his gospel of fascism. The Silver shirts, the Bund and a score of other fascist groupings take on a new lease in life. What is the answer? A United Labor Defense Committee with special squads in Akron is a partial solution. Union Defense Squads in Minneapolis was the quick answer of the labor movement to threats by the Silver Shirts that they would raid the union headquarters and run the union leaders out of town. Extension of the idea of Workers Defense Squads – in this alone is there a safeguard against fascist attacks.

There is another danger. Division of the workers and farmers is a major point in the strategy of the bosses. Wealthier farmers organize into Associated Farmers, Inc. on the West Coast and the Middlewest. They recruit vigilantes and propagandize against the unions. In reply, the unions in Minneapolis, Omaha, the West Coast, and the rubberworkers in Ohio, unite with the lower strata of farmers. They cooperate with the farmers in obtaining equitable prices. The CIO has a national tie-up with the Farmers Union. Unity against the common enemy, America's Sixty Families, has been the only effective slogan for rallying the farmers to the worker. Labor is rapidly learning that it must give leadership and support to the sharecroppers, the lower strata of farmers, and the agricultural workers. Otherwise, a valuable ally can easily be turned into a foe.

The Unemployed

Around 15,000,000 unemployed suffer in misery from conditions brought by the social crisis of American capitalism which offers starvation as the only permanent prospect for the working class, under this system. Of these, less than 100,000 pay dues into the Stalinist-controlled Workers Alliance, although it claims 400,000 membership. For the first time in its history, the AF of L took note of its unemployed members in convention reports. They number 1,400,000. The CIO has at least that many. Of great importance is the new attitude towards its unemployed members. Unemployment is considered as the problem of the union movement. The idea of a completely independent organization for the unemployed hasn't worked out in the last decade, whatever the reasons may be. The only permanent and really successful – in obtaining concessions from the government – unemployed organizations have been those allied directly to the union movement. This has been the experience of the Federal Workers Section of 544, in Minneapolis. It has been followed in Salem, Ohio, in Lynn, Mass. and has begun in Akron. The autoworkers in Detroit, steel lodges in the middle west: in fact, in many sections of the CIO, the union movement retains the unemployed as members in good standing, and takes up the problems. It gives the unemployed much greater power and prestige in fighting against present relief conditions when direct union affiliation has been retained. It unites more closely the employed and unemployed.

The recent national convention of the Workers Alliance consummated the final rites over this once large organization and turned it completely into another Stalinist stooge outfit. The progressive section in New York City broke away from the national organization. Other defections are on their way elsewhere. The Stalinists have but one hope left of covering up their criminal irresponsibility and actions in the Alliance that crippled it for life. For a year David Lasser, head of the Alliance, has been begging John L. Lewis for a CIO charter. Against this maneuver and its ruinous consequences, hundreds of CIO unions have written to the national office urging the CIO to coordinate its unemployed work on a national scale and itself form a CIO unemployed union, along industrial lines. Such a step would clearly be progressive, if the Stalinist wreckers are isolated and kept from capturing the proposed set-up. The question is coming before the national CIO convention. It must be noted, that the AF of L has been able to maintain high wage levels for its members on WPA projects, and is talking about organizing the unemployed. This much is certain for the future, no matter what particular organizational forms emerge. The trade union movement in America must definitely and to an ever increasing degree concern itself with the unemployment question.

Summary

In the midst of an epoch of triumphant world reaction marked by the ascendancy of fascism, the American workers made remarkable advances. The brilliant wave of sit-down strikes of 1936–37 shook American capitalism to its foundations. It established industrial unionism permanently. Young, inexperienced, and barely organized, the CIO carried on though it was plunged into the depths of a severe social crisis. And the American Federation of Labor found itself hammered by the blows of this same crisis. Yet, today the labor movement has held its own. In some respects it has made organizational gains. After the first shocks of mass unemployment, the labor movement steadied itself. American workers are groping around for an answer to the crisis that has brought such increased misery and insecurity for them. Proposals for $30 every Thursday, for an annual guaranteed wage, for a 30-hour week, for unemployment insurance, and a hundred other plans are advanced and experimented with by the labor movement.

There exists a certain inner cohesion in all these events. Inexorably, the American workers are moving towards class solidarity reflected in the trend towards unity in the labor movement. Dissatisfaction with capitalism is revealed in every proposal, good or bad, that the labor movement accepts against a continuation of the status quo. It is precisely this situation that offers unparalleled opportunities for the revolutionary movement. A program of transitional demands that express the desires of the workers in terms of tomorrow, a program that accelerates the development of class solidarity, a program that gives a better answer for today and prepares the workers for revolutionary advances tomorrow: This is a tremendous weapon held by the SWP.

The prospect of immediate world war in the recent European crisis threatened to cut short the opportunities of the revolutionary movement. The American labor movement would have been unprepared to meet that fundamental question except to fall victim to social patriotism. In the respite from war, history has given time as an ally to the revolutionary movement. Its agitation for a sliding scale of wages, for a 30-hour week, for turning over idle plants to workers, in a word, its program of transitional demands is on the order of the day. And war will not interrupt immediately. Our opportunity to cultivate the slender roots we have planted in the labor movement into a solid and broad base of the revolutionary movement is here now.

7 The Unions and Politics[21]

(1940, excerpts)

Farrell Dobbs

Beginning with the vast majority of the national leaders of the trade unions, reaching far down into the secondary stratum of the union leadership and including a section of the more privileged trade union membership, there exists a portion of the working class which looks with favor upon the system of individual enterprise. Compared with the conditions of the many poorly paid and unemployed workers, they find themselves in fairly comfortable circumstances. They see a bright side to things as they are. They are capable of viewing social and economic problems from the general point of view of the employers. Sincerely deploring the plight of the less fortunate workers, they are mentally incapable of taking decisive action to aid them. They decline to risk their own privileged position in the interests of this struggle.

The employers, understanding this, have pursued a conscious policy of nurturing a contented section in the official trade union movement. There are comparatively few communities in the country, including the smallest, that do not have a trade union group, based on the relatively better-paid skilled workers, which enjoys very good relations with the local Chamber of Commerce. These groups extend themselves into the gradually thinning ranks of the small minorities of skilled workers in the mass production industries.

AF of L Policy

The American Federation of Labor was built up into a substantial national organization primarily on this foundation. Its officialdom is dominated by those whose ideology and outlook is that of the individual who enjoys a certain degree of comfort and who therefore finds no serious fault with the present social structure.

---

21 Dobbs 1940.

This leadership continually reminds the workers that they 'must learn to crawl before they can walk'. Main emphasis is placed on lobbying for 'liberal' legislation as a means of struggle for improved wages and working conditions. Direct struggles against the employers through strike actions are subordinated to this program and, in general, discouraged if not sabotaged.

The traditional political policy of the AFL in promoting favorable legislation is to reward political 'friends' and punish political 'enemies' – by votes. The term 'friends' does not mean representatives of the workers. The 'friends' do not always vote for the bills endorsed by the unions. They are considered 'friendly' if they vote for the majority of them.

The AFL officialdom rejects independent working-class political action. They advise the workers to confine themselves solely to trade union activity and let the bosses organize the political parties and run the government. The 'friends' may be Republicans, Democrats or so-called 'Independents'.

Now that the mass production workers have broken the strangle-hold of the craft unions and have successfully established their industrial unions, a new pressure has developed on the political front. The bosses have few crumbs to offer to these great layers of the working class. The membership of the industrial unions find themselves in constant conflict with the bosses. They have the grave problems of low wages, poor housing, unemployment, industrial diseases in the most aggravated form. They are little impressed by the time-worn dictum about the 'long road' to the realization of their aims. Especially when those 'aims' are only a few cents more an hour or a few hours less work per week. There is little satisfaction in 'progressing' from starvation to mere malnutrition. They want action. And on the political as well as the economic front.

CIO and Labor's Non-partisan League

The leadership of the Congress of Industrial Organizations pretended to give the industrial workers a vehicle for independent working-class political action through Labor's Non-Partisan League. But it is only a pretense. The LNPL is not an independent working-class political party. It is nothing but a new method of applying the hoary AFL 'reward your friends and punish your enemies' policy.

…

An examination of the record does not speak well for these political 'friends' who are backed by the officialdom of the AFL and CIO. Few workers can remember a time when one of these 'friends' appeared before a union meeting to urge the workers to go on strike and use their economic power in the struggle for their rights. But many workers can recall incidents where the 'friends' have gone before meetings of the workers urging them not to go on strike, or to call off a strike already in progress, to say nothing about statements issued by them against the workers. They have many, many times helped the bosses to cram an unfair contract down the workers' throats or to force the workers to accept an insincere boss promise and no contract at all.

When the time comes for a showdown these 'friends' of labor show that their real allegiance is to the bosses. Their promises to the workers were not made in good faith.

In fact, the record shows that the policy of supporting 'friendly' politicians is in reality a matter of supporting those who are *least hostile*.

Some of the most serious defeats have been suffered where the unions depended on 'friendly' government officials instead of militant class struggle policy. For example, in Little Steel, the CIO workers got a large-scale demonstration of betrayal by the very people they had worked so hard to elect into posts in the government.

When a politician takes a more or less bold course in opposition to the workers or piles up too long a record of anti-labor actions the workers turn sharply against him. The alibi-artists in the trade union movement find it difficult to apologize for him and sometimes he does not survive the next election.

However, he is replaced not by a workers' representative, but by another slick politician who is also subservient to the bosses. He, too, is palmed off on the workers as their 'friend'. The union leadership must be put on record as approving or disapproving *all* action of these 'friendly' politicians. Nothing must remain unmentioned or covered up.

They will try to evade this responsibility, claiming that there is danger of embarrassing the 'friends' and risking the election of 'enemies'. The workers must insist upon an end to such 'friends' and the election of government officials from the workers' ranks by the workers' own party.

The workers do not elect bosses or boss stooges to lead the unions. Such an action would be patently foolish. It is done only in company unions. It is just as ridiculous for them to elect such people to political office. The theory that the workers are not capable of governing themselves is false to the core. Unthinking people in the trade unions who repeat this prevarication do an injustice to their class. Every worker who has participated in trade union life knows that the working class has a tremendous capacity for efficient administration.

Those parties which have represented themselves as labor parties are only substitutes for the real article. They confine themselves to competition for political posts of the lower rank. They do not seriously challenge the bosses' political parties for the key positions in the government. Occasionally they elect a mayor; very rarely a governor or a congressman. They avoid putting up workers as candidates. Lawyers, drug store proprietors and professional politicians have been more popular with them as standard bearers. They buckle under just like the Republicans and the Democrats when the bosses really turn on the heat.

For an Independent Labor Party

An independent labor party, sponsored and launched by the trade unions, will represent the political power, not only of the organized workers, but also of a broad strata of the unorganized industrial and agricultural workers who will give it their support.

Farmers, small merchants, professional people and other middle-class elements will also in large numbers follow the independent political leadership of a dynamic working class as opposed to the present leadership of a decaying boss class.

Class collaborationist leaders of the workers have been, and will continue to be, in political offices as timid before the bosses as they are in the unions. The independent labor party will no doubt elect to political office, among others, many class collaborationists. Their performance in office will help show them up in their true colors before the eyes of the workers. They can thus be compelled to change their policies or be eliminated entirely from leadership in the working-class movement in any capacity.

The class-conscious working-class leaders will fight as militantly in political office for the rights of the workers as they do in the unions. They will give a new meaning to the struggle of the workers for their rights. The workers will find powerful new weapons at their command.

The electing of workers' representatives to political offices will surely not solve the basic problems of the working class. But when the workers begin to participate in politics as a class, through an independent party of their own, they will have taken a long step forward toward their goal.

8 'If You are Afraid, You Lose Your Independence'[22] (*1940, excerpts*)

Leon Trotsky, James P. Cannon, Farrell Dobbs, Sam Gordon

Trotsky: ... I have a concrete suggestion, that we publish a letter to the Stalinist workers: during five years your leaders were protagonists of the democracies, then they changed and were against all the imperialisms. If you make a firm decision not to permit a change in line then we are ready to convoke a convention to support your presidential candidate. You must give a pledge. It would be a letter of propaganda and agitation to the Stalinist workers. We will see. It is probable that the line will change in some weeks. This letter would give you free possibilities without having to vote for their candidate

Cannon: They will probably make a change before we return.

Trotsky: Yes, it is quite likely.

Cannon: We must exercise great caution in dealing with the Stalinists in order not to compromise ourselves. Yesterday's discussion took a one-sided channel regarding our relations in the unions, that we act only as attorneys for the progressive labor fakers. This is very false. Our objective is to create our own forces. The problem is how to begin. All sectarians are independent forces – in their own imagination. Your impression that the anti-Stalinists are rival labor fakers is not quite correct. It has that aspect, but it has other aspects too. Without opposition to the Stalinists we have no reason for existing in the unions. We start as oppositionists and become irreconcilable. Where small groups break their necks is that they scorn maneuvers and combinations and never consolidate anything. At the opposite extreme is the Lovestone group.

In the SUP [Sailors Union of the Pacific] we began without any members, the way we usually begin. Up to the time of the war it was hard to find a more fruitful ground than the anti-Stalinist elements. We began with this idea, that it is impossible to play a role in the unions unless you have people in the unions. With a small party, the possibility to enter is the first essential. In the SUP we made a combination with syndicalist elements. It was an exceptional situation,

22 Trotsky 1940c.

a small weak bureaucracy, most of whose policies were correct and which was against the Stalinists. It was incomprehensible that we could play any role except as an opposition to the Stalinists who were the most treacherous elements in the situation.

We formed a tacit bloc with the one possibility to enter the union freely. We were weak numerically, strong politically. The progressives grew, defeated the Stalinists. We grew too. We have fifty members and may possess soon fifty more. We followed a very careful policy – not to have sharp clashes which were not necessary anyway so far, so as not to bring about a premature split – not to let the main fight against the Stalinists be obscured.

The maritime unions are an important section in the field. Our first enemy there is the Stalinists. They are the big problem. In new unions such as the maritime, which in reality surged forward in 1934, shattering the old bureaucracy, the Stalinists came to the fore. The old-fashioned craft unionists cannot prevail against the Stalinists. The struggle for control is between us and the Stalinists. We have to be careful not to compromise this fight. We must be the classical intransigent force.

The Stalinists gained powerful positions in these unions, especially in the auto union. The Lovestoneites followed the policy outlined by Trotsky yesterday – attorneys for the labor fakers, especially in auto. They disappeared from the scene. We followed a more careful policy. We tried to exploit the differences between the Martin gang and the Stalinists. For a while we were the left wing of the Martin outfit, but we extricated ourselves in the proper time. Auto is ostensibly CIO but in reality the Stalinists are in control. Now we are coming forward as the leading and inspiring circle in the rank and file that has no top leaders, that is anti-Stalinist, anti-patriotic, anti-Lewis. We have every chance for success. We must not overlook the possibility that these chances developed from experiments in the past period to exploit differences between the union tops. If we had taken a sectarian attitude we would still be there.

In the food unions there was an inchoate opposition to the Stalinists. There were office-seekers, progressives, former CPers. We have only a few people. We must link ourselves with one or the other to come forward. Later we will be able to come forward. Two things can compromise us: One, confusion with the Stalinists. Two, a purist attitude. If we imagine ourselves a power, ignoring the differences between the reactionary wings, we will remain sterile.

Dobbs: The general situation leads me to believe that we would lose more than we would gain from giving the impression that we are locking arms with the Stalinists. We have made connections with reactionary people but at the same time we have gained some very good trade union elements, bringing them closer to true Bolshevism. We have gained additional footholds. In steel we have

22 comrades in the rank and file movement. Some playing a very important role. At the last convention one comrade especially got the biggest ovation at the convention when he made his speech. Prior to the convention we had only a small nucleus. Since then we have grown among the rank and file.

Trotsky: Can we get them to go against Roosevelt?

Dobbs: Yes.

Trotsky: For whom will they vote?

Dobbs: I don't know. Maybe Roosevelt. For us to turn to the Stalinists will sow real confusion in their minds. It should not be rushed in any case.

Trotsky: I believe we have the critical point very clear. We are in a bloc with so-called progressives, not only fakers but honest rank and file. Yes, they are honest and progressive but from time to time they vote for Roosevelt – once in four years. This is decisive. You propose a trade union policy, not a Bolshevik policy. Bolshevik policies begin outside the trade unions. The worker is an honest trade unionist but far from Bolshevik politics. The honest militant can develop but it is not identical with being a Bolshevik. You are afraid to become compromised in the eyes of the Rooseveltian trade unionists. They on the other hand are not worried in the slightest about being compromised by voting for Roosevelt against you. We are afraid of being compromised. If you are afraid, you lose your independence and become half-Rooseveltian. In peacetimes this is not catastrophic. In wartimes it will compromise us. They can smash us. Our policy is too much for pro-Rooseveltian trade unionists. I notice that in the *Northwest Organizer* this is true. We discussed it before, but not a word was changed; not a single word. The danger – a terrible danger – is adaptation to the pro-Rooseveltian trade unionists. You don't give any answer to the elections, not even the beginning of an answer. But we must have a policy. It is not necessary now to vote for Browder. We are against Roosevelt. As for Norman Thomas, he is just a political misunderstanding. Browder, however, is a tremendous handicap because he has a 'revolutionary' attitude toward the imperialist war, etc. And our attitude? We turn our backs and give no answer. I understand that the situation is difficult.

What I propose is a manifesto to the Stalinist workers, to say that for five years you were for Roosevelt, then you changed. This turn is in the right direction. Will you develop and continue this policy or not? Will you let the leaders change it or not? Will you continue and develop it or not? If you are firm we will support you. In this manifesto we can say that you fix a sharp program for your candidate, then we will vote for him. I see no reason why we can't say this with these ifs. Does this signify that we have changed our trade union policy? Not at all. We continue to oppose them as before. We say, if you seriously consider your attitude to Roosevelt you would have such and such a policy in the trade unions. But you don't have such a policy there. We can't go along with you in the trade unions.

I would be very glad to hear even one single word from you on policy in regard to the presidential election.

Cannon: It is not entirely correct to pose the problem in that way. We are not with the pro-Roosevelt militants. We developed when the Stalinists were pro-Rooseveltian. Their present attitude is conjunctural. It is not correct that we lean toward Roosevelt. Comrade Trotsky's polemic is a polemic for an independent candidate. If we were opposed to that then his account would be correct. For technical reasons we can't have an independent candidate. The real answer is independent politics.

It is a false issue: Roosevelt vs. the Stalinists. It is not a bona fide class opposition to Roosevelt. Possibly we could support Browder against Roosevelt, but Browder would not only repudiate our votes, but would withdraw in favor of Roosevelt.

Trotsky: That would be the very best occurrence for us. After laying down our conditions for support, this capitulation would win us a section of the Stalinists. It is not a strategic policy but a policy for the presidential campaign only.

The fact is that they have developed this antiwar propaganda. We must consider this important fact in the life of the American workers. We begin with nothing being done about the Stalinists.

The 'progressive' rank and file are a kind of semi-fabrication. They have class struggle tendencies but they vote for Roosevelt. They are not formed politically. The rank and file Stalinists are not worse. They are caught in a machine. They are disciplined, political. Our aim is to oppose the Stalinist worker to the machine. How accomplish this? By leaving them alone? We will never do it. By postponing? That is not a policy.

We are for an independent labor ticket. But we don't even have this expressed in our press. Why? Because our party is embarrassed. It has no line on the elections. Last January we discussed a campaign in the unions to have our own trade union presidential candidate. We were to start in Minneapolis. We were to address Tobin. We were to propose to him that we would vote for him if he were nominated. Even Lewis. We were to begin the campaign for a labor president. But not a thing was done. Nothing appeared. Nothing in the *Northwest Organizer*.

…

I can't explain it by negligence. Nor just because it is a trade union paper with just a trade union policy. The members of the party could write letters to the editor. What do their trade union leaders believe? Why can't our comrades write to the *Northwest Organizer?* We discussed in detail the technical details. But nothing was done. Why? It signifies an immediate clash with the Rooseveltians – not the rank and file – but a clash with our allies, the machine, the conscious Rooseveltians, who would immediately attack, a clash with our own class enemies such as Tobin.

Cannon: It is necessary to counterpose trade union candidates in the field. That would retain our following. But what I can't accept is Browder as a symbol of the class struggle.

Trotsky: That is a bit of false polemics. In January I didn't propose Browder. But you are reduced to Browder or Roosevelt. Why this lack of initiative? Why were these six months not utilized? Why? It is not reduced to an individual fight, it has general reasons. I discussed with O'Shea two years ago on this same problem and this same necessity. With Dunne too. But the *Northwest Organizer* remains unchanged. It is a photograph of our adaptation to the Rooseveltians.

Understand, I don't believe that it would be advisable for important comrades to start such a campaign. But even totally unknown comrades could write such letters. He could write the executive board of the union, asking them what will be the fate of the workers. What kind of a president do we need? At least five months were not utilized. Completely lost. So we should lose two or three months more?

And Browder suddenly becomes an ideal political figure for me! A little false polemics!

How reach a compromise? I ask two or three hundred Stalinist workers. That is the minimum requirement. We can get them by holding their leaders to a class struggle policy. Are you ready to impose this class struggle line on your leader, we ask. Then we will find common grounds.

It is not just to write a manifesto, but to turn our political face to the Stalinist workers. What is bad about that? We begin an action against the Stalinists; what is wrong with that?

I propose a compromise. I will evaluate Browder 50 percent lower than I estimate him now in return for 50 percent more interest from you in the Stalinist party.

Cannon: It has many complications.

Gordon: On the question of adaptation to Roosevelt's program by our trade union comrades. Is it true? If so, it was necessary for our trade union work. The trade unionists are for Roosevelt. If we want to make headway we have to adapt – by not unfolding our full program in order to get a foothold for the next stage. We are still at the beginning despite all the work done. That is one thing, but to make it a permanent policy is another thing. We are against that. What is the right time to make the break? Have we exhausted the period of adaptation?

Cannon: The failure of the campaign to develop an independent ticket is due to inertia at the center, the faction fight, the tendency to wait in place of energetic application of policies, a feeling of smallness of the party – psychological faults rather than conscious or unconscious adaptation to the Rooseveltians. The bloc in the trade unions is not a political bloc but a bloc over trade union policy. It is possible to have an active policy in opposition. In 1936 we supported the Socialist Party, not Roosevelt, despite the trade unionists giving open support to Roosevelt. …

We should have started a campaign six months ago. During the faction fight there was a congressional campaign. Browder was running. Our policy was that it would be best to have our own candidate. We proposed this, but it was sabotaged by Abern. But to go out and campaign for Browder, just at the time of war, when we are trying to explain our policy –

Trotsky: It is precisely one of the elements of explaining that theirs is a false policy.

Cannon: Support for a labor candidate can be justified, but the CP is entirely different. The CP is not a genuine workers' party.

Dobbs: We are caught short. The criticisms are very pertinent. They will be productive of better results, you may be certain. But we feel that this policy would be completely disastrous. We would prefer to sacrifice the maneuver for Jimmy Higgins work[23] and put our own candidate on the ballot. It is not a question of Roosevelt. We will do anything short of supporting the Stalinists in order to go against Roosevelt.

Trotsky: Good. But why not write a manifesto, addressing them? Give them arguments understandable to them? But we don't have a candidate. It is now too late to have a candidate. What is your policy?

Good – we will abandon voting for Browder. We will abandon a manifesto. We will make a leaflet. You would agree with a leaflet on the above lines? We can state our differences with the CP: your party accepts the class struggle only on accidental grounds …

And if the Stalinist worker comes up to you and asks, will you vote for our candidate? We are a serious political party, where do you stand? We must give him a serious answer. We must say, yes, we will vote for him. No party is homogeneous, not even the Stalinist party. We cannot change the party but only introduce a wedge to start some of them moving toward us.

23 Jimmie Higgens was the hero of a socialist novel by Upton Sinclair and was commonly used to refer to activists or work that involved in practical, often mundane, activity required to make socialist political efforts successful.

Cannon: In 1920, in the first year of the CP in this country, we had a situation similar to this. We were in illegality. A few months before the election and impossible to run our own candidate. We openly boycotted the elections. It was completely ineffective. Lenin wrote us a letter. He held that we should have voted for Debs. But at that time there was a strong psychological separation from the SP. Lenin's statement produced quite a shock. And Debs was in prison – not a Browder.

Trotsky: Yes. Although Browder is condemned to prison.

Cannon: There has not been a direct attack or approach to the Stalinists for some years. Could it be possible?

CHAPTER 6

'The Negro Question'

Thomas Bias

A dilemma faced by the socialist movement in the United States, since its beginnings in the nineteenth century, had involved a failure to fully integrate the struggle of Black Americans into the struggle for a socialist future, a profound limitation reflected, and only partially overcome, in these selections. This is a problem afflicting a variety of radical and reform movements in the course of US history.[1]

Many socialists did recognise the special oppression African-Americans faced for well over a century before the United States came into existence as a republic, and in all the years that followed. Skin-colour prejudice directed against African-Americans has consistently been a big problem in the American working class and labour movement for generations, but by the 1930s – the period covered by this volume – socialists of all political tendencies rejected and actively opposed such attitudes. That also was not the issue. Socialists were especially instrumental in fighting against divisive race-hatreds in the Congress of Industrial Organizations (CIO) during its organising drives and strikes during the 1930s, and their work against racism in the unions was decisive in the CIO's success during those years. Yet this did not automatically translate into a recognition of the central importance of the African-American struggle for basic civil rights and later for a more fundamental liberation as a people.

The 1929 position presented by US Trotskyists on 'the Negro Question', a brief statement in *The Militant* entitled 'Work Among Negroes', was far in advance of what we find later. Framed in part as a critique of the US Communist Party, the article is consistent with positions articulated by Trotsky in the 1920s and early 1930s, and developed a decade later by CLR James. Possibly the general framework for the 1931 comments by James P. Cannon in 'Trifling with the Negro Question', it is remarkable that – far from being followed up and developed – the 1929 position appears to have been soon forgotten or quietly dropped.

One is struck by the relative paucity of articles devoted to the Black struggle in such US Trotskyist publications of this period as *The Militant*, *Socialist*

---

1 Allen 1974 and Foner 1977.

Appeal, and *New International*. There were some, and a representation of them is included here; however, there were not many. Furthermore, they are written from an intellectual and theoretical point of view, addressing the sociological and political issues posed by the special oppression of Black people. They do *not* address the strategy and tactics of day-to-day struggle to put an end to discrimination, poverty, and outright murder of Black people, and even more importantly, they do not reflect the point of view of people who faced racist oppression each day of their lives. It is revealing that the editors of *The Militant*, in presenting Hugo Oehler's three-part series in 1932, indicate that it comes from 'a commission to assemble material on the Negro question in America and to open a discussion in the [Communist] League', concluding that Oehler's contribution was 'a discussion article' whose views were only those of the author, and that 'others will follow on the same subject'. But there were no others published.

It is no less revealing that the draft of a pamphlet by Max Shachtman developed in the same period, *Race and Revolution* (advancing a line similar to that advanced by Oehler) was never published – until brought out by a socialist academic in 2003. The way Shachtman summed up the question uncompromisingly opposed racism, yet it somewhat mechanistically submerged the anti-racist struggle in the larger class struggle:

> The militant proletariat inscribes upon its banner in this country the uncompromising demand for full and equal rights for the oppressed Negro, so that he may rise out of the position of debasement and the backwardness to which he has been forced by a decadent ruling class to the level of human dignity and consciousness that will make him the invaluable comrade-in-arms of the white proletariat. In their joint struggle for the proletarian revolution, they will sweep away the abominable structure of imperialist capitalism, rooting out the barbarous remnants of slavery and serfdom, and abolishing the poisonous system of caste inequality, ostracism, misery and exploitation under which the millions of American Negroes suffer today. Any other road is a deception, leading through mirages to the brink of the precipice. The proletarian revolution is the road to freedom.[2]

While there is much of value in what was written in the Trotskyist publications in the 1930s, it shows that the Trotskyists at that time were not directly

2 Shachtman 2003, p. 102.

connected with the African-American people or their ongoing struggle against the horrific oppression they had faced for centuries. Even the remarkable CLR James (1901–89), usually writing under the pseudonym JR Johnson, wrote as an outsider. James, though he was himself Black, was Trinidadian and joined the socialist movement in Great Britain; he did not come to the United States until 1938. James contributed mightily to American Trotskyists' understanding of the Black experience and the Black struggle, to be sure, as readers will see in the articles in this section. Even so, he had little connection to the daily life and challenges faced by the masses of Black Americans as they struggled for survival during the 1930s, and his writing reflects that.[3]

In the articles included in this chapter, the reader will find little mention and no thorough analysis of the political debate within the Black struggle of the 1930s. The views of Booker T. Washington and Marcus Garvey are dismissed out of hand as 'reactionary', and indeed some aspects of their political orientation *are* antagonistic to a programme of working-class solidarity and working-class power. CLR James (writing as JR Johnson) says in his 'Preliminary Notes on the Negro Question':

> … Self-determination for the American Negroes is (1) economically reactionary and (2) politically false because no Negroes (except CP stooges) want it. For Negroes it is merely an inverted segregation. Yet it is not to be lightly dismissed without providing for what it aims at: the creation of confidence among the Negroes that revolutionary socialism does honestly and sincerely mean to stand by its promises. As so often with Marxists, the subsidiary psychological factors are not carefully provided for in the planning of political campaigns.

By 'self-determination' James means something very specific: the right to separate and form an independent self-governing political entity, and he rejects it. The Communist Party during the early 1930s, mechanically adapting the Bolsheviks' allowing of self-determination to the nationalities within the Tsarist Russian empire, had advocated the independence of the so-called 'Black Belt' of the deep South as an independent Black state.

When he participated with a number of other Socialist Workers Party members in a discussion with Trotsky in Coyoacán, Mexico, in 1938, his position was somewhat more nuanced. He said:

3 See Worchester 1995 and Rosengarten 2008.

> I therefore propose concretely: (1) That we are for the right of self-determination. (2) If some demand should arise among the Negroes for the right of self-determination we should support it. (3) We do not go out of our way to raise this slogan and place an unnecessary barrier between ourselves and socialism. (4) An investigation should be made into these movements; the one led by Garvey, the movement for the 49th state, the movement centering around Liberia. Find out what groups of the population supported them and on this basis come to some opinion as to how far there is any demand among the Negroes for self-determination.[4]

As to Washington, Joseph Vanzler, writing under the pseudonym John G. Wright, wrote: 'Booker T. Washington did what he could to discourage Negroes from putting their trust in working class unity'. That is true, as far as it goes. Vanzler went on to say:

> Booker T. Washington preached to the Negroes against class solidarity and tried to imbue them with self-degradation. He said, 'the wisest of my race understand that the agitation of questions of social equality is the extremest folly ...' He advocated an 'alliance' with the wealthy whites against the 'white trash', i.e., against the white workers who are the 'oppressors and scoundrels, who hold Negroes in contempt and lynch them'. The Negroes have been taught by the bourgeoisie to distrust and hate the white workers and vice versa. We must imbue the Negro with class solidarity.

Vanzler's polemic against Washington, brief as it is, is hardly an analysis. It fails to take into account the context in which Washington was doing his advocacy and organising, a context in which not knowing 'one's place' was life-threatening to Black people. It was also a context in which the danger of dispossession and starvation was clear and present to the Black sharecropper – and what else could Washington advocate but concrete and practical ways by which African-Americans could improve their economic condition? Obviously, no socialist could ever condone strikebreaking or even advocating strikebreaking, and, to be sure, Washington's strategy was far from a winning one for the African-American people. Nevertheless, it came from very practical considerations in the real world in which Black people lived, and one does not get an understanding of those considerations from what even the best revolutionary

4 George Breitman (ed.) 1978.

socialists were writing in the 1930s. Those socialists simply did not live in that same real world – Union Square in New York City was much further away from the Mississippi Delta than even the map would indicate. One can read voraciously and have a solid theoretical understanding, but it is still no substitute for direct personal experience.

Much of the Socialist Workers Party's attention – as well as the attention of the groups which preceded the SWP, such as the Communist League of America and Workers Party of the United States – was directed at the much larger Communist Party, and the CP's influence in the labour movement during the 1930s was strong and in many cases pernicious. The SWP in its 1939 convention resolution 'The SWP and Negro Work' noted correctly that the Communist Party had betrayed the trust of many Blacks who had joined it and had become 'another example of the use of Negroes by whites for political purposes unconnected with Negro struggles'. The resolution also noted that the New York State CP had lost 80 percent of its Black members between 1935 and 1939. Addressing the issues posed by this was of paramount importance in the 1930s.

CLR James, in his 1939 'Preliminary Notes on the Negro Question', which laid the basis for the convention resolution 'The SWP and Negro Work', summed up the problem faced by the SWP as shown by the articles included in this chapter:

> The Fourth International movement has neglected the Negro question almost completely. If even the Party personnel were not of a type to do active work among the Negro masses, the Negro question as an integral part of the American revolution can no longer be neglected. The Negro helped materially to win the Civil War and he can make the difference between success and failure in any given revolutionary situation. A Negro department of some sort should be organized (consisting, if need be, entirely of whites) which will deal as comprehensively with the Negro question as the Trade Union Department deals with the Trade Union Question. If the Party thinks the question important enough this will be done. The Party members and sympathizers must be educated to the significance of the Negro question. This is not a question of there being no Negroes in the Party. That has nothing to do with it at all. This work can begin immediately. The main question, however, that of organizing or helping to organize the Negro masses, is one of enormous difficulty for a party like the SWP. The main reasons for this are of course the discrimination against the Negro in industry by both capitalists and workers, the chauvinism of the white workers, and the political backwardness of the American movement. Each of these are fundamental causes inherent in the economic and social structure of the country.

James played a central role in the development of the SWP's perspectives on 'the Negro Question'. In 1939, he taught a course for the SWP on 'The Destiny of the Negro' whose outline (reproduced here) was serialised in *Socialist Appeal*, and also wrote the path-breaking essay 'Revolution and the Negro' (reproduced in Chapter 11 of this volume) which appeared in *New International*. James's study of African-American realities in the United States, as well as his discussions with Trotsky, also provided the basis for the resolution adopted by the SWP at its 1939 convention – 'The Right of Self-Determination and the Negro in the United States' – which provided a unique perspective on the US Left.

1 Work among Negroes[5]
(*1929*)

Militant

The Party as a whole has always greatly underestimated the tremendous importance of revolutionary work among the Negro masses. The American Negroes are destined to play a great role in the coming revolution. The Negro proletariat of the North, and the great mass of Negro peasantry in the South, form a tremendous reservoir of revolutionary force, which has hitherto remained untapped. What is needed is a recognition of the importance of this work, a correct policy in it and serious attention to it.

It must be the main task of the Party in this field to mobilize the white workers to fight for the rights of the Negro masses to full social, economic and political equality and to unite with them in their struggles. Not an attitude of liberal paternalism, but an attitude of comradely support in a common battle, will give an impetus to the movement of struggle and resistance among the Negroes and will pave the way for the expansion of Party influence among them. The organization of the Negro masses for struggle goes hand in hand with the mobilization of the white workers for the defense of the Negroes against persecution and discrimination.

A prerequisite for this is the persistent struggle against race prejudice (white chauvinism) which is sedulously cultivated by the ruling class and dominates large sections of the white workers. It is even reflected in certain sections of the Party. This can be rooted out only by a broad ideological campaign explaining the reactionary, anti-working class origin, nature and result of bourgeois 'theories' of 'white supremacy', and utilizing every concrete instance in this sense. Such a campaign has not yet even been begun in our Party press. The attempt to deal with the question by purely mechanical methods is false.

The Negro question is also a national question, and the Party must raise the slogan of the right to self-determination for the Negroes. The effectiveness of this slogan is enhanced by the fact that there are scores of contiguous counties in the South where the Negro population is in the majority, and it there that

5 *Militant* 1929.

they suffer the most violent persecution and discrimination. This slogan will be the means especially of penetrating these Negro masses in the South and of mobilizing them for revolutionary struggle. The Party must at the same time decisively reject the false slogan of a 'Negro Soviet Republic in the South' at this time, raised by Pepper.[6] This theory is being propagated in the Party press and in official Party literature despite its rejection even at the Sixth Congress of the Comintern.

The work among the Negro masses must from the very beginning be based on leadership by the Negro proletariat and not by the Negro petty-bourgeoisie. The Party's orientation in the past has been based more on the latter than the former. Only through the domination of the Negro proletariat in the movement will the Party be able to advance the work of organizing the Negro peasants, tenant farmers, share croppers, etc., in the South in an effective and revolutionary sense.

6 John Pepper, a Hungarian whose actual name was Jozsef Pogany, was influential among leading US Communists in the late 1920s. Associated with the Communist International, he had been close to ultra-left Communist Bela Kun, who had headed the short-lived Hungarian Soviet Republic of 1919. Most historians have viewed him as an audacious yet destructive figure.

2 Trifling with the Negro Question[7]

(1931)

James P. Cannon

In its struggle against the workers' emancipation movement capitalism plays upon all the dark sentiments of ignorance, prejudice and superstition. This is seen daily and hourly in its endeavors to divide the workers and oppressed people along national, racial and religious lines. The very air we breathe is saturated with these prejudices which arise from class society like foul odors from decaying matter. The revolutionary struggle for the solidarity of labor is also a struggle for knowledge and light on these questions.

These problems have a particular importance and acuteness in America where the proletariat, enslaved by bourgeois ideology, is inflamed against the foreigner, the Jew and the Negro. Communism cannot be other than the mortal enemy of these devastating prejudices, and the Communist party is charged with an irreconcilable struggle against them. In no small degree the party of the proletariat is to be judged by the vigor, and also by the wisdom, with which it conducts this struggle. And it is self-evident that the Negro question takes first place within it. Communist ideas, Communist teaching and practice must break down the artificial wall which bourgeois prejudice has reared between the races; the Communists must be the heralds of a genuine solidarity between the exploited workers of the white race and the doubly exploited Negroes.

This is no question to be played with. Its seriousness and its difficulty are enormous. The deep-seated prejudices of the white workers will not be extirpated by force or terror any more than the justified suspicions of the Negroes will be removed by cajolery. In this field education takes the first place – patient, unceasing and systematic explanation combined with a genuine policy of equality in practice. Such a policy must be as free from discrimination on the one hand as it is free from flattery and demagogy on the other. Only along this path will real progress be recorded.

During their career as leaders of the party, Lovestone, Minor & Co., did their best to spoil this work, as they did others. For discrimination against

7 Cannon 1931a.

the Negroes – the instinctive attitude of all petty-bourgeois elements, but an attitude formally impossible in the name of Communism – they substituted an unscrupulous demagogy, and a policy of flattery, condescension and bribery of Negro intellectuals and careerists on the make. By this they attracted not a few outright scoundrels and adventurers while they repelled the self-reliant type of proletarian militants of the Negro race – the type which is offended, and justly so, no less by discrimination than by its twin, condescension. Thereby they arrested the real work among the Negroes and transformed the whole question into a factional football.

The Foster leaders, who have set for themselves the historic task of matching the Lovestone regime in unworthy demagogy and combining it with a stupidity all their own, are now having their fling at the Negro question – and at the Negro. They seem to labor always under a psychological fixation that their time is short and that what they do must be done quickly. The eradication of racial antagonisms, like the creation of a new trade union movement, is a small task for these high-pressure people; a task to be accomplished between plenums, by command. Prejudice against the Negro, that ugly poison which has been injected into the veins of the white workers, is to be removed at one stroke.

The *Daily Worker* of February 24 features the announcement of this major operation. Comrade Yokinen, a member of the party in Harlem, is accused of manifesting a prejudicial attitude toward Negro workers. One might think – if this is really the case and not a frame-up as we knew of in the days of the Lovestone leadership – that the incident could be made the occasion for an education of the party on the concrete case. Education however, particularly on such a question, requires a calm atmosphere; an atmosphere free from demagogy, hypocrisy and incitement; an atmosphere created by teachers of the proletariat, not by terrorizers.

But such methods are alien to the blustering vulgarians who feel the need to shout down their own prejudices of yesterday. They are going to summon the offending comrade to a mass trial! This trial, they announce, must be packed with Negro and white workers. Workers' organizations are asked to send delegations to the sport. The mass trial, they say further, will be the forerunner of similar trials all over the country. And all this is to be done so that the Negro workers will know that the Communist party is in deadly earnest in its fight for the Negro masses. Otherwise they would not know.

Just a moment, gentlemen! Aren't you insulting the intelligence of the Negro masses just a little? Aren't you stultifying the party with this stupid campaign of terror? If you have been educating the party properly how does it happen that race prejudice among party members is manifested all over the country? For the Negro masses racial persecution is a bitter actuality that confronts them every moment of their lives. They have learned to recognize all forms of this reactionary poison, including that form of so-called freedom from it which protests too much. Take care, triflers, lest your indecent demagogy becomes a boomerang for the party. Take care lest the Negro masses ask: If your own conscience is clear, why do you shout so loud?

3 The Negro and the Class Struggle[8]
(*1932*)

Hugo Oehler

In modern Europe, where capitalism has long ago had its decisive battles with feudalism, there still linger remnants of the past, feudal carry-overs complicating the solution of the proletariat's problems. This complication does not confront the workers of America, but in its place we have a variety of more conflicting inheritances. One of these was the carry-over of chattel slavery, a more backward system which gained supremacy over attempted feudalist inroads in new America by its economic advantages in the south for large scale agriculture production. The race form of chattel slavery in America gave impetus to this development.

The period when economic systems were gaining a foothold in new America cannot be separated from the class struggles in Europe at that time. The discovery of America which gave the feudal kingdoms greater land rights only accelerated the internal contradictions between the feudal land property relations and the developing bourgeois property relations. The commercial system of Europe was on the upgrade and the race for America reflected this. The discovery of America accelerated bourgeois development in Europe and logically expressed its growth in the colonies.

In Europe, feudalism ruled by the monopoly of land through the feudal estates and the Catholic Church and by hindering the developing handicraft system, keeping it part of the feudal hand-tool production. Free land in America played havoc with feudal relations, not just because there was free land, but primarily because with this free land developed the bourgeois property relations. Bourgeois relations are made difficult by free land, but the presence of large tracts of usable free land in a new country smashes all feudal attempts at stability when capitalism moves in at the same time.

8 Oehler 1932.

The Problem of Labor Power

Labor power and its control was the burning problem of the rulers of the colonies, not only its scarcity but also its control once obtained. Wage workers would soon disappear as free farmers, hunters and trappers. The white slaves and indentured slaves from Europe enabled the merchant and commercial classes to retain a sufficient supply of cheap labor power, but this could only be kept up by a constant influx from Europe. The land to the west was an escape for this labor supply. At the same time, however, this resulted in developing bourgeois agriculture relations in the northern part of the colonies.

In Europe, where capitalism was already at work appropriating those who had escaped feudalism through the handicraft system or by free peasant farming, and turning them into an army of propertyless wage slaves, there was no further escape. Either work as wage slaves, starve to death, or be killed or imprisoned as beggars and thieves – these were the alternatives. In America the escape to the west was still open. But this 'escape' laid the basis for the further development and strengthening of bourgeois domination in America.

In the south conditions were different. The kinds of crops and the climatic conditions called for a different form. The crops demanded large-scale agriculture production, and, capitalist agriculture relations were yet in their infancy. Feudalism could answer this request but, it could not furnish Serfs tied to the land and accustomed to the hot climate, when livelihood could be obtained by hunting and fishing, and trapping and free land for farming. The only suitable alternative, that rising bourgeois relations could tolerate was chattel slavery; bringing in large scale agriculture production, labor power bound in slavery, suitable for the climate. It was proven that the Indian could not serve this purpose. The white man from Europe had too easy an escape, even if it were possible to brand him as a chattel slave. The Negro race answered the need. Indentured slavery was the closest form to chattel slavery possible for the white man of Europe. It sufficed for the recruitment of a supply of labor in the north, but was not suitable for cotton and tobacco production in the south.

The traffic in Negro slaves was just as profitable as the traffic in indentured slaves. The chattel slave was more profitable for the south under the conditions. But in the latter period of Slavery in America the bourgeois relation had far outstripped the other forces and had shown that the wage slave was by far the most profitable for the master class. The conflict of these two antagonistic systems reached its climax in the Civil War. The forceful expropriation of the chattel masters' property in the form of the slaves put an end to the most dangerous internal enemy of the bourgeois system. However, this did not remove all the obstacles and give a free hand for capitalist penetration. The carry-over was as heavy as a mountain, hindering all speedy solutions.

The expropriation of the chattel masters of their property in the slaves, opened up new avenues for capitalist development and new markets for penetration. The dictatorship which the capitalists set up in the south after the Civil War soon reduced the chattel masters to submission to the new rulers of America. In fact, the dictatorship was becoming a boomerang. The former slave was taking his liberty seriously in an increasing degree. The exploiters of the wage slaves were not long in learning they had a hundred times more in common with the former chattel masters than with the former slaves. The freedom taken by the slaves had to be checked; the dictatorship against the chattel masters was modified when their resistance was broken, when they came to terms – the terms of the northern capitalists. From then on the capitalist supremacy took on a form of democracy for the white rulers of the south, and a new form of dictatorship against the Negro masses who were driven into worse slavery than before.

The New Role of the Negro

The freeing of the Negro from chattel slavery opened the door to a tremendous supply of cheap labor for the American capitalist. In fact the supply was too great for developing capitalism to absorb. However, it remained in reserve, ever ready to be used as expansion would warrant. Although capitalist development in America was fairly fast, the influx of European wage slaves, already trained, kept in check the rapid transformation of former chattel slaves into wage slaves.

The slaves' 'freedom' turned out to be a bourgeois joke. The former slave found himself, free from his former master's obligation to feed, clothe and shelter him, and keep him well as property, but not free from the economic exploitation and political domination of the capitalists and plantation owners. Left 'free', without economic means for a livelihood (land and tools), the Negro was free to starve to death, to submit to his former master in worse economic subjection than before, or to become a wage slave, providing he could find an employer. The 'free' Negro, without land or tools, had only one road to travel as a class and race – to submit to the new forms of exploitation, since conditions were not ripe for a successful revolution to free themselves from their white masters and obtain the land and tools of production for themselves. As a race they adjusted themselves to the new condition – unassimilated as wage slave; not held as chattel slaves; reflecting the old and looking at the new, but representing neither. They started the process by eking out an existence on the land and as servants of the white rulers; part slave, part serf and part wage slave.

At the time of the transformation only the Marxists realized the historic significance of the 'freeing' of the chattel slaves. The history of American labor cannot be written properly unless this current is traced back and properly connected with the development of the white and Negro proletariat and their allies in the coming revolution.

Westward expansion, internal northern American development and colonial expansion could tolerate concessions to the white rulers of the south in return for their political support as plantation owners. Rule the Negroes in your own state as you like so long as you support your political hegemony, said the northern capitalist; and besides you can make more profits by your support than by resistance. And just as the freedom of the American Revolution amounted to so many words and pieces of paper for the workers and farmers, so much did the freedom of the Civil War amount to for the Negro masses.

Revolutions and civil wars are always followed by 'counter-revolution' (reaction, terror, etc. against the exploited) unless the workers are able to carry the civil war over to the point where they seize power for themselves. During the struggle, concessions are necessary to gain the support of the exploited for the exploiters' war. But once the former exploiter is defeated, the new exploiter makes haste to bring about a new alignment with the former enemy, under the hegemony of the new exploiter, against the exploited. The results of the civil war only confirmed this truth again.

The legal forms of capitalist rule were not sufficient for the needs of the plantation owners of the south. Lynch law was added – a necessary measure used against the whole exploited class whenever the formal legal means do not suffice to keep them in check. Lynch law exists for the Negro every minute of the day and night. But it is not the elimination of the lynch law that will free the Negro. Rather lynch law, as such, can only be done away with by the overthrow of capitalism. In the struggle to overthrow capitalism a necessary part is the constant struggle against lynch law and all forms of discrimination (discriminating law prohibiting admittance to public and private buildings, schools universities, parks, etc.; restrictions regarding jury service and civil service; disenfranchisement; prohibition of inter-marriage; lease system, chain gangs, etc., and admittance to working class organizations, trade unions etc.).

The Negro in America – bourgeoisie, petit-bourgeoisie, farmer and worker – stands as an oppressed racial minority, a national minority. Of course they are a minority of the nation; and in this sense, a mechanical one, they are a national minority. But in the political sense it is not so. A national minority are a people not only with racial differences, but a people with special differences of language, custom and religion, or with a separate national character or national interests. Politically speaking, national minorities always have the integral element of racial minority (race or branch of race). But a racial minority, in the hodge-podge of capitalist society, does not necessarily signify national minority. On the other hand, racial oppression does not always mean the oppression of a national minority. This oppression may be inflicted on a national majority, as in the case of China and India. One could give countless examples of this kind in the past history. America, the outstanding representative of Capitalism, is the best example to show the differences between a racial minority and a national minority. America is now a nation and its people take pride in their nationality, regardless of the descent, especially those Americans of the second and third generation of foreign descent. In the United States we find many racial groups making up the nation as 'Americans'. The Swedes, English, Spanish or French born in America, who may still have the 'pure blood' of their race, can be considered as a racial minority (races of Europe) of the population of the United States. In this way they are catalogued mechanically as part of a national group. But, in spite of this, they cannot be considered as a national minority in the political sense.

The Negro was brought from Africa, from a system of barbarism where nations as political states were only in the process of formation. He was hurried through the process and now is part of Capitalism. He brought with him racial characteristics, as well as traditions and modes of the past. However, his life in America has overbalanced that which was brought from the past, has modified it, has changed it. Capitalist America has forced him to adopt the language and religion and modes of the country and of the economic system as the *determining factors* of this part of his make-up. The more complicated economic structure here in America has swallowed up the past. And, although it cannot be eliminated and expresses itself in the new make-up, it is not the determining factor of the American Negro.

As an oppressed racial minority it is one question, and the question is the race form of the class struggle. As an oppressed national minority it is another question. The attempt to construe the Negro question this way can only result, not in nationalism for the Negro, but in national reformism for the 'Marxist'. The idea of self-determination for national minorities (which include races or racial groups) is a compromise and concession; it is a transitional measure, a weapon against capitalism, providing it is used at the proper time, where no other road out is possible. This is not the situation in America with the American Negro, as the Stalinites contend.

Objective conditions are still on the move for the Negro, and particularly since the world war. The shortage of labor in the War period, the stoppage of the immigration flow, and the development of capitalism at a faster pace in the South – all this moved the Negro into the stream of class struggle. The racial expression of the oppression of the Negro is no reason for a revolutionist to see the form (racial oppression) and enlarge this out of its true relation to the content of the class struggle.

The decisive section of the Negroes, in relation to the problem considered, is no longer the one which is 'half slaves-half serfs', it is not petty-bourgeois Negro. The decisive section in the class struggle, in the North as well as the South – in America as a whole, which is the proper way to look at the problem – is the Negro proletariat. His weight as a proletarian, if it is the decisive part (and even Stalinism does not deny this in words), will make up for his weakness in the 'South' where Stalinism says the slogan of self-determination is necessary.

The complicated race form of the class struggle for the Negro lays the main burden upon the Negro proletariat in relation to the rest of the Negroes, but not in relation to the white proletariat. The main burden of the relation of the Negro to the white proletariat rests upon the shoulders of the latter. The white worker must be ready to meet the Negro more than half way. He must go to the point – no matter how far – for the victory of the workers over capitalism. The Negro worker is a necessary part of this problem for the victory not of the *white* workers but of the *workers* regardless of their race.

But the solution cannot be brought closer by artificial slogans, such as the slogan of self-determination. We must minimize the desires of the Negro Petty-Bourgeoisie and enlarge the form of the proletarian interest of the Negro who is, like the white worker, choked with bourgeois ideology. National minorities must be won as allies to the proletariat, if they are oppressed minorities. But in winning them as allies we do not approach the workers of this nationality or race as such. This would be national opportunism. We approach these workers as workers. We know the bourgeois element of the national minorities under Czarism were no better and often worse than the dominating bourgeoisie against the workers. Likewise the Negro bourgeois elements have already proven they can outstrip their white masters. We want allies, but not on the basis of concessions and compromises on principles. But the Negro proletarian is no Negro ally – he is a worker. The cropper and dirt farmer are allies and must be won as such. But in this relation the Negro industrial and agriculture worker is decisive.

A compromise on principle means that the 'allies' have captured the proletariat. The program of the Communists (Marxists) is the only one possible for the American Negro for social, political and economic equality and freedom. The road is the road of class struggle, not that of 'preparation stages' – self-determination, democratic dictatorship of the Proletariat and Peasantry, four class party, workers and peasant parties, peoples revolution, etc. – which give the petty-bourgeois Negroes organizational and political control. Preparation stages in struggles are necessary, but not compromises on principle, passed off as preparation stages.

We must consider slogans and tactics for the race form of the class struggle. This is essential in order to defeat the bosses' policy of divide and rule. Slogans and tactics against the legal and extra-legal discrimination and lynch laws are the order of the day. A will to fight the battles of the Negro masses, as the party has already demonstrated, is a big step forward. Let us not step backward into the swamp of national reformism.

The Negro of America was not snatched from a state or nation in Africa with national aspirations and ideologies. Neither has America given the Negro as a Negro the material base for nationalism as such. The class struggle of the Negro is not cloaked in a national form (complicated with the national bourgeois influence) that calls for the slogan of self-determination at special stages and under special conditions in the struggle. It is cloaked in the race form. The American Negro bourgeoisie elements are no ally of ours. The problem is complicated enough without adding the national complex to it, which in this case can only result in national reformism.

The racial form of social conflicts has taken the national form where the racial group obtained an economic unit. This has been the case in the past. Blood ties, gens and clans in the process of development from primitive Communism through the stages to an exploiter's society, naturally crystallized as such. But the American Negro presents no such picture. His is a different and far more difficult problem.

The Socialist tells us in substance, that the workers must not seize power in backward countries. We must let the bourgeois revolution take its course develop its industries (nationalism), and then we will win it over. Stalinism tells us that we must move the American Negro into the feeling of national consciousness through the slogan of self-determination. Of course Stalinism will say, 'No, not national consciousness'. But we will answer: The slogan of self-determination for a racial group that does not have a material base for such has even less logic than the socialist position. At least, these non-Marxists speak of a material base for bourgeois power, in one form or the other, in backward sections.

When the proletariat takes power, the Negro worker will take his place as an equal with the white worker. Where the Negroes are the majority (parts of South, etc.), this majority will dominate the Soviets.

The Negro worker and farmer, being even more suppressed and exploited than his white brother requires special consideration from the revolutionary party, even though, economically, he is a worker or dirt farmer. This double exploitation and class suppression is carried out through the race form of the class struggle, which does not include the national form in the political sense. Stalinism says, because the Negro constitutes a doubly exploited racial minority, and regardless of the argument on nationalism, it is proper to present the slogan of Self-Determination for oppressed racial minorities as well as national minorities.

Let us consider it in this light for a moment, in spite of the arguments already presented. Adding to what has been said about the slogan of self-determination, we must say that it can only be realized, so far as the American Negro is concerned, after the overthrow of capitalism in the South, which means the overthrow of American imperialism as such. Is this transition step needed then? The victory of the proletariat includes within it the solution of the double exploitation of the Negro masses. As for the Negro bourgeoisie, the Negro and white workers will take care of them just as they will take care of the white exploiters. The Soviets of the South will solve this problem, even though special efforts will have to be leveled against reactionary ideological carryovers. But the main struggle against the reactionary ideology is not a problem of the Negroes, but of the whites.

But how about the slogan as a means of winning the Negro masses today for the proletarian revolution? Yes, the slogan will win over many petty-bourgeois elements on the basis of national reformism. But we don't want the Negro petty-bourgeoisie as allies on that basis. The Negro worker, industrial and agricultural, is not even in this problem, because we do not use a slogan of self-determination for workers. We win them as workers, even though different racial and sectional (youth and women, etc.) tactics are necessary.

4 The Negro Question in America[9]

(*1933*)

Leon Trotsky, Arne Swabeck, Pierre Frank

Swabeck: We have in this question within the American League no noticeable differences of an important character, nor have we yet formulated a program. I present therefore only the views which we have developed in general.

How must we view the position of the American Negro: As a national minority or as a racial minority? This is of the greatest importance for our program.

The Stalinists maintain as their main slogan the one of 'self-determination for the Negroes' and demand in connection therewith a separate state and state rights for the Negroes in the black belt. The practical application of the latter demand has revealed much opportunism. On the other hand, I acknowledge that in the practical work amongst the Negroes, despite the numerous mistakes, the [Communist] party can also record some achievements. For example, in the Southern textile strikes, where to a large extent the color lines were broken down.

Weisbord, I understand, is in agreement with the slogan of 'self-determination' and separate state rights. He maintains that is the application of the theory of the permanent revolution for America.

We proceed from the actual situation: There are approximately 13 million Negroes in America; the majority are in the Southern states (black belt). In the Northern states the Negroes are concentrated in the industrial communities as industrial workers, in the South they are mainly farmers and sharecroppers.

Trotsky: Do they rent from the state or from private owners?

Swabeck: From private owners, from white farmers and plantation owners; some Negroes own the land they till.

The Negro population of the North is kept on a lower level – economically, socially and culturally; in the South under oppressive Jim Crow conditions. They are barred from many important trade unions. During and since the war the migration from the South has increased; perhaps about four to five

---

9 Trotsky, Swabeck, Frank 1933.

million Negroes now live in the North. The Northern Negro population is overwhelmingly proletarian, but also in the South the proletarianization is progressing.

Today none of the Southern states have a Negro majority. This lends emphasis to the heavy migration, to the North. We put the question thus: Are the Negroes, in a political sense, a national minority or a racial minority? The Negroes have become fully assimilated, Americanized, and their life in America has overbalanced the traditions of the past, modified and changed them. We cannot consider the Negroes a national minority in the sense of having their own separate language. They have no special national customs, or special national culture or religion; nor have they any special national minority interests. It is impossible to speak of them as a national minority in this sense. It is therefore our opinion that the American Negroes are a racial minority whose position and interests are subordinated to the class relations of the country and depending upon them.

To us the Negroes represent an important factor in the class struggle, almost a decisive factor. They are an important section of the proletariat. There is also a Negro petty bourgeoisie in America but not as powerful or as influential or playing the role of the petty bourgeoisie and bourgeoisie among the nationally oppressed people (colonial).

The Stalinist slogan 'self-determination' is in the main based upon an estimate of the American Negroes as a national minority, to be won over as allies. To us the question occurs: Do we want to win the Negroes as allies on such a basis and who do we want to win, the Negro proletariat or the Negro petty bourgeoisie? To us it appears that we will with this slogan win mainly the petty bourgeoisie and we cannot have much interest in winning them as allies on such a basis? We recognize that the poor farmers and sharecroppers are the closest allies of the proletariat but it is our opinion that they can be won as such mainly on the basis of the class struggle. Compromise on this principled question would put the petty bourgeois allies ahead of the proletariat and the poor farmers as well. We recognize the existence of definite stages of development which require specific slogans. But the Stalinist slogan appears to us to lead directly to the 'democratic dictatorship of the proletariat and peasantry'. The unity of the workers, black and white, we must prepare proceeding from a class basis, but in that it is necessary to also recognize the racial issues and in addition to the class slogans also advance the racial slogans. It is our opinion that in this respect the main slogan should be 'social, political and economic equality for the Negroes', as well as the slogans which flow therefrom. This slogan is naturally quite different from the Stalinist slogan of 'self-determination' for a national minority. The [Communist] party leaders maintain that the Negro workers and farmers can be won only on the basis of this slogan. To begin with it was advanced for the Negroes throughout the country, but today only for the Southern states. It is our opinion that we can win the Negro workers only on a class basis advancing also the racial slogans for the necessary intermediary stages of development. In this manner we believe also the poor Negro farmers can best be won as direct allies.

In the main the problem of slogans in regard to the Negro question is the problem of a practical program.

Trotsky: The point of view of the American comrades appears to me not fully convincing. 'Self-determination' is a democratic demand. Our American comrades advance as against this democratic demand, the liberal demand. This liberal demand is, moreover, complicated. I understand what 'political equality' means. But what is the meaning of economic and social equality within capitalist society? Does that mean a demand to public opinion that all enjoy the equal protection of the laws? But that is political equality. The slogan 'political, economic and social equality' sounds equivocal and while it is not clear to me it nevertheless suggests itself easy of misinterpretation.

The Negroes are a race and not a nation: Nations grow out of the racial material under definite conditions. The Negroes in Africa are not yet a nation but they are in the process of building a nation. The American Negroes are on a higher cultural level. But while they are there under the pressure of the Americans they become interested in the development of the Negroes in Africa. The American Negro will develop leaders for Africa, that one can say with certainty and that in turn will influence the development of political consciousness in America.

We do, of course, not obligate the Negroes to become a nation; if they are, then that is a question of their consciousness, that is, what they desire and what they strive for. We say: If the Negroes want that then we must fight against imperialism to the last drop of blood, so that they gain the right, wherever and how they please, to separate a piece of land for themselves. The fact that they are today not a majority in any state does not matter. It is not a question of the authority of the states but of the Negroes. That in the overwhelming Negro territory also whites have existed and will remain henceforth is not the question and we do not need today to break our heads over a possibility that sometime the whites will be suppressed by the Negroes. In any case the suppression of the Negroes pushes them toward a political and national unity.

That the slogan 'self-determination' will rather win the petty bourgeois instead of the workers – that argument holds good also for the slogan of equality. It is clear that the special Negro elements who appear more in the public eye (businessmen, intellectuals, lawyers, etc.) are more active and react more actively against the inequality. It is possible to say that the liberal demand just as well as the democratic one in the first instance will attract the petty bourgeois and only later the workers.

If the situation was such that in America common actions existed between the white and the colored workers, that the class fraternization had already become a fact, then perhaps the arguments of our comrades would have a basis – I do not say that they would be correct – then perhaps we would separate the colored workers from the white if we commence with the slogan 'self-determination'.

But today the white workers in relation to the Negroes are the oppressors, scoundrels, who persecute the black and the yellow, hold them in contempt and lynch them. When the Negro workers today unite with their own petty bourgeois that is because they are not yet sufficiently developed to defend their elementary rights. To the workers in the Southern states the liberal demand for 'social, political and economic equality' would undoubtedly mean progress, but the demand for 'self-determination' a greater progress. However, with the slogan 'social, political and economic equality' they can much easier be misled ('according to the law you have this equality').

When we are so far that the Negroes say we want autonomy; they then take a position hostile toward American imperialism. At that stage already the workers will be much more determined than the petty bourgeoisie. The workers will then see that the petty bourgeoisie is incapable of struggle and gets nowhere, but they will also recognize simultaneously that the white Communist workers fight for their demands and that will push them, the Negro proletarians, toward Communism.

Weisbord is correct in a certain sense that the 'self-determination' of the Negroes belongs to the question of the permanent revolution in America. The Negroes will through their awakening, through their demand for autonomy, and through the democratic mobilization of their forces, be pushed on toward the class basis. The petty bourgeoisie will take up the demand for 'social, political, and economic equality' and for 'self-determination' but prove absolutely incapable in the struggle; the Negro proletariat will march crier the petty bourgeoisie in the direction toward the proletarian revolution. That is perhaps for them the most important road. I can therefore see no reason why we should not advance the demand for 'self-determination'.

I am not sure if the Negroes do not also in the Southern states speak their own Negro language. Now that they are being lynched just because of being Negroes they naturally fear to speak their Negro language; but when they are set free their Negro language will again become alive. I will advise the American comrades to study this question very seriously, including the language in the Southern states. Because of all these reasons I would in this question rather lean toward the standpoint of the [Communist] party; of course, with the observation: I have never studied this question and in my remarks I proceed from the general considerations. I base myself only upon the arguments brought forward by the American comrades. I find them insufficient and consider them a certain concession to the point of view of American chauvinism, which seems to me to be dangerous.

What can we lose in this question when we go ahead with our demands, and what have the Negroes today to lose? We do not compel them to separate from the States, but they have the full right to self-determination when they so desire and we will support and defend them with all the means at our disposal in the conquestion [conquest] of this right, the same as we defend all oppressed peoples.

Swabeck: I admit that you have advanced powerful arguments but I am not yet entirely convinced. The existence of a special Negro language in the Southern states is possible; but in general all American Negroes speak English. They are fully assimilated. Their religion is the American Baptist and the language in their churches is likewise English.

Economic equality we do not at all understand in the sense of the law. In the North (as of course also in the Southern states) the wages for Negroes are always lower than for white workers and mostly their hours are longer, that is so to say accepted as a natural basis. In addition, the Negroes are allotted the most disagreeable work. It is because of these conditions that we demand economic equality for the Negro workers.

We do not contest the right of the Negroes to self-determination. That is not the issue of our disagreement with the Stalinists. But we contest the correctness of the slogan of 'self-determination' as a means to win the Negro masses. The impulse of the Negro population is first of all in the direction toward equality in a social, political and economic sense. At present the party advances the slogan for 'self-determination' only for the Southern states. Of course, one can hardly expect that the Negroes from the Northern industries should want to return to the South and there are no indications of such a desire. On the contrary, their unformulated demand is for 'social, political and economic equality' based upon the conditions under which they live. That is also the case in the South. It is because of this that we believe this to be the important racial slogan. We do not look upon the Negroes as being under national oppression in the same sense as the oppressed colonial peoples. It is our opinion that the slogan of the Stalinists tends to lead the Negroes away from the class basis and more in the direction of the racial basis. That is the main reason for our being opposed to it.

We are of the belief that the racial slogan in the sense as presented by us leads directly toward the class basis.

Frank: Are there special Negro movements in America?

Swabeck: Yes, several. First we had the Garvey movement based upon the aim of migration to Africa. It had a large following but busted up as a swindle. Now there is not much left of it. Its slogan was the creation of a Negro republic in Africa. Other Negro movements in the main rest upon a foundation of social and political equality demands as, for example, the League [National Association] for Advancement of Colored People. This is a large racial movement.

Trotsky: I believe that also the demand for 'social, political and economic equality' should remain and I do not speak *against* this demand. It is progressive to the extent that it is not realized. The explanation of Comrade Swabeck in regard to the question of economic equality is very important. But that alone does not yet decide the question of the Negro fate as such, the question of the 'nation', etc. According to the arguments of the American comrades one could say for example that also Belgium has no right as a 'nation'. The Belgians are Catholics, and a large section of them speak French. What if France would annex them with such an argument? Also the Swiss people, through their historical connection, feel themselves, despite different languages and religion, as one nation. An abstract criterion is not decisive in this question, but much more decisive is the historical consciousness, their feelings and their impulses. But that also is not determined accidentally but rather by the general conditions. The question of religion has absolutely nothing to do with this question of the nation. The Baptism of the Negro is something entirely different from the Baptism of Rockefeller: These are two different religions.

The political argument rejecting the demand for 'self-determination' is doctrinarism. That we heard always in Russia in regard to the question of 'self-determination'. The Russian experiences have shown to us that the groups who live on a peasant basis retain peculiarities, their customs, their language, etc., and given the opportunity they develop again.

The Negroes are not yet awakened and they are not yet united with the white workers. 99.9 per cent of the American workers are chauvinists, in relation to the Negroes they are hangmen, and they are so also toward the Chinese. It is necessary to teach the American beasts. It is necessary to make them understand that the American state is not their state and that they do not have to be the guardians of this state. Those American workers who say: 'The Negroes should separate when they so desire and we will defend them against our American police' – those are revolutionists, I have confidence in them.

The argument that the slogan for 'self-determination' leads away from the class basis is an adaptation to the ideology of the white workers. The Negro can be developed to a class standpoint only when the white worker is educated. On the whole the question of the colonial people is in the first instance a question of the development of the metropolitan worker.

The American worker is indescribably reactionary. It is shown today that he is not even yet won for the idea of social insurance. Because of this the American Communists are obligated to advance reform demands.

When today the Negroes do not demand self-determination that is naturally for the same reason that the white workers do not yet advance the slogan of the proletarian dictatorship. The Negro has not yet got it into his poor black head that he dares to carve out for himself a piece of the great and mighty States. But the white worker must meet the Negroes half way and say to them: 'When you want to separate you will have our support'. Also the Czech workers came only through the disillusion with their own state to Communism.

I believe that by the unheard-of political and theoretical backwardness and the unheard-of economic advance the awakening of the working class will proceed quite rapidly. The old ideological covering will burst, all questions will emerge at once, and since the country is so economically mature the adaptation of the political and theoretical to the economic level will be achieved very rapidly. It is then possible that the Negroes will become the most advanced section. We have already a similar example in Russia. The Russians were the European Negroes. It is very possible that the Negroes also through the self-determination will proceed to the proletarian dictatorship in a couple of gigantic strides, ahead of the great bloc of white workers. They will then furnish the vanguard. I am absolutely sure that they will in any case fight better than the white workers. That, however, can happen only provided the Communist party carries on an uncompromising merciless struggle not against the supposed national prepossessions of the Negroes but against the colossal prejudices of the white workers and gives it no concession whatever.

Swabeck: It is then your opinion that the slogan for 'self-determination' will be a means to set the Negroes into motion against American imperialism?

Trotsky: Naturally, thereby that the Negroes can carve out their own state out of mighty America and with the support of the white workers their self-consciousness develops enormously. The reformists and the revisionists have written much on the subject that capitalism is carrying on the work of civilization in Africa and if the peoples of Africa are left to themselves they will be the more exploited by businessmen, etc., much more than now where they at least have a certain measure of lawful protection.

To a certain extent this argument can be correct. But in this case it is also first of all a question of the European workers: without their liberation the real colonial liberation is also not possible. When the white worker performs the role of the oppressor, he cannot liberate himself, much less the colonial peoples. The self-determination of the colonial peoples can, in certain periods, lead to different results; in the final instance, however, it will lead to the struggle against imperialism and to the liberation of the colonial peoples.

The Austrian Social Democracy (particularly Renner) also put before the [first world] war the question of the national minorities abstractly. They argued likewise that the slogan for 'self-determination' would only lead the workers away from the class standpoint and that such minority states could not live independently. Was this way of putting the question correct or false? It was abstract. The Austrian Social Democrats said that the national minorities were not nations. What do we see today? The separate pieces [of the old Austro-Hungarian empire, headed by the Habsburgs] exist, rather bad, but they exist. The Bolsheviks fought in Russia always for the self-determination of the national minorities including the right of complete separation. And yet, by achieving self-determination these groups remained with the Soviet Union. If the Austrian Social Democracy had before accepted a correct policy in this question, they would have said to the national minority groups: 'You have the full right to self-determination, we have no interest whatever to keep you in the hands of the Hapsburg monarchy' – it would then have been possible after the revolution to create a great Danube federation. The dialectic of the developments shows that where the tight centralism existed the state went to pieces and where the complete self-determination was proposed a real state emerged and remained united.

The Negro question is of enormous importance for America. The League must undertake a serious discussion of this question, perhaps in an internal bulletin.

5 Shifts in the Negro Question[10]
(*1934*)

John G. Wright (*Joseph Vanzler*)

Negroes in the United States in 1930 numbered about 11,900,000. About 80% live in 16 southern states and the District of Columbia.

Historically the Negro was rural and agricultural. He was primarily a cultivator of cotton. Since the center of the cotton area is in the South, the Negro population was from the very beginning concentrated there. In this sense it is still correct to speak of the Negro as primarily 'southern'. In approaching the Negro problem these historical aspects have been stressed more than sufficiently, but the profound changes that have taken place among the Negroes during the last few decades have been neglected almost completely.

Originally, the history of the Negro in America was the history of cotton. But today, it is an anachronism to view the Negro as primarily a backward farmer confined to cotton areas. In this sense it is no longer correct to speak of the Negro as primarily 'southern'. The history of the Negro has become directly linked with modern industry. He has been separated from the soil and suddenly placed in the midst of the complex modern industrial structure. This is a fact. And, obviously, it is necessary to establish this fact because a tendency still prevails to view the Negro, especially the southern Negro, in terms of those conditions that prevailed at the outbreak of the Civil War, and in the period immediately following. The Negro, especially the southern Negro, is no longer overwhelmingly agricultural.

In 1860 the Negroes were most densely concentrated in the South, particularly within the boundaries of six cotton-growing states, Mississippi, Georgia, Alabama, South Carolina, Louisiana and Arkansas. Naturally enough these states then could serve as a focus in any consideration of the Negro problem. In 1860 what was true of the Negroes in these states applied largely to the Negroes of the entire South, who comprised more than 92% of the total Negro population, and who were overwhelmingly agricultural. But to take these six states as our point of departure today can lead only to most grievous errors. The pro-

10 Wright 1934.

found economic changes that the South underwent following the Civil War met with the greatest inertia precisely in these states. To this day they have remained predominantly agricultural with cotton still the main crop. (They produced 63% of the cotton crop in 1930). Only within this area have the Negroes remained largely rural and agricultural.

The Negro population has been becoming urbanized (i.e. proletarianized) at an ever increasing tempo. For three decades following the Civil War, for the US as a whole, it remained rural and agricultural (in 1890, it was 80.6% rural and only 19.4% urban); in the three decades following, and particularly in the last decade the trend has been toward towns and cities. In 1920 the shift was to 66% rural and 34%; urban; in 1930 the shift was much more accentuated, 56.3% rural, 43.7% urban. The shift was by no means restricted solely to the North. In 1930 the number of Negroes living in southern cities exceeded those in northern cities. Concurrently, while the Negro population was growing in other states (southern as well as northern), the Negro population in this *Old South* area remained stationary over a period of decades. The Negro population of these six states was in 1910 – 5,087,000; in 1920 – 5,079,000; in 1930 – 5,073,000. During the same period the Negro population in the US had increased more than 20%. This clearly denotes an intense migration from these agricultural states into industrial sections. However, it should not be concluded that deep-going changes have not been occurring within the Old South itself. Here too, the industrial development has been making gigantic strides forward, breaking down the old economic structure, and the original economic differentiation between the industrial North and the agricultural South. The development has been uneven, but the same process has been going on here as elsewhere, only at a different rate. The historical, cultural and economic conditions of the Old South tended to retard the process. What has most tended to obscure its actual course is the fact that even today more than 42% of the total Negro population still lives within the boundaries of these six states. In 1910 the same area held 51.7% of the total Negro population.

More than two-thirds of the total Negro farmers in the South and almost three-fourths of the tenant farmers are to be found in these same six states. A study limited to this area must necessarily fail to reflect the fundamental changes in Negro life.

From the density of the Negro population within this area, conclusions have been drawn that are highly fallacious, particularly the conclusions that the Negro problem is primarily geographic, i.e., southern, and agricultural, and therefore a 'national' problem. Flowing from this, the attempt is made to reduce the entire problem to the analysis of only this particular section of the South, the famous 'Black Belt' sector. For the core of this sector stretches precisely over the states we have been discussing. Just as it is possible to draw any kind of a triangle within a circle, so it is possible to construct within this territory a particular 'well defined area' in which the Negroes would compose the majority of the population. But just as what applies to the inscribed triangle need not apply to the circle, just so what applies to this particular sector need not apply at all elsewhere. Such a sector may be, and in this case it actually is, arbitrary and artificial. In the first place the 'Black Belt' embraces a territory that has remained primarily rural and overwhelmingly agricultural; secondly, even according to the most sanguine estimates it includes only about 3,000,000 Negroes, or approximately one-fourth of the total Negro population. Even the Stalinists claim for it only 'some 3,320,000 Negroes'. The 'Black Belt' is a very arbitrary sort of a belt. The six states over which the core of it extends comprise about 500 counties, with a population of 8 million whites and 5 million Negroes, that is, 61.5% white. To obtain a 'solid area' in which the Negroes form the majority of the population, it is necessary to select particular counties which must be contiguous. Some 200 counties can be squeezed into this requirement. The most imposing picture of the Black Belt is painted by the Stalinists. Yet even they claim for it only that, 'In 192 counties they made up from 50% to 75% of the population; in 36 counties they comprise more than 75% of the population' (*Labor Fact Book*, p. 78. Figures based on 1920 census).

Leaving aside for the moment all other considerations it is obvious that one cannot equate even the actual area over which the bulk of the Negroes is spread – some 24 states including the District of Columbia – with a handpicked area of 192 counties, in which the whites compose an insignificant minority only in 36. Moreover such a belt, to be consistent, must exclude the remaining 300 counties in which there are *only* about 2 million Negroes. It also throws out of focus not only the millions of northern Negroes, but also a greater southern population than the one actually included, some 3,300,000 Negroes in the directly adjoining states of Texas, North Carolina, Tennessee, Virginia, and Florida, in which there are 11,460,000 whites. Needless to say, the constructors of 'Black Belts' do not and cannot remain consistent with their own premises. They include perforce within it counties that explode the premises of Negro majority, of contiguity and of 'well marked area'. No two maps drawn of the 'future' Negro State tally. The most appalling and ambitious ones include practically the entire South. The least pretentious would include the cities of Richmond, Memphis, Vicksburg, New Orleans and Savannah, which with the exception of Savannah are predominantly white.

By focusing our attention on the 'Black Belt' we cannot understand the significance of the decisive economic and social shifts in the South in general and among the Negroes in particular. By thinking in terms of the 'Black Belt' we can only think of the Negro problem in terms of conditions that prevailed in the middle of the 19th century. The basic factors in the Negro problem are not geographic divisions, or state boundaries, or county lines. The basic factors are economic. The so-called 'Black Belt' was and still remains predominantly rural and agricultural. In the meantime, the economic development has been surging over the old state and new county lines. Under the impact of economic forces the mass of the Negro population in and outside of the six states has been rapidly shifting from rural to urban, from agriculture to industry. This shift, which has been going on at an ever increasing rate, must continue to take place in accordance with the internal logic of American capitalist development. This process, which has already vitally affected the 'Black Belt' itself, although it has not yet disintegrated it, must proceed at an ever increasing tempo. The agricultural aspect of the Negro problem, particularly in this phase of it, provides the subject for an independent analysis. Suffice it to say that the entire agricultural base of the South as a whole is being disintegrated not only by the permanent crisis of American agriculture, and the industrialization of the South, but also by the mechanization of cotton farming. All these factors bear most directly and immediately upon the Negro farmer who is being driven from the land into urban centers and into the ranks either of the proletariat or the unemployed. In the period immediately before us we shall witness accelerated changes in the 'Black Belt' proper, precisely along the lines indicated by what has already happened elsewhere in the South. The Negro farmer is being driven from the land.

This movement has already penetrated deeply into the heart of the 'Black Belt' itself. We have already pointed out its stationary or declining population and also the fact that more than two-thirds of the Negro farms in the South and almost three-fourths of the tenant farmers are in the 'Black Belt' area. What holds true of the entire South bears most directly upon the Negro farmers in these six states. In the entire South, in 1920, there were about 980,000 Negro farmers of whom 714,000 or about three-fourths were tenants; in 1930 the Negro farmers dropped to 880,000 of whom 699,000 were tenants or more than three-fourths. At the same time, only 46.6% of the white farmers in the South were tenants. The pressure to which the agricultural Negro is being subjected is brought out still more clearly by comparing the trend among Negro farmers with that among white southern farmers. Between 1920 and 1930 the number of white farmers dropped also, but only 1.6% as compared with more than 7% for the Negroes. While the Negro tenants decreased absolutely, the number of white tenant farmers increased. At the same time the number of white share croppers almost approached that of the Negro croppers: white, 383,381; Negro, 392,897. The white farmer is being pauperized at a different rate from the Negro. But the pauperization of the white farmer accelerates the rate at which the Negro is being driven from the land. And in point of fact this has already crystallized itself definitely: the economic base of the Negro has already shifted from agriculture to industry. The crux of the Negro problem is in modern industry and not in the old agricultural South.

The movement of the Negroes to the North has been nothing but an integral part of the urbanization of the Negro. The movement northward began at the same time as the urban shift in the South. The growth of Negro population in the North from 9.4% in 1890 to 20.2% in 1930 is only an integral part of the shift to cities and towns of the Negro population as a whole from 19.4% of the total in 1890 to 43.7% in 1930. The sweep of this shift is apparent at a glance, if we examine some figures.

In 1930 there were more *adult* Negroes in towns and cities than remained on land. According to the last census, adult urban Negroes – in the entire US between 20 and 44 years of age – numbered 2,820,000; those who remained on the land numbered 2,197,000.[11]

Over 3,800,000 or almost two-thirds of those gainfully employed were engaged in occupations other than agriculture in which there had remained only 36.1%, a drop of almost a million from the number in 1910 when 84.6% of those gainfully employed were engaged in agriculture.

Equally illustrative of the intensity of the shift is the fact that the Negro population in 79 major cities increased over 60% in a single decade, 1920–1930, leaping from 1,920,000 in 1920 to 3,150,000 in 1930. Even in 1920, at the inception of the 'Black Belt' ballyhoo, this trend away from the land was clearly indicated, for already at that time only two-fifths of those gainfully employed were engaged in agriculture.

The consequences of this urbanization have been far-reaching. The relation of the Negro to industry has radically altered. Until as late as 1914, the Negro served as a reserve to draw on in times of labor shortage or strikes. By 1930

11 [Footnote by Wright] As the obverse phase of this shift, we naturally find that the bulk of children, adolescents as well as the aged remained behind on the land. Thus in 1930 there were:

	Negroes under 5	5–9	10–14	18–19	65 and over
Rural	802,000	900,000	843,000	803,000	233,611
Urban	427,000	468,000	407,000	447,000	139,108

the Negro had become an integral part of the labor force in practically every important industry.

In the movement away from the land, two peak waves are to be observed, one in 1916–1919, the other in 1921–24; but they were only a part of the continuous trend and not a sudden isolated exodus. Once again we stress that underlying the ebbs and flows of this movement are not geographic or 'sentimental' causes but profound economic forces. The labor agencies of large industries had a great deal more to do with it than the activities of the Ku Kluxers in the South.

The Negroes' function as a labor reserve led to their utilization as strikebreakers. But from this role of a labor reserve they have become transformed into integral parts of the industrial structure. Negroes compose 7.6% of the total labor force in the mining industry; 10.3% in transport; 7.2% in manufacturing and machine industry. Although they are only 9.7% of the US population, they composed in 1930, 28% of the unskilled workers in large meat packing concerns; 16.2% of the unskilled in the steel industry; and 22.7% of the laborers in building trades. Instances are not lacking of strikes in which the proletarianized Negro served as the backbone while the bosses depended upon Negro strikebreakers primarily recruited from rural districts. The Negro has definitely become an integral part of the proletariat, preponderantly unskilled and most intensely exploited.

The Negro problem is and will be to an ever increasing degree a working class problem; and the crucial criterion is the economic and not the geographic distribution of the Negro population. By themselves statistics are meaningless such as that in 1930 almost four-fifths of the Negro population still lived in the so-called South, or that the bulk of the Negro population is spread over 24 states and that almost 20% lives in eight northern states (Pennsylvania, New York, New Jersey, Ohio, Illinois, Michigan, Missouri, and Indiana), or any other assortment of vital statistics. What is decisive is the economic content of the figures. And in respect to the Negro this content is industrial. This does not mean that we disregard entirely, or intend to minimize the importance of the Negro farmer. The Negro agrarian problem is an acute and an important one. However, the American Negro is not predominantly agricultural. He is a proletarian.

From the revolutionary standpoint the Negro problem is primarily the problem of gaining over to the revolutionary platform the overwhelming majority of the Negro workers. The rural Negro can be gained as an ally only in the same manner, basically, as the rural white, and that is by being mobilized under the leadership of the proletariat.

From the very beginning the misleaders of the American working class as a whole and Negroes in particular have tried to drum into the heads of Negro and white that working class unity could not be achieved directly. Booker T. Washington did what he could to discourage Negroes from putting their trust in working class unity. And on the other hand, the reactionary trade union bureaucracy has drawn racial lines as rigidly as any Ku Kluxer. The unmasking of the class struggle will greatly facilitate the political development of American workers, Negro and white. But we will fail to unite them unless our fundamental approach to the Negro is the same as to any other worker, taking of course into consideration that they represent at present the most backward section of the backward working class, not because they were colored but because they stem directly from the most backward rural sections.

The elemental urge to class solidarity has manifested itself time and again. But these were and remained only episodic beginnings, in the absence of a genuine revolutionary party. Decades ago, in 1886, the old Knights of Labor had over 60,000 Negroes organized in its ranks. The IWW even in the darkest South was able to organize into a single organization Negroes and whites and lead them to successful strikes particularly in the lumber industry. In West Virginia, where the reactionary United Mine Workers of America tried to gain a foothold, two counties were more than half organized and most of the miners were Negroes; they were the backbone of the strike. But numerous as these instances are, they have remained episodic, and the base must be practically laid anew. One thing is certain: there are no 'national' shortcuts to organizing the Negro workers. The basic slogan is that of *class solidarity*, and not at all the slogan of 'self-determination'.

Booker T. Washington preached to the Negroes against class solidarity and tried to imbue them with self-degradation. He said, 'the wisest of my race understand that the agitation of questions of social equality is the extremest folly …'. He advocated an 'alliance' with the wealthy whites against the 'white trash', i.e. against the white workers who are the 'oppressors and scoundrels, who hold Negroes in contempt and lynch them'. The Negroes have been taught by the bourgeoisie to distrust and hate the white workers and vice versa. We must imbue the Negro with class solidarity. We must say,

> The wisest of the Negro race understand that the agitation of the question of class solidarity is the only way out for his race! Class conscious Negro and white workers must teach the Negro masses and the white that they have only one enemy – their real lynchers and oppressors – the capitalists.

6 Preliminary Notes on the Negro Question[12] (*1939*)

J.R. Johnson (C.L.R. James)

I

The 14 or 15 million Negroes in the USA represent potentially the most militant section of the population. Economic exploitation and the crudest forms of racial discrimination make this radicalization inevitable. We also have historical proof, first in the part played by the Negroes in the Civil War and in the response to a Marcus Garvey. Superficially, the Negro accepts, but that acceptance does not go very deep down. It is essentially dissimulation and a feeling of impotence, the age-old protective armor of the slave. It has been stated that the CP in organizing the Negroes in the South got such response that it had to check the campaign. The reason given was that owing to the number of Negroes joining and the fewness of the whites, the result would soon be a race-war between the Southern workers and sharecroppers.

II

The Negro responds not only to national but international questions. It is stated that during the Ethiopian crisis, thousands of Negroes were ready to go to Ethiopia as fighters and nurses. Since the trouble in the West Indies, Jamaicans in New York have formed a Jamaica Progressive Association. They drafted a memorandum demanding a democratic constitution for the West Indies, sent a delegate to meet the Royal Commission and to visit Panama and Colon to organize membership of the association.

12 Johnson 1939a.

III

Finally, I am informed that a new spirit is moving among the Negroes, in Harlem and elsewhere today. People who knew the Harlem Negro fifteen years ago and know him today state that the change is incredible. The Negro press today, poor as it is, is an immense advance on what it was five years ago. *The Pittsburgh Courier*, with a circulation of over 100,000 weekly, though a bourgeois paper, bitterly attacks the Roosevelt administration for its failure to deal with the Negro question. The younger generation in particular aims at equality, not to be discriminated against simply because they are black. To sum up then

a. The Negro represents potentially the most revolutionary section of the population.
b. He is ready to respond to militant leadership.
c. He will respond to political situations abroad which concern him.
d. He is today more militant than ever.

IV

The Fourth International movement has neglected the Negro question almost completely. If even the Party personnel were not of a type to do active work among the Negro masses, the Negro question as an integral part of the American revolution can no longer be neglected. The Negro helped materially to win the Civil War and he can make the difference between success and failure in any given revolutionary situation. A Negro department of some sort should be organized (consisting, if need be, entirely of whites) which will deal as comprehensively with the Negro question as the Trade Union Department deals with the Trade Union Question. If the Party thinks the question important enough this will be done. The Party members and sympathizers must be educated to the significance of the Negro question. This is not a question of there being no Negroes in the Party. That has nothing to do with it at all. This work can begin immediately. The main question, however, that of organizing or helping to organize the Negro masses, is one of enormous difficulty for a party like the SWP. The main reasons for this are of course the discrimination against the Negro in industry by both capitalists and workers, the chauvinism of the white workers, and the political backwardness of the American movement. Each of these are fundamental causes inherent in the economic and social structure of the country.

But an already difficult situation has been complicated by the funereal role of the CP, especially during the last few years. It is stated, and there is every reason to believe it, that the possibilities of a rapprochement between blacks and whites on a working class basis are today worse than they were ten years ago. The CP has lost 1,579 or 79% of its Negro membership during the last year in New York State alone. Since that time, there has taken place the split of the Workers Alliance, and New York is slated to be always symptomatic of developments in the Party as a whole. It was not always like this. I am informed that some years ago in Harlem, the Negro who was aware of politics might not join the CP, but he would say that of all the white parties, the CP was the only party which did fight for Negro equality and which tried to stick to its principles. Today that is gone. The chief reason for this is, of course, the new Popular Front turn of the CP. The CP cannot gain the allies it wants if it fights the difficult fight for Negro rights. The CP is now an American party, and the petty bourgeois supporters of democracy who are coming into it have nothing in common with the Negro, who, finding himself an outsider, has simply left the Party. I have had personal experience of the bitterness of ex-members of the CP toward the party, and unfortunately, to all white parties also.

But it is to be noted that the main grievance is political – the activity of the CP on the Ethiopian question. First of all, that Russia sold oil to Italy made a disastrous impression on the blacks. Yet many Negro party members remained. What seems to have been a decisive factor was the activity in regard to Spain and China and its lack of activity in regard to Ethiopia.

> Every day it is only Spain, Spain, China, Spain, but nothing done for Ethiopia except one or two meager processions around Harlem.

I have the impression that the CP could have gotten away with the Soviet selling of oil if it had carried on a vigorous campaign, collecting money, etc. for the Ethiopian cause. The contrast with Spain has been too glaring, and when the CP entirely neglected the West Indian situation, the Negroes became finally conscious that they were once more the dupes of 'another white party'.

The Ethiopian question and the West Indian question are still live questions for the politically minded Negroes. They will judge a Party on the international field by what it does or says on these issues.[13]

---

13 [Footnote by James]: The neglect of the Ethiopian question by the Fourth International (the British Section included) is a grave strategic error. The Ethiopians are in the field fighting and are going to be there for years. If there is any break in Italy during a war, these

Articles, leaflets, and even small meetings in Harlem are not beyond the Party today with a little effort. One party comrade has managed to make himself familiar with the Indian problem, to write articles in the *NI*, and to make valuable contacts. The same could surely be done nearer home.

France at the present time is the key to the world situation. How to awaken interest in the American Negroes on the critical situation in France, obviously of such importance to themselves? Obviously by the struggle for independence of the French colonies and particularly through the Negro organizations in Europe and Africa which are working towards this end. (The French party and with it the Belgian and British parties have their responsibility here). In France today there are African revolutionary organizations in contact with a similar organization in Britain. The Fourth International must determinately assist in building and strengthening its connections with this work, and the American Party has its part to play in this important means of educating and organizing the Negro movement in America.

The most difficult question is still to be faced. What will the Party aim at in its Negro work? There are certain things that every revolutionary party will do:

a. Fight for the Negroes' place and rights in the Trade Unions.
b. Seek to make as many Negroes as possible members.
c. Carry on a merciless struggle against White chauvinism.

About (c) a word should be said. The CP has been accused of fostering a black chauvinism. There have been exaggerations and absurdities and downright crimes against socialism, e.g. using white women to catch Negroes, but on the whole, the CP attitude of going to lengths in order to make the Negro feel that the CP looked upon him as a man and equal is not to be lightly dismissed. The general aim was correct. The Negro brought up in America or Africa is extremely sensitive to chauvinism of any kind. Lenin knew this and in his thesis to the Second Congress on the *Colonial Question*, he warned that concessions would have to be made to correct this justifiable suspicion on the part of the colonial workers. No principled concession can ever be made. But sensitiveness to 'black chauvinism' will gain nothing and will do a great deal of harm. It should be noted that this suspicious attitude is not directed

---

fighters will sweep the isolated Italian force out of the country. The African revolution today has a starting point in Africa. It is obvious what effect any such sweeping victory by the Ethiopian army will have on French black troops in Western Europe, and on Africans.

against whites only. Africans, and also to some degree Americans, are often hostile to educated West Indian Negroes who from their British education and the comparative absence of sharp racial discrimination in the West Indies are accused, and justly, of having a 'superior' and 'white' attitude. Organizations in London predominantly West Indian find it difficult to get African members, and in America, to get American members.

The party will base itself in the everyday needs of the Negroes. It must aim at being a mass organization or it would be useless and mischievous. The dangers of such an organization are obvious. But a recognition of these dangers does not solve two questions:

1. The great masses of Negroes are unorganized and no white party is going to organize them. They will not join the Fourth International. Is it worthwhile to assist in the formation of an organization which will rally Negroes, and, though reformist in character, must from the very nature of its membership develop into a militant organization? The Negro has poured his money into Garvey's coffers, and now into Father Divine's, has worked hard and been robbed. Is there a way out for him to fight unless he joins the Fourth International?
2. Though I may be wrong here, I think that such an organization is going to be formed whatever we do.

This question of the Negro organization is one that deserves the closest study. As far as I can see, no white leader or white organization is going to build a mass organization among the Negroes, either in Africa or in America. As recently as 1935, however, the Negroes have shown their capacity for mass political action under one of their own leaders. One, Sufi, a Southern Negro, masquerading as a man from the East, organized a party, picketed shops, and helped to force employers to give one-third of their jobs to Negroes. He was the leading figure in the riots which gained Harlem schools, more colored teachers, recreation grounds, etc. Sufi was a racketeering demagogue and was entangled into an Anti-Semitism which, I am informed, was no part of his creed, such as it was. But he was ready to fight for such things as the Negro understood and he got a strong response. The question, however, is pertinently asked: Why is it that intelligent Negroes with political understanding never attempt to lead Negroes but always leave them to men like Garvey and Sufi?

This, it seems to me, is one of the most important questions on which the party has to come to a decision. It is closely linked to the question of self-determination for American Negroes. Self-determination for the American Negroes is (1) economically reactionary and (2) politically false because no

Negroes (except CP stooges) want it. For Negroes it is merely an inverted segregation. Yet it is not to be lightly dismissed without providing for what it aims at: the creation of confidence among the Negroes that revolutionary socialism does honestly and sincerely mean to stand by its promises. As so often with Marxists, the subsidiary psychological factors are not carefully provided for in the planning of political campaigns.

The Negro must be won for socialism. There is no other way out for him in America or elsewhere. But he must be won on the basis of his own experience and his own activity. There is no other way for him to learn, nor for that matter, for any other group of toilers. If he wanted self-determination, then however reactionary it might be in every other respect, it would be the business of the revolutionary party to raise that slogan. If after the revolution, he insisted on carrying out that slogan and forming his own Negro state, the revolutionary party would have to stand by its promises and (similarly to its treatment of large masses of the peasantry) patiently trust to economic development and education to achieve an integration. But the Negro, fortunately for Socialism, does not want self-determination.

Yet Negroes, individually and in the mass, will remain profoundly suspicious of whites. In private and in public, they ask the question: 'How are we to know that after the revolution we shall not be treated in the same way?' Many who do not say this think it. The CP Negroes are looked upon as touts for Negro converts in exactly the same way as the Democratic and Republican Parties have touts for Negro votes.

What is the remedy? I propose that there is an obvious way – the organization of a Negro movement. That the Negro masses do certainly want – they will respond to that and therefore they must have it. They will follow such a movement ably and honestly led. They have followed similar movements in the past and are looking for a similar movement now.

The great argument for such a movement is that it has the possibility of setting the Negro masses in motion, the only way in which they will learn the realities of political activity and be brought to realize the necessity of mortal struggle against capitalism. Who opposes such a procedure must have some concrete suggestions for attaining this most important end: bringing Negro masses into the struggle.

What precise aims will such an organization have? What it must not at any cost do is to seek to duplicate existing white organizations so as to result in anything like dual unionism, etc. One of its main tasks will be to demand and struggle for the right of the Negro to full participation in all industries and in all unions. Any Negro organization which fought militantly for such an aim would thereby justify its existence.

There are many urgent issues: the struggle for the Negro right to vote, against social and legal discrimination, against discrimination in schools (and universities), against oppressive rents. The struggle against such things and the task of bringing the white workers to see to a concrete realization of their responsibility in these questions can be best achieved by a combination of the few politically advanced whites backed by a powerful Negro movement. To expect a continuous struggle by the whites on these Negro issues is absurd to lay down as a condition. For what it amounts to – that the Negro cannot struggle against these things unless he forms organizations predominantly white – is sectarian and stupid.

The Negro himself will have the satisfaction of supporting his own movement. The constant domination of whites, whether by the bourgeoisie or in workers' movements, more and more irks the Negro. That is why he followed a Marcus Garvey in such hundreds of thousands and would not join the CP. The Party's attitude towards such a movement should therefore be one of frank, sincere, and unwavering support. The white proletariat will have to demonstrate concretely its value to the Negro not once, but many times, before it wins the Negro's confidence.

The support of this movement by the Party should be frank, sincere, and unwavering. This is not as easy as it sounds. What the Party must avoid at all costs is looking upon such a movement as a recruiting ground for party members, something to be 'captured' or manipulated for the aims of the party, or something which it supports spasmodically at the time it needs something in return. The party should frankly and openly endorse such a movement, urge Negroes to join it, assist the movement in every way and, while pointing out the political differences and showing that revolutionary socialism is the ultimate road, work side by side to influence this movement by criticism and activity combined. It is in this way and on the basis of a common struggle, with the party always helping by never seeking to manipulate the movement, that the confidence of the Negro movement be gained by revolutionary socialism, without raising the impracticable slogan of self-determination.

What are the dangers of such a movement? The chief are: (a) the danger that it might be used by reactionary elements such as the Democratic Party or the Communist Party, (b) the danger of encouraging racial chauvinism. A fortunate combination of circumstances reduces these dangers to manageable proportions.

At the present moment, there is a sufficient number of capable Negroes ready and willing to lead such a movement who, while willing to cooperate with white parties, have no racial chauvinism.

While all Negroes will be admitted and racial discrimination against any Negro as a Negro will be fought, it is recognized by all with whom I have discussed this question, that such a movement must be a mass movement based on the demands of Negro workers and peasants. Much will depend on the leadership here. I see no reason, however, to have any doubts on this score. Such a leadership exists at the present time and needs only be mobilized. The Negro's right to his place in industry and the trade unions must be one of the main planks of the platform and one of the main fields of activity. The prospective leadership, as I see it, will be militantly opposed to the political line and organizational practice of the CP.

Yet this is not sufficient as a political basis. Sooner or later the organization will have to face its attitude towards capitalism. Is it to be a reformist or revolutionary organization? It will not start as a full-fledged revolutionary socialist organization. As Lenin pointed out to the pioneers of communism in Britain immediately after the war, it would be a mistake to flaunt the banner of revolution right at the beginning. The basis of the organization must be the struggle for the day-to-day demands of the Negro. But the American economy is already and will increasingly pose the question to every political organization fascism or communism. Here again the initial leadership will exercise a decisive influence. This is a question which will ultimately be decided by struggle within the organization.

However, many factors are in favor of a victory ultimately for those who support revolutionary socialism, when the Negro masses are ready for it. First there is the question of revolutionary struggle for the Negroes in Africa against imperialism. On this, most politically minded Negroes are agreed. Secondly, the International African Service Bureau, a British organization, issued a *Manifesto* during the Munich crisis which demands a joint struggle of British workers in Britain and colonials of the Empire for the overthrow of Imperialism. This *Manifesto* has been warmly welcomed among advanced Negroes in America, and the bureau and its paper, *International African Opinion*, have already a powerful influence, and this not only on account of its policy, but because it is run by Negroes.

Militant struggle for day-to-day demands must be the basis and constant activity of the movement, but in this period, action on this basis will drive the movement sharply up against the capitalist state and fascists or neo-fascist bands; and the transition to revolutionary socialism will not ultimately be difficult. As soon as this organization has achieved a firm basis, an international conference will most probably be called between the various militant Negro organizations and from my personal knowledge of them and their personnel, there is a probability that Socialism may be adopted. Such are the possibilities at the present time. And it is fortunate that they are so favorable. But it must be insisted upon that support of a Negro mass movement must not be conditional upon whether it is or soon will be socialist or not. It is the awakening and bringing into political activity of the large mass of Negroes which is the main consideration, and to this the party must give its frank, sincere, and unwavering support. The rest depends on the development of the whole international situation, the struggle of revolutionary parties, e.g. the growth of the SWP and the individuals who will constitute the leadership.

On the specific danger of racial chauvinism, I shall say little; in my view, it is for the movement of the kind projected a minor question. No movement which proclaims the Negro's right to his place in the trade unions can be deeply penetrated with chauvinism. The Negroes who are likely to lead this movement see the dangers of chauvinism as clearly as the whites do. In America, where the Negroes are in a definite minority, serious fear of black chauvinism on the part of white revolutionaries seems to me not only unnecessary but dangerous. In the concrete instance, black chauvinism is a progressive force, it is the expression of a desire for equality of an oppressed and deeply humiliated people. The persistent refusal to have 'self-determination' is evidence of the limitation of black chauvinism in America. Any excessive sensitiveness to black chauvinism by the white revolutionaries is the surest way to create hostilities and suspicion among the black people.

Such, in outline, it seems to me, should be the attitude of the party towards such an organization. It should actively assist the formation of such a movement. In any case, I have little doubt that such a movement is going to be formed sooner or later. But the party also has its own responsibility to the Negro question. The following are a few observations, based on a necessarily limited knowledge of the American situation, learned chiefly by discussion with Negro Socialists or near-Socialists.

a. Earlier I stated that the Party must form a section devoted entirely to the Negro question. This is urgent work, whether a Negro organization is formed or not. Our great weapon at the present moment is Marxism by which we illuminate every grave social and political problem of the day. The Party's first task, therefore, is to do what no organization, white or Negro, can do completely unless it is based on the principles of Marxism, study the Negro question in relation to the national and international situation.
b. The Negro Committee should embark on an unremitting study of the Negro question, and immediately make arrangements for the publication of articles regularly in the *Socialist Appeal* and the *New International*. The

Appeal should have a weekly column devoted to the Negro question. It will not be difficult to get regular information if contact is kept with Negroes. Not only accounts of lynchings, specific discriminations in industry, etc., but the presentation and analysis of various economic and social statistics issued, with special reference to the Negro, the colonial struggle in Africa, etc. This must now be a prominent and permanent section of the party's work, for Party members as well as Negro contacts.

Particularly urgent for the *New International* is an article or series of articles written from the inside and exposing the dealings of the American Communist Party with the Negro. The political line, the activities of Ford, Richard Moore, and Co., would be shown up, and their political corruption and degeneration traced in relation to the decline of the Comintern. The Negroes must be shown why the CP policy to the Negro has been what it has been at different times and why. The bureaucratic 'promotion' and 'demotion' of Negroes must be shown as a direct reflection of the bureaucratic degeneration of the Russian Revolution. A series of articles and a pamphlet relating the CP political and organizational policy towards Negroes with the zigzags of the Comintern would be of inestimable value. This should be done as a first task.

c. The numerous Negro organizations in Harlem and elsewhere must be contacted. This should be done very carefully, for the CP policy of 'penetration' or 'capturing from within' and generally of being concerned chiefly with bringing the organization under its influence, and not with helping in the Negro struggle, has borne bitter fruit, and the attitude towards any white is likely to be 'What have you come here to get?' That the party should encourage the formation of a Negro mass movement does not mean that it will in any way cease activity to gain membership among Negroes. What is to be avoided is the impression that it is interested in Negro activity solely for the purpose of getting members or influence, and not for the purpose of assisting Negro struggles. That would be a grave crime not only against Negroes but against the socialist movement. Yet the party will openly and frankly seek membership. It seems, however, that here certain dangers are to be avoided.

The NAACP, the Urban League, and other Negro organizations, weekly forums, etc., carry on a certain amount of activity. Mere condemnation of these as bourgeois is worse than useless. At present, in most areas, the party's appeal to most Negroes would chiefly be to those who are attracted by its superior understanding and analysis of the Negro question and the world situation. But these Negroes, when won, must not be immediately abstracted from their milieu and plunged into the struggle against Stalinism, etc. One of their main tasks at the present stage is to remain among the Negroes in their areas in the local organizations, carrying on an active fight for the party's ideas in a manner carefully adapted to their hearers' point of view. Broadly speaking, among whites there is a differentiation; revolutionaries circle around revolutionary organizations, and the petty-bourgeois democrats belong to the various petty bourgeois organizations. Among Negroes, especially in the provinces, it is not so. All types, instinctive revolutionaries and conservatives, can be found at the local Negro forums, YMCA etc. even though these meetings often begin with prayers. There is a vast field here for the winning of Negro members to the party if the party press and literature give them a weapon which they can use.

But at the same time, the party must beware of looking upon Negro work as to be done necessarily by Negroes. The clearance of the long road to socialist equality must begin at once. Certain white comrades can now begin to become experts on the Negro question. The method is easy to define, hard to carry out. It means a regular reading of the Negro press, Negro literature, regular attendance at Negro meetings, etc. The arguments for socialism are to be directed against the latest pronouncements of Kelly Miller, Mordecai Johnson, George Schulyer, the local Negro representatives of the Republican and Democratic parties, not against Stalin, Daladier, and Chiang Kai-Shek. And to attempt to do propaganda among Negroes on any other basis than attack, debate, exposition, etc. concerned with the writers, press etc. read by the Negroes, is to speak a language alien to them. This is of particular importance in areas where the Party is small. (For the moment I exclude organizations of the Negro unemployed etc. which would more properly be the problem of the Trade Union Section). A close attention by one or two white comrades to the discussion, literature, etc. of the various Negro groups in their community must bear fruit in the end owing to the superior power of the ideas we put forward. And while Negroes will do the main part of this work, even where the Party has Negro comrades, white comrades must take their part and will win great prestige for the party by showing themselves thoroughly familiar with Negro life and thought. We must work patiently in the rather restricted milieu to which even groups of educated Negroes are condemned by their position in American society.

The Committee should get into contact with the French, British, Belgian, and South African sections, get regular information about their work and contacts, a good supply of British and South African papers, especially those dealing with colonial questions, and circulate these and translations from the French among the Negro organizations and interested groups and persons. Every effort should be made to circulate the *Spark* widely among interested Negro contacts. The International African Service Bureau and its organ, *International*

African Opinion, should be popularized by the party among Negroes and whites alike. Negroes will welcome and appreciate this. This organization of Fourth International colonial activity in a manner to present it constantly and regularly to Negroes in America, is not only one of the most important means of drawing Negro contact ultimately into our party. It means also, and this is of immense importance in our period, that Negro organizations everywhere which are internationally minded or drawing towards internationalism will ultimately realize that the only genuine international organization in the world at the present time is the Fourth International.

7 The Right of Self-Determination and the Negro in the United States of North America[14]

(*1939*)

Socialist Workers Party, National Convention

In 1930 Negroes in America constituted nearly twelve million, or 10 percent of the American population. Of these, two-thirds were still in the South, despite the war and postwar emigration to the North. In the cities of the North and East, the Negroes form only a small minority of the population, generally less than 10 percent. In the cities of the South, the proportion is much higher, but in only one large city, Birmingham, Alabama, do the Negroes constitute as much as one-half of the white population. Similarly in the state areas of the South, they are outnumbered by the whites. In only one state of America, Mississippi, are the Negroes in a majority, and that of only 2 percent, though there are large county areas inhabited by a majority of Negroes.

Cut off for centuries from all contact with the continent and customs of his origin, the Negro is today an American citizen. In his daily work, language, religion, and general culture, he differs not at all from his fellow workers in factory and field, except in the intensity of his exploitation and attendant brutal discrimination. These discriminations are imposed by capitalism in the pretended name of the Negro's racial characteristics, but in reality to increase profit by cheapening labor and to weaken the workers and farmers by fostering racial rivalries.

The minority status of the Negro in the political divisions of capitalist America, even in the South, and the absence of a national Negro language and literature and of a differentiated political history, as in prewar Poland or Catalonia and the Ukraine of today, have caused in the past a too facile acceptance of the Negroes as merely a more than usually oppressed section of the American workers and farmers. This in turn has led to a neglect of the Negro's political past and a lack of historical imagination in envisaging his future political development.

---

14 Socialist Workers Party 1939a.

The American Negroes were among the earliest colonists of America, and for three centuries their history has been one of continual economic exploitation, social discrimination, and political expropriation by all classes of whites. Up to 1935, organized labor, as represented by the AFL, discriminated against the Negro as sharply as the capitalist class; today the poor whites of the South are the most savage of lynchers and the most rabid upholders of the theory of white superiority. The world economic crisis and consequent organization of the CIO including hundreds of thousands of Negroes, the organization of the Southern Tenant Farmers Union comprising both white and black, have shown that this division between the black and white workers is beginning to close under economic pressure. But not even a socialist revolution can immediately destroy the accumulated memories, mistrust, and suspicions of centuries; and today, in this period of capitalistic decline in America, the racial prejudices are more than ever based on economic privileges, possessed by one group of workers at the obvious and immediate expense of the other. Negroes today are being pushed out of jobs which, before the depression, whites disdained. Three centuries of property and privilege have used their wealth and power to make the Negroes feel that they are and must continue to be outcasts from all sections of American society, rich and poor; and the political backwardness of the American working-class movement has made it an easy victim to this propaganda, fortified by tangible if slight economic advantages. It is not improbable, therefore, that the bulk of the Negroes have absorbed their lesson far more profoundly than is superficially apparent and that on their first political awakening to the necessity of revolutionary activity they may demand the right of self-determination, i.e., the formation of a Negro state in the South. Thus, in their view, they would be free from that exploitation, discrimination, and arrogance, inseparable in their experience from any association with numerically superior whites. The desire to wipe out the humiliating political subservience and social degradation of centuries might find expression in an overpowering demand for the establishment and administration of a Negro state.

The past political history of the Negroes gives not insignificant indications that their political development may very well follow this course. The Garvey movement, one of the most powerful political mass movements ever seen in the USA, concealed behind its fantastic and reactionary slogan of 'Back to Africa' – the desire (revolutionary in its essence) for a Negro state. The Negroes no more desired to go to Africa of their own free will than German Jews before Hitler wanted to go to Palestine. The masses of Negroes, particularly in the South, dominated by the heritage of slavery and the apparently irresistible numbers and state power of the whites, did not dare to raise the slogan of a black state in America. But in a revolutionary crisis, as they begin to shake off the state coercion and ideological domination of American bourgeois society, their first step may well be to demand the control, both actual and symbolical, of their own future destiny. The question of whether the Negroes in America are a national minority to which the slogan of self-determination applies will be solved in practice. The raising or support of the slogan by the masses of Negroes will be the best and only proof required. It is inconceivable that propaganda by any American revolutionary party can instill this idea into their minds if they did not themselves consciously or unconsciously desire it. This desire may very well fall into the hands of reactionary leaders. But only the most energetic defense of the right of self-determination of the Negro masses can lead their movement into revolutionary channels.

Should the masses of Negroes raise this slogan, the SWP, in accordance with the Leninist doctrine on the question of self-determination and the imperative circumstances of the particular situation, will welcome this awakening and pledge itself to support the demand to the fullest extent of its power. The boundaries of such a state will be a matter of comradely arrangement between different sections of a revolution victorious over American capitalism and intent only on creating the best possible milieu for the building of the socialist commonwealth. The Fourth International aims at the abolition of the old and not at the creation of new national boundaries, but the historical circumstances and the stages of development of different sections of society will at given moments be decisive in the road to be followed at a particular historic moment. The demand for a Negro state in America, its revolutionary achievement with the enthusiastic encouragement and assistance of the whites, will generate such creative energy in every section of the Negro workers and farmers in America as to constitute a great step forward to the ultimate integration of the American Negroes into the United Socialist States of North America. The SWP is also confident that after a few years of independent existence the victories of the new regime in both states will lead inevitably to a unity, with the Negroes as anxious and willing partners, their justifiable suspicions and doubts weakened by the concrete manifestation of the desire for collaboration by the whites and the contrast between the capitalist and the socialist state. Such a development in America will have immediate and powerful repercussions not only among the millions of African Negroes but also among oppressed nationalities, particularly of color, everywhere, and will be a powerful step toward the dissolution of those national and racial antagonisms with which capitalism, particularly in this period of its desperate crisis, is poisoning and corrupting human society.

The SWP, while proclaiming its willingness to support the right of self-determination to the fullest degree, will not in itself, in the present stage, advocate the slogan of a Negro state in the manner of the Communist Party of the USA. The advocacy of the right of self-determination does not mean advancing the slogan of self-determination. Self-determination for Negroes means that the Negroes themselves must determine their own future. Furthermore, a party predominantly white in membership which, in present-day America, vigorously advocates such a slogan, prejudices it in the minds of Negroes, who see it as a form of segregation. But the SWP will watch carefully the political development of the masses of the Negroes, will emphasize their right to make this important decision themselves and the obligation of all revolutionaries to support whatever decision the Negroes may finally come to as to the necessity of a Negro state. The SWP recognizes that the Negroes have not yet expressed themselves on this important question. The opposition to a Negro state comes mainly from the articulate and vocal but small and weak class of Negro intellectuals, concerned with little else besides gaining a place for themselves in American capitalist society, and fanatically blind to its rapid decline. Negro members of the Fourth International, however, have every right to participate in the formation of the ideology of their own race, with such slogans and propaganda as correspond to the political development and revolutionary awakening of the great masses of the Negro people; and, while conscious of the ultimate aims of socialism, must recognize the progressive and revolutionary character of any demand unfolding among great masses of Negroes for a Negro state, and if necessary vigorously advocate it.

8 The Destiny of the Negro[15]

(1939)

J.R. Johnson (C.L.R. James)

To know where the Negro is going one must know where the Negro comes from. Capitalist history and capitalist science, taken as a whole, are designed to serve the needs of capitalist profit. Their studies of the Negro and his history have aimed at justifying his exploitation and degradation. They have excused the slave trade and slavery and the present position of Negroes as outcasts in capitalist society, on the ground that the Negro in Africa had shown himself incapable of developing civilization, that he lived a savage and barbarous life, and that such elements of culture as Africa showed in the past and shows today were directly due to the influence of Arabs and Europeans. All of this, from beginning to end, is lies.

Negroes in African Civilization

First of all, the capitalist scientist's attempts to isolate the 'pure' Negro from other African peoples are admitted today to be pure rubbish. Though there are broad differentiations, the Negroes in Africa are inextricably mixed. There are people of Hamitic stock who derive either from the Near East or the outermost peninsula of Africa (today British and Italian Somaliland). There are the short-statured Bushmen in the South and the supposedly 'pure' Negro is found on the West Coast alone. It is as if a scientist said that the 'pure' European was found only on the coast of Portugal. The truth is that even the Egyptians had a strong Negroid strain. There were Negro dynasties in Egypt. Queen Nefertiti, one of the great conquerors and rulers of Egyptian history, was reputedly a Negress. Among the modern Ethiopian ruling class can be seen types, ranging from the purely Semitic through the Mulatto to types indistinguishable from the Negro.

15 Johnson 1939c.

The chief object of these scientists is of course to deprive the Negro of any share in the famous civilizations of Egypt and Ethiopia. Today, ingenious Negroes call the Egyptians 'black men' and by this means place all Egyptian civilization to the credit of the Negro. Racial theories of this type, whether from white capitalist centers of learning or fanatical Negro nationalists, are neither history nor science, but political propaganda. This much is clear and for the time being sufficient: the Egyptian civilization began where it did and flourished because of favorable climactic and geographical conditions, and the Negroes had a great deal to do with it.

The attempt to deduce from history that Negroes are subhuman continually breaks down. The Bushmen are among the most primitive of peoples. Yet their drawings have been universally hailed as some of the most marvelous examples of artistic skill. And since when have monkeys been given to producing great artists? In South Africa the ruins of Zimbabwe are evidence of a great ancient civilization. Whose? Nobody knows, but numerous professors are racking their brains to prove that, whoever created it, it wasn't Negroes. Much good may it do them. They will not stop the world revolution that way.

But the greatest stumbling block in the way of the anti-Negro historians are the empires of Ghana, Songhay, Mos, and others, which flourished in the basin of the Niger. People who sneer at the Marxist phrase 'bourgeois ideology' simply have no conception of the dishonesty, corruption, and scope of capitalist lies and propaganda.

The Ghana Empire

For nearly a thousand years (300–1300), between the River Senegal and the Niger flourished the Ghana empire. We do not know how it was founded. Some people say that a Hamitic people from East Africa migrated there. Others say that they came from Syria. What we do know is that this empire at its zenith embraced many millions of people. It produced wool, cotton, silk, velvet; it traded in copper and gold. Many houses in the chief towns were built of stone. At one time its army consisted of 200,000 soldiers. Its schools, its lawyers, its scholars were famous all over the Mediterranean area. And this empire for nearly a thousand years was an empire of black men, of Negroes.

Another famous empire was that of Songhay (600–1500) with its dynasty of Askias. Askia Mohammed I (1443–1528) was not only a great ruler. He surrounded himself with scholars. Timbuktu and Gao were the centers of trade and learning.

The latest edition of the *Encyclopedia Britannica* says of these kingdoms,

> Long before the rise of Islam, the peoples of this Northern part of West Africa, consisting largely, as has been seen, of open plains watered by large and navigable rivers, had developed well-organized states, of which the oldest known, Ghana (or Ghanata) is thought to have been founded in the third century AD. Later arose the empire of Melle and the more famous and more powerful Songhoi (Songhoy) empire ... Marking the importance, commercial and political, of these states, large cities were founded.

The idea that Islamic influences founded these states is now exploded, and this is admitted by the Britannica writer. He follows, however, the theory of 'pure' and 'impure' Negroes. The Negroes on the coast were 'pure'. But even these, he notes, founded civilizations: '... the Yoruba, the Ashanti, the Dahomi, and the Beni created powerful and well organized kingdoms'.

The Beni, better known as the Benin, are famous today for their bronze sculpture, of artistic merit and technical skill unsurpassed by any people of ancient or modern times. When after many centuries they were 'discovered' in 1891, the impudent imperialists at once attributed these bronzes to 'Portuguese' influence. That theory has now joined the other in the waste-paper basket.

The High-water Mark

West Africa was the high-water mark. But all over Africa, organized civilizations flourished. The first Portuguese to visit East Africa some five hundred years ago did not remark any noticeable differences between the Africans and themselves; while less than fifty years ago, Emil Torday, the Belgian explorer, discovered in Central Africa the Bushongo people. A wise king, as far back as the seventeenth century, had prohibited all contact with Europeans, and, away in this interior, the tribe had survived. Torday found a free and happy people, living in villages well laid out, the huts beautifully decorated, their sculpture, textiles, and household objects of a rare beauty. Political organization was a perfect democracy. The king had all the honors, the council all the power. Representatives, two of them always women, were both regional and vocational. Today they are degraded savages.

Torday states that before the coming of the Europeans such civilizations, perfectly adapted to their environment, were widespread over Africa. The picture of warring tribes and savage cannibals is all lies.

As late as 1906, Frobenius traveling in the Belgian Congo, could still see the following:

> And on all this flourishing material, civilization then was abloom; here the bloom on ripe fruit both tender and lustrous; the gestures, manners, and customs of a whole people, from the youngest to the oldest, alike in the families of the princes and the well-to-do, of the slaves, so naturally dignified and refined in the smallest detail. I know no northern race who can bear comparison with such a uniform level of education as is found among the natives.

It was the slave trade that destroyed Africa, the depredations of Arabs and European imperialists. They ravaged the continent for three centuries. What the travellers of the nineteenth century discovered was the wreck and ruin of what had existed four centuries before, and even then enough remained to disprove the ideas of the subhuman Negro. Africa is a vast continent and many millions of people in varying degrees of civilization have lived there over the centuries. There was much ignorance, barbarism, and superstition, but the history and achievements of Negroes in art, literature, politics, empire-building, until Arab and European imperialism fell upon them in the twelfth and thirteenth centuries, is an incontrovertible refutation of the mountains of lies and slander built up by capitalist apologists in defense of capitalist barbarism. Africans worked in iron countless generations ago and many historians claim that it was they who introduced metal work to Europe and Asia.

Capitalism developing in Europe precipitated the discovery of America and sent its navigators and explorers to Africa. In the sixteenth century began the use of Negro slaves in the plantations of America. British capitalism drew one of the most powerful sources of wealth from the slave trade. The greatness of Liverpool, the second city of Great Britain, was founded on the trade. The wealth of the French bourgeoisie was based upon the slave trade. The rise of modern Europe is inexplicable without a knowledge of the economic ramifications of the slave trade.

Emancipation from Slavery and the Destruction of Feudalism

Here we shall make a political analysis of the role of the Negro in the phase of the development of Western civilization [that involved the revolutionary destruction of feudalism in England, France, and America].

First of all, what is feudalism? That is not easy to answer in a sentence. It is a form of society based on landed property and simple methods of cultivation.

They have a landowning class which rules; at the other end of the social scale you have the serfs, who get a part of their produce to feed themselves and contribute their surplus to the landowning aristocracy. Side by side with the landowning aristocracy is the clergy. The main characteristic of social life in feudal society is the fact that the aristocracy and clergy have great privileges, and the serfs and others have very few or none. This is not a question of custom, but a question of law. (In capitalist society, in theory, all men are equal before the law).

Feudal economy in Europe did not in any way have contact with Africa. It was essentially a subsistence economy; that is to say, it produced what it needed to feed and clothe itself. About the thirteenth and fourteenth centuries, however, there grew up in Europe a new class, the merchants. These were the first real capitalists.

Europe's First Dealings with Africa

Soon their business began to be of great importance in the state. With increasing wealth, they gradually changed the economies of certain countries from producing chiefly food and the simple things that the community needed, to the manufacture of goods on a large scale. This particular class was concerned as much with production for trade in other parts of the country and abroad as for use at home. It was this drive for trade, for raw materials, for markets, and for profit, that created the necessity for expansion, and in the fifteenth century finally sent expeditions to America and to Africa. Thus it was the development of capitalism in Europe that brought the millions of Africans into contact with Western civilization.

Capitalism demands above all else landless laborers. In Europe the capitalist class created a class of landless laborers by driving them off the land whenever possible, for if the serf or the peasant had land on which to work or earn his keep for himself, naturally he would not hire himself out to any capitalist for long hours and small pay.

When the capitalists discovered America, they tried to use the Indian as landless laborers. But the Indians died. There was so much land that it was impossible to get landless laborers from among the early colonists. Because of this, the capitalists in Europe and their agents in the colonies brought millions of Negroes as slaves to America and thereby provided the colonies with the necessary labor. By this means capitalism enormously expanded its capacity for making profit.

By means of these vast profits that they made at home and abroad, the capitalists in Britain and France, for example not only built up tremendous trade and business, but with the profits accumulated, they began to organize factories and extend the application of science to industry. The standard of civilization rose, and the power and profits of the capitalists increased also. But the governments of France and Britain still continued to be under the domination of the old feudal nobility. When came much trouble.

Capitalists Make Their Revolution

Trade and factories were more important than land. Yet the rulers of the countries were princes, dukes, lords, bishops, and archbishops. That was all very well when they had the economic power, but now it had passed from them. Not only were they proud and arrogant, but they tried to keep the laws and the government suitable to land ownership when, owing to the shift in the economic basis of the country, the laws and the government should have been organized to help trade and industry. It was no use pointing out to them that they should give way. It took revolutions to do it.

In Britain there were two revolutions. One took place in the seventeenth century and lasted off and on for nearly sixty years. In France, revolution began in 1789, and by the time it was over the power of the aristocracy and the clergy was wiped away completely.

What part did the Negroes play in all this? The capitalists who first profited by slavery were commercial capitalists and the planters in the colonies. These planters were partly capitalist in that they traded their produce far and wide, and partly feudal in that they kept their slaves in a state of subjection comparable to the old serfdom and built up a type of feudal society. But as capitalism developed, these commercial traders and the plantation owners collaborated closely with the aristocracy, and many of them became aristocrats themselves. By the time the industrial capitalists were busy developing their factories, the aristocrats, the planters, and the commercial capitalists formed, roughly speaking, one reactionary group.

An End to Slavery

Now one of the things that the industrial capitalists wanted to do was to finish with slavery. It was too expensive. Slave production was backward compared with modern methods and more highly developed capitalist production in agriculture. So that you had on one side the industrial capitalists determined to destroy the slave power of the aristocrats, the commercial capitalists, and the planters. It was in this political struggle that Negroes got their chance to fight for their freedom. They played a small part in the English political struggle, a larger part in the French struggle, and a decisive part in the American struggle. This was not accidental. A few figures will show us why.

In 1789 British colonial trade was five million pounds out of an export trade of 27 million. Britain had lost America in 1783 and had few slaves in the West Indies. We can therefore see that slavery was playing a very minor part in British economy. The British Negroes on the whole played little part in the destruction of British feudalism.

Negro in the French Revolution

In France in 1789 the export trade was 17 million pounds. The colonial trade was 11 million – two-thirds of it. The question of abolition was therefore of tremendous importance. It took a prominent part in the revolution. The Negroes fought magnificently and, being thousands of miles away, gained their independence. This is how Haiti came into being.

In America in 1861 this combination of the commercial bourgeoisie and the plantation owners was not a minor part of American economy. It was a major part. The combination was not a colony thousands of miles away. It occupied hundreds of thousands of square miles inside the country. To defeat this combination took the greatest Civil War in history, and the Negro's share was far greater than it had been in France.

This is the way we must look at history. People who only see black men in general being oppressed by white men in general, and are unable to trace the historical dialectic, do not understand anything and therefore cannot lead. That is the great value of being a genuine Marxist, an adherent of the Fourth International. You can study history and understand where we are today and why and where we are going tomorrow.

The Destiny of the Negro

Let us for a moment review our analysis of the Negro in his contact with Western civilization ... We established that the Negroes in Africa had built high if simple civilizations up to the fourteenth century. It was necessary to emphasize this, to destroy the imperialist-fostered conception of Africa as a land of eternal savagery and barbarism from which it has to some degree been raised by the gentle hand of the European invaders.

European contact with Africa began with the rise of European imperialism. A new continent, America, was discovered and Africa, which had always lain within easy reach of European ships, was penetrated. Commercial capitalism developed the mercantile system, which needed labor in the American tropical plantation. When the Indians proved unsatisfactory, slaves were brought from Africa. On the basis of the wealth created by the slave trade and the colonial trade directly dependent upon it, the commercial capitalists of Europe and America built up from their ranks a new section of the capitalist class, the industrial capitalists. These, whose chief function was the application of large-scale organization and science to industry, came inevitably into conflict with the planters: slave labor was too expensive, too backward for the new methods. This economic conflict was the basis for political conflict. The commercial bourgeoisie and the feudal aristocracy still had the political power their former economic predominance had given them, and for the new rising class of industrial bourgeoisie, to wrest it from them meant a struggle.

The Bourgeois Revolutions

This was a progressive struggle. It took place in great revolutions in France and in America, and in Britain it took not only the threat but the actual beginning of a revolution to break the power of the feudal aristocrats. In all these the Negro played a tremendous part. In America he was given the opportunity of doing this because his emancipation was in the interest of the Northern industrialist bourgeoisie. All these great movements of politics thrust the color question into subordination and unimportance. It is economics and politics, not color, that are decisive in history.

To see what happened after the industrialist bourgeoisie took power, it would be best to follow the course of one country, say Great Britain. The industrialists seized power in 1832. They struck a terrific blow at the landed aristocracy in 1847 by abolishing the 'corn laws'. Through these laws the feudal aristocrats had artificially maintained the price of grain by restricting foreign competition with the produce of their fields. Rising with the industrial bourgeoisie was a new class – the industrial working class, the proletariat. And by 1848 the Chartist Movement of the workers was feeling its way towards revolution.

But in this year began a great era of prosperity. So prosperous was the industrial bourgeoisie, thanks to the home market its victory had given it, that it treated the idea of colonies in Africa with scorn. Disraeli wrote in 1866 that the British had all that they wanted in Asia. For, he continued, 'what is the use of these colonial deadweights, the West Indian and West Africa colonies? ... Leave the Canadians to govern themselves; recall the African squadrons; give up the settlements on the southeast coast of Africa and we shall make a saving which will at the same time enable us to build ships and have a good budget'. In the year he wrote, only one-tenth or less of Africa was in the hands of European imperialists. They had devastated the continent, but now they wanted the slaves no longer. For a while it almost seemed that Africa would be left in peace.

A New Need for Africa

But capitalist production led inevitably to the concentration of wealth in the hands of a few and the corresponding increasing poverty of the masses. The workers cannot buy what they produce. The capitalists must find abroad new markets, sources of new materials, and places to invest their capital.

In 1885 Jules Ferry, the French statesman, used the famous words:

> Colonies for rich countries are one of the most lucrative methods of utilizing capital ... I say that France, which is glutted with capital, has a reason for looking on this side of the colonial question ... European consumption is saturated: it is necessary to raise new masses of consumer in other parts of the globe, else we shall put modern society into bankruptcy and prepare for social liquidation with the dawn of the twentieth century ...

Cecil Rhodes once told a friend, 'If you want to free civilization, become an imperialist'. With the glut in the home market, colonies were no longer 'deadweight'. While in 1880 only one-tenth of Africa was in the hands of European imperialists, by 1900 less than one-tenth of the land remained in the hands of the African people. That saturation of European consumption to which Ferry referred and the part that Africa played can be shown by the following simple calculation. Great Britain has invested abroad roughly twenty billion dollars. The total investment in Africa from all sources is roughly six billion dollars, and of this almost five billion is in British territory. That is to say, almost one-fourth of British foreign investment is to be found in Africa.

But this process of 'saturation' that forced the imperialists to expand to the colonies has now itself spread to the colonies. The increasing accumulation of great wealth in the hands of the few and the increasing poverty of the masses is now not only a European but world phenomenon. Imperialism, the highest stage of capitalism, is bankrupt. The war of 1914–18, the worldwide crisis since 1929, the new world war of 1939 – these are items from the ledger of imperialism. Only the overthrowing of the bankrupt class by a new class, only the triumphant proletarian revolution, can balance the budget of civilization.

And in the same way as the Negro played an important role in the revolution of the industrialists in unseating the feudal aristocracy, so tomorrow the Negroes will play a decisive role in the struggle between finance-capital and the working class. Against his declared intentions, Lincoln was forced to free the slaves. Revolutionary France had to recognize the revolution of the San Domingo blacks. In the stress of economic and political conflict, color was forgotten and the rising class took help wherever it could get it. The Negroes in Africa and America, wherever they are the most oppressed of people, are going to strike even more deadly blows for freedom, against the capitalist system of exploitation, in alliance with the white workers of the world.

9 The SWP and Negro Work[16]

(*1939*)

Socialist Workers Party National Convention

The American Negroes, for centuries the most oppressed section of American society and the most discriminated against, are potentially the most revolutionary element of the population. They are designated by their whole historical past to be, under adequate leadership, the very vanguard of the proletarian revolution. The neglect of Negro work and of the Negro question by the party is therefore a very disquieting sign. The SWP must recognize that its attitude to the Negro question is crucial for its future development. Hitherto the party has been based mainly on privileged workers and groups of isolated intellectuals. Unless it can find its way to the great masses of the underprivileged, of whom the Negroes constitute so important a section, the broad perspectives of the permanent revolution will remain only a fiction and the party is bound to degenerate.

The SWP proposes therefore to constitute a National Negro Department which will initiate and coordinate a plan of work among the Negroes and calls upon its members to cooperate strenuously in the difficult task of approaching this work in the most suitable manner. Our obvious tasks for the coming period are (a) the education of the party, (b) winning the politically more advanced Negroes for the Fourth International, and (c) through the work of the party among the Negroes and in wider fields influencing the Negro masses to recognize in the SWP the only party which is genuinely working for their complete emancipation from the heavy burdens they have borne so long. The winning of masses of Negroes to our movement on a revolutionary basis is, however, no easy task. The Negroes, suffering acutely from the general difficulties of all workers under capitalism, and in addition, from special problems of their own, are naturally hesitant to take the step of allying themselves with a small and heavily persecuted party. But Negro work is complicated by other more profound causes. For reasons which can be easily understood, the American Negro is profoundly suspicious of all whites and recent events have deepened that suspicion.

---

16 Socialist Workers Party 1939b.

Negroes Often Deceived

In the past, the Negro masses have had disastrous experiences with the Republican and Democratic parties. The benefits that the Negro as a whole are supposed to have received from the New Deal and the Democratic Party can easily be seen for the fraud that they are when it is recognized that it is the Democratic Party of Franklin Roosevelt which by force and trickery prevents the Negroes from exercising their votes over large areas in the South.

The CP of the USA from 1928 to 1935 did win a number of Negroes to membership and awakened a sympathetic interest among the politically more advanced Negro workers and intellectuals. But the bureaucratic creation of Negro 'leaders', their subservience to the twists and turns of the party line, their slavish dependence on the manipulations and combinations of the CP leadership, were seen by interested Negroes not as a transference of the methods and practices of the Kremlin bureaucracy to America, but merely as another example of the use of Negroes by whites for political purposes unconnected with Negro struggles. With its latest turn beginning in 1935, the CP has become openly a party of American bourgeois democracy. Not only to expand, but merely to exist in this milieu demanded that it imbibe and practice the racial discriminations inherent in that society. The Negroes, very sensitive to all such practices, have quickly recognized the new face of the CP beneath the mask of demagogy with which it seeks to disguise the predicament in which it finds itself, and the result has been a mass departure from the party (80% of the New York State Negro membership) and a bitter hostility to the CP which reached a climax when well-known former Negro members of the CP testified against it before the Dies Committee. Once more the Third International has struck a deadly blow at the American working class, this time by undermining the confidence that was being slowly forged between the politically advanced sections of the black and white workers.

Nationalist Tendencies

Furthermore, the awakening political consciousness of the Negro not unnaturally takes the form of a desire for independent action uncontrolled by whites. The Negroes have long felt and more than ever feel today the urge to create their own organizations under their own leaders and thus assert, not only in theory but in action, their claim to complete equality with other American citizens. Such a desire is legitimate and must be vigorously supported even when it takes the form of a rather aggressive chauvinism. Black chauvinism in America today is merely the natural excess of the desire for equality and is essentially progressive while white American chauvinism, the expression of racial domination, is essentially reactionary. Under any circumstances, it would have been a task of profound difficulty, perhaps impossible, for a revolutionary party composed mainly of whites to win the confidence of the American Negro masses, except in the actual crises of revolutionary struggles. Such possibilities as existed, however, have been gravely undermined by the CP. Today the politically minded Negroes are turning away from the CP, and Negro organizations devoted to struggle for Negro rights are springing up all over the North and East, particularly in Harlem. The nationalist tendencies of the Negroes have been fortified, and in addition to the poisoning of racial relations by capitalism, the SWP has now to contend with the heritage left by the CP and the pernicious course it is still actively pursuing.

For a Negro Organization

The SWP therefore proposes that its Negro members, aided and supported by the party, take the initiative and collaborate with other militant Negroes in the formation of a Negro mass organization devoted to the struggle for Negro rights. This organization will *not* be either openly or secretly a periphery organization of the Fourth International. It will be an organization in which the masses of Negroes will be invited to participate on a working-class program corresponding to the day to day struggles of the masses of Negro workers and farmers. Its program will be elaborated by the Negro organization, in which Negro members of the Fourth International will participate with neither greater nor lesser rights than other members. But the SWP is confident that the position of the Negroes in American society, the logic of the class struggle in the present period, the superior grasp of politics and the morale of members of the Fourth International, must inevitably result in its members exercising a powerful influence in such an organization. The support of such an organization by the SWP does not in any way limit the party's drive among Negroes for membership, neither does it invalidate the necessary struggle for the unity of both black and white workers. But that road is not likely to be a broad highway. Such an organization as is proposed is the most likely means of bringing the masses of Negroes into political action, which though programmatically devoted to their own interests, must inevitably merge with the broader struggles of the American working class movement taken as a whole. The SWP therefore, while recognizing the limitations and pitfalls of a mass organization without clearly defined political program, and while retaining its full liberty of action and criticism, welcomes and supports any attempt by Negroes themselves to organize for militant action against our common oppressors, instructs its Negro members to work actively towards the formation of such an organization, and recommends to the party members to follow closely all such manifestations of Negro militancy.

CHAPTER 7

Confronting Stalinism

Andrew Pollack

The Trotskyist movement was born in reaction to Stalinist degeneration and set itself the task of reversing course back to that of its revolutionary forebears. This of necessity created a constant tension between the tasks of restoration and strengthening the size, breadth and weight of the organisation taking up those tasks, i.e. of addressing the dialectical connection between the people and policies of the old and those of the new – a tension which could only be resolved by succeeding in reforming the old party or abandoning that hope and striking out anew as a new party challenging the old.

One aid in deciding at each step how to address this tension was the break with the unprincipled factional politics that had come to dominate both internal policymaking and relations with the international communist movement.

A particularly dramatic moment in that break is described by James P. Cannon in one of his letters to historian Theodore Draper (a portion of which makes up the initial selection here). Cannon describes reading for the first time documents of the Russian Left Opposition. That reading, which occurred at the Sixth Congress of the Communist International, awoke in Cannon and his closest factional allies a deep yearning for analysis and discussion of what had gone wrong.

In the most immediate sense, that meant abandoning participation in the factional manoeuvres going on at the congress. That in turn resulted in awakening suspicion among their former allies in the Foster-Cannon bloc, allies who were insisting that Cannon step up to the plate and rejoin the fight for position and preference within the Party and International. But that was not to be, as the political revelations in the Trotsky documents threw into glaring contrast the often-sordid factional manoeuvring which was everyday life in the US Communist Party (CP) in the 1920s. Such manoeuvring had included Cannon himself, who (although having earlier launched concrete efforts against factionalism) by his own admission had been only semiconscious of the depths to which the warfare within the Party had sunk and of his own role in it. Reading Trotsky's documents brought to the surface the political source of the faction fighting which had made Cannon and his closest allies uneasy but without quite knowing its source and therefore its remedy.

Of particular note in his letter to Draper is Cannon's description of how he fought against the temptation to stay silent in order to win positions from which, some of his allies told him, he would then be in a better position to launch an openly political fight – and his conclusion in the end that this would have disoriented potential followers and miseducated them on how to fight on a principled basis.

The second selection describes what it was like to be a Trotskyist during the movement's nadir, its 'Dog Days'. With few people and even fewer resources, the group of expellees, who had banded together as a public faction of the Party (as opposed to a new Party), had first and foremost to work out its programme, a task undertaken with the aid of international co-thinkers, and for the group to then, in Cannon's words, decide 'what shall be the nature of its activities, and what tasks it shall set itself, given the size and capacity of the group, the period of the development of the class struggle, the relation of forces in the political movement, and so on'.

A key part of that programme was the group's position on the Soviet Union. In this letter Cannon describes the criteria applied (later expounded at greater length in his 1947 'American Stalinism and Anti-Stalinism'). These included a principled and analytically balanced characterisation of the degenerating workers' state, and on that basis the proper approach toward on the one hand defending its remaining gains, while also criticising the backward steps taken by the consolidating Soviet bureaucracy which jeopardised those gains. That in turn meant not hunting for the easy pickings of elements who, seemingly shocked by one or another crime of Stalin, declared themselves the most anti-Stalinist of all – and who, because their critique was superficial, tended to end up as anti-Communists who abandoned revolutionary perspectives. For Trotskyists, in contrast, doing battle with Stalinism was a means to deepen the fight against capitalism at home and imperialism globally. The basis on which Stalinism was fought during these Dog Days created a template, for Cannon and his co-thinkers, in a subsequent factional struggle that erupted among US Trotskyists during the late 1930s (see Chapter 8 in this volume).

Accompanying the rush by some former CP oppositionists to declare the death of the Russian Revolution was an impatience among some in the Communist League to abandon the fight to reform the CP and declare a new party. Cannon and friends instead insisted on patient education of the revolutionary working-class vanguard, the overwhelming bulk of which was still inside the CP. But this approach meant putting up with the isolation and abuse – both verbal and physical – coming from the CP.

It also attracted unhealthy elements which, Cannon explained, was the inevitable fate of new groups swimming against the stream, i.e. to attract the loudest and longest talkers demonstrating the least interest in patient education and the organisational burdens involved. But in the end the patient approach won out, leaving the League ready to jump on new labour organising opportunities in Minneapolis and elsewhere, opportunities which yielded new recruits and prestige, which in turn made easier the coming break with the tactic of reforming the CP.

The next two articles are critiques of CP conventions, in 1934 and 1936, by Arne Swabeck and Albert Goldman respectively. Both describe how the degeneration of the International and its constituent parties led to interwoven methodological, strategic and tactical errors – whose negative results required further quashing of dissent, yielding less opening for correction by the membership based on their experience, and so on in an ever-downward spiral. The critiques cover the Party's mischaracterisation of the economic conjuncture, its international perspectives, as well as relationships to bourgeois and reformist parties and unions. The first article describes a convention held while the CP was still in its 'third period' mode. By the time of the second article, the turn toward the Popular Front had been made. Both are presented here to show how the new Stalinist methods could – in fact, had to – yield both sectarian and opportunist policies and practices.

The CLA not only criticised Stalinist ideology and its implementation, but was also required to defend itself from attacks by those same Stalinists – attacks which set new lows for slander, lies and miseducation. A key battlefront in this defence came after the Moscow Trials had begun, and the US wing of the worldwide Trotskyist movement took the lead in creating and facilitating the work of the Dewey Commission.

The summary presented here on the work of the Dewey Commission (its full name was the Commission of Inquiry into the Charges Made against Leon Trotsky in the Moscow Trials) explains why exposing such lies was not just a matter of fixing the historical record or clearing individuals' names; it was also intimately tied to the fight for revolutionary leadership of the workers' movement. A summary – probably composed by George Novack, who played a central role in organising the work of the Commission – states:

> The attack against the Commission is in no respect accidental. No question of our time is more crucial than that of the Moscow trials. In the issue of the trials is summed up in concentrated form the problem of the Russian revolution which in its turn sums up the problem of the international revolution and thus of the future of mankind.

An intended by-product of the Commission's work, by its insistence on upholding the traditional norms of honesty and fairness of the workers' movement, was the application of its methods to other battlefronts against Stalinism, e.g. frame-ups of various leftist trends in Spain, fighting the crushing of democracy within Stalinist-run unions and movements in the US, etc.

It is worth noting that the Dewey Commission's fight for truth paralleled the world movement's exposure of the obeisance of supposed 'friends of the Soviet Union' to the Stalin regime's policies and myths. In opposing capitalism and imperialism, it is not acceptable to condone heinous crimes carried out in the name of 'revolution', nor close one's eyes to whatever bizarre metamorphosis a presumably 'progressive' regime may undergo. Here, as with other methodological lessons to be drawn from the record of early Trotskyism, there is a more general applicability.

The 1938 survey by Max Shachtman – 'Revolution and Counter-Revolution in Russia' – presents the traditional perspective of the Trotskyist movement, defending the revolutionary origins and residual gains of the 1917 revolution, and as part of that defence uncompromisingly opposing the authoritarian-bureaucratic betrayals associated with the regime and policies represented by Stalin.

1 'At the Sixth World Congress'[1]

(1956)

James P. Cannon

Dear Sir:

There is very little I can add to what I have already written about the Sixth World Congress of the Comintern (1928) in the *History of American Trotskyism*. That report on the Congress as a whole is meager enough, and the reason for it is frankly explained there. The simple truth is that in the first period after our arrival in Moscow, I, like all the other American delegates, was far more concerned about the fight over the American question than the work of the Congress in general. Then, after I got hold of a copy of Trotsky's *Criticism of the Draft Program*, my interest and attention was concentrated on that and what I would do about it after I got back home.

Maurice Spector, a top leader of the Canadian party, read the *Criticism* at the same time and his reaction to it was the same as mine. Thereafter we lost interest in the official proceedings. We made a compact to fight for Trotsky's cause, but we knew that it would be futile and tactically unwise to begin our fight in Moscow. We held a continuous 'Congress' of our own about Trotsky's great document and its implications. As I said in the *History*, 'We let the caucus meetings and the Congress sessions go to the devil while we studied this document' …

Stalin evidently wanted to utilize the Congress as a final mopping-up operation against the Left Opposition before bringing the fight against Bukharin into the open. The American opposition delegates were cagey about getting out on a limb in connection with the internal affairs of the Russian party. They denounced the Lovestoneites as representatives of the right-wing tendency in the International without specifying who were the Russian leaders in this right wing. I cannot recall that Bittelman or any other member of the American opposition attacked Bukharin openly. I am pretty sure it didn't happen …

1 Cannon 1957.

What sticks in my mind is the report that Stalin, at a special session of the *Senioren Konvent*, had denied any conflict in the Russian leadership, and that this had a restraining influence on any delegates in the Congress who might have been inclined to press the question …

As far as I know, Stalin's devious method of political manipulation was absolutely unique. There was no criterion by which to estimate what he was driving at at any particular moment. In one of his comments about the early days of the struggle of the Left Opposition in the Russian party – perhaps it was in his autobiography – Trotsky said the party functionaries were kept in the dark as to what the majority faction intended by this or that action. They were required to 'guess' what it meant and to adapt themselves in time. Selections of people and promotions were made by the accuracy of their guesses at each stage of development in the factional struggle. Those who guessed wrong or didn't guess at all were discarded. This guessing game was played to perfection in the period of Stalin's preparation to dump Bukharin. I don't think many people knew what was really going on and what was already planned at the time of the Sixth Congress. Everybody was guessing, and it is quite evident that the Lovestoneites guessed wrong …

The main concern of Lovestone and Wolfe was not the general direction of policy in the Russian party and the Comintern, but their own stake in the leadership of the American party. When the showdown came at the party convention the following year, their attempt to propitiate Stalin by proposing the expulsion of Bukharin, was a revealing gesture. Their failure to cut loose from Bukharin at the time of the Sixth Congress really doesn't deserve to be considered as a sign of their quixotic devotion to Bukharin's cause. It was just a bad guess …

At the time we submitted the platform of the opposition on *The Right Danger* everything was still more or less normal in the opposition bloc. There was not the slightest sign of objection by the Fosterites to my participation, since there could be no hope of winning a majority in the party unless the bloc held together. The objection to me, rather, was that I was not sufficiently active and aggressive in the struggle before the American Commission. This discontent with my conduct became accentuated after I read Trotsky's *Criticism of the Draft Program*. Then I began to slow down and lose interest in the faction fight altogether. The others may have known, or suspected the reasons, but I am sure they could not bring themselves to believe that I would do anything foolishly impractical about it. They didn't care what anyone's secret thoughts might be as long as they were not compromised by some overt action.

The delegates of the 'Cannon group' were especially discontented with my increasing indifference to the factional struggle in Moscow and what it might portend; their own positions in the party stood to be affected adversely by my default. They started a pressure campaign to induce me to snap out of it and get back into the fight in earnest. The repudiation of Foster by his own faction had created a sort of vacuum in the leadership of the combined opposition and they felt, not without some justification, as things were at that time, that I was far better qualified to fill it than any of the other members of the Foster group. All this led to an incident which is perhaps worth reporting, since it compelled me to make the decision which was to have far-reaching consequences.

A meeting was called of all the members and sympathizers of our faction in Moscow. About a dozen, all told, were there, including our Congress delegates, the students in the Lenin School and a number of others. Spector was also present. There the proposition was flatly put to me – that if I would quit dragging my feet and go all-out in the factional struggle, they would pledge me their support all the way to the end as the logical candidate for the central position of leadership in the party when the Lovestone regime was overthrown.

I did not give a definite answer at the meeting. Spector and I held our own caucus on the question for a couple of days. We discussed it solely from the point of view of how best to serve the cause of Trotsky, to which we were by then fully committed. The proposal had an attractive glitter. In the first place, even though we were less optimistic than the others, we recognized that the objective outlined in the meeting was not unrealistic. If the indications of a Comintern swing to the left were fully developed there was good ground to think that the opposition's chances for gaining the majority in the party would steadily improve.

Secondly, with Foster discredited and repudiated by his own former supporters, it was obvious that my claim to a more important role as the central leader of the opposition, and eventually of the party, was far stronger than that of Bittelman or any of the others in the Foster faction. Bittelman suffered from a number of disqualifications, which he himself was well aware of. He was distinctively an internal party man, not a mass worker and orator suited to the role of public leader. Browder had no standing as a political leader and was not even thought of in that connection. The other people of the Foster group were of even lesser caliber. We speculated that if I could secure the central position in the official apparatus of the party, I would be in a position to swing far more substantial support for the International Left Opposition when the time came to make a decisive open break. The fly in the ointment was that in order to carry out such a maneuver I would have to adapt myself to the official Comintern line against Trotskyism, and even make up for previous derelictions by excessive zeal in this respect. I would, in effect, be winning the party for the program of Stalinism.

Could I then, at some indefinite future time, reveal my own secret program and overcome the effect of the miseducation which I had helped to disseminate? Was there not a danger that I myself would become compromised and corrupted in the process and find it impossible to extricate myself at some future time?

I must state frankly that Spector and I discussed the proposition between ourselves very seriously before deciding against it. Only after thorough consideration of the maneuver from all sides, did we finally decide to reject the proposition. We came to the conclusion that the cause of Trotskyism would be served better in the long run if we frankly proclaimed his program and started the education of a new cadre on that basis, even though it was certain to mean our own expulsion and virtual isolation at the start of the new fight.

The choice of alternatives would present no difficulties to people who have been raised and educated in the Trotskyist school of principled politics, which our movement has consistently represented since 1928. The decision we made at that time would seem to be an easy one, to be made out of hand. It was not so easy for us in those days. Since the death of Lenin, the politics of the Comintern had become a school of maneuverism, and we ourselves had been affected by it. Trotsky's document on the Draft Program was a great revelation of the meaning of principled politics. But for us at that time it was a new revelation. We were profoundly influenced by it, but we were only beginning to assimilate its full significance.

That accounts for our hesitation, for our toying for a day or two with the possibility of a self-deceiving maneuver which might well have gravely injured the cause of genuine communism in this country. And not only in this country, for the expelled and slandered defenders of the banner everywhere were then in their darkest hour. They needed to hear an American voice in their support. Our demonstrative action in publicly unfurling the banner of Trotsky in 1928 – at a time when he was exiled and isolated in Alma Ata – greatly encouraged the scattered forces of the International Left Opposition throughout the world …

The Fosterites in revolt were still dependent on Foster's name and prestige whether they liked it or not. At that time they had no prospect of playing a big role in the party without him. Foster, for his part, had nowhere else to go except to become a captive of the Lovestoneites, and that was impossible for him. So the whole stew blew up violently and then receded and continued to simmer and sizzle in the same pot. We, the 'Cannonites', stood aside and let the Fosterites fight it out among themselves. From a personal standpoint I felt a certain sympathy for the slaves in hysterical rebellion. But from a political standpoint I couldn't see any sense whatever in encouraging a split with a view to realignment in the form of a bloc between our faction and the Fosterites, minus Foster.

Foster's name and prestige, and his dogged persistence and outstanding ability as a mass worker, were always the bigger half of the assets of the Foster group, and remained so even after he had been defeated and isolated within the group. This was shown quite conclusively a short time later. When Stalin wanted to convey a message – with more than a hint of future support – to the American opposition, he sent for Foster and gave it to him personally ...

There is one small postscript to my recollections of this family fight among the Fosterites, which was soon swallowed up in my preoccupation with the immeasurably larger subject of Trotsky's *Criticism of the Draft Program*, and all that it implied for my own future course.

After the meeting, in a personal conversation with Bill Dunne and me, Foster complained of the treatment he had received and intimated – without saying so directly – that he would like to have better personal relations with us for collaboration in the future. But my own mind was already turning to far bigger things than the old factions and faction squabbles in the American party, and I couldn't get up any interest in them any more.

Yours truly,
James P. Cannon

2 The Dog Days of the Left Opposition[2]

(1944, excerpts)

James P. Cannon

Our last lecture brought us up to the first National Conference of the Left Opposition in May 1929. We had survived the difficult first six months of our struggle, kept our forces intact and gained some new recruits. At the first conference we consolidated our forces into a national organization, set up an elected leadership and defined our program more precisely. Our ranks were firm, determined. We were poor in resources and very few in numbers, but we were sure that we had laid hold of the truth and that with the truth we would conquer in the end. We came back to New York to begin the second stage of the struggle for the regeneration of American Communism.

The fate of every political group – whether it is to live and grow or degenerate and die – is decided in its first experiences by the way in which it answers two decisive questions.

The first is the adoption of a correct political program. But that alone does not guarantee victory. The second is that the group decide correctly what shall be the nature of its activities, and what tasks it shall set itself, given the size and capacity of the group, the period of the development of the class struggle, the relation of forces in the political movement, and so on.

If the program of a political group, especially a small political group, is false, nothing can save it in the end. It is just as impossible to bluff in the political movement as in war. The only difference is that in wartime things are brought to such a pitch that every weakness becomes exposed almost immediately, as is shown in one stage after another in the current imperialist war. The law operates just as ruthlessly in the political struggle. Bluffs do not work. At most they deceive people for a time, but the main victims of the deception, in the end, are the bluffers themselves. You must have the goods. That is, you must have a correct program in order to survive and serve the cause of the workers.

An example of the fatal result of a light-minded bluffing attitude toward program is the notorious Lovestone group. Some of you who are new to the

2 Cannon 1944a.

revolutionary movement may never have heard of this faction which once played such a prominent role, inasmuch as it has disappeared completely from the scene. But in those days the people who constituted the Lovestone group were the leaders of the American Communist Party. It was they who carried through our expulsion, and when about six months later, they themselves were expelled, they began with far more numerous forces and resources than we did. They made a much more imposing appearance in the first days. But they didn't have a correct program and didn't try to develop one. They thought they could cheat history a little bit; that they could cut corners with principle and keep larger forces together by compromises on the program question. And they did for a time. But in the end this group, rich in energies and abilities, and containing some very talented people, was utterly destroyed in the political fight, ignominiously dissolved. Today, most of its leaders, all of them as far as I know, are on the bandwagon of the imperialist war, serving ends absolutely opposite to those which they set out to serve at the beginning of their political work. The program is decisive.

On the other hand, if the group misunderstands the tasks set for it by the conditions of the day, if it does not know how to answer the most important of all questions in politics – that is, the question of what to do next – then the group, no matter what its merits may otherwise be, can wear itself out in misdirected efforts and futile activities and come to grief …

[T]he question confronting us at our first convention was whether we should continue to support the Soviet state, the Soviet Union, despite the fact that the direction of it had fallen into the hands of a conservative, bureaucratic caste. There were people in those days, calling themselves and considering themselves revolutionary, who had broken with the Communist Party, or had been expelled from it, and who wanted to turn their backs entirely on the Soviet Union and what remained of the Russian revolution and start over, with a 'clean slate' as an anti-Soviet party. We rejected that program and all those who urged it on us. We could have had many members in those days if we compromised on that issue. We took a firm stand in favor of supporting the Soviet Union; of not overturning it, but of trying to reform it through the instrumentality of the party and the Comintern.

In the course of development it was proved that all those who, whether from impatience, ignorance or subjectivity – whatever the cause might be – prematurely announced the death of the Russian revolution, were in reality announcing their own demise as revolutionists. Each and every one of these groups and tendencies degenerated, fell apart at the very base, withdrew to the side lines, and in many cases went over into the camp of the bourgeoisie. Our political health, our revolutionary vitality, were safeguarded, first of all, by the correct attitude we took toward the Soviet Union despite the crimes that had been committed, including those against us, by the individuals in control of the administration of the Soviet Union.

The trade union question had an extraordinary importance then as always. At that time it was particularly acute. The Communist International, and the Communist parties under its direction and control, after a long experiment with rightwing opportunist politics, had taken a big swing to the left, to ultra-leftism – a characteristic manifestation of the bureaucratic centrism of the faction of Stalin. Having lost the Marxist compass, they were distinguished by a tendency to jump from the extreme right to the left, and vice versa. They had gone through a long experience with right-wing politics in the Soviet Union, conciliating the kulaks and Nepmen, until the Soviet Union, and the bureaucracy with it, came to the brink of disaster. On the international arena, similar policies brought similar results. In reacting to this, and under the relentless criticisms of the Left Opposition, they introduced an ultra-leftist over-correction in all fields. On the trade union question they swung around to the position of leaving the established unions, including the American Federation of Labor, and starting a new made-to-order trade union movement under the control of the Communist Party. The insane policy of building 'Red Unions' became the order of the day.

Our first National Conference took a firm stand against that policy, and declared in favor of operating within the existing labor movement, confining independent unionism to the unorganized field. We mercilessly attacked the revived sectarianism contained in this theory of a new 'Communist' trade union movement created by artificial means. By that stand, by the correctness of our trade union policy, we assured that when the time arrived for us to have some access to the mass movement we would know the shortest route to it. Later events confirmed the correctness of the trade union policy adopted at our first conference and consistently maintained thereafter.

Faction or Party?

The third big important question we had to answer was whether we should create a new independent party, or still consider ourselves a faction of the existing Communist Party and the Comintern. Here again we were besieged by people who thought they were radicals: ex-members of the Communist Party who had become completely soured and wanted to throw out the baby with the dirty bath water; syndicalists and ultra-leftist elements who, in their antagonism to the Communist Party, were willing to combine with anybody ready to create a party in opposition to it. Moreover, in our own ranks there were a few people who reacted subjectively to the bureaucratic expulsions, the slander and violence and ostracism employed against us. They also wanted to renounce the Communist Party and start a new party. This approach had a superficial attraction. But we resisted, we rejected that idea. People who over-simplified the question used to say to us: 'How can you be a faction of a party when you are expelled from it?'

We explained: It is a question of correctly appraising the membership of the Communist Party, and finding the right tactical approach to it. If the Communist Party and its members have degenerated beyond reclamation, and if a more progressive group of workers exists either actually, or potentially by reason of the direction in which such a group is moving and out of which we can create a new and better party-then the argument for a new party is correct. But, we said, we don't see such a group anywhere. We don't see any real progressiveness, any militancy, any real political intelligence in all these diverse oppositions, individuals and tendencies. They are nearly all side-line critics and sectarians. The real vanguard of the proletariat consists of those tens of thousands of workers who have been awakened by the Russian revolution. They are still loyal to the Comintern and to the Communist Party. They haven't attentively followed the process of gradual degeneration. They haven't unraveled the theoretical questions which are at the bottom of this degeneration. It is impossible even to get a hearing from these people unless you place yourself on the ground of the party, and strive not to destroy but to reform it, demanding readmission to the party with democratic rights.

We solved that problem correctly by declaring ourselves a faction of the party and the Comintern. We named our organization The Communist League of America (Opposition), in order to indicate that we were not a new party but simply an opposition faction to the old one. Experience has richly demonstrated the correctness of this decision. By remaining partisans of the Communist Party and the Communist International, by opposing the bureaucratic leaders at the top, but appraising correctly the rank and file as they were at that time, and seeking contact with them, we continued to gain new recruits from the ranks of the Communist workers. The overwhelming majority of our members in the first five years of our existence came from the CP. Thus we built the foundations of a regenerated Communist movement. As for the anti-Soviet and anti-party people, they never produced anything but confusion.

The Propaganda Task

Out of this decision to form, at that time, a faction and not a new party, flowed another important and troublesome question which was debated and fought out at great length in our movement for five years – from 1928 until 1933. That question was: What concrete task shall we set for this group of 100 people scattered over the broad expanse of this vast country? If we constitute ourselves as an independent party, then we must appeal directly to the working class, turn our backs on the degenerated Communist Party, and embark on a series of efforts and activities in the mass movement. On the other hand, if we are to be not an independent party but a faction, then it follows that we must direct our main efforts, appeals and activities, not to the mass of 40 million American workers, but to the vanguard of the class organized in and around the Communist Party. You can see how these two questions dovetailed. In politics – and not only in politics – once you say 'A' you must say 'B'. We had to either turn our face towards the Communist Party, or away from the Communist Party in the direction of the undeveloped, unorganized and uneducated masses. You cannot eat your cake and have it too.

The problem was to understand the actual situation, the stage of development at the moment. Of course, you have to find a road to the masses in order to create a party that can lead a revolution. But the road to the masses leads through the vanguard and not over its head. That was not understood by some people. They thought they could by-pass the Communistic workers, jump right into the midst of the mass movement and find there the best candidates for the most advanced, the most theoretically developed group in the world, that is, the Left Opposition which was the vanguard of the vanguard. This conception was erroneous, the product of impatience and the failure to think things out. Instead of that, we set as our main task *propaganda*, not *agitation*.

We said: Our first task is to make the principles of the Left Opposition known to the vanguard. Let us not delude ourselves with the idea we can go to the great unschooled mass now. We must first get what is obtainable from this vanguard group, consisting of some tens of thousands of Communist Party members and sympathizers, and crystalize out of them a sufficient cadre either to reform the party, or, if after a serious effort that fails in the end – and only when the failure is conclusively demonstrated – to build a new one with the forces recruited in the endeavor. Only in this way is it possible for us to reconstitute the party in the real sense of the word ...

It is very easy for isolated people, gathered together in a small room, to talk themselves into the most radical proposals unless they retain a sense of proportion, of sanity and realism. Some of our comrades, disappointed at our slow growth, were lured by this idea that we needed only a program of mass work in order to go out and get the masses ...

We consumed an enormous amount of time and energy debating and fighting out this question. And not only with Weisbord. In those days we were continually pestered by impatient people in our ranks. The difficulties of the time pressed heavily upon us. Week after week and month after month we appeared to be gaining hardly an inch. Discouragement set in, and with it the demand for some scheme to grow faster, some magic formula. We fought it down, talked it down, and held our group on the right line, kept its face turned to the one possible source of healthy growth: the ranks of the Communist workers who still remained under the influence of the Communist Party.

'Third Period' Policies

The Stalinist 'left turn' piled up new difficulties for us. This turn was in part designed by Stalin to cut the ground from under the feet of the Left Opposition; it made the Stalinists appear more radical even than the Left Opposition of Trotsky. They threw the Lovestoneites out of the party as 'right wingers', turned the party leadership over to Foster and Company and proclaimed a left policy. By this maneuver they dealt us a devastating blow. The disgruntled elements in the party, who had been inclined toward us and who had opposed the opportunism of the Lovestone group, became reconciled to the party. They used to say to us: 'You see, you were wrong. Stalin is correcting everything. He is taking a radical position all along the line in Russia, America and everywhere else'. In Russia the Stalin bureaucracy declared war on the kulaks. All over the world the ground was being cut from under the feet of the Left Opposition. A whole series of capitulations took place in Russia. Radek and others gave up the fight on the excuse that Stalin had adopted the policy of the Opposition. There were, I would say, perhaps hundreds of Communist Party members, who had been leaning towards us, who gained the same impression and returned to Stalinism in the period of the ultra-left swing.

Those were the real dog days of the Left Opposition. We had gone through the first six months with rather steady progress and formed our national organization at the conference with high hopes. Then recruitment from the party membership suddenly stopped. After the expulsion of the Lovestoneites, a wave of illusion swept through the Communist Party. Reconciliation with Stalinism became the order of the day. We were stymied. And then began the big noise of the first Five Year Plan. The Communist Party members were fired with enthusiasm by the Five Year Plan which the Left Opposition had originated and demanded. The panic in the United States, the 'depression', caused a great wave of disillusionment with capitalism. The Communist Party in that situation appeared to be the most radical and revolutionary force in the country. The party began to grow and swell its ranks and to attract sympathizers in droves.

We, with our criticisms and theoretical explanations, appeared in the eyes of all as a group of impossibilists, hairsplitters, naggers. We were going around trying to make people understand that the theory of socialism in one country is fatal for a revolutionary movement in the end; that we must clear up this question of theory at all costs. Enamored with the first successes of the Five Year Plan, they used to look at us and say, 'These people are crazy, they don't live in this world'. At a time when tens and hundreds of thousands of new elements were beginning to look toward the Soviet Union going forward with the Five Year Plan, while capitalism appeared to be going up the spout; here were these Trotskyists, with their documents under their arms, demanding that you read books, study, discuss, and so on. Nobody wanted to listen to us.

In those dog days of the movement we were shut off from all contact. We had no friends, no sympathizers, no periphery around our movement. We had no chance whatever to participate in the mass movement. Whenever we tried to get into a workers organization we would be expelled as counterrevolutionary Trotskyists. We tried to send delegations to the unemployed meetings. Our credentials would be rejected on the ground that we were enemies of the working class. We were utterly isolated, forced in upon ourselves. Our recruitment dropped to almost nothing. The Communist Party and its vast periphery seemed to be hermetically sealed against us.

Then, as is always the case with new political movements, we began to recruit from sources none too healthy. If you are ever reduced again to a small handful, as well the Marxists may be in the mutations of the class struggle; if things go badly once more and you have to begin over again, then I can tell you in advance some of the headaches you are going to have. Every new movement attracts certain elements which might properly be called the lunatic fringe. Freaks always looking for the most extreme expression of radicalism, misfits, windbags, chronic oppositionists who had been thrown out of half a dozen organizations – such people began to come to us in our isolation, shouting, 'Hello, Comrades' …

Many people came to us who had revolted against the Communist Party not for its bad sides but for its good sides; that is, the discipline of the party, the subordination of the individual to the decisions of the party in current work. A lot of dilettantish petty-bourgeois minded people who couldn't stand any kind of discipline, who had either left the CP or been expelled from it, wanted, or rather thought they wanted to become Trotskyists. Some of them joined the

New York branch and brought with them that same prejudice against discipline in our organization. Many of the newcomers made a fetish of democracy. They were repelled so much by the bureaucratism of the Communist Party that they desired an organization without any authority or discipline or centralization whatever.

All the people of this type have one common characteristic: they like to discuss things without limit or end. The New York branch of the Trotskyist movement in those days was just one continuous stew of discussion. I have never seen one of these elements who isn't articulate. I have looked for one but I have never found him. They can all talk; and not only can, but ***will***; and everlastingly, on every question. They were iconoclasts who would accept nothing as authoritative, nothing as decided in the history of the movement. Everything and everybody had to be proved over again from scratch.

Walled off from the vanguard represented by the Communist movement and without contact with the living mass movement of the workers, we were thrown in upon ourselves and subjected to this invasion. There was no way out of it. We had to go through that long drawn-out period of stewing and discussing. I had to listen, and that is one reason my gray hairs are so numerous. I was never a sectarian or screwball. I never had patience with people who mistake mere garrulousness for the qualities of political leadership. But one could not walk away from this sorely beset group. This little fragile nucleus of the future revolutionary party had to be held together. It had to go through this experience. It had to survive somehow. One had to be patient for the sake of the future; that is why we listened to the windbags. It was not easy. I have thought many times that, if despite my unbelief, there is anything in what they say about the hereafter, I am going to be well rewarded – not for what I have done, but for what I have had to listen to.

Hard Times

That was the hardest time. And then, naturally, the movement slid into its inevitable period of internal difficulties, frictions and conflicts. We had fierce quarrels and squabbles, very often over little things. There were reasons for it. No small isolated movement has ever been able to escape it. A small isolated group thrown in upon itself, with the weight of the whole world pressing down upon it, having no contact with the workers mass movement and getting no sobering corrective from it, is bound in the best case to have a hard time. Our difficulties were increased by the fact that many recruits were not first class material. Many of the people who joined the New York branch weren't really there by justice. They weren't the type who, in the long run, could build a revolutionary movement – dilettantes, petty-bourgeois undisciplined elements. ...

And then, the everlasting poverty of the movement. We were trying to publish a newspaper, we were trying to publish a whole list of pamphlets, without the necessary resources. Every penny we obtained was immediately devoured by the expenses of the newspaper. We didn't have a nickel to turn around with. Those were the days of real pressure, the hard days of isolation, of poverty, of disheartening internal difficulties. This lasted not for weeks or months, but for years. And under those harsh conditions, which persisted for years, everything weak in any individual was squeezed to the surface ...

The greatest movement, with its magnificent program of the liberation of all humanity, with the most grandiose historic perspectives, was inundated in those days by a sea of petty troubles, jealousies, clique formations and internal fights. Worst of all, these faction fights weren't fully comprehensible to the membership because the great political issues which were implicit in them had not yet broken through. However, they were not mere personal quarrels, as they so often appeared to be, but, as is now quite clear to all, the premature rehearsal of the great, definitive struggle of 1939–40 between the proletarian and petty-bourgeois tendencies within our movement.

Those were the hardest days of all in the thirty years that I have been active in the movement – those days from the conference of 1929 in Chicago until 1933, the years of the terrible hermetically sealed isolation, with all the attendant difficulties. Isolation is the natural habitat of the sectarian, but for one who has an instinct for the mass movement it is the most cruel punishment.

The Old Print Shop

Those were the hard days, but in spite of everything we carried out our propaganda tasks, and on the whole we did it very well. At the conference in Chicago we had decided that at all costs we were going to publish the whole message of the Russian Opposition. All the accumulated documents, which had been suppressed, and the current writings of Trotsky were then available to us. We decided that the most revolutionary thing we could do was not to go out to proclaim the revolution in Union Square, not try to put ourselves at the head of tens of thousands of workers who did not yet know us, not to jump over our own heads.

Our task, our revolutionary duty, was to print the word, to carry on *propaganda* in the narrowest and most concentrated sense, that is, the publication and distribution of theoretical literature ...

Great sacrifices were made by the rank and file of our comrades all the time, but they were never greater than the sacrifices made by the leaders. That is why the leaders of the movement always had strong moral authority. The leaders of our party were always in a position to demand sacrifices of the rank and file – because they set the example and everybody knew it.

Somehow or other the paper came out. Pamphlets were printed one after another. Different groups of comrades would each sponsor a new pamphlet by Trotsky, putting up the money to pay for the paper. In that antiquated print shop of ours a whole book was printed on the problems of the Chinese revolution ...

And in spite of everything – I have cited many of the negative sides and difficulties – in spite of everything, we gained a few inches. We instructed the movement in the great principles of Bolshevism on a plane never known in this country before. We educated a cadre that is destined to play a great role in the American labor movement. We sifted out some of the misfits and recruited some good people one by one; we gained a member here and there; we began to establish new contacts ...

Those were cruel and heavy times. We survived them because we had faith in our program and because we had the help of Comrade Trotsky. Comrade Trotsky began his great work in exile for the third time. His writings and his correspondence inspired us and opened up for us a window on a whole new world of theory and political understanding. This gave us the strength to persevere and to survive, to hold the organization together and to be ready when our opportunity came ...

3 'The Decay of the Stalinist Party'[3] (1934)

Arne Swabeck

One of the great American contradictions finds its expression in the backward ideology of the working masses existing alongside of the advanced technology of the country. But the crowning height of this contradiction is attained by the official Communist party. An examination of its position made in the light of a comparison with the gigantic tasks of the American revolution will reveal it beyond a shadow of a doubt as the one party in the Stalinized Comintern which is the least equipped with the indispensable weapons of Marxism.

It is necessary to remember that Marxism both interprets the world and teaches how to change it. Without the Marxian interpretation and estimate of world events, there can be very little hope of finding the correct road for the change. Nor will there be a possibility of deepening and extending the revolutionary practice. Lacking these prerequisites the official party has already become a force of disorientation and working class defeats in the day to day struggles as well. Marxism does not exist in its theory or practice, neither in the sense of interpreting the world nor in the sense of teaching how to change it. It would be difficult to conceive of a party which more stupidly parrots the trite formulae, devoid of revolutionary realism, of Stalin, Manuilsky and Molotov. The pernicious mistakes of the Third International on a world scale it duplicates on the national scene – and in worse form. All that is needed to prove this is furnished by the party itself.

With the world crisis, American capitalism arrived at a fundamental turning point in its political history. The economic self-sufficiency formerly proclaimed and the American provincialism which resulted from it, together with the celebrated 'rugged individualism', are, historically speaking, at an end. In their place we will have a more centralized monopoly capitalism assisted by a definite system of attempted governmental control of class relations. This change is perhaps most clearly typified in the contrast between the Hoover regime and the Roosevelt regime. The Hoover regime was the last staunch representative of

3 Swabeck 1934.

the past while the Roosevelt regime represents the beginning of new methods in the course of American capitalism toward its more complete world hegemony.

From this the question arises: To what extent has the official party taken notice of or made a theoretical analysis of the deep going changes in class relations that this new situation presents? Has it taken notice of the vast new problems facing the working class vanguard? It has, of course, been cognizant of the increasing misery and lowered standard of living imposed on the working class by the crisis. It is true that it has also recognized the increasing and multiplying difficulties that now confront American capitalism. But that is still far short of a theoretical analysis of the fundamental changes involved. Such an analysis would be obligatory upon a revolutionary general staff, for without it there can be no correct conclusions at all for the tasks that are pending. This, however, cannot be expected from the official party which in all of its practice remains entirely true to the empiricist methodology of the epigones.

Instead of an analysis we have the pompous proclamation of the discovery of Fascism in both the Hoover and the Roosevelt regimes. In the Fascism of the Hoover regime was included, according to the seventh convention thesis of 1930, the AF of L, the Socialist party and the Muste group. The latter two, said the thesis, were covering their Fascism with pseudo-revolutionary phrases. It may be granted that the party is now trying to make a distinction by specifying the Fascist methods of the Hoover regime and the Fascist economic system of the Roosevelt regime. But that is only so much nonsense. Of course, the official party qualifies its 'theoretical' conclusions by saying that it is not speaking of developed Fascism, but Fascism nevertheless. In this respect the American party leaders only repeat the fatal errors of the German party and the Stalintern as a whole. And from such premises it would be impossible, even in the remotest sense, to make a sound estimate of what Fascism actually is, of the conditions under which it arises, its special characteristics as a social phenomenon of a certain epoch, or its historical role.

In view of this, the speech made by Browder to the party plenum in January 1934, is not at all surprising. After the usual attempt at justifying the capitulation of the German CP by explaining that the social democracy still held the majority of the working class under its influence, he projects the question, which he says has been asked by many: Why did the German party not lead the revolutionary section of the German working class in struggle against Fascism? And listen to the wisdom of his answer: To hold such a position, he says, would mean

> ... nothing but capitulation to the social democracy. It is a complete acceptance of the social democratic understanding of the significance

> of the rise of Fascism and of Hitler. Along with it necessarily goes the view that the victory of Hitler inaugurates a protracted period of Fascist reaction and long time defeat of the revolution.

Browder has no such view, and he could therefore declare nonchalantly to the Cleveland convention in discussing the question of the rise of Fascism in the United States,

> It [Fascism] destroys the moral base for capitalist rule, discrediting bourgeois law in the eyes of the masses; it hastens the exposure of all demagogic supporters of capitalism, especially its main support among the workers – the Socialist and trade union leaders. It hastens the revolutionization of the workers, destroys their democratic illusions, and thereby prepares the masses for the revolutionary struggle for power.

What is said here is full of false and dangerous propositions. It is the covering of one's tracks in the most treacherous manner. It is said to justify the criminal capitulation in Germany and to maintain the fiction that the German party is consolidating and strengthening itself as a political force. According to this statement, Fascism does not denote a new period existing on the ruins of the working class organizations, requiring entirely new methods of struggle, particularly the struggle for the democratic demands, and under much greater difficulties. Fascism is a mere incident. It is really not different from any preceding regime, except that it hastens disillusionment and speeds up the revolution. That the proletariat will conquer ultimately, even in spite of Fascism, is incontestable. But what Browder is attempting here is an advance justification of the capitulation of the party to Fascism. There is really no point to the Leninist demand for the united front to crush Fascism before it overcomes the proletariat and destroys its organizations.

In regard to the question of changing class relations in the United States the official party position is no less astounding and no less stupid. Already in 1930 it saw a 'revolutionary upsurge of the working masses of the United States', which was 'opening the road to the Communist party for organizing and leading these masses into struggles'. This was evidenced among many other things 'by increasing militancy of the workers in resisting the violent suppression of strikes and demonstrations … by the mass interest in revolutionary trade unionism' and 'by the rapid growth of the Communist party in membership and influence'. This is quoted from the seventh convention thesis presented in March 1930. But at the eighth convention, held recently, we are informed that the party at that time did not grow at all. And what the interest in the 'revolutionary unions' amounted to at the time might as well not be mentioned. It was nil. Suffice it to recall that the 'revolutionary upsurge' had been announced by Molotov when he inaugurated the 'third period' at the tenth Comintern plenum, and this upsurge therefore had to be discovered everywhere, including the United States. Such was the 'theoretical' analysis and evaluation of class relations made by the official party in 1930. Would we not be justified in assuming that conclusions for a general strategy should have been made therefrom which would be in accord with this perspective of revolutionary upsurge? Marxism would impose such a duty upon a revolutionary party leadership. But the perspective was false and Marxism was non-existent in the party. History completely refuted this perspective. Apparently, then, so much the worse for history. The adventurist commands which were issued for the 'capture of the streets' in the daily 'revolutionary' practice of the official party led only to futile and isolated exercises.

In the thesis of the eighth convention the official party outlines the same perspective as in 1930, even though in foundation it is stated a little more circumspectly. Meanwhile, gigantic events have intervened on a world scale: the conquests of Fascism in Germany and Austria, its growth elsewhere, and the collapse of the Second and the Third Internationals. However, in the eighth convention thesis this is not even mentioned. Not the least trace can be found to indicate that a single lesson has been learned from these world-shaking events. Again it is necessary to remember that Marxism both interprets the world and teaches how to change it. That is the weapon which is already forged. Actually applying Marxism, however, would mean first of all to learn the bitter lessons from all of the criminally false policies and the final capitulation which helped Fascism come into power and brought about the destruction of the workers' parties. The party bureaucracy could not even begin to permit that. It would have meant its own undoing. Therefore it pursued the opposite course and with worse consequences to the party.

In view of this it would be ludicrous to expect a correct theoretical analysis of the changes now taking place in class relations in the United States. The crisis has been a great leveling process, reducing economically the various working class strata much nearer to one common low level. The turn in the economic cycle finds the masses entering the trade unions in numbers running into hundreds of thousands with the unions extending into the very heart of the basic and the mass production industries. There is a surging revival of the AF of L unions, a radical change in its position and composition and new processes are beginning within its ranks. Back in 1930 the official party proclaimed the AF of L a company union and moribund. It had only one regret, that it 'did not sooner clearly analyze and characterize the open Fascism of the AF of L' (1930 convention thesis). From this it drew the conclusion that its 'most fundamental task in mass work is the building of the revolutionary unions of the Trade Union Unity League'.

The party had entirely forgotten the warning of the *Communist Manifesto* that: 'They [the Communists] do not set up any sectarian principles of their own, by which to shape and mould the proletarian movement'. History has made a mockery of the official party prognosis. A whole series of false policies foisted upon a party membership which has been denied the elementary right and privilege of inquiring into reasons, and has lost the ability to distinguish, has brought its cruel retaliation. While the mass unions are experiencing new growth and, regardless of the desires and policies of the reactionary leaders, are drawn into the vortex of new great class battles, the TUUL unions remain paper institutions, devoid of life, an obstruction in the path of working class advance. In the present sharpening of class lines in the United States events in the trade union field are of a decisive character. The question of correct trade union policy is at present the key to the working class problems. A workers' party which cannot approach a solution of this problem cannot be counted upon at all to lead the proletarian revolution in America. It will function instead as a brake and a force for disintegration and defeat.

Is it any wonder that the official party is now compelled to bewail the results of its handiwork in the following admission penned in the eighth convention thesis?

> The leadership of the party in the trade union work remains extremely weak despite the *Open Letter* and control tasks adopted by the CC and the Districts. The majority of the party members remain outside of the unions in most of the districts (including such concentration districts as Chicago, Detroit): in the party as a whole the important progress made was with but a small section of the party membership active in the economic struggles. Communist fractions, without which there can be no real leadership by the party in the work of the trade unions, remain weak and receive little attention.

Further proof – if further proof is needed – of the bankruptcy of the party is furnished in the *Open Letter* referred to above (July 7, 1933). There we are informed that:

> The clearest expression of the failure to carry out this concentration is the fact that during the past year the majority of strikes were led by reformists … In fact the reformists in Eastern Ohio, a concentration

> district of the party, succeeded in taking over the leadership of miners who had previously carried on a heroic strike under the leadership of the National Miners Union.

Finally it must be said that in the splendid class battles of most recent date, in Minneapolis and Toledo, the official Communist party was no political factor at all. The inspiring influence and conscious direction given came from other political forces in the country. The official party appeared as far as these battles are concerned only as a demoralizing and disorganizing factor.

A comparison today between Stalinism and social democracy will reveal that within the latter, including the American Socialist party, serious repercussions have been produced by recent world events. New tendencies and new groupings are emerging which acknowledge the defeats and the collapse of the workers' parties. Hazily some of these groups are beginning to draw conclusions in a revolutionary direction. Within the official Communist party, however, 'unanimity' prevails. Its theoretical level is unquestionably the lowest ever recorded. With implicit faith the celebrated 'general line' is adopted again and again no matter what history records. Utterly incapable of reasoning otherwise than according to its own bureaucratically constructed dogmas, alien to Marxism, but accepted by the membership in a spirit of religious fervor, the party stumbles into ever greater contradictions. While the American workers in ever greater numbers become attracted to Communism, thousands leave the official party ranks. From 1930 to February 1934, Browder admits in his eighth convention report, the party had recruited 49,080 new members, but the actual membership in this period rose only from 7,645 to 24,800. These figures attest the membership turnover. But there would be little grounds for accepting the announced gains at face value when we recall that the 1930 convention thesis estimated the party membership to be, not 7,540 but 'approximately 15,000'.

The bureaucratic triumph of the little epigones recorded at the eighth convention climaxed in the one and only infallible general secretary, apparently presents the party as having reached new and hitherto unknown heights. But stripped of all the pompous convention trimmings, the exact opposite is revealed. What remains is a picture of theoretical decline, bankruptcy and degeneracy. It is high time to clear the road for the new revolutionary party.

4 Communists Play 'Follow the Leader'[4]
(*1936*)

Albert Goldman

A convention in the life of a revolutionary working class party that believes in and practices the principle of democratic centralism is an extremely important occasion. It affords an opportunity for the membership of the party, through elected delegates, to express their views on questions confronting the party members and the working class and permits the reaching of a final decision on such questions. A convention is a convenient and necessary institution, giving a revolutionary party a chance to look back upon its progress or lack of it, evaluate the policies followed, correct mistakes and gather its forces for the march onward with substantial or slight changes in direction and tempo.

No one in the least acquainted with the life of the Communist party in this country or anywhere else expects any discussion prior to a convention or during a convention or expects any new policy to come out of a convention. That is, no one who thinks independently and is not a blind devotee of the 'beloved leader'. A convention is as necessary and useful for the Communist party as is the calling of Parliament by Hitler. A perfectly superfluous gesture to deceive the naive and credulous who think that to discuss whether a policy handed down has been executed correctly is identical with a discussion on the correctness of the policy itself.

Examine the publications of the Communist party and you will find no trace of any view contrary to the official viewpoint on any of the problems raised at the convention. All the policies were already decided upon before the convention by the 'beloved leaders' great and small, and all there was left for the followers was to accept with great enthusiasm. And the members of the CP have come to take the system for granted. In the 'Party Life' column of the *Daily Worker* of July 17, a worried comrade writes: 'There is an attitude which we have to break down in our educational work. The comrades in the Units feel that all the questions of the Party are settled in the higher Party bodies. Therefore they don't have to worry about it in the Unit; there'll be a statement in the *Daily*

4 Goldman 1936.

Worker on it anyhow. So why discuss it'. We can assure the comrade that the attitude will not be broken down.

Convention Adds Nothing New

Every one of the ideas embodied in every one of the resolutions placed before the agreeable delegates were contained in the utterances or writings of Browder long before the convention took place. The august gathering was simply for the purpose of placing a formal stamp of approval upon those ideas ...

There are some comrades who incline to say that this is too much; there will be a revolt amongst the intelligent Communists. But these comrades underestimate the power of a bureaucratic apparatus that has succeeded in establishing its authority over the minds of people who in all other respects seem to be of normal intelligence. Until the line is changed we can expect all the Communists even those who might read Lenin's *State and Revolution*, to preach the formation of a people's government ...

A Combination That Terrifies

Until such time as the American people can take over the government for themselves they must concentrate on that really dreadful combination of the Republican party, the Liberty League and Hearst. 'The chief political center of extreme capitalist reaction, which carries the threat of fascism today is the Republican Party–Liberty–League–Hearst combination'. Again: 'The Communist Party declares that the struggle against reaction and incipient fascism demands the utmost unification and concentration of all forces of the working class and its allies against the Republican–Liberty League–Hearst combination' (*Daily Worker*, June 16, 1936).

Does that mean that the CP has come out for supporting Roosevelt? Not in so many words. The Communists insist that Roosevelt is not fighting that combination as he should and that is why, it is to be presumed, they are not calling upon the masses openly to support Roosevelt. Of course Browder, in his report at the convention, was bold enough to state that there is no principle connected with refusing to vote for a bourgeois candidate like Roosevelt. And to support his boldness he had the temerity to cite Lenin on the necessity of the proletariat to support the democratic bourgeoisie in a bourgeois democratic revolution. Perhaps he thinks we need a bourgeois democratic revolution in this country.

Lenin pointed out that after the death of a great revolutionist the real essence of his revolutionary theories is emasculated and vulgarized by opportunists. And Lenin is now suffering the same fate. And out of seven hundred and fifty delegates there was not one with spirit enough to cry 'Shame' upon this disgusting effort to enlist Lenin in the work of betrayal.

It is true that the Communists formally are not endorsing Roosevelt, but in concentrating their attack on the Republican party as the bearer of fascism and in mildly chiding Roosevelt for his failure to come out more aggressively against the Liberty Leaguers they are practically advising the workers that to vote for Roosevelt is to vote for the lesser evil. The Stalinists have changed their policy since the German catastrophe but only to substitute the policy of the Social Democrats for the sectarian polices of the Third Period.

Recently they have called for a conference to stop Landon and have urged Lewis and Hillman to take the lead in such a conference. Since these labor leaders are heart and soul for the election of Roosevelt what would be the meaning of such a conference if not to whip it up for Roosevelt?

Bourgeois Democracy versus Fascism

The theoretical justification for concentrating the attack on the Liberty League–Hearst combination is the theory that the working class is at the present time faced with the alternative of bourgeois democracy or fascism. This theory of course is not the product of Browder's hard thinking but it goes back to Dimitroff and back of him to the beloved Stalin. Enunciated with great profundity at the Seventh Congress it is used to justify the most opportunistic policies.

In this respect the Socialist party is one hundred percent correct. To defeat fascism one must attempt to mobilize the masses for the destruction of the very system of capitalist democracy which gives rise to fascism. This does not mean that we urge the workers to be indifferent to their democratic rights. On the contrary we must mobilize the workers for a struggle for every democratic right which they possess and do not possess under the capitalist system. But that is simply for the purpose of strengthening their forces for the destruction of the capitalist system. When we say that the real alternative is fascism or socialism it does not mean that unless we get socialism in this election fascism will result. This is the way the Communists attempt to pose the question.

It means that revolutionary Socialists recognize that the development of capitalist society has reached a point where the capitalist democratic regime cannot function and if that regime is not destroyed by the forces of the proletariat it will be destroyed by the forces of fascist reaction. With that as a perspective we do not struggle to save the bourgeois *democratic regime* but we struggle for the *democratic rights of the workers*. The Communists also claim that they are struggling for democracy in order ultimately to bring in socialism. Whatever the intention of the Communist leaders may be, the effect of their incorrect theory is to demoralize both the workers and the middle class and open the way for fascism.

Much has been said and written about the reformist attitude on war which the Communists have adopted within the last year. The slogan of collective security accepted by the Stalinist regime as a safeguard for the Soviet Union and subsequently adopted by all the Communist parties was augmented in the Communist platform by the immediate demand for the 'complete prohibition of the sale or delivery of goods, or the granting of loans to nations engaged in a foreign war contrary to the provisions of the Kellogg Peace Pact'. The Marxist interpretation of the nature of imperialist war with its rejection of the idea of an aggressor nation is thrown over-board and in its stead we find ourselves scrutinizing a document drawn up by a former Republican Secretary of State to determine our attitude to a particular capitalist nation. Exactly who shall determine the question as to which particular nation was guilty of violating the Peace Pact is not stated. We presume the Communists will be guided by their investigators and lawyers ...

It is difficult to imagine that only a little over two years ago the same party held a convention in Cleveland at which convention ideas were expressed which are the exact opposite of the ideas presented at the last convention. The 8th convention of the CP held two years ago issued a Manifesto and the ideas found therein cannot possibly be harmonized with the concepts propounded at the 9th.

> There is no possible way out of the crisis in the interest of the masses except by breaking the control of the State power now in the hands of this small monopolist capitalist class. There is no way out except by establishing a new government of the workers in alliance with the poor farmers, the Negro people and the impoverished middle class.
>
> There is no way out except by the creation of a revolutionary democracy of the toilers, which is at the same time a stern dictatorship against the capitalists and their agents ... There is no way out in short except by the abolition of the capitalist system and the establishment of a Socialist society.

We can accept this portion of the Manifesto without qualification.

The eighth convention was held after Hitler came to power; after the brave struggle of the Austrian workers against Dolfuss; even after the general strike against the fascists of France. But the theory of social-fascism was still accepted. At that time a non-Communist was either a fascist, or a semi-fascist or a variety of social-fascist. That convention 'established the fact' that the New Deal was a 'program of fascization', that the 'fascization of the trade unions' had reached a dangerous stage and that 'in this trickery of the masses Roosevelt has the utmost support of the AF of L bureaucrats, Socialists and liberals'. The Socialist party was at that time the 'third party of capitalism' and a possible Farmer-Labor party would be a 'new left social-fascist party'.

Revolutionary Phrases Retained

Ideas, however, are very easily discarded in the life of the Communist movement. Without the slightest explanation and certainly without the least preparation in the form of discussion, the old stand-bys were dropped; the Socialist party became a brother party of the working class; the Farmer-Labor party the only hope of the working class; Roosevelt a mild liberal who was not calling upon the Communists in his struggle against the American fascists organized in the Liberty League.

It would be folly to expect that the old revolutionary phrases would disappear entirely from the resolutions and speeches. The tremendous appeal which the Communist movement has for the revolutionary workers lies in the fact that these workers sincerely think that the Communist International is still the revolutionary International of Lenin and that it is devoted to the effort of overthrowing the system which every advanced worker hates. For the Communists to discard altogether the revolutionary phraseology and cling to a consistent system of reformist ideas would mean the complete loss of their influence.

Not only can they not afford to get rid of the revolutionary word but they must actually assume the pose of critics of the Socialists as reformists. This fundamental necessity of playing a dual role in order to keep the good will of both the liberal bourgeoisie and the revolutionary workers explains the tactics of the Communists in France and in Spain. They have to talk 'left' once in a while; they must appear as the supporters of the workers' struggles ever so often. But in reality their activities have nothing at all to do with the interests of the proletarian revolution. And it is hardly likely that they will ever come out in the open as avowed revisionists of Marx and Lenin. They would thereby lose all their influence with the revolutionary section of the working class.

And so in the resolutions of the last convention and even in the platform there are tucked away suggestions about the necessity of establishing Socialism through the Soviet power. 'Such policies', states the resolution, 'will create favorable conditions for the overthrow of capitalist rule altogether, the establishment of Soviet Power and the building of Socialism'. A necessary insertion which has no relationship to the actual policies pursued.

Zig-Zag Policy

How long will this change last? There are Socialists who doubt the 'sincerity' of the Communists. Alas they are terribly in earnest. Their opportunism is not a cloak which is to be put on and taken off to please the liberals and some Socialists. It is basic to their whole conception built around the theory of building socialism in the Soviet Union – and only in the Soviet Union. Their previous sectarian ultra leftism is but a different form of their basic reformism. What attitude the Communists will take to the bourgeoisie of their own country will depend entirely upon the relationship of the Soviet Union to that particular country. The foreign policy of the Stalin regime will determine the particular garment which the Communists will don to cover their opportunist nakedness.

It is not at all excluded that in the future there will be a swing back to the most insane sectarianism. The alliances between the different imperialists are not yet stabilized and it is possible that the different imperialist rivals might succeed in making a temporary bargain, with the Soviet Union left out. In which case to 'protect and defend the Soviet Union' it might be necessary to designate every one who thinks it essential for the workers to develop their consciousness before calling on them for revolution – to designate such a person as a left or right social fascist.

The exigencies of Soviet diplomacy will determine the tactics of the Communist parties. And not the need for a revolutionary overthrow of the capitalist system to solve the problems of the whole working class including the workers of the Soviet Union.

5 The Dewey Commission[5]
(*1937*)

New International

The Commission of Inquiry into the charges made against Leon Trotsky at the Moscow trials has announced that it will deliver its final report at a public meeting called for December 12. We are not as yet, of course, acquainted with the content of the report. The character and abilities of the members of the Commission and our knowledge of the scientific thoroughness with which they have pursued their investigation, however, assures us in advance of the profound historical significance of the forthcoming document.

Probably no analogous Commission in the history of the labor movement has ever been confronted with such obstacles or subjected to so vicious, unabating and ruthless an attack. By every method, precedented and unprecedented, every agency of every form of reaction has brought its energies to bear on one sole aim: to prevent the truth about the Moscow Trials from being known. It is a vast tribute to the courage and integrity of the Commission members, and of its distinguished chairman, Professor John Dewey, that they have not been turned aside, but have carried their work to its completion.

The attack against the Commission is in no respect accidental. No question of our time is more crucial than that of the Moscow trials. In the issue of the trials is summed up in concentrated form the problem of the Russian revolution which in its turn sums up the problem of the international revolution and thus of the future of mankind. To suppose that the trials are 'out-dated', have sunk into the background against the lurid and mighty events of the intervening months, is to be merely blind.

The trials of Zinoviev-Kamenev and of Piatakov-Radek are the blue-prints of the full force of the reaction against the proletarian revolution, of the counter-revolution. In them the ideology, the methods and the implications of the counter-revolution are displayed in the purest and bluntest manner. These trials are the archetype upon which are modeled the entire series of lesser trials, purges, executions which have become a daily feature of the Soviet regime. No

5 Editorial, ***New International*** 1938.

one can even pretend to understand the meaning of the purge without first understanding the trials; and they are equally necessary to an understanding of the new Constitution, the developments in Soviet economy, and indeed of the entire present policy of Stalinism.

But the trials are not in the least a 'merely Russian phenomenon', as the philistines are so anxious to insist. Their effect was felt immediately by the entire world; in every nation the trials at once became, and remain, an inescapable issue. More directly and specifically, the method of the trials has already been introduced into country after country, on an international scale. What is the policy of the Stalinists in Spain but the trials transferred to Spanish soil? In Czechoslovakia, the first Moscow trial has already been attempted – to end in failure, for this first time. In France, the preparation is well under weigh. In this country also, the trials have already begun: the Stalinists in Minnesota are now endeavoring to transform the events surrounding the assassination of the labor leader, Corcoran, into a native American replica of the Moscow trials. It would be naïve to imagine that it will stop with this, whatever the immediate result. Stalinism and all of its henchmen, agents, and allies, are now irrevocably committed to the method of the trials; this method now sums up its political substance; and it can no longer draw back.

There is no avoiding the issue of the trials, and there is no middle ground. That is why it is a permanent issue, why it remains and cannot be thrust aside. For, in actuality, the issue of the trials is the issue of the revolution itself. If Stalin and Vishinsky are correct, those who made the revolution are traitors, fascists, counter-revolutionists, and the revolution in its own history proves that the goal of socialism is impossible and must be abandoned. But to understand the truth, to realize that the trials are the most gigantic frame-up in history and to realize why that frame-up was undertaken, is to see that it is Stalinism which is the counter-revolution, and to re-assert triumphantly the goal of socialism and the methods – the methods of Marx and Lenin and Trotsky – through which that goal will be achieved.

6 Revolution and Counter-revolution in Russia[6] (*1938*)

Max Shachtman

The twentieth anniversary of the Russian revolution has been greeted in monotonous dithyrambs by the liberals of almost every school. It is not so much the social revolution against capitalist society and private property to which they pay their belated respects. They hail what they consider the successfully established Great Power, the abandonment of all those childish notions of world revolution which they always regarded as Utopian and more than a little ill-mannered, and the maturing of the once rude youngster who has now come of age and is eminently fitted to join the society of the respectable and democratic nations of the earth.

This aspect of the twentieth anniversary is of no small symptomatic significance. In November 1917 and afterwards, the liberals regarded the Bolshevik revolution as an unwarranted intrusion upon the legitimate development of Russia towards their concept of democracy, under the aegis of Kerensky and his coalition government with the realistic and statesmanlike social-democrats. The withdrawal of the Soviets from the imperialist war which left the Allies all alone in the fight to make the world safe for democracy, and the subsequent overturn of all the economic power of the capitalistic class and their political retainers only added to the already mounting horror of the liberal intelligentsia. Their horror was not abated but intensified when the proletariat began to shatter the resistance of the counterrevolution with distinctly impolite weapons of ruthless warfare.

The dust stirred up by the intense class struggle in Russia blinded the liberals to the world-historical significance of the revolution which was laying the foundation stones for a hitherto only dreamed-of social order. Even years later they could not forgive the Bolsheviks their audacity. Grudgingly at first, and in the end enthusiastically, with a pitying if not angry glance at the Trotskyists who strike a discordant note at the ceremony, they joined in the now stylish endorsement of the Soviet regime. But their tardy recognition of the revolution

6 Shachtman 1938a.

of 1917 coincides not with its social triumph but with the period of its degeneration. Just as they once failed to see that the victory of the Bolsheviks marked the victory of the social revolution against capitalism, so they fail to see that the victory of the Stalinist bureaucracy marks the victory of a *political counter-revolution*. Yet that is precisely what is new in the development of the Russian revolution.

Not a single Bolshevik leader considered it possible for the Soviet power to endure for a long period of time, much less for Russia to achieve the classless socialist order, unless the workers of one or more advanced capitalist countries come to its aid.

> When we began the international revolution [said Lenin at the Third Congress of the Communist International in 1921] … we thought, either the international revolution comes to our aid and then our victory is quite assured, or else we do our modest revolutionary work and do it in the knowledge that in the event that we suffer defeat, we are thereby of use to the cause of the revolution, because we make it possible for other revolutions, made shrewder by our experiences, to do it better. It was clear to us that without the support of the international world revolution, the victory of the proletarian revolution is impossible. Even before the revolution and also afterwards, we reflected: either the revolution in the other countries, in the capitalistically more developed countries, comes immediately or at least in very swift succession, or we must succumb.

Neither the hope nor the prognosis was realized, as is known. Yet the Soviet state has not perished. At first blush, this seems to confirm Stalin's nationalistic thesis that a socialist society can be established within a single Country regardless of whether the revolution triumphs in other lands. But only at first blush. For while the Soviet state has not succumbed despite its enforced isolation, it has not only been unable to achieve its socialist goal but it has been corrupted from within by the deadly cancer of degeneration. The canal through which the poisons have flowed to the heart and head of the régime, is the Stalinist bureaucracy.

Even before it expropriated the economic power of the bourgeoisie, the Russian revolution deprived it of its political power. Its place was taken by the rule of the working class, a proletarian democracy, Lenin wrote, 'a million times more democratic than any bourgeois democracy, and the Soviet regime … a million times more democratic than the most democratic régime in a bourgeois republic'. The Soviet democracy was based on the abolition of a professional governmental bureaucracy divorced from the people, on the indivisibility of the legislative and executive bodies, on the direct rule of the toilers through their deputies to the Soviets, subject at all times to recall, on the armed people as against a professional body of armed men divorced from the masses, and on the privileged position of the proletariat as the vanguard of the toiling masses. While the Bolshevik party, as the tested and trusted revolutionary vanguard of the proletariat, was the ruling party, it maintained a live and sensitive contact with the toilers through the Soviets, the trade unions, the factory committees, the committees of poor peasants, the cooperatives, and similar institutions. The existence of a wide freedom of discussion and decision in all these bodies, of genuine workers' democracy, made of this interlocking system of institutions the living reality of the political rule of the proletariat – never ideal or flawless, to be sure, but decisive.

The counter-revolution of the Stalinist bureaucracy consists in nothing less than this: It has effectively destroyed all these institutions in the last fourteen years and thereby it has just as effectively expropriated the proletariat *politically*.

THE OLD GUARD OF THE PARTY. – Lenin attached, even if not uncritically, a tremendous significance to what was called the Old Guard of the Bolshevik party. He regarded those veterans who had passed through three revolutions, the World War and the civil war, as one of the main assurances that the revolution would continue along its indicated path. 'It must be recognized', he wrote to the Central Committee in March 1922, 'that at the present time the proletarian party policy is determined not so much by its membership as by the unlimited and powerful authority of that thin layer which we may name the old party Guard'. The Stalinist bureaucracy, in the course of its reaction to the revolution, its traditions and its ideology, has destroyed the Old Guard which embodied them.

Take but one example which comes to hand, the Central Committee elected at the 9th Congress in 1920: Artem, Dzerzhinsky, Lenin, Bukharin, Zinoviev, Kamenev, Krestinsky, Preobrazhensky, Rudzutak, Radek, Rakovsky, Rykov, Serebriakov, I.N. Smirnov, Tomsky, Trotsky, Andreyev, Kalinin and Stalin. The first three died of natural causes. Of the rest, Zinoviev, Kamenev, Serebriakov and I.N. Smirnov were murdered by the Stalinists; Tomsky was killed or driven to suicide; Trotsky is in Mexican exile; Bukharin, Krestinsky, Preobrazhensky, Rudzutak, Radek, Rakovsky and Rykov are imprisoned or disgraced – all thirteen of them as fascists or wreckers or assassins. Only Stalin, Kalinin and Andreyev remain, which is like saying that only Stalin remains.

Important to note in this devastating and uninterrupted purge is the fact that it is not only the generation of defenders of the October that has been crushed. The Trotskyists or Zinovievists – men like Trotsky, Zinoviev, Kamenev, Rakovsky, Mdvani, Piatakov, Smirnov, Smilga, Preobrazhensky, Bieloborodov, Muralov – were removed long ago by the Thermidorian generation that brought Stalin to power. Now even the men of the Thermidorian reaction have gone or are going: Bukharin, Rykov, Rudzutak, Tukhachevsky, Bubnov, Postyshev, and hundreds less well known. Their places are taken by entirely colorless unknowns like Beria, Eikhe, Zhdanov, Khrustchev who are not so much party leaders as Stalinist governor-generals who rule the provinces like old Turkish Walis; they are made or unmade in a day by simple decree, and their coming and going are like the shadows of a guttering candle flame.

THE BOLSHEVIK PARTY. – Whatever else it may be, a political organization that does not have a free and rich inner life is not a revolutionary proletarian party. In Lenin's time, even after the Mensheviks and Social Revolutionists had placed themselves outside the Soviet pale by their counter-revolutionary course and left the Bolshevik party with a monopoly of political rule, the party led an intense and active inner life, discussing freely at all times, debating all questions openly, electing, criticizing and removing its leadership and deciding the party line at will. Under the gun-fire of the Kronstadt mutiny and the echoes of the peasant risings in Tambov and elsewhere, the 10th Congress adopted the entirely exceptional and temporary emergency measure prohibiting separate factions with separate platforms. This unprecedented limitation on party democracy, however, was adopted with numerous significant reservations. The adopted resolution stated:

> It is necessary that every party organization takes rigorous care that the absolutely necessary criticism of the shortcomings of the party, all analyses of the general party direction, all appraisals of its practical experience, every examination of the carrying out of the party decisions and of the means of correcting the mistakes, etc. – shall not be discussed in separate groups standing upon any 'platform', but rather in the meetings of all the party members. Towards this end, the Congress decides to publish a periodical Discussion Sheet and special periodicals. Everyone who comes forward with a criticism must take into consideration the position of the party in the midst of its encircling enemies, and he must also strive, in his direct activity in Soviet and party circles, to correct the mistakes of the party in practice.
>
> *While the Congress orders the Central Committee to exterminate all factionalism, the conference declares at the same time that those questions which*

> *attract the special attention of the party membership – e.g., on the purging of the party of unproletarian, unreliable elements, on the struggle against bureaucratism, on the development of democracy and the broader participation of the workers, etc. – and in general all objective proposals, must be examined with the utmost possible scrupulousness and tested practically. All party members must know that the party cannot take all the required measures in these questions, since it encounters a whole series of the most varied obstacles, and that while the party decisively rejects an un-objective and factional criticism, it will continue tirelessly to test new methods, and to fight with all means against bureaucratism and for the extension of the democracy of the self-active masses, for the uncovering, exposure and expulsion of all unreliable elements from the party.*
>
> *Russische Korrespondenz, Nr. 5, May 1921, p. 323*

Not aimed at suppressing democracy, even the restrictions of the 10th Congress were designed to extend discussion and criticism, to organize it, to ferret out bureaucratism, and to do all this in a manner that would be less dangerous and factional under the concrete conditions. When, at the same congress, Riazanov moved an amendment prohibiting elections of delegates to coming congresses on the basis of factional platforms, Lenin, quick to sense the danger, replied:

> I think that the desire of comrade Riazanov is unfortunately not realizable. If fundamental disagreements exist on a question, we cannot deprive members of the Central Committee of the right to address themselves to the party. I cannot imagine how we can do this. The present congress can in no way and in no form engage the elections to the next congress. And if, for example, questions like the Brest-Litovsk peace arise? Can we guarantee that such questions will not arise? It cannot be guaranteed. It is possible that it will then be necessary to elect by platform. That's quite clear.
>
> *Minutes of the 10th Congress*, p. 292, Russ. ed.

And again, elsewhere, during the same period Lenin wrote:

> But if deep, fundamental disagreements of principle exist, we may be told: 'Do they not justify the sharpest factional action?' Naturally they justify it, if the disagreements are really deep, and if the rectification of the wrong policy of the party or of the working class cannot be obtained otherwise.
>
> *Works*, Vol. XVIII, Pt. 1, p. 47, Russ. ed.

In the period of acute danger to the Soviet regime, when it had to make the painful and hazardous transition to the New Economic Policy, and when the party imposed certain organizational restraints upon itself, Lenin nevertheless called for freedom of discussion and criticism, for internal discussion organs, and acknowledged the permissibility and even inevitability of factions, platforms and the 'sharpest factional action'. By this he was merely testifying to the existence of a *living party*.

The Stalinist bureaucracy has changed all that. It started with the Trotsky-Zinoviev Opposition. In 1927, it prohibited the publication of their *Platform*, arrested those leaders and militants who mimeographed it for circulation in a pre-congress discussion period, and expelled all those who defended it. It demanded not only that the Opposition supporters cease *advocating* the views in their *Platform*, but that they cease believing those views! In 1932, Stalin demanded the execution of the old Bolshevik, Riutin, for circulating a 'platform' which ended with Lenin's demand that Stalin be removed from his post; Riutin was 'merely' imprisoned by the GPU. In the last few years – the years of Stalinist domination – not one single word of criticism of the party leadership has been uttered; not one single proposal different from the proposals of the Führer. Nobody dares. Yet there are differences of opinion, whispered about and muttered in tiny grouplets. Only, the party does not decide these differences. The party is dead. The GPU decides them in accord with the instructions of the Secretariat.

The congress of the party is its highest and most authoritative instance, selecting the leadership to carry out the line of policy which the congress adopts. At least, so it was in Lenin's time. The question of seizing power, the Brest-Litovsk treaty, the New Economic Policy, the trade union question – all these were decided at party congresses, after the fullest discussion of all the conflicting standpoints. In the Stalinist epoch, congresses no longer take place. In their stead, the bureaucracy organizes palace assemblies of hand-picked lieges who listen without discussion to the Throne Speech of the Führer. The lesser bureaucrats appear only for the purpose of burning frankincense to Stalin and of giving him assurances of their blind fealty in terms reminiscent of the fawning speeches made by provincial princelings to an Oriental potentate.

Just think: In the days of illegality and thin purses, under Tsarist despotism, the Russian party nevertheless held four regular congresses between July 1903 and May 1907. (Of party conferences under Tsarism, there were eight, from the Tammerfors meeting in 1905 to the Poronino meeting in 1913). In the revolutionary period, between the overthrow of the Tsar and the death of Lenin, the party held eight regular party congresses (and seven conferences). The Stalinist record is quite different. The first real post-Lenin congress was the 14th, in December 1925; the 15th was held 2 years later; between it and the 16th, 2½ years were allowed to elapse; between the 16th and the 17th Congress – the last to be held, in January 1934 – more than 3½ years went by. The statutes adopted by the Stalinists themselves at the 17th Congress provided that 'regular congresses are convened no less than once in three years'. In cynical violation of its own statutes, the bureaucracy has let four years pass and the fiction of a party is not even allowed to hold its fiction of a congress. And what four years these have been! What drastic changes the bureaucracy has made without even going through the formality of consulting the party! Under the Stalinist bureaucracy, the Bolshevik party (if it may be called that) has been allowed to meet in congress (again, if it may be called that) only four times in more than thirteen years. The party met more often under the Tsar! The bureaucracy has crushed the old party.

THE TRADE UNIONS. – In the early days of the revolution, the Bolsheviks regarded the trade unions as a school of Communism, and as one of the institutions through which the workers ruled in the factories and the Soviets. The Bolsheviks did not fear debate and discussion, and as late as 1920, almost three years after the revolution, Dalin and Martov could still appear as the official representatives of the Menshevik party at the 3rd Congress of the trade unions to present their views and debate the Bolshevik spokesmen. But even more: the Bolsheviks regarded the trade unions as an indispensable instrument for the defense of proletarian interests from the transgressions, abuses and wantonness of the state itself, and especially of its bureaucracy. It was only in 1927 that Molotov put forward the bigoted, bureaucratic conception that since Russia is a workers' state there can be no question of defending the workers from it. Lenin had nothing in common with this bureaucratic idealism. Speaking before the party fraction of the 8th Soviet Congress on December 30, 1920, during the discussion on the trade union question, he said:

> Comrade Trotsky speaks of the workers' state. Permit me, that is an abstraction. When we wrote about the workers' state in 1917 that was understandable; but when it is said today: Why defend, defend the working class against whom, there's no longer a bourgeoisie, don't we have a workers' state – then an obvious error is being committed. The whole joke is that it is not quite a workers' state. That's where the basic mistake of comrade Trotsky lies! We have passed over from general principles to objective discussion and to decrees, but that's where we are being held back from practical objective work. That will not do! Our state is in reality no workers' state, but a workers' and peasants' state. A whole lot follows from that

> ... But still more. From our party program it follows that our state is a workers' state with bureaucratic deformations. We have to paste this – how shall we call it? – sorry label on it. That is the reality of the transition! ...
>
> *Our present state is such that the organized proletariat must defend itself and we must utilize these workers' organizations for the defense of the workers against their state and for the defense of the state by the workers.*
>
> *Der Kampf um die soziale Revolution*, pp. 593 f.

What a decisive role Lenin assigned to the trade unions in this profoundly dialectical concept of the interrelations between the economic organizations of the workers and the *real* – not idealistically perfect – workers' state, a concept beyond the grasp of superficial minds accustomed to abstract and absolute categories. The trade unions are an instrument for the defense of the workers' state and for the defense of the workers from that state! And if the latter was necessary seventeen years ago, how infinitely more urgent is it today that the trade unions defend the workers from a regime in which the bureaucratic cancer has grown to monstrous, undreamed-of proportions? What, for example, has happened to the right to strike, solemnly recognized by the party congress in Lenin's time? Most likely it has not been abolished by law; only, the exercise of that right is rewarded by a prompt visit by the GPU.

The right to intervene in the question of hiring and firing and of management in general was taken from the trade unions, from the factory committee and from the party nucleus in the factory, in September 1929. The trade unionists and the unions themselves are silent in the face of the most abominable abuses of the factory directors. The bitterness of the average worker against the growing disparity between his wages and the salary of the industrial bureaucrat or the labor aristocrat who carries the title of Stakhanovite, is felt in the heart and muttered in the most discreet privacy, but is not expressed in or through the trade unions.

The trade union leadership is composed of case-hardened bureaucrats, appointed from above and removed just as easily. They know they have neither obligations nor responsibilities to the ranks; nor are they under their control. As a result the Soviet press is compelled to print countless depressing reports of wantonness, irresponsibility, embezzlement, brutality and degeneration among the trade union officialdom. The worker does not know today who will be the head of his trade union tomorrow; he is not consulted and, knowing quite well that he has a union in name only, he cares precious little. He is aware that the armed guard who watches over him in the mine pit, as described by Kléber Legay elsewhere in this issue, is far more real and far more powerful than the empty shell that was once the Russian trade union movement.

The first All-Russian congress of the trade unions met in January 1918; the second early in 1919; the third in April 1920. The 9th Congress met towards the end of 1928; the 10th Congress early in 1932. Since then – that is for almost six crucial years – there has been no congress. If one knew nothing else about the Russian trade unions, the comparison between the two sets of dates would suffice to indicate the difference between a living movement, a real foundation stone in the structure of proletarian democracy – and a fiction. But behind the fiction stands the usurpatory bureaucracy.

THE SOVIETS. – The Russian revolution laid bare the Soviets – the councils of workers, soldiers, peasants – as the most natural, most democratic, most efficient form of proletarian state rule in the transition period between capitalism and communism. In all other countries where a revolutionary situation matured, Soviets, just like the Russian or slightly varied in form, developed spontaneously as the embryonic organs of insurrection and power, and not as a product artificially imported from Russia.

The original Soviets *were* a million times more democratic than any bourgeois republic precisely because they smashed the monopoly of the professional capitalist politician and bureaucrat whose relationship with the masses is confined to electoral campaigns once a year or less often. The Soviets made it possible for the masses to throw off the yoke of 'voting cattle' which bourgeois rule imposes upon them, and to act as the direct, independent administrators of their own affairs. Unsatisfactory representatives could be recalled at will and replaced by others. Lenin saw especially in the right of recall not only one of the main pillars of Soviet democracy but also a guarantee of the peaceful settlement of conflicts and disputes in the country. Four weeks after the Bolshevik uprising, he said at a session of the All-Russian Central Executive Committee of the Soviets:

> Various parties have played a dominant role among us. The last time, the passage of influence from one party to another was accompanied by an overturn, by a fairly stormy overturn, whereas a simple vote would have sufficed had we had the right of recall … The right of recall must be granted the Soviets, which are the most perfect carrier of the state idea, of coercion. Then the passage of power from one party to another will proceed without bloodshed, by means of simple new elections.
>
> *Izvestia*, No. 233, Dec. 6, 1917

The whole course of the Stalinist bureaucracy, climaxed by a 'democratic election under the new democratic Constitution' which is gruesomely mocked by the never-ceasing purge, has proceeded by trampling under foot every one of the conceptions of the place and function of the Soviets which prevailed in the early years of the revolution. From the local Soviets to the Central Executive Committee itself, the administrations are appointed and removed at will by the corresponding party apparatus-bosses, and without the slightest intervention of the masses themselves. The right of recall exists, to be sure, but it is exercised only by the Stalinist bureaucracy. What Soviet institution, what mass organization or movement intervened, for example, to remove the recently condemned People's Commissars of White Russia, of the Ukraine, of Georgia, of the RSFSR, of the Soviet Union, and to put others in their place? Only the GPU, acting as administrative agent of the party secretariat. What 'democratic' significance have the new constitutional rights of free speech, free press and free assembly when they are enjoyed exclusively (and even then limitedly) by the myrmidons of the bureaucracy who are themselves under the constant surveillance of the secret police? What value has the secret ballot when there is but one candidate to choose from, and he hand-picked by the apparatus? The elections to the Soviets and all other alleged legislative and executive bodies are classic examples of Bonapartist plebiscites; they are an abominable caricature of Soviet democracy, the very negation of it.

The bureaucracy has strangled the Soviets of the revolution. The political rule of the workers and peasants has been supplanted by the political rule of the bureaucracy and those social strata which are its direct props. What a revealing story there is in the social composition of the guaranteed-to-be-elected candidates to the Council of the Union! Of actual workers and peasants, there are none or next to none. The overwhelming majority of the candidates is made up of party officials, factory directors, labor aristocrats (Stakhanovites), GPU and army officers, well-to-do farmers, that is, the reactionary bureaucracy and its associated social layers. The Soviets were to make it possible, in Lenin's words, for any charwoman, for the lowest and most despised, to become the administrators of the state, so that it would no longer be, properly speaking, a state in the old sense of a bureaucratic apparatus of oppression with special bodies of armed men separate and apart from the people. The triumph of the Stalinist bureaucracy has been accomplished by the political expropriation of the charwomen, of the proletariat. It signifies the victory of the *political counter-revolution.*

THE FOREIGN POLICY. – At home, the bureaucracy has not yet been able to free itself from the confines of the economic basis achieved by the Russian revolution, about which more later. But abroad, it has a free hand, so to speak, and there its course is openly counter-revolutionary. It is the gendarme of law and order, of the *status quo* throughout the capitalist world. A comparison between the situation even in 1923, when the reactionary tumor was already apparent in the Soviet body, and 1937, when the totalitarian bureaucracy is celebrating its triumph, will indicate the profound change.

In 1923, when the German revolution was expected, the Soviet Republic stood at attention to aid it. The harbor of Petrograd was filled with grain ships ready to sail for Stettin so that the German Soviet republic would not be starved out by the Entente. Representatives of the Comintern and the Russian party were active on German soil, preparing for the uprising as best they could under the leadership of Brandler and Zinoviev. Specialists of the Red Army were assigned to give expert assistance to the German communists. The close diplomatic alliance existing at that time between the Soviets and the German bourgeois republic had not converted the International into the main prop of German capitalism – quite the contrary.

In 1937, all the diplomatic moves in Europe, all the aid sent by the Soviet Union to the Spanish loyalists (in the form of munitions, arms, military experts, GPU agents, etc.), are directed towards crushing the proletarian revolution in Spain, preserving Spanish bourgeois democracy as an instrument in the hands of Anglo-French imperialism. The policy of Stalin in Spain is distinguished from that of Noske and Scheidemann in the Germany of 1919 only by its more systematic savagery. *All* the policies of the Soviet bureaucracy are based upon its self-preservation. Abroad, at the very least, in the international labor movement and class struggle, it is indisputable that the interests of the Soviet bureaucracy come into head-on conflict with the interests of the working class. These interests produce not the policies of the Mensheviks of 1905, nor even of 1917, but of those Mensheviks who took up arms, in alliance with Anglo-French imperialism in 1918–1919, to overthrow the young Soviet republic. They are not just non-revolutionary policies, they are the policies of counter-revolution.

What remains of the Russian revolution? Why should we defend the Soviet Union in case of war?

A number of realities still remain. The conflict between German fascism (and fundamentally, also, of the capitalist world as a whole), and the Soviet Union, still remains no less a reality than, let us say, the conflict between fascism and social-democracy or the trade unions, regardless of how corrupt may be the leadership of the latter, regardless of how it may compromise and capitulate, regardless of how much it may seek to place itself under the protection of one capitalist force (as did the Austrian social democracy) against another. The conflict can be resolved only by the capitalist world being overturned by the working class, or by the Soviet Union, its present bureaucracy included, being crushed and reduced to the status of a colonial or semi-colonial country, divided among the world's imperialist bandits.

Another great reality is the economic foundation established by the October revolution. Despite bureaucratic mismanagement and parasitism, we have the prodigious economic advances made by Soviet industry, the great expansion of the productive forces in Russia (without which human progress is generally inconceivable) in a period of stagnation and retrogression in the capitalist world, the principle and practise of economic planning. All these were possible only on the basis of the abolition of socially-operated private property, of the nationalization of the means of production and exchange, their centralization in the hands of the state which is the main prerequisite of an evolution towards the classless society of universal abundance, leisure and unprecedented cultural advancement.

Outraged by the brutality of the reactionary usurpers, by their blood purges, by their political expropriation of the toilers, by their totalitarian regime, more than one class conscious worker and revolutionary militant has concluded that nothing is left of the Russian revolution, that there are no more grounds for defending the Soviet Union in a war than for defending any capitalist state. The professional confusionists of the various ultra-leftist grouplets prey upon these honest reactions to Stalinism and try to goad the workers into a reactionary position. Some of these philosophers of ignorance and superficiality prescribe a position of neutrality in a war between the Soviet Union and Germany; others, less timid, call for the strategy of defeatism in the Soviet Union. At bottom, the ultra-leftist position on the Soviet Union, which denies it any claim whatsoever to being a workers' state, reflects the vacillations of the petty bourgeoisie, their inability to make a firm choice between the camps of the proletariat and the bourgeoisie, of revolution and imperialism.

Class rule is based upon property relations. Bourgeois class rule, the bourgeois state, is based upon private ownership, appropriation and accumulation. The political superstructure of the bourgeois class state may vary: democratic republic, monarchy, fascist dictatorship. When the bourgeois can no longer rule directly politically, and the working class is still too weak to take power, a Bonapartist military dictatorship may arise which seeks to raise itself 'above the classes', to 'mediate' between them. But it continues to rule over a *bourgeois state* (even though, as in Germany, it has politically expropriated the bourgeoisie and its parties), because it has left bourgeois property relations more or less intact.

The October revolution abolished bourgeois property relations in the decisive spheres of economic life. By centralizing the means of production in the hands of the state, it created new property relations. The counter-revolutionary bureaucracy, although it has destroyed the political rule of the proletariat, has *not yet* been able to restore capitalist property relations by abolishing those established by the revolution. This great reality determines, for Marxists, the character of the Soviet Union as a workers' state, bureaucratically degenerated, it is true, usurped and therefore crucially imperilled by the Bonapartists, but still fundamentally a workers' state. This great remaining conquest of the revolution determines, in turn, our defense of the Soviet Union from imperialist attack *and* from its Bonapartist sappers at home.

Because it is not a simple question, Lenin pointed out at the 9th Congress of the party in 1920, we must be careful not to sink into the morass of confusion.

> Wherein consists the rule of the class? Wherein consisted the rule of the bourgeoisie over the feudal lords? In the constitution it was written: 'in freedom and equality'. – That is a lie. So long as there are toilers, the property owners are capable and, as such, even compelled, to speculate. We say that there is no equality there, and that the sated are not the equals of the hungry, the speculator is not the equal of the toiler. Wherein does the rule of the class express itself? The rule of the proletariat expresses itself in the abolition of landed and capitalist property. Even the fundamental content of all former constitutions – the republican included – boiled down to property. Our constitution has acquired the right to historical existence, we did not merely write down on paper that we are abolishing property, but the victorious proletariat did abolish property and abolished it completely. – Therein consists the rule of the class – primarily in the question of property. When the question of property was decided in practise, the rule of the class was thereby assured; thereupon the constitution wrote down on paper what life had decided: 'There is no capitalist and landed property', and it added: 'The working class has more rights than the peasantry, but the exploiters have no rights at all'. Therewith was written down the manner in which we realized the rule of our class, in which we bound together the toilers of all strata, all the little groups. The petty bourgeois proprietors were split-up. Among them those who have a larger property are the foes of those who have less, and the proletariat openly declares war against them when it abolishes property …
>
> *The rule of the class is determined only by the relationship to property. That is precisely what determines the constitution. And our constitution correctly*

> *set down our attitude to property and our attitude to the question of what class must stand at the head. He who, in the question of how the rule of the class is expressed, falls into the questions of democratic centralism, as we often observe, brings so much confusion into the matter that he makes impossible any successful work on this ground.*
>
> *Russische Korrespondenz*, Nr. 10, July 1920, p. 8

Liberal apologists have distorted Lenin's concepts into an argument for the compatibility of the bureaucratic dictatorship, and even a personal dictatorship, with a consistent development towards the new social order. 'So long as industry remains nationalized and the productive forces expand', runs their apology, 'what does it really matter if Stalin maintains a bureaucratic despotism, which we civilized liberals would not tolerate but which is good enough for backward Russians?' It is of course quite true that Lenin saw no absolute incompatibility between proletarian democracy and 'individual dictatorship' in industry under given conditions. A year before his quoted speech at the 9th Congress, he observed:

> That the dictatorship of single persons in the history of the revolutionary movements was very often the spokesman, the carrier and the executant of the dictatorship of the revolutionary classes, is evidenced by the incontestable experience of history ... If we are not anarchists, we must acknowledge the necessity of the state, i.e., of coercion, for the transition from capitalism to socialism. The form of coercion is determined by the degree of development of the given revolutionary class, furthermore, by such special circumstances as, e.g., the heritage of a long, reactionary war, furthermore, by the forms of the resistance of the bourgeoisie or of the petty bourgeoisie. Therefore there is not the slightest contradiction in principle between Soviet (i.e., socialist) democracy and the application of the dictatorial rule of individual persons.
>
> *Sämtliche Werke*, Bd. XXII, pp. 524f., Ger. ed.

But in order to make clear his real thoughts, he hastened to add the following indispensable supplementary statement, without which everything is one-sided and therefore false:

> The more resolutely we now come out in favor of a ruthlessly strong power, for the dictatorship of individual persons *in definite labor processes* during certain periods of *purely executive functions*, the more manifold must be the forms and methods of control from below in order to paralyze

> every trace of a possibility of distorting the Soviet power, in order to tear out, incessantly and tirelessly, the weeds of bureaucratism.
>
> Ibid., p. 532

It is precisely those manifold forms and methods of *democratic control from below* which the bureaucracy has destroyed in its development towards despotic rule. In destroying proletarian democracy and the political rule of the working class, the bureaucracy has lifted itself beyond the reach of the masses out of which it emerged. Having abandoned its original class base, it must find a new one, for it cannot last long as a thin bureaucratic stratum hanging, so to speak, in mid-air. The social layers with which it has linked itself are the well-to-do farmers, the factory directors and trust heads, the Stakhanovite aristocracy, the officialdom of the party, the Soviet apparatus, the Red Army and the GPU. But none of these, nor all of them taken together, represents a *class*, with a distinctive function in the productive life of the country, or with specific property forms upon which to build a firm class and firm class rule. Their whole *tendency* is to develop into a new property-owning class, that is, into a capitalist class based on private property. Blocking the road to the realization of this yearning stands the still powerful reality of the nationalization of the means of production and exchange, centralized planning, and the protection of nationalized industry which is afforded by the monopoly of foreign trade.

The bureaucracy, closely interlinked with these restorationist strata of Soviet society and embodying their social aspirations, is now driven by inexorable forces to take its next big step backward. Hitherto, the reaction has been confined essentially to the destruction of the whole political superstructure of the workers' democracy established by the revolution, and to the physical annihilation of all those who were the living connection between today and the revolutionary yesterday. From now on, the anti-Soviet bureaucracy will, and in a certain sense, must seek its self-preservation by an assault upon the economic foundations of the workers' state: nationalized property, planning, the monopoly of foreign trade.

In our opinion, it cannot and will not succeed in establishing the rule of an independent, new Russian capitalist class, even if we arbitrarily exclude the possibility, *by no means exhausted*, of the crushing of the counter-revolutionary bureaucracy by a resurgent proletariat. The new strata of society gathered around the ruling Soviet clique *may* prevail over the Russian proletariat in the period to come. But we do not believe that they are strong or solidly rooted enough to develop into a national neo-bourgeoisie capable of resisting, on a capitalist basis, the infinitely stronger bourgeoisie of the foreign imperialist countries.

In other words, the Stalinist bureaucracy and its satellites are doomed regardless of the outcome. They cannot develop into an independent ruling capitalist class in Russia. Either they are defeated by the proletariat which carries through a political revolution for the purpose of restoring workers' democracy and of safeguarding the economic basis of the workers' state which still exists. Or they are defeated by powerful foreign imperialism, which would wipe out that old economic basis, reduce the Union to a semi-colonial country, and convert the restorationist strata not into a ruling capitalist class for Russia but merely into a compradore agency of world imperialism, occupying a position not dissimilar from that of the Chinese national bourgeoisie.

The class conscious workers will place all their hopes and bend all their efforts towards the realization of the former outcome of the struggle. The building of the revolutionary party to lead the Russian masses in the battle to save the Russian revolution is dependent upon the success of the revolutionary movement in the capitalist world. The depression and reaction in the ranks of the Russian proletariat was created by the defeats of the working class in the rest of the world, by the feeling of the Russians that they had no powerful allies in the capitalist world. The growth and victories of the Fourth International will galvanize the latent revolutionary strength of the Russian masses and set it into irresistible motion. Everything depends on the speed with which we accomplish our indicated task.

The crisis of the Russian revolution has emboldened all the critics of Bolshevism, that is, of revolutionary Marxism – all of them, old and new. But all their hoary argumentation leaves the Marxist unrepentant for his solidarity with those principles and ideas which made the Russian revolution possible. For in abandoning these ideas, he would have to adopt others, and what others are there? Should he adopt those of the Mensheviks? It is true: had they triumphed, the proletarian revolution in Russia would not have degenerated into its Stalinist caricature for the simple reason that there would have been no proletarian revolution. Should he adopt those of the Western European *confrères* of the Mensheviks, the parties of the Second International? It is true: they did not let the proletarian revolution in Germany and Austria and Italy degenerate, and that by the simple device of crushing it in the egg and thus facilitating the consolidation of their famous bourgeois democracy which brought the working class directly under the knife of Hitler and Schuschnigg and Mussolini. Should he adopt those of the anarchist politicians who have become so clamorous of late, especially about the Kronstadt rebellion? But the lamentable collapse of anarchist politics in Spain, the servile collaboration with the bourgeoisie, the heaping of capitulation upon capitulation and the yielding of one position after another without a struggle, are not calculated to attract us away from Marxism.

It is not in place here to dwell on the flawlessness of Bolshevism and all its policies in the great period of the revolution. Its defects may be freely granted. But the oppressed and exploited of the world have not yet been offered a scientific guide to action in their struggle for freedom which can even remotely claim to serve as a substitute for the party and principles of Lenin. In the face of enormous obstacles – not the least of which were created, with arms in hand, by the present-day bourgeois and reformist critics – Lenin and the Bolsheviks carried through the first conscious proletarian revolution. They laid the economic foundation for the new society without class rule, without iniquity or exploitation or oppression. They – and nobody else – gave us a picture of the truly breath-taking prospects for human advancement and human dignity which are open to us as soon as capitalism is sent to the rubbish-heap.

Rash indeed would he be who forecast the immediate future of the Russian revolution. But whatever it may be, its historical achievements are already imperishable. The first steam engine may not have been much faster than the old-fashioned stage-coach, if it was able to move at all. But the country's network of rails is today skimmed by speedy, advanced, stream-line locomotives, while the stage-coach can be found only in museums. The creation of the steam-engine was a monumental contribution to human progress. The creation of the first Soviet republic was an even greater contribution. History will give little place to the period of Stalinist counter-revolution, for it will treat it as a passing historical episode. But the Bolshevik revolution of 1917 and its enduring achievements will never be wiped out of the consciousness of man, for it sounded the knell of all class rule, marked the beginning of the end of man's pre-history, the inauguration of a new era for a new man. In this sense, Lenin and his party of revolutionary Bolsheviks could say with Ovid:

> *Jamque opus exegi: quod nec Jovis ira, nec ignes, Nec poterit ferrum, nec edax abolere vetustas.*
>
> I have now completed a work which neither the wrath of Jove, nor fire, nor the sword, nor the corroding tooth of time, shall be able to destroy.

CHAPTER 8

Political Complications

Paul Le Blanc

In any political organisation and movement (and perhaps in any human organisation and movement), assuming a certain critical mass, there are bound to be dynamics in which personalities, ideas, and general orientations clash. It is the stuff of life and of politics. With a movement as politically intense and intellectually robust as that represented by US Trotskyism, this was very much the case.

Deeply rooted in this political current was the commitment to remain true to the revolutionary principles of Marx and Lenin – diluted, betrayed and abandoned by reformist Social Democrats on the one hand and Stalinists on the other. This could easily become entangled, of course, with sectarian and narrowly purist impulses even in the best of revolutionaries, and such tendencies certainly emerged among US Trotskyists, although this was often checked by countervailing tendencies within the organisation and even within the same individual.

But not always. Sociologist Daniel Bell once jocularly referred to 'the Law of Faction Formation and Fission' which afflicts particularly small left-wing groups, reflecting a purist and sectarian impulse gone cancerous:

> The main factional progeny of the [1930s] came from the Trotskyites – they who claimed the seal of purity and had the effulgent brilliance of the creator of the Red Army to sustain them. But even Trotsky could not guarantee unity; in fact, Trotsky alive was more likely to be the source of splits since it was a great lift to the revolutionary ego of the new sectarian leaders to have jousted with one of the original creators of the Russian Revolution.[1]

Among serious political activists were those resistant to such tendencies, but such tendencies flourished, nonetheless, described and lampooned in a brief article, included here, by Max Shachtman. It is hardly the case, however, that all those engaged in such dissident split-offs said or did or represented nothing of

1 Bell 1952, p. 366.

interest. The memoirs of two individuals associated with skewered split-offs, for example, went on to have substantial and serious impact within the intellectual and political life of the Left – Paul Jacobs (a one-time Fieldite) and Sidney Lens (a one-time Oehlerite) – are certainly worth consulting.[2]

A different set of complications – although perhaps not entirely unrelated – arose from the dynamics within powerful intellectual circles that overlapped with the Trotskyist movement. In the crisis-ridden 1930s, many intellectuals and artists – some of whom would have a powerful impact on US culture for the rest of the twentieth century – were naturally drawn to the Left, at least during that turbulent decade, and of these a significant number were drawn to the Trotskyist movement. Some observers have sometimes drawn the mistaken conclusion that the 'Trotskyites' were predominantly drawn from the non-proletarian intelligentsia, devoid of actual working-class members and influences. The element of truth in this distortion was that the influence of left-wing intellectuals was quite strong among the Trotskyists (just as the Trotskyists had a strong impact on the intellectuals). But as the disappointed hopes of the late 1930s began to pile up, the left-wing intellectuals increasingly pulled away from revolutionary ideas and commitments, a retreat that found reflection in the books and articles they produced, which increasingly questioned the revolutionary Marxism to which they had once been attracted.[3]

The second contribution offered in this section is an incredibly lengthy, detailed, but brilliant polemic co-authored by James Burnham and Max Shachtman, intensively analysing this development. Ironically, while applauding most of it, Trotsky perceived – in the article's shrugging off of dialectics – germs of the same affliction the authors were discussing.[4] It is not without interest that shortly afterward such issues would figure in a factional dispute, initiated by Shachtman and Burnham. Within two years, Burnham himself would speed along the trajectory away from Marxism that he and Shachtman wrote about in 1939. These are matters dealt with at greater length in Chapter 9.

---

2 Jacobs 1965; Lens 1980.

3 Wald 1987.

4 Burnham's critical view of dialectics was similar to that of his colleague and left-pragmatist philosopher Sidney Hook (see Hook 1940). On the more positive conception of dialectics prevalent within the SWP, see Novack 1971. Useful discussion of dialectics and Marxism can be found in a number of works – see Marcuse 1999, Lefebvre 2009, and Rees 1998.

1 Footnote for Historians[5]

(*1938*)

Max Shachtman

We do not envy the future historian of the American revolutionary movement when he faces the problem of tracing the course of the ephemeral sects. Out of consideration for him, we give here a brief factual outline of at least those sects that broke away from our movement. We preface it with the fact that in virtually every case, those who split away proclaimed themselves the only 'genuine Trotskyists' and unlike us, whom they doomed to disintegration, the possessors of sure-fire recipes for 'mass activity'.

Not falling into the above-described category, but first to separate from us were three Italian followers of Bordiga, since constituted as the New York group of the 'Italian Left Fraction of Communism'. Like their separation from us, their subsequent existence has been quiet, dignified, passive, fruitless and unruffled either by the departure of an old adherent or the acquisition of a new one. Score: no hits, no runs, no errors.

Next, chronologically, was Albert Weisbord, upon the size of whose hats the Passaic strike of 1926 had a most distressing effect. Although he never carried out his threat actually to join our organization, he broke conclusively all relations with it on March 15, 1931 – the historic date of the formation of his Communist League of Struggle. In the heraldic announcement of its birth, he wrote: 'Not an isolated sect, but a two-fisted hard group of communists is what we are forming'. Its seven years of existence were all lean; each one ended with the loss of another member, the last to go joining the Marxist Workers League (q.v.), leaving Weisbord in unchallenged charge of what he now calls the 'Friends of the Class Struggle'. The plural of 'Friends' has the same numerical significance as the imperial 'We'. Rewards offered by relatives for information leading to the whereabouts of the Weisbord group having gone unclaimed for years, the money has recently been placed in escrow.

Of the 8 original founders of the Field group, only 3 are left. It would be an exaggeration to say that B.J. Field has been strikingly successful in his favor-

5 Shachtman 1938c.

ite activity: uniting with other groups. In May 1933, the Workers Communist League was formed by Ben Gitlow and Lazar Becker, two Lovestoneite dissidents. Immediately after the New York hotel strike in 1934, the Fieldites had their first unity – with Gitlow et al. (et al. = Lazar Becker), under the name of 'Organization Committee for a Revolutionary Workers Party'. The two ex-Lovestoneites did not tarry long in the OCFARWP, but sped to the greener pastures of the Socialist Party, where Becker became a henchman of Altman and from which Gitlow retired later to voice his unique theory that 'Lenin was the first fascist'. A sadder but not wiser Field thereupon reduced the length of his group's name to 'League for Revolutionary Workers Party' and proceeded to 'unity negotiations' with Weisbord. These broke with Field concluding indignantly that 'it is impossible to see how such a group with such policies and leadership can contribute anything toward building a revolutionary International'. Weisbord reciprocated with a description which only further reduced the latter's faith in the sweetness of the former's lacteal glands. Whereupon Field tried his luck again, this time with the patient Bordigist trinity, themselves worn out by just finished luckless unity negotiations with Weisbord. In January 1936, Field titteringly announced that he had 'held a series of joint discussions with the Italian Left Fraction of Communism during the month of November. Eight fundamental questions of the revolutionary movement were discussed and complete political agreement has been arrived at'. It goes without saying that just because the two groups were in 'complete political agreement' does not mean that there was the slightest reason for uniting. Nor did they. Two months later, that man was at it again, announcing that 'negotiations have been proceeding between the Oehler group (RWL) and the LRWP of the US and promise to result in the fusion of the two organizations'. Naturally the promise was not kept and the fusion died in the egg. But as the old adage says, unlucky at fusions, lucky at splits. The last fusion attempt broke down right after the May 1936 split of the Field group in New York, when a majority of the membership outvoted the leader and joined with us. Since then, Field's first lieutenant succeeded in effecting a fusion of a more personal kind, the fruits of which he has been enjoying in a Greek villa overlooking the restful, jewelled Mediterranean. Sadder than ever, considerably aged, but not yet wiser, Field sends periodic letters to us for more 'unity negotiations', which we are deterred from entering into by his none-too-alluring experiences. Ditto for his counsel on how to win friends and influence masses.

Originally the most numerous of the sects, the Oehler-Stamm group broke from the then-Trotskyist Workers Party around November 1935 because of chaste opposition to our proposal to enter the Socialist Party and unite with its revolutionary wing. The splitters formed the Revolutionary Workers League whose dire predictions of our impending degeneration and absorption by reformism all but frightened us. Differing only in degree of virulence, the RWL, all its offspring, and all its predecessors have decayed to the level of Trotsky-baiting sects, hurling at us all the imprecations familiar since the days of 'Third Period' Stalinism. That so far as their political evolution goes. Organizationally, a no less dismal picture of splits and disintegration must be painted.

Barely split from us, the New York Oehlerite caucus chief, a turncoat named Mendelsohn, left his friends, joined the SP, and in it became the right wing's anti-Trotskyist finger-man. A few months after his defection, a whole series of leading Oehlerites, typified by Gordon and Gunta, returned to our ranks. In the period following, one Oehlerite after another came back to our movement, was expelled by Oehler for one heresy or another, or retired completely from activity (Kogan in California, Giganti and Garber in Chicago, Pierce in Cleveland, Hirsch in Philadelphia, Gaynor in Newark, Simmons in Kansas City, etc.). In addition to individual defections, the last three years have seen one splitlet after another.

First, early in 1936, came the 'Marxist Workers League' in New York which, after a sensational existence of both its members for 19 days, rejoined our movement. Then the RWL recorded the loss of its trade union 'specialist', Joseph Zack, who openly abandoned Marxism to form a new sect, or rather two at a clip: the 'One Big Union Club' and the 'Equalitarian Society'; in the latter enterprise he is associated with the eminent scholar, S.L. Solon, whose theoretical innovations have thrilled the readers of that political parasite's paradise, the *Modern Monthly*. Following this it lost a group around its theoretical Nestor, Paul Eiffel, adventurer in the movement and dubious figure in general, who advocated the sabotage of the Loyalist struggle against Franco.

Then came a dramatic breathing spell in the series of splits. An Oehlerite stooge group was formed in our ranks in Chicago by a young man named Beckett, who discovered that we were capitulating to Norman Thomas just at the time we were being expelled from the SP. He called himself the 'Marxist Policy Committee'. After making his bow with an apostolic denunciation of another ultra-leftist in our ranks, led by one Joerger, he announced to a trembling world, in his August 24, 1937 bulletin: 'Salemme-Joerger group fuses with MPC on Marxist basis', adding that 'in the course of negotiations the MPC found that the S-J group did not hold the position criticized in *MPC Bulletin* No. 2'. Hardly had the proletariat finished cheering itself hoarse at the momentous news, than it learned from Beckett, on October 1, 1937, that Salamme-Joerger were knaves after all and their line was 'not in essence different from that of Cannon, Shachtman, Abern, Glee, Glotzer, Goldman, Heisler, Most, Curtis, and all the other herdsmen of *khvostism*'. The tragically disconcerting atmosphere created by this declaration was only partly cleared by the heartening communiqué that Beckett – after the proper and necessarily exhaustive negotiations – was joining the Oehler group.

The RWL, meanwhile, had not stood breathlessly still while waiting for its first recruit. Alarmed at the prospect of the resultant over-expansion, a furious struggle broke out between Oehler and Stamm, perhaps the greatest dispute since the churchmen gathered for the Council of Nicaea in 325 AD to work out what became the Nicean Creed of Catholicism. One faction held that the description of Christ, or God the Son, should read '*homo'ousias*', or a being of identical substance with God the Father; the other faction held that the Greek word in question properly had another letter, making it read '*homoi'ousias*', or a being of similar substance with God the Father. Result: the split between the Roman Catholic and the Eastern (Greek Orthodox) churches. Of no less importance was the fight between Oehler and Stamm, the former holding, at the RWL's historic 3rd Plenum in October–November 1937, that Trotsky, 'after a sojourn of 17 years in the Marxist movement, reverted to Trotskyism' and degenerated in 1934, while the other insisted that Trotskyism degenerated along about 1928 (month not given). It seems that Oehler won, after assailing the rebels for their 'false position on democratic centralism [which] has its leader in Stamm, who combines errors of bourgeois democracy with bureaucracy', to say nothing of 'his ultra-left and false evaluation of Marxism'. But when he sought to put a cap marked 'Heresiarch' on Stamm's bloody but unbowed head, Stamm promptly upped and formed his own group, using the old name but with a new little paper which, if it does not differ from Oehler's organ in committing just as many sins of *lèse*-sanity, at least is not as guilty of *lèse*-grammar and *lèse*-syntax.

The idea of the schismatics proved contagious and the splits began all over again. First came another 'Marxist Workers League', led by a young soloist named Mienov, who announced in the initial issue of his inevitable bulletin that 'to be wrong on the Spanish war means to open the door wide open to social-patriotism in the coming world imperialist war. That is exactly what the Oehler group is doing ... We are proud that we split from such a centrist group'. All is not, however, what it should be in the MWL. Although the majority of the leadership, in its resolution on The Party, writes (Sec. VIII, Part D, Point 1a, §e): 'Trotskyism cannot be reformed but must be smashed', we learn that there is a minority of Stonne and Spencer, which replies, 'In 20 years of history, these comrades of the majority have learned nothing', to which the majority annihilatingly retorts: 'We were just informed that Spencer has joined the Trotskyists. Truly, there is no limit to degeneration'.

Second Oehlerite split-off (Series II) is the Leninist League, also formed at the beginning of the year. It is lead by George Marlen and is unique also in other respects. While definitely anti-gynaicocratic, and taking no formal position on exogamy or endogamy, it is based fundamentally on the primitive gens in so far as one must be a blood relation of the immediate family, or at least related to it by marriage, in order to qualify for membership. This has the unfortunate effect of somewhat reducing the arena for recruitment, but it does guarantee against contamination. Marlen is so exhausted by his literary efforts to prove that Trotsky is an agent of Stalinism, that he is able to do nothing else. His cool, balanced judgment is sampled by what he says of Field: 'The LRWP is an enemy of the international working class. It is a sabotaging agency in the struggle of exposure and destruction of the Stalinist reaction'. Oehler, Stamm, Mienov, Smith, Jones, and Robinson – all are contemptuously and severely dismissed as 'left Trotskyists'. Reminding one irresistibly of the story of the monkey and the elephant is the report current that Marlen is writing a book that will annihilate Trotsky politically. *Sic itur ad astra!* Or, freely translated, that's as good a way as any of getting into the headlines.

The last Oehlerite splinter to pierce the surface is composed of the remnants of the RWL in Philadelphia, led by a lad named Fleming who is followed by a membership not exceeding one. After a self-imposed novitiate in a 'Social Science Circle', it climaxed its liberation from what it calls 'ululating Oehlerism' by proclaiming the 'Revolutionary Communist Vanguard' – not of Philadelphia, not of the United States, not of the Western Hemisphere, but of the World. Its statutes insist on it. No new members, unfortunately, can be admitted, for the statutes require a two-thirds approval of applications and there are but two members now; however, a congress of the organization is possible, even now, for it 'can be assembled by determination of at least half the membership'. The RCV is the *reductio ad absurdum* of all the absurd and infantile ultra-leftist sects. The boys are having a fine time playing Revolution. They write in their bulletins (naturally, they have one) under ever so funny pseudonyms: Don Quickshot, Obadiah Fairfax, Robin Redbreast, Jerome Rembrandt, and Esther Paris. Just like Tom Sawyer and Huck Finn playing Pirates.

Finally, simple justice requires mention of the latest and most ferocious group, founded, built, and staffed by the somewhere above-mentioned Joerger. His public name is the thumping 'Revolutionary Marxist League' and he announces bellicosely in his initial literary production: 'We cannot emphasize too much our position that we have nothing in common with the Trotskyite brand of Stalinism or any other inverted form of Stalinism. The various types of Trotskyites (Oehler, Field, Marlen, et al.) …'. Stamm, Mienov, et al., to say nothing of Robin Redbreast, are apparently to be let off with a lighter sentence.

There are undoubtedly others, which have not come to our attention, but these will suffice to focus the ludicrous picture of sterility and futility to which ultra-leftist sectarianism condemns itself. In making the record, moreover, we have the feeling of pious satisfaction with a good deed done in easing the research pains of tomorrow's biographer of the movement.

2 Intellectuals in Retreat[6]
(*1939*)

James Burnham and Max Shachtman

Part I: Introduction

We are, in this article, writing particularly about the following persons:

Group I: Max Eastman, Sidney Hook, Charles Yale Harrison, James Rorty, Edmund Wilson, Philip Rahv, Benjamin Stolberg, James Farrell, Louis Hacker, and others.
Group II: John Chamberlain, Louis Adamic, Eugene Lyons, John Dewey, George S. Counts, Ferdinand Lundberg.

It may reasonably be asked in what sense we list these individuals as *groups*; and how we happen to direct our attention to the two groups in a single article. All of those in Group I have a similar political background. They are all what is known as 'radical intellectuals'. Most were once, for varying lengths of time, within the orbit of the Communist Party, several of them Party members. With the exception of Eastman and Stolberg, they continued as Communist Party sympathizers well into its Stalinist period. From five years to a year and a half ago, they broke sharply with Stalinism, and for a period were, in political sympathies and general political orientation, close to the revolutionary movement – that is, to the Fourth Internationalist or 'Trotskyist' movement. Indeed, they were and still for the most part are known to a considerable public as 'the Trotskyist intellectuals'. Within the past year or more, they have been steering away from the revolutionary movement.

Group II is of a different character, and will occupy us only incidentally. These intellectuals, also, were at one time closely associated with Stalinism. However, in contrast to Group I, they were – to employ a picturesque phrase which has become current in this country – 'Stalinist liberals'. Their support was always in terms of bourgeois, not of working class, politics. They have

6 Shachtman and Burnham 1939.

in recent years drawn away from Stalinism, though of them only Lyons and Dewey have broken sharply. For Group II, however, this change does not mean a decisive shift: their basic bourgeois liberal politics dominated their Stalinist associations, and now continues little altered without the Stalinist trimmings. Group II is herein included because its members with those of Group I are known as 'radical anti-Stalinist intellectuals'; and more especially because, from a different origin, some of Group I have coalesced politically with Group II, and others of Group I are now heading plainly toward that same outcome.

As we shall show, the ideas and actions of these persons whom we have grouped together are in many symptomatic respects similar, and the current *direction* (though not the speed) of their political evolution is the same. It is in addition worth noting that this group, considered as a political phenomenon, is by no means confined to this country. As prominent European analogues we may mention: Victor Serge, Willi Schlamm, Andre Gide, Charles Plisnier, Ignazio Silone, Eric Wollenberg, Anton Ciliga. The political background and present course of each of these corresponds closely with that of our Group I, except that Serge and Plisnier were never associated with Stalinism.

There seems, then, ample *prima facie* justification for treating our subjects as a group. It is true, of course, that they do not like to think of themselves as a collectivity, a group. In their own minds and in public they seem to stress that they are 'individuals', 'independent thinkers'; and this is related to a theoretic stress which they place upon Psychology, attacking revolutionists for 'disregarding psychology' and blindly 'reducing' everything to political terms. Indeed, this assertion of independent individuality and of the primacy of psychology is another of their *group* characteristics.

It is also true that it would be an over-simplification and indeed a serious error, to suggest that there are no important differences among them, to lump them together in a single mass. Harrison and Rorty, for example, are birds of a different political species, Harrison having now ended up unambiguously in the cage of the class enemy. Nor shall we maintain that each of these individuals, as individuals, will 'necessarily' finish up on the same spot. We are writing not psychology nor morality but politics. Our aim is to analyze the nature and direction of a political phenomenon; and politics is concerned with groups, not individuals. Having determined the political nature of a group, we can say of any given individual only that if he thinks and acts consistently as a member of the group such and such an outcome will follow. But individuals are, perhaps fortunately, often inconsistent; and individuals change.

The Frying Pan of the Intellectuals

We may notice at once about our subjects that as compared with the Stalinist intellectuals and with most of the bourgeois intellectuals they have outstanding abilities, talents and moral virtues. This should not surprise us. The foulness of Stalinism and imperialism can today breed only maggots; in particular is it impossible for *intellectuals* to avoid degeneration not merely of their characters as human beings but also of their minds if for any length of time they give their allegiance to these allied monsters of the lie.

The chief talent of the intellectuals in our list is that of writing well. This almost all of them do. How refreshing it is to compare their styles with the dull and dreary pages of *New Masses* or *Science And Society*!

However, we should also observe that those with whom we are dealing are primarily 'ideologists': they are critics, philosophers, sociologic-political writers. Only one of them (Farrell) is a creative artist; Harrison, Wilson, and Adamic have written novels in passing, and Rorty a number of poems, but these are a subordinate part of their work. None among all of them is a physical scientist. What pretensions they have to empirical science of any sort are to be found in the dangerous fields of history, sociology and politics, where it is so hard to distinguish a hypothesis from a prejudice; and even in these fields, Hacker and Lundberg only have done any substantial original research.

We may further record that all of these individuals, some of them outstandingly, have many good and progressive deeds to record. In some cases for more than a generation, they have been in the forefront of many of the most important cases in this country and internationally where civil and human rights were at stake. Their names are linked with the fight for Sacco and Vanzetti, for the recognition of the Soviet Union, for Fred Beal, for the Scottsboro boys and Tom Mooney. With the exception of Counts, everyone of them made the vast social and personal sacrifice which was involved in serving on the Committee for the Defense of Leon Trotsky, and three of them were members of the Commission of Inquiry into the charges against Trotsky in the Moscow Trials. The work of the Committee and the Commission remains as an enduring monument; its influence has been felt throughout the world. Nor are their good deeds of the past only. We continue to find their names in the majority of those cases where men have joined efforts toward some genuinely progressive end.

It is hardly to be expected that such activities can be carried on without trouble; and they have, indeed, plenty of trouble. The troubles are of several sorts. One type might be called 'craft troubles': they find heavy obstacles placed in the way of the fruitful exercise of their talents. The bourgeoisie and the Stalinists, controlling between them the press, the magazines, the publishing houses, are not eager to give recognition to these persons who proclaim themselves against the *status quo* and against Stalinism. A none-too-subtle sabotage, increasing in recent years, scuttles their work or at the least handicaps it.

To add to these craft hazards are pervasive and equally painful personal troubles. Psychologists and anthropologists teach us that the pressure of public opinion, of social approval and disapproval, praise and blame, is one of the most powerful forces molding the human personality; and the bourgeoisie and the Stalinists have learned the lesson. Our subjects find themselves to be modified pariahs in their community. Old friends cut them dead or throw vicious insults at them. Public and private denunciation becomes commonplace; the lurid prose of the Kremlin apologists holds them up to the world as fascists, counter-revolutionists, German or Japanese spies, even – last bitter indignity – as Trotskyists. When serving in such an enterprise as the Trotsky Committee, to these are added an unremitting plague of telephone calls, letters and telegrams, all designed for the harshest possible effect on the nervous system.

Yet, in this vale of tears, where at least some trouble is the lot of every man, and where therefore judgment of troubles must be relative, it would be possible to exaggerate the ills of our subjects. None of them is forced into the loneliness of the mountain eagle; none is compelled to be altogether silent; and none as yet is exactly starving. In fact, after ten years of economic crisis during which even brokers and bankers have gone bankrupt, some seem to do rather well by themselves. Especially is this true of those who have either remained throughout on the bourgeois side or who have gone over to it. Each one under Group II may be presumed to use the larger form for his income tax reports. Chamberlain's recognition by the owners of *Fortune* runs, it is said, well into five figures. Columbia University, second richest educational institution in the country, has given its fullest academic honors to Dewey and Counts, and their books are widely published and read. Lyons is able to combine public relations counsellorship with substantial freelance journalism and lecturing. The recent books of Adamic and Lundberg were not too badly treated by the general press. Though Eastman's earlier defenses of the revolution had to content themselves with modest appearance in little magazines, his recent attacks on the socialist ideal are featured on the covers of *Harper's* and *Liberty*. Hacker's defense of liberal capitalism in his *Graphic History* does not seem to have injured his academic standing (also at Columbia) nor his access to publication. We understand that Harrison's ringing break with Marxism (in the *New Leader*) was followed by negotiations for a well deserved appointment in the Federal Housing Administration …

Dewey has often and brilliantly explained how the conflicts with which human beings unavoidably find themselves confronted give rise to ideas and ideals which are projected as instruments for solving those conflicts. (There is, of course, no *a priori* assurance that the given idea or ideal will actually be capable of solving the given conflict.) Out of the troubled conflicts of our subjects, an ideal, a dream emerges. In a world pressing tumultuously, imperiously against every one of its inhabitants, grinding and battering them from every direction, they seek a little peace, quiet, a chance to cultivate and bring to harvest their talents. They ask for freedom, meaning by freedom what Eastman, who is usually several steps in advance, has written: 'Freedom is being in a position to do what comes into *your own* head, to act whether sooner or late on *your own* impulses'. Phrased somewhat differently: They ask to be able to do and write what they wish without having to accept the consequences when what they do and write affects others; they ask not to be pushed around by others who are sure of their ideas and intend to fight for them; they ask to be released from responsibility.

When is a Program a Program?

It is a literal and easily verifiable fact that not one of these intellectuals, in all the millions of words they have written and publicly spoken, has presented a new political program. Indeed, so far as *explicit* statement goes, we find in them very little reference to the concrete political issues of the day. It goes without saying that by 'political program' we do not mean a list of empty generalities such as those with which Eastman ends his *Harper's* article: 'Problems of being and of universal history ... should be acknowledged to exist ... The various components of the [socialist] ideal should be analyzed and considered separately ... Those obviously fantastic ... should be thrown out ...'; nor the apostrophes to Truth and Freedom by which Hook has lately taken to climaxing his essays. No one need bother to agree or disagree with such abstractions, because agreement or disagreement commits one to nothing. A political program means a set of doctrines, principles, rules or directives which gives the unambiguous answers, or from which the answers may be derived, to the chief *concrete* political problems of the present time: war, insecurity, fascism, unemployment, the struggle for (or against) socialism ...

Eastman, as so often, gives the show away. At the end of his polemic against Burnham (*New International*, August 1938) he confesses openly that he has no (conscious) program. 'If I live', he promises, 'I will complete my thesis'. But he 'would not hurry'. To him, 'it seems just now in America a period for deliberation'.

Let us pause for a moment to consider the meaning of this confession, assuming it to be true. What is Eastman (and almost any name on our list could be substituted for Eastman's) saying? What is he saying, for example, to the French worker standing today with the whip of fascism descending toward his back? to the American worker plunged into the misery and despair of permanent mass unemployment and swamped by the tidal wave of Roosevelt's armament preparations and his looming war? to his fellow-intellectuals? Eastman is saying: I, who am not a humble clerk in an office nor an obscure cog in an assembly line nor a timid teacher trying to keep a job in a high school, but a writer widely and publicly known, one who presumes to sit publicly in judgment on the great events of history, to publish my decrees on the Russian Revolution, the century-old struggles of the proletarian movement, the rise of fascism, the lot of humanity and its future, I who do not hesitate to attack and expose Lenin and Hitler and Stalin and Trotsky, I tell you: 'Sorry, there is nothing to do about it; I regret that at present I have no answer to give you; you will just have to wait patiently until I get around to completing my notes – a page or two seems to be missing from my files'. And if meanwhile fascism completes its conquest of Europe, if the war begins with no organization of the forces against it …? 'Sorry, that's not *my* responsibility …'.

But, our subjects uniformly reply, when we remind them that they have overlooked the detail of supplying us with a new program: 'That's not our affair. We are not politicians. Politics is not our field. We are – writers'.

We have heard this reply so often that we believe it, too, deserves a word of comment. In making this answer, we ask ourselves, whom are they trying most to fool? their general readers, us, or themselves? The truth of the matter is: with one or two partial exceptions, these are all *thoroughly political people*. They intervene *constantly* in political affairs; their interests, feelings, thoughts, conversations, personal relations, speeches, writings and actions are bound up predominantly with politics. Though members of no political parties, it is entirely safe to say that they are far more politically active than, for example, the median Socialist Party member, more active than many members even of such parties as the Communist Party or the Socialist Workers Party.

If they are not writing about politics most of the time, what in hell is it that they are writing about? About what are Hook's books, his articles in the *Modern Monthly*, in the *New Leader*, in the *Southern Review*, most of his reviews in a dozen periodicals, his hundred-and-one speeches in a score of courses and forums? What is Harrison's very novel about, if not politics? Where is politics absent from Stolberg's essay on the New Deal, his book on the CIO, his *ex cathedra* review of *The Revolution Betrayed* in the *Nation*? What is Counts writing about when he publishes his thick volume on democracy? or Lundberg on the Sixty Families, with its concluding defense of New Dealism?

or Chamberlain when he explains that Washington is 'our state' in *Common Sense*? or Adamic, the immigrant boy who made good, when he covers the whole field in *My America*? or Lyons in his book about Russia, his column, his speeches? or the whole bunch in their recent *New Leader* essays? You will have to search through Rahv's and Phillips' and Dupee's *Partisan Review* with a high-power microscope to find an article, whatever the alleged subject, that avoids politics. How about Hacker, now reviving evolutionary meliorism in his latest interpretations of American history? Or even such a one as Wilson, who is reported to say nowadays that 'Writers should not sign anything; they should merely write' – what does he deal with in his book about his Soviet journey, his discussions of proletarian literature, his essays on Marx and Engels and Marxism, his *New Republic* article on the Moscow Trials, his ballyhooing of Willi Schlamm?

Let us finish with this tommyrot about 'Not interested in politics; not politicians ...' once and for all. These are indeed 'political animals' in a sense far more complete than Aristotle had in mind when he first applied the characterization to men in general.

They are above all preoccupied with politics, they are in their own not obscure way *politicians*. The trouble is precisely that their politics are *negative, irresponsible and unprincipled.*

These adjectives may seem to be harsh, part of the 'insufferable Trotskyist tone' which our subjects are not the last to criticize. As is usual with us, however, we employ them not as mere careless emotive epithets, but as carefully meant description.

Their politics are *negative* in the sense that they are always and constantly criticizing and attacking everybody else's politics, often in the sharpest conceivable manner, on every type of question from the highest branches of theory to the latest move in the trade unions or the labor party, but seldom making concrete and positive proposals of their own. If anyone has any doubts about this generalization, he may remove them through acquaintance with their works.

Their politics are *irresponsible* in the sense that they do not lay their cards on the table, state and make explicit the premises from which they derive their particular conclusions (they do not even to themselves), and thus they can jump from one week to the next in and out of organizations, back and forth from one position to another, one attitude to another, without being checked up and called to account. If anyone has any doubts about this generalization, he may remove them by studying their actions during the past couple of years.

Their politics are *unprincipled* because their specific political actions and positions are not derived from consciously, explicitly recognized principles (whether such principles were right or wrong would be irrelevant to this point). If anyone has any doubts about this generalization, let him try to find such consciously and explicitly recognized principles in their writings.

Now, though our subjects have not presented – and, we may be confident, will not present – any new program, it would be very naive to suppose that they have no program at all. Like all those who intervene more than sporadically in politics, they of course have a program – if not a program openly stated, then a program which may be deduced from their actions and the positions they take on specific questions at issue. In fact, our group may be said to have not one but two programs: a 'formal', avowed or alleged program which has been developed at length in the writings of its more prominent spokesmen, to some extent in the writings of all of them; an 'actual', politically decisive program which we may piece together from their actions and specific positions on concrete questions. It is to these two programs that we turn.

Part II: The Formal Program of the Anti-Stalinist Intellectuals

A careful sifting of the large mass of evidence constituted by the writings of our subjects enables us to sum up what we have called their 'formal' program under three main heads: (1) Against dialectical materialism; (2) Against one-party dictatorship; (3) Leninism is the source of Stalinism. A fourth point crops up so frequently that, though of a different order, it almost deserves a separate heading: Against the harsh tone of revolutionary polemics. Before turning to examine each of these four separately, we wish to make certain preliminary remarks.

In the first place, we are compelled to notice that, even with the addition of the leading items on the positive side of the formal program – for Freedom, Truth and Science – this is not much of a program; nor do we think that we are being unfair or arbitrary in reducing the formal program to these elements. Even if we should grant that our subjects are 100% correct in everything they have written on all and each of these matters, we do not find that we would be very far along the road toward solving the issues of war, fascism and insecurity. In fact we can't see that we would even have left the starting post. The mountain of intellectual and nervous energy, to say nothing of the social labor of lumberjacks, paper manufacturers, linotype operators, printers, book salesmen and the rest, seems to have brought forth a pretty mouse-like theoretical offspring.

In the second place, we want to make clear that we regard none of these subjects as taboo: there are no theoretical Sacred Cows in our eyes, and we criticize no one merely for discussing no matter what subject. But there are a variety of ways in which discussion may be carried on. Simply to claim that 'we seek the truth' is not enough. Even in the highly developed physical sciences, the concept of truth, the adoption or rejection of the whole method of inquiry, must be in the end related to purposes which the inquiry is designed to serve. How much more dangerously is this the case with such less developed fields as sociology, history and politics! Historical and political inquiries do not occur in a social vacuum; they are immediately and crucially related to the political ends and aims of individuals, parties and classes, and function actively as weapons in the political struggle.

For our part, we state explicitly that we undertake historical and political inquiries for the sake of our socialist aim. This does not in the least mean that therefore we 'subordinate' truth, are willing to pervert it as a 'means to our end'; on the contrary, our conception of the socialist ideal teaches us that the truth is a decisive means for realizing it, is indeed a part of it. But it does mean that we refuse to argue about truth in the 'abstract', that in discussing theoretical questions in history and politics we establish a context which includes reference to the ends and aims and purposes which the given discussion, argument or inquiry serves. Truth, or rather truths, a necessary means and part of the socialist ideal, is yet short of the Godhead; it too can serve reactionary and vicious aims.

This last statement may seem surprising or shocking to those who are hypnotized by abstractions. However, it is verified daily. For example, the Dies Committee, among many lies, has also disclosed a substantial percentage of truths. Are we then to hail its work as progressive, and follow the example of cheap renegades like J.B. Matthews and Sam Baron in aiding it? Naturally not. Its truths, partial of course and intertwined with lies, are the instrument of reaction – and it is the truths, not the lies, which make the instrument effective. We, along with everyone else who is not a traitor, denounce and attack the Dies Committee, expose its reactionary purpose, demand its dissolution. We do not, of course, deny to the masses that its truths are true; that, the function of the Stalinists, would be treachery of another kind. But we insist that those truths must be acquired in another way and made to serve other ends.

On a more grandiose scale, we may make the same observations about fascism. The critique of bourgeois parliamentary democracy given by the leading fascist theoreticians is for the most part true; and this is one of the sources of the strength of fascism as a movement. Is it any the more progressive on that account? What would we say to a fascist who complained: 'Why do you keep attacking us? You yourselves agree with most of what we have to say about bourgeois democracy'.

We mention these things not to suggest that the 'formal program' of our subjects may in fact be true, but because in the present article we are not so much concerned with the isolated question of the factual truth or falsity of their opinions as with their nature as a political phenomenon, with the political ends and aims which their present writings and actions are serving. We could hardly expect to cover adequately the problems of dialectical materialism, party dictatorship and the origins of Stalinism in a single article. But it is not at all necessary to do this in order to complete the task we have set ourselves.

A Question of Tone

Our subjects are frequent critics of the 'bad tone' that they find in the political press of the working-class parties, including conspicuously that of our own party. Indeed, they find in our sharp tone so much to condemn that it can be done only by the sharpest tone on their part. As a rule they explain: 'It is not what you *say* to which we object, but the way in which you say it. You simply drive people from you. You don't understand psychology'. Stubbornly, perhaps, we are not able to take this explanation seriously. We believe that where questions of tone are raised in connection with political issues, it is ninety-nine times out of a hundred not the *manner* of saying but *what* is said that is being debated.

The 'question of tone' – which we also readily grant to be an important question – is obviously enough not a literary or stylistic problem. There is that problem too, but it is nothing to argue over: it is a matter of talent and technical training so that style will communicate just what is intended. We, certainly, recognize our literary lacks, and strive to overcome them.

But no one is getting embittered or impassioned over the literary difficulty. In politics and out, the more basic aspect of the issue of 'tone' is subordinated to content. Roughly, in general, one uses a harsh tone to those against whom one feels enmity, a friendly tone to friends, bitterness toward traitors, conciliation toward those whom one regards as misled, and so on. This follows quite automatically for many persons; their attitudes, almost without giving it a thought, govern their tone. We wish to make perfectly clear that, in so far as we are technically able, we are ourselves quite deliberate and conscious in our 'tone'; we regard tone also as a *political* instrument.

This does not mean that we are 'just like the fascists and Stalinists' in the use of tone. Not in the least. The Stalinists and fascists use 'tone' *demagogically*, to *hide* the truth and to *obscure* their aims: as when they call revolutionary militants 'fascist spies, counter-revolutionaries, mad dogs', or themselves 'socialists'.

We on the contrary employ tone to *clarify* the truth and our aims. When we write that Norman Thomas is a political colleague and defender of the butchers of the Barcelona workers, the phrase is no doubt harsh; but the harshness is that of literal truth. When we say that Stalin is a murderer, Roosevelt a warmonger, Hillman a reactionary labor bureaucrat, we mean exactly what we say. We do not think that politics is a polite parlor game; we understand it as the struggle for power, and a very rude and brutal struggle, for all that we might wish otherwise.

Now how is it with our subjects on the question of tone? True, they do not seem to be deliberate and conscious in their political use of tone; but their use of it is nonetheless political in spite of their blinders. We discover, for example, that in the history of American radical journalism, no one has written with sharper or harsher tone than they against the Stalinists. Consider Hook, Eastman, Stolberg, Lyons on the Stalinists and Stalinism; you could not match their invective from the pages of the Fourth Internationalist press.

Nor is their tone toward us exactly suitable for the drawing room. With what casualness they assure the world that on Kronstadt we are guilty of amalgams worthy of a Vishinsky (Serge and Macdonald), that in essence and origin we are identical with Stalinism (Hook, Eastman, Lyons, Harrison, Adamic, Counts) and even with fascism (Eastman in *Liberty*, Harrison in the *New Leader*), that, like all of Bolshevism, we are ever ready to lie as a means to our end, that our secret aim is to destroy all democracy and freedom for the sake of a clique dictatorship.

But, equally interesting, we find when we turn to recent writings of our subjects that deal with social-reformists or bourgeois liberals, the harsh, sharp, bitter tone quite disappears, and all is again sweetness and light. And, similarly, we find that we are never criticized by our subjects for 'tone' when we attack the Stalinists, but only when we attack social reformists and bourgeois liberals. And this little asymmetry is just what we object to.

The *New Leader* is 'so different' from the *Daily Worker*; it is so bright, informative, lively, readable, to be recommended and written for – in spite of the fact that in its somewhat politer way it spreads nine-tenths of the identical filthy lies and black reactionary proposals that smell up the sheet of the Stalinists. Norman Thomas, 'so different' from Earl Browder, even if a mite confused, must be treated with white gloves – in spite of the fact that he gives political support in Spain to the stranglers of the Revolution, international allegiance to the international organization that began its sell-outs and betrayals before the Third International came into existence and has changed since 1914 only to deepen its degeneration, in spite of the fact that in this country he proved his devotion to democracy by throwing out the revolutionists in his own party by dictatorial ukase, now is selling out what is left of his party to the Social-Democratic Federation, and for a generation has an unparallelled record of sowing disorientation on every major issue that has ever arisen here or anywhere else in the world. As for tone toward the bourgeois liberals, toward even 'left' bourgeois liberals like Chamberlain and Adamic – what should a serious person have but contempt and hatred for them who spend their lives trying to persuade the workers of America to accept the blessings of US imperialism?

Very revealing, tone. Over a period, the tone of political journalism reveals not the literary finesse nor psychological insight of writers, but, with surprising accuracy – the *political* attitudes and directions.

Dialectical Materialism as Whipping Boy

Eastman, Hook, Wilson, Lyons, Dewey, at some length, others on our list more sporadically, have set their lances against the 'theology' of dialectical materialism. We do not propose here to discuss the general theory of dialectical materialism; that would require a book, not a single section of an article. We are now interested only in certain features of our subjects' *attack* on dialectical materialism.

The two authors of the present article differ thoroughly on their estimate of the general theory of dialectical materialism, one of them accepting it and the other rejecting it. This has not prevented them from working for years within a single political organization toward mutually accepted objectives, nor has this required on the part of either of them any suppression of his theoretical opinions, in private or public. There is nothing anomalous in such a situation. Though theory is doubtless always in one way or another related to practice, the relation is not invariably direct or immediate; and as we have before had occasion to remark, human beings often act inconsistently. From the point of view of each of the authors there is in the other a certain such inconsistency between 'philosophical theory' and political practise, which *might* on some occasion lead to decisive concrete political disagreement. But it does not now, nor has anyone yet demonstrated that agreement or disagreement on the more abstract doctrines of dialectical materialism necessarily affects today's and tomorrow's concrete political issues – and political parties, programs and struggles are based on such concrete issues. We all may hope that as we go along or when there is more leisure, agreement may also be reached on the more abstract questions. Meanwhile there is fascism and war and unemployment.

During 1907–8, Lenin was, as is well known, carrying on a philosophical dispute with the Machists and also a sharp political fight against the Mensheviks.

Gorky inclined, on the philosophic questions, toward the Machists, and apparently considered that this might prevent him from making common *political* cause with Lenin against the Mensheviks on the concrete questions then at issue. On February 25, 1908, Lenin wrote to Gorky as follows:

> I believe I must tell you my view quite openly. A certain scrap among the Bolsheviks in the question of philosophy I now consider quite unavoidable. But to split up on that account would be stupid, in my opinion. We have formed a bloc for the carrying through of a certain tactic in the Social-Democratic Labor party. This tactic we have been and are continuing to carry through *without differences of opinion* (the only difference of opinion occurred in connection with the boycott of the Third Duma), but firstly it never reached such a sharp point among us even to hint at a split; secondly, it did not correspond to the difference of opinion of the materialists and the Machists, for the Machist Bazarov, for example, was, like myself, against the boycott and wrote about it (a large feuilleton in the *Proletarii* [the journal then under Bolshevik direction]).
>
> To obstruct the cause of the carrying through of the tactic of the revolutionary social democracy in the Labor party because of disputes over materialism or Machism, would be, in my opinion, an inexcusable stupidity. We must be at loggerheads over philosophy in such a way that the *Proletarii* and the Bolsheviks, as a faction of the party, *are not affected by it*. And that is entirely possible.

These wise, responsible and humane words are those, of course, of the real Lenin, not the sanctimonious Pope of the Stalinist fairy tales nor the one-party tyrant who is now being imaginatively constructed by Eastman, Hook and Harrison.

Shortly after the time of the above letter, interestingly enough, one of the Mensheviks declared in the *Neue Zeit* that the philosophical dispute was identical with the political dispute. *Proletarii* made the following editorial statement:

> In this connection, the editorial board of *Proletarii*, as the ideological representative of the Bolshevik tendency, deems it necessary to present the following declaration: 'In reality this philosophical dispute is not a factional dispute and, in the opinion of the editorial board, it should not be one; any attempt to represent these differences of opinion as factional is thoroughly erroneous. Among the members of both factions there are supporters of both philosophical tendencies'.

We wish to make, in the present circumstances, the following observations

1. Let us assume that the entire attack of our subjects on dialectical materialism is correct. Dialectical materialism is 'contrary to science', an 'idealistic metaphysics', a 'theology'. Then let us ask: So what? What follows, politically? To be even more concrete: From the destructive analysis of dialectical materialism by these critics, what conclusions may be derived as to changes in any section, paragraph, line or word of the Declaration of Principles of the Socialist Workers Party, the programmatic document upon which the Fourth Internationalist movement in this country is based, in its general conceptions identical with the Fourth Internationalist program throughout the world?

Not one of these critics, in spite of the many, many pages they have spent on the subject, has yet proposed any such *specific* changes. Even if they object to parts of our program, they have not pretended that their objection can be *deduced* from their attitude on dialectical materialism; but this is what it is incumbent upon them to show if they are justified in ascribing political importance to their formal theory, and if they excuse their failure to give unequivocal support to the Fourth International by appeal to their theory. Their inability to make any such deductions would go to prove, in fact, that politically their whole formal discussion of 'Marxist philosophy' is operationally meaningless, since no political conclusions follow from it. But it is not, in actuality, politically meaningless. The lack of political content in the formal doctrine is precisely the indication that this doctrine – the attitude toward dialectical materialism – is not at all what is at issue; that the whole 'philosophic discussion' is in practise a smokescreen for *political* positions which receive no explicit expression in the formal discussion proper, but must be analyzed out from other data.

2. The 'theory of the inevitability of socialism' is the chief bugaboo in this critique of dialectical materialism. Eleven years ago, in his book, *Marx and Lenin*, Max Eastman began his attack on this theory chiefly with the contention that it led to passivity on the part of those who believed in it, because they could permit the revolution to take care of itself. The same point was made by Hook in *Toward the Understanding of Karl Marx*, and more recently by Wilson and others. Once again we discover that our anti-metaphysicians are rationalist and *a priori* in their method of analysis, this time with charmingly ironic results.

Entirely apart from what may be the purely logical relation between a theory of inevitability and passivity, what are the empirical psychological and historical *facts*? Lenin and Trotsky, believing in inevitability, made a revolution. The Fourth Internationalists today and yesterday and tomorrow, a majority of whom doubtless believe in the theory of inevitability (if they are interested in the problem), spend their lives and energies in militant active political struggle. Eastman, who does not believe because it leads to passivity, announces his retirement for 'deliberation'. Hook has withdrawn from direct party political activity. Wilson is so non-inevitable about politics that he advises writers not even to sign anything any more.

3. Let us assume that the belief in 'the inevitability of socialism' is incorrect, that we should substitute the hypothesis that socialism is, to one or another extent, probable. Once more: what, directly and indirectly, is *politically* altered? But let us turn to other doctrines of our group. Having dismissed inevitability with a very airy gesture, they are now preaching, apparently – the *impossibility* of socialism (Eastman in his *Harper's* article), and the *inevitability* of … Thermidor (Stolberg in his *Nation* article on *The Revolution Betrayed*, Hook implicitly in his *Southern Review* article, 'Reflections on the Russian Revolution'). If 'the inevitability of socialism' is theology, then the 'impossibility of socialism' and the 'inevitability of Thermidor' are certainly no less theological. And, if we had to choose between theologies, we would say that the latter is surely the inferior brand: because the latter counsels the masses to despair and not to fight; and whatever the chances for socialism, we won't get it unless the masses fight.

4. Our subjects put up in opposition to dialectical materialism as their code and method: empirical science or, some of them, scientific empiricism. Let us examine briefly their pretensions to scientific empiricism. (We have already dealt with Eastman's utterly trivial conception and practises of what he naively imagines to be 'science' – *New International*, June and August 1938).

Is it not of some significance that from our entire list, only the politically insignificant Hacker and Lundberg have done any extensive original research to bring to light fresh historical and political data? (Hook's original researches have been almost entirely work of literary scholarship.) The function of the others has been almost solely one of interpretation – a far from unimportant function, but hardly one by itself to justify major claims to status as empirical scientists. Indeed, it becomes even suspicious when we observe it to be a *group* characteristic; when we note that this present attempt to re-interpret early Bolshevism is being accomplished with virtually no new data.

Again: scientific hypotheses are tested by the predictions that are made on their basis. We do not of course expect predictions in history or in politics to be made with the specificity or precision of those in the physical sciences, but we would like to inquire: What predictions of any kind about politics and history have our self-vaunted empiricists made to test for us their theories? We have been unable to discover a single one. In fact, we state quite soberly that so far as we can see, everything concrete and specific they know about modern politics, every reasonably concrete prediction they have made, has been learned from Trotsky and the press of the Fourth Internationalist movement.

Trotsky and the Fourth Internationalists generally, on their side, *test* their theories *daily* by specific analyses and by verifiable predictions – not mere vague predictions about a 'defeat' or 'victory', but careful predictions of the process and mechanism of what will happen; not merely in connection with large-scale historical crises, but likewise in the constant traffic of unions, parties, factions, Leagues. The predictions are occasionally in error, the time sequences are sometimes mis-stated; but by and large we can with not the slightest hesitation point to the past fifteen years as a triumphant reservoir of proof for the empirical superiority of our method of political analysis as against any other in the field. Our record, in small matters and great, is not even approximated by that of any other individual or group.

The truth *is* that in so far as our subjects are empiricists at all in politics and history, they are not scientific but *vulgar* empiricists. That is, they keep their political noses rubbing in the immediate fact and refuse or fear to state generalized hypotheses summing up the accumulated data of historical and political experience. This vulgar empiricism is, moreover, *directly* related to their specific political judgments and their political actions (which will be dealt with in detail in Part III). They 'are not sure' how entry of the POUM into the Spanish bourgeois government will work out; and therefore they refuse to characterize it politically. The infamous sham Keep America Out of War Committee 'might' turn into an effective instrument against war, so they hop into it (and after a burning, very shortly out again). 'You can't tell' just what the Social-Democratic Federation will do in case of war – after all some members in it say they are against collective security; so they write for the *New Leader*. The revolution 'might' lead to Thermidor everywhere; so we will be careful not to commit ourselves too thoroughly to the revolution.

5. Let us, finally, examine some empirical gems from our anti-theologians. And let no one imagine that these are arbitrarily selected. Their attacks on dialectical materialism end up with hymns to Freedom, Truth, Morality, and to empty abstract formulas that make the Platonic Ideas look like models of careful empirical observation.

In articles and speeches, Hook has recently adopted as his motto Lord Acton's well-known aphorism: 'Power breeds corruption; absolute power breeds absolute corruption'; and Hook draws many a conclusion from this 'hypothesis'. At first hearing, this pretty phrase sounds dignifiedly profound, and an audience is usually impressed. Yet let us consider. To begin with, the form of the aphorism is nothing but our old friend 'inevitability' once more. And whence comes this 'absolute' for an empiricist who by profession recognizes nothing as absolute? But these might be dismissed as quibbling objections? Think, then, of the completely absurd content of the aphorism, however interpreted. Power does, of course, sometimes breed corruption – certain kinds of power directed toward certain types of end. But power also breeds, and is the only breeder, of just the opposite of corruption – other powers directed toward other ends. If we went back over history and eliminated all power in order to get rid of all corruption, we would also have to get rid of all history and put man back where he started from. Hook's implicit advice to slaves, serfs, villeins would be: do not exercise power against your masters, because then you will be corrupted (they heard exactly the same advice at the time – from the priests). His implicit advice to workers today would have to be: do not use your trade union power against the bosses, because that will corrupt you; do not use political power to overthrow the bosses' government and set up your own government, because that will lead only to the triumph of Thermidor. In *concrete* meaning, this 'anti-power' preaching, which is now a feature of this whole school (the quotation from Acton is merely a minor symptom), is on the one hand empirically simply ridiculous, on the other politically *reactionary*. In sum, it, like the doctrine of 'the inevitability of Thermidor', is just a fancy way of putting the time-honored precept of class collaboration.

'Problems of being and of universal knowledge ... should be acknowledged to exist, but not solved by the device of pretending to know what is not known' (Eastman in *Harper's*). A juicy morsel for the semantic analysis of young empiricists.

Or let us listen to Eugene Lyons, at the close of his book, summing up the lessons of his mighty experiences, coming finally to grips with the problems of the day:

> The 'coming struggle' – and it is not coming, it is already here – is not between communism and fascism. It is the struggle for the moral and ethical ideals [the distinction between 'moral ideals' and 'ethical ideals' would be a little obscure in our minds if we didn't understand that the whole business were reduplicating bombast] which have been renounced by both these movements.
>
> *Assignment in Utopia*, p. 622

> I left Russia and Europe convinced that the immediate [*sic*] task for those who have the urge to participate consciously in the historic processes of their lifetime – is to defend the basic concepts of freedom, humaneness, intellectual integrity, respect for life ... [And then at last the abstractions get down on the ground:] They must be defended from Bolshevik onslaughts no less than fascist or capitalist onslaughts.
>
> Ibid., p. 623

Against 'One-Party Dictatorships'

The broad attack on 'one-party dictatorship', in which nearly all of our subjects have participated, has reached a new climax in Hook's article, 'Reflections on the Russian Revolution', published in the current (Winter 1938–9) issue of the *Southern Review*. A full discussion of this presumptuous essay will have to wait for another occasion. Now, as with the other doctrines, we are primarily interested in the *political* motivation of the attack taken as a whole.

It might be expected that these empiricists, who regard the question of 'one-party dictatorship' as so crucial that, in Hook's thesis, it is by itself *the* cause of the degeneration of the Russian Revolution, would at least bother to be wholly unambiguous as to what they meant by 'one-party dictatorship'. This, however, is not the case. Do they mean a regime in which a single party administers the apparatus of government? Sometimes the context shows that this is what they mean – which would make the United States a one-party dictatorship. Or do they mean a regime in which all parties but one are *illegal*? Presumably this should be consistently their meaning, and we will interpret them in this sense.

They maintain: (a) that 'one-party dictatorship' is an integral and essential part of Bolshevik theory as held by Lenin, Trotsky and Stalin alike; (b) that one-party dictatorship leads to dictatorship of a clique or individual *over* the party and thereby to brutal totalitarian Thermidor; (c) this is the causal explanation of the Russian Thermidor: 'the explanation of the present political regime in Russia is to be found in its natural evolution from party dictatorship to dictatorship of the secretariat'.

It is interesting to observe how conclusion (b) is reached. It is not in the least by an empirical examination of the facts of the Russian Revolution or analogies from other historically similar events, but almost exclusively by a purely *rational deduction* from 'the nature of dictatorship' – e.g. the nature of the *concept* of dictatorship; a deduction, that is, of a Hegelian, 'theological' variety (cf., *Southern Review* article, pp. 452f.). '... The dictatorship of a political party cannot for long be effective without its own internal organization becoming dictatorial'. Why not? 'The necessity [*sic*] of *controlling* the mass of the population ... compels [*sic*] the party to assume a military, sometimes called a monolithic, structure'. In passing, what disingenuous sophistry so casually to identify 'military' with 'monolithic' structure – two altogether different conceptions. 'But the dictatorship of the party cannot [*sic*] be effectively wielded ...', etc. 'To conceal this division ... the ruling group in the party must [*sic*] regulate ...' etc. 'Now in order to exercise the proper supervision the leading group must [*sic*] itself be unified. Dissidents are isolated, gagged into silence, exiled, deported, and shot'. Notice again – unity of the leading group so casually identified with exiling and shooting all dissidents. 'The rule of the leading group must [*sic*] be fortified by a mythology …'. But this process, for our empiricist, is of course only probable? Pause, dear reader: 'Historical variations may appear in *some points* [our italics] in this evolution …'; but the iron law of the general pattern, the necessary inevitability of the degeneration rises supreme above all minor variations! This, and all these 'musts' and 'compels' and 'necessities' from our oh-so-empirical anti-inevitabilityists!

∴

Notes on Morality: It would be farcical to regard Hook's article as a scientific treatise. It is actually a *moral* essay, attempting to fix moral responsibility, moral praise and blame. Taken in its entirety we declare quite bluntly: it is an ideological *deception* serving to direct moral onus against the Bolsheviks and to alibi the crimes of the Mensheviks, SRs, Kerensky, and indeed the imperialist interventionists themselves. In a brilliant polemic against Corliss Lamont, Hook once showed how support of a big-scale frameup led to one's commission on one's part of minor frameups. Something dangerously like this occurs in the *Southern Review* article. In citing a few details, we must keep in mind that Hook's article was written for a magazine most of whose readers are not acquainted in detail with revolutionary history and conceptions.

1. As to the scientific pretensions, a single and major example: Hook maintains that the advances in Russian economy during the past 20 years prove nothing about the comparative possibilities of socialized as against capitalist economy, because we can come to different conclusions by shifting our standard of comparison. Historically speaking, he claims, it is equally significant to compare the present Russian economy with Russian economy 20 years ago; or with US economy today. And, says Hook, the US workers are much better off. (Therefore, any unsuspecting reader might naturally conclude, US economy is 'better', more worth defending, than Russian). The point is not dissimilar to that made by the National Chamber of Commerce, which uses the argument to reconcile the US workers to eternal misery and insecurity (cf., news dispatch published December 28 in the general press).

What conceivable historical significance, to any but a purely Platonic or theological theory of history, could there be to a static comparison between the Russian standard of living today and its development during the past 20 years to the US standard of living today (incidentally, Hook of course omits any reference to the *development* of US economy during these 20 years, which has sent it *back* to the early years of the century)? Or to that of any of the advanced capitalist powers which got an early monopoly of the imperialist field? There is a far more suitable comparison which evaluates Russian economy in terms of what was the sole historical alternative in Russia of 1917–18 to workers' power and socialized economy: namely reduction of Russia to a semi-colonial nation. The comparison, of course, is with *China*. Recognizing this, as any conscientious historian of any school must do, Hook's facile generalizations go up at once in smoke. As a matter of fact, what Hook here and throughout the article is interested in is to display the *moral* heinousness of Stalin's totalitarian regime, and his 'science' comes in only for decorative effect.

2. Hook's central thesis is that one-party dictatorship is *the* cause of the degeneration because it was 'the only *controllable factor*'. What in the world does he or can he mean? If he is inquiring into questions of historical causation, how does he exempt himself from discovering what *causal* factors brought about restrictions and finally suppression of democracy, brought about the one-party dictatorship which he is presumably investigating? Surely it was not, like an act of God's, self-caused. But Hook is prohibited from such an analysis, not by any scientific demands (which would lead to just that analysis) but by implicit but unrecognized *political aims*, since that analysis would not turn out so well for the objects of his present apologies, the SRs, Mensheviks and Kerensky.

But, apart from this, taking the perspective of 1917, in what specifiable sense was the extent of democracy more 'controllable' than a dozen other factors? The seizure of power by the Bolsheviks and their subsequent agitation and actions certainly exercised a causal influence, which might have been a 'controlling' influence, on revolutions elsewhere. Unfortunately, the workers' movement in Germany turned out to be under the control of the social democrats and not of the Bolsheviks – a little item that is omitted from Hook's 'Reflections'. Hook will hardly tell us that successful revolutions in other nations would have had no important effects on the internal Russian conditions, including the political regime.[7]

7 [Footnote by Burnham and Shachtman]: Even Benjamin Stolberg, though less trained in scientific method than Sidney Hook, does not go so far as to tell us that there would have been no effect. By no means. He writes: 'It may be true that the pre-revolutionary backwardness of a country determines the degree of its Thermidorian savagery; that is only saying that the past of a culture patterns its future. But that does not mean that if a series of Octobers had rapidly occurred in Berlin and Paris and London, Thermidorean reactions could not have followed. On the contrary, the far more powerful counter-revolutionary forces in the West – so powerful that after all they were able to abort all social revolutions – could have been defeated, if at all, only by a revolutionary terror so strenuous and complex that it might have ended in an international Thermidor, less cruelly Byzantine, but far more hopeless than Stalinism'. (*The*

The peace negotiations with Germany, the delay in formulating an industrial plan (so disastrous in its consequences), the Polish campaign, the agricultural policy, the policy of the CI in the Balkans or China, the adoption of a perspective of national Bolshevism or of world revolution, were all not less 'controllable' in Hook's sense than the alleged position on party dictatorship.

What Hook seems really to be holding against the Bolsheviks is that they didn't exercise their 'control' over their own actions to abdicate, and abandon the state power to the only possible alternative – restoration or imperialist reduction to semi-colonial status, so that Russia might have become another China. This, of course, they might have done; and had they done so, it is also true that there would have been no Stalinism.

3. Hook 'proves' that 'the Bolsheviks considered the dictatorship of the proletariat to be the dictatorship of the Communist party' in the sense that this involves also the complete suppression of democracy and the illegalization of both opposition parties and inner-party factions, by a process which is a neat little lesson in the mechanism of deception.

Item 1: His first two categories of evidence (out of five) are – the accusations of the opponents of Bolshevism! Giving important weight to such evidence, we could say that Hook is quite probably a Nazi-Japanese agent, and that Roosevelt is a Communist.

Item 2: The third category of evidence – 'their oppressive treatment of other working-class organizations' – has not the slightest bearing on the question until we examine specifically what the basis for and circumstances of this treatment were. All States 'oppress' those who seek to overthrow them.

Item 3: The fifth category: 'Most important of all, as far as this specific point is concerned, the program of the Communist International, which left no room for doubt that the Communist parties or respective countries would liquidate at the first opportunity other working-class parties'. Triumphantly, he quotes, in a footnote, the relevant passage of the program. We hope that all readers take the trouble to glance at the footnote. *The quotation says absolutely nothing about liquidating other working-class parties*, nor could the smartest logician possibly deduce such a conclusion from it. The passage discusses several possible types of government, ending with one which the Communist party exclusively administers. Hook italicizes the following: 'Only the workers' government, consisting of Communists, can be the true embodiment of the dictatorship of

---

Nation, April 10, 1937) Conclusion? If you're crazy enough to want a revolution at all, the only guarantee against its Thermidorean degeneration – and that a very shaky one – would be to start it in Andorra or Wake Island, and then fight like hell to keep it from spreading beyond the borders.

the proletariat'. What in the world has this to do with liquidating anything or anybody? This simply embodies the theory and aim of *every* political party of any kind which is worth its weight in salt. *Every* serious political party, including the Republican and Democratic parties of the US, aims at the administration of State power and asserts that it alone can administer it properly in the interests of whomever it claims to represent.

For if Hook considers his perfectly commonplace quotation from the program of the Comintern's 4th Congress in 1922 to be such crushing proof of his argument that totalitarianism is inherent in Bolshevism, what will he say about the following (equally commonplace) quotations?:

> In a *real* Labour revolution, which breaks out where the workers as a class have captured political power, the Communist party, which constitutes a mere sect, will no longer play any part. Victory will fall to the Social Democratic party, *which is wide enough to include all the class-conscious workers*, and it will be its task to employ the political power thus acquired to carry out a socialistic transformation ...

> ... no socialist would prefer a coalition Government, if given the choice of a Socialist Government. *Only* the latter type of Government can pave the way to Socialism, and proceed energetically and systematically to the socialization of the capitalist process of production. (*The Labour Revolution*, pp. 27, 52. Our emphasis).

Who wrote these terribly totalitarian words, according to which the 'real' proletarian revolution, and the transitional period during which the way to socialism is paved, can be directed 'only' by a government consisting exclusively of members of a single party? Karl Kautsky, the theoretical Pope of international social democracy! Should not, then, the rights of paternity require the re-naming of at least five contemporaries with his patronymic, i.e., Vladimir I. Kautsky, Leon D. Kautsky, Joseph V. Kautsky, Benito Kautsky, Adolf Kautsky? For according to Hook's argumentation, Kautsky is, as much as anybody, the ideological father of totalitarian Leninism, Trotskyism, Stalinism, Fascism and Nazism.

Item 4 (the payoff): To clinch his point finally, Hook ends with a quotation from – William Z. Foster in 1932! 1932, when the process of Stalinization was complete, is used as *proof* for Hook's thesis that original (Lenin's) Bolshevism held the theory and that therefore Lenin and Stalin are one in their attitude toward democracy! Needless to say, no word of warning is included by Hook for his uninstructed *Southern Review* readers.

Item 5: Perhaps the most decisive test for a scientist is his scrupulous inclusion of all *negative* evidence. In arguing for his thesis, Hook includes not one word of mention of the negative evidence well known to him and *not* to the bulk of those who will read the article. Not a word of *State and Revolution*, Lenin's magnificent formulation of workers' democracy, written on the very eve of October in order to explain to the masses not merely of Russia but of the world and for the future (as a guide if the Bolsheviks should that time fail in achieving their aims) the meaning of workers' democracy. Not a word of Lenin's constant struggle, from the first year of the revolution until his death, against the bureaucratization of the party and state apparatus. Not a word on the great discussions over Brest-Litovsk, the Polish campaign, trade union policy. Not a word to indicate to the reader that the Bolsheviks invited the Mensheviks and SRs to form the government jointly with them, and that the Mensheviks and right wing SRs, standing on the basis of the Constituent Assembly, declined of their own will. Not a word to recall that those of the left SRs who had not meanwhile fused with the Bolsheviks voluntarily and deliberately withdrew from the government because of their disagreement with the Brest-Litovsk Treaty, and publicly announced themselves against the Soviet state power. Not a word of the fact that in 1923 Trotsky *began* the struggle of the Opposition on the issue of workers' democracy nor of the continuous struggle of the Opposition against Stalin's anti-democracy from then onward. And of course not a word of the economic and military conditions nor the actions of the opposition parties in the early years which compelled the restrictions of democracy.

Democracy, also, like truth, is not an empty abstraction. Democracy is a part, an essential part, of the socialist ideal, but it alone is not the whole of socialism. And it must always be understood in a context, with its concrete historical content. Democracy for a beleaguered regime in the midst of civil war cannot mean the same thing as democracy for an established regime at peace and prosperous. What the Bolshevik aim and ideal is, on the question of the right of other parties to free functioning, is summed up for the masses and for the Hooks of the future by two resolutions of the Central Committee of the party passed shortly after the conquest of power:

> The Central Committee declares that it is excluding nobody from the Second All-Russian Soviet Congress and is entirely ready, also now, to admit those who departed and to recognize a coalition *with* them inside the Soviets, that, consequently, the assertions that the Bolsheviks do not want to share the power with anybody are absolutely false.
>
> *Resolution on the Question of an Agreement with the Socialist Parties, Pravda,* Nov. 15, 1917

> In Russia the Soviet power has been conquered and the transfer of the government from the hands of one Soviet party into the hands of another Soviet party is possible without any revolution, by means of a simple decision of the Soviets, by means of simple reelection of the Soviets.
>
> *Declaration to All Party Members and to All the Toiling Classes of Russia, Pravda,* Nov. 20, 1917

4. Another little bit of deception: Says Hook, to the Bolsheviks, '*all* who made the demand for democratically elected Soviets, including the heroic Kronstadt sailors, were regarded as counter-revolutionists'. Why is this a 'deception'? To most of those who will read Hook's article, having only general acquaintance with history, 'heroic Kronstadt sailors' can only mean: those sailors who were the backbone of the revolution in 1917 and the first part of 1918. Now, Trotsky recalled that the Kronstadters of the days of the suppression of Kronstadt were *not* the same sailors as those of 1917–18; no one has contradicted his evidence on this point because everyone with any direct knowledge recognizes it as true. It may be argued that the neo-Kronstadtians were also 'heroic' and that the suppression was incorrect; but that is not at issue. The deception occurs through Hook's hiding from his readers what he himself knows to be the case, and by sliding an emotive attitude directed toward one set of people in 1917 to an entirely different set in 1921.[8]

5. And another: 'For every act of violence against Bolshevik leaders, there were hundreds committed against their political opponents ... All others [except those who agreed with them on specific points] were simply classified as bandits and subjected to a ruthless reign of terror'. Now notice: 'It is quite true that some of the activities of the non-Bolshevik working-class parties exceeded the limits of Soviet legality, but it is even truer to say that the Bolsheviks themselves defined and changed these limits at will'. What would the average reader understand by these statements? So far as the *facts* alleged about the Bolsheviks go, Hook is stating merely the most irresponsible lies. But there is more than this. The Bolsheviks are murderers and slanderers. The non-Bolsheviks – 'exceeded the limits of Soviet legality ...'. That will call up, doubtless, pictures of an unlicensed speech, a meeting without a permit, agitation against some important military decree ... Now what did the non-Bolsheviks actually do? Mensheviks fought in the White Armies and worked directly with the imperialist interventionists; so also with the right SRs; the left SRs attempted the assas-

8 [Foonote from Burnham and Shachtman]: Sidney Hook in June, 1935 (*Modern Monthly*, p. 218): 'the Kronstadt rebellion – an uprising of a local soviet representing a comparative handful of sailors against the entire Soviet regime ...'.

sination of the leaders of the government, and publicly boasted about their armed struggle against the Soviet power, giving a political motivation.[9] Yes, just a touch beyond the limits of Soviet legality. Again the dominating political function of Hook's moral charade comes to the surface: to direct moral indignation against Bolshevism, *and to turn it away from the centrists and reformists.*

∴

What are the facts about 'one-party dictatorship'? So far as the *scientific* problem of understanding the events in Russia goes, that is to be settled by sober investigation into the specific conditions which in Russia did in the end eventuate in the extermination of democracy, an investigation by no means yet completed, but which has been most fully made in the literature of the Fourth International. The '*theory* of one-party dictatorship' has nothing to do with what happened, because Bolshevism does not and did not hold such a theory;[10] to the extent that it may be suggested in some of the writings of Bolshevik leaders in the early '20s, these were *ad hoc* generalizations from the specific Russian occurrences.

As, however, to the *practice* of one-party dictatorship, we must observe: (1) a difference of opinion is permissible; (2) no *a priori* conclusion can be reached; (3) in any case there is no necessary connection between one-party dictatorship and the evolution of Thermidor.

Let us consider: At the time of a revolution the line between parties is drawn not by complicated theories but by the barricades. A dual power arises, one power based on the old state apparatus, one on the Soviets or some similar class organizations of the workers and peasants. Fighting occurs upon the issue of which depends what power will be sovereign. It is sometimes hard to be sure about logical deductions, but it is simpler to tell one end of the rifle from the

9 [Foonote from Burnham and Shachtman]: Sidney Hook in October, 1934 (*Modern Monthly*, p. 539): 'It is well to remember that the Bolshevik party led the October Revolution in a coalition with the left Social Revolutionists who were later suppressed only when they took up arms against the Soviet state'. And speaking of morality, aren't we moralists usually a little opener about the whys and wherefores of our *changes* in views – and in facts?

10 [Foonote from Burnham and Shachtman]: 'While the Workers' State will necessarily reserve to itself the indispensable right to take all requisite measures to deal *with* violence and armed attacks against the revolutionary regime, it will at the same time assure adequate civil rights to opposition through the allotment of press, radio, and assembly facilities in accordance with the real strength among the people of the opposition groups or parties'. From the *Declaration of Principles of the Socialist Workers Party*.

other. The parties who line up with their members' rifles pointed at you are the enemy. In war, the enemy is by the fact of being an enemy 'illegal'. Those who point their rifles in the same way you do are your comrades or at least your allies. If this includes other parties, then according to Bolshevik theory and practice such parties have equal rights with the Bolsheviks to democracy and legality.

Will there be parties other than the Bolsheviks pointing guns in the same direction – i.e., defending the same State? This cannot be settled by deduction, but only by practice. In Russia there were for a while, and then those parties were all legal; but the non-Bolshevik parties turned their guns around.

Consider what might have happened in Spain in connection with the Barcelona events. Let us assume that there had been a strong Bolshevik party also present, and that the workers had been successful in taking power. In Barcelona, the barricades drew the lines of legality. On one side were republicans, socialists and Stalinists; on the other the anarchists, POUM, and our assumed strong Bolshevik party. Now does Hook want to accord democratic rights to the republicans, socialists and Stalinists? But they have illegalized themselves by shooting in the wrong direction. Then it would seem that three parties – POUM, anarchists and Bolsheviks – would be legal, all basing themselves on the correct, the workers' side of the barricades.

That *might* have happened, but our assumptions may be too artificial. *If* there had been a strong Bolshevik party, which had not made the fatal errors of the POUM and anarchists, had not entered or given political support to the government, it would perhaps more probably have drawn off during the preceding months all the most progressive and militant of the membership of the POUM and the anarchists (as in 1917 and 1918 the Bolsheviks *did* from the Mensheviks and SRs); the POUM and the anarchists would have had their proletarian ranks excised and would have remained as bureaucratic apparatuses. If that had been the case, then either at the time of the Barcelona events or subsequent to it, they might well have gone to the other side of the barricades – where in fact their truer interests would be. Then there would have been 'one-party dictatorship', only one legal party. But such a party would be under such circumstances the most democratic possible expression of the interests and will of the broadest strata of the masses, of workers' and peasants' democracy. Nor would there be the least *necessary* reason why their political monopoly would bring about suppression of inner-party democracy. The conditions of such a development as hypothetically outlined, in fact, might well tend toward a richer democracy than in a pre-revolutionary situation, granted a few good breaks. Later on, with the workers regime consolidated, with at all favorable circumstances internally and internationally, the one-party dictatorship might most naturally develop into many parties, the new parties (perhaps beginning as factions) arising on the basis of the *new* problems of the new economy and social structure.

These are not idle speculations, based on fancy. In Russia, immediately following the victory in the Civil War, tendencies at once appeared working toward the breakup of the Bolshevik party. These were expressed as faction struggles. The factions were, however, at least in embryo, *separate political parties*. They had different programs and different tactics. They carried their struggle to one or another extent *outside* of the framework of the party (in 1918, it will be remembered, the Bukharin faction functioned quite independently, with its own public press, officially endorsed by the Moscow region of the party). For a while we might say that the Bolshevik party was somewhat like the Trinity – 'one substance and three persons': it was from one point of view a coalition of three parties, the Stalin and Bukharin and Trotsky 'parties'. In 1929, the SR Chernov, who, unlike Hook, was looking at realities and not forms, wrote an essay most significantly entitled: *Russia's Two Parties* (i.e. the Stalin party and the Bukharin party).

How simply might such developments as these – granted other external developments (the success of the Chinese revolution, for example) or different internal circumstances (the advanced productive plant of the United States) – have issued in a number of freely competing parties. But even if this would *not* be the case, it would not prove that 'one-party dictatorship' is necessarily incompatible with democracy. If we are interested not in juridical abstraction but in actualities, it is possible that the workers' state will find in some cases that a one-party *form* is the most *democratic* political structure. Such a party would be in effect a *coalition* of many parties, a federated party; and full democratic expression might be given, publicly and freely, through it. (The Democratic party of the US is at this moment close to such a coalition party on a bourgeois foundation).

But does the revolutionary party, the Bolshevik party, claim that only it can *adequately* represent the interests of the masses, administer the workers' state effectively and through its leadership open the road for socialism? Does it aim to act as the 'government party' and the sole such party? Certainly. And there is not the slightest incompatibility between such claims and such a purpose, and the fullest possible democracy short of the liquidation of the state – which is also part of the purpose of the revolutionary party.

∴

Why all this fuss from our subjects about 'one-party dictatorship'? If it were a 'purely scientific question', if it were actually only a study in historical causation, or the attempt to study and predict the political forms of the workers' state, we may be sure that it would not be so passionate a point of dispute. There is such a fuss because behind the 'purely scientific dispute' lurks as usual the political objective, because the scientific dispute is only the screen for the attack not on 'the theory of one-party dictatorship' but on the practical objective of *class dictatorship, of* the workers' state to be achieved by the overthrow of the bourgeois state, on the sole historical means available for carrying through the socialist transformation of society. This is not yet explicit in Hook, though suggested by the trend of his recent argumentation, but it rises plainly to the surface in those of his *confréres* who have outstripped him – in Eastman, Lyons, Harrison, and of course all of those included in our 'Group II'. Let us, however, present it in the words of an old master at the 'inevitable deduction': '"Class dictatorship" necessarily means party dictatorship. Dictatorship by a party inevitably becomes dictatorship within the party – the dictatorship of a leader and his clique'. (Algernon Lee, *New Leader*, Feb. 6, 1937).

And there is a second reason, which is betrayed most naively in Hook's article, for the fuss. Near the end he points out, what is unquestionably true, that '*every* working-class party considers itself to be the vanguard not only of the class but of the new society it is striving to achieve' and that all parties are sometimes or at least might be mistaken. The incidence of his argument makes clear that the only sufficient explanation for his dragging in these two flat and obvious truths is to provide a justification for failing to make a firm choice among the political parties actually on the field, to give loyalty and allegiance unambiguously to one camp or the other. The justification is of course absurd. The first point is completely irrelevant: making a claim doesn't prove a claim; Voliva claims his flat-earth theory is correct, but that doesn't entitle us to make no choice between it and the theory of scientific astronomy and geography. Do we balance witch doctors against John Hopkins on the basis of their *claims*? The second point is equally unimportant since the problem is not one of infallibility but the general course of one party *as compared with* that of others. What Hook is trying to do is to spin himself a theory which would enable him to be 'impartially' and paternally a 'friend' equally of the Social Democratic Federation and of the Socialist Workers Party – after all, they both claim[11] to be the vanguard and both make mistakes. He is trying to give a

11 [Foonote from Burnham and Shachtman]: Yes, even the *New Leader* makes its claim, and in such bold and sweeping terms that Hook may be forced to include it in his next attack on one-party dictatorship: 'Dangerous as all the economic trends are, they provide rich material for interpreting the new capitalism in terms of the basic aims of democratic

rational basis to the dream of our group that we mentioned in Part I: the dream of peace, freedom, release from responsibility.

Lenin is the Father of Stalin

The final major contention of our subjects, the remaining plank in their 'formal program', is that Leninism is the source of Stalinism. This theory has been put forward in one form or another by Lyons, Eastman, Hook (in the *Southern Review* article), Stolberg, Harrison, and by all in Group II except Lundberg (who hasn't discussed the matter). Eastman, in his recent *Liberty* article carries the theory to its conclusion by stating that Leninism is the source not only of Stalinism but also of fascism.

Since this theory is based exclusively on the related theory about 'one-party dictatorship', it will not require extended additional discussion. We wish to make three points:

1. As in other instances but here more grossly, our subjects do not bother at all to define *what* the point is that they are trying to make. At times they seem to be saying no more than that Leninism in Russia preceded in time Stalinism. Granted. Or that a continuous state power underwent the transformation from Leninism to Stalinism. Obviously. Or that Leninist politics is the 'cause' (whatever they mean by historical cause, which they do not state) not only in Russia but as a general law of the subsequent transformation to Stalinism. Or that Leninism 'must' under any and all circumstances result in Stalinism – which is what, as a matter of fact, they all do say, these anti-inevitabilityists. Or that there were juridical features of the party and state structure under Lenin which Stalin was able to utilize for his own purposes, in consolidating his totalitarian power. Which last, again, is known to everyone.

The ambiguity here is not unimportant. Since many of these interpretations of their vaguely worded thesis are almost self-evidently true, they are able to carry over the favorable emotive attitude which a reader grants to a recognized truth, to their general central thesis that Leninism is simply a stage in a necessary process which must eventuate in Stalinist totalitarianism.

2. As with all the rest of their formal program, the reasoning of our subjects here is entirely formalistic, *a priori*: Leninism means by definition one-party

socialism. The Social Democratic Federation is the only organization in this country with a program and philosophy that presents a solution of the problems implied by these startling changes'. (Issue of Dec. 24, 1938). But perhaps they are saved by the next sentence: 'Due to internal conflicts, its voice in these matters has not been heard'.

dictatorship – which is besides its 'essential' and causally crucial doctrine; one-party dictatorship by a necessary process leads to dictatorship of a clique or Führer and the murder of all opposition; Q.E.D. Simple enough.

Let us observe what our empiricists are doing. For the sake of their *a priori* syllogism they are simply throwing all the events of history into the scrap heap. For instance, by making the alleged theory of one-party dictatorship the quintessence of Leninism in the most approved scholastic manner, they are committed to the conclusion that all of Lenin's concrete policies on the hundred and one questions of colonial revolt, trade unions, united front, war, the soviet organization of society, etc., etc., are mere subordinate 'accidents' of no decisive importance.

Or, second, how explain that Stalin, in order to consolidate a totalitarian power, had to abandon all the policies of Lenin (cf. Eastman, *The End of Socialism in Russia*!), and murder all of Lenin's colleagues.

Or again: In any conceivable sense that Leninism is the source of Stalinism it is at least as true that it is also the source of 'Trotskyism'. But for fifteen years, on a Soviet and world scale, on every major economic and social and political question, the adherents of Trotskyism have been in diametric opposition to the adherents of Stalinism, an opposition expressed equally in program and in practical human struggle. Nevertheless, the theory of our subjects commits them to the view that Trotskyism and Stalinism are fundamentally *twins* – a view which each of them step by step approaches and which many (Lyons, Harrison, and Hook by implication in the next to last paragraph of the *Southern Review* article) already express openly – that the entire struggle is at bottom nothing but a sham, motivated only by the personal bureaucratic desire for posts – the outs wanting to be in, the ins wanting to stay in. This incredibly vulgar conclusion is the only possible logical consequence of their thesis – as they indeed increasingly recognize. Vulgar as it is, we have met the theory often before, from many other sources.

3. Several of the more prominent of our subjects, including Hook outstandingly, broke with Stalinism about five years ago primarily on the issue of 'social-fascism'. Memory of this will serve as an ironic, even amusing, comment on the fact that their thesis of today commits them to the *theory of communo-fascism*. In the early stages of their present development, it might have been thought that the new theory was only that of 'Stalino-fascism', but today they have gone from Stalino-fascism to communo-fascism. There is no way for them to avoid this without abandoning their present theses.[12]

---

12 [Foonote from Burnham and Shachtman]: And, by the way, the original inventors of the

The theory of social-fascism was based on the theoretical premise summed up in Stalin's famous aphorism to the effect that social democracy and fascism are not antipodes but twins. The third-period Stalinist tactics toward reformists and reformist organizations followed naturally from this premise. But this premise is exactly that now formulated by our subjects with respect first to Stalinism and now to communism in general. Isolating totalitarian dictatorship as the determinative feature, the 'essence' of a social regime, they first identify Stalinism with fascism. (Already in this first step, Stalinism and fascism have been proved to be not antipodes but twins). They then trace Stalinism back to Leninism as its root, source, or cause, and thus, since Trotskyism is also the child of Leninism, communism in its Leninist and Trotskyist form as well as in its Stalinist perversion is shown to be the twin of fascism. The implicit logic becomes fully expressed in Eastman's *Liberty* article where he says quite bluntly that Leninism is the source both of Stalinism *and of fascism*:

> To some it may seem almost fantastic to say that the communist parties are thus becoming fascist parties. Fascism originated, out of communism in exactly this way. Mussolini was a revolutionary socialist. He learned all he knew from the Bolsheviks ... Mussolini learned it from Lenin, Hitler learned it from Mussolini. In origin that is what fascism is.

Our empiricists once more reveal themselves to be moralistic Platonists under the skin. Leninism, Stalinism, Trotskyism, fascism, all 'participate' in and derive their reality from the Platonic Idea of Dictatorship; and therefore they are all 'essentially', in the Realm of Being, 'the same thing'. A lot of trouble is thereby saved. No more need for careful analysis of modes of economy, class relationships, social origins, concrete conflicting interests. All such matters are only a part of the World of Becoming, with no more than a secondary, shadow reality. All we require is a formal syllogism of two to reach Q.E.D.S.

The practical political consequences, if their theory is taken seriously, will, of course, have to be just the same as those of the theory of social-fascism except that the communist and Stalinist movements will be substituted for reformism.

---

theory of communo-fascism were who but our old friends the social democrats. When we – and our present subjects – attacked the Stalinists in 1930–3 for the theory of social-fascism and the failure to make a united front with the social democrats, that was not implicit approval of the social democrats. Knowing them well from the past, we were aware in advance that they held the theory of communo-fascism, were against any united front, and could only be *forced* into it.

To begin with, for example, they must abandon altogether the defense of the Soviet Union; there is no possible justification in their present theory for the policy of defense of the Soviet Union. We suspect that Hook, Eastman and Lyons have been aware of this consequence for some time. So far as we know, none of them has yet declared himself publicly on the issue – which is so obviously raised by their writings of the last year. Whence this silence? Are not these the moralists who so diligently proclaim their devotion to Truth and so zealously attack the a-moralism of the Bolsheviks? Can it be part of their morality to hide or obscure the practical meaning of their theories from the masses?

We take this occasion, therefore, to demand from Hook, Eastman and Lyons unambiguous declarations on the question of defense of the Soviet Union from attack by Hitler or Japan – or for that matter by England – *declarations motivated by the theories which they are now putting publicly forward.*

But, of course, much more than this follows. It follows that one must be equally against both communism and fascism, against dictatorships whether of the left or of the right; it follows that communism and fascism are the Siamese twin main danger; it follows, in fact, as it did from the theory of social-fascism, that a united front with any communist organization is as impermissible as a united front with a fascist organization. Of course, our subjects do not as yet draw out all of these conclusions, even in their own minds. But that is because they are as we have mentioned before *irresponsible* politicians; if they take their program seriously they will have to draw them in time, or else abandon their program. Toward the end of his *Southern Review* article, Hook writes as follows: 'They [political parties] may offer a program and leadership, but just as soon as they reach out for a monopoly of political power, education, and propaganda behind the back of representative political institutions of the producers and consumers [and this is just what Hook in the preceding section of his article claims to have *proved* that all communist parties whether Leninist, Trotskyist or Stalinist, do], it *is time to build barricades against them*'. (Our italics). Hook will doubtless explain that he means the italicized phrase in a merely metaphorical sense – i.e., barricades of education and propaganda. But the particular metaphor chosen, as so often with metaphors, reveals more than the author consciously intends: for from Hook's present theory, if taken seriously, the statement follows with entire literalness.

In Summary

It is time to summarize briefly certain general features of what we have called 'the formal program'. It is, taken at its face value and as a whole: stale, abstract, negative, and preoccupied with the past.

1. Our subjects take great pride in believing that they are contributing something 'fresh', that they are 'reevaluating in the light of new experiences', that they 'are not dogmatists who refuse to reexamine their "basic assumption"', etc. What a pathetic self-deception! None of them has brought to light any new facts, given any new understanding of the present or future. As Freud put it once in a polemic: 'They are now disputing things which they, themselves, formerly defended and what is more, this dispute is not based on new observations, which might have taught them something fresh, but rather on a different interpretation which makes them see things in a different light than before'. In this case, the 'different interpretation' is different political aims which for justification require the violent re-arrangement of the past. New experience and events are 'teaching' them and not the dogmatists? All that they say in their formal program can be found long, long ago in the pages of Kautsky and put far more brilliantly, consistently and *openly*.

2. The abstract and formal character of their program has already been demonstrated, and is besides sufficiently obvious. They are occupied with a realm distantly removed from hard, cold events: with 'method', with 'nature dialectic', the concept of the inevitability of socialism, the essential nature of one-party dictatorship ..., with Truth and Freedom and Morality in caps.

3. And entirely negative also: *Against* dialectical materialism, *against* one-party dictatorship, *against* Stalinism ... But what *for*? For Truth, for Freedom, for Morality ...

4. And, where actual events are referred to in a decisive manner, we discover that these are always events of the past: Kronstadt, how Kerensky was overthrown, the outlawing of party factions in 1920, the illegalization of the opposition parties ... What of the present, and the future?

These pervasive features of the 'formal program' as developed by them all – stale, abstract, negative, concerned with the past – are sufficient indication by themselves that this formal program, taken at its face value, is *not* the actual political program of this group in the sense of that set of ideas and directives, explicit or implicit, which actually indicates the direction and aims of their intervention in the political arena. These features show us that the formal program functions not to *express* clearly and unambiguously the group's political nature, but to *veil and obscure* its political nature. It is a flank movement, to direct attention *away* from the main strategic maneuver.

However, specific analysis of even the formal program has already disclosed the actual politics to which it is indirectly related: An attack on revolutionary Marxism, on Bolshevism, and a growing *rapprochement* with reformism of both social-democratic and bourgeois varieties. It is politics of a group tendency in motion from revolutionary Marxism toward reformism: that is, of a centrist tendency.

We shall now proceed to establish this same conclusion by reference in some detail to the concrete political *acts* of our subjects.

Part III: The Actual Program

There are only five significant and clearly defined programs in present-day society, supported and acted upon with a more or less continuous tradition by organized social groups. Each of these offers a distinctive solution of the devastating crisis that threatens civilization itself. In the ranks of the working class: revolutionary Marxism, or the Fourth International, commonly referred to as the Trotskyist movement; Stalinism, the theory and practice of internationally projected anti-Soviet totalitarianism; and reformism, or the social democracy of the Second International.[13] In the ranks of the bourgeoisie: liberalism, whose

13 [Foonote from Burnham and Shachtman]: For a number of reasons, we do not list independently the anarchist or anarcho-syndicalist movement. In Spain, where alone it stepped out of the pages of Kropotkin and Bakunin and into the arena of the real class struggle, it revealed itself as little more than a variety of reformism, with overtones of verbal radicalism. If the anarchists in Spain did not 'outstrip' their social-democratic partners in the People's Front, they at least 'caught up with' them. As for the first French edition of anarcho-syndicalism, personified by M. Leon Jouhaux, it does not even have the Spanish version's literary devotion to revolution to recommend it. The pitiful bankruptcy of anarchism in action – in the only country where it has assumed the proportions of a mass movement – and the mushroom growth of a bureaucracy at its head which has little to learn from its social-democratic contemporary, have not left its official spokesmen and defenders here unembarrassed. All the louder do they clamor in their press against 'Trotsky, the butcher of Kronstadt' and against the unspeakable immorality of all Bolsheviks. Neither this noise, nor the demagogic references to the exemplary heroism of the anarchist workers, can dispel what is so obvious to the naked eye: the political collapse of anarchism in action. It is at the moment when this conclusion has become indisputable that Jean Mendez, who considers that the Trotskyism followed a sectarian line in Spain, abandons her Marxism to assume the post of an editor of a New York anarchist paper. It goes without saying that the editors of the paper who, unlike the Bolsheviks, are upright and forthright, speak of the disconcerting conduct of the FAI-CNT bureaucracy with all

left wing merges with the labor reformists, and which is concerned with keeping capitalism alive by 'making democracy work'; and fascism, which is concerned with keeping capitalism alive by putting an end to bourgeois democracy.

Stalinism has drawn increasingly close to social democracy. As far back as a dozen years ago, the Stalinists functioned as stand-in for the absent social democracy in the Chinese revolution. In the last three years especially, even theoretical and reminiscential distinctions have been abandoned, and no important differences exist between the two movements in any important practical political question. Their different origins, bases and functions – as well as narrower 'job' interests – militate against their complete fusion or even unmarred collaboration; nor do we identify the two. But what is of paramount importance in connection with the point we are discussing is the common position they hold on such vital questions as: the class nature of the state; bourgeois democracy and socialist revolution; democracy and fascism; class struggle and class collaboration; independent political action and People's Frontism or coalition government; class war and 'war for democracy'; colonial independence; etc., etc. We shall have occasion to refer to this similarity of positions more concretely later on.

As for liberalism, it represents a period of capitalist development which, where it is not already outlived and irretrievable, is in rapid decay. Where it continues to subsist, it is on its last legs. There is no power on earth that can make it endure, which may well be why so many liberals have taken to prayer since Munich. If it is not replaced by workers' rule that can reorganize society socialistically, it will be crushed inexorably by fascism. Not even those liberals who, like Max Lerner, rebaptize themselves 'democratic collectivists', can, we fear, redeem it from its fate. Even if it should be restored later in the now totalitarian countries – the post-1931 events in Spain show that it is not absolutely excluded – its resurrection can only be episodic, again as shown by the events in Spain.

So far as the working class movement goes, experience shows that all programs and tendencies that seek or claim to be independent and distinct from the two main streams – revolutionary Marxism and reformism (social-democratic or Stalinist) – merely move back and forth among them, never acquiring either stability or consistency, and coming to rest finally in one or the other. This holds true even of the sterile and miniscular sects which seem

---

the painful delicacy and incoherence of, let us say, a Louis Fischer writing in *The Nation* to explain away the Kremlin's anti-abortion ukase. Malicious tongues might even refer to them in the terms applied by Eugene Lyons to the Bolsheviks: 'devotees of the theory of multiple truths'. But only malicious tongues.

to accomplish the biological miracle of existing outside of life itself. Nobody has yet succeeded in holding together a centrist movement for any length of time. Depending on its point of departure and the direction in which it moves, it ends up sooner or later in the camp of revolution or reformism. It is the classic fate of Hamlet politics – centrism.

To the extent that it has a real program – and it has one – the group of radical intellectuals we have been discussing is *centrist*. Protests at this political characterization on the grounds of our 'label-mania' can already be heard. More than anyone else, the centrist, who shows a cavalier lack of discrimination in ticketing everybody else, has a congenital dislike for being properly and bluntly designated by the name of his tendency. Yet there is no other way of describing politically a group made up of individuals who, in virtually every case, have been moving from a revolutionary Marxian position, or one close to it, *towards* reformism, or a little beyond it to bourgeois liberalism (or in some instances, scarcely concealed passivity). Factual evidence that has been accumulating throughout the recent past substantiates this conclusion.

Straws in the Wind

We will not dwell here on the apparently trivial and unconnected incidents of the past year, except to point out that running through them all like a thread has been a series of 'dissociations from Trotskyism'. They began during the period when the Commission of Inquiry was rendering its verdict on the Moscow Trials and the case of Leon Trotsky – for example, at the public meeting in December 1937 when several of the Commissioners went out of their way to assure the audience that they had nothing to do with Trotskyism. They have continued down to the present day. Oddly enough, the 'dissociations' were made public on the most inappropriate and unwarranted occasions; the announcement never seemed to have any germane relationship to the context or the circumstances in which it was delivered. But lest we seem to insist too much on punctilio, we hasten to add that everyone has a right to pronounce himself on a program or a movement and even to choose an inauspicious moment in which to do it. We would go further: one who is not a supporter of 'Trotskyism', or who has convinced himself to cease being one, not only has the right to proclaim his opposition to this movement, but also the duty to do so. We would not be the last to urge him to fulfill it. Thus, we can only be grateful when Mr. Charles Yale Harrison writes in the *New Leader* that 'as for myself, I must dissociate myself' from the Trotskyist movement, after he discovered the distilled essence of Truth in the pages of a posthumous brochure by Julius

Martov. It is a blow hard to survive, but at least it is delivered in the open. (But then, it had to be delivered openly if the unemployment crisis in the United States was to be solved, at least so far as Mr. Harrison is concerned).

We have said that if a person is sufficiently known to warrant being listened to, if only for a moment, on political questions, or even if that is not the case and he wants to express himself on such questions, he has both the right and duty to declare what program and movement he repudiates or opposes. But that is not always very interesting; certainly it is not his most important obligation. He must also state in one way or another the program or movement he *advocates*, especially in these times when everybody is looking for guidance to a way out of a situation widely acknowledged to be untenably bad. For it is not so much by what is *opposed*, but by what is *proposed* that a political tendency may be established. From the actions taken and proposals made by the group under consideration, it is not difficult to establish the political tendency of its component parts-more developed in some, less in others, to be sure – as one of *rapprochement with the social democracy* or even bourgeois liberalism. And a tendency which is in general *away from* revolutionary Marxism and *towards* social democracy, we are justified in designating as *centrist*. A few examples, so that we may follow the scriptural injunction of knowing people by their acts:

Item: Several months ago, the Thomasites and Lovestoneites launched their private imitation and would-be rival of the Stalinist anti-war farces under the name of the 'Keep America Out of War' Committee. Such movements were inaugurated about a dozen years ago, and since produced in kaleidoscopic series, by Stalin-Münzenberg, as a petty bourgeois-pacifist substitute for independent working class struggle against imperialist war. Nowadays, whether of the frankly patriotic Stalinist variety or of the more subdued pacifist type established by Norman Thomas, they all proceed from the fatal premise that the fight against war is an independent task, above, outside of and separate from the class struggle and to be conducted with 'special' (i.e. petty bourgeois) methods. It goes without saying that the KAOW included the standard quota of pacifist ladies of uncertain age and sure-fire nostrums (yesterday's stand-bys for similar set-ups managed by the Stalinists), to say nothing of Hamilton Fish, Maj.-General Rivers (Retired) and Mr. Frederick J. Libby, who has the ingenious idea of warding off another war by dividing more equitably among the imperialist powers the present world's colonies – without, of course, consulting the god-damn niggers who inhabit them. It goes without saying, also, that the founding conference of the KAOW endorsed the Roosevelt 'good neighbor' policy – could it do less? – and adjured the government to show that it was really worthy of the name 'democracy' by exerting America's economic pressure upon the fascist 'armament economy' nations (i.e. the policy of government sanctions which, when advocated by the Stalinists in slightly altered terms, arouses the horrified indignation of the *Socialist Call* and *Workers Age*). In a word, we had here a less lurid variety, but only a variety, of the familiar social-democratic-Stalinist-pacifist trap. Yet, among the signatories to the call for the first KAOW meeting in New York's Hippodrome were to be found Sidney Hook, James Rorty, James T. Farrell, Anita Brenner, Dwight Macdonald, Suzanne LaFollette, Ben Stolberg, John Chamberlain, Liston Oak, etc. That many of the signatories subsequently withdrew from the KAOW – naturally without explaining publicly why they had gone in or why they pulled out – is a tribute to the effects of the predictable policies of the KAOW on their conscience. That they sponsored it in the first place is not so complimentary to their foresight.

Item: Several weeks ago, the country voted in local elections. In New York, the ALP, the Stalinists and the Lovestone group, not being sectarians, supported No. 18 of the Sixty Families, Herbert H. Lehman, Democratic party candidate for governor. But there were two labor candidates for the office. The Socialist party nominated Norman Thomas; the Socialist Workers party conducted a write-in campaign for James P. Cannon. Norman Thomas and the SP are social-democratic; Sidney Hook, presumably, is not. James P. Cannon and the SWP are revolutionary Marxists; so, presumably, is Sidney Hook. But Sidney Hook endorsed the candidate of the SP, without even a statement to show that he was not a supporter of Thomas and the SP in general. Since this was not a private, confidential matter, but a public political act, may we ask, also publicly, why? Surely Thomas was not supported on the 'good man' theory. Surely also, he was not supported because he had a chance of being elected, whereas Cannon didn't. Surely, again, he was not supported because his party's program was superior from the revolutionary standpoint to the SWP's. Surely, finally, the choice was not made by tossing a coin. Wasn't Hook running the risk of letting the uninitiated conclude that he feels a closer political affinity with the party of social democracy than with the party of revolutionary Marxism?

The *New Leader*'s Dress Parade

Let us look a bit further into the matter of political affinities.

In the last few months, there has been a veritable parade of new but not unknown contributors across the pages of the *New Leader*, the New York weekly edited by James Oneal. About half of the newcomers wrote an article apiece as the private guests, so to speak, of Eugene Lyons, for whom they substituted as 'columnist' during his absence on a speaking tour; the other half appeared under more general editorial auspices. The political significance of their appearance cannot be denied. It is not a matter of an article written by one individual or two, which might therefore be dismissed as accidental or incidental. But the *number* of individuals involved, and above all their common characteristics (virtually all of them, regardless of other differences, have been avowed opponents of the Second International and what it stands for), make it possible and necessary to draw certain political conclusions. The writers include Leon Dennen, Charles Yale Harrison, Sidney Hook, Max Nomad, James Rorty, Ben Stolberg, Philip Rahv, James T. Farrell and Stephen Naft.

What is wrong, some will say, with writing for the *New Leader* if an invitation is extended by its editors? We pinch-hit for Lyons, others will say, as a personal favor to him while he was touring. These explanations for the sudden and concerted appearance of this group of radical intellectuals on the pages of the *New Leader* seem to us too simple and, in fact, irrelevant.

The *New Leader* is not an 'ordinary' periodical, like, let us say, *The Nation* and the *New Republic*, or even the *Saturday Evening Post* and *Liberty*. It is a distinct *party paper*, the official organ of the Social Democratic Federation, American section of the Second International. As such, it has a distinct political line, and avowed political and organizational objectives. As a consequence, literary collaboration with it is willy-nilly an act of solidarity with the organization for which it speaks, and an aid to it.

What is this organization? The Social Democratic Federation is composed of the self-styled 'Old Guard' of the split-up Socialist party. On every important political question of the day, the Federation and its paper take the position of the extreme right wing of the Second International. To them, Norman Thomas is (or rather, was!) the incarnation of Bolshevism. To them, in the words of the late Hillquit, the Russian Revolution has always been 'the greatest disaster and calamity that has ever occurred to the socialist movement'; and they have never given up their vicious fight against it. This has not prevented them – quite the contrary! – from taking a position which is substantially indistinguishable from that of the Stalinists, on all the important questions of the day.

The *New Leader* is for the Popular Front because it is for class collaboration, and was for it long before the Stalinists adopted it. It stands for 'collective security' and is for the holy crusade of 'democracy against fascism'. It is for Rooseveltism and the New Deal with at least as much vigor and even more sincerity than the *Daily Worker*. It can give the Stalinists cards and spades in licking the boots of the trade union bureaucracy and still come out ahead of the game. Wherein does it differ on any urgent political question from totalitarian Stalinism – which, by the way, is not an abstract concept but a system of concrete policies and actions on concrete issues? It does not, it is true, entirely cover up or justify the crimes of the Stalinist bureaucracy in Russia, but it does its best to defend or conceal the no less reprehensible crimes of the social-democratic bureaucracy in Europe – including the deals it makes with the same Stalinism. And if it does not use the Stalinist formula of 'Drive the Trotskyists and Lovestoneites out of the labor movement', it is only because it believes that the slogan is too restricted: the Stalinists should be driven out too! (The *New Leader* has just heartily endorsed the Red-baiting resolution of the Minnesota Farmer-Labor Party bureaucracy, which calls for the automatic expulsion of all advocates of proletarian revolution).

The *New Leader* is, however, respectable, ever so respectable. In its pro-war propaganda, it is not quite so blatant and clamorous as, let us say, the *Daily Worker*, but that does not lessen its comparative effectiveness as a recruiting sergeant in the coming imperialist war 'for democracy'. Two of its chief editorial writers are Charles Edward Russell and William E. Bohn, a couple of social-patriotic renegades from socialism and the SP in 1917, who served their country in the last World War, even if at a safe distance (i.e. 3,500 miles) from the trenches. They are no doubt ready to serve again in the coming war, even if every able-bodied citizen must again be drafted. By pure chance, Messrs. Russell and Bohn are past 60; Mr. Oneal is 63, Mr. Algernon Lee is 65.

In brief, the *New Leader* is a rotten social-democratic sheet from which so overpowering an odor has emanated that even Norman Thomas, not so long ago, found it too much for him. A spray of respectability that will reduce the pungency of the odor has therefore become pretty much a physical necessity for the editors. To get it, they have laid a not unclever trap for incautious people. The paper has not only been given a snappier typographical dress, but the splenetic and hysterical abuse Oneal used to heap on everything radical has been given a somewhat primmer polish. Above all, a systematic, deliberate effort is made to draw into the paper especially those radical writers who were at one time connected with the communist movement and whose personal and even political probity is so high that when the eye focuses on their names, the name and repute of Oneal and Co. are automatically excluded from the field-scope of vision. All this helps to retrieve the political fortunes of the *New Leader*. It is able to point with pious pride to the unselfish hospitality it vouchsafes 'all radicals', even those who 'disagree with us', provided they aren't 'totalitarians'. It is enabled to foster the pernicious myth that the 'decent' alternative to Stalinism is the right wing social democracy. It is enabled to fortify itself as a rallying ground for all 'radicals', and especially for those who are disillusioned with Stalinism, which the *New Leader* would like to equate with a disillusionment with revolutionary Marxism. These are the obvious *political motives* behind the invitations so generously extended by Oneal and Levitas, and not some weak-boned sentimental desire to convert their paper into a broad, all-inclusive 'radical forum'. In a word, it is a political trap for wandering radicals.

– But in heaven's name! are you so bitterly and narrow-mindedly sectarian that you cannot conceive of a revolutionary article being written in a social-democratic paper, whose editors, whatever their private motives, invite you to write whatever you please, without censorship?

This rejoinder has, unfortunately, more indignation in it than critical thoughtfulness, as may be seen from an examination of *what* the new crew of contributors has written in the *New Leader*.

Emily Post in the House of the Hanged

Take Eugene Lyons, for example. And a very good example he is, our anti-sectarian objector will retort. Don't the editors allow him full freedom of expression, even when he writes in opposition to the official editorial standpoint of the paper? Hasn't Lyons attacked 'collective security', whereas Oneal and Co. defend it? How then dare you call him a social-patriot, as you have?!

Softly, softly, friends. Let us see by taking a typical 'column' by Lyons. On October 8, he does indeed assail 'collective security' and with vigor. 'In effect, the Stalinists and other collective security advocates were saying: "Trust your government, despite the fact that it is a capitalist government. Declare a moratorium on your larger grievances in this hour of emergency"'. Good. Very good. A telling blow at the Stalinists. But who might the '*other* collective advocates' be? Why, unlike the Stalinists, are they relegated to anonymity? Lyons couldn't possibly be referring to the Second International, could he? Or to the editor of his paper and the Federation for which it speaks? Yessir, they are exactly the ones to whom he is referring! But not by name, either in this or any other of his columns, so that the 'uninitiated' reader would never know from Lyons (who, however, knows it perfectly well!) that at least so far as the 'collective security' doctrine is concerned, the social democracy is just as guilty of the crime as the Stalinists, Oneal as much as Browder.

In his *Assignment in Utopia*, Lyons stoutly inveighs against the 'devotees of the theory of multiple truths'. Moreover, he has a whole, moving chapter called 'To Tell or Not to Tell', in which he describes the psychologically painful process by which he 'overcame those inhibitions' against giving a complete picture of Soviet reality; 'I decided, for myself, that I must tell the truth as I saw it. The decision in time assumed the magnitude of a pressing moral obligation'. Bravo! None too soon, but ... Bravo! Now, would it be asking too much of an 'uncensored' contributor to a *social-democratic* paper to write a polite and restrained footnote to his next column saying, in substance: 'I must apologize to my readers for having omitted an important element in my criticism of "collective security". In this respect, as in most others, the official international social, democracy, including my good friends who edit this paper, are just as despicable a gang of war-mongering flunkies of imperialism as are the Stalinists'.

What is there to prevent him from writing this down and thereby clarifying his own position? Can the moral obligation to tell the truth which Lyons writes about so eloquently, refer only to the truth about Stalin? Surely, also, there is no 'censorship' for the 'independent' writers in the *New Leader*, such as prevented Lyons from telling 'the truth as I saw it' while he was correspondent in Moscow (and, shall we add, while he was publicity director for Messrs. Rose and Antonini of the ALP?).

Or can the nasty and uncapitalized truth be, as Germans say: *Im Hause des Gehenkten spricht man nicht vom Strick* – You don't talk of the rope in the house of the hanged!

Or take the case of Stephen Naft, who also substituted for Lyons in one issue of the *New Leader*. A social democrat? Not for a minute. He's far more radical than that. So he writes on a 'neutral' subject, that is, he attacks the Stalinists, doing both a good and timely job. Two solid columns of unanswerable evidence are devoted to excoriating the Stalinists for their united Popular Front with the fascists in the recent Chilean election. Conclusion? 'The two totalitarian parties, the Stalinist and the Nacistas of Chile, were thus again united against another totalitarian competitor ....'. All right. But Naft mentions *only in passing and without any commentary* the fact that the Chilean *social democrats* were also in this bastard united front. Now, why does he exempt them from his contempt and his denunciations? Why does he flay the Stalinists and not even murmuringly chide the social democrats? One might think that an anti-social democrat, writing in a social-democratic paper untrammelled by censorship, would make a point of clarifying his position in the manner we indicated. Is it possible that, like so many others, he is so absorbed in an effort to identify Bolshevism and fascism that he simply cannot find time or space for a gentle criticism of social democratic abominations? Or is it a point of honor with the Association of Friends of Morality and Truth not to offend a hospitable host? *Im Hause des Gehenkten spricht man nicht vom Strick!*

Or take the case of Sidney Hook, another of Lyon's substitutes. His article on the conduct of the Kremlin and the Stalinists towards the Jewish refugees is not merely a fine polemic; it is as savagely eloquent and moving a political indictment as has been written in a long time. It is hard to imagine even a Stalinist reading it without involuntarily blushing with shame at the shame which Hook so bitterly pillories. Yet there is something missing in his two full newspaper-columned article. Hook proclaimed himself not so long ago an exponent of the principles of communism as set forth by Marx, Engels, Lenin and Trotsky. This would lead one to believe that in spite of the fact that he now calls himself a 'democratic socialist' (in distinction from the 'totalitarian socialists'!), he nevertheless has little if anything in common with 'the' social democracy, that is, the Second International. For did he not say, only a few years ago, that the objective observer cannot deny 'that the historic function of social democracy since 1918 has been to suppress or abort all revolutionary movements throughout the world independently of whether it shared power in a coalition government or not'?

Would it be too much, then, to conclude that once Hook has decided to risk creating confusion about his politics by accepting the invitation-without-strings to write for the *New Leader*, he would improve on the occasion by dissociating himself just the teeniest bit from the social democracy? Just the teeniest bit – so that while 'using' a social-democratic paper as a tribune for the presentation of his own views, it would be amply clear to the reader that *his* criticism of Stalinism has nothing in common with the reactionary *social-democratic* criticism of communism. Would it not, therefore, have been in place, after his excoriation of the Stalinist regime for not opening Russia's doors to a single Jewish refugee, to add just a few words – a paragraph, a sentence – not to condemn but, let us say, to … deplore the fact that the social-democratic governments of the three Scandinavian countries haven't thrown open their doors either? After all, one cannot expect much from the totalitarian Kremlin. But Oneal's comrades-in-the-government of Norway, Sweden and Denmark, who are so completely immune to the virus of Bolshevism – shouldn't they be called upon to give an account of themselves? Why this gentleness and even silence about the social-democratic criminals? *Im Hause des Gehenkten spricht man nicht vom Strick!*

Not only *don't* you speak of rope in the house of the hanged, but we make bold to assert that you *may not*. The truth of our assertion should not be hard to test. We propose that Hook, Farrell, Stolberg and Dennen each submit a series of articles to the *New Leader*: Hook on the crimes of the German social democracy from 1914 to 1933, along the lines of his theory of the 'historic function' of this movement; or the more topical subject of the Second International's preparations for the new war; Farrell on the strangling of the French labor movement by Leon Blum and associates of the People's Front; Stolberg on the shady and reactionary role played in the American trade union movement by the 'Old Guard' socialists; Dennen on the role played by the Russian Mensheviks and Social Revolutionists as agents of Kerensky and foreign imperialism in the early years of the October revolution. Do they have any doubt about the editorial reception of such articles? Do they not know that when Listen Oak was invited by Managing Editor Levitas to contribute to the *New Leader*, and replied that while he was neither a Trotskyist nor a Stalinist he was also not a social democrat, and that in any article he wrote he would condemn the social democracy as strongly or even more strongly than Trotskyism or Stalinism – that was the last, he heard of Levitas and his invitation?

The Oneal-Levitas invitations to 'write freely' in the *New Leader* are a characteristic fraud, a trap for wandering radicals. But the fact that the latter fell into it so easily, and that when they wrote their articles for the *New Leader* they neglected the little detail of indicating any differences between themselves and their hosts, has, when taken together with what we have written earlier in this article, a strong symptomatic political significance. It is evidence of the fact that while they have all established the irreconcilability between their views and those of Stalinism (which many of them now equate with Bolshevism), *they seem to find no such irreconcilability between their views and those of social democracy*. By their political writings and activities, therefore – and not their artistic or cultural work, which we do not even wish to consider in this connection – they occupy the position of *centrism*, a centrism which brings them continually closer to social democracy, which, unless checked and re-directed, will end by transforming them from revolutionary radicals into ordinary petty bourgeois radicals.

The League of Abandoned Hopes

Lasciate ogni speranza, voi ch'entrate

– DANTE

This process of transformation is best exemplified in the preparations now being made in this circle to launch the 'League Against Totalitarianism', sponsored by Sidney Hook.

The League is opposed, according to its draft manifesto, equally to the totalitarianism of Italy, Germany and the Soviet Union, that is, of Fascists, Nazis and Stalinists. What is it *for*? That detail is omitted; in its place there is a *meaningless* reference to the need of protecting artists and scientists from totalitarianism, and to the desirability of Freedom and Truth. The formula cannot be construed otherwise than as an *evasion*, which automatically opens the doors of the League not only to all sorts of conservatives and reactionaries, but reactionary policies as well.

Why?

On the face of it, so to speak, the projected League aims to be a united front organization. By its very nature, every united front is calculated to *include* different individuals or groups and at the same time to *exclude* those individuals or groups against whom the front is erected or directed. The united proletarian front aims to include all labor organizations in a common struggle against the capitalists. A united front for Tom Mooney aims to include those who stand for his freedom against those who stand for his imprisonment; it would not include Sidney Hook *and* ex-Governor Merriam. A united front to ferret out the truth about the Moscow Trials would include John Dewey and exclude Stalin-Browder-Lamont. The limits of any united front are established by its objectives.

Now, generally speaking, a united front against fascism could take one or more of three forms. It might be limited to giving material aid to the victims of fascism – political prisoners' relief and defense, aid to refugees, etc. – and, by virtue of its specific, concrete and yet 'broad' aims, would include people of the most divergent views. The League does not claim to be such a movement. The united front might be a movement of action against fascism in the strictest sense of the word, that is, for the organization of workers' defense guards against fascist assaults. Such a movement, without committing itself to the program of any one 'faction' in the working class, would nevertheless scrupulously and impartially defend from attack the newspapers and institutions of the trade unions, the social democrats, the Stalinists, the anarchists, the Trotskyists, etc., etc., and if need be, go over to the offensive against the fascist bands. The League does not claim to be such a movement, either; in all likelihood, it would disclaim such a program in the most vigorous terms. Finally, the joint organization or movement might be an 'ideological united front'. That is precisely what the League is – an organization for combatting the ideology of totalitarianism.

But an ideology can be combatted only from the standpoint of another ideology, and in the given case, certainly, by a contrary ideology. Totalitarianism, especially if the term is applied both to the Italo-German and the Soviet regimes, represents a complex of political ideas, and not a social system. To capitalism, one can counterpose feudalism or socialism. To totalitarianism, one can counterpose democracy – bourgeois democracy or workers' democracy. This restriction is all the more compelling in the case of the League, for the conflicting *social* views of those who make it up render impossible the presentation of anything more than a common *political* alternative to totalitarianism. The League makes no *social* distinction between Russia and Germany-Italy; it says not a word against the social order of capitalism or for the social order of socialism. That it may claim to concern itself with the supra-class interests of artists, intellectuals and scientists, does not alter the fact that it is confined to the question of alternative political regimes.

The League obviously would exclude avowed supporters of the German-Italian and Soviet regimes, that is, Nazis, fascists and Stalinists. But it would be interesting to learn on what grounds other than personal taste it would exclude Mr. Martin Dies who has spoken out categorically against totalitarianism of the fascist or communist variety and who champions 'Americanism', i.e. American capitalist democracy. On what grounds, further, would it exclude Mr. Matthew Woll, head of the newly-formed League for Human Rights, Freedom and Democracy, whose 'faith is expressed in the Constitution of the United States and the Bill of Rights contained therein'? Woll adds: 'Specifically included in the threats to this faith we feel it imperative to name those forms of autocracy known as communism, fascism and Nazism. To those we are implacably opposed, to the one as vigorously as to the others. Democracy can make no compromise with autocracy'. On what grounds would the League exclude Dorothy Thompson and Walter Lippman, who also oppose all three 'totalitarianisms' and favor 'democracy', but go further than Hook in arguing that Rooseveltism personifies the encroachment of totalitarianism in America?

It would be enlightening to hear answers to these questions, for, on the basis of the League's program, we can see no logical reason why the above-named reactionaries should be excluded.

Let us look a little closer at the League.

On what grounds would Max Eastman, opponent of Stalinist as well as Hitlerite totalitarianism, be excluded from the League? None, so far as we can see; on the contrary, there is every reason why his membership should be earnestly solicited. But if the League accepted Eastman's conception of the struggle against totalitarianism in the United States – which is the only country in which he writes and acts on his beliefs – it would mean that at least its main efforts would have to be directed against the official Communist party, which, according to Eastman, represents in this country 'the real menace of fascism' (the theory of Stalino-fascism at its worst!). But not only against the Stalinist party – according to Eastman, logically, also, against the Trotskyists who have their origin in communism (i.e. Leninism) together with Mussolini and Hitler.

On what reasonable grounds, further, would John Dewey, anti-totalitarian, be excluded from the League and on what grounds could he fail to take the position that the League must combat, not merely Stalinism, but communism (i.e. revolutionary Marxism) which, according to him, helps produce fascism? That Dewey is a man of outstanding intellectual probity, that he is among the last of the classic democrats – we do not even pretend to challenge. But we are concerned with his political position. His opposition to Stalinism is only *derivative*. He bases it upon his more fundamental opposition to what he believes it proceeds from: communism, Leninism, revolutionary Marxism. Thus:

> Communism, then [the communism of Marx, Engels, Lenin and Trotsky which you once espoused, comrade Hook, and not merely 'Stalinist totalitarianism'!], with its doctrine of the necessity of the forcible overthrow of the State by armed insurrection, with its doctrine of the dictatorship of the proletariat, with its threats to exclude all other classes from civil rights, to smash their political parties, and to deprive them of the rights of freedom of speech, press and assembly – which communists *now* claim for themselves under capitalism – communism is itself, an unwitting, but nonetheless, powerful factor in bringing about fascism. As an unalterable opponent of fascism in every form, I cannot be a communist.
>
> JOHN DEWEY, *Modern Monthly*, Apr. 1934, p. 136f.

Dewey *should* not be excluded from the League. Nor is he. He is one of its sponsors. And that is fitting. It is proper.

On what grounds would Eugene Lyons be excluded from the League? He is already imbued with a 'detestation of the soul of Bolshevism – its cruel, morbid, Jesuitical soul', and there is little doubt as to what ideological line he would contribute to and support in the organization. A few samples:

> We had gone to Russia believing there were good dictatorships and bad. We left convinced that defending one dictatorship is in fact defending the principles of tyranny.
>
> LYONS, *Assignment in Utopia*, p. 621

> The talk of New Deal regimentation sounded absurd against my experience of totalitarian practices. Though I had given many years to the defense of political prisoners and civil liberties in America, I now found myself angered by glib and off-hand denunciations of American democracy by people who could not even imagine what total annihilation of democratic processes and civil rights meant.
>
> Ibid., p. 624

> The very basic elements of the Leninist-Trotskyist-Stalinist methods of revolution are in disrepute. The cumulative and gigantic sacrifice may be

> justified ultimately, when history's record is clearer, chiefly as an object lesson *how not to make revolutions*.[14]
>
> Ibid., p. 639

In light of these views, Lyons' membership in the League should be assured. And so indeed it is. He is already one of its moving spirits.

From all the facts adduced, the unavowed but quite implicit program of the League is the *defense of bourgeois democracy* from fascism, Stalinism and ... Marxism, which is the theory and practice of the revolutionary proletariat. Whose 'traditional' program is this? Who has always stood for the 'struggle on two fronts', against the 'dictatorships of the left or the right', for the hopeless not-so-golden mean? Hook, at least, is more than sufficiently aware of the fact that this is the classic outlook of the middle classes. The program of the League is nothing but a program of *middle-class radicalism*.

But it may be objected, however, whatever may be the individual views of this or that member of the League, do you not show your own totalitarian inclinations by your contempt for the struggle to preserve democracy from totalitarian extermination? The objection is based on a misunderstanding.

---

14 Do not conclude from this pontifical judgment that Lyons has any idea of how a revolution *should* be made. Or for that matter, any idea as to what to do right now, today, to thrust the knife of fascism from our throats. In his *New Leader* column of October 22, 1938, he gives a good example of his complete demoralization and helplessness: 'Questions pound at one's conscience these days – as Hitlerism marches roughshod across Europe – but answers there are none [*sic*] ... In what direction shall we look for hope and for help? Perhaps to Great Britain?' No, he answers, quite accurately. To France? Again, no. To Russia? 'The cemetery of our epoch's greatest hope'. To Germany? Of course not. To 'the socialist and internationalist ideals perhaps?' Alas, again no. Then where in heaven's name are we to look and what are we to do? Look into the distant future. 'A reorientation of socialist theory and socialist practice in the light of the last three decades of history is essential – and is taking place under the surface of the various socialist movements. It may be generations, for all we know, before a new and clearer and more effective pattern of thought will emerge'. Generations! Excuse our seeming impatience, but we fear that fascism is not obliging enough to wait with its headsman's ax and concentration camp for 40–50–60 years while we produce a 'new and clearer and more effective pattern of thought'. By virtue of the above declaration of bankruptcy, Lyons seems to us a fitting leader in the struggle of the League against totalitarianism. His may not know 'in what direction' to look, or what to do, but he can repeat what Ezra Pound wrote of A.E. Housman's message:

O Woe, woe,
People are born and die,
We also shall be dead pretty soon
Therefore let us act as if we were dead already.

The revolutionary Marxists are not only the staunchest partisans of a socialist republic. They are also the only consistent defenders of democracy in a very concrete and meaningful sense. Of 'democracy' as an abstraction, or some absolutist conception? Not at all. Of the vicious fraud which is bourgeois democracy, that is, the social dictatorship of the bourgeoisie? Not at all. But we are fierce partisans of those democratic rights which capitalism has been compelled in the course of decades of bitter struggle to grant the masses: democratic popular representation, the right of free speech, assembly and press, the right to organize and strike, etc., etc. Circumscribed as all these concrete democratic rights are under capitalism, we are not only for their preservation but for their extension, for converting them into genuine and not crippled rights, for anchoring them in *social* democracy – the socialist society.

We are anything but indifferent to the attempts of fascism to abolish these rights, and are ready to join with any progressive force to defend them, even in their present crippled state, from reactionary assault, as is confirmed concretely by our position in the Spanish civil war. But in our position there is a little 'reservation', which distinguishes us from all brands of liberals and social democrats and Stalinists. It is this: not only socialism, but even the defense of the democratic rights of the masses is impossible of attainment without the methods of the proletarian class struggle. Those who have not learned this elementary lesson, have learned nothing from the tragic but instructive experience in Germany, Austria, Spain and Czechoslovakia. Middle-class politics, class collaboration with the 'progressive' bourgeoisie (and under its domination!), are perfectly fitted for paralyzing the masses and facilitating the victory of fascist totalitarianism. The attempt to ward off fascism by defending bourgeois democracy-made over and over again in the recent past with calamitous and not unknown results – is in direct conflict with the policy for the struggle against fascism and defense of democratic rights which revolutionary Marxists advocate – a policy confirmed by all recent events, both negatively and positively.

It is for this reason also – and not only because the 'orthodox Trotskyists' are regarded by the League founders as totalitarian – that the revolutionary Marxists are neither invited nor desired as members of the new organization. For among the first questions we would raise in its as yet unimpressive ranks, would be included these:

Where does the League stand on the question of 'Stalino-fascism'? Are there no differences between Stalinism and fascism, between Germany and the Soviet Union, and if there are, why are they not indicated in the League's program? If a war broke out between Germany and France, we assume that the League would not feel called upon to take a position in favor of one or the other belligerent. But suppose Germany were to launch a war against the Soviet Union in order – as a beginning! – to detach the Ukraine, would the League also refrain from taking a position or would it declare itself neutral? In a word, is it for the defense of the Soviet Union from imperialist attack, regardless and in spite of the Stalinist regime? Whatever the answer, why does not the League say so? What is more, what position does the League take on the question of a war between 'democracy' and fascism? (The League draft is simplicity itself on this score: It hasn't a word – not one word – on war or imperialism or their direct relation to totalitarianism, thus leaving the membership doors open to supporters of 'democratic' wars or imperialism). Is it not mandatory, even for artists and intellectuals and scientists, to express themselves on this most vital question?

To be sure, these are concrete and far from remote or unreal questions; nor are they academic and abstract. It is far more important and interesting to have an anti-totalitarian League express itself unambiguously on these urgently real matters than to proclaim ever so sonorously its attachment to Truth, Freedom and Justice. But even if the League or its collective sponsors could ever be prevailed upon to give precise answers to these questions, the result would make it perfectly clear to everybody, we are convinced, that – regardless of their individual protestations – we are dealing with an association of democrats working on a program of middle-class radicalism. Or, to put it differently, these anti-Stalinists are forming a typically Stalinist People's Front – without the Stalinists.

Where the Road Ends

It is their evolution (at different speeds, to be sure) towards futile middle-class radicalism that is bringing so many of the members of 'Group I' progressively closer to these whom we have classified in 'Group II', that is, to those who, we gratefully recall, never pretended to be Marxists, revolutionary or otherwise. Sidney Hook is now in a political alliance with John Dewey. Harrison, out of not such ideological considerations, has become an enthusiastic barker for the ALP and presumably, like it, he is at least as enthusiastic a partisan of the New Deal as, let us say, Ferdinand Lundberg. The difference between Eastman's estimate of the Russian Revolution and Lyons' is rapidly approaching the political vanishing point, and such an estimate involves all the fundamental questions of Marxism.

Dewey's views of communism, Marxism and class collaboration as against class struggle are too well known to require repetition here. John Chamberlain has recently written (in *Common Sense*) an exposition of his view that the degeneration of the Russian Revolution has its original source not so much in Stalinism or even in Leninism but in the pernicious and false doctrine of the class nature of the State which was set forth by Karl Marx. The State is not theirs, it is ours as well, it belongs to all of us, declaims Chamberlain. The point of view is not merely class-collaborationist but, fundamentally, patriotic. Hence he is able to write, more concretely, that 'Sweden has a swell civilization, which is enough for me. I want a mixed economy under coalition rule …'. Adamic is frankly for the preservation of capitalism 'for I have become convinced that labor cannot abolish capital if it would …'.

You would imagine that in our critical times, when the most paralyzing poison in the labor movement is the spirit and practise of class collaboration, of bourgeois or social-patriotism, the main fire of even the 'dissident Marxists' would be directed at the ruinous doctrines disseminated by the Lundbergs and Adamics and Chamberlains and Deweys and Oneals and Lees, as well as against the Stalins and Browders who, in abandoning revolutionary socialism, have really taken over these doctrines from the former. We dare say that if any one of the members of 'Group I' could now be persuaded to write a political criticism of the partisans of bourgeois democracy who compose 'Group II', it would be couched in the most conciliatory manner imaginable and would not generate one-fiftieth as much heat as is contained in their sharp polemics against Marxism. But the first group has simply forgotten to criticize the second. Virtually all the fire of our backsliding 'Marxists' is aimed in the other direction, and they are so active in abandoning the revolutionary position that they have retreated, many without noticing it, towards the camp of the apostles of bourgeois democracy.

The centrism which develops in the course of a departure from Marxism moves, if not deliberately checked, gradually but inexorably to the program of social reformism, of middle-class radicalism. To the extent that they act politically, that is the actual program of the group we have been discussing.

Part IV: What to Do?

An analysis of the position of the radical intellectuals would be incomplete without tracing the social causes of the movement we have been discussing. In turn, an understanding of the causes is a prerequisite to a correction of the tendency to which they have yielded and a *return* to the position which will enable them to make their authentic and positive contribution to the revolutionary class struggle.

The main sociological cause of this movement is to be found in the long list of defeats suffered by the revolution in Europe and Asia, and the failure of the revolutionary movement here to grow rapidly enough to cope adequately with its great problems. It is obvious, also, that the Russian Revolution, which had such a powerful effect in restoring revolutionary Marxism to its rightful place in the ranks of the working class movement as well as among the radical intellectuals, had the contrary effect in the period of its degeneration under Stalinism.

The revolutionary socialists, however, could not and cannot see in any of these developments a reason for abandoning Marxism. Quite the contrary. Marxism was verified not only on the triumph of the October Revolution but also negatively in the defeats and decay that followed. Who other than those who applied the methods of Marxism to the realities of the class struggle were able to predict the setbacks suffered by the world proletariat, to explain the phenomena of the revolutionary ebb and the rise of fascism, to outline the only policy that would enable the proletariat to turn the tide of defeat into an irresistible wave of victory? The Marxists did not require the *post hoc* lucubrations now dished up on 'one-party dictatorship' in order to explain the causes of the revolution's degeneration. As early as 1906, in a fundamental way, the Marxist Trotsky already analyzed the danger of reaction inherent in a revolution confined to a single country. From 1917 onward, Lenin, Trotsky and all the other Bolsheviks repeated 'a thousand times' that without the world revolution the Soviet republic would succumb to counter-revolutionary forces. Beginning with 1923, the Trotskyist Opposition, basing itself upon a political analysis which has never been excelled or even matched, launched the struggle against the Thermidorean degeneration of the Soviet power and the Communist International. Every important event in the last twenty years has only emphasized the irreplaceability of revolutionary Marxism as an instrument of analysis and a weapon of struggle for social emancipation.

Every period of reaction that follows a revolutionary defeat produces a variety of superficial and transient 'new' and 'stylish' doctrines, which eschew Marxism as 'outlived'. It would be instructive to compare the history of the 'factional struggles' following the defeat of the Russian revolution of 1905 with their analogues of the last decade or more. It is the present reactionary moods of depression, discouragement, loss of confidence in the recuperative powers of the proletariat and its revolutionary movement, which are rationalized into the widespread attacks against revolutionary Marxism. The radical intellectuals, by the very nature of their social position, are generally the first to yield to these moods, to capitulate to them instead of resisting them deliberately. In an entirely different degree, to be sure, they are as much the victims of our prolonged period of reaction as the Stalinist degeneration of the Russian Revolution and the temporary rise of fascism are its products.

The main intellectual disease from which these intellectuals suffer may be called Stalinophobia, or vulgar anti-Stalinism. The malady was super-induced by the universal revulsion against Stalin's macabre system of frame-ups and purges. And the result has been that most of the writing done on the subject since then has been less a product of cold social analysis than of mental shock, and where there is analysis, it is moral rather than scientific or political.

It is interesting to note in this connection that virtually all our subjects have for years taken us to task for what they considered our exclusive preoccupation with the fight against Stalinism, 'Why don't you ever attack anybody or anything besides Stalinism?' they used to complain. If we were not deeply stirred by their criticisms then, it was because they were based on a misapprehension of our fundamental position. Now times have changed to the point where the roles seem to be shifted; but in a very peculiar way. There is hardly an article written by our critics, or a speech delivered, without the fiercest attacks on Stalinism which they increasingly and undiscriminatingly identify with revolutionary Marxism. Their vulgar anti-Stalinism consists in this: they condemn Stalinism in reality for precisely those policies which – and this is what the critics of Bolshevism do not realize! – have brought it steadily closer to the fundamental policies of social reformism and bourgeois democracy; and at the same time they have adopted a conciliatory attitude towards reformism and democracy. They abstract Stalinism out of its concrete historical context, its relation to declining world imperialism. Thus their opposition is opportunistic, since it is divorced from the basic struggle against imperialism itself. This leads them into the most peculiar combination with people who profess some sort of 'anti-Stalinism' even when they represent views no less reactionary than Stalin's.

The 'Trotskyist' movement was insured against such a conciliatory attitude by the objective political position it adopted from the very beginning. It began the struggle against the Soviet Thermidoreans fifteen years ago not on the grounds that they were the legitimate heirs of Leninism, but because they were a bastard product; and it always related this struggle to the general fight against imperialism and for world socialism. The struggle against Stalinism was launched, Trotsky insisted, because it represented a capitulation to social democracy, because it was the channel through which flowed the forces of capitalist restoration. The policy of the Second International is the policy of surrender to the bourgeoisie. Stalinism differs from that policy in no important particular. The methods by which Stalinism rules were not invented by it: it copied them from the bourgeoisie and the social democracy – frame-ups, massacres of revolutionists and all the rest of it, merely giving to these methods a more totalitarian character. If the political genealogy of Stalinism were to be honestly established, it would be found that while it is neither the son of Leninism nor the brother of fascism, it is the totalitarian offspring of the bourgeois and social democracies.

Once this is understood, the struggle against Stalinism assumes a solid and objective political character. It can be conducted progressively only from the standpoint of revolutionary Marxism. It is in this way that anti-Stalinism acquires a positive significance, and is prevented from being vulgarized to the point of reconciliation with reformism and bourgeois democracy. (We dismiss entirely that brand of 'anti-Stalinism' which leads to, or is only a cloak for, complete retirement from the struggle).

For a Reorientation

Our aim in writing this article is not to abuse or disparage our critics among the radical intellectuals, but to address ourselves seriously (even if sharply!) to the problems they themselves have raised. As Max Eastman has observed, this is indeed 'a time for deliberation'. But would it not be well for these intellectuals and those who incline towards their ideas to ask themselves: In what direction are we traveling? Eastman has already announced that his deliberations will take place in retirement. Harrison has already proclaimed his conversion to social democracy. Others have already taken steps in their direction. The deliberate purpose of our article is, by presenting sufficiently convincing arguments, to stop their further drift towards an anti-Marxist position and to bring about a change of direction.

We are intransigently hostile to the attitude of the Stalinists towards the intellectual fellow-travelers of the working class; it is repugnant to a revolutionist. The combination of flattery, bribery and intimidation with which they keep 'their' intellectuals 'in line', that is not our method. We do not demand of the writer that his creative work – under penalty of being denounced as worthless – be imbued with the philosophy of dialectic materialism, for we believe with Lenin that a work of art can be great and of value to the working class even if it is 'imbued' with an idealistic philosophy, or for that matter without any systematic philosophy whatever. We do not demand of the singer that his poems be written in line with the latest or the last-but-latest turn in party policy. Towards the intellectual we have neither the contemptuous attitude expressed in 'Stick to your last and keep your nose out of politics', nor the desire to buy his praise of our party and its policies (or its Leaders!) in return for 'official' party praise of his creative products.

The intellectual genuinely concerned with advancing the socialist movement has a multitude of opportunities to put his energy and talents at its service. There is the work or making possible continued life and activity of the revolutionary refugees from persecution; there is the work of defending the class war prisoners. There is above all the work of popularizing the ideas of revolutionary Marxism, if not among the proletariat, then at least among the now conservative or reformist-minded members of their own circles. And for those who are prepared to participate more actively and directly in the movement, who understand that without a consciously organized vanguard party the working class cannot win its war and consolidate its victory, there is membership in the world party of the social revolution – the Fourth International, which needs and welcomes serious intellectuals in its ranks. Such action is not proposed as a substitute for critical articles on no matter what fundamental question, for free and candid exchange of opinions, for the right to join in the discussion of every revolutionary problem. Not at all and just the contrary. It is only by such action that criticism and discussion acquire richness and reality and fruitfulness and purpose. Without it, they become common intellectual perambulations in midair, a spurious *substitute* for positive activity.

The intellectuals have also an autonomous and far from unimportant role to play in the cultural field. Entirely justified and necessary is a union of intellectuals – writers, scientists, philosophers, teachers – regardless of their divergent 'factional' views, but only on the basis of specific and concrete action against specific abuses, of which there are a growing number under 'democracy' to say nothing of the totalitarian regimes (Teacher's Oaths, censorship, sabotage of publication, reactionary intolerance in schools and universities, etc., etc.). Such alliances or united fronts have a positive and progressive significance, in contrast to the anti-Marxist 'ideological' political unions typified by the League Against Totalitarianism.

What a contrast is presented to the latter by the international movement which André Breton and Diego Rivera have in their manifesto proposed to launch! They, too, call for an association of artists and intellectuals. While they do not propose that it be tied to a political party, they take just as firm and infinitely clearer a position against both fascist and Stalinist totalitarianism, but they also make the indispensable distinction between the two. They do not take a mouthful of hot potatoes when they are called upon to express themselves flatly on the question of bourgeois and social democracy, on the question of imperialist war, on the question of capitalism and socialism.

Why have not the radical intellectuals responded to their call which was prominently displayed in the *Partisan Review*? Is it perhaps because they object to the references to Freudianism? Or to some minor formulation? Or to the style? But those are scarcely of real importance. Rivera-Breton have explained that they consider the manifesto to be simply a draft. Obviously, what is important and decisive is the main line of thought and action which it proposes. That line, while boldly describing the sphere of freedom and independence which the artist and intellectual must take for themselves, is unambiguously revolutionary – not Stalinist, not social-democratic, not middle-class radicalism.

Is it possible that the reply to our question will be the one we have heard so often in the past? 'The line is none too radical for me, you understand, but it will repulse 'the others' whom we want to win'. It is the answer of the psychologists and not of the revolutionists – and not of such good psychologists. The only way we, or anyone else, have learned to win people to a revolutionary position is by standing on that position. To start out by adopting or adapting yourself to the present (i.e. conservative) position of those you seek to win over – which is the alternative – means that you will win nobody over for the simple reason that *you* have already been won over yourself. The not at all imaginary quotation we have cited was the basis of the argument in the editorial board of the late *Marxist Quarterly*, which is one of the reasons why the adjective must now be affixed to it; it is heard often enough in the *Partisan Review*; it was not absent in the days of the American Committee for the Defense of Leon Trotsky; it was the argument used to trap so many into going along (for a time) with the muddle known as the Keep America Out of War Committee.

But its shallowness is revealed by a single glance at the totality of those who employ it. *Each* of them uses it, with a vague toss of the head in the direction of those who 'have to be won over', so that all of them, taken together, finally end up by being less 'radical' than each of them taken individually! Yet, united, and shedding their conservative rationalizations, they already represent a sufficiently imposing force which, together with those who would be immediately attracted to them, would bring to life in the United States such a movement as is outlined by Breton and Rivera.

∴

If the 'subjects' of this article have been a group of radical intellectuals, the matters we have dealt with far exceed them in political importance, and only thereby make possible a justification of this essay's length. The devastating crisis of capitalism is accompanied by a no less devastating crisis in the labor movement. Reflecting it is a turbulent discussion of proletarian principles, tactics, strategy, theory, ideology, history. Our article is a summary of the most important points in this discussion and a contribution to it in the form of a criticism of critics.

For us political criticism is worth the time spent on it only if it lays the basis for action. Action has positive significance for the socialist movement only if it is directed towards its historic goal. Not merely by doctrines handed down to us by those great minds which founded our movement, but by the endless variety of events which we have experienced in our own lifetime, the conviction has deepened in us that if the socialist revolution is not triumphant, society will end in self-destruction. And if the socialist revolution is to be realized by the working class, an indispensable prerequisite of this victory is the building up and consolidation of that party which stands on the program of revolutionary Marxism. The wisdom of man has supplied no effective substitute for it in the great struggle for freedom; the less effective, we see no reason for accepting. The confirmation which history has given this program gives us the right to call upon the revolutionary intellectuals as well as the class-conscious workers for support to the party which is its champion.

CHAPTER 9

Ruptures, 1939–40

Andrew Pollack

In the early 1930s, the Communist League of America had fought against the bureaucratisation, the over-centralisation and consequent abandonment of revolutionary principle and strategy, of the Stalinised Communist Party (see Chapter 7). At end of the 1930s the CLA cadre, now gathered in the newly-founded Socialist Workers Party, had to face a seemingly opposite phenomenon: internal demands for a loosening of party practices and structures, culminating in a challenge to the Leninist model itself. This was part of a major factional conflict that ruptured the SWP, with James P. Cannon leading a slim majority and Max Shachtman (along with Martin Abern and James Burnham) leading a substantial minority out of the party in 1940, founding the rival Workers Party.

The SWP majority sought to maintain traditional Leninist forms of functioning – as they saw it, a democratic, revolutionary leadership chosen by a membership that was in control of the party, a party guided by the Marxist method. The record of this factional battle is contained in two books produced in 1939–40: Cannon's *The Struggle for a Proletarian Party* and Trotsky's *In Defense of Marxism*. Both volumes were for years considered essential educational material for new SWP cadre; typically after reading Cannon's *The History of American Trotskyism*, new recruits would delve into *Struggle* and *In Defense* for a deeper look at Leninist organisational norms – primarily via the former book – and the Marxist philosophical method – via the latter.

This topical division of labour was of necessity not a rigid one, given the dialectical dependence of organisation on ideology, politics and strategy, and vice versa. In fact, a defence of the dialectic itself was at the heart of the dispute. This may seem surprising given, for instance, that the primary practical result of the dispute, once the split with the ex-minority was finalised, was a shifting of cadre into particular unions and workplaces. Getting from the seemingly abstract dialectical method to the details of individual cadre's assignments – from the standpoint of the SWP majority – dovetailed with the goal of developing a Leninist party, as the Trotskyists made the transition from a period of entry in the Socialist Party back toward an independent existence – a transition which seemed least understood by those with the most objection to dialectics.

This conflict erupted as the Second World War was beginning to unfold, and a central focus of the opposition was on the nature of Stalinism and the USSR. The majority, with Trotsky, continued to define the USSR as a bureaucratically degenerated workers' state. For them, the still-existing gains from the 1917 Revolution – a nationalised, planned economy which brought some cultural and material benefits to the working class – must be defended by overthrowing the Stalinist bureaucratic-dictatorship through a political revolution; at the same time, they must also be defended from any external assaults on the part of any of the capitalist powers. In the wake of the 1939 German-Soviet Nonaggression Pact, and subsequent Soviet military incursions into Poland and Finland, the minority concluded that Stalinism had destroyed anything that might have been worth defending. Shachtman and Burnham developed the argument that a new political-economic system – what they termed *bureaucratic collectivism* – had crystallised, no better than capitalism in either its democratic or fascist variants.

Along with this shift away from the traditional Trotskyist 'critical defence' of the USSR, within the ranks of the new minority there developed a deepening scepticism (or outright rejection) of Marxism's dialectical method and Leninism's organisational norms. Aspects of this were related to the Trotskyists' earlier entry into the 'all-inclusive' Socialist Party. The SP entry had attracted some new members to the SWP who, while partially recoiling from the bureaucratic practices of the SP leadership, had not really fully grasped revolutionary organising norms. It was the battle described in these two books by Cannon and Trotsky that finished, for those who stayed, that stage of their education, while for others it led to their departure from the SWP.

Although Cannon's apparent focus is organisational methods, his bottom line in *Struggle* is that politics must dictate organisation and not the other way round. The same method is illustrated in *In Defense*, as the bottom line flowing from Trotsky's philosophical discussion and his materialist analysis of the class nature of the Soviet Union is the same set of organisational proposals made by Cannon, e.g. sending cadre into industries and their unions (or new organising drives) and strengthening the party's democratic centralist norms.

The minority, in contrast, separated philosophy, politics, and organisation. This made possible a bloc between supporters and opponents of the dialectic. It also meant that the minority's main organisational complaint – the allegation of 'bureaucratic conservatism' practiced by Cannon and his 'regime' – was never traced back to underlying social pressures or class forces responsible for such a regime. Cannon responded that if the program and policies of a leadership were good but its organisational methods bad, that was a situation amenable to fixing; the reverse, however – a bad program grafted onto a supposedly more 'democratic' regime – would leave the party on the road to perdition.

The majority's refusal to budge on the contested issues – the source of the minority's 'bureaucratic conservatism' accusation – was related to the belief that even bigger shocks (including repression by the US ruling class) were likely in store. At the same time, Trotsky's influence on Cannon contributed to flexibility toward the minority, with offers of compromise on organisational issues. They both agreed on the need to focus the attention of the party ranks on the theoretical and political issues under dispute, avoiding any distractions from the roots of the conflict.

While we have avoided including Trotsky's writings in most of this volume, to do so in this section would distort the reality, so central were his interventions into the 1939–40 dispute. It is also instructive to note how he interweaves the various aspects of the debate. Trotsky illustrates his stated purpose of defending the dialectic by using it to analyse the Kremlin's changing diplomacy and military moves. He rejects liberal and social-democratic characterisations of such shifts as being down to 'evil' individuals or ideologies, instead tracing them to attempts to defend the material interests of the Soviet bureaucracy. Only such an approach, he insisted, could leave supporters of the Bolshevik Revolution in a position to clarify, for vanguard workers around the world, how to fight the bureaucracy as an essential, integral part of the fight against capitalism within each country and its global manifestations.

1 The Struggle for a Proletarian Party[1]

(1940, excerpts)

James P. Cannon

1 What the Discussion Has Revealed

… At the present time the pressure of alien class forces upon the proletarian vanguard is exceptionally heavy. We must understand this first of all. Only then can we approach an understanding of the present crisis in the party. It is the most severe and profound crisis our movement has ever known on an international scale. The unprecedented tension in the ranks signalizes a conflict of principled positions which is obviously irreconcilable. Two camps in the party fight for different programs, different methods and different traditions.

What has brought the party to this situation in such a short space of time? Obviously it is not a suddenly discovered personal incompatibility of the individual leaders involved; such trifles are symptoms of the conflict, not causes. Nor can a conflict of this depth and scope be plausibly explained by the flaring up of old differences of opinion on the organization question. In order to understand the real significance of the crisis it is necessary to look for profounder causes.

For those who understand politics as an expression of the class struggle – and that is the way we Marxists understand it – the basic cause of the crisis in the party is not hard to find. The crisis signifies the reaction in our ranks to external social pressure. That is the way we have defined it from the outset of the crisis last September, immediately following the signing of the Soviet-Nazi pact and the beginning of the German invasion of Poland. More precisely, we say the crisis is the result of the pressure of bourgeois-democratic public opinion upon a section of the party leadership. That is our class analysis of the unrestrained struggle between the proletarian and the petty-bourgeois tendencies in our party.

We define the contending factions not by such abstract general terms as 'conservative' and 'progressive'. We judge the factions not by the psychologic traits of individuals, but by the program they defend. The discussion has revealed not

1 Cannon 1940.

a difference of opinion about the application of the program – such differences frequently occur and usually have a transitory significance – but an attempt to counterpose one program to another. This is what has divided the party into two camps. Naturally, these terms, which we have used from the beginning of the discussion to characterize the two tendencies in the party, are meant as definitions and not epithets. It is necessary to repeat this in every debate between Marxists and petty-bourgeois politicians of all types; the one thing they cannot tolerate is to be called by their right name.

The leaders of the opposition consider it outrageous, a malicious faction invention, for us to place this class signboard above their faction, when their only offence consists in the simple fact that they turn their backs on the Soviet Union and deny it defense in the struggle against world imperialism. But our definition and description of such an attitude is not new. Back in the days when Shachtman was paraphrasing Trotsky and not Burnham, he himself wrote:

> At bottom, the ultra-leftists' position on the Soviet Union, which denies it any claim whatsoever to being a workers' state, reflects the vacillations of the petty bourgeois, their inability to make a firm choice between the camps of the proletariat and the bourgeoisie, of revolution and imperialism.

This quotation, from an article written in the *New International* by Shachtman two years ago, can be accepted as a scientific definition of the opposition combination and its present position, with only one small amendment. It is hardly correct to describe their position as 'ultra-leftist'.

The leaders of the opposition in the past have written and spoken a great deal along the lines of the above quotation. Year in and year out in innumerable articles, documents, theses and speeches the leaders of the opposition have been promising and even threatening to defend the Soviet Union – 'In the hour of danger we will be at our posts!' – but when the hour drew near, when the Soviet Union almost began to need this defense, they welched on their promise.

So with the program in general, with the doctrine, the methods and the tradition of Marxism. When all this ceased to be the subject for literary exercises in times of tranquility and had to be taken as a guide to action in time of war, they forgot everything that had been said and written and started a frantic search for 'new and fresh ideas'. In the first half-serious test they revealed themselves as 'peacetime Trotskyists'.

And this shameful performance, this betrayal of Marxism, has taken place in the American section of the Fourth International even before the formal entry of American imperialism into the war. In the bible of the opposition, their document on 'The War and Bureaucratic Conservatism', we are assured that the party crisis 'was provoked by the war'. That is not precisely accurate. America has not yet formally entered into the war, and thus far we have only a faint intimation of the moral and material pressure which will be brought to bear against the proletarian vanguard under war conditions. Not the war, but merely the shadow of the approaching war was enough to send Burnham, Shachtman and Abern on their mad stampede ...

In the proletarian majority of the party there is not a trace of pessimism. On the contrary, there is universal satisfaction that the defection of a section of the party leadership revealed itself in time, before the war, and under conditions where it could be combated openly and in free discussion and beaten down. The virtual unanimity with which the proletarian cadres have rallied to the defense of the party and the Fourth International, the militancy and irreconcilability with which they have met the attack of Burnham, Abern and Shachtman is living proof of the vitality and indestructibility of our movement. That is a good omen for the future. It gives us confidence that it will stand up against the real test of war when it comes. It gives grounds for the most optimistic calculation that the Fourth International will not only 'survive', but conquer in struggle ...

In the course of a few months' discussion the differences between the majority and the opposition have reached such depth and scope as to completely overshadow all questions of party regime. If all the alleged faults of the regime were true, and then multiplied 10 times over, the whole question would pale into insignificance beside the principled differences which now clearly separate the two contending factions. The struggle of the opposition ostensibly began as a struggle against the 'Cannon regime', and as a defense, or at any rate as an anticipation, of the 'changing' position of Trotsky. But in a short time it unfolded as a fundamental conflict with the Fourth International over all the questions of our program, our method and our tradition.

Abern, who voted at the plenum [of October 1939] for the principled resolution of the majority on the Russian question and accuses us of inventing and exaggerating differences, ended up, by the logic of his unprincipled combination, in the revisionist camp of Burnham. Shachtman, who at the plenum could only be accused of building a bridge to Burnham, became his attorney, writing 'open letters' to Comrade Trotsky in his behalf, and directing the most venomous attacks against the proletarian majority of the party who remind him of his yesterday. Burnham, in his latest document on 'Science and Style', speaks the language of a hate-inspired enemy of the proletarian revolutionary movement and of all those who remain faithful to it.

This is what has been revealed in a few months of political discussion.

2 A New Stage in the Development of American Trotskyism

The body of doctrine and methods known as 'Trotskyism' is indubitably the genuine Marxism of our time, the heir and continuator of the Bolshevism of Lenin and the Russian revolution and the early Comintern. It is the movement known as Trotskyism and no other that has developed Bolshevism in analyzing and interpreting all the great events of the post-Lenin period and in formulating the program for the proletarian struggle and victory. There is no other movement, there is no other school that has answered anything. There is no school that is worthy of a moment's consideration by the proletarian revolutionists. Trotskyism, embodied in the Fourth International, is the only revolutionary movement.

But the road from the elaboration of the program to the organization of firm cadres, and from that to the building of mass parties of the Fourth International, is difficult and complicated. It proceeds through various stages of evolution and development as a continuous process of selection, attracting new forces and discarding others who fail to keep step. The American section of the Fourth International is right now in the midst of a crisis in this evolutionary process. If, as all signs indicate, we are moving toward a radical solution of the crisis, it is to be accounted for by the speed at which world events are marching and the immensity of their scope and the sensitivity of our party to their impact.

The Second World War, no less than the First, strikes all organizations and tendencies in the labor movement with cataclysmic force. Our own organization is no exception. Like all others, it is being shaken to its foundations and compelled to reveal its real nature. Weaknesses which remained undisclosed in time of peace are rapidly laid bare with the approach of war. Numerous individuals and whole groupings, whether formally members of the Fourth International or sympathizers, are being submitted to the same tests. There will be casualties, which may seem to indicate a weakening of the movement. But that is rather the appearance of things than the reality. Trotskyism is the veritable doctrine and method of proletarian revolution; it reveals its true substance most unfailingly in times of crisis, war and revolutionary struggle. Those who have assimilated the program, the doctrine, the method and the tradition into their flesh and blood, as the guiding line of struggle, cling all the more firmly to the movement under the pressure of the crisis.

It is only those who took Bolshevism as a set of literary formulas, espousal of which gave one a certain distinction in radical circles without incurring any serious responsibilities; those who adopted Trotskyism as a form of 'extreme radicalism' which never went beyond the bounds of sophisticated debate – it is such people who are most inclined to falter and to lose their heads under the pressure of the crisis, and even to blame their panic on that same 'Trotskyism' which simply remains true to itself.

Everybody knows the crisis has dealt heavy blows to the imposing movement of Stalinism. With the signing of the Soviet-Nazi pact the flight of the Stalinist fellow-travellers began. They could stomach the Moscow trials but not the prospect of coming into collision with the democratic government of US imperialism. After the Soviet invasion of Poland and then of Finland, the flight of the fellow-travellers became a rout. This wild migration attracted wide attention and comment. We ourselves contributed our observations and witticisms on this ludicrous spectacle. Up to now, however, we have remained silent on an analogous phenomenon in our own 'periphery'. The flight of the more sophisticated, but hardly more courageous, intellectual fellow-travellers of American Trotskyism has been scarcely less precipitate and catastrophic.

With the approach of the war Trotskyism as a doctrine and as a movement began to lose its 'respectability'. Many of the intellectuals, sniffing danger, arranged a somewhat hasty and undignified departure. In truth, there is not much left of that considerable army of drawing room heroes who used to admire Trotsky's literary style and confound the less intelligent periphery of Stalinism with nuggets of wisdom mined from Trotsky's writings. The collapse of the Trotskyist 'cultural front' was taken by some people, especially the ex-fronters themselves, to signify a collapse of our movement. In the journals of the class enemy to which they promptly attached themselves some of them have already worked up courage to write about Trotskyism as an 'outmoded sectarian tendency'. However, it is they who are 'outmoded', not the movement of the proletarian vanguard, Trotskyism.

The petty-bourgeois intellectuals are introspective by nature. They mistake their own emotions, their uncertainties, their fears and their own egoistic concern about their personal fate for the sentiments and movements of the great masses. They measure the world's agony by their own inconsequential aches and pains. Insofar as our party membership consists in part of petty-bourgeois elements completely disconnected from the proletarian class struggle, the crisis which overtook the periphery of our movement is transferred, or rather, extended, into the party.

It is noteworthy that the crisis struck the New York organization of the party, thanks to its unfavorable social composition, with exceptional force and virulence, while the proletarian centers of the party remained virtually unaffected. The tendency of the petty-bourgeois elements to flee from our program and to repudiate our tradition is counterposed to a remarkable demonstration of loyalty to the program and to the party on the part of the proletarian membership. One must indeed be blind not to understand the meaning of this differentiation. The more our party revealed itself as a genuine proletarian party, the more it stood firmly by principle and penetrated into the workers' mass movement, the better it has withstood the shock of the crisis. To the extent that our party has sunk its roots in proletarian soil it has gained, not lost, during this recent period. The noise we hear around and about our movement is simply the rustling of the leaves at the top of the tree. The roots are not shaking.

The evolution and development of American Trotskyism did not proceed according to a preconceived plan. It was conditioned by a number of exceptional historical circumstances beyond our control. After the initial cadres had accustomed themselves to withstand the attacks and pressure of the Stalinists, the movement began to take shape as an isolated propaganda society. Of necessity it devoted an inordinate amount of its energy to the literary struggle against Stalinism. World events, one after another, confirmed our criticisms and prognoses. After the collapse of the Comintern in Germany, the failure of the successive five-year plans to bring 'socialism' in Russia, the monstrous excesses of the forced collectivization and the man-made famine, the murderous purges and the trials – after all this, which Trotsky alone had explained and analyzed in advance, Trotskyism became more popular in petty-bourgeois intellectual and half-intellectual circles. For a time it even became the fashion. Party membership conferred a certain distinction and imposed no serious hardships. Internal democracy was exaggerated to the point of looseness. Centralism and discipline existed only in the program, not in practice. The party in New York was more like a sophisticated discussion club than a combat party of the proletariat.

The fusion with the Muste organization, and later the entry into the Socialist Party, were carried out with the deliberate aim of breaking out of propagandistic isolation and stagnation and finding a road to wider circles. These actions brought hundreds of new recruits to the party, and gave us the possibility of expanding our activities. But the successes also brought their own contradictions. The membership of the Socialist Party in New York, including its left wing and its youth organization, was primarily petty-bourgeois in composition, and, despite their goodwill, were not easy to assimilate. If our party organization in New York had been much larger, and predominantly proletarian in composition, the task would have been much easier. As it was, some of the new forces from the SP complicated the problem of proletarianizing the party and contributed fresh recruits to the petty-bourgeois clique of Abern.

At the same time, thanks to our deliberate orientation toward trade union work, the party in other centers of the country was developing in a proletarian direction. Penetration into the trade unions was bringing into the party fresh elements of proletarian fighters; and the contrast between the proletarian centers and the New York organization flared up in numerous skirmishes before it finally exploded in the present party crisis.

The approach of the war, with its forewarning of heavy difficulties and sacrifices for members of the party, brought with it a restlessness and dissatisfaction among many of the petty-bourgeois elements. These sentiments found authentic expression in a section of the leadership. They began to translate their own nervousness into exaggerated criticism of the party and demands upon it which could not be fulfilled in the circumstances. After the signing of the Stalin-Hitler pact, the opposition became more articulate. It began to express itself in the form of a fight against our program and, eventually, in a revolt against the whole doctrine, tradition and method of Marxism and Bolshevism.

It would be utterly absurd, however, to characterize the party crisis as the result merely of political differences of opinion. We would not touch the core of the problem if we confined ourselves to a 'political' characterization of the fantastic proposals and flip-flops of the opposition. Serious political struggles, such as these, are an expression of the struggle of classes; that is the only way to understand them. The leaders of the opposition, and a very large percentage of their followers, have shown that they are capable of changing their opinions on all fundamental questions of theory and politics overnight. This only demonstrates quite forcibly that their opinions in general are not to be taken too seriously.

The driving impulses behind the opposition as a whole are petty-bourgeois nervousness at the prospect of impending struggles, difficulties and sacrifices, and the unconscious desire to avoid them at all costs. For some, no doubt, the frenzied struggle against our program and our tradition is simply a device to mask a capitulatory desertion of the revolutionary movement in a cloud of dust and controversy. For others, their newly discovered 'political position', and their endless talk about it and around it are an unconscious rationalization of the same inner compulsion. In such cases it is not sufficient to stop at a political characterization of the outlandish propositions of the oppositionists. It is necessary to expose their class basis.

The present crisis in the party is no mere episode. It is not to be explained by simple differences of opinion such as have occurred at times in the past, and will always occur in a free and democratic party. The crisis is the direct reflection of alien class pressure upon the party. Under this pressure the bulk of the petty-bourgeois elements, and the petty-bourgeois leaders, lost their heads completely, while the proletarian sections of the party stand firm and rally around the program with a virtual unanimity.

From this we can and must draw certain conclusions:

1. It is not sufficient for the party to have a proletarian program; it also requires a proletarian composition. Otherwise the program can be turned into a scrap of paper overnight.
2. This crisis cannot be resolved simply by taking a vote at the convention and reaffirming the program by majority vote. The party must proceed from there to a real proletarianization of its ranks. It must become obligatory for the petty-bourgeois members of the party to connect themselves in one way or another with the workers' movement, and to reshape their activities and even their lives accordingly. Those who are incapable of doing this in a definite and limited period of time must be transferred to the rank of sympathizers.

We stand at a decisive stage in the evolution of American Trotskyism from a loosely organized propaganda circle and discussion club to a centralized and disciplined proletarian party rooted in the workers' mass movement. This transformation is being forced rapidly under pressure of the approaching war. This is the real meaning of the present party struggle.

3 Their Method and Ours

… [I]t is clear that the question stands not organizationally in the first place, but politically. The political line is and must be the determining factor. It is and must be placed in the center of discussion. We held to this method in spite of everything, even at the cost of losing the votes of comrades who are interested primarily in secondary questions, because only in that way is it possible to educate the party and consolidate a reliable base of support for the program.

What is the significance of the organization question as such in a political party? Does it have an independent significance of its own on the same plane with political differences, or even standing above them? Very rarely. And then only transiently, for the political line breaks through and dominates the organization question every time. This is one of the first ABC lessons of party politics, confirmed by all experience.

In his notorious document entitled 'Science and Style', Burnham writes: 'The second central issue is the question of the regime in the Socialist Workers Party'. In reality the opposition tried from the beginning of the dispute to make the question of the 'regime' the *first* issue; the basic cadres of the opposition were recruited precisely on this issue before the fundamental theoretical and political differences were fully revealed and developed.

This method of struggle is not new. The history of the revolutionary labor movement since the days of the First International is an uninterrupted chronicle of the attempts of petty-bourgeois groupings and tendencies of all kinds to recompense themselves for their theoretical and political weakness by furious attacks against the 'organizational methods' of the Marxists. And under the heading of organizational methods, they included everything from the concept of revolutionary centralism up to routine matters of administration; and beyond that to the personal manners and methods of their principled opponents, which they invariably describe as 'bad', 'harsh', 'tyrannical', and – of course, of course, of course – 'bureaucratic'. To this day any little group of anarchists will explain to you how the "authoritarian" Marx mistreated Bakunin.

The 11-year history of the Trotskyist movement in the United States is extremely rich in such experiences. The internal struggles and faction fights, in which the basic cadres of our movement were consolidated and educated, were, in part, always struggles against attempts to replace principled issues by organizational quarrels. The politically weak opponents resorted to this subterfuge every time.

This was the case from the first days. In the early years of our movement, from 1929 almost uninterruptedly up until 1933, Abern-Shachtman conducted a furious war of words against the "bureaucratic apparatus" of Cannon-Swabeck, which consisted at the time of one typewriter and no stenographer and no regularly paid functionary. The same hue and cry was raised by the faction of Abern-Muste against the Cannon-Shachtman 'regime'. Then Shachtman, who writes with equal facility on either side of any question, defended the "regime" – the same regime – in an eloquently written and needless to say lengthy document.

In our battle with the centrist faction of Symes-Clement in the Socialist Party of California, the latter controlled the state committee and cheated and persecuted us by every possible bureaucratic trick, resorting finally to our expulsion; this did not stop them from protesting all the time against the 'organizational methods' of Cannon. In the dispute over the Russian question, after our expulsion from the Socialist Party and preceding the formal constitution of the SWP, Burnham and Carter raised the organization question against us in a special resolution inspired by the conception of Menshevism. Shachtman, who was on the Bolshevik side that season, collaborated with me in the drafting of a counter-resolution on the organization question and defended the 'regime'.

In the present party conflict, the most fundamental of all, the question of the regime is again represented as a 'central issue'. This time Shachtman is on the side of Burnham, attacking the regime which he defended yesterday and attacked the day before. The times changed, the attorney changed clients, but the war against 'bureaucratism' in the most democratic party in the world is conducted in the same way and for the same ends as before. These 'internal problems', says Abern in his letter to Trotsky of February 16 [1940], 'have never been resolved satisfactorily'. He should know. He has been conducting the war without cessation for 10 years – in the open when he could find prominent allies, by secret intrigues and sniping from ambush when he and his group stood alone. But he never yet got 'satisfaction'. His numerous organizational combinations, for the sake of which he was always ready to sacrifice any principle, always collapsed at the critical moment. In each case, a new stratum of party members who had mistakenly followed him, learned an instructive if painful lesson in the superiority of principled Marxist politics over organizational combinationism.

All the experience of our rich past has shown that no matter what temporary successes an organizational combination may have in the beginning, in recruiting inexperienced comrades by fairy tales about the regime, the political line always breaks through in the end and conquers and subordinates the organization question to its proper place. It is this absolute law of the political struggle that has frustrated and defeated Abern every time and left him and his clique isolated and discredited at the end of every struggle.

Abern and his intimate circle of petty-bourgeois gossipmongers never learned. But conscientious comrades whose inexperience and ignorance he exploited, who had no axe to grind, and who took his expositions of the organization question for good coin, have learned. That is the great gain from the past struggles. Those comrades of our younger generation who have had bad experiences with the attempt, under the tutelage of Abern, to substitute the organization question for the political line, and even to raise it to first place above the political line – it is precisely these comrades who are most immune to this kind of factional trickery in the present dispute. From their unfortunate experiences, and supplementary study, they have learned to brush aside the claptrap about the regime at the beginning of every dispute; they have learned to probe to the bottom of the political differences, and to take their positions accordingly …

We, from the beginning of the present conflict, steadfastly refused to conduct the battle on this ground. We were determined at all costs to bring out the political and theoretical essence of the dispute. Many comrades objected to this strategy. They complained that inexperienced comrades were being disoriented by this story and that story, by one alleged grievance and another, and lined up in caucus formation before they had begun to seriously consider the political questions. In spite of that, instructed by the experience of the past, we stuck to our method. The subsequent development of the party discussion confirmed its correctness. The issues are pretty clear now. That is a great gain.

There is no doubt that quite a few comrades have been disoriented and won over to the opposition because, in the early stages of the discussion, we refused to be diverted from the fundamental political and theoretical struggle and allowed most of the gossip and chitchat about the 'regime' to go unanswered. The opposition is welcome to the supporters gained by these means; this must be said in all seriousness and frankness.

We are living in serious times. We stand on the eve of grave events and great tests for our movement. People who can be disoriented and swept off their feet by rumors and gossip and unsupported accusations will not be very reliable soldiers in the hard days coming. The petty-bourgeoisie, after all, do everything on a small scale. The gossip and slander campaign of our opposition is not a drop in the bucket compared to the torrents of lies, misinformation and slander that will be poured over the heads of the revolutionary fighters in the coming days of the war crisis through the mighty propaganda mediums of the class enemy. And it is to be expected that for long periods of time we will be gagged and bound hand and foot and have no means of communication with each other. Only those who have thought out their principles and know how to hold to them firmly will be able to sustain themselves in such times. It is not difficult to foresee that those who succumbed already at the feeble anticipation of this campaign inside our own party can be engulfed by the first wave of the real campaign. Such comrades need not simply a reassurance about this or that fairy tale. They need a re-education in the principles and methods of Marxist politics. Only then will it be possible to rely upon them for the future battles.

4 The Organization Question

As long as the real scope of the political and theoretical disputes remained undetermined the talk about the organization question contributed, and could contribute, nothing but confusion. But, now that the fundamental political issues are fully clarified, now that the two camps have taken their position along fundamental lines, it is possible and perhaps feasible to take up the organization question for discussion in its proper setting and in its proper place – as an important but subordinate issue; as an expression in organizational terms of the political differences, but not as a substitute for them.

The fundamental conflict between the proletarian and the petty-bourgeois tendencies expresses itself at every turn in questions of the party organization.

But involved in this secondary conflict are not little incidents, grievances, personal friction and similar small change which are a common feature in the life of every organization. The dispute goes deeper. We are at war with Burnham and the Burnhamites over the fundamental question of the character of the party. Burnham, who is completely alien to the program and traditions of Bolshevism, is no less hostile to its 'organizational methods'. He is much nearer in spirit to Souvarine and all the decadents, skeptics and renegades of Bolshevism than to the spirit of Lenin and his terrible 'regime'.

Burnham is concerned first of all with 'democratic guarantees' against degeneration of the party after the revolution. We are concerned first of all with building a party that will be capable of leading the revolution. Burnham's conception of party democracy is that of a perpetual talking shop in which discussions go on forever and nothing is ever firmly decided ... Consider his 'new' invention – a party with two different public organs defending two different and antagonistic programs! Like all the rest of Burnham's independent ideas, that is simply a plagiarism from alien sources. It is not difficult to recognize in this brilliant scheme of party organization a rehabilitation of Norman Thomas' ill-fated 'all-inclusive party'.

Our conception of the party is radically different. For us the party must be a combat organization which leads a determined struggle for power. The Bolshevik party which leads the struggle for power needs not only internal democracy. It also requires an imperious centralism and an iron discipline in action. It requires a proletarian composition conforming to its proletarian program. The Bolshevik party cannot be led by dilettantes whose real interests and real lives are in another and alien world. It requires an active professional leadership, composed of individuals democratically selected and democratically controlled, who devote their entire lives to the party, and who find in the party and in its multiform activities in a proletarian environment, complete personal satisfaction.

For the proletarian revolutionist the party is the concentrated expression of his life purpose, and he is bound to it for life and death. He preaches and practices party patriotism, because he knows that his socialist ideal cannot be realized without the party. In his eyes the crime of crimes is disloyalty or irresponsibility toward the party. The proletarian revolutionist is proud of his party. He defends it before the world on all occasions. The proletarian revolutionist is a disciplined man, since the party cannot exist as a combat organization without discipline. When he finds himself in the minority, he loyally submits to the decision of the party and carries out its decisions, while he awaits new events to verify the disputes or new opportunities to discuss them again.

The petty-bourgeois attitude toward the party, which Burnham represents, is the opposite of all this. The petty-bourgeois character of the opposition is shown in their attitude toward the party, their conception of the party, even in their method of complaining and whining about the 'grievances', as unfailingly as in their light-minded attitude toward our program, our doctrine and our tradition.

The petty-bourgeois intellectual, who wants to teach and guide the labor movement without participating in it, feels only loose ties to it and is always full of 'grievances' against it. The moment his toes are stepped on, or he is rebuffed, he forgets all about the interests of the movement and remembers only that his feelings have been hurt; the revolution may be important, but the wounded vanity of a petty-bourgeois intellectual is more important. He is all for discipline when he is laying down the law to others, but as soon as he finds himself in a minority, he begins to deliver ultimatums and threats of split to the party majority.

The leaders of the opposition are running true to type. Having recited the whole dolorous catalogue of their petty and inconsequential and mostly imaginary grievances; having been repulsed by the proletarian majority in their attempt to revise the program; having been called in sociological and political terms by their right names – having 'suffered' all these indignities – the leaders of the opposition are now attempting to revenge themselves upon the party majority by threats of split. That will not help them. It will not prevent us from characterizing their revisionist improvisations, and showing that their attitude on the organization question is not disconnected from their petty-bourgeois conceptions in general, but simply a secondary expression of them.

Organization questions and organizational methods are not independent of political lines, but subordinate to them. As a rule, the organizational methods flow from the political line. Indeed, the whole significance of organization is to realize a political program. In the final analysis there are no exceptions to this rule. It is not the organization – the party or group – which creates the program; rather it is the program that creates the organization, or conquers and utilizes an existing one. Even those unprincipled groups and cliques which have no program or banner of their own, cannot fail to have a political program imposed upon them in the course of a struggle. We are now witnessing an illustration of the operation of this law in the case of those people in our party who entered into a combination to fight against the 'regime' without having any clearly defined political program of differences with it.

In this they are only reproducing the invariable experience of their predecessors who put the cart before the horse, and formed factions to struggle for 'power', before they had any clear idea of what they would do with the power after they got it.

In the terminology of the Marxist movement, unprincipled cliques or groups which begin a struggle without a definite program have been characterized as political bandits. A classic example of such a group, from its beginning to its miserable end in the backwaters of American radicalism, is the group known as 'Lovestoneites'. This group, which took its name from the characterless adventurer who has been its leader, poisoned and corrupted the American Communist movement for many years by its unprincipled and unscrupulous factional struggles, which were carried on to serve personal aims and personal ambitions, or to satisfy personal grievances. The Lovestoneites were able and talented people, but they had no definite principles. They knew only that they wanted to control the party 'regime'. As with Abern, this question always occupied first place in their calculations; the 'political' program of the moment was always adapted to their primary aim of 'solving the organization question satisfactorily' – that is, in their favor.

They were wild-eyed radicals and ultra-leftists when Zinoviev was at the head of the Comintern. With the downfall of Zinoviev and the violent right swing of the Comintern under Bukharin, they became ardent Bukharinites as quickly and calmly as one changes his shirt. Due to an error in calculation, or a delay in information, they were behindhand in making the switch from Bukharin to Stalin and the frenzied leftism of the Third Period. To be sure, they tried to make up for their oversight by proposing the expulsion of Bukharin at the party convention they controlled in 1929. But this last demonstration of political flexibility in the service of rigid organizational aims came too late. Their tardiness cost them their heads.

Their politics was always determined for them by external pressure. At the time of their membership in the Communist Party it was the pressure of Moscow. With their formal expulsion from the Comintern a still weightier pressure began to bear down upon them, and they gradually adapted themselves to it. Today this miserable and isolated clique, petty-bourgeois to the core, is tossed about by bourgeois-democratic public opinion like a feather in the breeze. The Lovestoneites never had any independent program of their own. They were never able to develop one in the years since their separation from the official Communist Party. Today their paper, the *Workers' Age*, is hardly distinguishable from a journal of left liberalism. A horrible example of the end result of unprincipled 'organizational' politics.

The most horrible case of all, with the most immeasurably tragic final consequences, is that of the 'anti-Trotskyist' faction of the Russian Communist Party. It is unquestionable that the Stalin-Zinoviev-Kamenev combination began its factional struggle against Trotsky without any clearly defined programmatic aim. And precisely because it had no program, it became the expression of alien class influences. The ultimate degeneration of the Stalinist faction into a helpless tool of imperialism and a murderous opponent of the true representatives of the Russian revolution is not, as our enemies say, the logical development of Bolshevism. It is rather the ultimate outcome of a departure from the Bolshevik-Marxist method of principled politics.

All proportions guarded, the degeneration of the Abern clique, from formal adherents to the program and doctrine of Marxism into factional supporters of revisionism, has followed the same pattern as the other examples cited. The present ideological and political hegemony of Burnham in the opposition bloc is the most striking proof of the political law that groups and cliques which have no program of their own become the instruments of the program of others. Burnham has a program of a sort. It is the program of struggle against the doctrine, the methods and the tradition of our movement. It was only natural, indeed it was inevitable, that those who combined with Burnham to fight against the 'regime' should fall under the sway of his program. The speed with which Abern accomplished this transformation can be explained in part by the fact that he has had previous experience in ideological betrayal in the service of picayune organizational ends, and in part by the fact that the social pressure upon our party is much heavier today than ever before. This pressure accelerates all developments.

5 The Intellectuals and the Workers

The outspoken proletarian orientation of the majority is represented by Burnham as an expression of antagonism to 'intellectuals' as such, and as an ignorant backwoods prejudice against education in general. In his major document, 'The War and Bureaucratic Conservatism', he writes: 'Above all, an "anti-intellectual" and "anti-intellectuals" attitude is drummed into the minds of party members. The faction associates are taught, quite literally, to despise and scorn "intellectuals" and "intellectualism"'. For reasons best known to themselves, Shachtman and Abern sign their names to this protest and take sides in a conflict where they have every right to proclaim neutrality …

The question at issue is the attitude of proletarian revolutionists to educated members of the petty-bourgeois class who come over to the proletarian movement. This is an important question and deserves clarification. Burnham is indubitably an intellectual, as his academic training, profession and attainments testify. There is nothing wrong in that, as such, and we cannot have the slightest reason to reproach him for it. We are quite well aware, as Marx said, that 'ignorance never did anybody any good', and we have nothing in common with vulgar prejudices against 'educated people' which are cultivated by rascally demagogues to serve their own ends. Lenin wrote to Gorky on this point: 'Of course I was not dreaming of "persecuting the intelligentsia" as the stupid little syndicalists do, or deny its necessity for the workers' movement'. It is a slander on the Marxist wing of the party to attribute such sentiments to us. On the other hand, we are not unduly impressed by mere 'learning' and still less by pretensions to it. We approach this question, as all questions, critically.

Our movement, the movement of scientific socialism, judges things and people from a class point of view. Our aim is the organization of a vanguard party to lead the proletarian struggle for power and the reconstitution of society on socialist foundations. That is our 'science'. We judge all people coming to us from another class by the extent of their real identification with our class, and the contributions they can make which aid the proletariat in its struggle against the capitalist class. That is the framework within which we objectively consider the problem of the intellectuals in the movement. If at least 99 out of every 100 intellectuals – to speak with the utmost 'conservatism' – who approach the revolutionary labor movement turn out to be more of a problem than an asset it is not at all because of our prejudices against them, or because we do not treat them with proper consideration, but because they do not comply with the requirements which alone can make them useful to us in our struggle.

In the *Communist Manifesto*, in which the theory and program of scientific socialism was first formally promulgated, it was already pointed out that the disintegration of the ruling capitalist class precipitates sections of that class into the proletariat; and that others – a smaller section to be sure, and mainly individuals – cut themselves adrift from the decaying capitalist class and supply the proletariat with fresh elements of enlightenment and progress. Marx and Engels themselves, the founders of the movement of scientific socialism, came to the proletariat from another class. The same thing is true of all the other great teachers of our movement, without exception.

Lenin, Trotsky, Plekhanov, Luxemburg – none of them were proletarians in their social origin, but they came over to the proletariat and became the greatest of proletarian leaders. In order to do that, however, they had to desert their own class and join 'the revolutionary class, the class that holds the future in its hands'. They made this transfer of class allegiance unconditionally and without any reservations. Only so could they become genuine representatives of their adopted class, and merge themselves completely with it, and eliminate every shadow of conflict between them and revolutionists of proletarian origin. There was and could be no 'problem' in their case.

The conflict between the proletarian revolutionists and the petty-bourgeois intellectuals in our party, as in the labor movement generally in the whole world for generation after generation, does not at all arise from ignorant prejudices of the workers against them. It arises from the fact that they neither 'cut themselves adrift' from the alien classes, as the *Communist Manifesto* specified, nor do they 'join the revolutionary class', in the full sense of the word. Unlike the great leaders mentioned above, who came over to the proletariat unconditionally and all the way, they hesitate halfway between the class alternatives. Their intelligence, and to a certain extent also their knowledge, impels them to revolt against the intellectual and spiritual stagnation of the parasitic ruling class whose system reeks with decay. On the other hand, their petty-bourgeois spirit holds them back from completely identifying themselves with the proletarian class and its vanguard party, and reshaping their entire lives in a new proletarian environment. Herein is the source of the 'problem' of the intellectuals.

The revolutionary workers' movement, conscious that it 'holds the future in its hands', is self-assured, imperious, exacting in the highest degree. It repels all flirtations and half-allegiances. It demands from everyone, especially from leaders, 'all or nothing'. Not their 'education', as the Lovestoneite sympathizers of our party opposition maintain, brings the intellectuals into conflict with the proletarian cadres of the party, but their petty-bourgeois spirit, the miserable halfness, their absurd ambition to lead the revolutionary labor movement in their spare time.

It is not true that the advanced militant workers are hostile to education and prejudiced against educated people. Just the contrary. They have an exaggerated respect for every intellectual who approaches the movement and an exaggerated appreciation of every little service he renders. This was never demonstrated more convincingly than in the reception accorded to Burnham when he formally entered our movement, and in the extraordinary consideration that has been given to him all this time. He became a member of the National Committee without having served any apprenticeship in the class struggle. He was appointed one of the editors of our theoretical journal. All the recognition and the 'honors' of a prominent leader of the party were freely accorded to him.

His scandalous attitude toward the responsibilities of leadership; his consistent refusal to devote himself to party work as a profession, not as an avocation; his haughty and contemptuous attitude toward his party co-workers; his disrespect for our tradition, and even for our international organization and its leadership – all this and more was passed over in silence by the worker elements in the party, if by no means with approval. It was not until Burnham came out into the open in an attempt to overthrow our program that the worker elements of the party rose up against him and called him to order. His attempt now to represent this revolutionary action as an expression of ignorant prejudice against him because of his 'learning' is only another, and most revealing, exhibition of his own petty-bourgeois spirit and petty-bourgeois contempt for the workers.

A proletarian party that is theoretically schooled in the scientific doctrines of Marxism cannot be intimidated by anybody, nor disoriented by a few unfortunate experiences. The fact that the learned Professor Burnham revealed himself as just another petty bourgeois may possibly engender a little more caution in regard to similar types in the future. But it will not change anything in the fundamental attitude of the workers' vanguard toward the intellectuals from the bourgeois world who approach the movement in the future. Instructed by this experience it is possible that the next one who comes along will have to meet stiffer conditions. It is hardly likely that in the future anyone will be permitted to make pretensions to leadership unless he makes a clean break with his alien class environment and comes over to live in the labor movement. Mere visiting will not be encouraged.

The American movement has had very bad experience with intellectuals. Those who have appeared on its horizon up to date have been a pretty shabby crew. Adventurers, careerists, self-seekers, dilettantes, quitters-under-fire – that is the wretched picture of the parade of intellectuals through the American labor movement as painted by themselves. Daniel De Leon stands out as the great exception. He was not merely an intellectual. He was a man and a fighter, a partisan incapable of any divided allegiance. Once he had decided to come over to the proletarian class, the stale atmosphere of the bourgeois academic world became intolerable for him. He departed from the university, slamming the door behind him, and never once looked back. Thereafter, to the end of his life, he identified himself completely with the socialist movement and the struggle of the workers. Revolutionary workers of the present generation remember him with gratitude for that, without thereby overlooking his political errors. Other, and we hope, greater De Leons, will come to us in the future, and they will receive a wholehearted welcome from the party of the proletarian vanguard. They will not feel sensitive if we scrutinize their credentials and submit them to a certain apprenticeship. They will not be offended if we insist on an explicit understanding that their task is to interpret and apply the proletarian science of Marxism, not to palm off a bourgeois substitute for it. The new De Leons will readily understand that this preliminary examination is simply a precaution against the infiltration of intellectual phonies and does not signify, in any way whatever, a prejudice against intellectuals who really come to serve the proletarian cause.

The genuine Marxist intellectuals who come to us will understand the cardinal point of our doctrine, that socialism is not simply a 'moral ideal', as Burnham tries to instruct us in the year 1940 – 92 years after the *Communist Manifesto* – but the necessary outcome of an irreconcilable class struggle conducted by the proletariat against the bourgeoisie. It is the workers who must make the revolution and it is workers who must compose the proletarian vanguard party. The function of the Marxist intellectual is to aid the workers in their struggle. He can do it constructively only by turning his back on the bourgeois world and joining the proletarian revolutionary camp, that is, by ceasing to be a petty bourgeois. On that basis the worker Bolsheviks and the Marxist intellectuals will get along very well together.

2 The War and Bureaucratic Conservatism[2] (*1940, excerpts*)

Max Shachtman, James Burnham, and Martin Abern

1 The Origin of the Party Crisis

… Whatever the background of an internal crisis, however much it may be implicit in the general situation within a party, it very often comes first into the open in a leading committee. This is the case with the present crisis in our party, and the place and date of its breaking into the open can be precisely fixed. It occurred in the Resident Political Committee at a special meeting held on the evening of the day when the German army invaded Poland; that is, the first day of the Second World War. Between the end of the July convention and that day there had been no crisis and no 'crisis atmosphere' in the Resident Committee. From that day, there has been an uninterrupted and deepening crisis.

The crisis was precipitated by a statement and series of motions presented by Gould. Gould's statement condemned the sluggishness and inactivity of the Committee, and its failure to respond adequately to the war situation which had been signaled by the announcement of the German-Russian agreement and the subsequent mobilizations of the European powers. His motions, practical in character, called for a drastic re-orientation of the party's activities and attitude in order to meet the demands of the war: cancellation of all leaves; more frequent publication of the *Appeal*, and of pamphlets, leaflets and manifestos; the holding of public meetings and demonstrations; the immediate convocation of a full plenum of the National Committee. He proposed that the agenda of the plenum should include an analysis of the war, the preparation of the party's organization to meet the war, and the 'Russian question' in the light of the new developments …

It is of the first importance to recall that the 'Russian question' played a completely subordinate role at this meeting, as it had in all previous meetings, including those following the announcement of the German-Russian agreement. Gould did not motivate his demand for an immediate plenum only or

2 Shachtman, Burnham, Abern 1940.

mainly on the Russian issue. All of the committee, without exception, recognized that discussion of the Russian question ought properly to be part of the business of the plenum. And the committee at that meeting voted unanimously to appoint Burnham to make a verbal report on the Russian question to the next meeting, as preparation for the plenum ...

A great event – the greatest since the beginning of the Fourth Internationalist movement, the start of the Second World War, occurred. This great event precipitated a major crisis in our party, in the first instance in the leadership. One part of the leadership held that this great event called for a drastic change in the organization and activity of the party, and a change in our policy toward Stalinism in the war along the lines already dealt with by Johnson, Shachtman and Carter, prior to the German-Soviet pact, at the July convention of the party. Another section (the majority of the committee) held that no change was necessary.

The view that the crisis broke out over the 'Russian question' is entirely false, and is disproved by the record, the essential parts of which are cited in Shachtman's speech to the New York membership discussion meeting and *all* of which will be presented verbatim in the Internal Bulletin. The crisis broke out over the war, not over the Russian question. The Russian question entered and became acute, only as one phase of the more general question of the war ...

The minority kept pressing along three lines: 1. for concrete answers to the specific questions being raised by the war – in particular the Red Army's invasion of Poland, which was then the outstanding immediate issue; 2. for action on the reorganization of the party's structure and activities to meet the war; 3. for the opening of a discussion in the party, and the holding of a plenum ...

The plenum, when finally held, revolved around the Russian question and the reorganization of the Political Committee. The first session, held nominally on 'the party and the war', was hardly more than a formality, and has besides led to nothing. At the plenum there were presented for vote: 1. the resolution of Shachtman, which characterized the war in its present phase and the role of Russia in the war, and drew the conclusions from this characterization as to our attitude in such cases as that of the Polish invasion; and 2. a motion of Cannon reaffirming our basic position, but not in any way characterizing either the war or the role of Russia or the Polish invasion ...

2 The War and the Party Crisis

... Wars and revolutions are the most decisive of all events in the lives of political parties. In 1914, the outbreak of the war had a shattering effect upon every working-class party in the world. In their bulk, the parties went over to their respective imperialists. But even within the left, ostensibly revolutionary wings, the Russian Bolsheviks not excluded, the outbreak of the war provoked the most profound crises. In spite of all that had been written and foretold, no one – neither Lenin nor anyone else – had anticipated the actual effect which the outbreak of the war would have. New groupments and regroupments were to be found within every party, the Bolshevik Party included. Nor was a definitive solution to the various crises found in a day or a week. During the course of the entire war, even among those who stood committed to struggle against the war, a constant and changing debate went on as to just what struggle against the war meant concretely (Lenin, Liebknecht, Trotsky, Luxemburg, Debs ...) ...

These questions are the background and foundation of the present dispute in the party, whatever form it may seem at a given moment to take. The Russian question became a center for a while not merely because of its own independent merits – and it is a very serious question indeed – but because in the first stage of the war the party leadership has shown itself incapable of meeting the political challenge of the wax on the issues where that challenge first became acute – namely on the issues raised by Russia's actions. But the organizational problems could not be left out, even temporarily, because the leadership was simultaneously showing that it was not meeting the challenge of the war organizationally ...

It is the contention of the opposition that the position which the Cannon group has taken in the present dispute is the manifestation or expression of a type of politics which can be best described as bureaucratic conservatism. We hold that this bureaucratic conservative tendency has existed in the party for some time; that during the course of a number of years it gradually solidified, manifesting itself at first sporadically and then more and more continuously; and that the outbreak of the war crystallized this tendency and brought it to a head. The outstanding representative of this tendency in the party, we hold, is Comrade Cannon. The importance of Cannon, however, is not primarily as an individual but precisely as the embodiment of bureaucratic conservatism; and when we refer to him in what follows we do so in no personal sense but simply as the outstanding representative of a tendency.

The crisis in the party occurred fundamentally, it follows, because of the resistance by one section of the party, in the light of the war, to the solidification of the entire party on a bureaucratic conservative basis. The resolution of the crisis, therefore, must be sought in the definite ascendancy in the party as a whole of either bureaucratic conservatism or of the opposition which stands for party democracy and collective leadership …

4 The Nature of Bureaucratic Conservatism

It is a fact that from the outset in the present dispute there have been raised questions of 'organization' and 'regime'. The majority has accused the minority of having been 'responsible' for raising these questions, and in addition has made the mutually contradictory accusations that: (a) the minority has been using the question of 'regime' as a cover for a false and revisionist position on the Russian question; and (b) the minority has been using the Russian question as a cover for an underhanded attack on the 'regime'.

In his letter of October 22 to Comrade Stanley (Internal Bulletin, 11, 2, p. 14), Comrade Crux [Trotsky] writes as follows:

> … 4. You state in your letter that the main issue is not the Russian question but the 'internal regime'. I have heard this accusation often since almost the very beginning of the existence of our movement in the United States. The formulations varied a bit, the groupings too, but a number of comrades always remained in opposition to the 'regime'. They were, for example, against the entrance into the Socialist Party (not to go further into the past). However it immediately occurred that not the entrance was the 'main issue' but the regime. Now the same formula is repeated in connection with the Russian question.
>
> 5. I, for my part, believe that the passage through the Socialist Party was a salutary action for the whole development of our party and that the 'regime' (or the leadership) which assured this passage was correct against the opposition which at that time represented the tendency of stagnation.
>
> … 9. Thus in two most important issues of the last period comrades dissatisfied with the 'regime' have had in my opinion a false political attitude. The regime must be an instrument for correct policy and not for false. When the incorrectness of their policy becomes clear, then its protagonists are often tempted to say that not this special issue is decisive but the general regime. During the development of the Left Opposition and the Fourth International we opposed such substitutions hundreds of times. When Vereecken or Sneevliet or even Molinier were beaten on all

> their points of difference, they declared that the genuine trouble with the Fourth International is not this or that decision but the bad regime.

A correct understanding of Cannon's bureaucratic conservatism will enable us to understand both how and why the question of 'organization' and 'regime' immediately entered, and also the falsity of the accusations made by the majority on the one side and by Crux on the other ...

Assuming a correct policy, it is not merely possible, but it frequently happens, that this policy is carried through in a bad or false organizational manner: e.g. bureaucratically, by manipulation of the 'apparatus', by arbitrary fiat, by removals from posts or expulsions, without education of the membership to the correctness of the policy, etc. When this occurs (and there are hundreds of examples in political history: the records of the Frey group in Austria and the Molinier group in France are but two instances in the history of the Left Opposition alone), a certain paradox arises within the given organization, especially acute for those who agree with the policy but object to the 'methods'. Ideally and in the abstract, this paradox can be solved by separating the two questions (policy and regime) carefully, and by supporting the policy but taking steps to alter the regime and methods. In practice the solution is not so simple, since the bureaucratic regime exploits its allegedly correct (or rather generally false) policy to uphold its regime and methods. Indeed, a bureaucratic regime, seeing its methods about to be attacked, often provokes a political dispute to turn aside the organizational attack. No absolute rule can be given in advance for meeting these problems in practice. At a particular time the failure to alter the regime may have a more damaging long-term effect even than the adoption, temporarily, of a false or inadequate policy, especially in those cases where policy is only a secondary consideration in the mind of the regime.

We make these remarks not to suggest that the majority has in the present a correct policy – which it most certainly does not have, but to combat the loose and empty formalism of the conception that regime and policy are mechanically, necessarily and automatically united, and particularly against the conception that regime flows directly and harmoniously from policy.

5. However, bureaucratic conservatism is unique among all political tendencies in precisely the relation that holds, in *its* case, between regime and policy. In its case, there is a necessary relation between regime and policy; and this relation is the reverse of the normal. In the case of bureaucratic conservatism, policy is subordinated to regime, not the other way around. Let us see what this means.

Bureaucratic conservatism is, put crudely and bluntly, apparatus politics. Its chief base, in any organization or movement, large or small, is the 'apparatus'.

Objectively considered, the goal and purpose and aim of a bureaucratic conservative tendency is *to preserve itself*. To this aim all else is, in the last analysis, subordinated. To this aim, policy and political issues are subordinated.

It is for this reason that the policies adopted by the bureaucratic conservative tendency tend always toward being conservative. It is the defender of the status quo – until the point where its own preservation becomes incompatible with the preservation of the status quo. Normally a bold move, an abrupt change, a reorientation, the intrusion of something new, upset things as they are: that is, tend to undermine the established regime. That is why, to Cannon and his central core of supporters, those who propose bold and new steps, changes and reorientations, are almost invariably characterized out of hand, without even consideration or discussion, as 'irresponsible ... lightminded', 'yielding to pressure', etc. ...

No, here as elsewhere we must seek a political explanation for the speedy appearance of the organization question in every dispute. And that explanation is found in the political character of the Cannon faction, in the fact that it is a bureaucratic conservative tendency, a tendency for which every serious political proposal with which it differs (and this includes virtually all proposals which involve something new) is interpreted as an attack on its regime. It replies always by raising, openly or implicitly, the question of 'confidence'. Its tone takes on the bitterness of the apparatus defending its control of the leadership ...

From the point of view of the minority, therefore, it is not in the ordinary sense that it raises the question of 'regime'. When we call the Cannon faction 'bureaucratic conservative', we are giving a political characterization. But this particular political tendency manifests itself at one and the same time as conservative in its politics, and bureaucratic in its regime – these are the two sides of the same coin ...

5 Bureaucratic Conservatism in Action

Now the minority contends that the war which is going on is not entirely the war that we foresaw and that the role of Russia in it is not what we expected; and therefore that we must make new analyses related to the reality of today's events and give new answers, and that among other things we must also revise our slogan of 'unconditional defense of the Soviet Union'. The minority, concretely and clearly, has made the new analyses, given new answers, and proposed the revision of the slogan. This again is why we say that the policy of the majority has been conservative ...

Cannon, upon all occasions without exception, accepts the politics of Trotsky, accepts them immediately and without question. Since Trotsky's politics are, as a rule, correct and progressive, this tends often to make Cannon's politics appear correct and progressive – that is, the opposite of conservative …

The Cannon group, we have said, accepts automatically, in words at least, the politics of Trotsky. But this does not mean that it accepts all the views of Trotsky. We have defined the Cannon group as bureaucratic conservative, and have pointed out that for a bureaucratic conservative group, politics is subordinate to regime. The independence of the Cannon group, what keeps it alive and makes it possible for it to be a group, is not its political policies – which, in the last analysis, are wholly secondary for it – but its central object of the maintenance of itself. On questions of regime, or 'organizational methods', Cannon is not in the least the 'follower of Trotsky', but, on the contrary, though willing to listen to Trotsky's opinion, pursues an assured and independent course. Political or theoretical questions can be left to others – to Trotsky, or even, on 'normal' occasions, to Burnham, or Shachtman. But Cannon will keep a firm and guiding hand on 'organization'. This difference in attitude is infinitely revealing of the true nature of bureaucratic conservatism. Politics, programs, are more or less routine matters for others to take care of; the business of the 'real Bolshevik' is to cinch up the majority and retain party control. Yes: Trotsky or Burnham, or Shachtman writes the 'political resolutions' for plenums and conventions; but the organization resolutions come from the firm Bolshevik hand of Cannon. From the end of the Chicago convention in November 1937 to June 1939 not one word of Cannon's appears in the public political press of the party; but his articles on 'organization' feature the preconvention discussion …

… We have already pointed out that the Cannon group is in a state of development. Its bureaucratic conservatism is not the product of a day or a year. It has become crystallized, become a system, only gradually, over a long period. It is our conviction that the outbreak of the war is what precipitated it clearly and crassly. It was difficult to attack before the party as a whole what was primarily a threat, a tendency, an embryo. Nor would this have been justified. By taking things as they came, a point at a time, the tendency might be corrected in time; at least we might 'muddle through'. …

7 The Clique and Its Leader

The leading members of the Cannon faction are well known as such. They are not new recruits, either to the party or to the faction. They include such comrades as Lewit, Gordon, Dunne, Skoglund, Weber, Turner, Clarke, Cochran,

Morrow, Wright, Weiss, etc. We have called this faction a clique. We do so not for the sake of employing an epithet with unpleasant associations against our opponents, but, as always, in the effort to give an exact and scientific political description.

The Cannon faction is a clique because it is a grouping that exists, that has a continuous existence, without any principled political foundation so different from the policies of others as to warrant a separate (and secret) formation.

Cannon has stated, in the present party discussion, that for two years there was no 'Cannon faction', but that now there is; and there is one now because a serious political dispute arose (over the Russian question) and a faction representing an identical point of view took shape on the foundation of that political view. This claim is put forward only to pull wool over the eyes of the innocent. It is quite true that, in the present dispute, many supporters and members of the present (temporary) 'Cannon faction' are not members of the (permanent) Cannon clique. But the clique itself has a lasting life …

The Cannon faction is a bureaucratic conservative clique, not a group built on a commonly accepted political platform. But what, then, holds it together, if not a political platform? It, like all such groupings, if it is to endure, has only one resort: to group itself around an individual, a leader. The 'platform' of the grouping becomes – the leader. It could not be otherwise.

It is natural, in politics, that individuals who have shown talent and ability should come to occupy somewhat special places in the minds of their associates, and that some or many persons will put considerable confidence in what the talented individuals do and say. It is natural that these leading individuals should carry weight as persons and not merely as embodiments of political ideas. There need be nothing wrong with this, though it contains undoubted dangers in the best of circumstances. But the relation of the followers of a clique to its 'leader' is something very different; and the 'cult of the leader' is not at all the same thing as confidence in an outstanding, tried, and talented comrade. It is in this latter sense, that we say that Cannon is regarded as a leader by his followers. He is the substitute for a political platform …

A clique with a leader-cult has its own laws of development, and the Cannon faction cannot escape the operation of these laws. In order to keep the leader in his niche, all other leading comrades must be toppled. Consequently, a systematic undercover campaign to poison the minds of party members is conducted, in terms often of the most fantastic slanders. An 'anti-New York' propaganda is spread, which is at bottom a catering to prejudices that are not always healthy. This campaign was especially whipped up by Cannon at the last convention of the party in the most artificial manner and to such an extreme point that it was carried over to the public mass meeting celebrating the convention. It served the interests of the clique to do so at the national convention. But, at the New York city convention a few mouths later, when it served the clique's interests to laud to the skies everything Cochran, the city organizer, had done and to deny violently that anything was wrong or deficient in his administration, the New York organization was suddenly presented as an all but perfect section of the party – at least that section of it which supported the Cannon group.

Above all, an 'anti-intellectual' and 'anti-intellectuals' attitude is drummed into the minds of party members. The faction associates are taught, quite literally, to despise and scorn 'intellectuals' and 'intellectualism'. A loud laugh is guaranteed for a joke or story about an intellectual. Such symptoms, though they have been rare in the 'Trotskyist' movement, are familiar enough. Some of us will remember a prominent appearance of them in the American movement some six years ago: Within the AWP the struggle against fusion with the CLA was conducted by Hardman under the banner of 'anti-New York', 'anti-intellectual' (not unlike many of the present campaigners, the banner-carrier was himself a New York intellectual). The self-avowed 'trade-union' faction of Foster and Co. in the old Communist Party fights distinguished itself in the same way, although in those days Cannon combated Fosterite demagogy with all his strength.

Rudeness and harshness, of a personal rather than a political kind, more and more make their appearance. At the very beginning of the present dispute, before positions and lines were even clearly drawn, Cannon and his associates were referring to the opposition constantly as 'traitors', 'sniveling' this and 'stinking' that. Not on the floor of the plenum, but during its sessions Dunne described the minority as 'sniveling strikebreakers' (our quotations are, as always, literal). The opposition has since become 'agents of imperialism', 'scabs' and 'strikebreakers'. Vocabulary, too, is caught in the bureaucratic conservative trap ...

8 Cannon's 'Theory of Crises'

We have explained to the party, consistently and openly, our *political analysis* of the party crisis. It is our duty to do so. It is no less Cannon's duty to give *his* theory, *his* political analysis. It is not without significance that since the beginning of the present crisis, he has shifted back and forth among no less than four different theories of the party crisis; and only one of these four, the one to which he has devoted least attention, is a political analysis.

1. Cannon's first theory was that the leaders of the opposition are 'irresponsible', 'light-minded', 'subjective', and using their own inner doubts to 'throw the party into a crisis'. This, it may be observed, is what Cannon has said at the outset of every even minor conflict in the party during the past several years.

2. The second theory of Cannon was that the position of the minority is an expression of 'the pressure of democratic imperialism': that is, that the minority's position on the question immediately under dispute is social-patriotic. This is Cannon's sole attempt at a political analysis. But apparently he senses the weakness of this analysis, for he mentions it only occasionally and in passing. He never, so far, has dwelt on it, never attempted to prove it.

To prove it convincingly, it will not be enough for him to give an abstract analysis of the minority's position on 'the Russian question'. He must bolster his proof with evidence from other actions – motions, speeches, writings – of the leaders of the minority during this period and before it, must show that these too reveal the tendency toward democratic imperialist patriotism. But everyone knows that he cannot do this. Everyone knows that the leaders of the minority have consistently and day-by-day upheld the internationalist, anti-patriotic position of the party, above all on the question of war, where it means most. Everyone knows that they have been not the last but the first in the party in this all-important task.

Our party, true enough, is subject to the pressure of democratic patriotism, and we must guard against it. Fortunately, this pressure has not yet had serious and crystallized results in our ranks. Where it has been manifested concretely – when Cochran in Cleveland jumped head over heels into the Keep America Out of War Committee, when the comrades in Toledo slipped reformist versions of our transition slogans into the unemployment pamphlet they sponsored, when a couple of months ago our Minneapolis comrades supported a resolution at the Minnesota State AF of L convention hailing William Green as a fighter against war – in these concrete cases we find that it was never members of the present minority who were primarily involved, or involved at all.

3. The third theory of Cannon, advanced at a New York membership meeting, is that the present minority constitutes a 'stinking office bureaucracy' (the adjective was very much insisted upon). As proof of this he offered flat falsifications of three incidents in party history. We shall not here counter these with the truth, though if the falsifications are persisted in or committed to paper we shall take occasion to do so, and do so conclusively. But we wish now only to observe, as in theory 1, how this reply is typically bureaucratic. 'You call me a bureaucrat? You are yourselves not only bureaucrats, but stinking bureaucrats'. Again: a *substitute* for a political answer.

4. The fourth theory of Cannon is as follows: The present dispute in the party is the expression of a conflict between the petty-bourgeois, middle-class elements (the minority) and the proletarian elements (the majority). A luscious and satisfying theory indeed! What we – the majority says to itself, licking its chops – have in the party is: the class struggle. Thus the majority can get compensation by participation in 'its own' class struggle for the party's inadequacies in the real struggle which is proceeding in its own way in the outside world.

This theory also is not political, but sociological. If it were true – and significant – it would still be necessary to characterize the position reached by the 'petty-bourgeois current' politically. It is not enough just to call it 'petty-bourgeois' …

Cannon's 'class struggle' theory of the party crisis is a very dangerous fraud. Its concrete meaning is to encourage the trade union comrades to free themselves – not from 'petty-bourgeois elements' – but from political control by the party. The talk about 'petty-bourgeois elements' serves them as a rationalization to excuse rejection of political control by the party when that control seems to (and sometimes, necessarily, does) interfere with local or temporary advantages in trade union work. In this fundamental respect it is identical with the 'theory' and agitation of the Foster faction in the CP years ago, often condemned by our movement in the past and meriting the same condemnation today.

9 The Sterility of Bureaucratic Conservatism

A political party cannot continue as a living organism in a period of crisis, above all of war crisis, merely with a policy of 'reaffirming our past position'.

More and more we find that the Cannon faction resists every new idea, every experiment. Let us grant that half at least of the new ideas and proposed experiments are wrong. Still: we can better afford to make mistakes than to do nothing. What is revealing is that the Cannon associates always have as their first response to a new idea – 'hysteria', 'romanticism', 'light-mindedness'. In small things as in great: Whether it is the attempt actually to do something about building a 'workers' guard' or even to hold, in New York, an out-of-door May Day meeting (which Goldman and Cannon opposed as not feasible and sure to flop – though, as usual with experiments we try, it far more than justified itself when carried out). We must not 'rush into' taking concrete positions on concrete questions of the day-the embargo or the invasion of Poland or municipal ownership of New York subways or what is going on in India –

because, forsooth, we 'might be mistaken' or 'might violate our fundamental position' or 'involve ourselves in speculation'.

Bureaucratic conservatism, by its very nature, is sterile. Its self-preserving objective allows it to be skillful in organizational maneuvers, but blocks the outward road; if it tries the outward road, it is only because its inner difficulties have compelled it to seek external solution; and its expansion is also therefore conservative and bureaucratic.

The growing sterility of the Cannon faction is shown most clearly of all by its attitude toward the youth, and by its inability to assimilate the best of the youth. It has never even noticed the youth except to smash down on its leaders for an alleged 'anti-party' attitude and, characteristically, for their alleged 'ultra-leftism' and 'adventurism' – which is in reality only the resistance of the youth to the Cannon clique's bureaucratic conservatism and to its leader-cult. It is not yet a decided question in our party that failure to adulate Cannon as infallible leader constitutes an anti-party attitude.

Entirely prepared for the easy bureaucratic charge of 'flattering the youth' and well recognizing the distinct weaknesses in our youth organization, we say without hesitation that our youth – the YPSL organization itself and those comrades recently come from the YPSL to the party – are in every essential respect the most progressive force in the movement, and 90% of its hope for the future. The approach of war only makes this truth the more weighty. The youth carry the burden of the work of the party as well as of the YPSL; in responsible organization they put the party to shame; in receptivity to new and experimental ideas they are a standing lesson; they supply the party with most of its new members; and it is they alone who have actually done something to put themselves in readiness for work under war conditions. And it is this force, the potential force of the revolution, which Cannon, instead of educating and assimilating, brutally dismisses as 'irresponsible petty-bourgeois triflers', 'Lovestoneites' and 'traitors to the party'!

What, we ask, *is* the perspective of the Cannon group? We know very well what are its intentions with regard to the coming special convention. It has become increasingly plain that the Cannon regime is preparing a split. The party must not be taken in for a moment by solemn 'unity resolutions' which Cannon presents and has adopted for the sake of the record. Despite the 'unity resolution' the line and the conduct of the Cannon group have already made it abundantly clear that if they are in the majority at the convention, they will wipe out the opposition (that is, one form of a split); and if they are in the minority, they have no intention of abiding by the discipline of the party (that is, another form of a split). Whichever variant materializes, that is, no matter how the annoying opponents and critics are disposed of, the Cannon group will still have before it the question: What is its perspective? To continue forever 'reaffirming our old position' in answer to the political questions of the day, and to reply to all proposals for new organizational steps by denouncing them as 'hysteria'?

The truth is that the Cannon group has no perspective beyond that proper to it as a bureaucratic conservative-grouping: self-maintenance; hanging on.

This is the truth: If bureaucratic conservatism completes its crystallization and engulfs the party as a whole, then the party cannot survive the war. It will not, as a whole, capitulate to the war. But it will simply be lost, swamped by great events that leave it helpless, to which it cannot respond. That is the destiny of bureaucratic conservatism in the crises of war and revolution.

10 The Alternative

What has led to the spreading growth of this evil of bureaucratic conservatism that now threatens the very life of the party? The general causes are clear: It is a consequence of long years of isolation, defeat, uphill struggle, fighting always against the stream; of the weariness, discouragement, even cynicism and despair that these engender in the hearts of men. Bureaucratic conservatism, creeping stealthily up, seems a last desperate means of somehow 'hanging on', and refuge against a better day …

We shall, in an independent document, present to the party a specific program of action, the initial steps in the cure. What is needed is, in its general outline, clear enough: In place of conservative politics, we must put bold, flexible, critical and experimental politics – in a word scientific politics. In place of bureaucracy in the regime, not an abandonment of centralism naturally, but democracy also, democracy to the utmost permissible limit. Wherever there is a doubt, resolve the doubt on the democratic side. Only a truly democratic inner life can develop the initiative, intelligence and self-confidence without which the party will never lead the masses. All the formal democracy enjoyed by the party today – and it is abundant – is worse than meaningless, it is a mockery, if the real policies and the leadership and the regime of the party are continuously determined only by a clique which has no distinctive political foundation. The removal of party control from the hands of this clique is a precondition to the establishment of genuine party democracy and progressive policy. In place of a leader-cult, not another leader (we propose none and want none) but a collective leadership, genuinely collective, coordinating and integrating by a real exchange of opinion and an efficient division of labor the best talents of the party. If there is one in the party who is outstanding from all others in his abilities and devotion and political insight, he will be known and recognized; but let him be primus intra pares – first among equals. In place of 'reaffirming old positions', let us like free and intelligent men use our mighty programmatic concepts to meet the living problems of history, to foresee and to guide in action. A maximum of branch and local initiative! Comradely education, not brutal and disloyal attacks, for those in error. A warm, if critical, welcome for every new idea, even a doubtful idea, not a denunciation for 'irresponsibility'. Comradely criticism, encouragement, help, praise for the youth – even when the youth errs on the side of exaggeration or over-zealousness. And let us be less terrified of mistakes! Only the dead make no mistakes ...

3 Speech on the Russian Question[3]
(*1939*)

James P. Cannon

The Russian question is with us once again, as it has been at every critical turning point of the international labor movement since November 7, 1917. And there is nothing strange in that. The Russian question is no literary exercise to be taken up or cast aside according to the mood of the moment. The Russian question has been and remains the question of the revolution. The Russian Bolsheviks on November 7, 1917, once and for all, took the question of the workers' revolution out of the realm of abstraction and gave it flesh and blood reality.

It was said once of a book – I think it was Whitman's *Leaves of Grass* – 'who touches this book, touches a man'. In the same sense it can also be said: 'Who touches the Russian question, touches a revolution'. Therefore, be serious about it. Don't play with it.

The October Revolution put socialism on the order of the day throughout the world. It revived and shaped and developed the revolutionary labor movement of the world out of the bloody chaos of the war. The Russian revolution showed in practice, by example, how the workers' revolution is to be made. It revealed in life the role of the party. It showed in life what kind of a party the workers must have. By its victory, and its reorganization of the social system, the Russian revolution has proved for all time the superiority of nationalized property and planned economy over capitalist private property and planless competition and anarchy in production.

A Sharp Dividing Line

The question of the Russian revolution – and the Soviet state which is its creation – has drawn a sharp dividing line through the labor movement of all countries for 22 years. The attitude taken toward the Soviet Union throughout

3 Cannon 1939.

all these years has been the decisive criterion separating the genuine revolutionary tendency from all shades and degrees of waverers, backsliders and capitulators to the pressure of the bourgeois world – the Mensheviks, social-democrats, anarchists and syndicalists, centrists, Stalinists.

The main source of division in our own ranks for the past 10 years, since the Fourth Internationalist tendency took organized form on the international field, has been the Russian question. Our tendency, being a genuine, that is, orthodox, Marxist tendency from A to Z, has always proceeded on the Russian question from theoretical premises to political conclusions for action. Of course, it is only when political conclusions are drawn out to the end that differences on the Russian question reach an unbearable acuteness and permit no ambiguity or compromise. Conclusions on the Russian question lead directly to positions on such issues as war and revolution, defense and defeatism. Such issues, by their very nature, admit no unclarity, no compromise, because it is a matter of taking sides! One must be on one side or another in war and revolution.

The Importance of Theory

But if the lines are drawn only when political conclusions diverge, that does not at all signify that we are indifferent to theoretical premises. He is a very poor Marxist – better say, no Marxist at all – who takes a careless or tolerant attitude toward theoretical premises. The political conclusions of Marxists proceed from theoretical analyses and are constantly checked and regulated by them. That is the only way to assure a firm and consistent policy.

To be sure, we do not decline cooperation with people who agree with our political conclusions from different premises. For example, the Bolsheviks were not deterred by the fact that the left SRs were inconsistent. As Trotsky remarked in this connection: 'If we wait till everything is right in everybody's head there will never be any successful revolutions in this world' (or words to that effect). Just the same, for our part we want everything right in our own heads. We have no reason whatever to slur over theoretical formulas, which are expressed in 'terminology'. As Trotsky says, in theoretical matters 'we must keep our house clean'.

Our position on the Russian question is programmatic. In brief: the theoretical analysis – a degenerated workers' state. The political conclusion – unconditional defense against external attack of imperialists or internal attempts at capitalist restoration.

Defensism and Defeatism

Defensism and defeatism are two principled, that is, irreconcilable positions. They are not determined by arbitrary choice but by class interests.

No party in the world ever succeeded in harboring these two antipathetic tendencies for any great length of time. The contradiction is too great. Division all over the world ultimately took place along this line. Defensists at home were defeatists on Russia. Defensists on Russia were defeatists at home.

The degeneration of the Soviet state under Stalin has been analyzed at every step by the Bolshevik-Leninists and only by them. A precise attitude has been taken at every stage. The guiding lines of the revolutionary Marxist approach to the question have been: See the reality and see it whole at every stage; never surrender any position before it is lost; the worst of all capitulators is the one who capitulates before the decisive battle.

The International Left Opposition which originated in 1923 as an opposition in the Russian party (the original nucleus of the Fourth International) has always taken a precise attitude on the Russian question. In the first stages of the degeneration of which the Stalinist bureaucracy was the banner bearer the opposition considered it possible to rectify matters by methods of reform through the change of regime in the Communist Party of the Soviet Union. Later, when it became clearer that the Communist Party of Lenin had been irremediably destroyed, and after it became manifest that the reactionary bureaucracy could be removed only by civil war, the Fourth International, standing as before on its analysis of the Soviet Union as a workers' state, came out for a political revolution.

All the time throughout this entire period of 16 years, the Bolshevik-Leninists have stoutly maintained, in the face of all slander and persecution, that they were the firmest defenders of the workers' state and that in the hour of danger they would be in the front ranks of its defense. We always said the moment of danger will find the Fourth Internationalists at their posts defending the conquests of the great revolution without ceasing for a moment our struggle against the Stalinist bureaucracy. Now that the hour of danger is at hand – now that the long-awaited war is actually knocking at the door – it would be very strange if the Fourth International should renege on its oft-repeated pledge.

'Conservatism' on the Russian Question

Throughout all this long period of Soviet degeneration since the death of Lenin, the Fourth Internationalists, analyzing the new phenomenon of a degenerating workers' state at every turn, striving to comprehend its complications and contradictions, to recognize and defend all the progressive features of the contradictory processes and to reject the reactionary – during all this long time we have been beset at every new turn of events by the impatient demands of 'radicals' to simplify the question. Thrown off balance by the crimes and betrayals of Stalin, they lost sight of the new system of economy which Stalin had not destroyed and could not destroy.

We always firmly rejected these premature announcements that everything was lost and that we must begin all over again. At each stage of development, at each new revelation of Stalinist infamy and treachery, some group or other broke away from the Fourth International because of its 'conservatism' on the Russian question. It would be interesting, if we had the time, to call the roll of these groupings which one after another left our ranks to pursue an ostensibly more 'revolutionary' policy on the Russian question. Did they develop an activity more militant, more revolutionary, than ours? Did they succeed in creating a new movement and in attracting newly awakened workers and those breaking from Stalinism? In no case.

If we were to call the roll of these ultra-radical groups it would present a devastating picture indeed. Those who did not fall into complete political passivity became reconciled in one form or another to bourgeois democracy. The experiences of the past should teach us all a salutary caution, and even, if you please, 'conservatism', in approaching any proposal to revise the program of the Fourth International on the Russian question. While all the innovators fell by the wayside, the Fourth International alone retained its programmatic firmness. It grew and developed and remained the only genuine revolutionary current in the labor movement of the world. Without a firm position on the Russian question our movement also would inevitably have shared the fate of the others.

The mighty power of the October Revolution is shown by the vitality of its conquests. The nationalized property and the planned economy stood up under all the difficulties and pressures of the capitalist encirclement and all the blows of a reactionary bureaucracy at home. In the Soviet Union, despite the monstrous mismanagement of the bureaucracy, we saw a tremendous development of the productive forces – and in a backward country at that – while capitalist economy declined. Conclusion: nationalized and planned economy, made possible by a revolution that overthrew the capitalists and landlords, is infinitely superior, more progressive. It shows the way forward. Don't give it up before it is lost! Cling to it and defend it!

The Class Forces

On the Russian question there are only two really independent forces in the world. Two forces who think about the question independently because they base themselves, their thoughts, their analyses and their conclusions, on fundamental class considerations.

Those two independent forces are:

1. The conscious vanguard of the world bourgeoisie, the statesmen of both democratic and fascist imperialism.
2. The conscious vanguard of the world proletariat.

Between them it is not simply a case of two opinions on the Russian question, but rather of two camps. All those who in the past rejected the conclusions of the Fourth International and broke with our movement on that account, have almost invariably fallen into the service of the imperialists, through Stalinism, social and liberal democracy, or passivity, a form of service.

The standpoint of the world bourgeoisie is a class standpoint. They proceed, as we do, from fundamental class considerations. They want to maintain world capitalism. This determines their fundamental antagonism to the USSR. They appreciate the reactionary work of Stalin, but consider it incomplete, insofar as he has not restored capitalist private property.

Their fundamental attitude determines an inevitable attempt at the start of the war, or during it, to attack Russia, overthrow the nationalized economy, restore a capitalist regime, smash the foreign trade monopoly, open up the Soviet Union as a market and field of investments, transform Russia into a great colony, and thereby alleviate the crisis of world capitalism.

The standpoint of the Fourth International is based on the same fundamental class considerations. Only we draw opposite conclusions, from an opposite class standpoint.

Purely sentimental motivations, speculation without fundamental class premises, so-called 'fresh ideas' with no programmatic base – all this is out of place in a party of Marxists. We want to advance the world revolution of the proletariat. This determines our attitude and approach to the Russian question. True, we want to see reality, but we are not disinterested observers and commentators.

We do not examine the Russian revolution and what remains of its great conquests as though it were a bug under a glass. We have an interest! We take part in the fight! At each stage in the development of the Soviet Union, its advances and its degeneration, we seek the basis for revolutionary action.

We want to advance the world revolution, overthrow capitalism, establish socialism. The Soviet Union is an important and decisive question on this line.

Our standpoint on the Russian question is written into our program. It is not a new question for us. It is 22 years old. We have followed its evolution, both progressive and retrogressive, at every stage. We have discussed it and taken our position anew at every stage of its progressive development and its degeneration. And, what is most important, we have always acted on our conclusions.

The Decisive Criterion

The Soviet Union emerged from the October Revolution as a workers' state. As a result of the backwardness and poverty of the country and the delay of the world revolution, a conservative bureaucracy emerged and triumphed, destroyed the party and bureaucratized the economy. However, this same bureaucracy still operates on the basis of the nationalized property established by the revolution. That is the decisive criterion for our evaluation of the question.

If we see the Soviet Union for what it really is, a gigantic labor organization which has conquered one-sixth of the Earth's surface, we will not be so ready to abandon it because of our hatred of the crimes and abominations of the bureaucracy. Do we turn our backs on a trade union because it falls into the control of bureaucrats and traitors? Ultra-leftists have frequently made this error, but always with bad results, sometimes with reactionary consequences.

We recall the case of the International Ladies' Garment Workers Union here in New York. The bureaucrats of this union were about as vile a gang of labor lieutenants of the capitalist class as could be found. In the struggle against the left-wing in the middle twenties they conspired with the bosses and the AFL fakers. They expelled the left-wing locals and used hired thugs to fight them and to break their strikes. The difference between them and Stalin was only a matter of opportunity and power. Driven to revolt against the crimes of these bureaucrats the left-wing, under the influence of the Communist Party in the days of its Third Period frenzy, labeled the union – not merely its treacherous bureaucracy – as a 'company union'.

But this same 'company union', under the pressure of the workers in its ranks and the increasing intensity of the class struggle, was forced to call a strike to defend itself against the 'imperialist' attack of the bosses. Workers who had kept their heads, supported ('defended') the strike against the bosses. But the Stalinists, trapped by their own hastily improvised theory, having already denounced the union as a company union, renounced support ('defense') of the strike. They denounced it as a 'fake' strike. Thus their ill-considered radicalism led them to a reactionary position. They were denounced, and rightly, throughout the needle trades market as strikebreakers. To this day they suffer the discredit of this reactionary action.

To defend the Soviet Union as a gigantic labor organization against the attacks of its class enemies does not mean to defend each and every action of its bureaucracy or each and every action of the Red Army which is an instrument of the bureaucracy. To impute such a 'totalitarian' concept of defense to the Fourth International is absurd. Nobody here will deny defense of a bona fide trade union, no matter how reactionary its bureaucracy. But that does not prevent us from discriminating between actions of the bureaucracy which involve a defense of the union against the bosses and other actions which are aimed against the workers.

The United Mine Workers of America is a great labor organization which we all support. But it is headed by a thoroughgoing scoundrel and agent of the master class who also differs from Stalin only in the degrees of power and opportunity. In my own personal experience some years ago, I took part in a strike of the Kansas miners which was directed against the enforcement of a reactionary labor law, known as the Kansas Industrial Court Law, a law forbidding strikes. This was a thoroughly progressive action on the part of the Kansas miners and their president, Alex Howat. Howat and the other local officials were thrown into jail. While they were in jail, John L. Lewis, as president of the national organization, sent his agents into the Kansas fields to sign an agreement with the bosses over the head of the officers of the Kansas district. He supplied strikebreakers and thugs and money to break the strike while the legitimate officers of the union lay in jail for a good cause. Every militant worker in the country denounced this treacherous strikebreaking action of Lewis. But did we therefore renounce support of the national union of mine workers? Yes, some impatient revolutionaries did, and thereby completely disoriented themselves in the labor movement. The United Mine Workers retained its character as a labor organization and only last Spring came into conflict with the coal operators on a national scale. I think you all recall that in this contest our press gave 'unconditional defense' to the miners' union despite the fact that strikebreaker Lewis remained its president.

The Longshoremen's Union of the Pacific Coast is a bona fide organization of workers, headed by a Stalinist of an especially unattractive type, a pocket edition of Stalin named Bridges. This same Bridges led a squad of misguided longshoremen through a picket line of the Sailors' Union in a direct attempt to break up this organization. I think all of you recall that our press scathingly denounced this contemptible action of Bridges. But if the Longshoremen's

Union, headed by Bridges, which is at this moment conducting negotiations with the bosses, is compelled to resort to strike action, what stand shall we take? Any ordinary class-conscious worker, let alone an educated Marxist, will be on the picket line with the Longshoremen's Union or 'defending' it by some other means.

Why is it so difficult for some of our friends, including some of those who are very well educated in the formal sense, to understand the Russian question? I am very much afraid it is because they do not think of it in terms of struggle. It is strikingly evident that the workers, especially the more experienced workers who have taken part in trade unions, strikes, etc., understand the Russian question much better than the more educated scholastics. From their experiences in the struggle they know what is meant when the Soviet Union is compared to a trade union that has fallen into bad hands. And everyone who has been through a couple of strikes which underwent crises and came to the brink of disaster, finally to emerge victorious, understands what is meant when one says: No position must be surrendered until it is irrevocably lost.

I, personally, have seen the fate of more than one strike determined by the will or lack of will of the leadership to struggle at a critical moment. All our trade union successes in Minneapolis stem back directly to a fateful week in 1934 when the leaders refused to call off the strike, which to all appearances was hopelessly defeated, and persuaded the strike committee to hold out a while longer. In that intervening time a break occurred in the ranks of the bosses; this in turn paved the way for a compromise settlement and eventually victorious advance of the whole union.

How strange it is that some people analyze the weakness and defects in a workers' organization so closely that they do not always take into account the weakness in the camp of the enemy, which may easily more than counterbalance.

In my own agitation among strikers at dark moments of a strike I have frequently resorted to the analogy of two men engaged in a physical fight. When one gets tired and apparently at the end of his resources he should never forget that the other fellow is maybe just as tired or even more so. In that case the one who holds out will prevail. Looked at in this way a worn-out strike can sometimes be carried through to a compromise or a victory by the resolute will of its leadership. We have seen this happen more than once. Why should we deny the Soviet Union, which is not yet exhausted, the same rights?

The Danger of a False Position

We have had many discussions on the Russian question in the past. It has been the central and decisive question for us, as for every political tendency in the labor movement. That, I repeat, is because it is nothing less than the question of the revolution at various stages of its progressive development or degeneration. We are, in fact, the party of the Russian revolution. We have been the people, and the only people, who have had the Russian revolution in their program and in their blood. That is also the main reason why the Fourth International is the only revolutionary tendency in the whole world. A false position on the Russian question would have destroyed our movement as it destroyed all others.

Two years ago we once again conducted an extensive discussion on the Russian question. The almost unanimous conclusion of the party was written into the program of our first convention:

1. The Soviet Union, on the basis of its nationalized property and planned economy, the fruit of the revolution, remains a workers' state, though in a degenerated form.
2. As such, we stand, as before, for the unconditional defense of the Soviet Union against imperialist attack.
3. The best defense – the only thing that can save the Soviet Union in the end by solving its contradictions – is the international revolution of the proletariat.
4. In order to regenerate the workers' state we stand for the overthrow of the bureaucracy by a political revolution ...

Our motion calls for unconditional defense of the Soviet Union against imperialist attack. What does that mean? It simply means that we defend the Soviet Union and its nationalized property against external attacks of imperialist armies or against internal attempts at capitalist restoration, without putting as a prior condition the overthrow of the Stalinist bureaucracy. Any other kind of defense negates the whole position under present circumstances. Some people speak nowadays of giving 'conditional' defense to the Soviet Union. If you stop to think about it we are for conditional defense of the United States. It is so stated in the program of the Fourth International. In the event of war we will absolutely defend the country on only one small 'condition': that we first overthrow the government of the capitalists and replace it with a government of the workers.

Does unconditional defense of the Soviet Union mean supporting every act of the Red Army? No, that is absurd. Did we support the Moscow Trials and the actions of Stalin's GPU in these trials? Did we support the purges, the wholesale murders of the forces in Spain which were directed against the workers? If I recall correctly, we unconditionally defended those workers who fought on the other side of the barricades in Barcelona. That did not prevent us from supporting the military struggle against Franco and maintaining our position in defense of the Soviet Union against imperialist attack.

It is now demanded that we take a big step forward and support the idea of an armed struggle against Stalin in the newly occupied territories of old Poland. Is this really something new? For three years the Fourth International has advocated in its program the armed overthrow of Stalin inside the Soviet Union itself. The Fourth International has generally acknowledged the necessity for an armed struggle to set up an independent Soviet Ukraine. How can there be any question of having a different policy in the newly occupied territories? If the revolution against Stalin is really ready there, the Fourth International will certainly support it and endeavor to lead it. There are no two opinions possible in our ranks on this question. But what shall we do if Hitler (or [British Prime Minister Neville] Chamberlain) attacks the Sovietized Ukraine before Stalin has been overthrown? This is the question that needs an unambiguous answer. Shall we defend the Soviet Union, and with it now and for the same reasons, the nationalized property of the newly annexed territories? We say, yes!

That position was incorporated into the program of the foundation congress of the Fourth International, held in the summer of 1938. Remember, that was after the Moscow Trials and the crushing of the Spanish revolution. It was after the murderous purge of the whole generation of Bolsheviks, after the People's Front, the entry into the League of Nations, the Stalin-Laval pact (and betrayal of the French workers). We took our position on the basis of the economic structure of the country, the fruit of the revolution. The great gains are not to be surrendered before they are really lost. That is the fighting program of the Fourth International.

The Stalin-Hitler Pact

The Stalin-Hitler pact does not change anything fundamentally. If Stalin were allied with the United States, and comrades should deny defense of the Soviet Union out of fear of becoming involved in the defense of Stalin's American ally, such comrades would be wrong, but their position would be understandable as a subjective reaction prompted by revolutionary sentiments. The 'defeatism' which broke out in our French section following the Stalin-Laval pact was undoubtedly so motivated and, consequently, had to be refuted with the utmost tolerance and patience. But an epidemic of 'defeatism' in the democratic camp would be simply shameful. There is no pressure on us in America to defend the Soviet Union. All the pressure is for a democratic holy war against the Soviet Union. Let us keep this in mind. The main enemy is still in our own country.

What has happened since our last discussion? Has there been some fundamental change in Soviet economy. No, nothing of that kind is maintained. Nothing happened except that Stalin signed the pact with Hitler! For us that gave no reason whatever to change our analysis of Soviet economy and our attitude toward it. The aim of all our previous theoretical work, concentrated in our program, was precisely to prepare us for war and revolution. Now we have the war; and revolution is next in order. If we have to stop now to find a new program it is a very bad sign.

Just consider: There are people who could witness all the crimes and betrayals of Stalin, which we understood better than anybody else, and denounced before anybody else and more effectively, they could witness all this and still stand for the defense of the Soviet Union. But they could not tolerate the alliance with fascist Germany instead of imperialist England or France!

The Invasion of Poland

Of course, there has been a great hullaballoo about the Soviet invasion of Polish Ukraine. But that is simply one of the consequences of the war and the alliance with Hitler's Germany. The contention that we should change our analysis of the social character of the Soviet state and our attitude toward its defense because the Red Army violated the Polish border is even more absurd than to base such changes on the Hitler pact. The Polish invasion is only an incident in a war, and in wars borders are always violated. (If all the armies stayed at home there could be no war.) The inviolability of borders – all of which were established by war – is interesting to democratic pacifists and to nobody else.

Hearing all the democratic clamor we had to ask ourselves many times: Don't they know that Western Ukraine and White Russia never rightfully belonged to Poland? Don't they know that this territory was forcibly taken from the Soviet Union by Pilsudski with French aid in 1920?

To be sure, this did not justify Stalin's invasion of the territory in collaboration with Hitler. We never supported that and we never supported the fraudulent claim that Stalin was bringing 'liberation' to the peoples of the Polish Ukraine. At the same time we did not propose to yield an inch to the 'democratic' incitement against the Soviet Union on the basis of the Polish events. The democratic war-mongers were shrieking at the top of their voices all over town. We must not be unduly impressed by this democratic clamor. Your National Committee was not in the least impressed.

In order to penetrate a little deeper into this question and trace it to its roots, let us take another hypothetical example. Not a fantastic one, but a very logical one. Suppose Stalin had made a pact with the imperialist democracies against Hitler while Rumania had allied itself with Hitler. Suppose, as would most probably have happened in that case, the Red Army had struck at Rumania, Hitler's ally, instead of Poland, the ally of the democracies, and had seized Bessarabia, which also once belonged to Russia. Would the democratic war-mongers in that case have howled about 'Red Imperialism'? Not on your life!

I am very glad that our National Committee maintained its independence from bourgeois democratic pressure on the Polish invasion. The question was put to us very excitedly, point-blank, like a pistol at the temple: 'Are you for or against the invasion of Poland?' But revolutionary Marxists don't answer in a 'yes' or 'no' manner which can lump them together with other people who pursue opposite aims. Being for or against something is not enough in the class struggle. It is necessary to explain from what standpoint one is for or against. Are you for or against racketeering gangsters in the trade unions? – the philistines sometimes ask. We don't jump to attention, like a private soldier who has met an officer on the street, and answer: 'against!' We first inquire: who asks this question and from what standpoint? And what weight does this question have in relation to other questions? We have our own standpoint and we are careful not to get our answers mixed up with those of class enemies and pacifist muddleheads.

Some people – especially affected bosses – are against racketeering gangsters in the trade unions because they extort graft from the bosses. That side of the question doesn't interest us very much. Some people – especially pacifist preachers – are against the gangsters because they commit violence. But we are not against violence at all times and under all circumstances. We, for our part, taking our time and formulating our viewpoint precisely, say: We are against union gangsterism because it injures the union in its fight against the bosses. That is our reason. It proceeds from our special class standpoint on the union question.

So with Poland: We don't support the course of Stalin in general. His crime is not one incident here or there but his whole policy. He demoralizes the workers' movement and discredits the Soviet Union. That is what we are against. He betrays the revolution by his whole course. Every incident for us fits into that framework; it is considered from that point of view and taken in its true proportions.

The Invasion of Finland

Those who take the Polish invasion – an incident in a great chain of events – as the basis for a fundamental change in our program show a lack of proportion. That is the kindest thing that can be said for them. They are destined to remain in a permanent lather throughout the war. They are already four laps behind schedule: There is also Latvia, and Estonia, and Lithuania, and now Finland.

We can expect another clamor of demands that we say, pointblank, and in one word, whether we are 'for' or 'against' the pressure on poor little bourgeois-democratic Finland. Our answer – wait a minute. Keep your shirt on. There is no lack of protests in behalf of the bourgeois swine who rule Finland. The *New Leader* has protested. Charles Yale Harrison has written a tearful column about it. The renegade Lore has wept about it in the *New York Post*. The President of the United States has protested. Finland is pretty well covered with moral support. So bourgeois Finland can wait a minute till we explain our attitude without bothering about the 'for' or 'against' ultimatum.

I personally feel very deeply about Finland, and this is by no means confined to the present dispute between Stalin and the Finnish Prime Minister. When I think of Finland, I think of the thousands of martyred dead, the proletarian heroes who perished under the white terror of Mannerheim. I would, if I could, call them back from their graves. Failing that, I would organize a proletarian army of Finnish workers to avenge them, and drive their murderers into the Baltic Sea. I would send the Red Army of the regenerated Soviet Union to help them at the decisive moment.

We don't support Stalin's invasion only because he doesn't come for revolutionary purposes. He doesn't come at the call of Finnish workers whose confidence he has forfeited. That is the only reason we are against it. The 'borders' have nothing to do with it. 'Defense' in war also means attack. Do you think we will respect frontiers when we make our revolution? If an enemy army lands troops at Quebec, for example, do you think we will wait placidly at the Canadian border for their attack? No, if we are genuine revolutionists and not pacifist muddleheads we will cross the border and meet them at the point of landing. And if our defense requires the seizure of Quebec, we will seize it as the Red Army of Lenin seized Georgia and tried to take Warsaw.

Foreseen in Program of Fourth International

Some may think the war and the alliance with Hitler change everything we have previously considered; that it, at least, requires a reconsideration of the whole question of the Soviet Union, if not a complete change in our program. To this we can answer: War was contemplated by our program. The fundamental theses on 'War and the Fourth International', adopted in 1934, say:

Every big war, irrespective of its initial moves, must pose squarely the question of military intervention against the USSR in order to transfuse fresh blood into the sclerotic veins of capitalism …

Defense of the Soviet Union from the blows of the capitalist enemies, irrespective of the circumstances and immediate causes of the conflict, is the elementary and imperative duty of every honest labor organization …

In the existing situation an alliance of the USSR with an imperialist state or with one imperialist combination against another, in case of war, cannot at all be considered as excluded. Under the pressure of circumstances a temporary alliance of this kind may become an iron necessity, without ceasing, however, because of it, to be of the greatest danger both to the USSR and to the world revolution.

The international proletariat will not decline to defend the USSR even if the latter should find itself forced into a military alliance with some imperialists against others. But in this case, even more than in any other, the international proletariat must safeguard its complete political independence from Soviet diplomacy and thereby also from the bureaucracy of the Third International.

A stand on defense was taken in the light of this perspective.

A slogan of defense acquires a concrete meaning precisely in the event of war. A strange time to drop it! That would mean a rejection of all our theoretical preparation for the war. That would mean starting all over again. From what fundamental basis? Nobody knows.

There has been much talk of 'independence' on the Russian question. That is good! A revolutionist who is not independent is not worth his salt. But it is necessary to specify: Independent of whom? What is needed by our party at every turn is class independence, independence of the Stalinists, and, above all, independence of the bourgeoisie. Our program assures such independence under all circumstances. It shall not be changed! …

4 From a Scratch – To the Danger of Gangrene[4] (*1940, excerpts*)

Leon Trotsky

… A considerable proportion of the membership of the American section as well as our entire young International, came to us either from the Comintern in its period of decline or from the Second International. These are bad schools. The discussion has revealed that wide circles of the party lack a sound theoretical education. It is sufficient, for instance, to refer to the circumstance that the New York local of the party did not respond with a vigorous defensive reflex to the attempts at light-minded revision of Marxist doctrine and program but on the contrary gave support in the majority to the revisionists. This is unfortunate but remediable to the degree that our American section and the entire International consist of honest individuals sincerely seeking their way to the revolutionary road. They have the desire and the will to learn. But there is no time to lose. It is precisely the party's penetration into the trade unions, and into the workers' milieu in general that demands heightening the theoretical qualification of our cadres. I do not mean by cadres the 'apparatus' but the party as a whole. Every party member should and must consider himself an officer in the proletarian army.

'Since when have you become specialists in the question of philosophy?' the oppositionists now ironically ask the majority representatives. Irony here is completely out of place. Scientific socialism is the conscious expression of the unconscious historical process; namely, the instinctive and elemental drive of the proletariat to reconstruct society on communist beginnings. These organic tendencies in the psychology of workers spring to life with utmost rapidity today in the epoch of crises and wars. The discussion has revealed beyond all question a clash in the party between a petty-bourgeois tendency and a proletarian tendency. The petty-bourgeois tendency reveals its confusion in its attempt to reduce the program of the party to the small coin of 'concrete' questions. The proletarian tendency on the contrary strives to correlate all the partial questions into theoretical unity. At stake at the present time is not

4 Trotsky 1940b.

the extent to which individual members of the majority consciously apply the dialectic method. What is important is the fact that the majority as a whole pushes toward the proletarian posing of the questions and by very reason of this tends to assimilate the dialectic which is the 'algebra of the revolution'. The oppositionists, I am informed, greet with bursts of laughter the very mention of 'dialectics'. In vain. This unworthy method will not help. The dialectic of the historic process has more than once cruelly punished those who tried to jeer at it …

To view as the cause of the present party crisis – the conservatism of its worker section; to seek a solution to the crisis through the victory of the petty-bourgeois bloc – it would be difficult to conceive a mistake more dangerous to the party. As a matter of fact, the gist of the present crisis consists in the conservatism of the petty-bourgeois elements who have passed through a purely propagandistic school and who have not yet found a pathway to the road of class struggle. The present crisis is the final battle of these elements for self-preservation. Every oppositionist as an individual can, if he firmly desires, find a worthy place for himself in the revolutionary movement. As a faction they are doomed. In the struggle that is developing, Shachtman is not in the camp where he ought to be. As always in such cases, his strong sides have receded into the background while his weak traits on the other hand have assumed an especially finished expression. His Open Letter represents, so to speak, a crystallization of his weak traits.

Shachtman has left out a trifle: his class position. Hence his extraordinary zigzags, his improvisations and leaps. He replaces class analysis with disconnected historical anecdotes for the sole purpose of covering up his own shift, for camouflaging the contradiction between his yesterday and today. This is Shachtman's procedure with the history of Marxism, the history of his own party, and the history of the Russian Opposition. In carrying this out, he heaps mistakes upon mistakes. All the historical analogies to which he resorts, speak, as we shall see, against him …

On May 25, 1937, I wrote to New York concerning the policy of the Bolshevik-Leninist faction in the Socialist Party:

> … I must cite two recent documents: (a) the private letter of 'Max' about the convention, and (b) Shachtman's article, Towards a Revolutionary Socialist Party. The title of this article alone characterizes a false perspective. It seems to me established by the developments, including the last convention, that the party is evolving, not into a 'revolutionary' party, but into a kind of ILP, that is, a miserable centrist political abortion without any perspective.

> The affirmation that the American Socialist Party is now 'closer to the position of revolutionary Marxism than any party of the Second or Third Internationals' is an absolutely unmerited compliment: the American Socialist Party is only more backward than the analogous formations in Europe – the POUM, ILP, SAP, etc. … Our duty is to unmask this negative advantage of Norman Thomas and Co., and not to speak about the 'superiority (of the war resolution) over any resolution ever adopted before by the party …' This is a purely literary appreciation, because every resolution must be taken in connection with historical events, with the political situation and its imperative needs …

In both of the documents mentioned in the above letter, Shachtman revealed excessive adaptability toward the left wing of the petty-bourgeois democrats – political mimicry – a very dangerous symptom in a revolutionary politician! It is extremely important to take note of his high appraisal of the 'radical' position of Norman Thomas in relation to war … in Europe. Opportunists, as is well known, tend to all the greater radicalism the further removed they are from events. With this law in mind it is not difficult to appraise at its true value the fact that Shachtman and his allies accuse us of a tendency to 'capitulate to Stalinism'. Alas, sitting in the Bronx, it is much easier to display irreconcilability toward the Kremlin than toward the American petty bourgeoisie.

… To believe comrade Shachtman, I injected the question of comrade Abern's faction as a concentration of petty-bourgeois individuals artificially and without any basis in fact. Yet on October 10, 1937, at a time when Shachtman marched shoulder to shoulder with Cannon and it was considered officially that Abern had no faction, I wrote to Cannon:

> The party has only a minority of genuine factory workers … The non-proletarian elements represent a very necessary yeast, and I believe that we can be proud of the good quality of these elements … But … Our party can be inundated by non-proletarian elements and can even lose its revolutionary character. The task is naturally not to prevent the influx of intellectuals by artificial methods, … but to orientate practically all the organization toward the factories, the strikes, the unions …
>
> A concrete example: We cannot devote enough or equal forces to all the factories. Our local organization can choose for its activity in the next period one, two or three factories in its area and concentrate all its forces upon these factories. If we have in one of them two or three workers we can create a special help commission of five non-workers with the purpose of enlarging our influence in these factories.

> The same can be done among the trade unions. We cannot introduce non-worker members in workers' unions. But we can with success build up help commissions for oral and literary action in connection with our comrades in the union. The unbreakable conditions should be: not to command the workers but only to help them, to give them suggestions, to arm them with the facts, ideas, factory papers, special leaflets, and so on.
>
> Such collaboration would have a tremendous educational importance from one side for the worker comrades, from the other side for the non-workers who need a solid re-education.
>
> You have for example an important number of Jewish non-worker elements in your ranks. They can be a very valuable yeast if the party succeeds by and by in extracting them from a closed milieu and ties them to the factory workers by daily activity. I believe such an orientation would also assure a more healthy atmosphere in side the party.
>
> One general rule we can establish immediately: a party member who doesn't win during three or six months a new worker for the party is not a good party member.
>
> If we established seriously such a general orientation and if we verified every week the practical results, we will avoid a great danger; namely, that the intellectuals and white collar workers might suppress the worker minority, condemn it to silence, transform the party into a very intelligent discussion club but absolutely not habitable for workers.
>
> The same rules should be in a corresponding form elaborated for the working and recruiting of the youth organization, otherwise we run the danger of educating good young elements into revolutionary dilettantes and not revolutionary fighters.

From this letter it is obvious, I trust, that I did not mention the danger of a petty-bourgeois deviation the day following the Stalin-Hitler pact or the day following the dismemberment of Poland, but brought it forward persistently two years ago and more. Furthermore, as I then pointed out, bearing in mind primarily the 'non existent' Abern faction, it was absolutely requisite in order to cleanse the atmosphere of the party, that the Jewish petty-bourgeois elements of the New York local be shifted from their habitual conservative milieu and dissolved in the real labor movement. It is precisely because of this that the above letter (not the first of its kind), written more than two years before the present discussion began, is of far greater weight as evidence than all the writings of the opposition leaders on the motives which impelled me to come out in defense of the 'Cannon clique'.

… On June 1, 1938, I wrote comrade Shachtman: 'It is difficult to understand here why you are so tolerant and even friendly toward Mr. Eugene Lyons. He speaks, it seems, at your banquets; at the same time he speaks at the banquets of the White Guards'.

This letter continued the struggle for a more independent and resolute policy toward the so-called 'liberals', who, while waging a struggle against the revolution, wish to maintain 'friendly relations' with the proletariat, for this doubles their market value in the eyes of bourgeois public opinion …

The Philosophic Bloc against Marxism

… In his Open Letter, Shachtman refers particularly to the fact that comrade Vincent Dunne expressed satisfaction over the article on the intellectuals. But I too praised it: 'Many parts are excellent'. However, as the Russian proverb puts it, a spoonful of tar can spoil a barrel of honey. It is precisely this spoonful of tar that is involved. The section devoted to dialectic materialism expresses a number of conceptions monstrous from the Marxist standpoint, whose aim, it is now clear, was to prepare the ground for a political bloc. In view of the stubbornness with which Shachtman persists that I seized upon the article as a pretext, let me once again quote the central passage in the section of interest to us:

> … nor has anyone yet demonstrated that agreement or disagreement on the more abstract doctrines of dialectic materialism necessarily affects (!) today's and tomorrow's concrete political issues – and political parties, programs and struggles are based on such concrete issues.
>
> *The New International*, January 1939, p. 7

Isn't this alone sufficient? What is above all astonishing is this formula, unworthy of revolutionists: '… political parties, programs and struggles are based on such concrete issues'. What parties? What programs? What struggles? All parties and all programs are here lumped together. The party of the proletariat is a party unlike all the rest. It is not at all based upon 'such concrete issues'. In its very foundation it is diametrically opposed to the parties of bourgeois horse-traders and petty-bourgeois rag patchers. Its task is the preparation of a social revolution and the regeneration of mankind on new material and moral foundations. In order not to give way under the pressure of bourgeois public opinion and police repression, the proletarian revolutionist, a leader all the more, requires a clear, far-sighted, completely thought-out world outlook.

Only upon the basis of a unified Marxist conception is it possible to correctly approach 'concrete' questions.

Precisely here begins Shachtman's betrayal – not a mere mistake as I wished to believe last year; but, it is now clear, an outright theoretical betrayal. Following in the footsteps of Burnham, Shachtman teaches the young revolutionary party that 'no one has yet demonstrated' presumably that dialectic materialism affects the political activity of the party. 'No one has yet demonstrated', in other words, that Marxism is of any use in the struggle of the proletariat. The party consequently does not have the least motive for acquiring and defending dialectic materialism. This is nothing else than renunciation of Marxism, of scientific method in general, a wretched capitulation to empiricism. Precisely this constitutes the philosophic bloc of Shachtman with Burnham and through Burnham with the priests of bourgeois 'Science'. It is precisely this and only this to which I referred in my January 20 letter of last year …

The Abstract and the Concrete; Economics and Politics

The most lamentable section of Shachtman's lamentable opus is the chapter, The State and the Character of the War.

'What then is our position?' asks the author. 'Simply this: It is impossible to deduce directly our policy towards a specific war from an abstract characterization of the class character of the state involved in the war, more particularly, from the property forms prevailing in that state. Our policy must flow from a concrete examination of the character of the war in relation to the interests of the international socialist revolution'. (*Loc. cit.*, p. 13. My emphasis).

What a muddle! What a tangle of sophistry! If it is impossible to deduce our policy directly from the class character of a state, then why can't this be done non-directly? Why must the analysis of the character of the state be abstract whereas the analysis of the character of the war is concrete? Formally speaking, one can say with equal, in fact with much more right, that our policy in relation to the USSR can be deduced not from an abstract characterization of war as 'imperialist', but only from a concrete analysis of the character of the state in the given historical situation. The fundamental sophistry upon which Shachtman constructs everything else is simple enough: In as much as the economic basis determines events in the super-structure not immediately; inasmuch as the mere class characterization of the state is not enough to solve the practical tasks, therefore … therefore we can get along without examining economics and the class nature of the state; by replacing them, as Shachtman phrases it in his journalistic jargon, with the 'realities of living events'. (*Loc. cit.*, p. 14).

The very same artifice circulated by Shachtman to justify his philosophic bloc with Burnham (dialectic materialism determines our politics not immediately, consequently ... it does not in general affect the 'concrete political tasks'), is repeated here word for word in relation to Marxist sociology: Inasmuch as property forms determine the policy of a state not immediately it is possible therefore to throw Marxist sociology overboard in general in determining 'concrete political tasks'.

But why stop there? Since the law of labor value determines prices not 'directly' and not 'immediately'; since the laws of natural selection determine not 'directly' and not 'immediately' the birth of a suckling pig; since the laws of gravity determine not 'directly' and not 'immediately' the tumble of a drunken policeman down a flight of stairs, therefore ... therefore let us leave Marx, Darwin, Newton, and all the other lovers of 'abstractions' to collect dust on a shelf. This is nothing less than the solemn burial of science for, after all, the entire course of the development of science proceeds from 'direct' and 'immediate' causes to the more remote and profound ones, from multiple varieties and kaleidoscopic events – to the unity of the driving forces.

The law of labor value determines prices not 'immediately', but it nevertheless does determine them. Such 'concrete' phenomena as the bankruptcy of the New Deal find their explanation in the final analysis in the 'abstract' law of value. Roosevelt does not know this, but a Marxist dare not proceed without knowing it. Not immediately but through a whole series of intermediate factors and their reciprocal interaction, property forms determine not only politics but also morality. A proletarian politician seeking to ignore the class nature of the state would invariably end up like the policeman who ignores the laws of gravitation; that is, by smashing his nose.

Shachtman obviously does not take into account the distinction between the abstract and the concrete. Striving toward concreteness, our mind operates with abstractions. Even 'this', 'given', 'concrete' dog is an abstraction because it proceeds to change, for example, by dropping its tail the 'moment' we point a finger at it. Concreteness is a relative concept and not an absolute one: what is concrete in one case turns out to be abstract in another: that is, insufficiently defined for a given purpose. In order to obtain a concept 'concrete' enough for a given need it is necessary to correlate several abstractions into one – just as in reproducing a segment of life upon the screen, which is a picture in movement, it is necessary to combine a number of still photographs.

The concrete is a combination of abstractions – not an arbitrary or subjective combination but one that corresponds to the laws of the movement of a given phenomenon.

'The interests of the international socialist revolution', to which Shachtman appeals against the class nature of the state, represent in this given instance the vaguest of all abstractions. After all, the question which occupies us is precisely this, in what concrete way can we further the interests of the revolution? Nor would it be amiss to remember, too, that the task of the socialist revolution is to create a workers' state. Before talking about the socialist revolution it is necessary consequently to learn how to distinguish between such 'abstractions' as the bourgeoisie and the proletariat, the capitalist state and the workers' state.

Shachtman indeed squanders his own time and that of others in proving that nationalized property does not determine 'in and of itself', 'automatically', 'directly', 'immediately' the policies of the Kremlin. On the question as to how the economic 'base' determines the political, juridical, philosophical, artistic and so on 'superstructure' there exists a rich Marxist literature. The opinion that economics presumably determines directly and immediately the creativeness of a composer or even the verdict of a judge, represents a hoary caricature of Marxism which the bourgeois professordom of all countries has circulated time out of end to mask their intellectual impotence.[5]

As for the question which immediately concerns us, the interrelationship between the social foundations of the Soviet state and the policy of the Kremlin, let me remind the absent-minded Shachtman that for seventeen years we have already been establishing, publicly, the growing contradiction between the foundation laid down by the October Revolution and the tendencies of the state 'superstructure'. We have followed step by step the increasing independence of the bureaucracy from the Soviet proletariat and the growth of its dependence upon other classes and groups both inside and outside the country. Just what does Shachtman wish to add in this sphere to the analysis already made?

However, although economics determines politics not directly or immediately, but only in the last analysis, nevertheless economics does determine politics. The Marxists affirm precisely this in contrast to the bourgeois professors and their disciples. While analyzing and exposing the growing political independence of the bureaucracy from the proletariat, we have never lost sight of the objective social boundaries of this 'independence'; namely, nationalized property supplemented by the monopoly of foreign trade.

It is astonishing! Shachtman continues to support the slogan for a political revolution against the Soviet bureaucracy. Has he ever seriously thought out the meaning of this slogan? If we hold that the social foundations laid down

5 To young comrades I recommend that they study on this question the works of Engels (*Anti-Dühring*), Plekhanov and Antonio Labriola. – *L.T.*

by the October Revolution were 'automatically' reflected in the policy of the state, then why would a revolution against the bureaucracy be necessary? If the USSR, on the other hand, has completely ceased being a workers' state, not a political revolution would be required but a social revolution. Shachtman consequently continues to defend the slogan which follows (1) from the character of the USSR as a workers' state and (2) from the irreconcilable antagonism between the social foundations of the state and the bureaucracy. But as he repeats this slogan, he tries to undermine its theoretical foundation. Is it perhaps in order to demonstrate once again the independence of his politics from scientific 'abstractions'?

Under the guise of waging a struggle against the bourgeois caricature of dialectic materialism, Shachtman throws the doors wide open to historical idealism. Property forms and the class character of the state are a matter of indifference to him in analyzing the policy of a government. The state itself appears to him an animal of indiscriminate sex. Both feet planted firmly on this bed of chicken feathers, Shachtman pompously explains to us – today in the year 1940 – that in addition to the nationalized property there is also the Bonapartist filth and their reactionary politics. How new! Did Shachtman perchance think that he was speaking in a nursery ...

What does 'degenerated workers' state' signify in our program? To this question our program responds with a degree of concreteness which is wholly adequate for solving the question of the defense of the USSR; namely: (1) those traits which in 1920 were a 'bureaucratic deformation' of the soviet system have now become an independent bureaucratic regime which has devoured the soviets; (2) the dictatorship of the bureaucracy, incompatible with the internal and international tasks of socialism, has introduced and continues to introduce profound deformations in the economic life of the country as well; (3) basically, however, the system of planned economy, on the foundation of state ownership of the means of production, has been preserved and continues to remain a colossal conquest of mankind. The defeat of the USSR in a war with imperialism would signify not solely the liquidation of the bureaucratic dictatorship, but of the planned state economy; and the dismemberment of the country into spheres of influence; and a new stabilization of imperialism; and a new weakening of the world proletariat.

From the circumstance that the 'bureaucratic' deformation has grown into a regime of bureaucratic autocracy we draw the conclusion that the defense of the workers through their trade unions (which have undergone the self-same degeneration as the state) is today in contrast to 1920 completely unrealistic; it is necessary to overthrow the bureaucracy; this task can be carried out only by creating an illegal Bolshevik party in the USSR.

From the circumstance that the degeneration of the political system has not yet led to the destruction of planned state economy, we draw the conclusion that it is still the duty of the world proletariat to defend the USSR against imperialism and to aid the Soviet proletariat in its struggle against the bureaucracy.

Just what in our definition of the USSR does Shachtman find abstract? What concrete amendments does he propose? If the dialectic teaches us that 'truth is always concrete' then this law applies with equal force to criticism. It is not enough to label a definition abstract. It is necessary to point out exactly what it lacks. Otherwise criticism itself becomes sterile. Instead of concretizing or changing the definition which he claims is abstract, Shachtman replaces it with a vacuum. That's not enough. A vacuum, even the most pretentious vacuum, must be recognized as the worst of all abstractions – it can be filled with any content. Small wonder that the theoretical vacuum, in displacing the class analysis, has sucked in the politics of impressionism and adventurism.

'Concentrated Economics'

Shachtman goes on to quote Lenin's words that 'politics is concentrated economics' and that in this sense 'politics cannot but take primacy over economics'. From Lenin's words Shachtman directs at me the moral that I, if you please, am interested only in 'economics' (nationalized means of production) and skip over 'politics'. This second effort to exploit Lenin is not superior to the first. Shachtman's mistake here assumes truly vast proportions! Lenin meant: when economic processes, tasks and interests acquire a conscious and generalized ('concentrated') character, they enter the sphere of politics by virtue of this very fact, and constitute the essence of politics. In this sense politics as concentrated economics rises above the day-to-day atomized, unconscious and ungeneralized economic activity.

The correctness of politics from the Marxist standpoint is determined precisely to the extent that it profoundly and all-sidedly 'concentrates' economics: that is, expresses the progressive tendencies of its development. That is why we base our politics first and foremost upon our analysis of property forms and class relationships. A more detailed and concrete analysis of the factors in the 'superstructure' is possible for us only on this theoretical basis. Thus, for example, were we to accuse an opposing faction of 'bureaucratic conservatism' we would immediately seek the social, i.e. class roots of this phenomenon. Any other procedure would brand us as 'Platonic' Marxists, if not simply noisy mimics.

'Politics is concentrated economics'. This proposition one should think applies to the Kremlin too. Or, in exception to the general law, is the policy of the Moscow government not 'concentrated economics' but a manifestation of the bureaucracy's free will? Our attempt to reduce the politics of the Kremlin to nationalized economy, refracted through the interests of the bureaucracy, provokes frantic resistance from Shachtman. He takes his guidance in relation to the USSR not from the conscious generalization of economics but from 'observing the realities of living events'; i.e. from rule of thumb, improvisations, sympathies and antipathies. He counterpoises this impressionistic policy to our sociologically grounded policy and accuses us at the same time of … ignoring politics. Incredible but true! To be sure, in the final analysis Shachtman's weak-kneed and capricious politics is likewise the 'concentrated' expression of economics but, alas, it is the economics of the declassed petty bourgeoisie.

Comparison with Bourgeois Wars

Shachtman reminds us that bourgeois wars were at one time progressive and that in another period they became reactionary and that therefore it is not enough to give the class definition of a state engaged in war. This proposition does not clarify the question but muddles it. Bourgeois wars could be progressive only at a time when the entire bourgeois regime was progressive; in other words, at a time when bourgeois property in contradistinction to feudal property was a progressive and constructive factor. Bourgeois wars became reactionary when bourgeois property became a brake on development. Does Shachtman wish to say in relation to the USSR that the state ownership of the means of production has become a brake upon development and that the extension of this form of property to other countries constitutes economic reaction? Shachtman obviously does not want to say this. He simply does not draw the logical conclusion to his own thoughts.

The example of national bourgeois wars does indeed offer a very instructive lesson, but Shachtman passes it by unconcernedly. Marx and Engels were striving for a unified German republic. In the war of 1870–71 they stood on the side of the Germans despite the fact that the struggle for unification was exploited and distorted by the dynastic parasites.

Shachtman refers to the fact that Marx and Engels immediately turned against Prussia upon the annexation of Alsace-Lorraine. But this turn only illustrates our standpoint all the more lucidly. It is impermissible to forget for a moment that what was in question was a war between two bourgeois states. Thus both camps had a common class denominator. To decide which of the two sides was the 'lesser evil' – insofar at as history generally left any room for choice – was possible only on the basis of supplementary factors. On the German side it was a question of creating a national bourgeois state as an economic and cultural arena. The national state during that period was a progressive historical factor. To that extent Marx and Engels stood on the side of the Germans despite Hohenzollern and his junkers. The annexation of Alsace-Lorraine violated the principle of the national state in regard to France as well as Germany and laid the basis for a war of revenge. Marx and Engels, naturally, turned sharply against Prussia. They did not thereby at all incur the risk of rendering service to an inferior system of economy as against a superior one since in both camps, we repeat, bourgeois relations prevailed. If France had been a workers' state in 1870, then Marx and Engels would have been for France from the very beginning, inasmuch as they – one feels abashed again that this must be mentioned – guided themselves in all their activity by the class criterion.

Today in the old capitalist countries the solving of national tasks is no longer at stake at all. On the contrary mankind is suffering from the contradiction between the productive forces and the too narrow framework of the national state. Planned economy on the basis of socialized property freed from national boundaries is the task of the international proletariat, above all – in Europe. It is precisely this task which is expressed in our slogan, 'For the Socialist United States of Europe!' The expropriation of the property owners in Poland as in Finland is a progressive factor in and of itself. The bureaucratic methods of the Kremlin occupy the very same place in this process as did the dynastic methods of Hohenzollern – in the unification of Germany. Whenever we are confronted with the necessity of choosing between the defense of reactionary property forms through reactionary measures and the introduction of progressive property forms through bureaucratic measures, we do not at all place both sides on the same plane, but choose the lesser evil. In this there is no more 'capitulation' to Stalinism than there was capitulation to Hohenzollern in the policy of Marx and Engels. It is scarcely necessary to add that the role of Hohenzollern in the war of 1870–71 justified neither the general historical role of the dynasty nor so much as its existence.

Conjunctural Defeatism, or Columbus and the Egg

... Lenin deduced the policy of defeatism from the imperialist character of the war; but he did not stop there. He deduced the imperialist character of the war from a specific stage in the development of the capitalist regime and its ruling class. Since the character of the war is determined precisely by the class character of society and the state, Lenin recommended that in determining our policy in regard to imperialist war we abstract ourselves from such 'concrete' circumstances as democracy and monarchy, as aggression and national defense. In opposition to this Shachtman proposes that we deduce defeatism from conjunctural conditions. This defeatism is indifferent to the class character of the USSR and of Finland. Enough for it are the reactionary features of the bureaucracy and the 'aggression'. If France, England or the United States sends airplanes and guns to Finland, this has no bearing in the determination of Shachtman's politics. But if British troops land in Finland, then Shachtman will place a thermometer under Chamberlain's tongue and determine Chamberlain's intentions – whether he aims only to save Finland from the Kremlin's imperialistic politics or whether in addition he aims to over throw the 'last conquest of the October Revolution'. Strictly in accordance with the readings of the thermometer, Shachtman, the defeatist, is ready to change himself into a defensist. This is what it means to replace abstract principles with the 'realities of living events'.

Shachtman, as we have already seen, persistently demands the citation of precedents: when and where in the past have the leaders of the opposition manifested petty-bourgeois opportunism? The reply which I have already given him on this score must be supplemented here with two letters which we sent each other on the question of defensism and methods of defensism in connection with the events of the Spanish Revolution. On September 18, 1937, Shachtman wrote me:

> ... You say, 'If we would have a member in the Cortes he would vote against the military budget of Negrin.' Unless this is a typographical error it seems to us to be a non-sequitur. If, as we all contend, the element of an imperialist war is not dominant at the present time in the Spanish struggle, and if instead the decisive element is still the struggle between the decaying bourgeois democracy, with all that it involves, on the one side, and fascism on the other, and further if we are obliged to give military assistance to the struggle against fascism, we don't see how it would be possible to vote in the Cortes against the military budget ... If a Bolshevik-Leninist on the Huesca front were asked by a Socialist comrade why his representative in the Cortes voted against the proposal by Negrin to devote a million pesetas to the purchase of rifles for the front, what would this Bolshevik-Leninist reply? It doesn't seem to us that he would have an effective answer ... (My emphasis)

This letter astounded me. Shachtman was willing to express confidence in the perfidious Negrin government on the purely negative basis that the 'element of an imperialist war' was not dominant in Spain.

On September 20, 1937, I replied to Shachtman:

> To vote the military budget of the Negrin government signifies to vote him political confidence ... To do it would be a crime. How we explain our vote to the anarchist workers? Very simply: We have not the slightest confidence in the capacity of this government to conduct the war and assure victory. We accuse this government of protecting the rich and starving the poor. This government must be smashed. So long as we are not strong enough to replace it, we are fighting under its command. But on every occasion we express openly our non-confidence in it: it is the only one possibility to mobilize the masses politically against this government and to prepare its overthrow. Any other politics would be a betrayal of the revolution ...

Having revealed such odd perspicacity in understanding the events in Poland, Shachtman descends upon me with redoubled authority in connection with events in Finland. In my article A Petty-Bourgeois Opposition, I wrote that 'the Soviet-Finnish War is apparently beginning to be supplemented by a civil war in which the Red Army finds itself at a given stage in the same camp as the Finnish petty peasants and the workers ...'. This extremely cautious formula did not meet with the approval of my unsparing judge. My evaluation of events in Poland had already taken him off balance. 'I find even less (proof) for your – how shall I put it? – astonishing remarks about Finland', writes Shachtman on page 16 of his Letter. I am very sorry that Shachtman chooses to become astonished rather than think things out.

In the Baltic states the Kremlin confined its tasks to making strategical gains with the unquestionable calculation that in the future these strategic military bases will permit the sovietization of these former sections of the Czarist empire too. These successes in the Baltic, achieved by diplomatic threat, met with resistance, however, from Finland. To reconcile itself to this resistance would have meant that the Kremlin placed in jeopardy its 'prestige' and thereby its successes in Estonia, Latvia and Lithuania. Thus contrary to its initial plans the Kremlin felt compelled to resort to armed force. From this fact every thinking person posed to himself the following question: Does the Kremlin wish only to frighten the Finnish bourgeoisie and force them to make concessions or must it now go further? To this question naturally there could be no 'automatic' answer. It was necessary – in the light of general tendencies – to orient oneself upon concrete symptoms. The leaders of the opposition are incapable of this.

Military operations began on November 30. That very same day the Central Committee of the Finnish Communist Party, undoubtedly located in either Leningrad or Moscow, issued a radio manifesto to the toiling people of Finland. This manifesto proclaimed: 'For the second time in the history of Finland the Finnish working class is beginning a struggle against the yoke of the plutocracy. The first experience of the workers and peasants in 1918 terminated in the victory of the capitalists and the landlords. But this time … the toiling people must win'.

This manifesto alone clearly indicated that not an attempt to scare the bourgeois government of Finland was involved, but a plan to provoke insurrection in the country and to supplement the invasion of the Red Army with civil war.

The declaration of the so-called People's Government published on December 2 states: 'In different parts of the country the people have already risen and proclaimed the creation of a democratic republic'. This assertion is obviously a fabrication, otherwise the manifesto would have mentioned the places where the attempts at insurrection took place. It is possible, however, that isolated attempts, prepared from without, ended in failure and that precisely because of this it was deemed best not to go into details. In any case, the news concerning 'insurrections' constituted a call to insurrection. Moreover, the declaration carried information concerning the formation of 'the first Finnish corps which in the course of coming battles will be enlarged by volunteers from the ranks of revolutionary workers and peasants'. Whether there were one thousand men in this 'corps' or only one hundred, the meaning of the 'corps' in determining the policies of the Kremlin was incontestable. At the same time cable dispatches reported the expropriation of large landholders in the border regions. There is not the slightest ground to doubt that this is just what took place during the first advance of the Red Army. But even if these dispatches are considered fabrications, they completely preserve their meaning as a call for an agrarian revolution. Thus I had every justification to declare that 'The Soviet-Finnish War is apparently beginning to be supplemented by a civil war'. At the beginning of December, true enough, I had at my disposal only a part of these facts. But against the background of the general situation, and I take the liberty to add, with the aid of an understanding of its internal logic, the isolated symptoms enabled me to draw the necessary conclusions concerning the direction of the entire struggle. Without such semi-*a priori* conclusions one can be a rationalizing observer but in no case an active participant in events. But why did the appeal of the 'People's Government' fail to bring immediate mass response? For three reasons: first, Finland is dominated completely by a reactionary military machine which is supported not only by the bourgeoisie but by the top layers of the peasantry and the labor bureaucracy; secondly, the policy of the Kremlin succeeded in transforming the Finnish Communist Party into an insignificant factor; thirdly, the regime of the USSR is in no way capable of arousing enthusiasm among the Finnish toiling masses. Even in the Ukraine from 1918 to 1920 the peasants responded very slowly to appeals to seize the estates of the landlords because the local soviet power was still weak and every success of the Whites brought about ruthless punitive expeditions. All the less reason is there for surprise that the Finnish poor peasants delay in responding to an appeal for an agrarian revolution. To set the peasants in motion, serious successes of the Red Army are required. But during the first badly prepared advance the Red Army suffered only failures. Under such conditions there could not even be talk of the peasants rising. It was impossible to expect an independent civil war in Finland at the given stage: my calculations spoke quite precisely of supplementing military operations by measures of civil war. I have in mind – at least until the Finnish army is annihilated – only the occupied territory and the nearby regions. Today on January 17 as I write these lines dispatches from a Finnish source report that one of the border provinces has been invaded by detachments of Finnish émigrés and that brother is literally killing brother there. What is this if not an episode in a civil war? In any case there can be no doubt that a new advance of the Red Army into Finland will confirm at every step our general appraisal of the war. Shachtman has neither an analysis of the events nor the hint of a prognosis. He confines himself to noble indignation and for this reason at every step he sinks deeper into the mire.

The appeal of the 'People's Government' calls for workers' control. What can this mean! exclaims Shachtman. There is no workers' control in the USSR; whence will it come in Finland? Sad to say, Shachtman reveals complete lack of understanding of the situation. In the USSR workers' control is a stage long ago completed. From control over the bourgeoisie there they passed to management of nationalized production. From the management of workers – to the command of the bureaucracy. New workers' control would now signify control over the bureaucracy. This cannot be established except as the result of a successful uprising against the bureaucracy. In Finland, workers' control still signifies nothing more than crowding out the native bourgeoisie, whose place the bureaucracy proposes to take. Furthermore one should not think that the Kremlin is so stupid as to attempt ruling eastern Poland or Finland by means of imported commissars. Of greatest urgency to the Kremlin is the extraction of a new administrative apparatus from among the toiling population of the occupied areas. This task can be solved only in several stages. The first stage is the peasant committees and the committees of workers' control.

Shachtman clutches eagerly even at the fact that Kuusinen's program 'is, formally, the program of a bourgeois "democracy"'. Does he mean to say by this that the Kremlin is more interested in establishing bourgeois democracy in Finland than in drawing Finland into the framework of the USSR? Shachtman himself doesn't know what he wants to say. In Spain, which Moscow did not prepare for union with the USSR, it was actually a question of demonstrating the ability of the Kremlin to safeguard bourgeois democracy against proletarian revolution. This task flowed from the interests of the Kremlin bureaucracy in that particular international situation. Today the situation is a different one. The Kremlin is not preparing to demonstrate its usefulness to France, England and the United States. As its actions have proved, it has firmly decided to sovietize Finland – at once or in two stages. The program of the Kuusinen government, even if approached from a 'formal' point of view does not differ from the program of the Bolsheviks in November 1917. True enough, Shachtman makes much of the fact that I generally place significance on the manifesto of the 'idiot' Kuusinen. However, I shall take the liberty of considering that the 'idiot' Kuusinen acting on the ukase of the Kremlin and with the support of the Red Army represents a far more serious political factor than scores of superficial wise acres who refuse to think through the internal logic (dialectics) of events.

As a result of his remarkable analysis, Shachtman this time openly proposes a defeatist policy in relation to the USSR, adding (for emergency use) that he does not at all cease to be a 'patriot of his class'. We are happy to get the information. But the trouble is that Dan, the leader of the Mensheviks, as far back as November 12 wrote that in the event the Soviet Union invaded Finland the world proletariat 'must take a definitive defeatist position in relation to this violation' (*Sozialisticheski Vestnik*, No. 19–20, p. 43). It is necessary to add that throughout the Kerensky regime, Dan was a rabid defensist; he failed to be a defeatist even under the Czar. Only the invasion of Finland by the Red Army has turned Dan into a defeatist. Naturally he does not thereby cease to be a 'patriot of his class'. What class? This question is not an uninteresting one. So far as the analysis of events is concerned Shachtman disagrees with Dan who is closer to the theater of action and cannot replace facts with fiction; by way of compensation, where the 'concrete political conclusions' are concerned, Shachtman has turned out to be a 'patriot' of the very same time as Dan. In Marxist sociology this class, if the opposition will permit me, this class is called the petty bourgeoisie …

5 Open Letter to James Burnham[6]

(1940, excerpts)

Leon Trotsky

Dear Comrade:

You have expressed as your reaction to my article on the petty-bourgeois opposition, I have been informed, that you do not intend to argue over the dialectic with me and that you will discuss only the 'concrete questions'. 'I stopped arguing about religion long ago', you added ironically …

Is There Logic in Identifying Logic with Religion?

As I understand this, your words imply that the dialectic of Marx, Engels and Lenin belongs to the sphere of religion. What does this assertion signify? The dialectic, permit me to recall once again, is the *logic of evolution*. Just as a machine shop in a plant supplies instruments for all departments, so logic is indispensable for all spheres of human knowledge. If you do not consider logic in general to be a religious prejudice (sad to say, the self-contradictory writings of the opposition incline one more and more toward this lamentable idea), then just which logic do you accept? I know of two systems of logic worthy of attention: the logic of Aristotle (formal logic) and the logic of Hegel (the dialectic). Aristotelian logic takes as its starting point immutable objects and phenomena. The scientific thought of our epoch studies all phenomena in their origin, change and disintegration. Do you hold that the progress of the sciences, including Darwinism, Marxism, modern physics, chemistry, etc., has not influenced in any way the forms of our thought? In other words, do you hold that in a world where everything changes, the syllogism alone remains unchanging and eternal? The Gospel according to St. John begins with the words: 'In the beginning was the Word', i.e. in the beginning was Reason or the Word (reason expressed in the word, namely, the syllogism). To St. John the syllogism is one of

6 Trotsky 1940b.

the literary pseudonyms for God. If you consider that the syllogism as immutable, i.e. has neither origin nor development, then it signifies that to you it is the product of divine revelation. But if you acknowledge that the logical forms of our thought develop in the process of our adaptation to nature, then please take the trouble to in form us just who following Aristotle analyzed and systematized the subsequent progress of logic. So long as you do not clarify this point, I shall take the liberty of asserting that to identify logic (the dialectic) with religion reveals utter ignorance and superficiality in the basic questions of human thought …

'Science' against Marxism and 'Experiments' against Program

Accusing your opponents of 'bureaucratic conservatism' (a bare psychological abstraction insofar as no specific social interests are shown underlying this 'conservatism'), you demand in your document that conservative politics be replaced by 'critical and experimental politics – in a word, scientific politics' (p. 32). This statement, at first glance so innocent and meaningless with all its pompousness, is in itself a complete exposure. You don't speak of Marxist politics. You don't speak of proletarian politics. You speak of 'experimental', 'critical', 'scientific' politics. Why this pretentious and deliberately abstruse terminology so unusual in our ranks? I shall tell you. It is the product of your adaptation, comrade Burnham, to bourgeois public opinion, and the adaptation of Shachtman and Abern to your adaptation. Marxism is no longer fashionable among the broad circles of bourgeois intellectuals. Moreover if one should mention Marxism, God forbid, he might be taken for a dialectic materialist. It is better to avoid this discredited word. What to replace it with? Why, of course, with 'science', even with Science capitalized. And science, as everybody knows, is based on 'criticism' and 'experiments'. It has its own ring; so solid, so tolerant, so unsectarian, so professorial! With this formula one can enter any democratic salon.

Reread, please, your own statement once again: 'In place of conservative politics, we must put bold, flexible, critical and experimental politics – in a word, scientific politics'. You couldn't have improved it! But this is precisely the formula which all petty-bourgeois empiricists, all revisionists and, last but not least, all political adventurers have counterpoised to 'narrow', 'limited', 'dogmatic' and 'conservative' Marxism.

Buffon once said: The style is the man. Political terminology is not only the man but the party. Terminology is one of the elements of the class struggle. Only lifeless pedants can fail to understand this. In your document you painstakingly expunge – yes, no one else but you, comrade Burnham – not only such terms as the dialectic and materialism but also Marxism. You are above all this. You are a man of 'critical', 'experimental' science. For exactly the same reason you culled the label 'imperialism' to describe the foreign policy of the Kremlin. This innovation differentiates you from the too embarrassing terminology of the Fourth International by creating less 'sectarian', less 'religious', less rigorous formulas, common to you and – oh happy coincidence – bourgeois democracy.

You want to experiment? But permit me to remind you that the workers' movement possesses a long history with no lack of experience and, if you prefer, experiments. This experience so dearly bought has been crystallized in the shape of a definite doctrine, the very Marxism whose name you so carefully avoid. Before giving you the right to experiment, the party has the right to ask: What method will you use? Henry Ford would scarcely permit a man to experiment in his plant who had not assimilated the requisite conclusions of the past development of industry and the innumerable experiments already carried out. Furthermore experimental laboratories in factories are carefully segregated from mass production. Far more impermissible even are witch doctor experiments in the sphere of the labor movement – even though conducted under the banner of anonymous 'science'. For us the science of the workers' movement is Marxism …

Theoretical Bewilderment and Political Abstentionism

Throughout all the vacillations and convulsions of the opposition, contradictory though they may be, two general features run like a guiding thread from the pinnacles of theory down to the most trifling political episodes. The first general feature is the absence of a unified conception. The opposition leaders split sociology from dialectic materialism. They split politics from sociology. In the sphere of politics they split our tasks in Poland from our experience in Spain – our tasks in Finland from our position on Poland. History becomes transformed into a series of exceptional incidents; politics becomes transformed into a series of improvisations. We have here, in the full sense of the term, the disintegration of Marxism, the disintegration of theoretical thought, the disintegration of politics into its constituent elements. Empiricism and its foster-brother, impressionism, dominate from top to bottom. That is why the ideological leadership, comrade Burnham, rests with you as an opponent of the dialectic, as an empiricist, unabashed by his empiricism.

Throughout the vacillations and convulsions of the opposition, there is a second general feature intimately bound to the first, namely, a tendency to refrain from active participation, a tendency to self-elimination, to abstentionism, naturally under cover of ultra-radical phrases. You are in favor of overthrowing Hitler and Stalin in Poland; Stalin and Mannerheim in Finland. And until then, you reject both sides *equally*, in other words, you withdraw from the struggle, including the civil war. Your citing the absence of civil war in Finland is only an accidental conjunctural argument. Should the civil war unfold, the opposition will attempt not to notice it, as they tried not to notice it in Poland, or they will declare that inasmuch as the policy of the Moscow bureaucracy is 'imperialist' in character 'we' do not take part in this filthy business. Hot on the trail of 'concrete' political tasks in words, the opposition actually places itself outside the historical process. Your position, comrade Burnham, in relation to the Dies Committee merits attention precisely because it is a graphic expression of this same tendency of abstentionism and bewilderment. Your guiding principle still remains the same: 'Thank you, I don't smoke'.

Naturally, any man, any party and even any class can become bewildered. But with the petty bourgeoisie, bewilderment, especially in the face of great events, is an inescapable and, so to speak, congenital condition. The intellectuals attempt to express their state of bewilderment in the language of 'science'. The contradictory platform of the opposition reflects petty-bourgeois bewilderment expressed in the bombastic language of the intellectuals. There is nothing proletarian about it.

The Petty-Bourgeoisie and Centralism

In the organizational sphere, your views are just as schematic, empiric, non-revolutionary as in the sphere of theory and politics. A Stolberg, lantern in hand, chases after an ideal revolution, unaccompanied by any excesses, and guaranteed against Thermidor and counter-revolution; you, likewise, seek an ideal party democracy which would secure forever and for everybody the possibility of saying and doing whatever popped into his head, and which would insure the party against bureaucratic degeneration. You overlook a trifle, namely, that the party is not an arena for the assertion of free individuality, but an instrument of the proletarian revolution; that only a victorious revolution is capable of preventing the degeneration not only of the party but of the proletariat itself and of modern civilization as a whole. You do not see that our American section is not sick from too much centralism – it is laughable even to talk about it – but from a monstrous abuse and distortion of democracy on the part of petty-bourgeois elements. This is at the root of the present crisis.

A worker spends his day at the factory. He has comparatively few hours left for the party. At the meetings he is interested in learning the most important things: the correct evaluation of the situation and the political conclusions. He values those leaders who do this in the clearest and the most precise form and who keep in step with events. Petty-bourgeois, and especially declassed elements, divorced from the proletariat, vegetate in an artificial and shut-in environment. They have ample time to dabble in politics or its substitute. They pick out faults, exchange all sorts of tidbits and gossip concerning happenings among the party 'tops'. They always locate a leader who initiates them into all the 'secrets'. Discussion is their native element. No amount of democracy is ever enough for them. For their war of words they seek the fourth dimension. They become jittery, they revolve in a vicious circle, and they quench their thirst with salt water. Do you want to know the organizational program of the opposition? It consists of a mad hunt for the fourth dimension of party democracy. In practice this means burying politics beneath discussion; and burying centralism beneath the anarchy of the intellectual circles. When a few thousand workers join the party, they will call the petty-bourgeois anarchists severely to order. The sooner, the better.

Conclusions

Why do I address you and not the other leaders of the opposition? Because you are the ideological leader of the bloc. Comrade Abern's faction, destitute of a program and a banner, is ever in need of cover. At one time Shachtman served as cover, then came Muste with Spector, and now you, with Shachtman adapting himself to you. Your ideology I consider the expression of bourgeois influence in the proletariat.

To some comrades, the tone of this letter may perhaps seem too sharp. Yet, let me confess, I did everything in my power to restrain myself. For, after all, it is a question of nothing more or less than an attempt to reject, disqualify and overthrow the theoretical foundations, the political principles and organizational methods of our movement.

In reaction to my previous article, comrade Abern, it has been reported, remarked: 'This means split'. Such a response merely demonstrates that Abern lacks devotion to the party and the Fourth International; he is a circle man. In any case, threats of split will not deter us from presenting a Marxist analysis of the differences. For us Marxists, it is a question not of split but of educating the party. It is my firm hope that the coming convention will ruthlessly repulse the revisionists.

The convention, in my opinion, must declare categorically that in their attempts to divorce sociology from dialectic materialism and politics from sociology, the leaders of the opposition have broken from Marxism and become the transmitting mechanism for petty-bourgeois empiricism. While reaffirming, decisively and completely, its loyalty to the Marxist doctrine and the political and organizational methods of Bolshevism, while binding the editorial boards of its official publications to promulgate and defend this doctrine and these methods, the party will, of course, extend the pages of its publications in the future to those of its members who consider themselves capable of adding something new to the doctrine of Marxism. But it will not permit a game of hide-and-seek with Marxism and light-minded gibes concerning it.

The politics of a party has a class character. Without a class analysis of the state, the parties and ideological tendencies, it is impossible to arrive at a correct political orientation. The party must condemn as vulgar opportunism the attempt to determine policies in relation to the USSR from incident to incident and independently of the class nature of the Soviet state.

The disintegration of capitalism, which engenders sharp dissatisfaction among the petty bourgeoisie and drives its bottom layers to the left, opens up broad possibilities but it also contains grave dangers. The Fourth International needs only those emigrants from the petty bourgeoisie who have broken completely with their social past and who have come over decisively to the standpoint of the proletariat.

This theoretical and political transit must be accompanied by an actual break with the old environment and the establishment of intimate ties with workers, in particular, by participation in the recruitment and education of proletarians for their party. Emigrants from the petty-bourgeois milieu who prove incapable of settling in the proletarian milieu must after the lapse of a certain period of time be transferred from membership in the party to the status of sympathizers.

Members of the party untested in the class struggle must not be placed in responsible positions. No matter how talented and devoted to socialism an emigrant from the bourgeois milieu may be, before becoming a teacher, he must first go to school in the working class. Young intellectuals must not be placed at the head of the intellectual youth but sent out into the provinces for a few years, into the purely proletarian centers, for hard practical work.

The class composition of the party must correspond to its class program. The American section of the Fourth International will either become proletarian or it will cease to exist.

∴

Comrade Burnham! If we can arrive at an agreement with you on the basis of these principles, then without difficulty we shall find a correct policy in relation to Poland, Finland and even India. At the same time, I pledge myself to help you conduct a struggle against any manifestations whatsoever of bureaucratism and conservatism. These in my opinion are the conditions necessary to end the present crisis.

With Bolshevik greetings,
L. TROTSKY

6 Science and Style: A Reply to Comrade Trotsky[7]

(1940, excerpts)

James Burnham

Dear Comrade Trotsky:

I find the Open Letter which you have addressed nominally to me more than a little disarming. It is not easy, I confess, for me to undertake an answer.

In reading it I was reminded of a conversation I had some while ago with one of our good comrades from Central Europe. We were discussing, in that idle and profligate way we intellectuals have, the possible conflicts between the aesthetic sense, the feeling for beauty, and the demands of political action. He told me a story.

A number of years ago, the country in which he lived was going through a period of social crisis. The masses were surging forward, heading, it seemed, toward revolt. One morning, near the height of the movement, a crowd of many thousand workers gathered on one side of the wonderful great square of the capital city of that country. Our comrade was assigned as captain to direct one wing of the workers' detachments.

The sky was dark blue, with the white morning sun throwing across the square the shadows of the buildings that lined its sides. From the side of the square opposite the workers, the troops of the police filed out and took formation: in straight rows, mounted on their tense horses, equipment gleaming. At the shout of command, in a single swift gesture their sabers were drawn, and flashed in the rays of that white sun. The second command came: forward against the workers.

The instant had come for reply: for our comrade, to launch his wing of the workers into a driving counter-attack. But for a long moment he found his will paralyzed and his voice stopped by the sensuous beauty of the unfolded scene. And all that day, while the bitter struggle lasted – more than fifty were killed that day, hundreds wounded, our comrade among them – he could not forget that sun, those shadows, that blue sky, those whirling horses and flashing sabers.

7 Burnham 1940a.

So, too, on this verbal battleground, pale reflex – and indispensable spark – of the battles in the streets, I, when all my will should be concentrated in launching my ranked arguments into counter-attack against your letter (so wrong, so false, so very false), find I must stop awhile in wonder: at the technical perfection of the verbal structure you have created, the dynamic sweep of your rhetoric, the burning expression of your unconquerable devotion to the socialist ideal, the sudden, witty, flashing metaphors that sparkle through your pages.

How unpleasant and thankless a duty to submit that splendid structure to the dissolving acids from those two so pedestrian, so unromantic flasks: logic and science!

Comrade Trotsky, while reading and thinking about this Letter, I recalled also the first time that I had ever given really serious attention to your work: in a lengthy review of the first volume of your *History*, published in the July 1932 issue of *The Symposium*. I re-read that review, which I had not done for many years. There, too, I found that I had been compelled to discuss first of all your style, your wonderful style, which in fact I analyzed at considerable length. And I saw more clearly than ever before what is, in my eyes, an important truth: that you have a too literary conception of proof, of evidence; that you deceive yourself into treating persuasive rhetoric as logical demonstration, a brilliant metaphor as argument. *Here, I believe, is the heart of the mystery of the dialectic, as it appears in your books and articles: the dialectic, for you, is a* device of style *– the contrasting epithets, the flowing rhythms, the verbal paradoxes which characterize your way of writing*.

Comrade Trotsky, I will not match metaphors with you. In such a verbal tournament, I concede you the ribbon in advance. Evidence, argument, proof: these only are my weapons.

The Skeleton Undraped

I will now summarize your argument:

With reference to your own position, you assert the following:

a. The philosophy of dialectical materialism is true.
b. Marxian sociology, in particular the Marxian theory of the state, is true.
c. Russia is a workers' state.
d. A tactic of defense of the Russian state in the present war is correct.

With reference to the position of the opposition – or, more exactly, of Burnham who you claim expresses the 'essence' of the opposition – you assert the following:

1. Burnham is a bourgeois democrat.
2. Burnham rejects dialectics.
3. Burnham rejects Marxian sociology, in particular the Marxian theory of the state.
4. Burnham denies that Russia is a workers' state.
5. Burnham's practical politics are 'abstentionist'.
6. Burnham rejects Bolshevik organization theories and methods.

But you not merely assert these individual propositions. You are even more concerned to assert certain connections which you allege hold among these propositions.

With reference to your own position, you thus assert the following additional propositions:

a. From dialectical materialism, it follows that Marxian sociology, in particular the Marxian theory of the state, is true.
b. From the Marxian theory of the state, it follows that Russia is a workers' state.
c. From Russia's being a workers' state, it follows that a tactic of defense of the Russian state in the present war is correct.

With reference to Burnham's position, you assert the following connections:

1. From Burnham's being a bourgeois democrat, it follows that he rejects dialectics.
2. From his rejection of dialectics, it follows that he rejects Marxian sociology, in particular the Marxian theory of the state.
3. From his rejection of the Marxian theory of the state, it follows that he denies that Russia is a workers' state.
4. From his denial that Russia is a workers' state (and from 1 and 2), it follows that his practical politics are 'abstentionist'.
5. From his being a bourgeois democrat and his rejection of dialectics, it follows that he rejects Bolshevik organization theories and methods.

So far as I have been able, I have been scrupulously fair in presenting here your central argument. These 18 propositions constitute that 'unified conception' whose absence you so deplore in the point of view of the opposition. But as soon as these propositions are made explicit, as soon as they are brought to the surface from beneath the shrouds of metaphor and rhetoric, it is clear that each of them stands on its own feet, that each would have to be proved independently of the others. Moreover, the structure of your argument, of your 'unified conception' and 'explanation', stands or falls on the truth of all of these propositions. And who, even of your most ardent supporters, would be so brash as to claim that you have proved all of them to be true?

Examination shows, more specifically, that these 18 propositions are either trivial or irrelevant or obviously false or at the least unproved. It would be wearisome, and unnecessary, to demonstrate this with reference to each of these propositions; every comrade has, indeed, material at his disposal to carry out the analysis for himself. I shall confine my attention to only a few of those which raise special problems.

Dialectics as a Red Herring

... I find about 75 per cent of what Engels wrote in these latter fields to be confused or outmoded by subsequent scientific investigation – in either case of little value. It seems to me (and as a Marxist I do not find it astonishing) that in them Engels was a true son of his generation, the generation of Herbert Spencer and Thomas Huxley, of the popularizers of Darwin who thought that by a metaphorical extension of the hypothesis of biological evolution they had discovered the ultimate key to the mysteries of the universe. Nevertheless, Engels made a real effort to acquaint himself with the philosophy, logic and science of his day, and wrote with this acquaintance in mind.

You, however, serve up to us only a stale re-hash of Engels. The latest scientist admitted to your pages is – Darwin; apart from Aristotle, the only 'logic worthy of attention' is that of – Hegel, the century-dead arch-muddler of human thought. Comrade Trotsky, as we Americans ask: where have you been all these years? During the 125 years since Hegel wrote, science has progressed more than during the entire preceding history of mankind. During that same period, after 2300 years of stability, logic has undergone a revolutionary transformation: a transformation in which Hegel and his ideas have had an influence of exactly zero.

You ask me: 'Do you hold that the progress of the sciences, including Darwinism, Marxism, modern physics, chemistry, etc., have not influenced in any way the forms of our thought?' But it is to yourself that you should address this question, not to me. Of course I hold that they have (and one way that they have influenced it is to show that Hegelian dialectics has nothing whatever to do with science). How the sciences have influenced the forms of thought no one will ever discover by spending even a lifetime on the tortuous syntax of the reactionary absolutist, Hegel, but only by studying modern science and mathematics, and the careful analysts of modern science and mathematics.

In a most sarcastic vein, you keep asking me to 'take the trouble to inform us just who following Aristotle analyzed and systematized the subsequent progress of logic', 'perhaps you will call my attention to those works which should supplant the system of dialectic materialism for the proletariat ...' as if this demand were so obviously impossible of fulfillment that I must collapse like a pricked balloon before it. The sarcasm is misplaced, for the demand is the easiest in the world to fulfill. Do you wish me to prepare a reading list, Comrade Trotsky? It would be long, ranging from the work of the brilliant mathematicians and logicians of the middle of the last century to one climax in the monumental *Principia Mathematica* of Russell and Whitehead (the historic turning point in modern logic), and then spreading out in many directions – one of the most fruitful represented by the scientists, mathematicians and logicians now cooperating in the new *Encyclopedia of Unified Science*. For logic in its narrower sense, C.I. Lewis' *Survey of Symbolic Logic* is an excellent, though not easy, introduction. I am afraid, however, that in all of these works you will find scarcely a single reference to Hegelian (or Marxian) dialectics; nor will you in those of a single reputable contemporary scientist – except the Soviet scientists, whose necks depend upon such references, or one or two Kremlin hangers-on, like J.B.S. Haldane, in other nations. The study of these works would be not uninteresting; but I am afraid that when we finished we would be not much nearer the solution of the question of the role of Russia in the war ...

You tell us that workers, proletarians, are 'naturally inclined to dialectical thinking'. Where are these workers, Comrade Trotsky? It seems to me that you are presenting a very damaging advertisement for dialectics. The only workers I, or anyone else, know anything about are these human beings found in the mines of Kennecott Copper, the mills of US Steel, the ships of the merchant marine ... These workers, in spite of what has been happening in the world, continue to trust John L. Lewis and Citrine and Jouhaux and Stalin, continue to vote Democratic or Republican, continue to believe in capitalism. I think they will change their thinking, perhaps one day very quickly. But I find their thought, for the most part, false or where not false, confused. If this is what you mean by 'dialectical thinking', I can agree with you ...

What are the Issues?

The dominant issues dividing the ranks of our party and the International are not dialectics or sociology or logic. To pose the question in this manner is an evasion or a fraud. It is with the greatest impatience and reluctance that I have written on them to the extent that I have.

The dominant, the fundamental issues, in the present dispute are two, one involving the entire International, the other particularly concerning the Socialist Workers Party.

The first is the central political issue. This has been clarified and simplified by the course of events and the discussion. What it concerns is the problem of the strategical orientation of the Fourth International in the present phase of the Second World War. It is an issue which every single party member can understand clearly, without any obfuscation from Hegel and dialectical foxes.

The practical politics of every active and serious political organization is normally governed by what might be called a strategical focus, an axis around which the major part of agitation and action revolves. The Popular Front, for example, constituted such a focus, or axis, for the Stalinist movement during a number of years: the agitation, actions, proposals, analyses of the CI and its sections revolved around this strategic center. For our movement, during several years, the orientation toward the Second International was such a focus.

Today there are two tendencies in the Fourth International. They are differentiated by the fact that they propose two sharply different strategical orientations, different axes to govern our practical politics.

Trotsky-Cannon propose the strategy of defense of the Stalinist bureaucracy as the lesser evil. It doesn't make any difference what Trotsky-Cannon say about their policies; this is what it comes down to in practice. This focus governs their major specific proposals, their agitation, their interpretation of events, their predictions (not always, not consistently, but on the whole – sufficiently to determine the practical direction), their weighting of agitation (in the *Appeal*, for example), and so on. Let any party member re-trace in his mind the events of the past months, let him read the party press and internal documents, remember the speeches and committee proposals; and he will see for himself how an understanding of this underlying strategical orientation provides a clear pattern which makes the events intelligible.

The opposition, nationally and internationally (for the dispute has of course already spread beyond the borders of our party, as it should), proposes the strategy of the third camp. Any party member who makes a similar review of the actions of the opposition during this period, their proposals and speeches and articles, their interpretations of what is happening in the world, their emphases and stresses, will similarly see for himself how an understanding of this opposed strategical orientation provides an adequate pattern and guide.

The second central issue is the question of the regime in the Socialist Workers Party. This question has been thoroughly treated in the document, The War and Bureaucratic Conservatism. No reply has been made to this document; and it is safe to predict that no serious reply will be forthcoming ...

7 Resolutions of the SWP National Convention[8]

(1940, after the breakaway of the minority)

A The Organizational Principles upon Which the Party was Founded

The third convention of the Socialist Workers Parity reaffirms the resolution adopted by the Founding Convention of the SWP 'On the Internal Situation and the Character of the Party', as follows:

The Socialist Workers Party is a revolutionary Marxian party, based on a definite program, whose aim is the organization of the working class in the struggle for power and the transformation of the existing social order. All of its activities, its methods and its internal regime are subordinated to this aim and are designed to serve it.

Only a self-acting and critical-minded membership is capable of forging and consolidating such a party and of solving its problems by collective thought, discussion and experience. From this follows the need of assuring the widest party democracy in the ranks of the organization.

The struggle for power organized and led by the revolutionary party is the most ruthless and irreconcilable struggle in all history. A loosely-knit, heterogeneous, undisciplined, untrained organization is utterly incapable of accomplishing such world-historical tasks as the proletariat and the revolutionary party are confronted with in the present era. This is all the more emphatically true in the light of the singularly difficult position of our party and the extraordinary persecution to which it is subject. From this follows the party's unconditional demand upon all its members for complete discipline in all the public activities and actions of the organization.

Leadership and centralized direction are indispensable prerequisites for any sustained and disciplined action, especially in the party that sets itself the aim of leading the collective efforts of the proletariat in its struggle against capitalism. Without a strong and firm Central Committee, having the power to act promptly and effectively in the name of the party and to supervise, coordinate and direct all its activities without exception, the very idea of a revolutionary party is a meaningless jest.

---

8 Cannon 2008.

It is from these considerations, based upon the whole of the experience of working class struggle throughout the world in the last century, that we derive the Leninist principle of organisation, namely, democratic centralism. The same experience has demonstrated that there are no absolute guarantees for the preservation of the principle of democratic centralism, and no rigid formula that can be set down in advance, a priori, for the application of it under any and all circumstances. Proceeding from certain fundamental conceptions, the problem of applying the principle of democratic centralism differently under different conditions and stages of development of the struggle, can be solved only in relation to the concrete situation, in the course of the tests and experience through which the movement passes, and on the basis of the most fruitful and healthy interrelationship of the leading bodies of the party and its rank and file.

The Responsibilities of Leadership

The leadership of the party must be under the control of the membership, its policies must always be open to criticism, discussion and rectification by the rank and file within properly established forms and limits, and the leading bodies themselves subject to formal recall or alteration. The membership of the party has the right to demand and expect the greatest responsibility from the leaders precisely because of the position they occupy in the movement. The selection of comrades to the positions of leadership means the conferring of an extraordinary responsibility. The warrant for this position must be proved, not once, but continuously by the leadership itself. It is under obligation to set the highest example of responsibility, devotion, sacrifice and complete identification with the party itself and its daily life and action. It must display the ability to defend its policies before the membership of the party, and to defend the line of the party and the party as a whole before the working class in general.

Sustained party activity, not broken or disrupted by abrupt and disorienting changes, presupposes not only a continuity of tradition and a systematic development of party policy, but also the continuity of leadership. It is an important sign of a serious and firmly constituted party, of a party really engaged in productive work in the class struggle, that it throws up out of its ranks cadres of more or less able leading comrades, tested for their qualities of endurance and trustworthiness, and that it thus insures a certain stability and continuity of leadership by such a cadre.

Continuity of leadership does not, however, signify the automatic self-perpetuation of leadership. Constant renewal of its ranks by means of additions and, when necessary, replacements, is the only assurance that the party has, that its leadership will not succumb to the effects of dry-rot, that it will not be burdened with deadwood, that it will avoid the corrosion of conservatism and dilettantism, that it will not be the object of conflict between the older elements and the younger, that the old and basic cadre will be refreshed by new blood, that the leadership as a whole will not become purely bureaucratic 'committee men' with a life that is remote from the real life of the party and the activities of the rank and file.

Responsibilities of Membership

Like leadership, membership itself in the party implies certain definite rights. Party membership confers the fullest freedom of discussion, debate and criticism inside the ranks of the party, limited only by such decisions and provisions as are made by the party itself or by bodies to which it assigns this function. Affiliation to the party confers upon each member the right of being democratically represented at all policy-making assemblies of the party (from branch to national and international convention), and the right of the final and decisive vote in determining the program, policies and leadership of the party.

With party rights, the membership has also certain definite obligations. The theoretical and political character of the party is determined by its program, which forms the lines delimiting the revolutionary party from all other parties, groups and tendencies in the working class. The first obligation of party membership is loyal acceptance of the program of the party and regular affiliation to one of the basic units of the party. The party requires of every member the acceptance of its discipline and the carrying on of his activity in accordance with the program of the party, with the decisions adopted by its conventions, and with the policies formulated and directed by the party leadership.

Party membership implies the obligation of 100% loyalty to the organization, the rejection of all agents of other, hostile groups in its ranks, and intolerance of divided loyalties in general. Membership in the party necessitates a minimum of activity in the organization, as established by the proper unit, and under the direction of the party; it necessitates the fulfillment of all the tasks which the party assigns to each member. Party membership implies the obligation upon every member to contribute materially to the support of the organisation in accordance with his means.

A Party of Revolutionary Workers

From the foregoing it follows that the party seeks to include in its ranks all the revolutionary, class conscious and militant workers who stand on its program and are active in building the movement in a disciplined manner. The revolutionary Marxian party rejects not only the arbitrariness and bureaucratism of the Communist Party, but also the spurious and deceptive 'all-inclusiveness' of the Thomas-Tyler-Hoan Socialist Party, which is a sham and a fraud. Experience has proved conclusively that this 'all-inclusiveness' paralyses the party in general and the revolutionary left wing in particular, suppressing and bureaucratically hounding the latter while giving free rein to the right wing to commit the greatest crimes in the name of socialism and the party. The SWP seeks to be inclusive only in this sense: that it accepts into its ranks those who accept its program and denies admission to those who reject its program.

The rights of each individual member, as set forth above, do not imply that the membership as a whole, namely, the party itself, does not possess rights of its own. The party as a whole has the right to demand that its work be not disrupted and disorganized, and has the right to take all the measures which it finds necessary to assure its regular and normal functioning. The rights of any individual member are distinctly secondary to the rights of the party membership as a whole. Party democracy means not only the most scrupulous protection of the rights of a given minority, but also the protection of the rule of the majority. The party is therefore entitled to organize the discussion and to determine its forms and limits.

All inner-party discussion must be organized from the point of view that the party is not a discussion club, which debates interminably on any and all questions at any and all times, without arriving at a binding decision that enables the organization to act, but from the point of view that we are a disciplined party of revolutionary action. The party in general not only has the right, therefore, to organize the discussion in accordance with the requirements of the situation, but the lower units of the party must be given the right, in the interests of the struggle against the disruption and disorganization of the party's work, to call irresponsible individuals to order and, if need be, to eject them from the ranks.

The decisions of the national party convention are binding on all party members without exception and they conclude the discussion on all these disputed questions upon which a decision has been taken. Any party member violating the decisions of the convention, or attempting to revive discussion in regard to them without formal authorization of the party, puts himself thereby in opposition to the party and forfeits his right to membership. All party organizations are authorized and instructed to take any measures necessary to enforce this rule.

B The Organizational Conclusions of the Present Discussion

The Bolshevik party of Lenin is the only party in history which successfully conquered and held state power. The SWP, as a combat organization, which aims at achieving power in this country, models its organization forms and methods after those of the Russian Bolshevik party, adapting them, naturally, to the experience of recent years and to concrete American conditions.

The SWP as a revolutionary workers' party is based on the doctrines of scientific socialism as embodied in the principal works of Marx, Engels, Lenin and Trotsky and incorporated in the basic documents and resolutions of the first four congresses of the Communist International and of the conferences and congresses of the Fourth International.

The SWP rejects the contention of social democrats, skeptics and capitulators disillusioned in the Russian revolution, that there is an inevitable and organic connection between Bolshevism and Stalinism. This reactionary revision of Marxism is a capitulation to democratic imperialism. It is capable of producing only demoralization and defeat in the critical times of war and revolution.

The rise of reaction on a world scale, accompanied and produced by the disastrous course of Stalinism in the working class movement, has catapulted all centrist groups and parties (Lovestoneites, Socialist Party, London Bureau) away from Bolshevism and in the direction of social democracy. In whole or in part, all of these groups attempt to identify Bolshevism with Stalinism. Without exception these groups are all in a state of collapse and passing over to the side of the class enemy.

Petty Bourgeoisie Transmits Skepticism

This tendency (Souvarinism) has manifested itself in leading circles of our party (Burnham) and in certain sections of the membership. Their skeptical criticisms of Bolshevism express their petty-bourgeois composition and their dependence on bourgeois public opinion. The petty bourgeoisie is a natural transmission belt carrying the theories of reaction into the organizations of the working class.

Those who seek to identify Bolshevism with Stalinism concern themselves with a search for guarantees against the Stalinist degeneration of the party and the future Soviet power. We reject this demand for insurance as completely undialectical and unrealistic. Our party, in the first instance, is concerned with the struggle for state power, and therefore with creating a party organization capable of leading the proletarian struggle to this goal. There are no constitutional guarantees which can prevent degeneration. Only the victorious revolution can provide the necessary preconditions for preventing the degeneration of the party and the future Soviet power. If the party fails to carry through and extend the revolution the degeneration of the party is inevitable.

Insofar as any guarantees are possible against the degeneration of the proletarian party, these can be obtained only by educating the party in firm adherence to principles and by a merciless struggle against all personal and unprincipled clique combinations within the party. The outstanding example of this clique formation is the Abern group which is based solely on personal loyalties and on rewards of honor and place within the party for those whose primary loyalty is to the clique. The history of the Fourth International in this country amply reveals that such a clique, with its utter disregard for principles, can become the repository for alien class influences and agents of enemy organizations seeking to disrupt the Fourth International from within. The SWP condemns the Abern clique as hostile to the spirit and methods of Bolshevik organization.

Revolutionary Centralism

To overthrow the most powerful capitalist ruling class in the world, the SWP must be organized as a combat party on strong centralist lines. The resolution adopted at the founding convention gave a correct interpretation of the principle of democratic centralism. Its emphasis was placed on the democratic aspects of this principle. The party leadership has faithfully preserved the democratic rights of the membership since the founding convention. It has granted the widest latitude of discussion to all dissenting groups and individuals. The duty of the incoming National Committee is to execute the decisions of the convention, arrived at after the most thorough and democratic discussion, and to permit no infringement upon them.

Conditions, both external and in the internal development of the party, demand that steps now be taken towards knitting the party together, towards tightening up its activities and centralizing its organization structure. For the work of penetrating into the workers' mass movement, for the heavy struggles to come against capitalism, for the onerous conditions of war, it is imperative that a maximum of loyalty be required of every leader and every member, that a maximum of activity be required, that a strict adherence to discipline be demanded and rigidly enforced.

The Press

The party press is the decisive public agitational and propagandist expression of the Bolshevik organization. The policies of the press are formulated on the basis of the fundamental resolutions of the congresses and conferences of the International, the conventions of the party, and decisions of the National Committee not in conflict with such resolutions. Control of the press is lodged directly in the hands of the National Committee by the convention of the party. The duty of the editors is loyally to interpret the decisions of the convention in the press.

Control of Public Discussion

The opening of the party press to discussion of a point of view contrary to that of the official leadership of the party or of its programmatic convention decisions must be controlled by the National Committee which is obligated to regulate discussion of this character in such a way as to give decisive emphasis to the party line. It is the right and duty of the National Committee to veto any demand for public discussion if it deems such discussion harmful to the best interests of the party.

The petty-bourgeois opposition in our party demonstrates its hostility to Bolshevik organization by its demand that the minority be granted the right to transform the press into a discussion organ for diametrically opposite programs. By that method it would take the control of the press out of the hands of the National Committee and subordinate it to any temporary, anarchistic combination which can make itself heard at the moment.

By the same token, the demand of the petty-bourgeois opposition for an independent public organ, expounding a program in opposition to that of the majority of the party, represents a complete abandonment of democratic centralism and a capitulation to the Norman Thomas type of 'all-inclusive' party which is inclusive of all tendencies except the Bolshevik. The granting of this demand for a separate organ would destroy the centralist character of the party, by creating dual central committees, dual editorial boards, dual treasuries, dual distribution agencies, divided loyalties and a complete breakdown of all discipline. Under such conditions the party would rapidly degenerate into a social democratic organization or disappear from the scene altogether. The convention categorically rejects the demand for a dual organ.

Leadership

To build the combat organization capable of conquering state power, the party must have as its general staff a corps of professional revolutionists who devote their entire life to the direction and the building of the party and its influence in the mass movement. Membership in the leading staff of the party, the National Committee, must be made contingent on a complete subordination of the life of the candidate to the party. All members of the National Committee must devote full-time activities to party work, or be prepared to do so at the demand of the National Committee.

In the struggle for power, the party demands the greatest sacrifices of its members. Only a leadership selected from among those who demonstrate in the struggle the qualities of singleness of purpose, unconditional loyalty to the party and revolutionary firmness of character, can inspire the membership with a spirit of unswerving devotion and lead the party in its struggle for power.

The party leadership must, from time to time, be infused with new blood, primarily from its proletarian sections. Workers who show promise and ability through activity in the union movement and its strike struggles should be elevated to the leading committees of the party in order to establish a more direct connection between the leading committee and the workers' movement, and in order to train the worker-Bolshevik for the task of party direction itself.

The party must select from its younger members those qualified, talented and promising elements who can be trained for leadership. The road of the student youth to the party leadership must not and cannot be from the class room of the high school and college directly into the leading committee. They must first prove themselves. They must be sent without high-sounding titles into working class districts for day-to-day work among the proletariat. The young student must serve an apprenticeship in the workers' movement before he can be considered as candidate for the National Committee.

Proletarianize the Party

The working class is the only class in modern society that is progressive and truly revolutionary. Only the working class is capable of saving humanity from barbarism. Only a revolutionary party can lead the proletariat to the realization of this historic mission. To achieve power, the revolutionary party must be deeply rooted among the workers, it must be composed predominantly of workers and enjoy the respect and confidence of the workers.

Without such a composition it is impossible to build a programmatically firm and disciplined organization which can accomplish these grandiose tasks. A party of non-workers is necessarily subject to all the reactionary influences of skepticism, cynicism, soul-sickness and capitulatory despair transmitted to it through its petty-bourgeois environment.

To transform the SWP into a proletarian party of action, particularly in the present period of reaction, it is not enough to continue propagandistic activities in the hope that by an automatic process workers will flock to the banner of the party. It is necessary, on the contrary, to make a concerted, determined and systematic effort, consciously directed by the leading committees of the party, to penetrate the workers' movement, establish the roots of the party in the trade unions, the mass labor organizations and in the workers' neighborhoods and recruit worker militants into the ranks of the party.

Steps to Proletarianize the Party

To proletarianize the party, the following steps are imperative:

1. The entire party membership must be directed towards rooting itself in the factories, mills, etc., and towards integrating itself in the unions and workers' mass organizations.

2. Those members of the party who are not workers shall be assigned to work in labor organizations, in workers' neighborhoods and with the worker-fractions of the party – to assist them and learn from them. All unemployed members must belong to and be active in organizations of the unemployed.

Those party members who find it impossible after a reasonable period of time to work in a proletarian milieu and to attract to the party worker militants shall be transferred from party membership to the rank of sympathizers. Special organizations of sympathizers may be formed for this purpose.

Above all the student and unemployed youth must be sent into industry and involved in the life and struggles of the workers. Systematic, exceptional and persistent efforts must be made to assist the integration of our unemployed youth into industry despite the restricted field of employment.

Lacking connection with the workers' movement through failure or inability to get jobs in industry or membership in unions, the student and unemployed youth are subject to terrific pressure from the petty-bourgeois world. A large section of the youth membership of the SWP and YPSL adopted the program of the Fourth International, but brought with them the training and habits of the social-democratic movement, which are far removed from the spirit of the proletarian revolution.

These student elements can transform the program of the Fourth International from the pages of books and pamphlets into living reality for themselves and for the party only by integrating themselves in the workers' movement and breaking irrevocably from their previous environment. Unless they follow this road they are in constant danger of slipping back into their former social democratic habits or into complete apathy and pessimism and thus be lost for the revolutionary movement.

3. To attract and to hold workers in the ranks of the party, it is necessary that the internal life of the party be drastically transformed. The party must be cleansed of the discussion club atmosphere, of an irresponsible attitude toward assignments, of a cynical and smart aleck disrespect for the party.

Organizing Real Campaigns

Party activity must be lifted out of dragging, daily routine and reorganized on the basis of campaigns which are realistically adjusted to the demands and direction of the workers' movement. These campaigns must not be sucked out of the thumb of some functionary in a party office, but must arise as a result of the connections of the party with the workers' movement and the indicated direction of the masses in specific situations.

All party agitation campaigns, especially in the next period, must be directed primarily at those workers' groups and organizations in which we are attempting to gain a foothold and attract members. General agitation addressed to the working class as a whole or the public in general must be related to those specific aims.

The press must gear its agitation into the activity conducted among specific workers' groups so as to transform the party paper from a literary organ into a workers' organizer. The integration of the party into the workers' movement, and the transformation of the party into a proletarian organization, are indispensable for the progress of the party. Successful achievement of this internal transformation is a thousand times more important than any amount of empty phrases about 'preparation of the party for war'. This transformation is, in fact, the only real preparation of the party for war, combined of course with the necessary technical adjustments in organization forms.

The SWP must adhere to the principles and program of the Fourth International, transform itself into a democratically centralized Bolshevik organization, integrate itself into the workers' movement. On that basis, and on that basis alone, can the party meet the test of the war, survive the war and go forward to its great goal – the establishment of a workers' republic in the United States.

C Resolution on Discipline

Having heard the declaration made to the convention by the representative of the minority to the effect that, regardless of the decision of the convention, the minority will publish a paper of its own in opposition to the press of the party, the convention states:

1. The threat is an attempt of a petty-bourgeois minority to impose its will upon the party in opposition to the principles of democratic centralism which alone can assure the unity of a revolutionary combat party. The convention categorically rejects the ultimatum of the minority and declares that any attempt on the part of any individual or group to execute it and to issue or distribute

any publication in opposition to the official press of the party is incompatible with membership in the party.

2. All party organizations are instructed to expel from the party any member or members violating this convention decision.

The National Committee or its Political Committee are empowered and instructed by the convention to expel any regular or alternate member or members of the NC or PC who may participate in any such violation. The NC or PC is instructed to immediately expel and reorganize any party unit or executive committee failing to act promptly in the execution of the above instructions in regard to any member or members under its jurisdiction who may violate the convention decisions.

D Supplementary Resolution on the Organizational Question

In order to assure the concentration of the party membership on practical work under the most favorable internal conditions, to safeguard the unity of the party and to provide guarantees for the party rights of the minority, the convention adopts the following special measures:

1. The discussion in the party branches on the controversial issues is to be concluded with the convention decisions and the reports of the delegates to their branches. It may be resumed only by authorization of the National Committee.

2. In order to acquaint the party sympathizers and the radical labor public with all aspects of the disputes, and the opinions of both sides, the NC shall publish in symposium form the most important articles on the Russian question and the organization question. These symposia shall be jointly edited and each side may select the articles it wishes to publish.

3. As an exceptional measure in the present circumstances, the discussion may be continued in literary form if the representatives of either side, or both, so desire. Articles dealing with the theoretical-scientific aspects of the disputed questions may be published in the *New International*. Political discussion articles are to be published in a monthly *Internal Bulletin*, issued by the NC, under joint editorship of the convention majority and minority.

4. The NC shall publish all resolutions considered by the convention, those rejected as well as those adopted. Editorial comment shall be restricted to defense of the adopted positions.

5. The decisions of the party convention must be accepted by all under the rules of democratic centralism. Strict discipline in action is to be required of all party members.

6. No measures are to be taken against any party member because of the views expressed in the party discussion. Nobody is obliged to renounce his opinion. There is no prohibition of factions. The minority is to be given representation in the leading party committees and assured full opportunity to participate in all phases of party work.

8 Post-convention Reports and Decisions[9]

(*1940*)

A The Convention of the Socialist Workers Party [Report]

… Our convention had more than national significance. The Fourth International, as a whole, like all other organizations in the labor movement, was put to a decisive test by the outbreak of the war. Fortuitous political circumstances have delayed the entry of US imperialism into the war. This provided our party with a more favorable opportunity for a free and democratic discussion of the issues posed by the war crisis than was enjoyed by any other section of our International. Our party was also the best equipped by past experience and training to carry out this discussion in all its implications, from all sides, and to the very end. In addition, outstanding representatives of several other important sections of our International were able to participate directly in the literary discussion in our party. The discussion in the SWP became in effect a discussion for the entire Fourth International and was followed with passionate interest by the members of all sections.

It was clear from the beginning that the issues at stake were international in character and that our decisions would have fateful consequences for our movement on a worldwide scale. Thus our convention, formally and nominally a convention of the Socialist Workers Party, was in its political import a veritable congress of the Fourth International. Under war conditions, and the consequent illegality of many of the sections, a formally organised World Congress, composed of representative delegations, could not be held. Our convention had to serve as temporary surrogate for the World Congress. Politically, there can be no doubt that it had this meaning for all the other sections.

The discussion initiated in our party was transferred into the other sections; and one after the other, they began to take positions on the dispute. In every case where we have been able to establish communication under war conditions, and have direct knowledge of their position, the sections have supported the majority of our party. The international report at our convention disclosed that the Canadian, Mexican, Belgian, German, Argentine, Chinese, Australian

9 Cannon 2008.

and Russian sections have all declared categorically in support of the position of the majority of our party. The other sections, with whom communication is faulty or who have not formerly recorded their position, indicate the same tendency. After our convention there can no longer be the slightest doubt that the overwhelming majority of the members and sections of the Fourth International remain true to their banner – to the doctrine and program of revolutionary Marxism. The decision is made. The revisionist movement of Burnham and Co. can no longer hope for success in our movement, nationally or internationally. The Fourth International remains, after the first test of the war, firm in its programmatic position – the only revolutionary organization of the workers' vanguard in the entire world …

The report and discussion on the trade union question and mass work dealt a knockout blow to the calamity howlers, pessimists and quitters who have been attributing to the movement their own weakness, cowardice and futility. The convention resounded with proletarian optimism and confidence in the party. The trade union report and discussion, following the decisive reaffirmation of the proletarian program, engendered a remarkable enthusiasm. It was clear from this discussion that the turn of the party toward mass work is already well under way and that the proceedings of the convention could not fail to give it a powerful acceleration …

The majority did everything possible to preserve unity, and even made extraordinary concessions to induce the minority to turn back from their splitting course before it was too late. Their party rights as a minority were guaranteed by a special resolution at the convention. This resolution went to the extreme length of sanctioning a continuation of discussion of the decided questions in the *Internal Bulletin*, and a discussion of the theoretical aspects of the question in the *New International*. At the same time, the convention resolution decreed that discussion in the branches must cease, and that all attention and energy of the party membership be concentrated on practical mass work in the next period.

The minority was given proportional representation on the National Committee and a period of time to make up their minds whether to remain in the party or not under the terms and conditions laid down. The minority leaders rejected the convention decision, launched their own publication, and began a public attack on the program of the party and the Fourth International. Thus, by their own decision and actions, they placed themselves outside the ranks of the party and the Fourth International. Their political degeneration is inevitable; nobody has ever yet found a revolutionary road outside the Fourth International. But that is their own affair. Our discussion with them, which was fully adequate, is now concluded.

We are looking forward, not backward. Our task is a deeper penetration of the workers' mass movement on the basis of the convention decisions. That is our way to prepare for the war. In this course we are assured of the support of the overwhelming majority of the sections of the Fourth International. With a correct program, and the assurance of international collaboration and support, we have every reason to be confident of our future.

B The Suspension of the Burnham-Shachtman-Abern Group (Statement of the National Committee)

The readers of the *Appeal* are already familiar with the resolutions adopted by the recently concluded national convention of our party.

These resolutions (published last week) made extremely liberal provisions for the participation of the leaders of the minority in party work. The resolutions offered them the opportunity to continue the discussion in defense of their point of view in the *Internal Bulletin* and in the *New International*, on the condition that they refrain from issuing an independent publication in opposition to the press of the party.

These decisions of the convention have been rejected by the leaders of the minority. This conduct left the National Committee no alternative, under the instructions of the convention, but to suspend the minority leaders from the party until such time as they signify their readiness to abide by the convention decisions. This action was taken by the National Committee, at its meeting held on April 16, in order to protect the party against disruption. At the same time the terms of the suspension leave the way open for the suspended members to reconsider the question and return to their places in the party leadership and in its editorial boards on the basis of the convention decisions.

C The Expulsion of the Shachtman-Abern Group [Report]

By decision of the April 1940 convention of the party, the National Committee was instructed to take disciplinary action against the Burnham-Shachtman-Abern group if that group failed to abide by the decisions of the convention.

In accordance with those instructions, the National Committee on April 22 suspended those members of the Burnham-Shachtman-Abern group who, following the convention, refused to accept the decisions of the convention. The National Committee by suspending rather than expelling the undisciplined members of the petty-bourgeois opposition, gave them an opportunity to reconsider their refusal to abide by convention decisions and to return to the party. In the course of the ensuing months a number of the suspended comrades have reconsidered their refusal, have declared their adherence in action to convention decisions while remaining free to defend their political views in subsequent party discussions, and have on this basis been restored to full membership rights.

The Emergency Conference of the Fourth International, convened in May 1940, endorsed the decisions of the April convention of the SWP. It recommended to our party that only a limited period should remain in which suspended members would have time to reconsider their refusal. At the end of that period those still refusing to accept the convention decisions should be unconditionally expelled from the party.

The period recommended by the Emergency Conference has now elapsed. Meanwhile, since their suspension, the Burnham-Shachtman-Abern group has undergone a political evolution which has widened the chasm between them and the Fourth International. Burnham has drawn the final conclusion to the position he elaborated for his group, and has openly deserted to the class enemy.

Shachtman and Abern lead a petty-bourgeois semi-pacifist sect. After the passage of nearly six months it is, therefore, time to draw a conclusion to this question and put an end to any possible ambiguity or confusion.

The plenary session of the National Committee declares that those suspended members who have not up to this time signified their willingness to abide by the decisions of the April convention are hereby unconditionally expelled from the party.

9 Exit Letter[10]

(1940, excerpts)

James Burnham

May 21, 1940
To the National Committee of the Workers Party:

The faction fight in the Socialist Workers Party, its conclusion, and the recent formation of the Workers Party have been in my own case, the unavoidable occasion for the review of my own theoretical and political beliefs. This review has shown me that by no stretching of terminology can I any longer regard myself, or permit others to regard me, as a Marxist.

Of the most important beliefs, which have been associated with the Marxist movement, whether in its reformist, Leninist, Stalinist or Trotskyist variants, there is virtually none which I accept in its traditional form. I regard these beliefs as either false or obsolete or meaningless; or in a few cases, as at best true only in a form so restricted and modified as no longer properly to be called Marxist …

I reject, as you know, the 'philosophy of Marxism', dialectical materialism. I have never, it is true, accepted this philosophy. In the past I excused this discrepancy and compromised this belief with the idea that the philosophy was 'unimportant' and 'did not matter' so far as practice and politics were concerned. Experience, and further study and reflection, have convinced me that I have been wrong and Trotsky – with so many others – right on this score; that dialectical materialism, though scientifically meaningless, is psychologically and historically an integral part of Marxism, and does have its many and adverse effects upon practice and politics.

The general Marxian theory of 'universal history', to the extent that it has any empirical content, seems to me disproved by modern historical and anthropological investigation.

Marxian economics seems to me for the most part either false or obsolete or meaningless in application to contemporary economic phenomena. Those

10 Burnham 1940b.

aspects of Marxian economics which retain validity do not seem to me to justify the theoretical structure of the economics.

Not only do I believe it meaningless to say that 'socialism is inevitable' and false that socialism is 'the only alternative to capitalism'; I consider that on the basis of the evidence now available to us a new form of exploitive society (what I call 'managerial society') is not only possible as an alternative to capitalism but is a more probable outcome of the present period than socialism.

As you know, I do not believe that Russia can be considered a 'workers state' in any intelligible sense of the term. This opinion, however, is related to far more basic conclusions: for example, that Stalinism must be understood as one manifestation of the same general historical forces of which fascism is another manifestation. There is still doubt in my mind as to whether this conclusion applies also to Leninism and Trotskyism.

I disagree flatly and entirely, as Cannon has understood for a long while, with the Leninist conception of a party ... The Leninist type of party seems to me incompatible with genuine scientific method and genuine democracy ...

CHAPTER 10

Holding the Line: Smith Act Trial

Bryan Palmer

The Socialist Workers' Party [SWP] was formed in Chicago at a national gathering convening immediately before and on New Year's Day, 1 January 1938. It was born of the Trotskyist realisation that the Stalinist policies that had consolidated over the course of the mid-to-late 1920s, and that had produced such disastrous consequences for the international revolutionary movement in the 1930s, had to be challenged with the formation of a new communist international and its constituent national sections and parties. But many developments fed into the revolutionary imperatives of this period, with their appreciations of the need for a party formation such as the SWP.

One critical component of early American Trotskyism was the victory that had been achieved in three 1934 International Brotherhood of Teamsters [IBT] strikes, led by the Minneapolis forces of the Communist League of America (Opposition) [CLA]. Supported and sustained by the leading cadre of the CLA, especially James P. Cannon and Max Shachtman, Minneapolis militants such as Vincent Ray Dunne, Miles Dunne, Grant Dunne, Carl Skoglund, and Farrell Dobbs built IBT Local 544, the General Drivers' Union, into a force nationally recognised as a vanguard in the industrial union mobilisations of the mid-to-late 1930s.[1]

Local 544 expanded the ranks of organised Teamsters in Minneapolis from less than 200 to 7,000, breaking the old craft union mould that restricted entry in the union to supposedly skilled and respectable drivers. So-called unskilled 'inside workers' in the trucking industry were brought into the General Drivers' Union, which under Trotskyist leadership now included coal heavers and those working the loading docks at markets. The union also linked the interests of the employed workers and their unemployed counterparts, setting up a Federal Workers Section [FWS] that encouraged the jobless to make common cause with striking workers, rather than crossing picket lines and breaking the organisational momentum of labour resistance. This defiant, militant, and broadened industrial union defeated recalcitrant local employers and their advocates in a backward-looking anti-labour Citizens Alliance. Minneapolis's

1 See Dobbs 1972; Korth 1995; Palmer 2013.

trade union Trotskyist leadership also battled the foot-dragging resistance of Teamster bureaucrat Dan Tobin and the hierarchy of the international union. This officialdom did everything it could to undermine class struggle unionism and its impressive initiatives.[2]

Later, in 1938, as a Silver Legion movement attempted to mobilise in Minnesota, targeting Local 544 in its fascistic attacks on Jews, religious and ethnic minorities, and progressive politics in general, the General Drivers' Union led the way in creating a Union Defense Guard [UDG]. Headed by Local 544 member, former SWPer, and Sioux Nation member Ray Rainbolt, the UDG was a broad-based workers' defence corps that brought together trade unionists (including many who were neither Trotskyists nor members of the General Drivers' Union) in Minneapolis to defend the labour movement from physical assault and right-wing intimidation.[3]

In the summer of 1939, Minneapolis-St. Paul Trotskyists and Local 544's FWS also played a pivotal role in a nationwide strike of Roosevelt's Works Progress Administration [WPA]. Ten thousand of these WPA relief strikers walked off their government-funded works projects in the Twin Cities, protesting conditions and inadequate entitlements. As tensions mounted, confrontations escalated: a police officer was killed, a relief officer shot, a striker stabbed, and more than a dozen people injured. Women working at a WPA sewing project, unaccustomed to public protest, nonetheless played a leading role on the militant picket lines, which often erupted in violence. Lasting more than two weeks, the confrontation led to a Justice Department-authorised Grand Jury investigation, in which hearings handed down scores of indictments resulting in three trials and a number of convictions. Two SWP members, Max Geldman and Edward Palmquist, co-chairs of the FWS described as the 'very fountainhead of the Minneapolis WPA strike conspiracy', were sentenced to a year-and-a-day in the federal penitentiary at Sandstone, Minnesota.[4]

Finally, over the course of the late 1930s, Local 544 and its leading SWP figures (Dobbs, V.R. Dunne, and Skoglund) pioneered the technique of 'leapfrogging', through which the organised and militant teamster base in Minneapolis was used to force employers from other centres in the mid-west who needed to truck goods into their cities to concede union wages and conditions in their distant operations. Dobbs nurtured the North Central District Drivers' Council

2 Palmer 2013; Dobbs 1972; Millikan 2001, pp. 264–88.

3 Allen 2012; Dobbs 1975, pp. 139–48; Haverty-Stacke 2015, pp. 24–6; Palmer 2013, pp. 227–8.

4 Dobbs 1973, pp. 77–86, Dobbs 1975, pp. 177–240; Haverty-Stacke 2015, pp. 9–24; Faue 1991, pp. 156–64.

(NCDDC) into being, a vehicle that would drive the Teamster interstate organisation of over-the-road truckers to success after success. As particular core metropolitan hubs were brought under union control, such as Chicago and Kansas City, they were then used to leverage other cities, such as Omaha and St. Louis, where recalcitrant employers were holding out against conceding contracts to the IBT. Late in 1939, the IBT signed a contract with a group of interstate trucking firms, covering 250,000 drivers and affiliated workers in 11 states. Mainstream labour historian Irving Bernstein concluded that the Trotskyist leaders of the Minneapolis General Drivers' Union had 'with the imagination and drive they had evidenced during the strikes [of 1934], expanded the organization of over-the-road drivers in the Upper Mississippi Valley as the foundation for mass unionism on a semi-industrial basis'. Left Oppositionists, then, had initiated an expansive industrial union drive in the mid-western trucking sector that resulted in an unprecedented explosion of IBT membership from roughly 75,000 to over 400,000 in the space of half a decade (1934–9). Not only did the Teamsters expand phenomenally in this period, but this technique was also used to create networks of labour solidarity, as Minneapolis initiatives proved indispensable in supporting unionisation campaigns among relatively low-skilled workers in spheres such as laundering, baking, clerking, and other traditionally difficult-to-organise occupational sectors.[5]

This was a formidable achievement. It placed Trotskyism in the public eye and, arguably, in the sights of various opponents. And it did so at a most threatening moment.

Trotsky understood that the gains registered by the Minneapolis Left Oppositionists in the unions over the course of the 1930s were crucial to the ongoing work of the revolutionary movement. But he also appreciated that such success could condition a certain complacency. A willingness to adapt somewhat to trade unionism's compromises with the progressive wing of American capitalism had to be countered. This tendency to let down a certain revolutionary guard, to collapse the independence of the revolutionary movement into conciliatory relations with those in the labour movement hierarchy inclined to temporarily accommodate revolutionaries as long as they were filling the dues coffers of the IBT, but who were fully committed to the Democratic Party's Franklin Delano Roosevelt and his New Deal policies, was an ever-present problem. Moreover, in its public propaganda, the SWP could follow such a trajectory by failing to adequately elucidate its actual policies with respect to rank-and-file militant workers who, like their leaders, tended to be insufficiently critical

5 Dobbs 1973; Palmer 2013, pp. 230–2; Bernstein 1969, pp. 250–2.

of Roosevelt, voting for him *en masse*. In peacetime, Trotsky told SWP leaders, such an 'adaptation to the pro-Rooseveltian trade unionists' might not be fatal, but if war broke out, he warned prophetically, a failure to prepare the working class for the repressive onslaught of the bourgeoisie could well have disastrous consequences. 'They can smash us. Our policy is too much for pro-Rooseveltian trade unionists'. The fact that, as of 22 June 1941, with the German invasion of the Soviet Union and the implosion of the Hitler-Stalin pact, the SWP was virtually the only voice on the communist left opposing the war, placed Trotskyists very much on the radar screen of American domestic repression.[6]

Trotsky's warning was delivered in mid-June 1940 to an SWP contingent made up of Cannon, Dobbs, Joe Hansen, Harold Robins, Sam Gordon, and veteran Left Oppositionist, Dr. Antoinette Konikow. This group met with Trotsky in Mexico. Approximately two weeks later, on 29 June 1940, with the war in Europe raging, but with the United States still not officially involved as a belligerent, Roosevelt signed into law the so-called Smith Act, anti-sedition legislation that criminalised speech and acts pertaining to overthrowing the government by force and agitation of a disloyal kind within the armed forces. Printing, publishing, or distributing material advocating this kind of ostensible sedition was criminalised, and belonging to any organisation that engaged in the dissemination of such documents or ideas was likewise made illegal. Although not entirely unprecedented, the Smith Act was arguably the most draconian peacetime prosecutorial initiative in modern United States history, with Donna Haverty-Stacke concluding that it went far beyond any legislative undertaking since the Alien and Sedition Acts of 1798.

As Haverty-Stacke shows, in the most sustained inquiry into the use of the Smith Act against Trotskyists in the early 1940s, the hounds of repression were unleashed against the Minneapolis trade union Trotskyists and their counterparts in the national leadership of the SWP. This attack consolidated over the course of a period reaching from June 1940 to June 1941, although different streams of varied currents that would come to be directed against the SWP had complicated histories reaching back into the struggles of the 1930s. A small contingent of Local 544 factional dissidents, some of whom were disgruntled former SWP members with an opportunistic eye on trade union office, aligned and indeed conspired with Dan Tobin and the Federal Bureau of Investigation [FBI], providing often uncorroborated reports of Trotskyist 'fifth column intrigue', which included outrageous and patently false allegations of the stockpiling of weapons and utterances of the intent to overthrow the government by

6 Trotsky 1969; International Bolshevik Tendency 1998, pp. 106–14.

force. As Tobin moved to strip Local 544 of its autonomy, putting the American Federation of Labor [AFL]-affiliated General Drivers' Union under receivership, Vincent Ray Dunne and the Trotskyist leadership secured the membership's approval to jump ship to the rival Congress of Industrial Organizations [CIO]. John L. Lewis offered a charter in the United Construction Workers Organizing Committee [UCWOC], which had been mobilising drivers and warehouse workers into an industry-wide union, later christened the Motor Transport and Allied Workers Industrial Union. This unleashed an acrimonious, and at times quite violent struggle in the streets and alleyways of the Minneapolis warehouse district, as Tobin and IBT muscle orchestrated by Jimmy Hoffa conducted an often physically violent 'caravan mop-up' in which they 'persuaded' drivers and helpers to forego the CIO for the old IBT AFL-affiliate. This battle for the streets had the de facto blessing of an array of powerful state structures/officials at the municipal, state, and federal levels.[7]

With this internecine intra-union war unfolding, J. Edgar Hoover and the FBI as well as IBT-head Tobin were pressuring Roosevelt to address the supposed threat the Trotskyists and Local 544 posed to national security. As early as September 1940 the Bureau had placed Vincent Ray Dunne on a custodial detention list, and Dobbs was added to the same designation of those the FBI thought should be detained in the event of a 'national emergency'. Reports on Trotskyist claims that the SWP was preparing to sabotage government and industry in preparation for a revolutionary seizure of power were filtered from the FBI to St. Paul US Attorney Victor Anderson, who in turn passed the 'information' on to the Department of Justice in Washington. By June of 1941 Tobin in the IBT, Minnesota's Governor Stassen, the Roosevelt Administration's Department of Justice, National Labor Relations Board, and Immigration and Naturalization service, not to mention J. Edgar Hoover's Federal Bureau of Investigation all had Minneapolis trade union Trotskyists in their sights, targeted for possible prosecution under the Smith Act. If Trotskyists like Dobbs and Dunne remained unaware of exactly what measures of surveillance the FBI was undertaking against them and Local 544, they were certainly cognisant, as early as 1940, that the Bureau was monitoring trade unionism with the purpose of curbing any possibility of a working-class upheaval.

7 Accepting much of Haverty-Stacke's account, Palmer 2013, pp. 223–48, provides a rejoinder of sorts. It emphasises not the importance of a dissident anti-communist faction in Local 544, or the extent to which Tobin's opposition to the Trotskyist leadership of the Minneapolis teamsters was somehow less important than the actions of the FBI, but rather the plethora of forces pitted against the established militant leadership of the union, which was a formidable set of interlocking state agencies. See also Dobbs 1977.

On 27 June 1941 Acting Attorney General Francis Biddle moved against the SWP and its Minneapolis trade union leadership, the Department of Justice/FBI raiding Party offices in both Minneapolis and St. Paul. Correspondence, copious documents, and a vast array of ephemera, including photographs, flags, banners, and the like were confiscated, later to be burned. Convening a Grand Jury, summoning 49 witnesses, and orchestrating the proceedings to secure indictments against 29 individuals, the prosecution alleged that the defendants had engaged in an 'unlawful conspiracy … to destroy by force the government of the United States' in violation of Section 6 of Title 18 of the US Code, a Civil War era insurrection statute. The accused, according to the charges, had placed themselves in pivotal positions throughout the country's major industries; infiltrated the army to undermine its effectiveness; and created the Union Defense Guard, an alleged nucleus of the proletarian army that would overthrow the government by force and violence. Also charged under the Smith Act, the defendants were claimed to have advised and counseled insubordination in the armed forces and the violent overthrowing of the duly constituted government. Printing, publishing, and disseminating by various means literature of the same purpose, including the *Communist Manifesto* (which had circulated freely in the US since the late nineteenth century), had also been undertaken by the indicted, who managed, as well, to organise societies known to spread the same revolutionary ideas. The 29 indicted – James Cannon, Grace Carlson, Jake Cooper, Oscar Coover, Harry DeBoer, Farrell Dobbs, Grant Dunne, Miles Dunne, Vincent Ray Dunne, George Frosig, Max Geldman, Albert Goldman, Walter Hagstrom, Clarence Hamel, Emil Hansen, Carlos Hudson, Karl Kuehn, Felix Morrow, Ray Orgon, Edward Palmquist, Kelly Postal, Ray Rainbolt, Alfred Russell, Oscar Schoenfeld, Dorothy Schultz, Rose Seiler, Carl Skoglund, Harold Swanson, and Nick Wagner – were leaders/members of the SWP or prominent figures in the General Drivers Union, with some, albeit not all, of the accused being active in both the Trotskyist party and Local 544.

The indictments drew immediate criticism from bodies like the CIO's Labor Non-Partisan League and the American Civil Liberties Union, while articles in liberal publications such as the *New Republic* and the *Nation* deplored how the Smith Act was criminalising 'mere expression of opinion'.[8] A Civil Rights Defense Committee [CRDC], chaired by James T. Farrell, author of the *Studs Lonigan* trilogy, highlighted how the 29 accused were victims of Dan Tobin's relentless persecution, which included fomenting a disgruntled faction within

8 See, for instance *New Republic*, 28 July 1941; Stone 1941.

Local 544 and appealing directly to President Roosevelt, urging him to utilise the FBI and the Justice Department to squelch the SWP, which opposed the war drive.[9]

Trotskyists in the SWP and in Local 544 were under no illusions about the forces arrayed against them. They very quickly saw the writing on the prosecutorial wall. The Judge in charge of the case, Matthew M. Joyce, had been a general counsel for railroad interests from 1917–32, when he was appointed to the US District Court by Herbert Hoover. He presided over the convictions of SWP members Geldman and Palmquist in the 1939 WPA relief strikers' trial, and was well known as a judicial advocate of utilising federal authority against the perceived threat of subversion. In September 1941 he rejected all of the defence's pre-trial motions. Approximately three weeks before the trial commenced, in October 1941, one of the indicted, Grant Dunne, committed suicide. This left 28 accused to face trial before a jury that contained not a single trade union member; only one of the impaneled 12 jurors was a resident of Minneapolis, the remainder coming from surrounding rural counties.[10]

Shaping up, in the words of CRDC spokesperson George Novack [William F. Warde], as a 'capitalist frame-up', the 1941 trial nonetheless ended in outright exoneration of fully ten of the accused. Walter Hagstrom, Dorothy Schultz, Rose Seiler, George Frosig, and Nick Wagner were discharged during the trial, with Judge Joyce forced to acknowledge that there was insufficient evidence indicating that they had knowledge of any conspiracy to overthrow the government by force or that they participated in any activities/writing/speeches to that end. Furthermore, at the end of the trial, on 1 December 1941, after a 56-hour deliberation, five of the accused – Miles Dunne, Ray Rainbolt, Roy Orgon, Harold Swanson, and Kelly Postal – were acquitted on all charges associated with both of the counts under the antiquated Civil War statute and under the Smith Act. These exonerated contingents, in 1941, often had tenuous connections to the SWP, their memberships having lapsed or, in the case of Frosig, never having been formally registered. Yet they were adamant in statements of solidarity with their co-defendants, and in insisting that the ordeal of a sedition trial had done nothing to dampen their commitment to militant, class struggle industrial unionism that they associated with Local 544 and its leadership. (Postal, Secretary-Treasurer of Local 544 had the briefest of reprieves: acquitted in 1941, he faced other charges and was promptly convicted of embezzlement because he refused to turn over dues and union property to Tobin's IBT, his loyalties remaining with the CIO-affiliated Motor Transport and Allied

9 Wald 1987, p. 249.

10 Haverty-Stacke 2015, pp. 22–4, 83–94, 107.

Workers Industrial Union. Sentenced to a draconian five-year prison term, he was released after 12 months, due in large measure to a spirited campaign launched by the CRDC). Of the 18 remaining defendants, all were also acquitted of charges under Section 6/Title 18 of the Civil War insurrection statute. But the Smith Act charges of advising and counseling the violent overthrow of the duly constituted government were upheld against these 18 indicted figures, with an important group of SWP leaders (James P. Cannon, Vincent Ray Dunne, Grace Carlson, Farrell Dobbs, Carl Skoglund, Max Geldman, Felix Morrow, and Albert Goldman) receiving sentences of 16 months. The jury, somewhat tepid in its enthusiasm for the prosecution's zeal, recommended leniency for the convicted, the Smith Act charges carrying a possible maximum sentence of ten years in jail and a $10,000 fine.[11]

Throughout the trial, the SWP conducted itself as a principled defender of civil rights and freedom of expression, holding firm to the notion that advocating the 'right of revolution' was not tantamount to sedition. Cannon, in particular, testified at length and accented adroitly that while Marxists understood well that the bourgeoisie was unlikely to give up its power without a violent fight, it was nevertheless the case that revolutionaries did not advocate or foment violence so much as recognise the likelihood of its inevitability. Against ultra-left critics within the Trotskyist Fourth International, such as Grandzio Munis, Cannon, Goldman, and others who crafted the SWP's defence strategy utilised the trial to expose the repressive nature of the capitalist state and to educate workers in Marxist understandings of class struggle and the necessity of building and expanding the revolutionary organisation of the working class. If, at times, Cannon and other SWP witnesses bent the stick of testimony too far in the direction of passivity, seemingly adapting to the conservative consciousness of the American working class, they erred, understandably, on the appropriate side of a divide that separated them from Munis's adventurist fetishisation of unrealistic 'calls to action'.[12] The CRDC worked relentlessly to defend the convicted 18 SWP members, campaigning against what it called the 'Gag Act' convictions. By the summer of 1942, Trotskyists could claim that scores of unions representing roughly one million workers had voiced protests of the Minneapolis trial and FBI interference in the internal, democratic affairs of the labour movement.[13]

---

11 Haverty-Stacke 2015, pp. 109–38; Palmer 2013, p. 247. Postal's persecution is detailed in Dobbs 1977, pp. 247–63.

12 See the discussion by Chris Knox, which first appeared in *Workers Vanguard*, 1973 in International Bolshevik Tendency 1998, pp. 116–18.

13 Haverty-Stacke 2015, p. 146.

The Minneapolis 18 were sentenced one day after the Japanese bombed Pearl Harbor, plunging the United States into World War II. In this climate, vengeance against anti-capitalist, anti-war revolutionaries was a *fait accompli*. Appeal of the December 1941 convictions, supported by the American Civil Liberties Union, worked its way through legal channels only to confirm the original judicial findings. The Supreme Court refused three defense petitions pleading for a rehearing of the case. In this it received support from an unlikely quarter.

From the moment Trotskyists and trade unionists first faced the repressive onslaught of criminal proceedings around seditious conspiracy in 1941, the Communist Party had been a voice on the ostensible left calling for their conviction and suppression. The *Daily Worker* equated the SWP with Hitler's 'National Socialist Workers Party', and likened Trotskyists' refusal to support what they claimed was an imperialist war as a dangerous aid to Hitler's aggressions. As the appeal campaign culminated in the Supreme Court petitions for a reconsideration of the Minneapolis trial convictions in 1943, the Communist Party prepared a series of exhibits for the Department of Justice, which included an inflammatory 24-page typescript, 'The Fifth Column Role of the Trotskyites in the United States'. This document described the SWP as a 'sabotage organization, concentrating upon the disruption of the war effort', calling on the state to remove this small core of saboteurs, thereby wrecking 'a strong fascist weapon in America'.[14] This kind of rhetoric, emanating from an ostensible communist organisation, revealed just what the 18 Trotskyists convicted under the Smith Act in 1941 were up against in a climate of war-induced xenophobia. Ironically enough, it would not be very long before Communist Party members would themselves be subject to Smith Act repression, and among their staunch defenders would be the same Trotskyists the Stalinists were advocating be jailed in 1941–3.[15]

Surrendering to authorities on 31 December 1943, the convicted Smith Act Trotskyists went to jail and served their time. As Cannon noted and Goldman confirmed in his contribution to the 'Farewell Speeches' of the 18, the Trotskyists had 'set no limit on what they will do for their ideas', and this is why they were imprisoned.[16] When they returned to the SWP over the course of the next 13 months they largely reentered a revolutionary movement strengthened by their resolve and principled stand.[17] To be sure, long-term prices were paid: a

14 Jaffe 1975, pp. 50–2.

15 Belknap 1977; Haverty-Stacke 2015, p. 201.

16 Cannon 1944c, pp. 10–15.

17 Le Blanc 1996, pp. 27–31.

part of the factional dissension in the SWP over the course of the 1940s can be attributed to differences arising precisely because of the tensions and difficulties that understandably emerged amidst state repression, trial, and imprisonment. Committed comrades such as Albert Goldman and Grace Carlson were lost to the Trotskyist movement in the decade after their Smith Act convictions, the former through factional exit, the latter by a return to the Catholic Church.[18]

Others, such as Carl Skoglund and Farrell Dobbs, remained loyal to the SWP. Years of state harassment dogged these revolutionary Trotskyists. The Smith Act, a particularly sordid instance of a broader state repression of the left that reaches back to the nineteenth century and forward into our times, revealed the extent to which the capitalist state was prepared to go to suppress dissent. In its refusal to bend to this repressive onslaught, and in its principled defence and ongoing campaigns to challenge those who would 'gag' the revolutionary party, US Trotskyists wrote an important chapter in the history of resistance to repression. Their orientation revealed a strategic sense of what can be done in decidedly non-revolutionary times, providing a concrete example of how to conduct a campaign of political labour defence against threats to fundamental civil liberties. The Smith Act trial of 1941 and its immediate aftermath remains instructive for revolutionaries concerned with how to conduct class struggle politics outside of the arena of production, defending freedoms essential to the preservation of liberties and the possibilities of revolutionary social change.

18 Albert Goldman's factional exit from the SWP will be the subject of a later chapter in the second installment of this volume. On Carlson see Cannon 1952.

1 The FBI and the Unions[19]

(*1941*)

Farrell Dobbs

The trade union movement today is today the victim of the most thoroughgoing governmental attack since the days of the Palmer raids. This assault, carefully planned and conducted in a most deliberate manner, daily becomes broader in scope and the methods utilized become more brazen. Its purpose is to prepare the American workers for docile submission to regimentation in industry and service in the military machine when Roosevelt, acting for Wall Street, plunges the United States into World War II. The ground for the campaign was prepared by Congressman Martin Dies and his 'Committee on Un-American Activities'. He is now preparing to go back over the same ground and plow a little deeper. A pretense was made at investigation of fascist groups. Dies now announces that this phase of the work of his Committee has been satisfactorily cleaned up. Few people are so naive as to accept this statement at face value. The truth is that Dies has made a few motions in this direction for the record and that he is now prepared to get down to serious business in the attacks on the workers' organizations. According to his own announcement, these are his intentions in the next stage of the campaign. The task of the Dies Committee is to stir up public suspicion toward union leaders and militant rank and filers through a mud-throwing campaign. The real job is to be done by Roosevelt's political police, the Federal Bureau of Investigation, which is the spearhead of the entire anti-union drive. Thurman Arnold, head of the anti-trust division of the United States Department of Justice, is Roosevelt's number one hatchet-man in the courtrooms. It is their ambition to make full preparations for M-Day, which is the War Department's name for the day on which the American worker will be compelled to go to war.

Present-day appropriations for the Federal Bureau of Investigation are roughly fifteen times as large as they were in 1917, the year of United States entry into World War I. The FBI operates in all fields, finding grounds on whatever

19 Dobbs 1941.

slender pretext for federal jurisdiction in labor cases. When this is not possible, the FBI gives full aid to the local police and courts.

J. Edgar Hoover, head of the FBI, testified before the House Appropriations Committee in November, 1939, that the FBI has organized a 'general intelligence division' which has compiled extensive records of individuals, groups and organizations engaged in what he calls 'subversive activity'. All of these are earmarked for arrests in mass when Roosevelt plunges the country into war. The immediate objective of the government is to cull out of the trade union movement in advance of the war as many of the militant elements as possible. By this action they aim to terrorize the workers, and especially the working class leaders, so that there will be a minimum of resistance to the war plan. The record of government action against the unions shows what Roosevelt-Arnold-Hoover consider as 'subversive activities' and just who they intend to terrorize.

The social outlook of J. Edgar Hoover is quite aptly characterized by his speech at the meeting of the International Association of Chiefs of Police in July, 1935, in which he termed as 'enemies of society' even those who are advocates of the prison parole system. This federal fink-herder wrote Chairman Matson of the National Labor Relations Board in November 28, 1939, complaining that a Board field examiner was speaking in favor of a pardon for an imprisoned labor leader. The case in question was one in which the FBI had no jurisdiction, but Hoover is interested in keeping all labor leaders in jail no matter how they are put there.

The FBI has on several occasions sent out public requests that it be given notice of all working class meetings, parades and demonstrations so that they may have snoopers present. There have already been cases, for example, the Minneapolis WPA strike, where they sent agents-provocateur as well as snoopers. They have requested the trade unions to advise them of any 'known subversive elements'. This is their not too subtle method of trying to make stool-pigeons out of the workers.

Industrial mishaps of whatever nature are today followed immediately by noisy FBI investigations of 'sabotage'. When an old scow capsized in the Hudson River, Hoover thought it was the work of enemies of the US government. These are dress rehearsals for the spy scare. It is only a short step from this to the branding of strikes as 'industrial sabotage' and the prosecution of strike leaders as 'agents of foreign powers'.

Thurman Arnold, during the early stages of his 'antitrust' campaign, sent a letter to the Indianapolis Central Labor Union of the AFL, setting forth a list of what he called unquestionable violations of the Sherman Anti-Trust Law. These boil down in their essence to a demand for docile acceptance by the workers of all employer methods and practices which Arnold can force down the throats of the trade-unionists. Federal grand juries have returned wide-scale indictments against trade unions and trade union officials on charges of 'criminal conspiracy in constraint of trade', 'interference with inter-state commerce' and any other charge which the FBI can dig up which will give Arnold an opportunity to wield the axe upon the trade union movement through the courts.

The Sherman Anti-Trust Law was enacted by Congress in 1890 as a result of the pressure from the workers and farmers who demanded that the huge trusts and monopolies be curbed by the government. It was first used, not against the trusts, but against the American Railway Union in 1894. Thereafter, the courts often invoked it against the unions, acting under pressure from the employers. The worker-farmer revolt against this practice became so strong that in 1914 Congress passed the Clayton Act specifically exempting labor from the 'conspiracy' charge which the courts were justifying on the basis of the Sherman Law.

Today, under the 'great liberal' Roosevelt, who is the real head of the FBI, the Department of Justice and its anti-trust division, the old practices are again revived. Workers are already in the federal prisons as a result of this drive. Others are under heavy bond pending appeal of convictions to higher courts; still others are now on trial or are under bond awaiting trial. A considerable number are under probation to federal officers with jail sentences hanging over their heads.

The first union victory in the fight against the 'anti-trust' campaign was recorded on May 6 when a Federal District Court ordered a verdict of acquittal in a case against the Washington, D.C. local union of the AFL Teamsters. According to the latest reports Roosevelt-Arnold-Hoover were 'undecided' whether an appeal would be taken to a higher court in a further attempt to jail these trade unionists.

The workers have little fear of the city police or any other local police agency against whose acts of violence they have had to defend themselves in strikes. Above all, they have little or no confidence in the cop as being in any way their friend. It is different with the FBI. There is much confusion in the minds of the workers on this point. Roosevelt understands this and is taking full advantage of the fact.

A feeling of awe towards all federal authority is drilled into the minds of the workers during their school days and then carefully nurtured by clever propaganda throughout their adult life. This is the primary advantage of the FBI as an instrument for the campaign against the unions. There has been a careful special buildup to augment the standing of the FBI in the eyes of the workers. The highly dramatized campaign against Dillinger, Machine-gun

Kelly, etc., provided the stage for the buildup. A series of movie plays glorifying the 'G-Men' has reinforced the drive. News reels of the 'G-Men' in training, accompanied by the inevitable sadist speech by J. Edgar Hoover, have been a powerful supplement. The radio has contributed its share through the *Gang Busters* serial and through numerous other devices. These factors have been a big help to Roosevelt in his anti-union drive.

The methods employed by the FBI in arresting workers and bringing them to trial are deliberately calculated to create the general public impression that they are dangerous characters. The most popular hour for the arrest of trade unionists by the FBI is between 3 a.m. and 5 a.m. in the morning. The daily press is often tipped off in advance of the arrest so that they may obtain pictures of the 'G-Men' herding the workers off to jail handcuffed and fastened together by a chain. Put in jail and still half asleep, the workers are given the old tough-cop/good-cop act. The first 'G-Man' who talks to them acts very hard-boiled; a little later another 'G-Man' comes in who pretends to be friendly and wants to 'help' the worker. If he doesn't get a 'confession' he then tells the worker hair-raising stories about what happens to those arrested by the FBI who do not 'tell all'. A companion action to this phase of the program is the frequent searching of workers' homes without even so much as the formality of a warrant.

Bail bond for workers arrested by the FBI has been uniformly high and, not satisfied with this, the FBI has in many cases interfered with the efforts of the unions to secure bond. And, once presented, the bond is submitted to a super-technical scrutiny; if any technicality can be found to justify the action, the bond is rejected. Another popular practice of the FBI is to prevent the arrested worker from establishing contact with a lawyer until the last minute before he is arraigned for hearing, so that he has little time to confer with his counsel to prepare a defense.

A good example of FBI methods is the case of the arrests and convictions of seven officers of local unions of the AFL Teamsters in Federal court at Sioux City, Iowa. In this case the FBI made minute measurements of a stretch of highway at the boundary between Minnesota and Iowa in order to establish jurisdiction for the Federal Court. High bail was set for the accused workers and all manner of interference was put in the way of their efforts to obtain the bail bond. Almost a year and a half had elapsed since the time of the alleged unlawful act. During this period the FBI had taken all of the time it considered necessary to prepare its case. The seven trade unionists were rushed to trial without opportunity to prepare adequate defense. One defendant had less than 48 hours from the time he was first able to see a lawyer until he was brought to trial. The men were all sentenced to two years in a Federal penitentiary and are now under bond pending an appeal to the higher court.

A part of the whole plan is for the FBI, both by example and by direct collaboration, to stir up similar actions by the local police and prosecuting attorney. A chain of interrelated actions against the workers is thus set in motion, both by the federal cops and the local cops. One agency supplements the other. A typical example of this is the case of Republican presidential aspirant Thomas E. Dewey's attempt to smear the Building Service Employees International Union of the AFL through the George Scalise case. The Building Service workers do not need the help of the cops-and-robbers minded Dewey to administrate their union. However, Dewey insists that they shall have his full interference whether they want it or not. During the second day of the proceedings of the union convention just held at Atlantic City, Dewey's henchmen broke into a session, placed four officials of the union under technical custody and disrupted the meeting so badly that it was necessary to adjourn. When W.L. McFetridge, one of the four, was later elected to succeed Scalise as president of the union, the New York *Daily News* came out on May 8 with the headline: 'Man Sought by Dewey Heads Scalise Union'. A swarm of FBI agents snooped around the convention headquarters, eavesdropping on conversations and spreading malicious gossip among the delegates.

There has been a veritable epidemic of seizures of the books and records of trade unions by the FBI and local police and prosecuting attorneys. In all parts of the country bosses serving on federal and county grand juries have been eagerly poking their long noses into the records of the unions that have been brought into the grand jury room.

The employers are rapidly falling into step with Roosevelt's anti-union drive on their own initiative and by their own methods, to say nothing of the wholehearted cooperation they give to the FBI and the local cops. Damage suits are instituted against the trade unions at every opportunity. Finks are planted in the unions to institute suits for accounting and then the union records are dragged into court and pried into by attorneys and accountants, hired and paid for by the employers' association.

The boldness of the drive against the leading officials of trade unions demonstrates Roosevelt's urgent desire to get the job done. It is also unmistakable evidence of his contempt for those very leaders who give him their unconditional support. The next item on the Roosevelt-Arnold-Hoover agenda will be a sweeping follow-up campaign directed against a much broader strata of the trade union movement.

Some trade unionists seek reasons to consider Roosevelt innocent of any complicity in this campaign. They point out that he did not appoint Thurman Arnold to the post of attorney-general when Frank Murphy was elevated to the United States Supreme Court. They credit Roosevelt when the Department of

Justice does not always get the full appropriation which it requests. But they are only deceiving themselves and others. These little incidents do not affect the general line. Make no mistake about it. Roosevelt is the head man of this anti-union drive.

The AFL is at present bearing the main brunt of this attack. But this does not mean that the CIO can afford to remain silent or hope to escape it. Fines and sentences have already been imposed upon leaders of the CIO Fur Workers Union. This is only a beginning. There seems to be a general belief in the CIO that it is safe to stand aside and permit the AFL to stand up as best it can against these attacks. This attitude is obviously motivated by factional considerations resulting from the struggle inside the trade union movement. Such a policy will in the end bring grave consequences to the CIO movement. Even in the AFL, although additional unions are constantly falling into the line of fire, there is a strong tendency on the part of those unions not involved to ignore the whole matter more or less. They will pay heavily for this ostrich policy.

The trade union movement is confronted by a vital threat to its very existence. Roosevelt is preparing to sterilize the unions. There are many willing hands to help him. The failure of the movement to defend itself can only intensify the attack and result in the unions becoming tied hand and foot by the government. Then they will be unable to perform their natural functions as independent organizations of the workers.

The carefully planned anti-union drive of the government must be met head-on. The defense of the unions must be just as carefully and thoroughly worked out as the attack. Facts must be recognized. Every section of the movement is affected. The independence of the labor movement is at stake. A powerful united campaign of defense must be launched with the full participation of all trade unions.

2 Witch Hunt in Minnesota[20]
(1941)

George Novack

On July 15, 1941 twenty-nine people were indicted by a Federal Grand Jury in St. Paul, Minnesota, on charges of 'seditious conspiracy'. The indictment had been drawn up by the US Department of Justice.

Among these indicted were the national and local leaders of the Socialist Workers Party and the officers of Motor Transport and Allied Workers Industrial Union, Local 544-CIO.

This prosecution is the most sweeping government attack upon the democratic rights of labor in many years. For its parallel, one would have to go back to the mass trials of the I.W.W. during the last World War.

The Minnesota 'seditious conspiracy' case has become an issue of national importance. Hundreds of publications throughout the country have featured and commented upon the Federal indictments. News of the arrests was flashed around the world. The case has aroused vast sections of the American trade union movement.

Forces are lining up on both sides. The Roosevelt administration's action has been backed up by the conservative press, Democratic and Republican leaders, certain reactionary AFL officials and the Communist Party. The prosecution has been vigorously denounced as a serious threat to civil liberties and organized labor by the CIO's Labor Non-Partisan League, the United Auto Workers, the American Civil Liberties Union, *The Nation, The New Republic* and other outstanding labor organizations and liberal spokesmen.

What is the true story behind this unprecedented Federal prosecution? Why were the officers and members of Local 544-CIO indicted at this particular time? Who prompted the prosecution? What are the real views and activities of the Socialist Workers Party? Is there any basis to the charge that the defendants were 'conspiring' to overthrow the US Government by force and violence? What is the significance of this case for civil liberties and labor's rights? …

---

20 Novack 1941.

Teamsters Local 544 Makes Minneapolis a Union Town

The 'seditious conspiracy' prosecution has arisen directly out of the influence of the Trotskyists, the Socialist Workers Party, in the trade union movement in Minneapolis. The storm center of the struggle is Teamsters Local 544, in which members or sympathizers with the policies of the Socialist Workers Party have played a leading role. Local 544 has been the spearhead and stronghold of the most militant and progressive sections of the labor movement in Minneapolis and the Northwest, ever since it consolidated itself as a powerful union organization by winning a series of strenuously fought strikes in 1934. These strikes made the Minneapolis Teamsters Union and its leadership nationally famous.

The leaders of 544 became known throughout the Northwest as hard-hitting fighters, uncompromising trade-unionists, and tough opponents. Under their inspiration and guidance Minneapolis, in a few years, became transformed from the leading open-shop city in the US to one of the most strongly organized union centers.

In the process of building their own union and extending trade unionism, the leaders of Local 544 had to engage in an uninterrupted series of battles and controversies with employers and their agents, city officials, police, National Guardsmen, strike-breakers, Silver Shirts, etc. This is not the first time members of 544 have been charged with 'conspiracy' by the Department of Justice. During the 1939 WPA strikes 162 workers, led by 544's Federal Workers Section, were arrested en masse and held for 'conspiracy'. After 32 strike leaders had been convicted, nation-wide labor protest forced the government to release the other 130 defendants.

544's First Fights with Daniel Tobin

In the course of their struggles the 544 leaders made many bitter enemies inside as well as outside the labor movement. Not least amongst these was the President of their own International organization, Daniel Tobin. Tobin opposed the militant policies which had enabled the Teamster leaders of Minneapolis to establish their union and defend it against all kinds of attacks. During the 1934 strikes, he publicly denounced the leaders of the union as 'Reds' and branded their strike action as 'illegal'.

In 1935 Tobin expelled the Local from the International Brotherhood of Teamsters and tried to set up a rival local. A year later, however, although he had declared its leaders would never again be permitted to head a union in his International, Tobin had to readmit the local. The CIO was growing and was about to break away from the AFL. Tobin took back the local as a lesser evil. 544's leaders were also advised by CIO officials they consulted at that time to return to the AFL.

During the next five years, Local 544 was instrumental in building the teamsters movement in Minneapolis and the entire North-Central area into the most powerful labor force in the Northwest. The 11-state North-Central Area Committee, inspired and directed by 544's leadership, brought over 200,000 over-the-road drivers into the Teamsters International under a closed-shop area-wide contract signed in the fall of 1937. Although he knew that Farrell Dobbs belonged to the Socialist Workers Party, Tobin had to appoint Dobbs, Secretary-Treasurer of Local 544, as International Organizer in charge of this area. When Dobbs, one of the 29 now under indictment, resigned as International Organizer in January 1940 to become Labor Secretary of the Socialist. Workers Party he informed Tobin of his decision. Tobin assured Dobbs that he could always return as an International Organizer. At that juncture Tobin was more interested in the dues-paying members Local 544's leadership could bring into his International than he was in hounding the Trotskyists for their anti-war stand.

At the last Teamsters' International Convention in September 1940 – I.B.T. conventions are held only once every five years – the 544 delegates led the fight against two important measures sponsored by Tobin. They defeated a proposal that Tobin be given powers to enforce arbitration upon affiliated locals in any dispute with the employers. They fought against raising Tobin's annual salary from $20,000 to $30,000 a year, but Tobin won that pot. The convention battles ended in an uneasy truce between Tobin and Local 544.

In the Spring of 1941, immediately after the Local 544 elections a 'Committee of 99', composed of a small group of disgruntled union members, but backed by Tobin from the start, filed charges against the elected officers of Local 544 with the Executive Board of the IBT. They accused 544's leaders of being 'Communists' and 'radicals' and therefore unworthy to head the union. The charges were the same as those made three years before by five discredited members of the union, who, abetted by the open-shop employers' organization, the Associated Industries, had instituted a legal action against 544. Local 544 had successfully fought and defeated this suit in the courts. After the most thorough examination of the books, records and activities of the union, District Judge Carron ruled that the union's leadership had carried on the affairs of the union in a legal, efficient and honest manner.

The earlier accusers in the so-called 'Fink Suit' had called upon the Court to remove 544's leadership and appoint a receiver for the union. Now the 'Committee of 99' appealed to Tobin to take this same step. On the basis of their charges, Tobin ordered a Committee of 544 leaders to attend a hearing held before International officers on April 8, 1941 in Chicago. At that hearing, the 544 delegation presented its refutation of the charges leveled against them.

Tobin Moves against 544

Fortune Magazine for May, 1941 appeared with an article on the International Brotherhood of Teamsters which emphasized the racketeering prevalent in Tobin's International and taunted him about the Trotskyist leadership of Local 544 in Minneapolis. Tobin, sensitive to the criticism of Big Business, answered that he was going to rid his organization of such elements. But he acted, not against the racketeers, but solely against the 'Reds'.

In the May, 1941 issue of his *Teamsters Journal*, Tobin published an editorial, stating that some Minnesota teamsters were 'known advocates of the Socialist Workers Party' and threatened that anyone who would not resign from the party would be removed from the ranks of the IBT. Other editorials in the *Teamsters Journal* warned all members who did not loyally support President Roosevelt's policies, particularly his policy toward the war that they had no place in the Teamsters International and would be liable to disciplinary action by Tobin. The official organ of the Minneapolis Teamsters, the *Northwest Organizer*, had persistently opposed Roosevelt's labor and war policies.

Upon the appearance of 544's delegation at the meeting of the International Executive Board at Washington the first week in June, Tobin asked that they agree to his appointment of a dictator-receiver over the union, with absolute powers, including the power to expel anyone. Local 544 rejected this proposal that same week.

For a month before, negotiations between 544 and the Minneapolis employers for the renewal of the union contracts which expired on June 1st, had produced no results. It was stated in the Minneapolis press that the employers were awaiting the outcome of the June meeting with Tobin, when they confidently expected that the leadership of 544 would be ousted and replaced by Tobin appointees.

544 Goes CIO

At a regular membership meeting held on June 9th, 544's delegation to Washington and its officers presented these facts in reports to the nearly 4,000 members present of the more than 5,000 in the union. By a well-nigh unanimous vote, the members decided to disaffiliate from the IBT and to apply for a charter from the United Construction Workers Organizing Committee of the CIO. After thoroughly investigating the union and the record of its leadership, this charter was granted by A.D. Lewis, President of the United Construction Workers Organizing Committee, who announced that it was the first step in a 'streamlined CIO organizing campaign among the Motor Transport and Allied Workers of the entire midwest area to bring them into a modern, progressive industrial union'. The Minneapolis Ice-Drivers Local 21, the Austin (Minn.) Drivers Union, the Ottumwa (Iowa) Teamsters Local voted to follow 544's example in leaving the AFL for the CIO. Teamsters' locals elsewhere were considering similar action. This was demonstrated a short time later in Michigan when 5,000 teamsters in Detroit and entire AFL Drivers Locals in Flint, Pontiac, Lansing, Monroe and other cities went over to the CIO.

Tobin Asks Roosevelt for Help against 544-CIO

Four days after Local 544 voted to join the CIO, as the movement it initiated was gaining momentum and extensive support, Tobin telegraphed President Roosevelt, appealing to the Government to take action in this matter. Tobin's statement said in part: 'The withdrawal from the International Union by the truck drivers' union, Local 544 and one other small union in Minneapolis, and their affiliation with the CIO is indeed a regrettable and dangerous condition. The officers of this local union ... were requested to disassociate themselves from the radical Trotsky organization ... we feel that while our country is in a dangerous position, those disturbers who believe in the policies of foreign, radical governments, *must be in some way prevented from pursuing this dangerous course ...*' (*NY Times*, June 14, 1941).

Upon receipt of this message from Tobin, the President's secretary, Stephen Early, issued the following statement to the White House press conference:

> Mr. Tobin telegraphed from Indianapolis that it is apparent to him and to the other executives of his organization that because they have been and will continue to stand squarely behind the government, all subversive organizations and all enemies of our government, including Bundists, Trotskyists and Stalinists are opposed to them and seeking to destroy loyal trade unions which are supporting democracy.
>
> Mr. Tobin goes into considerable detail and states that he is going to issue a statement from the Indianapolis office of the teamsters union.

> When I advised the President of Tobin's representations this morning, *he asked me to immediately have the Government departments and agencies interested* in *this matter notified*, and to point out that this is no time, in his opinion, for labor unions, local or national, to begin raiding one another for the purpose of getting-memberships or for similar reason.
>
> *NY Times*, June 14, 1941

Roosevelt Sends the FBI to Minnesota

Within a few days after Tobin's appeal and the President's statement, Henry A. Schweinhaut, Special Assistant Attorney General of the Department of Justice, was sent to Minneapolis with several aides to prepare the raids and the indictments which followed. On June 27th, FBI agents raided the Socialist Workers Party headquarters in Minneapolis and St. Paul, seizing books by Marx, Lenin and Trotsky, copies of the party's publications (although these were on public sale in many places), red flags and photographs.

Acting Attorney General Biddle announced from Washington that same day: 'the principal Socialist Workers Party leaders, against whom prosecution is being brought, are also leaders of Local 544-CIO in Minneapolis ... and have gained control of a legitimate labor union to use it for illegitimate purposes' (*Minneapolis Star-Journal*, June 28, 1941).

Frank Barnhart, Regional Director of the CIO's United Construction-Workers Organization Committee and personal representative of John L. Lewis, immediately denounced the raids as 'a smear campaign against the CIO'. He charged that President Roosevelt had instigated the action in payment of his political debt to Tobin, a member of the Democratic Party National Committee and head of the Democratic Labor Committee in the 1940 Presidential election. He accused the US Department of Justice with intervening on behalf of the AFL against the CIO in their dispute over the Minneapolis teamsters.

Indictments by the Score!

On July 15th the Department of Justice obtained from a Federal Grand Jury in St. Paul indictment of 29 people on charges of 'seditious conspiracy'. Among those indicted were the officers and most active members of Local 544-CIO and national and local leaders of the Socialist Workers Party. Bail was first set at $5,000 each. Upon protest by attorneys, bail for the sixteen 544-CIO members was reduced to $3,500 each. This was provided by the National CIO.

The bail of ten others was reduced to $2,500 each. This was provided by the Civil Rights Defense Committee. Three of the defendants were released on their own recognizance.

A hailstorm of additional indictments has been heaped upon the officers of 544-CIO. On July 14th the Hennepin County Grand Jury, on a Tobin complaint, indicted Miles Dunne, President, and Kelly Postal, Secretary-Treasurer of 544-CIO, for 'embezzling funds' claimed by the AFL.

On July 18, Carl Skoglund, organizer of 544-CIO, was arrested and held for deportation on $25,000 bail. On Monday, July 28th, the Hennepin County Grand Jury voted four new indictments against Secretary-Treasurer Kelly Postal and Organizer Moe Hork for 'first degree larceny'. *This makes a total to date of 66 charges against those connected with this case!*

The Government's aim in heaping these indictments upon the officers and members of Local 544-CIO is plain. By crushing the union beneath the enormous burden of expensive and prolonged litigation involved in fighting the cases and by terrorizing its members, the Government helps Tobin throttle his CIO rival.

The CIO union has also had to contend with hostile actions on the part of State and local authorities. On September 19th, 1941 State Labor Board administrator Blair denied Local 544-CIO's petition for elections to determine which union represents the workers and certified the AFL without elections as bargaining agent for the Minneapolis motor transport workers. Local 544-CIO has appealed Blair's outrageous decision both in the courts and to the National Labor Relations Board.

Local 544-CIO Fights On

The spirit with which Local 544-CIO faces this fight was expressed in the following speech by Frank Barnhart, Regional Director of the UCWOC, at a membership meeting on August 11, 1941.

> The United Mine Workers is a great and powerful organization. It has had members and leaders in every jail in America. But labor's enemies were never able to break the United Mine Workers.
>
> The CIO organized the steel workers and the auto workers. The CIO has never tackled a fight it didn't finish. The CIO came to Minneapolis to stay until this Local 544-CIO fight is won.
>
> *The Industrial Organizer*, August 14, 1941

The fight on behalf of the 29 defendants in this case is thus part of the CIO's struggle to maintain democratic trade unionism amongst the Minneapolis teamsters and to build a powerful industrial union of motor transport workers throughout the nation.

Prosecution Rushes Case

On September 11th Federal Judge Joyce overruled the demurrers of the defendants and set the date of the trial for October 20th in the Federal Court in Minneapolis. The request of the defendants for more time to prepare for the trial was vehemently opposed by the prosecution.

The Federal prosecutors are obviously hurrying the case along, anxious to obtain quick convictions.

Convictions of the Minneapolis CIO leaders will not only signally assist Tobin in crushing his competitor but, as both Labor's Non-Partisan League and *The Nation* have pointed out, will also set a precedent for further government prosecutions against other militant trade unionists. This was clearly indicated by Assistant US Attorney-General Schweinhaut, who was quoted in the *St. Paul Dispatch* of June 28, 1941 as saying: 'We cracked down here first. Mr. Biddle has said this is only a start. So you can expect other actions to follow shortly'.

Political Motives for the Prosecution

This case, however, is by no means a simple trade union affair. It is essentially a *political* prosecution. This was pointed out by the American Civil Liberties Union in its letter of protest to Attorney-General Biddle on August 20, 1941: 'It seems more reasonable to conclude that the government injected itself into an inter-union controversy in order to promote the interests of the one side which supported the administration's foreign and domestic policies'.

Tobin is a 100% supporter of Roosevelt's policies. He is also among the most prominent members of Fight for Freedom, Inc., the foremost pro-war organization in the United States. In many recent public statements, Tobin has declared that opposition to the President's war policies is 'un-American' and incompatible with membership in his Teamsters International.

Local 544's weekly, *Northwest Organizer* (now *The Industrial Organizer*) on the other hand, has been a severe critic of Roosevelt's anti-labor actions and a resolute opponent of his war policies. For example, in an editorial on May 29, 1941 against Roosevelt's use of troops as strike-breakers, *The Northwest Organ-*

izer said: 'The forces most belligerently determined to put this nation into the "war for democracy" are the very forces who imitate Hitler by taking away what democracy we still possess, and would beat down and crush labor … American labor doesn't want any part of this war. American labor is determined to defend its unions and its rights, including the right to strike'.

Tobin moved to expel the 544 leaders at this particular time because, among other things, they refused to recant their avowed anti-war stand. This was affirmed in a statement issued on June 28th by Frank Barnhart, Regional Director of the UCWOC: 'Not long ago Tobin issued an ultimatum to the officers and members of the AFL Teamsters Union ordering them to give unequivocal support to Roosevelt's war policy under threat of reprisals against them by Tobin if they failed to comply … A great majority of the membership of the AFL Teamsters Union is opposed to Tobin's high-handed methods and moth-eaten organizational policies. There are also many who are opposed to the war, especially in the northwest area. This is not Hitler Germany. The US is still a democracy. The people of this country still express their opinions about the policies of Roosevelt'.

Socialist Workers Party Opposes War

The political basis of the prosecution is unmistakable in the proceedings against the Socialist Workers Party. The Socialist Workers Party has consistently and uncompromisingly opposed Roosevelt's policies as 'imperialist war policies'. That the government acted against the Socialist Workers Party because of its anti-war position was explicitly acknowledged by Acting Attorney-General Biddle, who was quoted in the *Minneapolis Tribune* of June 28th, 1941 as saying: 'The principal basis for the prosecution is found in the Declaration of Principles adopted by the Socialist Workers Party in December, 1938'. The pertinent phrases mentioned by Biddle include the following: 'If in spite of the revolutionists and the militant workers, the US Government enters a new war, the Socialist Workers Party will not, under any circumstances support that war but will, on the contrary, fight against it'. According to Biddle, 'the 1938 Declaration says the Party would use a war crisis to overthrow capitalism in this country and substitute for it socialism'.

The administration's inclination to stamp even the mildest critics of its war course as 'seditious' is exemplified in Secretary of War Stimson's charge of treason against Senator Wheeler. If one member of the Cabinet can stigmatize an isolationist Senator as a traitor for sending to a few conscripts postcards expressing opposition to entering the war, surely Roosevelt's Attorney-General would not hesitate to treat the revolutionary anti-war position of the Socialist Workers Party as 'seditious activity'.

Rights of Free Speech Violated

... The Socialist Workers Party does not deny its revolutionary views nor its uncompromising opposition to war. It does deny, however, that the Government has any right to prosecute on that account. The Socialist Workers Party has the same legal and constitutional rights as any other political party to advocate its ideas and propagate them. This position fully accords with our best democratic traditions and with the Bill of Rights. The right to express one's own ideas by speech or in writing or through assembly is an elementary democratic right. Rights of opinion are specifically protected against Federal violation by the First Amendment to the Constitution which states that Congress 'shall make no law abridging the freedom of speech or of the press or the right of the people peaceably to assemble and to petition the Government for a redress of grievances'.

This right of free speech is unrestricted and unconditional. It cannot be denied on the ground that the doctrines advocated are revolutionary or displeasing to the administration in power. The Government's attempt to deprive the Socialist Workers Party of its right of free opinion and expression clearly encroaches upon this provision of the Constitution.

The prosecution has already been condemned and will be fought on this ground by the American Civil Liberties Union. The violation of law in this instance is not on the part of the Socialist Workers Party but on the part of the Federal prosecutors.

Real Ideas of the Socialist Workers Party

Nor is the Socialist Workers Party a secret, conspiratorial organization as the Government attempts to depict it. It is a legal political organization which has for years openly conducted political activities and participated in the labor movement. Its program has been published in numerous books and pamphlets, its views are currently expressed and discussed in various publications, its indicted leaders have long been active as prominent personalities in working class circles.

The accusation that the Socialist Workers Party is guilty of 'advising, counseling and urging insubordination, disloyalty and mutiny' in the armed forces of the US is based entirely upon the political ideas propagated by the party. No overt acts are specified in the indictment to back up this charge. In fact, the avowed military policy of the Socialist Workers Party provides no basis for such activities or allegations. For example, the Socialist Workers Party does not seek to gain control of the naval and military forces of the US, as alleged in the indictment. The Party's program calls for 'military training of workers financed by the government and under control of the trade unions'. There is nothing illegal in this proposal to place trade unions in charge of military training. The Plattsburg training camps, which the US Government approved and subsidized, were organized and controlled by private agencies and individuals for the purpose of training business and professional men in military science. The Socialist Workers Party proposes that this same right be extended by the Government to the trade unions.

What was the Union Defense Guard?

The only overt act allegedly committed by the defendants, which is specified in the indictment, is the formation of the Union Defense Guard, organized three years ago by members of Local 544. According to the prosecution, this Union Defense Guard was the instrument the Socialist Workers Party plotted to use for overthrowing the Government by force and violence. A brief account of the formation and functions of the Union Defense Guard will suffice to dispose of this absurd accusation.

The Minneapolis Union Defense Guard was organized as an outgrowth and answer to a series of threats of violence against Local 544 and of actual vigilante attacks upon unions in other parts of the nation during the summer of 1938.

On June 22, 1938, Ralph H. Pierce, one of the leaders of the 'Associated Independent Unions', launched by Minneapolis employers to fight organized labor, told officials of Local 544 and the Minneapolis Central Labor Union that George K. Belden, head of the Associated Industries, had raised $35,000 to import gunmen to assassinate three leaders of Local 544. Eight months earlier Patrick Corcoran, Secretary-Treasurer of the Minneapolis Teamsters Joint Council, had been assassinated by unknown gunmen. The day after Pierce said the murders were to be committed, Minneapolis police found a car containing two high-powered rifles with telescopic sights near the Central Labor Union headquarters. This lent credence to Pierce's story.

During 1938 the Fascist Silver Shirts were extremely active in the Twin Cities. Roy Zachary, National Organizer, openly called at Silver Shirt meetings for gangster bands to raid the General Drivers Hall. The Minneapolis papers disclosed the fact that Belden, head of the Associated Industries, had attended these Silver Shirt meetings. This tie-up between the Silver Shirts and the Associated Industries, which included the leading anti-union employers in Minneapolis, convinced the members of Local 544 that measures should be taken to protect the Union hall and leaders from attack.

Numerous acts of anti-labor violence by fascist and vigilante gangs at that time in other parts of Minnesota and in New Orleans, Westwood, California, Steubensville, Ohio, New York City and Jersey City, crystallized this conviction.

Activities of the Defense Guard

The formation of the Minneapolis Union Defense Guard was announced in the September 8, 1938 issue of the *Northwest Organizer*, the official organ of the Teamsters Joint Council. The functions of the Union Defense Guard were described in this story as 'defense of the Union's picket lines, Union headquarters and members against anti-labor violence'.

The activities of the Union Defense Guard demonstrate that such was its sole function. At meetings held in the basement of the Drivers Hall general discussions took place on methods of repelling attacks by fascist gangs. None of the guard members carried or possessed arms.

One of the two allegations of overt acts in the indictment charges the defendants with collecting arms and ammunition to overthrow the Government. The Union Defense Guard purchased two 22-A caliber single shot target rifles, two 22-caliber single shot target pistols, and some ammunition for target practice in the basement of the General Drivers Headquarters. These four practice rifles and ammunition were purchased from funds raised through the sale of tickets to dances and public entertainments held at the Drivers Hall.

I.F. Stone wrote in *The Nation* of July 26, 1941 that the Government was especially alarmed by a test mobilization of Guard members held one evening during September, 1938 in downtown Minneapolis. 'What did they do when they got there?' Mr. Schweinhaut, the Department of Justice prosecutor, was asked. Schweinhaut said they went to the Gaiety, a local burlesque house. He said that each admission cost 75 cents and 'the Government wants to know who paid for the tickets'. 'This was told me in all seriousness', was the caustic comment of *The Nation* reporter. 'I have heard of the Gunpowder Plot. Maybe this will go down in history as the G-String Conspiracy!'

The show of strength of the Union Defense Guard drove the Silver Shirts into hiding and inactivity. With the disappearance of the Silver Shirts the Union

Defense Guard discontinued its target practice and drills and its sole functions thereafter were dances, and acting as ushers at union picnics and affairs. It last functioned in December 1940 when Guard members acted as ushers at the Christmas party for children sponsored by the Minneapolis Teamsters Joint Council!

Such is the record of the 'armed forces' which were supposedly planning to march on Washington and take over the government. Who does the prosecution expect to believe that story? Indeed, this accusation had already been dismissed as baseless in the 544 'Fink Suit', when Judge Paul S. Carroll stated in his findings: 'According to the Union's position these so-called "defense guards" were organized "to meet the threat of Silver Shirt leaders and other anti-labor gangsters" and to defend armed raids against union halls. It was not shown that these men were ever armed or did other than general policing at their picnics and things of that sort'.

Indicted under Reactionary Smith 'Omnibus Gag' Act

The indictment has been drawn up under the provisions of two laws. One is a new law, the Smith 'Omnibus Gag' Act, introduced by a Poll-Tax Congressman, Howard W. Smith of Virginia, and passed in 1940. The Smith Act is the most reactionary piece of anti-labor legislation ever enacted in the US and was so characterized during the debates in Congress. 'This bill is an attempt to put an end to this trend toward real democracy', said Representative Geyer of California. 'It is an attempt to break the labor movement ... It is an attack on a minority group'.

'It is enough to make Thomas Jefferson turn over in his grave', said Representative Martin of Colorado. 'It is without precedent in the history of labor legislation. It is an invention of intolerance contrary to every principle of democracy'.

The American Civil Liberties Union pleaded with President Roosevelt to veto the Smith Bill on the ground that it was unconstitutional and 'would become an instrument of oppression against unpopular minorities and organized labor'. President Roosevelt nevertheless signed it.

The American Civil Liberties Union's prediction has now been fulfilled in the Minnesota case. According to *The Nation*, the Department of Justice itself has no confidence in the constitutionality of the Smith Act: 'Off the record, at least one official engaged in the prosecution is prepared to admit that the Supreme Court may find the sedition provisions of the Smith Act unconstitutional. For the first time in peace, since the Alien & Sedition Laws of John Adams, a mere expression of opinion is made a Federal crime. Under these provisions, a man might be sent to jail for ten years because he circulated such un-American documents as the Declaration of Independence and Lincoln's Second Inaugural, for both "advocate, abet, advise, or teach the duty, necessity, desirability or propriety of overthrowing or destroying any government" by force'.

The other law, Section 6 of Title 18 of the US Code governing 'seditious conspiracy', was passed in July, 1861 during the Civil War to be used against the Confederacy. Since no particle of evidence can be presented in this case of any such open armed rebellion against the government, this law obviously cannot apply. As *The Nation* points out: 'The rebellion of which the Trotskyist leaders of Local 544 are guilty was leaving the AFL for the CIO'. It is not a penal offense for American workers to quit one labor organization for another.

The Real Facts in This Case

Our review of the facts in this case has irrefutably established the following points.

1. After Local 544 had voted to disaffiliate from the AFL and join the CIO, Roosevelt responded to Tobin's plea for assistance by setting in motion the machinery of the Department of Justice which resulted in the raids and indictments. This intervention of the Federal authorities on behalf of one labor organization in its controversy with another constitutes a rank abuse of the legal functions of the Government.
2. The Socialist Workers Party does not conspire to overthrow the government by force and violence. Its object is to educate the majority of the people to accept the idea that a change in the social system is necessary to solve their economic and social problems.
3. There was no conspiracy whatsoever on the part of the defendants to overthrow the government by force and violence. The attempt to depict the Minneapolis Union Defense Guard as an armed band organized for this purpose is fantastic.
4. The Government is violating the free-speech provisions of the Constitution by instituting this repressive criminal action against the Socialist Workers Party.
5. Through this prosecution the Government is attempting to crush militant and independent unionism and to stifle the anti-war forces in the ranks of labor.

Roosevelt seeks to imprison the leaders of the Socialist Workers Party because of their anti-war views, as Woodrow Wilson jailed Eugene V. Debs and other socialists for opposing the last war. Attorney General Biddle is today prosecuting the militant unionists of Local 544-CIO as Attorney General Palmer prosecuted the members of the IWW.

Civil Liberties and Labor's Rights Imperiled

Will the American people and the American labor movement fight to maintain their civil liberties and democratic rights? Or will the Roosevelt administration, under pretext of wartime emergency and in defiance of the Constitution, abrogate and deny them? This is the central issue posed by this case.

The Administration's attitude toward civil rights today has been bluntly expressed by the prosecutor. During the Senate Judiciary Committee hearings on his nomination early in September, in defense of FBI tapping of Harry Bridges' wires, Attorney General Biddle declared: 'It is a dirty business, of course ... but we have abandoned civil rights before in times of war' (*New York Times*, Sept. 5, 1941).

Nation-Wide Protest against the Prosecution

Labor's Non-Partisan League, the political arm of the CIO of which John L. Lewis is Chairman, has emphasized the menace of the prosecution to the union movement. 'Witch-hunting tactics of the Justice Department under A. Mitchell Palmer in World War I are being revived here as history repeats itself in World War II. This is a clear case of Justice Department interference in a trade union matter. The incident is regarded generally as an attempt by the Justice Department to establish a precedent. If it is successful, many informed observers are expecting other indictments of labor figures who do not toe the mark'.

'This is one of the most serious issues involving civil liberties to arise in the US in many years', wrote *The New Republic* on July 28, 1941. 'That the Minneapolis case is tremendously important goes without saying. President Roosevelt and Acting Attorney General Francis Biddle have repeatedly promised that there would be no such violations of civil liberties as stained the honor of America in the last war. For a country preparing to fight for the principles of democracy, now to violate these principles ... would be unforgivable; it would be worth ten divisions to Hitler'.

The thousand delegates to the last annual Convention of the United Auto Workers held at Buffalo in August not only pledged full support to Local 544 in its fight but unanimously protested against this use of the FBI 'to oppress or harass any labor organization in the pursuit of their legitimate activities'.

'Even the language of the indictment has the peculiar twist of Stalin's famous frame-ups in Moscow', writes John Dos Passos in an article condemning the prosecution in *The Nation* of September 6, 1941. 'If the defendants are convicted', he says, 'a precedent will have been set that bodes ill for this country's liberties'.

The American Civil Liberties Union has publicly protested the prosecution and is cooperating with the defense in fighting the case. These labor and liberal organizations have realized that a successful prosecution of the Socialist Workers Party and the leaders of. Local 544-CIO would become the forerunner of an 'all-out' attack upon other trade union militants and political groups.

That is why the 29 defendants in this case are today the front-line fighters in the cause of civil liberties in this country. That is why they merit wholehearted moral and material support from every progressive organization and individual genuinely concerned with maintaining our democratic and constitutional rights. That is why the Civil Rights Defense Committee has been organized. That is why their fight against the prosecution must be won.

3 Capitalist Frame-Up: 1941 Model[21]
(1941)

William F. Warde (George Novack)

The Government has concluded its case against the leaders of the Socialist Workers Party and of Local 544-CIO. The presiding judge discharged five of the defendants on the ground of insufficient evidence. He refused to free the entire 28 as the defense attorneys requested.

For, in their haste to smash the progressive union movement headed by Local 544-CIO and to jail the revolutionary opponents of their war policy, Roosevelt's agents have not even bothered to contrive a credible case nor to conceal the crudely reactionary character of their frame-up.

The Judge Upholds the Prosecution

In denying the defense motion to dismiss the case, Judge Joyce upheld the contention of the prosecution that, as revolutionary socialists, the men and women on trial were 'outside the law' and were not entitled to any of the rights and protection guaranteed to all citizens by the Constitution. He stated that, under conspiracy statutes, 'it is not necessary to prove that the defendants actually agreed in terms to adopt the unlawful purpose and to pursue it by common means …'. The mere maintenance of their political opinions is cause for conviction. Finally, in language more familiar to Moscow than Minneapolis, Judge Joyce compared the Socialist Workers Party to Hitler's followers. These remarks, read from a prepared statement which completely disregarded the defense attorney's arguments, indicated the spirit in which Judge Joyce intends to instruct the jury.

The Federal prosecutors represent two different types of officials in the Roosevelt bureaucracy. One, the local prosecutor, Victor A. Anderson, is an aggressive and unbridled reactionary. Some of the defendants have confronted Anderson before in this same Minneapolis courtroom during the trials

21 Warde 1941.

of WPA workers who struck for higher relief in 1939. The other is Assistant Attorney-General Henry A. Schweinhaut, sent from the Department of Justice in Washington to direct the prosecution. Like his boss, Francis Biddle, Schweinhaut used to masquerade as a protector of civil liberties. He was formerly the chief of the Civil Liberties Division of the Department of Justice, which was nominally set up to guard against violations of the Bill of Rights. What better person could Roosevelt call upon to strike this blow at civil liberties than this ex-liberal? Schweinhaut showed his true colors when he repudiated the liberal doctrine of 'clear and present danger' advocated as the test of free speech by Justices Holmes and Brandeis against reactionary Supreme Court opinion.

The defense attorneys were not permitted to question the talesmen for prejudice. Most of these middle-class citizens, including big and small business men, come from the rural districts outside of Minneapolis. There is not a trade unionist or industrial worker amongst them, although Minneapolis is a strongly organized city.

Months before, Biddle promised 'startling revelations' regarding the defendants' armed plot to overthrow the government, 'which goes far beyond public knowledge'. These were not forthcoming at the trial. Instead, as newspaper commentators pointed out, the government's evidence was distinguished above all by its dullness. The bombshell of sensational revelations which the government promised to set off fizzled out at the trial. The government presented no more about the ideas and activities of the defendants than was already matter of common knowledge. It was no secret that the Socialist Workers Party was a revolutionary socialist political organization, based upon the teachings of Marx, Lenin and Trotsky. The only 'startling' revelation was that this could be considered proof of 'seditious conspiracy'.

Biddle and his associates had previously boasted that they possessed ample proofs of overt acts on the part of the defendants and that no restriction of civil liberties was involved or intended. The blunt-spoken Anderson swept aside this pretence in his opening statement to the jury by declaring that the prosecution was not obliged to prove the commission of any overt acts in order to establish that the defendants had engaged in 'seditious conspiracy'. In plain language, they could be convicted for the mere expression of their opinions. The very existence of the Socialist Workers Party, its propaganda and work for socialism, constituted a plot against the US Government. According to the government's own statement, the constitutional rights of free speech, free press, and freedom to assemble were to be explicitly denied to the people on trial, and their exercise of them constituted a criminal offense.

Expression of Opinion is – 'Seditious Conspiracy'

This was made plain as Prosecutor Anderson cited the allegedly criminal activities of the defendants. They organized an avowedly revolutionary socialist party; 'it was a part of the plan and purpose of this party to appeal to mass groups and psychology, largely among the workers, the more unfortunate workers ... and farmers who were small operators, to join this party'. They carried on all the normal functions of a political organization; collected dues, had headquarters, held public meetings, ran candidates for office, etc. The members of the SWP were instructed to be active in the trade unions. They believed that organized labor had the right and duty to defend itself from fascist attacks whether they came from at home or from abroad. They therefore advocated the formation of union defense guards and military training under the control of the trade unions. All this, according to the prosecutor, formed the basis of their plot to overthrow the government by force.

Their crimes did not stop there. The SWP, the prosecutor charged, was inspired by the teachings of Leon Trotsky and of 'the first executive head of the Soviet Union, V.I. Lenin, and wanted to establish a workers' state not only in the former Kingdom of Russia and its possessions but throughout the world'. The party also espoused not only the doctrines of Marx, but those of 'a more recent writer by the name of Engels'. As Fourth Internationalists, they sought to 'further the international revolution against organized society'.

Not least of their misdeeds was the fact that some of the defendants had visited Trotsky in Mexico City and furnished protection to him. That is, they were guilty of helping to prolong Trotsky's life against the attempts of Stalin's assassins.

The anti-labor character of the prosecution was laid bare as Anderson climaxed his charges by accusing the defendants of the 'crime' of urging workers to distrust arbitration and to demand higher wages. 'Every time there was an arbitration, labor surrendered something and labor should never surrender', Anderson said of the Trotskyists, 'that was a part of the program for carrying on successfully the program of this Socialist Workers Party – labor leaders should always demand, demand, demand. For instance, if it was a question of labor pay per hour, ask for an increase; if that was received, then don't stop there ... Always agitate and demand to cause a condition of unrest in order that there might be a breach between the employing class and the employed'.

Union Activity Now a Crime

The scope of the alleged conspiracy is wide enough to embrace all the ordinary activities of organized labor as well as the ideas of the revolutionary and socialist movement. All the democratic rights guaranteed under the constitution, all the hard-won rights of union labor embodied in the Wagner Act and other recent labor legislation are trampled underfoot by the government prosecutors.

If a trade union should ask for improved working conditions or strike for higher wages, this can hereafter be construed as a conspiracy to overthrow the government. If a labor organization should try to defend itself against unlawful vigilante attacks, then its members can be accused of armed insurrection. If anyone should venture to criticize Roosevelt's war policies or to call his regime imperialistic or capitalistic, he can be liable to 10 years in jail and $10,000 fine. Even a proposal for a popular referendum vote on war similar to the Ludlow Bill was admitted as evidence of 'sedition' by Judge Joyce on the ground that such a demand was not meant seriously since it could only be obtained by armed force. There is hardly a labor activity or progressive and radical idea which could not be outlawed by convictions in this case. This prosecution is a gigantic conspiracy on the part of the Roosevelt administration against the Bill of Rights and the rights of American labor.

The 23 on trial are only the first Roosevelt's witch-hunters will place on trial for their activities on behalf of the working class. The Southern Poll-Tax Congressmen who accused the striking shipyard workers of San Diego of trying 'to overthrow the Government by force and violence', and the errand boys of the steel magnates who are branding John L. Lewis a 'traitor' for insisting upon a closed shop agreement in the captive coal mines are preparing the political atmosphere for further prosecutions of this type. In the eyes of the imperialist war mongers and the profiteers, whoever defends the interests of the workers today is an enemy of the state, and must be punished accordingly.

Chief Defense Attorney and defendant Albert Goldman spoke out boldly for the defense. He stated that a political movement was on trial and that great principles and great social theories were involved. It was true that the members of the Socialist Workers Party were disciples of Marx, Lenin and Trotsky, but it was false that the Marxist movement was in any way a conspiracy. This was impossible, for the SWP aimed to win through education and propaganda a majority of the people of the US to its program. Socialism was the sole solution for the ills of mankind.

Goldman reaffirmed all the principal points in the program of the SWP: its opposition to the imperialist war, its struggle for democracy in the trade unions, its policy of military training under trade union control, its internationalism, its advocacy of union defense guards, its approval of the workers' revolution of 1917, etc. He denied that the Socialist Workers Party practices sabotage or advocates insubordination in the army, and declared that the prosecution's attempt to depict the union defense guard as an armed band for overthrowing the government was 'nothing but a frame-up'. He denied that the defendants advocated the violent overthrow of the government. The SWP members preferred a peaceful transition to socialism, but on the basis of their scientific knowledge of the class struggle in modern society, they predicted that the reactionary minority would employ force to prevent the majority from establishing socialism.

'We had a constitutional and legal right to say what we said and to do what we did', Goldman concluded. 'And we did everything openly. The evidence will show that we still continue our meetings, that we still publish and distribute our papers. It is a peculiar kind of criminals that you have, who insist upon their rights to do what they are doing and to say what they are saying'.

Marxist Classics Now Evidence of 'Conspiracy'

A considerable part of the government's evidence consisted in the introduction of the classic writings of the Marxist movement, beginning with the Communist Manifesto and rounded out with the current pamphlets and publications of the Socialist Workers Party. These writings were all openly distributed and publicly sold. They can be found in most libraries and book stores. They are discussed in thousands of class rooms, forums, and constantly referred to in the press. Suddenly, in 1941 these writings become converted into flaming bombs for blowing up the Capitol at Washington! Thus the Roosevelt regime joins the procession of reactionary capitalist governments which have proscribed the theories, history and principles of the revolutionary socialist movement. The Smith Act is the American equivalent of the Japanese law forbidding 'dangerous thoughts'. While Roosevelt is about to war upon Hitler, who burns the works of Marx, Lenin and Trotsky, and upon Mussolini, who bans them, he duplicates their destruction of the democratic rights of free expression.

When a benighted Tennessee legislature tried to outlaw Darwin's doctrines of organic evolution in the notorious Scopes 'Monkey Trial', the liberal world shivered with horror and indignation. The Minneapolis 'Sedition Trial' is a far more serious threat to progressive thought. This time, not an isolated group of hillbilly Baptists, but the United States Government is seeking to suppress all radical social criticism and to set back the scientific knowledge of society a century or more. The Roosevelt administration will have a capitalist Index to place beside the Catholic Church Index. The writings of the masters of Marxism upon social and political subjects, hitherto regarded as indispensable to modern education, are to become contraband, and their possession and circulation a criminal offense, punishable by 10 years in jail and $10,000 fine. This is evidence, not of the defendants' guilt of the charges against them, but of the thoroughly reactionary and repressive character of their prosecution.

The only other evidence introduced by the government to back up its contentions was presented by witnesses who gave accounts of alleged private conversations with the defendants. It is important to note the character of the 35 witnesses called by the government. Only seven came from outside the opposition group to the 544 leadership in its inter-union struggle with AFL Teamsters President, Daniel J. Tobin. Two of the seven are FBI agents. Sixteen government witnesses were members of Tobin's Committee of 99, six or seven more are relatives and friends of Committee members. About a dozen of these are on Tobin's pay roll. One of the witnesses was employed by the bosses' association, Associated Industries, which since 1934 has tried to smash Local 544 and frame up its leaders. It is these hostile witnesses with material interests at stake or with personal grudges against the defendants who provided the main testimony against them.

Frame-up Artists at Work

Most of these carefully coached hirelings of Tobin stated at some point that they had held private conversations with one or another of the defendants when no one except themselves was present, and that they were then initiated into the secret aim of the party to overthrow the government by violence. According to the government's star witness, James Bartlett, V.R. Dunne kept pulling him aside into a corner of a dark room and repeating the parrot-like phrase: 'We must overthrow the Government by force and violence'. Walter Stultz, another government witness who had clashed with Al Russell as an ex-official of the Omaha Teamsters Union, declared that Russell once confided to him: 'We have to grab a rifle and go after it'. Obviously, since these confidences were imparted in private, they had to remain uncorroborated. In fact they are sheer lies.

Here we see the classic formula of the frame-up in operation. The pattern is always the same. The technique of Roosevelt's frame-up is no different from Stalin's. The prosecutors claim that the defendants did and said one thing for public consumption while they meant and did the opposite in private. In the

Moscow trials, for example, Trotsky, who worked openly for the international socialist revolution and advocated the defense of the Soviet Union, was accused of secretly plotting the restoration of capitalism in the Soviet Union in alliance with Hitler and the Mikado. So the Trotskyists on trial in Minneapolis were supposed to have camouflaged their real activities and hidden their true views. The SWP, according to the prosecution, participated in political campaigns not to win people to its program but as a blind for armed revolt. The party inspired the organization of union defense guards, ostensibly to protect the union against vigilante attacks, but actually to march on Washington and take over the government. The party advised its members to submit to conscription but only the better to foment discontent in the armed forces. All this is to be believed upon the unsupported testimony of hostile witnesses, most of whom are materially dependent upon Daniel J. Tobin, the original instigator of the prosecution and its immediate beneficiary!

A Man Named Rube

One witness gave the slightest substance to the government charge that the SWP was preparing an armed uprising. A pathetic individual of subnormal mentality who worked on Tobin's goon-squads, John Novack, testified that a fellow named 'Rube' told him: 'We have guns and ammunition planted in the walls of churches; we have bullets that will go through an inch and a half of armor plate, which is better than the US Army can do'. He couldn't, however, recall what Rube's name was, where he met him or when. Nor did the government produce a specimen of these marvelous bullets. The best they could produce, after this, was an even more degraded witness whose testimony was so completely irrelevant that the Judge ordered it struck from the record.

The government witnesses said far more to support the position of the defense than the charges of the prosecution. There was almost unanimous agreement that the Union Defense Guard was organized against the 'real and present danger' of Silver Shirt attacks. *This is the defense explanation of the formation of the Guard.* The witnesses testified that they had never heard any incitement to armed rebellion at SWP meetings nor read any such advocacy in the party literature. All understood by the so-called 'armed revolt' simply the Marxist prediction concerning prospective social revolution when the masses would be driven to adopt the socialist program as a result of the horrors of war and economic catastrophe.

Several of the government's own witnesses paid tribute to the irreproachable character of the defendants. Thomas Smith, ex-secretary-treasurer of the

Omaha Teamsters Union, testified that he joined the SWP because 'I saw the good work of Local 544, the leaders were labor-minded; they helped out the smaller locals and were for the poor, so I figured that if the Socialist Workers Party produced those kind of people it was good enough for me!'

Under cross-examination, some of the principal government witnesses became entangled in direct contradictions and obvious lies. Typical of many such instances was Novack's assurance that he had discussed the armed conspiracy with defendant Ed Palmquist in August 1940, although Palmquist was in Sandstone Prison at that time.

The government failed utterly to show that the SWP engaged in any action tending to subvert the loyalty of the US armed forces. This was one of the two main charges in the indictment. Not a single member of the armed forces was placed upon the stand to testify that the party had urged him to overthrow the government. However, it should be remembered that under the Smith Act, incredible though it may be, the government need not prove that any one in the armed forces had ever read any of the party's literature, become convinced by it or acted upon it for the defendants to be found guilty. The mere expression of criticism of the armed forces or the publication of revolutionary ideas are in themselves evidence of incitement to insubordination. Under this law, CIO President Philip Murray could be indicted for his statement in the *CIO News* of Nov. 17th: 'There is widespread and wholly justified discontent in the army' and urging higher wages for American soldiers. Negro leaders could likewise be jailed for protesting against discrimination in the armed forces.

The Tobin-FBI Conspiracy

Under skillful cross-examination, Defense Attorney Goldman exposed one of the most sinister aspects of the government prosecution – the conspiracy between Tobin, Biddle and the FBI against the leaders of Local 544. Time and again Biddle has declared that the Department of Justice and the FBI acted independently of Tobin who played no part in promoting the prosecution. But the secrecy which up to now had screened the actual mechanism of collaboration between Tobin, Biddle and the FBI was shattered by the government's own witnesses.

The Committee of 100 (later the Committee of 99) was the agency Tobin organized and used in his fight to oust the leadership and gain control of Local 544. Herbert Harris, one of Tobin's lieutenants and a government witness, revealed that this Committee was organized in consultation with the FBI. The Committee of 100, said Harris, 'went to the FBI when the fight started in the union', last December or January. Tommy Williams, leader of the Committee of 100, instructed Harris to admit agent Thomas Perrin of the St. Paul office of the FBI to the first meeting of the Committee at the Hotel Nicolette. Perrin sent Harris to Carl Skoglund, Ex-President and Trustee of Local 544, with an offer to obtain citizenship for Skoglund if he 'would break with the Dunnes and side with the Committee of 100'. Skoglund rejected the government's bribe. For refusing to sell out the Minneapolis drivers for the sake of personal security and become an informer for the FBI, for refusing to kneel down before Dictator Tobin, Skoglund was not only indicted along with the others but later arrested and held for deportation. Here is disclosed the filthy role of the FBI acting under cover as provocateurs and as frame-up artists against honest trade union leaders. After such disclosures, can there be any doubt about the identity of the real conspirators in this case? They are not the 23 working men and women on trial but Roosevelt's lackey Biddle, the FBI and Tobin who schemed in secret to frame them up and railroad them to jail!

The fantastic nature of this frame-up and the discharge of five defendants by no means signifies that there will be no convictions. The cases of Tom Mooney, Sacco and Vanzetti, the Scottsboro boys and others demonstrate that the mere exposure of a frame-up is insufficient to prevent it from being put over.

The Minneapolis trial is not an ordinary criminal proceeding; it is from start to finish a political prosecution. These working men and women are being tried in a capitalist court under reactionary anti-labor laws for daring to oppose Roosevelt's war-policies and for defending the rights and interests of the working class. Their struggle against the official forces of reaction is an integral part of the fight of the American people and of organized labor to maintain their democratic rights. Only the mass protest of labor backed up by the pressure of liberal opinion can force the government to free these victims of capitalist persecution and prevent further assaults upon labor organizations and the Bill of Rights.

4 Socialism on Trial: The Official Court Record of James P. Cannon's Testimony[22]

(*1942*)

James P. Cannon

Courtroom Testimony, James P. Cannon, 19 November 1941

Imperialist War

Q **(By Mr. Goldman):** Mr. Cannon, will you tell us the position of the Socialist Workers Party on the causes of modern war?

A: Modern wars, in the opinion of our party, are caused by the conflict of imperialist nations for markets, colonies, sources of raw material, fields for investment, and spheres of influence.

Q: What do you mean by 'imperialist', Mr. Cannon?

A: Those capitalist nations which directly or indirectly exploit other countries.

Q: What is the party's position on the inevitability of wars under the capitalist system?

A: As long as the capitalist system remains, and with it those conditions which I have mentioned, which flow automatically from the operation of the capitalist and imperialist system, wars, recurring wars, are inevitable.

Q: And can anybody's opposition, including the opposition of the Socialist Workers Party to war, prevent wars under the capitalist system?

22 Cannon 1942a.

A: No. Our party has always stated that it is impossible to prevent wars without abolishing the capitalist system which breeds war. It may be possible to delay a war for a while, but eventually it is impossible to prevent wars while this system, and its conflicts of imperialist nations, remains.

Q: Then is it true that the party is of the opinion that wars are caused by international economic conflicts, and not by the good will or bad will of some people?

A: Yes. That does not eliminate the possibility of incidental attacks being caused by the acts of this or that ruling group of one country or another; but fundamentally wars are caused by the efforts of all the capitalist powers to expand into other fields. The only way they can get them is by taking them away from some other power, because the whole world has been divided up among a small group of imperialist powers. That is what leads to war, regardless of the will of the people.

We do not maintain that the ruling groups of any of the imperialist powers now at war really desired the war. We have stated many times that they would have been glad to have avoided it; but they could not avoid it and maintain the capitalist system in their country.

Q: What is the attitude of the party towards a war which it designates as an imperialist war?

A: Our party is unalterably opposed to all imperialist wars.

Q: And what is meant by opposition to imperialist wars?

A: By that we mean that we do not give any support to any imperialist war. We do not vote for it; we do not vote for any person that promotes it; we do not speak for it; we do not write for it. We are in opposition to it.

Q: How does the Socialist Workers Party oppose the idea of the United States entering into the war?

A: We do it as every other political party promotes its ideas on any foreign policy. We write against it in the paper; we speak against it; we try to create sentiment in any organization we can approach, to adopt resolutions against the war. If we had members in Congress, they would speak in Congress, in the Senate, against it. In general we carry on public political agitation against the entry of the

United States into war, and against all measures taken either by the Executive or by Congress which in our opinion lead towards active participation in the war.

Q: What do you mean by 'active'?

A: For example, all those measures which have been taken, which put the United States into the war, in effect, without a formal declaration to that effect.

Q: What was the party's position with reference to amending the Constitution to give the people the power to declare war?

A: For quite a while now we have supported the proposal that was introduced into Congress, I think by Representative Ludlow, and is known as the Ludlow Amendment, for an amendment to the Constitution requiring a referendum vote of the people for the declaration of a war. Our party supported this proposal and at times has carried on a very energetic agitation in favor of such an amendment to require a referendum vote of the people before war could be declared.

Q: And that is still the position of the party, Mr. Cannon?

A: Yes, that is incorporated as one of the points of practical daily policy, in the editorial masthead of our paper. If I am not mistaken, it appears on the editorial page as one of our current principles, and every once in a while there appears an editorial or an article in the paper attempting to revive interest in this idea.

Q: If the United States should enter into the European conflict, what form would the opposition of the party take to the war?

⁖

A: ... we would not become supporters of the war, even after the war was declared. That is, we would remain an opposition political party on the war question, as on others. ... Insofar as we are permitted our rights, we would speak against the war as a false policy that should be changed, in the same sense from our point of view, that other parties might oppose the foreign policy of the government in time of war, just as Lloyd George, for example, opposed the Boer War in public addresses and speeches. Ramsay MacDonald, who later became prime minister of England, opposed the war policy of England during the World War of 1914–1918. We hold our own point of view, which is different from the point of view of the two political figures I have just mentioned, and so far as we are permitted to exercise our right we would continue to write and speak for a different foreign policy for America.

∴

Q: Would the party try to sabotage the conduct of the war in any way?

A: No. The party has specifically declared against sabotage. We are opposed to sabotage.

Q: What is that – what do you mean by 'sabotage'?

A: That is, obstruction of the operation of the industries, of transportation, or the military forces. Our party has never at any time taken a position in favor of obstruction or sabotage of the military forces in time of war.

Q: And will you explain the reasons why?

A: Well, as long as we are a minority, we have no choice but to submit to the decision that has been made. A decision has been made, and is accepted by a majority of the people, to go to war. Our comrades have to comply with that. Insofar as they are eligible for the draft, they must accept that, along with the rest of their generation, and go and perform the duty imposed on them, until such time as they convince the majority for a different policy.

Q: So, essentially your opposition during a war would be of the same type as your opposition prior to the war?

A: A political opposition. That is what we speak of.

Q: Did the party ever, or does the party now, advise its members or any of its sympathizers, or any workers that it comes in contact with, to create insubordination in the United States armed forces or naval forces?

A: No.

Q: Will you explain the reason why?

A: Fundamentally the reason is the one I just gave. A serious political party, which aims at a social transformation of society, which is possible only by the consent and support of the great mass of the population – such a party cannot attempt while it is a minority to obstruct the carrying out of the decisions of the majority. By sabotage and insubordination, breaking discipline and so on, a party would absolutely discredit itself and destroy its possibilities of convincing people, besides being utterly ineffective so far as accomplishing anything would be concerned.

Q: Will you state the reasons why the party would not support a war conducted by the present government of the United States?

A: In general, we do not put any confidence in the ruling capitalist group in this country. We do not give them any support because we do not think they can or will solve the fundamental social problems which must be solved in order to save civilization from shipwreck.

We believe that the necessary social transition from the present system of capitalism to the far more efficient order of socialism can only be brought about under a leadership of the workers. The workers must organize themselves independently of the capitalist political parties. They must organize a great party of their own, develop an independent working-class party of their own, and oppose the policy of the capitalist parties, regardless of whether they are called the Democratic or Republican, or anything else.

∵

Q: What is the party's position on the claim that the war against Hitler is a war of democracy against fascism?

A: We say that is a subterfuge, that the conflict between American imperialism and German imperialism is for the domination of the world. It is absolutely true that Hitler wants to dominate the world, but we think it is equally true that the ruling group of American capitalists has the same idea, and we are not in favor of either of them.

We do not think that the Sixty Families who own America want to wage this war for some sacred principle of democracy. We think they are the greatest enemies of democracy here at home. We think they would only use the opportunity of a war to eliminate all civil liberties at home, to get the best imitation of fascism they can possibly get.

Q: What is the position of the party with reference to any imperialist or capitalist enemy of the United States, like Germany or Italy?

A: We are not pro-German. We absolutely are not interested in the success of any of the imperialist enemies of the United States.

Q: In case of a conflict between the United States and Germany, Italy, or Japan, what would the party's position be so far as the victory or defeat of the United States, as against its imperialist enemies?

A: Well, we are certainly not in favor of a victory for Japan or Germany or any other imperialist power over the United States.

Q: Is it true then that the party is as equally opposed to Hitler as it is to the capitalist claims of the United States?

A: That is uncontestable. We consider Hitler and Hitlerism the greatest enemy of mankind. We want to wipe it off the face of the earth. The reason we do not support a declaration of war by American arms is because we do not believe the American capitalists can defeat Hitler and fascism. We think Hitlerism can be destroyed only by way of conducting a war under the leadership of the workers.

Q: What method does the party propose for the defeat of Hitler?

A: If the workers formed the government I spoke of, if the workers' form of government were in power, we would propose two things:

One, that we issue a declaration to the German people, a solemn promise, that we are not going to impose another Versailles peace on them; that we are not going to cripple the German people, or take away their shipping facilities, or take away their milk cows, as was done in the horrible Treaty of Versailles, starving German babies at their mothers' breasts, and filling the German people with such hatred and such demand for revenge that it made it possible for a monster like Hitler to rally them with the slogan of revenge against this terrible Treaty of Versailles. We would say to them:

'We promise you that we will not impose any of those things upon the German people. On the contrary, we propose to you a reorganisation of the world on a fair socialist basis, where the German people, with all their recognised ability and their genius and labor, can participate equally with us'. That would be our party's first proposal to them.

Second, we would also say to them, 'On the other hand, we are going to build the biggest army and navy and air force in the world, to put at your disposal, to help smash Hitler by force of arms on one front, while you revolt against him on the home front'.

I think that would be the program, in essence, of our party, which the workers' and farmers' government of America would advance so far as Hitler is concerned, and we believe that is the only way Hitlerism will be destroyed …

Q: And the party's position is that there will be no obstruction of ways and means taken by the government for the effective prosecution of its war?

A: No obstruction in a military way, or by minority revolution; on the contrary, the party has declared positively against any such procedure.

War and Revolution

Q: What is the opinion of the party as to the relationship between war and a possible revolutionary situation?

A: Wars frequently have been followed by revolution; wars themselves are the expression of a terrible social crisis, which they are unable to solve. Misery and suffering grow at such a tremendous pace in war that it often leads to revolution.

The Russo-Japanese war of 1904 produced the Russian revolution of 1905. The World War of 1914 produced the Russian Revolution of 1917, the Hungarian revolution, near-revolution in Italy, and the revolution in Germany and Austria; and in general, a revolutionary situation developed over the whole continent of Europe, as the result of the First World War.

I think it is highly probable that if the war in Europe continues, then the mass of the people, especially in Europe, will undertake to put a stop to the slaughter by revolutionary means.

Q: So that it would be correct to say that a revolutionary situation is created by a war, and not by the Socialist Workers Party, if a revolutionary situation will arise?

A: I would say it is created by the privations of the capitalist system, which are tremendously accelerated by a war.

Q: What is the policy of the party with reference to permitting various opinions and interpretations of current events in the party's publications?

A: Well, it is not prohibited. Usually, individual members of the party write articles with a certain slant on current events that is not necessarily shared by the majority of the Committee.

Q: With reference to predictions or opinions about future occurrences, would you say the party is more liberal in granting that freedom?

A: Yes, it must necessarily be, because predictions are not verifiable, completely, until after the event, and different opinions arise. We have had in the party, especially since the outbreak of the World War, conflicting opinions as to when the United States would make formal entry into the war, or whether or not the United States would enter the war. There were not very many who doubted that it would, but I heard some people in the party express such opinions.

Q: And would you say that the opinions of party members with reference to a possible future revolutionary situation is in that category of opinion, concerning which there are many differences of opinion?

A: Yes, there must necessarily be.

Q: Do you include in that category also predictions as to whether the revolution would not be accompanied by force or not?

A: Well, within limits, within limits. There is more agreement among the educated leaders of the party who have studied history and Marxism – there is more agreement on that question, than on such a question as the prospect of entry into the present World War.

Q: But there can be, and there are differences of opinion as to the exact time of the revolutionary situation and the approximate development of it?

A: As to the time of a revolution, that is absolutely speculative. There isn't anybody in the party who has anything more than a tentative opinion on that question.

∴

Party's Proletarian Military Policy

Q: Now will you please explain what is called the military policy of the party?

A: The military policy of the party is incorporated in the decisions of the conference a year ago, in September 1940. At that time we called a special conference of the party, in connection with a plenary meeting of the National Committee, to consider this particular question, our attitude towards conscription and the further progress of the war situation, and there we adopted a resolution substantially as follows:

Point 1: As long as conscription has been adopted as the law, and once it was the law, referring to the Selective Service Act, all party members must comply with this law, must register and must not oppose the registration of others. On the contrary, the party specifically opposes the position of such groups as conscientious objectors. While we admire the courage and integrity of a rather high order that it takes to do what the conscientious objectors have done, we have written against their policy and said it is wrong for individuals to refuse to register when the great mass of their generation are going to war. So far as we are concerned, if the young generation of American workers goes to war, our party members go with them, and share in all their dangers and hardships and experience.

Point 2: Our resolution says that our comrades have got to be good soldiers, the same way that we tell a comrade in a factory that he must be the best trade unionist and the best mechanic in order to gain the confidence and respect of his fellow workers. We say, in the military service, he must be the best soldier; he must be the most efficient in the use of whatever weapons and arms he is assigned to, and submit to discipline, and be concerned about the welfare of fellow soldiers in order to establish his position in their respect and confidence.

∴

Q: Now, were there any other points discussed and adopted at that conference with reference to the military policy of the party?

A: Yes. We came out in favor of the idea of conscription, universal military training. That is predicated on the idea that at the present time the whole world is in arms, that all decisions nowadays are being made by arms, or with the threat of arms. In such a situation we must recognize that the workers must also become trained in the military arts.

We are in favor of universal military training, according to our official decision; but we are not in favor, that is, we do not give political support to the method that is used by the present capitalist government.

We propose that the workers should get military training in special camps under the direction of the trade unions; that the government should furnish a part of its military funds in appropriations to equip those camps with the necessary arms and materials and instructors, but the camps should be under the auspices of the trade unions.

There should be also special camps set up under the auspices of the unions, for the training of workers to become officers. Government funds should be appropriated for this purpose, so that a condition can be created to remove one of the greatest defects and sources of dissatisfaction in the present military apparatus, that is, the social gulf between the worker or farmer-soldier, and the officer from another class, who does not have an understanding of the soldier's problem and does not have the proper attitude towards him.

We believe the workers are entitled to have as officers men out of their own ranks whom they have learned to respect in the course of their work and common struggle with them, such as picket captains, leaders of unions, men who have distinguished themselves in the affairs of workers' organizations, and who come from the rank and file of the workers. Such men as officers would be much more concerned about the welfare of the rank and file of soldiers than a college boy from Harvard or Yale, who never saw a factory, and never rubbed elbows with the worker, and considers him an inferior being. That is, I would say, the heart of our military proposal, of our military policy.

Q: What is the position of the party with reference to civil rights in the army?

A: We stand also for soldier citizens' rights. We do not agree with the idea that when you take a million and a half young men out of civil life, that they cease to have the rights of citizens. We think they should have all the rights of citizens. They should have the right to petition Congress; they should have the right to vote; they should have the right to elect committees to present their grievances; they should have the right to elect their own officers, at least the minor officers; and in general they should have the democratic rights of citizens, and we advocate that. We advocate legislation to confer upon the soldiers those rights, and doing away with the present inefficient military setup.

Q: Did the party officially, or to your knowledge, did any party member now in the service, ever attempt to create insubordination in the ranks of the armed forces?

A: Not to my knowledge.

Q: In your opinion, if there have been such incidents, what is the cause of them?

A: I think there are a number of causes of discontent and dissatisfaction in the conscript army. That is a matter of public comment in all the newspapers and magazines, and various opinions and theories have been expressed as to the reasons for it

Q: How does the party propose to realize the demands for compulsory training under trade-union control?

A: Our program is a legislative program. Everything that we propose we would have incorporated into law. If we had a delegation in Congress they would introduce a bill, or a series of bills, providing for the incorporation in the law of the country of these proposals, these military proposals of ours.

Q: Did any authoritative leader of the party ever refer to Plattsburg as an example?

A: Yes. In fact, that was part of the origin of the idea. As I said before, the chief sore point in the military setup is the class distinction between the officers and the ranks. We know that in the period prior to the First World War, special camps were set up for the training of business and professional men to be officers in the army. Plattsburg was one of these. This was a part of the so-called preparedness campaign, before the United States finally got into the war. The government appropriated some funds, and some businessmen donated funds. The government provided instructors and furnished the necessary equipment for the training of a large number of business and professional men who were ultimately to be officers in the army.

We cannot see why the workers should not have the same rights. We think it is perfectly fair and reasonable, certainly it is compatible with the existing laws. As I said before, it is a legislative proposal on our part. We would, if we could, incorporate that into the law of the country.

∴

Q: I call your attention, Mr. Cannon, to the testimony of some witnesses for the prosecution to the effect that certain party members told them to join the army, and then to start to kick about the food and create dissatisfaction. What can you say with reference to the party policy about that? ...

A: The policy is not to support or to initiate any agitation about food. I want to tell you the reason. So far as our knowledge goes, from members of the party who have been drafted and whom we have seen on furlough, and from other investigation, there is not much dissatisfaction with the food in the present setup.

Q: And if there is any dissatisfaction with food, what would you say it was caused by?

A: So far as our information goes, there are only isolated cases now. We do not propose to kick about the food if the food is satisfactory. If the food is bad, the soldiers will kick about it themselves, and they should kick about it. ... I do not know of anything in the party program or party literature that proposes to incite grievances without foundation. Where causes for dissatisfaction exist, they create the dissatisfaction, not the party.

• •
•

Q: Now, on the question of military training under trade union control – you were speaking about Plattsburg at the time of the recess. Will you continue and explain further the policy on that?

A: I used that as an illustration of how special camps were instituted and government instructors provided to train business and professional men in the period shortly prior to our entry into the last World War. In the Spanish Civil War all the parties and unions not only had their own training camps authorized by the government, but even supplied their own regiments in the fight against the fascist army of Franco.

Q: Now, the present trade unions are not under the control of the party, are they?

A: No, they are under the control, essentially or practically completely, of leaders who are in harmony with the present Roosevelt administration.

Q: As I understand, the party favors military training under trade-union control?

A: Yes. The idea is to give to the unions, as they are, a wider authority and supervision over their people.

Q: And that policy is not dependent upon the party controlling the trade unions?

A: No. We can only take our chances that we will be in the minority in those training camps, as we are in the unions.

Q: What measures do you propose in order to effectuate the policy of military training under trade-union control?

A: As I think I said before, it is a proposal for a legislative program. We would have such a bill introduced into Congress and passed, if we had the power, or if we could gain the support of congressmen who are opposed to us on other grounds, but who would agree to this. This is a program that is not necessarily socialist.

Attitude to the Russian Revolution

Q: Does the party have an official position on the Russian Revolution, Mr. Cannon? ...

A: We support the Russian Revolution of 1917. We consider that it embodies the doctrines and the theories of Marxism which we uphold.

Q: How many revolutions were there in Russia in 1917?

A: There was a revolution in February according to the Russian calendar, in March according to the modern calendar, which developed into the proletarian revolution of November 7 according to the modern calendar.

Q: What is the general position taken by Marxists with reference to the Russian Revolution? ... The theory of Marxism in our opinion was completely vindicated in the Russian Revolution, and the theory of Marxism, which is the establishment of a government of workers and peasants, which undertakes to bring about a social transformation from capitalism towards socialism – all this was undertaken in the Russian Revolution.

Q: Now, can you tell us anything about the legality of that revolution? …

A: The czar and czarism were overthrown in March by an uprising of the masses, of the people in the big cities, and the peasants.

Q: Was the Bolshevik Party responsible for that uprising in any way?

A: No. The Bolshevik Party was a very infinitesimal group at the time of the March revolution.

Q: What is the meaning of 'Bolshevism'?

A: The world *Bolshevik* is a Russian word meaning *majority*. It acquired a political meaning in the Russian Social-Democratic Labor Party. In the Congress of 1903 a controversy developed which divided the party into groups, the majority and the minority, the majority called the Bolsheviks and the minority called Mensheviks.

Q: Those are Russian words meaning minority and majority?

A: Yes. They split up and divided into parties. Each called itself the Russian Social-Democratic Labor Party and in parentheses on the end 'Bolsheviks' or 'Mensheviks', as the case might be.

Q: Now, will you proceed and tell the jury what happened during the October Revolution, or in our calendar in November 1917.

A: Well, to show the chronology: When czarism was overthrown by the masses of the people, the whole structure of that tyranny was destroyed. A new government was constituted, but the new government machinery was based on the Soviets, which sprang up spontaneously in the revolutionary upheaval. Soviets of workers and soldiers were established everywhere. In Petrograd, the workers and soldiers sent delegates – deputies – to the central council or, as they called it, the Soviet; similarly in Moscow and other places. This body was recognized as authoritative.

The government that was constituted after the overthrow of the czar was headed by Prince Lvov, with Miliukov as foreign minister; it derived its authority from the Soviets of Workers' and Soldiers' Deputies and the Soviets of Peasants' Deputies. In April they had a National All-Russian Conference of the Workers' and Soldiers' Soviets, and there they elected an All-Russian Central Executive Committee of the Workers' and Soldiers' Soviets. In May, the peasant Soviets had an All-Russian Congress and elected an All-Russian Central Executive Committee of the peasants.

Q: What proportion of the population did those Soviets represent?

A: They represented the people, the great mass of the people. I think it was impossible even to speak in terms of majorities or minorities. They were the masses themselves. The peasants and the soldiers and the workers were the people; those two bodies, the All-Russian Central Executive Committee of the Workers' and Soldiers' Soviets and the All-Russian Central Executive Committee of the Peasant Soviets, formed a joint body which was recognized as the most authoritative and representative body in Russia. It was by their consent that the government cabinet ruled.

The All-Russian Executive Committee of the Soviets repudiated Miliukov, who was the leader of the bourgeoisie. The Soviet body opposed him because of his foreign policy, involving secret treaties that had been exposed. He therefore had to resign, because without the support of the Soviets, authority was lacking; and I think that could be likened, as an analogy, to the French system of the resignation of the prime minister when there is a no-confidence vote in the Chamber.

Q: So that the Soviets constituted the authority of the people of Russia?

A: That is right.

Q: In what way did the Bolsheviks progress to power?

A: I wish to go on with the chronology, if you will permit me. Following the fall of Miliukov, Kerensky rose – there is a popular impression in this country that he became premier with the fall of the czar. That is not so. Kerensky became premier in July. He was made a minister and eventually premier because he was a member of the Social Revolutionary Party. That was the peasant party, which then led the Soviets. He was also supported by the worker element, because he had been a labor lawyer. That was the basis of Kerensky's office; that is, his authority was derived directly from the Soviets.

Now in this period the Bolsheviks were a small minority. They did not create the Soviets. The Soviets were created by the masses; they were initiated by the masses. Neither the Bolshevik Party nor any other party could do anything without the support of the Soviets. In the midst of the revolution of 1905 and again in the overthrow of the czar in 1917, the Soviets sprang up simultaneously.

The most influential one naturally was in Petrograd, which was the seat of government. The Bolsheviks were a small minority in this Soviet at the time of the overthrow of the czar. When Kerensky became premier, the combination of his Social Revolutionary Party and the Menshevik Socialist Party – those two parties together had an overwhelming majority in the Soviets, and ruled by virtue of that. The Bolsheviks were an opposing faction.

During that time Lenin, as the spokesman for the Bolsheviks, said over and over again, 'As long as we are in the minority in the Soviets, all we can do is patiently explain'. The Bolshevik Party opposed any attempt to seize power by a putsch.

Q: What is a 'putsch'?

A: An armed action of a small group. The Bolshevik Party demanded, with Lenin as their spokesman, that the Social Revolutionary Party and the Menshevik Party take complete control of the government by removing the bourgeois ministers and make it a completely labor and peasant government, and they issued the promise that, 'If you do that we promise that as long as we are in the minority, we will not try to overthrow you. We will not support you politically, we will criticize you, but we will not undertake to overthrow the government as long as we are in the minority'. That was the policy of the Bolsheviks in the March days of the revolution against the czar, and into July.

In July the workers in Petrograd staged a demonstration with arms, against the advice of the Bolsheviks. The Bolsheviks advised against it on the ground that it might unduly provoke the situation, and tried to persuade the workers in Petrograd not to go into that action. It was not a rebellion; it was simply a parade with arms. This action, carried out by the Petrograd workers against the advice of the Bolsheviks, brought repressions against the workers on the part of the Kerensky government.

Then the Kerensky government undertook to discredit and frame up the Bolshevik Party. They accused Lenin and Trotsky of being German spies. This was the predecessor of Stalin's Moscow trials. They accused Lenin and Trotsky and the Bolsheviks of being German spies. Trotsky was thrown into jail, Lenin was forced into hiding, and repressions continued against the Bolsheviks, but it did not do any good, because the policy and slogans of the Bolsheviks were growing in popularity. One by one the great factories and soldiers' regiments began to vote in favor of the Bolshevik program.

In September an attempt at counterrevolution was made under the leadership of General Kornilov, who could be properly described as a Russian monarchist-fascist. He organized an army and undertook to overthrow the Kerensky government in Petrograd, with the idea of restoring the old regime.

The Kerensky government, that had put Trotsky in jail, had to release him from prison to get the support of his party to fight down the counterrevolutionary army of Kornilov.

Trotsky was brought from prison and went directly to the Military Revolutionary Committee, in which government men also sat, and there drew up with them plans for a joint fight against Kornilov. Kornilov was crushed; the counterrevolution was crushed primarily by the workers under the inspiration of the Bolshevik Party. They tied up his railroad trains, he could not move his troops; his best troops were induced to fight against him, and his counterrevolution was crushed.

As this was going on, the Bolsheviks became more popular all the time, as the genuine representatives of the revolution. They gained the majority in the Petrograd Soviet, the most influential Soviet in the country, and in Moscow and others. The Kerensky government was losing ground because it was not solving any of the problems of the people. The Bolsheviks' slogans of 'Bread', 'Peace', 'Land', and other slogans – those were the slogans that the masses wanted.

On November 7 was held the Congress of the All-Russian Soviets of Workers and Soldiers. The Bolsheviks had a majority there, and simultaneously with the meeting of the Soviets, where the Bolsheviks had a majority, they took the governmental power.

Violence and the Russian Revolution

Q: And was there any violence connected with the gaining of the majority by the Bolsheviks?

A: Very little – just a little scuffling, that's all. …

Q: And subsequent to the gaining of the majority by the Bolsheviks what violence, if any, occurred? …

A: That began following the armed struggle against the government.

Q: Who began it?

A: The czarists, the white guard Russian element, the bourgeoisie generally, the deposed capitalists and others. They undertook a counterrevolution, and the civil war that ensued lasted until almost 1921. The civil war lasted so long because the white guard and bourgeois elements received the support, first of the Germans, and then of England and France, and even the United States sent an expedition.

The Soviet government had to fight against the whole capitalist world, on top of fighting against their own opposition at home; and the fact that the Bolsheviks represented the great majority of the people was best evidenced by the fact that they were victorious in this civil war, not only against their opponents at home, but also against the outside powers who supplied the opposition with arms, soldiers and funds.

Q: How were the Soviets in those days elected?

A: They were elected in the factory-workers' meetings; that is, the factory workers would gather to elect their delegate. Each Soviet constituted a unit of government and the combination of Soviets constituted the government.

In the Soviet system, the factories select delegates, according to their number, one for each thousand or whatever the proportion may be. The soldiers' regiments do the same; the peasants or dirt farmers do the same, so that the government established in that way, by those Soviets, represents the whole mass of the people who are involved in productive activity.

Q: What was the number of members of the Bolshevik Party at the time of the Russian Revolution in November 1917?

A: The most authoritative figure I have seen given is 260,000, or a quarter of a million. That seems to be the figure that has the best authority.

Q: And what proportion of the population supported the Bolshevik Party at that time?

A: In my opinion, the great majority of the workers, peasants and soldiers supported them at the time they took power and afterwards.

Q: From which group or class of society did the Bolshevik Party get most of its members?

A: From the workers. It was a workers' party, a party of industrial workers and agricultural laborers. There were some peasants in the party, but the party was primarily constituted of industrial workers in the cities, agricultural laborers, and some intellectuals, some educated people who had put themselves at the service of the workers in the party.

Q: What is the best authority as to the number of workers in Russia at the time of the revolution – by 'workers' meaning industrial workers?

A: Five million.

Q: And the majority of the population consisted of peasants?

A: Peasants, yes.

∵

Differences between Stalin and Trotsky

Q: Will you describe briefly the fundamental differences that arose between Stalin and Trotsky subsequent to the revolution?

A: I mentioned the other day that the fight originated in the struggle over democracy. That was the origin of the fight, really inspired by Lenin during his last illness, in collaboration with Trotsky. Lenin did not survive to take part in the fight, and Trotsky had to lead it. This soon developed further.

It soon became apparent to critical observers, this tendency of Stalin to crush democracy in the party and in the life of the country generally. It was based on Stalin's desire to change the program and the course of direction of the revolution, which could only be done by this means. Trotsky struggled for free discussion of the problem, with the confidence that the majority of the workers in the party would support his program. Stalin and his group represented, in our opinion, the conservative tendency, based upon a certain stratum of the party and the government that had acquired official positions and privileges and wanted to stop there.

Q: Stalin then represented in your opinion the party of the bureaucratic?

A: The bureaucratic and conservative. As a matter of fact, Trotsky designated it as the bureaucratic-conservative faction, at one stage in the struggle. ... It assumed the form of crushing democracy inside of the Communist Party and establishing a dictatorial regime there.

∴

Q: What is the position of the party on the Soviet Union at present? ...

A: The characterization we make of the Soviet Union, as it is today, is of a workers' state, created by the revolution of November 1917, distorted by the bad present regime, and even degenerated, but nevertheless retaining its basic character as a workers' state, because it is based on nationalized industry and not on private property.

Q: Now, what is the position of the party towards the defense of the Soviet Union, and why?

A: We are in favor of defending the Soviet Union against imperialist powers for the reason I just gave, because we consider it a progressive development, as a workers' state, that has nationalized industry and has eliminated private capitalism and landlordism. That is the reason we defend it.

Q: That is, you consider the Russian or the Soviet state, a state based on the expropriation of private industry from the capitalists?

A: Yes, the operation of industry as a nationalized industry.

Q: And you are defending that kind of a state?

A: Yes.

Q: Isn't it a fact that Stalin has killed most all of the so-called Trotskyists in Russia?

A: Yes. We are against Stalin, but not against the Soviet form of industrial production.

Marxism – A Guide to Action

Q: What is the position that the party gives to Karl Marx and his doctrines?

A: Karl Marx was the originator of the theories and doctrines and social analyses, which we know as scientific socialism, or Marxism, upon which the entire movement of scientific socialism has been based since his day.

In the *Communist Manifesto* of 1848 his ideas were sketched and then in other big volumes, notably in *Capital*, he made a most exhaustive scientific analysis of the laws governing the operation of capitalist society, showed how the contradictions within it would lead to its downfall as a social system, showed how the conflict of interests between the employers and the workers would represent an uninterrupted class struggle until the workers gained the upper hand and instituted the society of socialism.

So Karl Marx can be viewed not only as the founder of our movement, but as [its] ... most authoritative representative ...

Q: Does the party accept all of the statements found in all of the books written by Karl Marx?

A: No, the party has never obligated itself to do that. We do not consider even Marx as infallible. The party accepts his basic ideas and theories as its own basic ideas and theories. That does not prohibit the party or members of the party from disagreeing with things said or written by Marx which do not strike at the fundamental basis of the movement, of the doctrine.

Q: And you interpret Marx, or you apply the Marxian theories, under conditions that prevail at the present time, is that right?

A: Yes. You see, we don't understand Marxian theory as a revelation, as a dogma. Engels expressed it by saying our theory is not a dogma but a guide to action, which means that it is a method which the students of Marxism must understand and learn how to apply. One can read every letter and every line written by Marx and still not be a useful Marxist, if one does not know how to apply it to the conditions of his own time. There have been such people, whom we call pedants.

Q: You are acquainted with the *Communist Manifesto*, are you not?

A: Yes.

Q: And you remember – I think it is the last clause of the *Manifesto*, where Marx and Engels, co-authors, say: 'We disdain to conceal our aims', and mention something to the effect about violent revolution. Do you remember that?

A: Well, it says, 'We disdain to conceal our aims. We openly say that they can be achieved only by the forcible overthrow of all existing social institutions'.

Q: When was the *Communist Manifesto* written?

A: 1848.

Q: Subsequent to the writing of the *Communist Manifesto*, did Marx ever write anything with reference to the possibility of a peaceful revolution in democratic countries?

A: Yes.

Q: Where was that written, and explain to the jury what was said.

A: Well, the most authoritative place where it is stated and explained is in the introduction to the first volume of Marx's masterwork, called *Capital*, the introduction by Frederick Engels, who was his co-worker, who was the co-author of the *Communist Manifesto*, and is recognized universally in the movement as completely identified with all of Marx's ideas and theories. Engels as a matter of fact edited and compiled the second two volumes of *Capital*, after the death of Marx.

Q: What did he say in that introduction?

A: This was the English translation of *Capital* and the introduction was presenting the volume to the English public. Engels stated – I think I can quote almost literally – that he thinks the work of a man who during his entire life was of the opinion that the social transformation in England, at least, could be effected by purely peaceful and legal means – he thought such a book should have a hearing from the English public. That is very close to a literal report of what he stated in this introduction.

Q: And why did Marx have that opinion with reference to England?

A: Well, he had that opinion with reference to England as distinct from the autocratic countries, because of its parliamentary system, its democratic processes, and civil libertarian method of political procedure.

Q: So at the time that Marx and Engels wrote the *Communist Manifesto* in 1848, there was no democracy in existence on the European continent, is that right?

A: The whole of Europe was seething with revolutions at that time.

Q: And no democratic processes were available?

A: At least not in the stable system that had been established in England. I think I should add, to get the whole picture of this introduction which I am speaking of, that Engels said, after he had made this remark which I have reported, he said: 'To be sure, Marx did not exclude the possibility of a proslavery rebellion on the part of the outmoded and dispossessed ruling class'. That is, after the transfer of power. … I think he had in mind the American Civil War. Marx and Engels attentively followed the American Civil War, wrote extensively about it in the *New York Tribune*. A collection of those writings, both political and military, has been published as a book, which is a classic in our movement. And what Marx undoubtedly had in mind when he spoke of a 'proslavery rebellion', was an analogy with the American Civil War, which he had characterized as a proslavery rebellion on the part of the Southern slave owners. Of course, he did not maintain that the English bourgeoisie are slaveholders in the same sense, but that they exploit the workers.

Q: Now what, in your opinion, is the relationship between the Declaration of Principles of the Socialist Workers Party and the theories of Karl Marx?

A: I would say that insofar as we understand Marxism and are able to apply it, it is an application of the Marxian theories and doctrines, his whole system of ideas, to the social problem in America.

Q: That is, the Declaration of Principles is based then upon the fundamental theories of Karl Marx?

A: Yes, we consider it a Marxist document.

Party's Attitude to Lenin

Q: What is the position that the party gives to Lenin?

A: Lenin, in our judgment, was the greatest practical leader of the labor movement and the Russian Revolution, but not on the plane of Marx in the theoretical field. Lenin was a disciple of Marx, not an innovator in theory. To be sure he contributed very important ideas, but to the end of his life he based himself on Marx, as a disciple in the Marxist movement of the world. He holds a position of esteem on a level with Marx, with this distinction between the merits of the two.

Q: Does the party, or do party members agree with everything that Lenin ever wrote and published?

A: No. The same attitude applies to Lenin as to Marx. That is, the basic ideas and doctrines practiced, promulgated, and carried out by Lenin, are supported by our movement, which does not exclude the possibility of differing with him about this or that particular writing, or of individual members of the party differing with Lenin in important respects, as has been the case more than once in our party. ... [For example], Socialism and communism are more or less interchangeable terms in the Marxist movement. Some make a distinction between them in this respect; ... Lenin used the expression socialism as the first stage of communism, but I haven't found any other authority for that use. I think that is Lenin's own particular idea. I, for example, consider the terms socialism and communism interchangeable, and they relate to the classless society based on planned production for use as distinct from a system of capitalism based on private property and production for profit.

Q: Could there be a socialist society and a dictatorship like Stalin has at the present time?

A: No. According to Marx and Engels, as you approach the classless socialist or communist society, the government, instead of becoming more of a factor in human affairs, becomes less and less and eventually withers away and disappears, and is replaced or evolves into an administrative body that does not employ repression against the people.

So the very term government implies, in our terminology, a class society – that is, a class that is dominant and a class that is being suppressed. That holds true whether it is a capitalist government, which in our views oppresses or suppresses the workers and the farmers and represents the interests of the big capital, or a workers' and farmers' government immediately following a revolution which represents the interests of the workers and farmers and suppresses any attempt of the displaced capitalist class to resist its authority or to reestablish its rule.

But once the resistance of the old outlived exploiting class is broken and its members become reconciled to the new society and become assimilated in it, find their place in it, and the struggle between classes which is the dominating factor in all class societies is done away with, because of the disappearance of class distinctions, then the primary function of government as a repressive instrument disappears and the government withers away with it. This is the profound conception of Marx and Engels that is adhered to by all their disciples.

Q: Did Lenin ever use the term 'Blanquism' to designate a certain type of movement? …

A: Yes, he wrote more than one article in the course of the Russian Revolution, … 'We are not Blanquists'. … Blanqui was a figure in the French revolutionary movement who had followers in the Paris Commune of 1871. Blanqui had his own conception of party and of revolution, and his ideas are known among the students of the history of the labor movement as Blanquism. [The] idea … that a small group of determined men, tightly disciplined, could effect the revolution with a coup d'État.

Q: What is a 'coup d'État'?

A: That is a seizure of power, a seizure of state power by armed action of a small, determined, disciplined group; they would, so to speak, make the revolution for the masses.

Q: And what did Lenin say about that?

A: Lenin opposed this view and his articles were written in answer to opponents who had accused the Bolsheviks of aiming to seize power without a majority. He said, 'We are not Blanquists. We base ourselves on mass parties and mass movements, and as long as we are in the minority our task is to patiently explain the problems and issues until we gain the majority, and as long as we are in the minority we will not try to overthrow you. You let us have our freedom of speech and press, give us the opportunity to expound our ideas, and you don't need to fear any Blanquist putsch on our part'. Putsch, as I explained before, is an attempt of a small group to seize power by surprise tactics.

Q: So Lenin depended upon mass parties and upon gaining a majority for those mass parties, did he?

A: Yes, in the early days of the Communist International – it is a period that I am familiar with through close study and personal participation in the movement – he hammered at this idea all the time, not only against his critics in Russia, but against various individuals and groups who came toward support of the Russian Revolution, and had some distorted ideas.

In Germany, for example in March 1921, the German party, which had been organized, attempted an insurrection without having the support of the masses; this became famous in the literature of our international movement, as 'the March Action'. The tactics embodied in it, the conception of some of the German leaders that they could force the revolution by their own determination and sacrifices – this whole idea, the March Action, and all the ideas embodied in it were condemned by the Third Congress of the Communist International at the insistence of Lenin and Trotsky. They refuted this theory, and they counterposed to it mass parties, mass movements, gaining the majority.

They put out the slogan to the German party that it should aim to have a million members. Zinoviev, who was chairman of the Comintern, made that one of his leading ideas on the German question, that the task of the German party was not to get impatient or to try to force history but to be busy with agitation and propaganda and have the goal of a million in the party.

Q: These million members would not by themselves make any revolution, would they?

A: Naturally not – Lenin did not expect to have a majority of the population become members of the party, but to support the party. But the very fact that he proposed – or rather Zinoviev, who was the lieutenant of Lenin, acting as chairman of the Communist International proposed – as a slogan, 'A million members in the German Party', certainly was a powerful indication that they did not expect to get a majority of the people until they had a numerically powerful party.

5 A Criticism of the Minneapolis Trial[23]

(*1942*)

Grandzio Munis

The initiation on the part of the United States government of a prosecution of the Socialist Workers Party and of the leaders of the Drivers Union of Minneapolis made us fear a decapitation, even though temporary, of our American movement. It filled us with a joyful hope at the same time, sure that the persecution by the bourgeois tribunals would popularize our revolutionary ideas when it gave our militants the opportunity to expound them completely and valiantly. It has been the norm and pride of the world revolutionary movement since the ringing reply of Louise Michel to her judges and of Karl Marx to the Bismarckian tribunal, to convert the accused into accusers and to employ the witness stand as a fortress from which to attack the reactionary powers. This attitude has been one of the principal forces of attraction of the revolutionary movement.

I experienced the first uneasiness that these results would be wasted totally or partially on reading the first published statement ... that seems to have set the tone for all the following statements. ... I again considered as lost a goodly part of the political benefits of the trial on reading the fundamental speeches and questionings of Comrade Cannon by Comrade Goldman .... It was there, replying to the political accusations – struggle against the war, advocacy of violence, overthrow of the government by force – where it was necessary to have raised the tone and turn the tables, accuse the government and the bourgeoisie of a reactionary conspiracy; of permanent violence against the majority of the population, physical, economic, moral, educative violence; of launching the population into a slaughter also by means of violence in order to defend the Sixty Families. On the contrary, it is on arriving at this part that the trial visibly weakens, our comrades shirk themselves, minimize the revolutionary significance of their ideas, try to make an honorable impression on the jury without taking into consideration that they should talk for the masses. For moments they border on a renunciation of principles. A few good words by Goldman in

23 Munis 1942.

his closing speech cannot negate the lamentable, negative impression of his first speech and of the interrogation of Cannon.

... Goldman, in his opening statement to the jury: 'I **repeat:** *The objective and the aim of the party was to win through education and through propaganda a majority of the people of the United States*'.

... It is hardly necessary to indicate the error of such a statement. It is understood by all, beginning by the one who made the statement, that our objective can in no way be only propaganda, nor will we win the majority by means of it. We are a party of propaganda in the sense that our numerical proportion prevents us or limits us to a minimum of action. But we are a party of revolutionary action – economic, political, and educative – in essence and potentially, because our propaganda itself can tend only to action and only through action will we conquer the majority of the exploited and educate them for the taking of power. ...

1 The Struggle Against Imperialist War

Cannon ... replying to Goldman: 'A decision has been made, and is accepted by a majority of the people, to go to war. Our comrades have to comply with that' ...

In the first place, the decision to go to war has *not* 'been made and accepted by a majority of the people'. This statement can be criticized very strongly, a statement that we would censure very energetically if it were made by a centrist. In the place of accusing the government of leading the American people to the slaughter against the will of the majority, instead of accusing it emphatically before the masses and of demonstrating to them how the parliamentarian majority acts against the majority of the people, Cannon endorses Roosevelt's decision as if it really corresponded to the majority of the people.

Yes, we submit to the war and our militants go to war, but not because it is a decision of the majority, but rather because it is imposed upon us by the violence of bourgeois society just as wage exploitation is imposed. As in the factory, we should take advantage of all the opportunities to fight against the war and against the system that produces it, just as we fight against the boss in a factory, as a function of the general struggle against the capitalist system. ...

The equivocation and inexactness are permanent. It seems that we are platonic opponents of the war and that we limit ourselves to statements and propaganda, written or verbal, without action of any kind. To say that 'we do not support a declaration of war because we do not believe the American capitalists can defeat Hitler and fascism', is to give the understanding that we would support it if we believed in that defeat; this induces those who believe in the victory of the United States to support it. Our rejection of the war is based on the character of the social regime that produces it, not on this or that belief about the defeat of fascism.

Immediately comes another equivocation: 'We think Hitlerism can be destroyed, etc.'. Uniting that to the reiterated statements to the effect that we will not agitate among the soldiers, that we are a 'political opposition' to the war, and to the, until now, limping exposition of military training under union control, can induce one to believe that we will be for the war *when* the control has been given to the unions. I believe it is necessary to clarify this, without leaving room for equivocation and I pronounce myself, for my part, against the war, even if control of the military service is achieved by the unions. ...

This does not merely deal with an omission, but with a statement of passivity in the face of the imperialist war; something which at best is a bad education for the workers who have become interested in the trial and does not grant us any credit for tomorrow when the masses begin to act against the war.

Forced by statements of this sort – decidedly opportunist; I do not hesitate to say – Cannon sees himself obliged to ask for the expulsion from the party of the militants who organize protests in the army. He is carried to the incredible, to reject Lenin, Trotsky and Cannon himself ...

I am wholeheartedly behind Cannon in his speech; but I categorically condemn Cannon before the jury, deforming himself, minimizing, reducing to words with revolutionary action of the party. And I will be equally behind and I propose that the party be behind the militants and soldiers who carry out acts of protests in the army, remembering that they do not deal with 'putsches, premature movements'.

Revolutionary action in time of war is absolutely impossible without obstructing a greater or less degree of military service. Therefore, the principle of revolutionary defeatism, which the American party and the International have and cannot renounce. ... I believe our comrades have lost a good opportunity to make the workers understand why they should act always by means of the word and by means of collective actions. The questioning of Cannon presented a completely false perspective to the workers, of comfortable propaganda, where it deals with a terrible struggle by all means from small protests to insurrections by groups, from partial fraternizations to wiping out the fronts. But from an error of perspective, one passes to an error of fact: therefore the defendants saw themselves forced to condemn sabotage in general, as though it dealt with something criminal. I believe that sabotage is a method for tactical use whose application at certain moments can be productive of contrary effects to what is intended but which is absolutely indispensable in the critical moments of struggle. …

Sabotage and defeatism will unite at a certain moment as the two main elements in the reactions of the masses against the imperialist war. The party should not and cannot renounce defeatism without condemning itself to perpetual sterile chat against the war.

What seems even more lamentable to me is that one can intuit from the trial that it is not only a question of something said especially for the jury. For the moment there is evidence that the defendants really consider sabotage a crime. If I am not mistaken – and I hope I am – this is a dangerous moral predisposition. Sabotage will be the reaction of the masses against the imperialist war. Why be ashamed of it? Why be ashamed that the masses react, as they can against the monstrous crime of the present war? It would have been easy to defend it as a principle and throw the responsibility on the leaders of the present war. Can we condemn the future sabotage of the masses when the war is a gigantic sabotage of the bourgeoisie against the masses, against civilization and humanity? Instead of receiving this idea, the workers who heard our comrades will have been left burdened with a prejudice against sabotage.

2 Transition to Socialism, Advocating and Employing Violence

Says Goldman: '… we prefer a peaceful transition to socialism; but that we analyze all the conditions in society, we analyze history, and on the basis of this analysis we predict, *we predict*, that after the majority of the people in the United States will want socialism established, that the minority, organized by the financiers and the capitalists, will use violence to prevent the establishment of socialism. That is what we predict'.

Why not ask forgiveness, besides, for seeing ourselves painfully obliged to employ violence against the bourgeoisie? Even neutralizing oneself to a mere diviner, the prediction is completely false. It is not necessary to poke into the future to discover the violence of the reactionary minority throughout society. The accusation lends itself ideally to launching a thorough attack against capitalist society and to show the American workers that the so-called American democracy is no more than a dictatorship of the bourgeoisie. Among the workers who have experienced the daily violence of bourgeois society, during strikes, demonstrations, meetings; all of them without exception experience the normal violence of either working for a wage established in the labor market or of perishing; a violence much more lamentable is the imposition of the war; educative violence; informative violence imposed by the newspaper trusts. Far from receiving a notion of the environment in which they live and far from preparing their spirit for rebellion against this environment, the workers watching the trial have been pacified in respect to the present. Only in the future will the bourgeoisie employ violence. …

I do not find in the long pages of the interrogation of Cannon anything else than propaganda, propaganda, and more propaganda, as if it dealt with recommending a patent medicine for baldness. … the line that our comrades have followed in not taking advantage of the trial to indicate to the masses how and why they should exercise their own violence is incorrect. … All the revolutionary, violent process, the *civil war* that must precede the establishment of a Workers' and Farmers' Government and the proletarian state, is palmed away. …

… The workers today need an indication of the dynamics of the class struggle, the forms of organization, methods of struggle up to the civil war, slogans, and included there is a need for proud valor against the class enemy, something which has been rare in the trial. The general tone has not been to accuse but to apologize to a point that makes one feel embarrassed at times; not to indicate and propose actions and immediate means for the struggle against the bourgeoisie and against the war, but rather to dilute our ideas into humanitarianism and to veil their *active* value with predictions of knowledge as if it were not honorable to employ violence against the present corrupted bourgeois democracy.

Something completely demonstrative of the foregoing is that our comrades have cited as witnesses in their defense – Jefferson, Lincoln, the Bible, Lloyd George, MacDonald; but when Marx, Lenin, Trotsky, and even Cannon appear, they are rejected as non-official mouthpieces of our organization. This attitude, not very valiant, cannot conquer sympathy, or at least cannot conquer as much as the opposite attitude would conquer. …

I consider it a very grave error to substitute maneuvers for principles in moments so important for the political future of the party. I believe and propose as a general principle that in similar trials our responsible militants accept all responsibility for the practical action of our ideas. This is worth more than a light sentence at the price of a pretty and deceptive polish.

6 Defense Policy in the Minneapolis Trial[24]

(1942, excerpts)

James P. Cannon

1 Our Strategy in the Trial

In the Minneapolis 'sedition' trial, as in the months-long trade-union battle which preceded and led up to it, the American Trotskyists were put to the test and compelled to show what stuff they are made of. In both instances they conducted themselves in a manner befitting disciples of Trotsky and met the test in all respects.

In the fight with the trade-union bureaucracy, which attracted national attention, it was clearly shown who the real leaders of militant labor, the real men of principle, really are. In the trial before the bourgeois court the party, by the conduct of all its members involved, earned the right to the confidence of the revolutionary workers. The two struggles, which in reality were two sides of one and the same struggle, marked a climactic point in the activity of the American movement which had developed in a restricted circle since its inception thirteen years before.

During that time the party, with some local exceptions, had gained the attention only of the vanguard of class-conscious workers. At the trial we had the opportunity, for the first time, to speak to the masses – to the people of the United States. We seized upon the opportunity and made the most of it and applied in practice without a serious fault the basic principles which had been assimilated in a long preparatory period. Since then the movement in the United States stands on higher ground.

A critical study and discussion of the trial cannot fail to be of the highest value to the Fourth International, especially to those sections which have yet to reach the turn in the road which leads from the propaganda circle to mass work. For our part we welcome the discussion and will do our best to contribute something useful to it.

24 Cannon 1942b.

From the first moment after the indictment was brought against us in the Federal Court at Minneapolis last July we recognized that the attack had two aspects, and we appraised each of them, we think, at their true significance. The prosecution was designed to outlaw the party and deprive it perhaps for a long time, of the active services of a number of its most experienced leaders. At the same time it was obvious that the mass trial, properly handled on our part, could give us our first real opportunity to make the party and its principles known to wide circles of workers and to gain a sympathetic hearing from them.

Our strategy, from the beginning, took both sides of the problem into account. Naturally, we decided to utilize to the fullest extent each and every legal protection, technicality and resource available to us under the law and the Constitution. A party leadership hesitating or neglecting to do this would frivolously jeopardize the legality of the party and show a very wasteful attitude indeed toward party cadres. Such a leadership would deserve only to be driven out with sticks and stones.

On the other hand, we planned to conduct our defense in court not as a 'criminal' defense but as a propaganda offensive. Without foolishly disregarding or provoking the jury or needlessly helping the prosecutor, it was our aim to use the courtroom as a forum to popularize the principles of our movement. We saw in this second proposition our main duty and opportunity and never for a moment intended to let purely legalistic considerations take precedence over it. Therefore we sternly rejected the repeated advice of attorneys – some who assisted Goldman in the trial of the case as well as others who were consulted about participation – to eliminate or play down our 'propaganda' program and leave the defense policy to the lawyers.

From the rather unhappy experiences of past trials of militants in the courts of the United States we knew what following such advice would mean: Deny or keep quiet about the revolutionary principles of the movement; permit the lawyers to disavow and ridicule the defendants, and pass them off as somewhat foolish people belonging to a party which is not to be taken seriously; and depend on spread-eagle speeches of the lawyers to the jury to get the defendants off some way or other.

The October plenum-conference of the party unanimously endorsed the National Committee's recommendations on courtroom policy. The resolution of the conference laid down the policy as follows:

'The policy of the party in defending itself in court, obligatory for all party members under indictment, can only be one that is worthy of our movement and our tradition; no attempt to water down or evade our revolutionary doctrine, but on the contrary, to defend it militantly. At the same time we maintain that we have a legal right under the Bill of Rights to propagate our principles'.

That is the policy we took with us to the trial. It guided us at every step in the proceedings. And we think it can be safely said that the policy has been amply vindicated by the results. Our principles were widely popularized, a hundred or a thousand times better than ever before, and our conduct before the court has met with approval and sympathy from the militant workers who followed the trial and read the testimony.

The trial was by far our greatest propaganda success. Moreover, even those workers who disagree with our program, have approved and applauded our conduct in court as worthy of people who take their principles seriously. Such is the testimony of all comrades who have reported on the reaction of the workers to the trial. On a recent tour across the country from branch to branch of the party we heard the same unvarying report everywhere.

Naturally, our work in the trial was not perfect; we did only the best we could within the narrow limits prescribed by the court. More qualified people can quite easily point out things here and there which might have been done more cleverly. We can readily acknowledge the justice of such criticisms without thereby admitting any guilt on our part for socialism does not require that all be endowed with equal talent, but only that each give according to his ability. It is a different matter when Comrade Munis – and other critics of our policy – accuse us of misunderstanding our task and departing from Marxist principles in the trial. To them we are obliged to say firmly: No, the misunderstanding is all on your side. The correct understanding of our task in the courtroom and the sanction of the Marxist authorities, are on our side.

In undertaking to prove this contention we must begin with a brief analysis of a point overlooked by Munis as well as by the others: the social environment in which the trial was conducted. Our critics nowhere, by so much as a single word, refer to the objective situation in the United States; the political forms still prevailing here; the degree of political maturity – more properly, immaturity – of the American proletariat; the relation of class forces; the size and status of the party – in short to the specific peculiarities of our problem which should determine our method of approach to workers hearing us for the first time from the sounding board of the trial.

Our critics talk in terms of trials in general and principles in general, which, it would appear, are always to be formulated and explained to the workers in general in precisely the same way. We, on the contrary, dealt with a specific trial and attempted to explain ourselves to the workers as they are in the United States in the year 1941. Thus we clash with our critics at the very point of departure – the analysis, the method. Our answer to their criticism must take the same form.

We shall begin by first setting forth the concrete environmental circumstances in which our party functioned in the United States at the time of the trial and the specific tasks and propaganda techniques which, in our opinion, were thereby imposed. Then we shall proceed to submit our position, as well as that of our critics, to the criterion which must be decisive for all of us: the expressions of the Marxist teachers on the application of the points of principle under discussion.

2 The Setting of the Trial

The United States, where the trial took place, is by far the richest of all the capitalist nations, and because of that has been one of the few such nations still able to afford the luxury of bourgeois democratic forms in the epoch of the decline and decay of capitalism. Trade unions, which have been destroyed in one European country after another in the past decade, have flourished and more than doubled their membership in the United States in the same period – partly with governmental encouragement. Free speech and free press, obliterated or reduced to travesty in other lands, have been virtually unrestricted here. Elections have been held under the normal bourgeois democratic forms, traditional in America for more than a century, and the great mass of the workers have freely participated in them. The riches and favored position of bourgeois America have also enabled it, despite the devastating crisis, to maintain living standards of the workers far above those of any other country.

These objective circumstances have unfailingly affected both the mentality of the workers and the fortunes of the revolutionary political movement. The revolutionary implications of the shaken economy, propped up for the time being by the armaments boom, are as yet but slightly reflected in the consciousness of the workers. In their outlook they are far from revolutionary. 'Politics' to them means voting for one or another of the big capitalist parties. The simple fact that the organized labor movement has not yet resorted to independent political action, even on a reformist basis, but remains in its political activity an appendage of the Roosevelt political party – this simple fact in itself shows conclusively that the American workers have not yet begun to translate their fierce militancy in the field of economic strikes, directed at individual employers, into terms of independent politics directed against the employers as a class. As for the Marxist party, with its program of the revolutionary transformation of society, it has been able in such an environment to attract the attention of only a few thousands to its message and to recruit into its ranks a still smaller number of the most advanced and class-conscious militants.

The forty million American workers, casting an almost solid labor vote for Roosevelt, remain in the first primitive stages of class political development;

they are soaked through and through with bourgeois democratic illusions; they are discontented to a certain extent and partly union-conscious but not class-conscious; they have a fetishistic respect for the federal government as the government of all the people and hope to better conditions for themselves by voting for 'friendly' bourgeois politicians; they hate and fear fascism which they identify with Hitler; they understand socialism and communism only in the version disseminated by the bourgeois press and are either hostile or indifferent to it; the real meaning of socialism, the revolutionary Marxist meaning, is unknown to the great majority.

Such were the general external factors, and such was the mentality of the American workers, confronting our party at the time of the Minneapolis trial, October, November, and December 1941. What specific tasks, what propaganda techniques were imposed thereby? It seems to us that the answers are obvious. The task was to *get a hearing* for our ideas from the forum of the trial. These ideas had to be simplified as much as possible, *made plausible* to the workers and illustrated whenever possible by familiar examples from American history. We had to address ourselves to the workers not in general, not as an abstraction, but as they exist in reality in the United States in the year 1941. We had to recognize that the forms of democracy and the legality of the party greatly facilitate this propaganda work and must not be lightly disregarded. It was not our duty to facilitate the work of the prosecuting attorney but to make it more difficult insofar as this could be done without renouncing any principle. Such are the considerations which guided us in our work at the trial.

Our critics do not refer to them; evidently they did not even think of them. Our method is a far different method than the simple repetition of formulas about 'action' which requires nothing but a good memory. More precisely, it is the Marxist method of applying principles to concrete circumstances in order to popularize a party and create a movement which can lead to action in the real life of the class struggle, not on the printed page where the 'action' of sectarian formalists always begins and ends.

The accomplishment of our main task – to use the courtroom as a forum from which to speak to those American workers, as they are, who might hear us for the first time – required, in our judgment not a call to arms but patient, schoolroom *explanations* of our doctrines and ourselves, and a quiet tone. Therefore we adapted, not our principles but our propaganda technique to the occasion as we understood it. The style of propaganda and the tone which we employed are not recommended as a universally applicable formula. Our propaganda style and tone were simply designed to serve the requirements, in the given situation, of a small minority Marxist party in a big country of democratic capitalism in the general historic circumstances above described.

Comrade Munis accuses us of popularizing our propaganda and defending ourselves (and the party's legality) at the expense of principle. Our statements at the trial are held to be 'decidedly opportunist'; to 'border on a renunciation of principles'. Following such and similar assertions we are informed that 'it is a very grave error to substitute maneuvers for principles'. This maxim – not entirely original in our movement – can be accepted with these provisos: that the maxim be understood; that a distinction be made between 'maneuvers' which serve principle and those which contradict it; and that it be applied to actual and not imaginary sacrifices of principle. This is the gist of the whole matter. The Marxist teachers did not change their principles, but in explaining them they frequently changed their manner and tone and points of emphasis to suit the occasion. We had a right and a duty to do the same. An examination of our testimony from this standpoint will bring different conclusions from those which our critics have so hastily drawn.

3 Violence and the Transition to Socialism

We were charged in the first count of the indictment with 'conspiracy to overthrow the government by force and violence' in violation of the statute of 1861 which was originally directed against the slaveholders' rebellion. In the second count we were charged, among other things, with 'conspiracy to *advocate* the overthrow of the government by force and violence' in violation of the Smith Act of 1940.

In our defense we flatly denied we had either 'conspired' or 'advocated' violence, and by that we did not in the least intend to deny or repudiate any principle of Marxism. We claimed the right to *explain* our position. We testified that we prefer a peaceful social transformation; that the bourgeoisie takes the initiative in violence and will not permit a peaceful change; that we advise the workers to bear this in mind and prepare to *defend themselves* against the violence of the outlived reactionary minority class.

This formula – which is 100 percent correct in the essence of the matter and unassailable from the standpoint of Marxist authority – did not coincide with the contentions of the prosecuting attorney, nor help him to prove his case against us. But that was not our duty. From entirely opposite considerations our exposition does not meet with the approval of Comrade Munis nor coincide with his conceptions. That is not our duty either, because his conceptions are arbitrary and formalistic – and therefore false.

The prosecutor wanted to limit the whole discussion of socialism to the single question of 'force and violence'. We on the other hand – for the first time in an American courtroom – tried to make an exposition, if only a brief and sketchy one, of the whole range of Marxist theory, as in an elementary study class for uninitiated workers, to the extent that this was possible within the narrow framework prescribed by the court's rules and the repeated objections of the prosecutor, assigning the question of force in the social revolution to its proper proportionate place and putting the responsibility for it where it properly belongs – on the shoulders of the outlived class.

We carried out this task to the best of our ability at the trial. Of course, thesis precision and full-rounded explanation are hardly possible in a rapid-fire impromptu dialogue, with answers compressed to extreme brevity by time limitations, prosecutor's objections and court rulings. We cannot claim such precision and amplitude for our answers, and reasonable people should not demand it of us. Even Trotsky admitted the possibility of flaws in testimony which he gave in somewhat similar but more favorable circumstances before the Dewey Commission. …

In such an atmosphere a witness is under constant pressure to condense his answers and to omit explanations which may be necessary for full clarity but which are not interesting to the court. … By and large, making all due acknowledgement of imperfections, omissions and inadequacies in the oral testimony, we accomplished our propagandistic aims at the trial, and we stand on the record. The court record, published in thousands of copies, became and will remain our most effective propaganda document. It is an honest and forthright revolutionary record. Nobody will succeed in discrediting it.

What did we say about violence in the transformation of society from capitalism to socialism? This is what we said:

1) The Marxists prefer a peaceful transition. 'The position of the Marxists is that the most economical and preferable, the most desirable method of social transformation, by all means, is to have it done peacefully'.
2) 'It is the opinion of all Marxists that it will be accompanied by violence'.
3) That opinion 'is based, like all Marxist doctrine, on a study of history, the historical experiences of mankind in the numerous changes of society from one form to another, the revolutions which accompanied it, and the resistance which the outlived classes invariably put up against the new order. Their attempt to defend themselves against the new order, or to suppress by violence the movement for the new order, has resulted in every important social transformation up to now being accompanied by violence'.
4) The ruling class always initiates the violence, 'always the ruling class; always the outlived class that doesn't want to leave the stage when the

time has come. They want to hang on to their privileges, to reinforce them by violent measures, against the rising majority *and they run up against the mass violence of the new class*, which history has ordained shall come to power'.

5) That is our prediction. But 'of course, we don't limit ourselves simply to that prediction. We go further, and advise the workers to bear this in mind and prepare themselves not to permit the reactionary outlived minority to frustrate the will of the majority'.

Q: What role does the rise and existence of fascism play with reference to the possibility of violence?

A: Well, that is really the nub of the whole question, because the reactionary violence of the capitalist class, expressed through fascism, is invoked against the workers. Long before the revolutionary movement of the workers gains the majority, fascist gangs are organized and subsidized by millions in funds from the biggest industrialists and financiers, as the example of Germany showed – and these fascist gangs undertake to break up the labor movement by force, raid the halls, assassinate the leaders, break up the meetings, burn the printing plants, and destroy the possibility of functioning long before the labor movement has taken the road of revolution.

I say that is the nub of the whole question of violence. If the workers don't recognize that and do not begin to defend themselves against the fascists, they will never be given the possibility of voting on the question of revolution. They will face the fate of the German and Italian proletariat and they will be in the chains of fascist slavery before they have a chance of any kind of a fair vote on whether they want socialism or not.

It is a life and death question for the workers that they organize themselves to prevent fascism, the fascist gangs, from breaking up the workers' organizations, and not to wait until it is too late. That is the program of our party.

That is all any Marxist really needs to say on the question of violence in a capitalist court or at a propaganda meeting for workers at the present time in the United States. It tells the truth, conforms to principle, and protects the legal position of the party. The workers will understand it too. To quote Shakespeare's Mercutio: ''Tis not so deep as a well nor so wide as a church-door; but 'tis enough, 'twill serve'.

Comrade Munis, however, is not satisfied with our 'lamentable dialogue', allegedly 'destined to pacify the easily frightened conscience of the jury about who initiates the violence'. The above-quoted answer advising the workers to 'bear in mind' the violent course of the ruling class and 'prepare themselves', is not 'sufficiently explicit and energetic'. (He underestimates the acuteness of the workers). 'Why not', says Comrade Munis, 'raise the voice at this point and call upon the workers to organize their own violence against the reactionary violence?'

Why not? Because it was not necessary or advisable either to raise the voice or issue any call for action at this time. We were talking, in the first place, for the benefit of the uninitiated worker who would be reading the testimony in the paper or in pamphlet form. We needed a calm and careful exposition in order to get his attention. This worker is by no means waiting impatiently for our call to violent action. Quite the contrary, he ardently believes in the so-called democracy, and the first question he will ask, if he becomes interested in socialism, is: 'Why can't we get it peacefully, by the ballot?' It is necessary to *patiently explain* to him that, while we would prefer it that way, the bosses will not permit it, will resort to violence against the majority, and that the workers must *defend* themselves and their *right* to change things. Our *defensive* formula is not only legally unassailable, 'for the jury', as our critics contemptuously remark – as though twenty-eight indicted people in their right senses, and a party threatened with illegality, can afford the luxury of disregarding the jury. It is also the best formula for effective propaganda.

These defensive formulas are not our invention; they come directly from the great Marxists who did not believe in the good will of the class enemies and knew how to organize action, that is, *mass* action, against them. And these same teachers and organizers of mass actions likewise never failed to appreciate the value of democratic forms and party legality and to hang onto them and utilize them to the fullest extent possible. Our teachers did not shrink from force; they never deluded the workers with the promise of a peaceful, democratic transformation of society. But they didn't speak of violence always in the same way, in the same tone and with the same emphasis. Always, in circumstances in any way comparable to ours, they have spoken as we spoke at the trial. Proof of this is abundant and overwhelming.

The first formulated statement of the communist position on the question of violence and the transition to socialism appears in Engels' 'Principles of Communism', a 'catechism' written in 1847 which is generally regarded as the first draft of the *Communist Manifesto*. Engels wrote:

> *Q[uestion] 16:* Will it be possible to bring about the abolition of private property by peaceful methods?
>
> *A[nswer]:* It is to be desired that this could happen, and Communists certainly would be the last to resist it.

Engels didn't promise such a solution and he didn't forget to add: 'Should the oppressed proletariat at long last be goaded into a revolution, the communists will rally to the cause of the workers and be just as prompt to act as they are now to speak'.

The *last* statement of Marxist authority, expressed by Trotsky ninety-three years later, follows the same pattern as that of Engels. In the summer of 1940 the Dies Committee conducted a raid on a comrade's house in Texas and carried off some party literature. Anticipating an attack on the legal position of the Socialist Workers Party, Comrade Trotsky wrote us a letter, advising us how to formulate our propaganda and defend ourselves 'from the legal point of view' and warning us 'not to furnish any pretext for persecutions'. ... He knew the value of party legality and did not want us to jeopardize it needlessly. Do not, he said almost in so many words, accept the prosecuting attorney's accusation that we advocate conspiratorial violence by a minority. Present the question in a way which 'corresponds to historical reality' and which is, at the same time, by its defensive formulation, 'juridically unattackable' ...

All four of the great Marxist authorities – Marx, Engels, Lenin and Trotsky – are united in an uninterrupted continuity of experience reflected in Marxist thought. For us, Lenin is Marx in the epoch of the First World War and the October Revolution. Trotsky is Lenin in the epoch of Stalinist degeneration and the struggle against it, the epoch of fascism and the Second World War and the preparation of the new rise of the international revolution of the proletariat ...

Our frank avowal before the court that we are disciples of Lenin is not enough to satisfy Munis. Our statement that in our movement 'he holds a position of esteem on a level with Marx'; that 'the basic ideas and doctrines, practiced, promulgated and carried out by Lenin, are supported by our movement' – these declarations, in the judgment of our critic, are not sufficient to constitute an acceptance of Lenin. He seems to think it is necessary to repeat and accept as gospel every word Lenin said on every occasion regardless of what Lenin himself may have said on the same subject on other occasions.

He cites the question of Mr. Schweinhaut the prosecutor, reading a sentence from Lenin's *The Revolution of 1905*: '"It is our duty in time of an uprising to exterminate ruthlessly all the chiefs of the civil and military authorities". You disagree with that?'

Naturally we denied that this is a statement of party policy here and now, modifying it as follows: 'We do not agree with the extermination of anybody unless it is in case of an actual armed struggle, when the rules of war apply'. In reality this was saying, out of deference to Lenin, a great deal more than needs to be said on the subject of extermination before a capitalist court or in a propaganda speech in the United States at the present time. ...

Our business is to help get everything possible done to make sure the 'last' chance for a peaceful development of the revolution, to help by the presentation of our program, by making clear its national character, its absolute accord with the interests and demands of a vast majority of the population.

Thus, Lenin proposed to fight 'the civil and military chiefs' in three different ways, according to the circumstances, on three different occasions – by 'extermination', by 'arrest' and by 'peaceful propaganda'. All were equally revolutionary. The occasions and the circumstances in each case were different. Lenin took such variations into account and changed his proposals accordingly. He never made a strait jacket out of his tactical formulas. Neither should we – if we want to be genuine Leninists.

That 'force is the midwife of every old society pregnant with the new' – this is an axiom known to every student of Marxism. It is wrong to entertain or disseminate illusions on this score, and we did not do so at the trial. But it is a great mistake to conclude from this that violence and the talk about violence serve the revolutionary vanguard advantageously at all times and under all conditions. On the contrary, peaceful conditions and democratic legal forms are most useful in the period when the party is still gathering its forces and when the main strength and resources, including the resources of violence, are on the other side. Lenin remarked that Engels was 'most correct' in 'advocating the use of bourgeois legality' and saying to the German ruling class in 1891: 'Be the first to shoot Messrs. Bourgeois!'

Our party, which must still strive to *get a hearing* from the as yet indifferent working class of America, has the least reason of all to emphasize or to 'advocate' violence. This attitude is determined by the present stage of class development and the relation of forces in the United States; not as Munis so generously assumes, by our exaggerated concern for a 'light sentence'. As a matter of fact the question of violence was given ten times more proportionate mention in our testimony at the trial than it has been given in the propaganda columns of our press during the past ten years, including the voluminous contributions of Comrade Trotsky.

Expressing disdain for our repeated painstaking explanations 'about who initiates the violence', and our 'general tone', which, he says, 'makes one feel embarrassed at times', Munis offers us 'proud valor' as a substitute. Had we been gifted with this rare attribute we should have said, according to Munis: 'The workers and farmers should respond to the daily violence of the bourgeoisie with majority and organized violence of the poor masses. We do not predict but rather we assure, we ask, we advocate temporary violence of the majority against the permanent organic violence of the reactionary minority'.

We don't know much about 'proud valor' and had no need of it; we did not appear at the trials as posturing actors but only as party militants with a practical political task to carry out. Naturally, it is a good thing for a revolutionary militant to have ordinary human courage enough to take those risks which are implicit in the struggle against capitalism. And we can add: He should also have enough prudence to avoid unnecessary sacrifices. The lack of either of these qualities can be a serious personal deficiency. But the possession of both, and in good working order at that, still does not suffice to answer the most important question confronting us at the trial; namely, what formulations, what tone, what emphasis on the question of violence could best serve our cause under the given conditions? The answer to the question must be political, not theatrical. …

If these ideas are correct and we believe they are, then it is certainly reasonable to conclude that the Socialist Workers Party in the United States has some long, hard days of propaganda work, of *patiently explaining*, ahead of it. By such means it must secure a mass support before it can afford the luxury of much talk about action. Lenin drew these conclusions for the Bolshevik Party, and laid down precise instructions accordingly, only six months before it was to become the majority. The same resolution says in another paragraph:

The slogans of the moment are: (1) To *explain* the proletarian policy and proletarian way of ending the war; (2) To *criticize* the petty-bourgeois policy of placing trust in the government of the capitalists and compromising with it; (3) To carry on propaganda and agitation from group to group *in every regiment*, in *every* factory, and, particularly, among the most backward masses, such as domestic servants, unskilled laborers, etc., since it was their backing in the first place that the bourgeoisie tried to gain during the crisis; (4) To *organize, organize* and once more *organize* the proletariat, in every factory, in every district and in every city quarter.

∴

Marxism, without a doubt, is the doctrine of revolutionary action. But it has nothing in common with 'violence practiced by individuals', 'local action of small groups', or any other form of 'action' wherein individuals or minorities attempt to substitute themselves for the masses. In other words Marxism is not anarchism or Blanquism; it wages irreconcilable war against such tendencies. The revolutionary action which Marxism contemplates is the action of the masses, of the proletarian majority, led by the vanguard party. But this action, and the party's leading role in it must be, and can only be, *prepared by propaganda*. That is the central lesson of the development of the Bolshevik Party after the March revolution and the eventual transformation of its slogans from propaganda to action. That was Lenin's method. It was less romantic than that of impatient people who dream of short cuts and miracles to be evoked by the magic word 'action'. But, in compensation, Lenin's method led to a mighty and victorious mass action in the end.

A party which lacks a mass base, which has yet to become widely known to the workers, must approach them along the lines of propaganda, of patient explanations, and pay no attention to impatient demands for 'action' which it is unable to organize and for exaggerated emphasis on 'violence' which, in the given conditions, can only react to its disadvantage. When one considers how persistently careful and even *cautious*, was Lenin's party to avoid provocation and cling to its formula of *peaceful propaganda* while it remained a minority, the merest suggestion that our party, at the present time, with its present strength, take a 'bolder' course appears utterly fantastic, like a nightmare separated from living reality. …

From the foregoing it should be clear that our disavowal of 'responsibility' for violence in the testimony before the court at Minneapolis was not a special device invented by us 'to reconcile the jury', as has been alleged; our formulation of the question, taken from Lenin, was designed to serve the political aims of our movement in the given situation. We did not, and had no need to, disregard legality and 'advocate' violence as charged in the indictment.

But neither did we represent ourselves as pacifists or sow pacifist illusions. Far from it. We elucidated the question of violence and the socialist transformation of society in the same way that our great teachers, who organized a revolution, elucidated it. More than that, we gave a sufficiently frank and precise justification of the defensive violence of the workers in the daily class struggle this side of the revolution. The court record bulges with proof that we had indeed advocated the organization of workers defense guards. The testimony goes further – and this is a not unimportant detail – and reveals that we translated the word into deed and took a hand in the actual organization and activities of defense guards and picket squads when concrete circumstance made such actions possible and feasible.

We are not pacifists. The world knows, and the prosecutor in our trial had no difficulty in proving once again, that the great Minneapolis strikes, led by the Trotskyists, were not free from violence and that the workers were not the only victims. We did not disavow the record or apologize for it. When the prosecutor, referring to one of the strike battles in which the workers came out victorious, demanded: 'Is that Trotskyism demonstrating itself?' he received a forthright answer. The court record states:

A: Well, I can give you my own opinion, that I am mighty proud of the fact that Trotskyism had some part in influencing the workers to protect themselves against that sort of violence.

Q: Well, what kind of violence do you mean?

A: This was what the deputies were organized for, to drive the workers off the street. They got a dose of their own medicine. I think the workers have a right to defend themselves. If that is treason, you can make the most of it.

With this testimony we said all that needs to be said on the question of violence in the daily class struggle, as in the previously quoted testimony we said enough about violence and the transition to socialism. If this method of presentation did not help the prosecutor, we can say again: That was not our duty. If it is objected that even in this example of the Minneapolis strike, dealing with an indubitable case of working-class violence, we insisted on its *defensive* nature, we can only reply: In real life the difference between careful defensive formulation and light-minded 'calls for action' is usually, in the end result, the difference between real action and mere talk about it.

4 Is it Correct to Say We Prefer a Peaceful Transition?

Our repeated insistence at the trial that we *prefer* a peaceful transition to socialism, and that we resort to violence only as a defensive measure, brings objection and ridicule from our critic. 'Why not', says Munis – 'why not ask forgiveness, besides, for seeing ourselves painfully obliged to employ violence against the bourgeoisie?' It is possible that others may regard our formulation as lacking in aggressiveness and militancy but, being more indulgent than Munis, pass it off as a legal euphemism, justifiable under the circumstances. To be sure, our formulation helped our position from a legal standpoint and we did not hesitate to emphasize it in this respect. Also, in our opinion, the declaration that we, the Trotskyists, prefer a peaceful change of society, is a good propaganda approach to the democratic-minded American workers. These two considerations are very important, but we are quite ready to agree that they would not justify the use of a false or hypocritical statement or a statement contradicting principle.

We were guilty of no such dereliction. Our formula in this case also is the formula of the Marxist teachers. They not only insisted on the *desirability* of a peaceful change of society, but in certain exceptional circumstances, considered such a peaceful revolution possible. We, on our part, rejected any such prospect in the United States, but at the same time declared our preference for it and accused the ruling bourgeoisie as the instigators of violence. In this we were completely loyal to Marxist doctrine and tradition. …

In *Terrorism and Communism*, a book aimed from beginning to end at the bourgeois-democratic fetishism of Kautsky, Trotsky defended the violence of the proletarian revolution as a weapon *forced upon it* by the violence of the counterrevolutionary bourgeoisie; never did he renounce a preference for the peaceful way. In his introduction to the Second English Edition, published in England under the publishers' title, *In Defense of Terrorism*, he explains the position as follows:

> From the Fabians we may hear it objected that the English proletariat have it quite in their own hands to come to power by way of Parliament, to carry through peacefully, within the law and step by step, all the changes called for in the capitalist system, and by so doing not only to make revolutionary terrorism needless, but also to dig the ground away under the feet of counter-revolutionary adventurers. An outlook such as this has at first sight a particular persuasiveness in the light of the Labor Party's very important successes in the elections – but only at first sight, and that a very superficial one. The Fabian hope must, *I fear*, be held from the very beginning to be out of the question. *I say 'I fear', since a peaceful, parliamentary change over to a new social structure would undoubtedly offer highly important advantages from the standpoint of the interests of culture, and therefore those of socialism.* But in politics nothing is more dangerous than to mistake what we wish for what is possible.

We tried to say the same thing at the trial in our own words and in our own way, suited to the circumstances. In this classic formulation of the question, the legal and propagandistic advantages of our 'preference for a peaceful transition' fall into their proper place beside, and subordinate to, the most weighty considerations of all: 'The interests of culture, and *therefore* those of socialism' …

[The] … words of the two greatest leaders of Marxism in action should have an instructive value for all revolutionary militants. Lenin's sincere and earnest talk about a 'peaceful development of the revolution'; his offer to 'make compromises' to assure 'the last chance' for it; Trotsky's summary statement that the 'key to the Bolshevik policy' had been the simple prescription: 'patiently explain' – in all this it is shown that Lenin and Trotsky were completely free from radical bombast about violence. But in return, they organized a victorious proletarian revolution.

And they had prepared so well that the transfer of power did indeed take place in Petrograd without any large-scale violence. We did not falsify the historical fact at the trial when we said there was 'just a little scuffling, that's all'. The violence came afterward, initiated by the 'proslavery rebellion' which was eventually crushed by the mass force of the people led by the Bolshevik Party. These impressive facts give the explanations and formulas of Lenin and Trotsky a certain authority for those who want to be Marxists.

5 'Submitting to the Majority'

Comrade Munis is dissatisfied with our assertions at the trial that 'we submit to the majority'. The Oehlerites also are scornful of this declaration and represent it as some kind of capitulatory repudiation of our principles in order to impress the jury. All these assumptions are without foundation. Our 'submission to the majority' was not first revealed at the trial. We said it before the trial and continue to repeat it after the trial. It is a correct statement of our position because it conforms both to reality and necessity. Moreover, our Marxist teachers said it before us; we learned it from them.

What else can we do but 'submit to the majority' if we are Marxists, and not Blanquists or anarchist muddleheads? It is a timely occasion to probe into this question because we believe any ill-considered talk about some kind of mysterious 'action', presumed to be open to us while we remain not only a minority, but a very small, numerically insignificant minority, can lead only to a dangerous disorientation of the party. An exposition of the Marxist position on this question can also be useful as an antidote for any remnants of the half-Blanquist tradition of the early years of the Comintern in America.

The pioneer communists in the United States (and not only here) heard of the Bolshevik victory in Russia long before they learned about the political method and propaganda techniques whereby the Bolsheviks gained the mass support which made the seizure of power possible. Their first impressions were undoubtedly colored by the capitalist press accounts which represented the revolution as a coup d'État engineered by a small group. This distorted conception was epitomized by the title given to the American edition of Trotsky's classic pamphlet *Terrorism and Communism*, which was published here by the party's publishing house in 1922 under the completely misleading title: *Dictatorship versus Democracy*. We took the 'dictatorship', so to speak, and generously handed over to the bourgeoisie all claim to 'democracy'.

This was far too big a concession, perhaps pardonable in a young movement lacking adequate knowledge about the democratic essence of the Bolshevik program, but by far out of date today. The bourgeoisie have always tried to picture communism as a 'criminal conspiracy' in order to alienate the workers who are profoundly democratic in their sentiments. That was the aim once again in the Minneapolis trial. It was our task at the trial to go out of our way to refute this misrepresentation and emphasize the democratic basis of our program; not in order to placate our enemies and persecutors, as is assumed, but in order to reveal the truth to our friends, the American workers.

We cannot eat our cake and have it too. We must either 'submit' to the majority and confine ourselves to propaganda designed to win over the majority – or, we must seize power, more correctly, *try* to seize power and break the neck of the party, by minority 'action'.

Marxist authority is clear and conclusive in choosing between these alternatives. When we took our stand in court regarding 'submission' to the majority we were not 'folding our arms' and making 'opportunistic' statements of 'passivity in the face of the imperialist war', as we are accused. Nothing of the sort. The testimony states, repeatedly, and with sufficient emphasis, that, while 'submitting to the majority' – that is, making no minority insurrections or putsches – we are organizing, speaking, writing, and 'explaining'; in other words, carrying on *propaganda* with the object of winning over the *majority* to our program, which is the program of social revolution.

Neither were we simply trying to 'make an honorable impression on the jury without taking into consideration that we should talk for the masses'. To be sure we did not stupidly disregard the jury which held the fate of twenty-eight comrades, not to mention the legality of the party, in its hands. But we were speaking also, and *especially*, 'for the masses'. We testified primarily for publication. It was our deliberate aim to convince those who would read the testimony in printed form of the *truth* that the proletarian movement which we aspire to lead is a *democratic* movement, and not a 'conspiracy', as the prosecutor and the whole of the capitalist press would picture it, and as loose talkers would unconsciously aid them to so picture it; not a scheme to transfer power from one clique to another, but a movement of the majority in the interest of the majority.

In addition, it may as well be said candidly that this testimony was also deliberately designed as an educational shock to such members and sympathizers of our movement as may still, at this late day, be dabbling with the idea of a shorter cut to socialism by some mysterious prescription for 'action' …

The communist political method and strategy follow ineluctably from this basic premise. Nowhere and never have the authoritative representatives of Marxism formulated the question otherwise. The Marxists aim to make the social transformation *with* the majority and not *for* the majority. The irreconcilable struggle of Marx and Engels against the Blanquists revolved around this pivot …

Not once or twice, but repeatedly and almost continually, so that neither friend nor foe could possibly misunderstand him, in the months directly preceding the October Revolution, Lenin limited the Bolshevik task to the propaganda work of 'criticizing', 'exposing errors' and 'advocating' in order to 'win the majority to their side'. This was not camouflage for the enemy but education for the workers' vanguard. He explained it theoretically as we, following him, tried to explain it in popular language at the trial. …

Naturally, when Lenin, or any other Marxist, spoke of the necessity of the revolutionary party having the support of the majority he meant the real majority whose sentiments are ascertainable in various ways besides the ballot box of the bourgeois state. On the eve of the insurrection he wrote his devastating attack on Zinoviev and Kamenev, who opposed the insurrection on the ground, among other things, that 'we do not enjoy a majority among the people, and in the absence of that condition insurrection is hopeless'.

Lenin, in 'A Letter to the Comrades', written on October 29–30, scornfully dismissed the authors of this statement as 'either distorters of the truth or pedants who want an advance guarantee that throughout the whole country the Bolshevik Party has received exactly one-half of the votes plus one, this they want at all events, without taking the least account of the real circumstances of the revolution'. Nevertheless, he took pains to prove the Bolsheviks had the majority by 'facts': 'the August 20 elections in Petrograd' … 'the district council elections in Moscow in September' … 'the new elections to the Soviets' … 'a majority of the peasant Soviets' who had 'expressed itself *against* the coalition' … 'the soldiers are passing *en masse* over to the side of the Soviets' … 'Last, but not least … *the revolt of the peasantry*'. He concluded his argument on this point by saying: 'To doubt now that the majority of the people are following and will follow the Bolsheviks is shameful vacillation'. …

On September 25–27 Lenin called upon the Bolshevik Party to take power. In this famous letter, addressed 'to the Central Committee, the Petrograd and Moscow Committees of the Russian Social-Democratic Labor Party', Lenin, with the logic and directness which characterized him, states his premise and his conclusion in the first sentence: 'The Bolsheviks, having obtained a majority in the Soviets of Workers' and Soldiers' Deputies of both capitals, can and *must* take state power into their own hands'.

He was not worried about a 'formal' majority; 'No revolution ever waits for *that*'. But he was sure of the *real* majority. He insisted upon the revolution '*at this very moment*', as he expressed it, not sooner and not later, because:

> The majority of the people are *on our side*. ... The majority gained in the Soviets of the metropolitan cities *resulted* from the people coming over *to our side*. The wavering of the Socialist-Revolutionaries and Mensheviks, and the increase in the number of internationalists within their ranks prove the same thing.

The prosecution at the Minneapolis trial attempted to convict us, as charged in the indictment of an actual 'conspiracy to overthrow the government by force and violence'. We successfully refuted this accusation, and the indictment covering this point was rejected by the jury. The most effective element of our refutation of this absurd charge against our small party was our exposition of the democratic basis of the proletarian program, of the party's reliance on the majority to realize its program, and its corresponding obligation, while it remains in the minority, to 'submit to the majority'. In making this exposition we had a legal purpose, but not only a legal purpose, in mind. As with all the testimony, it was designed primarily to explain and simplify our views and aims to the workers who would be future readers of the published court record.

6 Marxism and War

Our insistence at the trial that we undertake revolutionary action only with the support of the majority and not over their heads has brought a criticism also in connection with our attitude toward war, but this criticism is no more valid than the others and has no more right to appeal to the authority of Lenin.

Comrade Munis quotes with sharp disapproval the following answer to a hypothetical question concerning what our attitude would be in the event of the United States entering the war (this was before the declaration of war): 'A decision has been made, and is accepted by the majority of the people, to go to war. Our comrades have to comply with that'.

Munis widens the gap between his understanding of revolutionary policy and ours by strongly objecting to this, as it appears to us, obviously correct and necessary statement. ... [His] impassioned rhetoric contains neither logic, nor Leninism, nor understanding of my statement nor an answer to it. 'In the first place', I didn't '*endorse* Roosevelt's decision, as if it really corresponded to the majority of the people'. I said, 'the decision (hypothetically) is *accepted* by a majority of the people', the decision which has been '*made*' by others, for obviously one does not 'accept' a decision which he has made himself. But that is only a small point which illustrates that the testimony was carelessly read before it was even more carelessly criticized.[25]

In the essence of the matter, the majority do in fact *accept* and *support* either actively or passively, the 'decision to go to war'. This is an incontestable fact, as shown by the complete absence of mass opposition. It is this attitude of the majority which we have to contend with. The fact that the decision was *made* by others does not help us. It is the attitude of the masses toward the decision that we must contend with.

What can and what should we, as Leninists, do while the masses maintain their present attitude? – that is the question. To make our position clear it is necessary to complete the answer given in the testimony which Munis broke off in the middle. He stops with our statement that 'our comrades have to comply' without adding the sentences which explain what is meant by 'compliance'. Here are the explanatory sentences: 'Insofar as they are eligible for the draft, they must accept that, along with the rest of their generation, and go and perform the duty imposed on them, *until such time as they convince the majority for a different policy*'.

When the quotation is restored in full text it begins to look somewhat different than Munis hastily pictured it. It is nothing more or less than a warning to individual workers of the vanguard, who may be drafted, to 'go with the rest of their generation' and not waste their energy and militancy on individual resistance, refusal of military service, etc. Was this warning correct? And was it necessary? As to the correctness of the warning, from the standpoint of Leninism, it will suffice to give two authoritative quotations. The first is a representative extract from Lenin's writings during the First World War:

> The idea of refusing to serve in the army, of strikes against the war, etc., is mere foolishness, it is the miserable and cowardly dream of an unarmed struggle against an armed bourgeoisie, it is a weak yearning for the abolition of capitalism without a desperate civil war or series of wars.

---

25 [Footnote by Cannon]: From similar carelessness in reading the testimony, Munis blithely represents us as 'asking the expulsion from the party of the militants who organize *protests* in the army', and 'of disauthorizing agitation and protests in the army'. On the contrary, we defended the right of such agitation and protests, as a not too hasty reading of the testimony will convince anyone who is interested. What we 'disauthorize' is futile and suicidal individual acts of insubordination and obstruction by members of our small party, acts which could only isolate them from the soldier mass under the given conditions and operate against the aim of winning over the majority. That is not the same thing as 'disauthorizing agitation and protests in the army'.

The second quotation is from the fundamental theses, 'War and the Fourth International':

> If the proletariat should find it beyond its power to prevent war by means of revolution-and this is the only means of preventing war-the workers, together with the whole people, will be forced to *participate in the army and in war*.

This truth is presumably known to all revolutionists. But it was not always known. During the First World War many of the best proletarian militants in the United States knew no other way to express their principled opposition to the imperialist war than by individual resistance to conscription, objection to and refusal of military service, etc. Much precious energy and courage were wasted that way. In testifying before the court, with a view to the publication of the testimony, we assumed that rank-and-file worker militants, to whom Lenin's tactics are as yet unknown, might read and be influenced by this warning to 'accept' with the masses – 'until such time as they convince the majority for a different policy'. Our words were primarily directed to them.

We were not even dreaming either of 'endorsing Roosevelt's decision' or of having to defend this ABC formulation within our own movement. We simply intended to say, in words and tone which we thought most efficacious from a propagandistic standpoint in the situation, what Lenin said ....

Munis quotes a sentence in the testimony: 'We would not support the war in a political sense'. Now, this single sentence, even standing by itself, is perfectly correct. But Munis is greatly dissatisfied with it.

'Why, then, equivocate so dangerously?' he asks.

> I see no other reason but that our comrades have committed the very grave error of talking for a petty-bourgeois jury for the more immediate present not foreseeing the future struggles. Would it not have been better to state: 'We submit to your war, American bourgeois, because the violence of your society imposes it on us, *the material violence of your arms*. But the masses *will* turn against you. From today on, our party is *with* the masses in an irreconcilable struggle against your regime of oppression, misery and butchery. Therefore we will fight against your war with *all means*.' (Our emphasis).

This agitational substitute for the position we elucidated at the trial is false from beginning to end ... The testimony explains what we mean by 'political opposition' ...

Trotsky, who was an internationalist to his heart's core, explained that a socialist party, which was in the minority at the outbreak of the First World War, was required to and *could only*, take up a position of *political opposition* until such time as 'the change in the feeling of the working masses came about'. That is the way he expounded the problem in *War and the International*. This book, written during the First World War and published in the United States under the publisher's title, *The Bolsheviki and World Peace*, is one of the classics upon which our movement has been raised and educated. Trotsky wrote:

> The advance guard of the Social Democracy feels it is in the minority; its organizations, in order to complete the organization of the army, are wrecked. Under such conditions there can be no thought of a revolutionary move on the part of the Party. And all this is quite independent of whether the people look upon a particular war with favor or disfavor. In spite of the colonial character of the Russo-Japanese war and its unpopularity in Russia, the first half year of it nearly smothered the revolutionary movement. Consequently it is quite clear that, with the best intentions in the world, the Socialist parties cannot pledge themselves to obstructionist action at the time of mobilization, at a time, that is, when Socialism is more than ever politically isolated. And therefore there is nothing particularly unexpected or discouraging in the fact that the working-class parties did not oppose military mobilization with their own revolutionary mobilization …

The same idea was explained over again by Trotsky twenty-two years later in his testimony before the Dewey Commission in 1937. He still prescribes 'political opposition' as a revolutionary method. At that time France had a military alliance with the Soviet Union and he was asked the hypothetical question by Stolberg:

> You are a responsible revolutionary figure. Russia and France already have a military alliance. Suppose an international war breaks out … What would you say to the French working class in reference to the defense of the Soviet Union? 'Change the French bourgeois government' would you say?

Trotsky's answer is especially interesting to us, since the United States today stands in the position of France of 1937 in relation to the Soviet Union, and the hypothetical war has become a reality:

> This question is more or less answered in the theses, 'The War and the Fourth International', in this sense: In France I would remain in opposition to the Government and would develop systematically this opposition. In Germany I would do anything I could to sabotage the war machinery. They are two different things. In Germany and in Japan, I would apply military methods as far as I am able to fight, oppose, and injure the machinery, the military machinery of Japan, to disorganize it, both in Germany and Japan. In France, it is political opposition against the bourgeoisie, and the preparation of the proletarian revolution. Both are revolutionary methods. But in Germany and Japan I have as my immediate aim the disorganization of the whole machinery. In France, I have the aim of the proletarian revolution.

In his 'April Theses', which is a sufficiently authoritative document since it was the program for the revolutionary struggle of the Bolsheviks in Russia under conditions of war, Lenin thought it enough, in dealing with the question of war and the government to say: 'not the slightest concession must be made to "revolutionary defencism"'; 'No support must be given to the Provisional Government' because it is 'a government of capitalists'; power must be transferred to the Soviet. …

> In view of the undoubted honesty of those broad sections of the mass believers in revolutionary defencism who accept the war only as a necessity, and not as a means of conquest, in view of the fact that they are being deceived by the bourgeoisie, it is necessary with particular thoroughness, persistence and patience to explain their error to them.

Political opposition ('No support to the Provisional Government') and *propaganda* ('patiently explain') – these are the weapons with which Lenin and Trotsky prepared and finally carried through the proletarian revolution. They will suffice for us too. Our propagandistic explanations of our war policy in the Minneapolis courtroom are neither 'opportunistic' nor 'equivocal'. They contain the essence of the teachings and practice of Lenin and Trotsky.

The alternative formulas of Comrade Munis, however, contain one error after another. According to him, we should have said: 'We submit to your war, American bourgeois, because the violence of your society imposes it on us, the material violence of your arms'.

That is not correct. If that were so we would have no right to condemn acts of individual resistance. When militant workers are put in fascist prisons and concentration camps because of their socialist opinions and activities they submit, but only through compulsion, to 'the material violence of arms'. Consequently, individuals or small groups are encouraged and aided to 'desert' to make their escape whenever a favorable opportunity presents itself, without waiting for and without even consulting the majority of the other prisoners in regard to the action. The revolutionary movement gains by such individual 'desertions' because they can restore the prisoner to revolutionary effectiveness which is largely shut off in prison. Trotsky, for example, twice 'deserted' from Siberia without incurring any criticism from the revolutionists.

Compulsory military service in war is an entirely different matter. In this case we submit primarily to *the majority of the workers* who accept and support the war either actively or passively. Since we cannot achieve our socialist aims without the majority we must go with them, share their hardships and hazards, and win them over to our side by propaganda on the basis of common experiences. To accept military service under such circumstances is a revolutionary necessity. Individual resistance, objection, desertion, etc. in this case – directly contrary to that of prisoners escaping from 'the violence of arms' – constitute desertion of class duty. The party, which applauds and aids the escaping prisoner, condemns draft dodgers and deserters. The escaped prisoner frees himself to resume revolutionary work. The individual deserter from the military service cuts himself off from the mass who have to make the revolution and thereby destroys his value.

'From today on', Munis would have us say, 'our party is with the masses in an irreconcilable struggle against your regime of oppression, misery and butchery. Therefore we will fight against your war with all means' ...

It would appear that Munis' erroneous explanation of the primary reason why a minority revolutionary party 'submit' to the war, his tendency to skip a stage in the workers' development and his lack of precision in speaking of the struggle against the war by 'all means' – these errors lead him to slide over to equally loose and ill-considered formulations as to those means of struggle which are open, and advantageous, to the minority party of revolutionary socialism.

7 Marxism and Sabotage

The everlasting talk about 'action', as if a small minority party has at its disposal, besides its propaganda – its 'explanations' – some other weapons vaguely described as 'actions' but not explicitly defined, can only confuse and becloud the question and leave the door open for sentiments of an anarchistic and Blanquist nature. We, following all the Marxist teachers, thought it necessary to exclude such conceptions in order to safeguard the party from the danger of condemning itself to futility and destruction before it gets a good start on its real task at this time: to *explain* to the masses and win over the majority.

That is why we utilized the forum of the trial to speak so explicitly about our rejection of sabotage. That is why we denied all accusations in this respect so emphatically. Not – with Munis' permission – for lack of 'valor', but because, as Marxists, we do not believe in sabotage, terrorism, or any other device which substitutes the actions of individuals or small groups for the action of the masses. …

Sabotage was once the fashion in this country – in the politically primitive days before the First World War. Imported from France where it was advertised as a miraculous remedy by the anarchists and anarcho-syndicalists, sabotage was taken up by the IWW, the left socialists, and the radical intellectuals, who in those days had a decidedly anarchistic hue. It seemed for a time to offer a wonderful short cut to victory for a movement which wasn't doing so well with the humdrum job of educating and organizing the workers for mass action.

The consequences of this anarchistic folly were disastrous for the IWW. The advocacy of sabotage only repelled the masses and left the IWW members in a legally indefensible position. To avoid complete alienation from the workers, and for sheer self-preservation of the organization in the face of prosecutions during the war, the IWW was compelled to drop the 'weapon' of sabotage overboard with the most unseemly haste. …

Lenin wrote: 'Not *sabotage* of the war, not separate, individual actions in that spirit, but *mass propaganda* (not only among "civilians") leading to the transformation of the war into a civil war … *Not sabotage of the war*, but the struggle against chauvinism …' (our emphasis).

Munis is especially indignant at our rejection of sabotage in the testimony, but he is wrong in his criticism and wrong even, it would appear, in his understanding of the question …

Sabotage, to us, means individual acts of obstruction and destruction, substituted for mass action. That is the way Marxism defines it and, thereby, condemns it. Similarly, individual terrorism. But it is necessary to understand that such actions have one quality when employed as *substitutes* for mass action and another quality when subordinated to and absorbed by mass action. Marxism is opposed to terrorist assassinations, for example, but not to wars of liberation waged by the oppressed masses, even though wars entail some killing of obnoxious individuals. So, also, with acts of obstruction and destruction as *part of* and *subordinate* to wars waged by the masses, not as substitutes for them. 'Terrorism' and 'sabotage' are then no longer the same things. Everything changes, including the attitude of Marxists, according to what is *dominant* and what is *subordinate* in the circumstances. …

Comrade Munis seems to invest sabotage with a virtue in its own right. We, on the other hand, admit 'sabotage' only as a minor auxiliary factor in mass actions; that is, when it is no longer sabotage in the proper sense of the term. The difference is quite fundamental.

Munis writes: 'I believe that sabotage is a method for tactical use whose application at *certain moments* can be productive of contrary effects to what is intended' (our emphasis) … Munis' formulation, contrasted to that of Trotsky in his article, 'Learn to Think', shows a great difference of conception. Trotsky wrote:

> The proletarian party does not resort to artificial methods, such as burning warehouses, setting off bombs, wrecking trains, etc., in order to bring about the defeat of its own government Even if it were successful on this road, the military defeat would not at all lead to revolutionary success, a success which can be assured only by the independent movement of the proletariat … The methods of struggle change, of course, when the struggle enters the openly revolutionary phase. Civil war is a war, and in this aspect has its particular laws. In civil war, bombing of warehouses, wrecking of trains and all other forms of military 'sabotage' are inevitable. Their appropriateness is decided by purely military considerations – civil war continues revolutionary politics but by other – precisely military – means.

Sabotage is admissible as a weapon of the proletarian movement only 'in quotation marks' as elucidated by Trotsky. That is, when, strictly speaking, it is no longer sabotage, but a minor military measure supplementing mass action. Whoever speaks of sabotage in any other framework does not speak the language of Marxism.

8 Defensive Formulations and the Organization of Action

In general, it may be said that the source of all the criticism of our expositions at the Minneapolis trial is to be found in the apparent rejection of defensive formulations, and in counterposing 'offensive action' to them. But the essence of the whole question consists in this, that defensive formulations prepare and help to create genuine mass actions, while 'calls to action', not so prepared, usually echo in the void. It is not by accident that those revolutionists who understand this are precisely the ones who have shown the capacity to organize actions when the conditions for them are present. The ultra-left sectarians, meantime, who do not understand the best mechanism for the organization of actions – that is, precisely, defensive formulations – always remain alone and isolated with their impatient slogans and their self-imagined intransigence. ...

Also, defensive formulations are an indispensable medium for teaching the masses, who will not be convinced by theory but only by their own experience and propaganda related thereto. This experience of the masses proceeds in the main along the line of defensive actions. That is why defensive formulations are most easily comprehensible and represent the best approach of the revolutionary Marxists to the masses. Finally, it is a tactical and legal consideration of no small importance in a bourgeois-democratic country that defensive formulas partially disarm the class enemy; or in any case, make their attacks more difficult and costly. Why should such advantages be thrown away? ...

Every strike leader worth his salt knows, however, that strikers are not mobilized and sent into action against strikebreakers, thugs and law-breaking cops by lecturing them on the virtues of violence and 'calling' them to take the 'offensive'. The workers, militant and courageous as they may be, prefer victory by peaceful means; and in this they only show good sense. In addition strikers, at the beginning, almost invariably entertain illusions about the impartiality of the public authorities and tend to assume that they, as well as the bosses and their hirelings, will respect the rights of the strikers and the justice of their cause.

... Strike leaders who seek not self-expression but victory in the strike, who understand that it can be won only by means of mass solidarity and mass action, must take these illusions and sentiments of the workers into account as the point of departure. Strike leaders can in no case begin with loose-mouthed 'calls' for violent offensive action by the strikers. The first task is to *explain* the implacable nature of the struggle in which the self-interest of the bosses excludes fair play, and the role of the public authorities as political servants of the bosses; the second task is to *warn* the workers to expect violent attacks; and the third task is to prepare and organize the workers to *defend themselves and their rights*. Along these lines, and as a rule only along these lines, the struggle can be consciously developed in tempo and scope The most effective mass action of the strikers, as every experienced organizer of mass actions knows, is organized and carried out under *defensive slogans*.

Matters are no different when the workers' mass action ascends from the elementary field of the economic strike to the topmost peak of the class struggle – the open fight for political power. Here also the action proceeds under defensive slogans and, to a very large extent also under cover of legality. Trotsky has demonstrated this so convincingly in his monumental *History of the Russian Revolution* that there remains no ground for serious debate in our ranks on the subject. …

Trotsky painstakingly explains how the October Revolution was developed by defensive formulations from link to link over a period of thirteen or sixteen days during which 'hundreds of thousands of workers and soldiers took direct action, defensive in form, but aggressive in essence'. At the end of that time, the masses being fully mobilized, there remained 'only a rather narrow problem' – the insurrection, the success of which was assured[.] …

After these explanations of Trotsky about the defensive slogans whereby the Bolsheviks organized their victorious struggle for power it should not be necessary to say anything more on the subject. The method here acquires unimpeachable authority by virtue of the fact that it was not only expounded, but also successfully applied to the greatest revolution in history. In this light the defensive formulations employed by us in the Minneapolis trial, far from being repudiated, must be underscored more decisively. They are the right formulations for a propagandistic approach to the American workers. And they are the best methods for the mobilization of the workers for mass action throughout all stages of the development of the proletarian revolution in the United States.

7 Farewell Statement[26]

(1944)

Albert Goldman

Seven legal questions were raised in the petition which [our] attorneys filed before the US Supreme Court asking it to review the decision of the Circuit Court of Appeals affirming the conviction of the 18 Minneapolis defendants. … [A]t Ieast six of these legal questions not only justified but demanded that the Supreme Court grant a review, consider oral and written arguments and render its opinion [as to why it affirmed the decision of the Circuit Court of Appeals]. I offer for the consideration of the layman only two of the legal questions raised by the defense ….

One section of the Smith 'Gag' Act, under which the defendants were convicted, makes it unlawful 'to advise, counsel, urge, or in any manner cause insubordination, disloyalty, mutiny, or refusal of duty by any member of the military or naval forces of the United States'. The Espionage Act of 1917 makes it unlawful 'willfully to cause, or attempt to cause insubordination, disloyalty, mutiny, or refusal of duty, in the military or naval forces of the United States …'. Now I admit that the language is not exactly alike because the act under which we were convicted speaks of 'advising and urging' insubordination, while the Espionage Act uses the expression 'causing insubordination'. Sensible people would agree, I think, that causing insubordination must necessarily involve in some way or other advising and urging. … To all intents and purposes the two statutes are the same.

It was in interpreting the Espionage Act that the Supreme Court, in 1919, laid down the rule that, before anyone can be convicted for making oral or written statements, the government must prove that 'a clear and present danger' exists, that these statements might actually result in creating insubordination in the armed forces. The government contended that this rule does not apply to that section of the Smith Act which is almost identical with the Espionage Act. … the question is of such importance and the similarity of the statutes is so great, that the Supreme Court was obligated to discuss it and present reasons for its decisions.

---

26 Goldman 1944.

Another important question involved in the case which can be readily understood without any special training is: What constitutes urging insubordination in the armed forces? This does not involve the question whether the government witnesses testified against us truthfully. ... The question is whether, as a matter of law, the facts presented by the government constitute urging insubordination.

Stupid Invention

Some of the government witnesses testified that a few of the defendants told them that, if drafted, they should try to create dissension in the army by kicking about the food and bedding. This is obviously the invention of stupid people ... [Even if] it is true, [d]oes this constitute a conspiracy to create insubordination in the army? Suppose it turned out that the food and bedding were excellent and there was nothing to kick about on that score? Suppose they were bad, would it be wrong to kick about them?

It was also shown by the government that the Socialist Workers Party favors military training under the control of the trade unions and democracy in the military forces. Does that constitute urging insubordination?

A Supreme Court motivated purely by legal obligations would have considered at least the two questions that I have mentioned and would have presented reasons for its decision. It is possible to come to either one of two conclusions with reference to the failure of the Supreme Court to grant a review. It is possible to say that the Court considered all legal questions raised by the attorneys for the defendants and decided not to grant a review because these questions were not sufficiently important or were already settled in some previous case. Such a conclusion is ruled out for the reason that the questions raised were novel ones, and most people will agree that they are important.

The other conclusion, and the correct one, is that the Supreme Court did not want to interfere with the conviction in this case and was not interested in discussing the legal questions that were raised. It is on this assumption that one can best explain the failure of the Court to grant a review. This was the simplest and easiest way out. It obviated the necessity of discussing the questions and presenting reasons for a decision, something that would have been embarrassing for those judges who claim to be liberal. ...

Weapon for Reaction

Everyone in the labor and progressive movement must clearly realize the implications of the decision by the Circuit Court of Appeals, which the Supreme Court has approved by virtue of its refusal to review it. It not only permits a viciously reactionary law, the Smith 'Gag' Act, to remain on the stature books. It has strengthened that law by interpreting it in a manner which gives the widest possible scope for its use by prosecutors against anyone who stands for the right of workers to defend themselves against reactionary violence and who raises his voice on behalf of any democratic rights for men in the military service.

What more perfect weapon can a prosecutor expect than a stature so interpreted as to permit an indictment and conviction for any statement criticizing anything connected with the military regime? All that he need do is frame an indictment in the words of the statute. The method of choosing juries in the federal courts practically guarantees a conviction. What a paradise for a prosecutor aiming to convict revolutionists if no more is required to make a conviction stick than to introduce a copy of the *Communist Manifesto*. The courts have opened wide the gates of the federal penitentiaries for victims of the Smith 'Gag' Law to be driven in.

Whether or not the government will set the prosecutors into motion does not depend solely on the fact that a reactionary law has been interpreted in a reactionary manner, and that the conviction of eighteen Trotskyists has been affirmed. For the present government may well be satisfied to have a powerful weapon at its disposal which can be used whenever it becomes necessary, not only against revolutionists but against any and all militant unionists and progressives.

The weapon may again be used when the European masses take their fate into their own hands and refuse to take orders from Stalin, Roosevelt, and Churchill. It undoubtedly will be used when the workers of this country will become more militant in their demands to curb the war profiteers and will refuse to assume all the burdens of the war.

Motives for the Conviction

Undoubtedly it will be asked why the Supreme Court refused to interfere with the conviction. I explained why it chose the method of refusing to grant a review but that in itself does not explain why the judges decided to permit the conviction to stand.

Every individual having anything to do with the prosecution had his own particular reason for his desire to get us convicted. Tobin wanted to run the Minneapolis teamsters' union as he pleased without the interference of men who fought for honest, militant and democratic unionism. He asked his friend Roosevelt to do something for him. Our 'great' and 'democratic' President was more than willing to have us indicted and convicted in order to do his friend Tobin a favor. And once the machinery of what is called justice is set in motion, every individual connected with that capitalist justice is anxious to do his part faithfully and well ...

Basically, however, the special and particular reasons motivating the various personalities connected with the prosecution play a minor role. To find the basic motives of Tobin and Roosevelt and prosecutors and judges one must look to the fundamental ideas which the defendants represent and in the activities which the defendants pursue for the realization of their ideas.

Imprisoned for Our Ideas

Let me once more assure you that the charge of advocating violence to overthrow the government and the accusation of creating insubordination in the armed forces are only flimsy pretexts to confuse the backward and fool the gullible. In fact it is because we are opposed to a social order which condemns mankind to the physical violence of war and fascism and to the spiritual violence of poverty and ignorance that we have been sentenced to prison terms. They who boast about the number and quality of weapons produced to kill human beings by the thousands and tens of thousands, accuse us of advocating violence because, on the basis of an analysis of social forces and a study of history, we conclude that the ruling class will not yield its wealth and power without resorting to violence.

It is because we have been indicted, convicted, and are being sent to prison for holding and propagating advanced social ideas that the labor and liberal movements are obligated, in their own interests, to struggle for a pardon on our behalf and to erase the Smith 'Gag' Act from the statute books. Too many liberals and labor leaders are so interested in supporting Roosevelt in what they consider to be a struggle against German fascism, that they have forgotten that right here in this country men are being railroaded to jail because they are struggling for a new social order. Let those who want democracy to prevail and are indifferent to our case, beware. By their failure to struggle on our behalf they are helping to create a monster that will ultimately destroy them also.

Some people, I hope, have learned a lesson in this case. They have learned that no reliance can be placed in a so-called "liberal" Supreme Court to guard essential democratic rights. A 'liberal' Supreme Court can interfere with a lower court to protect the right of an unimportant and unpopular religious sect to distribute its literature. It has been shown in our case that it will not interfere with the jailing of people who seriously advocate a fundamental change in the social order.

In the last analysis, only a politically conscious working class will be able to guard the democratic rights of the people. The attention of all who are devoted to these rights must be centered on the masses, on educating them to the significance of our case as a violation of their rights. All of us can and must agree on one thing – that democracy is absolutely essential for the working class. It is essential for its struggle for better conditions under the present system. It is essential for its struggle for a new social order. It is essential for the building of the new social order.

To struggle for our pardon, for the appeal of the Smith 'Gag' Act and for the nullification of the decision of the Circuit Court of Appeals and of the Supreme Court is essentially a struggle for the democratic rights of the masses.

Full well do we know that the sacrifice which we are compelled to make by virtue of our imprisonment is nothing in comparison with the sacrifices which revolutionists of other lands and different times were forced and are still forced to suffer. We do not at all consider ourselves in the categories of martyrs. We have done our bit in the cause of working-class emancipation. We go to prison confident that the struggle for our ideas and for the democratic rights of the American masses will continue. Upon our liberation we shall together with you continue the struggle for socialism which will bring freedom and equality to all mankind.

CHAPTER 11

History and Theory

Paul Le Blanc

Permeating other contributions in this volume, practical as well as analytical, is an intensive engagement and utilisation of history and theory. The items in this chapter, however, are focused precisely on seeking to convey to the reader an understanding of historical events as well as the specifics and development of Marxist theory.

Felix Morrow and George Novack were two of the most prominent intellectuals in the Trotskyist movement, with keen interest in the history of the United States as developed by such influential 'progressive historians' as Charles Beard and V.L. Parrington. Both are eager to challenge a 'democratic' romanticising that had crept into the historiography of Communist Party writers (under the impact of Stalin's Popular Front that sought alliances with the 'democratic bourgeoisie'). They gave emphasis instead to the long history of the capitalist class advancing its interests at the expense of both democracy and the 'lower classes'. More recent scholarship updates the specifics but also largely corroborates the essentials in their accounts in the two selections offered here.[1]

Albert Goldman was an outstanding left-wing lawyer with a strong intellectual bent, and proved to be an outstanding popular educator in Trotskyist ranks. A three-part lecture series, designed to convey a relatively sophisticated and at the same time comprehensible understanding of Marxist theory, was published in a widely-distributed pamphlet. The second portion of *What is Socialism?* is reproduced here. Its focus, not surprisingly, is on problems and dynamics of class consciousness and class struggle.

Responding to what he saw as a false counterposition of Rosa Luxemburg to Vladimir Ilyich Lenin, Max Shachtman wrote what has been considered a classic essay (approvingly cited years later by sociologist C. Wright Mills) that explores common ground between them as well as differences between the two. In that essay, reproduced here, Shachtman attributes some of the key differences, interestingly, to the different contexts in which they were active. One of Luxemburg's younger comrades, Paul Frölich, would soon produce a major biography presenting a similar analysis.[2]

---

1 Hofstadter 1970; Countryman 2003; Nash, 2006; Blackburn 2011; Levine 2014.

2 Mills 1962, p. 150; Frölich 2010.

Among the most brilliant figures in the Trotskyist movement was the Afro-Caribbean intellectual C.L.R. James, the author of two groundbreaking histories – *World Revolution* and *Black Jacobins*.[3] Moving from England to the United States in 1939, he offered his comrades another groundbreaking work, reprinted here, under the party name J.R. Johnson. While the massive layer of humanity living in or originating from Africa was generally presented as a marginal element in world history or – at best – as passive victims, James argues powerfully that they are a central and active component in the transformative revolutions of the past, going on to emphasise the meaning of this for revolutionary struggles of the present and the future.

The final essay in this chapter, by George Novack (using the name William F. Warde), produces a stirring defence of revolutionary perspectives in the face of the government's Smith Act prosecutions, demonstrating that 'the right to revolution' is integral to the entire history of the United States.

3 James 1937; James 1989.

1 The Spirit of the US Constitution[4] (*1936*)

Felix Morrow

'The Supreme Court was never given the power it wields. It has usurped that power'. This cry, now being raised by the Rooseveltian liberals, has been on other occasions also a useful plank for demagogues. LaFollette ran his 1925 presidential campaign on that issue. Borah raised it in 1923. Teddy Roosevelt toyed with it on occasion and, of course, Jefferson and Jackson made excellent political capital out of it. So often has this cry of usurpation been raised, that one might well ask its present trumpeters: how is it that the Supreme Court has always bobbed up, unscathed and with ever growing power, after every 'assault' upon it?

This cry of usurpation is, indeed, a very dangerous piece of demagoguery. It implies that an otherwise pure democratic system of government has been perverted by the unnatural powers usurped by the Supreme Court, and that the pure stream of democracy may be restored by removing the Supreme Court. The notion of usurpation reeks of parliamentary cretinism: it is blind to the class role of the government as a whole – including the most representative organ, Congress – and the dependence of all governmental phenomena upon the real relation of forces outside in the world of capitalist ownership and class struggle.

But this 'blindness' is itself a class phenomenon. That the Supreme Court is but one of a host of instrumentalities and principles embodied in the Constitution by its makers to thwart forever the possibility of majority rule; that the Founding Fathers had as their fundamental aim the erection of such permanent barriers; that the hostility to majority rule is, in fact, the very essence of the Constitution – such ideas are repugnant to the ruling class, which prefers to perpetuate the myth that the Constitution is a democratic document. 'The ruling ideas of the epoch are the ideas of the ruling class'. In their very 'dissent', therefore, the Roosevelt liberals reveal their class loyalty and continue to perpetuate this democratic myth, the classless theory of the state.

4 Morrow 1936.

Clio's voice is muted by such powerful forces. The true history of the writing of the Constitution is available enough in the libraries for the student; but in the main it is the democratic myth which prevails in the textbooks and the universities, not to speak of the movies, radio and politics.

And now poor Clio may well despair, for – no doubt after re-reading the press-clippings of LaFollette's 1924 campaign – the communist party has issued a manifesto (*Daily Worker*, Jan. 11) and numerous 'historical' articles, embracing the 'usurpation' theory; the Stalinists have, indeed, become the chief purveyors of this anti-Marxian and factually-discredited theory.

The question of the powers given to the Supreme Court is, however, but one aspect of a much broader question that needs to be answered first: what is the nature of the Constitution? To answer this question at all, one must recall the main characteristics of the historical epoch which produced the Constitution.

When imperial Britain's leading strings began to turn into fetters on colonial America's further development, and the New England merchants and the Southern planters took to the road of independence, they faced the fact that the struggle against England involved serious dangers at home. The strong hand of England had upheld the oligarchical rule of merchant and planter over small farmer and artisan. What would happen when this strong hand was gone?

Nor was it merely that merchant and planter would now have to rule without England's aid. To fight England required the drawing into political life of the workingmen and farmers; once the colonies were free, would merchant and planter be able to dismiss the lower classes back to their subordinate role? The events of 1764–1766, when the workingmen backed up by mob violence frightened the merchants off for years. They wondered 'whether the Men who excited this seditious Spirit in the People have it in their power to suppress it'. Many of those who became Tories did so, like Joseph Galloway of Pennsylvania, because they 'feared the tyranny of mob rule more than the tyranny of Parliament'. Even James Otis roundly denounced mob riots, saying that 'no possible circumstances, though ever so oppressive, could be supposed sufficient to justify private tumults and disorders'. The merchants and planters would have preferred to fight England by methods which did not require drawing the masses into the struggle. The formation, by Boston and New York workingmen, of the Sons of Liberty, which performed the actual work of violence in 1764 and 1765, and which did not grow into a revolutionary inter-colonial organization at that time only because the Stamp Act was repealed, was an alarming sign that the masses might go forward for their own objectives once the fight with England was over.

The menace of farmers' demands was even more disturbing. In New England, the wealthier families had been able to take the lion's share of the coastal lands only by suppressing the demands of the poorer farmers and the former indentured servants. The tidewater planters had pre-empted the rich tobacco lands, forcing former servants into the backwoods. The struggle over taxation found the same classes in opposition, the farmers particularly complaining that they paid on their whole estate while merchants easily concealed assets. Especially bitter was the struggle over paper money, the debtors desiring to pay off debts and taxes with progressively depreciating paper money, while the prospering merchants wanted stable currency; uprisings of debtors threatened, and Riot Acts were passed against them; it was only Parliament's prohibition of paper money (1763), that turned the farmers' attack from their home merchants to England. These economic oppositions naturally also found expression in a struggle over representation. Under the colonial charters, office-holders were required to have larger properties than voters, thus weeding out many representatives of the lower classes; property franchises were general throughout the colonies, leaving mechanics and artisans, and some of the farmers, especially former indentured servants, voteless; even more irksome was the inequitable representation of the "back country" as against the coastal counties, which was one of the most bitterly contested issues throughout the colonial period.

Class stood arrayed against class. This is the main explanation for the hesitation and dilatoriness of merchant and planter in launching the final struggle against England. But they finally had to plunge.

The exigencies of revolutionary warfare gave more and more power to the artisans and backwoods farmers. Not only England's restraining hand disappeared, but a large part of the upper classes – British placemen, commercial agents, great landowners and merchants – sided with England, and had to be suppressed. The local Committees of Safety took over most governmental powers. They took charge of providing armed forces for the struggle. But, since the loyalists were far more numerous than the British army ever became, the apparatus for suppressing the loyalists was even more important. It was, in fact, civil war; and to wage it successfully meant political activization of the masses. Disarming parties went from house to house to seize loyalist weapons. Terrorization of loyalists by mob violence, tarring and feathering, arbitrary arrest, forcible exile, suspension of all their civil rights, forced confessions or recantations, confiscation of property, and not a few executions; 'the patriot organization for holding in check and destroying loyalism was fully as systematic, elaborate and far-reaching as the military establishment which Washington and his generals directed against the British regular army', says a noted authority, Fisher. The local committees had, of course, no legal basis; they had no status other than revolutionary necessity. As the revolution progressed, however, they had grown so accustomed to dealing with the loyalists, that they regarded it as an established and legalized procedure; an account of tars and feathers inflicted on a New Jersey loyalist closes with the words: 'The whole was conducted with that regularity and decorum that ought to be observed in all public punishments'.

The astute leaders of the merchants and planters were clearly aware of the dangers involved in thus drawing in the masses into state power. Alexander Hamilton tried to check confiscation of property and expulsion of loyalists but was powerless, even after the treaty of peace of 1783. In 1784 the loyalists in New York were disfranchised and disqualified from holding office, and debts due them were cancelled on condition that one-fortieth was paid into the state treasury. Hamilton saw his natural allies driven out by an agrarian majority who were his natural enemies. Earlier in the struggle, contemplating the 'rule of the mob', John Adams was so troubled that he asked:

> Is this the object for which I have been contending, said I to myself ... are these the sentiments of such people, and how many of them are there in the country? Half the nation, for what I know; for half the nation are debtors, if not more; and these have been in all countries the sentiments of debtors. If the power of the country should get into such hands, and there is a great danger that it will, to what purpose have we sacrificed our time, health and everything else?
>
> *Works*, Vol. II, p. 420

The masses had their way, too, about issuance of a progressively depreciating currency. Having 'commonly pledged the half or whole of their estates for the preservation of their sacred liberties', the provincial bodies evinced a uniform determination to pass the sacrifice on by way of a depreciating currency. Any opposition to this course was frustrated by the need of mass support for the struggle. As the currency depreciated and men refused to sell lands, houses or merchandize for nearly worthless paper, their stores were closed or pillaged, merchants mobbed, fined and imprisoned, as the agrarian-controlled legislatures declared the Continentals legal tender. Congress, if anything, outdid the state legislatures, for after a solemn declaration that the Continentals would not be depreciated – 'A bankrupt, faithless republic would be a novelty in the political world, and appear among respectable nations like a common prostitute among chaste and respectable matrons' – Congress adopted six months later a plan to redeem the money at one-fortieth of its nominal value. Progressive depreciation enabled the farmers to pay off debts and taxes; the last years of the war was a debtors' paradise. Madison is authority for the statement that the paper-money laws and the 'stay-laws' against foreclosures were the primary reason for calling the Constitutional Convention.

The small farmers controlled the revolutionary state governments which superseded the colonial charters. They did not do away with property qualifications for suffrage, so that a large part of the mechanics and artisans, as well as some former indentured servants, remained voteless, a condition for which the agrarians were to pay dearly when the Constitution was submitted to the electorate; but the new state governments gave sufficiently more equitable representation to the back country to enable the farmers to hold consistent majorities.

The form of government introduced by the agrarian majorities confirmed all the fears of the conservatives. The colonial governments had been, generally, subordinated to a royal- or proprietary-appointed governor who appointed the members of the upper legislative house, convened and dissolved the legislature, had an unqualified veto power over it, and appointed the judges and all other civil and military officers. In sharp contrast to this, the new state governments were based on the principle of legislative supremacy. The governor's veto power was entirely abolished in all but two states, his appointive power taken away or restricted, his term of office cut to one year in ten states, in New York and New England he was elected by the voters, in the other eight states by the legislature. The supremacy of the legislature is also shown by its powers over the judiciary; in nine states the judges were elected by the legislature, in the others they were controlled by the legislature's hold on governor and council who did the appointing. Annual elections of judges in three states, removal in six states by the executive on an address from the legislature, and simple methods of impeachment by the legislature, guaranteed considerable direct control over the judiciary. Most important of all, the judges had no power of voiding laws of the legislature, The theory of division of powers among legislative, executive and judicial departments, the system of checks and balances, embodied later in the Constitution, find no semblance in the constitutions of the revolutionary state governments.

The first federal constitution, the *Articles of Confederation*, framed under the impulse of the revolution, is also a democratic document. All the powers were vested in a single legislative body, the Continental Congress, which was unchecked by an executive or judiciary.

Fiercely opposed to the leveling doctrines of these governments, merchant and planter nevertheless submitted for the duration of the revolution; for the brunt of the struggle lay on the farming masses and the artisans, who took seriously the democratic implications of the theory of natural rights by which the revolution was justified. The sailors' and workers' interests were directly bound up with perpetuation and expansion of colonial commerce, and the farmers of the Northern and Middle Colonies were dependent for cash incomes on the sale of their cereals and meats to the West Indies and Europe; this provided common ground with the merchants and planters. But the masses had their own grievances against England: prohibition of paper currency, vetoing of debtor legislation, raising of cost of goods by duties, levying of direct taxes, and these were the issues which made the revolution *popular*. The literature of the time shows, too, that the masses understood that further liberty could come only after England was out of the way. In their opposition to the democratic state governments, their paper money and stay-laws, merchant and planter dared not come into fundamental opposition to the objectives for which the masses were laying down their lives. As one contemporary put it:

> Thoughtful patriots, who deplored the confusion, the turmoil and the mobs, nevertheless felt satisfied that it was a phase through which we must pass, a price which we must pay for independence. The long years of anarchy were trying, terrible and disgusting; but to remain the political slaves of England was, they said, infinitely worse.

They bided their time.

Once the treaty of peace was signed in 1783, the conservatives began to fight back. One of the main issues was depreciating paper money. In 1785 seven legislatures emitted new paper money, and the atmosphere of the struggle against it was one of impending civil war. When an armed mob in New Hampshire demanded unlimited paper money; when mobs in Massachusetts prevented the courts from sitting on foreclosure cases, and Daniel Shays attempted to close the courts altogether by armed force; when event after event showed merchant and planter that only a decisive transformation of the situation would insure their domination, there was talk among them of a military dictatorship, if necessary.

In the ensuing struggle from which they emerged so victorious, they were aided by the historical impotence of the agrarian population, with its narrow, provincial outlook. The agrarian opposition remained locked up in each state, often unconnected within the boundaries of one state; of a tendency toward a national coordination or organization of the agrarian forces, there was not a sign. The agrarians proved incapable of understanding the need of a centralized government for the further development of commerce and industry. The only opposition to merchant and planter which might have been successful was one which could combine democratic demands with centralized governmental power. Such a program could not come from the agrarians, with their hopelessly local outlook. They opposed every attempt to increase the powers of the government while it was still under the democratic Articles of Confederation. They levied duties on goods transported from one state to another, and carried on commercial wars of retaliation with each other, so that shipping and manufacturing were handicapped by multiple and conflicting tariff policies. The finances of the Confederation were dependent on payments by the agrarian legislatures, which held them back, with the result that even the interest on foreign obligations was unpaid, the revolutionary soldiers did not receive the funds voted them, and the government was paralyzed. Rival claims of the states, the inability of the government to provide protection and facilities for settlement, kept the Western lands closed. The lack of a national currency was an impediment to national commerce and industry. These various needs provided the conservatives with powerful arguments in favor of the Constitution; actually they were arguments only in favor of a strong national government, and in no way justified the anti-democratic character of the Constitution. But this was a distinction which the agrarians were incapable of making.

So long as the revolutionary struggle provided a common objective for all classes, and the national army and navy and the Continental Congress (permitted wide powers during the struggle) provided a national framework, the farmers had, by their local assumption of power against the loyalists, constituted the flesh and blood of a powerful, national state power. But when the classes went their separate ways, the power of the farmers frittered itself away in petty local struggles; they even lost control of some of the state legislatures. This incapacity for large-scale common action is all the more damning as a characteristic of the agrarian population, if one takes into consideration that the American agrarians were not subsistence farmers, but commercial farmers dependent in large measure on cash crops. Money payment of taxes, that sure index to the development of a highly-developed commercial agriculture, was established in Massachusetts as early as 1694 and soon became universal. Under the leadership of the bourgeoisie, they had fought against the England which closed its ports to their cereals and meats and hampered trade with the foreign West Indies and Europe; but when England, after the Revolution, continued to close its ports to their produce, they would not give the national government the necessary powers to institute retaliatory measures. Further development of commercial agriculture clearly depended on a strong state power, the growth of cities, the development commerce and industry; the agrarians could see no further than their county seats.

The largest section of the population, then, the freehold farmer, was incapable of bringing forward a program which combined the necessary national centralization with democratic forms of government. The artisans and mechanics in the towns, resembling more the prototype of the manufacturing *entrepreneur* than the proletarian, earning comparatively good wages, and daily aware of the dependence of his well-being on the development of capitalist enterprise, constituted too small and rapidly changing a class to bring forward the necessary program.

The former revolutionary vanguard, the ideologists like Samuel Adams and Josiah Warren, Jefferson, Madison and Patrick Henry who had rallied the farming masses against England with their passionate enunciations of the rights of man, not only did not come forward to provide leadership to the masses in the new situation but sided with their enemies. This significant fact is obscured the struggles which came *after* the Constitution, and therefore deserves emphasis. Adams, Warren and their associates from the commercial bourgeoisie returned after the Revolution to their class allegiance, and played no further role; this is sufficiently indicated by the fact that Samuel Adams, in the debates over the Constitution, supported the principle of judicial supremacy.

Jefferson, Madison and Henry represented the interests of planting aristocracy of the tidewater regions of the South, large scale commercial farmers producing one main cash crop (tobacco). They were scarcely the bearers of a democratic tradition; they were then passing from the use of dictatorially-treated indentured servants to chattel Negro slaves as their main labor supply; they had pre-empted the best growing lands and driven the smaller farmers back into the piedmont region; in the state legislature they were fighting the representatives of the back-country. Before the Revolution one of their chief links to the small farmer New England and the middle colonies had been their common interest in depreciating paper currency; for the peculiar business relations between the planters and their British agents (who extended credit before selling the crop, resulting in chronic over-buying by the planters) made the planters perennial debtors; British claims after the war were almost entirely against plantation provinces. But having successfully repudiated debts to England, the planters had become terrified during the war at the effects of paper money, and joined now with the merchants to prohibit it. Indeed, the sole link between the Southern planters and the small farmers was a reactionary one: the provincial demand for states rights against centralized government. But the planters were also the chief speculators in Western lands, and could not cash in without the aid of a centralized government. Concessions were made to them, in the constitution (three-fifths) of slaves to be counted for representation and taxation; importation of slaves not to be forbidden before a lapse of twenty years; as a check on commercial agreements detrimental to the planters a two-third Senate vote for ratifying treaties; equal representation of states (in the Senate) but they had nothing to do with democracy.

The planters were later to fall out with the commercial bourgeoisie, when Hamilton's bold and far-seeing policy of developing commerce and industry showed by its first fruits that the planters were eventually to become subordinate; and then the planter ideologists, seeking the agrarian masses as allies, reverted to the democratic slogans of the Revolution. But on the main issues *against the agrarian masses*, the planter ideologists joined the mercantile aristocracy in drafting the Constitution.

Merchant and planter vied with each other in denouncing legislative supremacy and finding ways and means to do away with it in the Constitution. Randolph of Virginia, seeking a 'cure for the evils under which the United States labored', declared that 'in tracing these evils to their origin, every man had found it in the turbulence and follies of democracy; that some check therefore was to be sought for against this tendency; and a good Senate seemed most likely to answer the purpose'. Another planter ideologist, Madison, declared the problem before the Constitutional Convention was to secure private rights 'against majority factions', and warned:

> An increase of population will of necessity increase the proportion of those who will labor under all the hardships of life and secretly sigh for a more equal distribution of its blessings. These may in time outnumber those who are placed above the feelings of indigence. According to the equal law of suffrage, the power will slide into the hands of the former. No agrarian attempts have yet been made in this country, but symptoms of a leveling spirit, as we have understood, have sufficiently appeared, in a certain quarter, to give notice of the future danger.
>
> *Debates*, ELLIOT, Vol. V, p. 243

Such was this great democrat's conclusions from Shays' Rebellion!

The banner-bearer of 'Jeffersonian Democracy' was American Minister in Paris during the Constitutional Convention. In a letter to Madison, dated December 20, 1787, Jefferson wrote:

> I like the organization of the government into Legislative, Judiciary and Executive ... And I like the negative given to the Executive with a third of either house, though I should have liked it better had the Judiciary been associated for that purpose, or invested with a separate and similar power.

In other letters of that year Jefferson said the bill of rights was needed 'to guard liberty against the legislative as well as the executive branches' and was to be favored because of 'the legal check which it puts into the hands of the judiciary'.

That his later quarrel with the Federalist-controlled Supreme Court was not as the champion of democracy, but as the reactionary defendant of states rights, is seen from a letter of 1798 in which Jefferson, speaking of his own state of Virginia, writes that 'the laws of the land, administered by upright judges, would protect you from any exercise of power unauthorized by the Constitution of the United States' (*Writings*, Vol. IV, p. 475; Vol. V, p. 76; Vol. VII, p. 281).

Patrick Henry, though he was not at the Constitutional Convention, declared that it was 'the highest encomium of this country, that the acts of the legislature, if unconstitutional, are liable to be opposed by the judiciary'.

The position of the planter ideologists is here emphasized because their later struggle with the Federalists has tended to obscure their essential agreement with the Federalists on the drafting of an anti-democratic Constitution.

How thoroughly did the Convention extirpate the democratic conquests won by the masses in the Revolution! So long as the Constitution endured, there would never again be a 'debtor majority' that could legally have its way. The so-called division of powers, of checks and balances, had no other function except to prevent such a majority. No matter how far the suffrage would be extended, the majority would never rule. 'Who would have thought, ten years ago, that the very men who risked their lives and fortunes in support of republican principles would now treat them as the fictions of fancy?' declared an agrarian at the New York ratifying convention. The Constitutional Convention combined its anti-democratic aims with political astuteness, however; democratic ideas had made sufficient progress among the masses to put an insurmountable obstacle in the way of any plan of government which did not pretend to confer the form of political power upon the people; this form was provided in the House of Representatives, for as Elbridge Gerry nicely put it, 'the people should appoint one branch of the government in order to inspire them with the necessary confidence'. It was a wise move and has served to obscure the essentially undemocratic character of the Constitution ever since.

Having given the people the semblance of power, the representatives of property reserved for themselves the reality: A small Senate. Executive control over the Congress. Judicial supremacy over the Congress.[5] Presidential power

5 The numerous ignorant and mendacious statements on this question recently made by the Stalinists would require too much space to correct. But one must expose their fantastic assertion that the Constitutional Convention three times voted down proposals to delegate to the Supreme Court the power of judicial review (*Sunday Worker*, Jan. 19). What the Convention thrice voted down was a proposal that the judges be associated with the President in the exercise of the *veto power*. Madison, who supported the proposal, as 'an additional opportunity [for the court] of defending itself against legislative encroachments', neverthe-

to send troops into states to suppress domestic insurrection. Overwhelming obstacles to amendment of the Constitution. Various limitations on the power of the states, especially a prohibition against emission of paper currency. In masterly fashion and with eyes ever on their objective of safeguarding property rights and forever preventing majority rule, merchant and planter ideologists wrote a document which has effectively served their descendants for a hundred and fifty years.

To a Marxist, it is obvious that the relationship of forces made inevitable the forcing through of the planter-merchant plan of government. With an extraordinary cadre of leadership, easily the equal of that available in any bourgeois revolution; with the two different sections of the ruling class united harmoniously for the struggle to establish the Constitution; with the working class, the only possible class which could oppose the anti-democratic program and yet propose a program of national centralization, as yet present only, one might say, in the interstices of commercial capitalism; with the vast majority, the agrarian masses, dispersed over a large territory with no facilities for common action and with no understanding of the national tasks – it was a foregone conclusion that the Constitution would be imposed.

Nevertheless, it is interesting to note with what intelligent strategy the conservatives moved. The Constitutional Convention itself was called ostensibly to suggest amendments to the Articles of Confederation, which would be submitted to the state legislatures, the unanimous consent of which was required under the Articles. Circumspection was necessitated by the often-voiced opposition of the agrarians to any considerable overhauling and strengthening of the Articles. By every means at their command, the merchants and planters managed to send their best minds to the Convention. When the fifty-five delegates met, they boldly put aside the Articles and prepared an entirely new document. Instead of submitting it to the Confederation and the agrarian-controlled state legislatures for further revision and perhaps total rejection, they embodied in the Constitution itself the means of its adoption, that it be

less hesitated to extend the court's jurisdiction to every and all cases under the Constitution. On the other hand, those who spoke against the proposal were among the most outspoken advocates of judicial supremacy; Elbridge Gerry, for example, in opposing it declared that the judges already had the power to pass on the constitutionality of all legislation. The debate on the veto power proposal is significant, in actuality, as proof of the opposite of the Stalinist claim; for in the debate was clearly enunciated the principle of judicial supremacy. The interested reader should consult Charles A. Beard, *The Supreme Court and the Constitution* (1912), which, to any serious student, conclusively proves that the framers of the Constitution intended to give such powers to the Supreme Court, and that this was generally understood.

submitted to special state conventions and go into force as soon as nine conventions approved it. The lack of legal continuity between the Confederation and the Constitution has been a source of embarrassment to constitutional commentators; Professor Burgess, more forthright than the rest, terms it a *coup d'état.*

The ablest pens in America deluged a literate population with dire threats of total chaos if the Constitution were not adopted. The agrarians complained truly enough that if they only had equally talented spokesmen they might have a fairer chance of victory. The opposition, in fact, was left largely in the dark. The Constitutional Convention had not only carried on its deliberations behind doors closed to the public, but had kept no official minutes of the proceedings and debates. It was not until fifty years later, after Madison's death and the publication of his journals, that any real insight into the deliberations became public property.

Without leadership and without an alternative program, the agrarians fought desperately but hopelessly. They had short-sightedly failed to abolish property qualifications for suffrage; they paid for it now by losing the possible votes of the lower classes in the towns. The conservatives put forward their ablest men for the special conventions, including the honored names of the Revolution; poured enormous funds into the election; flooded the country with literature and newspapers and talked the agrarian delegates to exhaustion in the conventions. With a clear vision of their objectives, they made a single mighty effort; after Shays' Rebellion many of them had declared themselves ready to use military force and we may be sure they would have had they failed to carry the Constitution; but, though by a narrow-enough margin, they carried it and thereby riveted its principles on the American masses for as long as the masses continue to play within the rules laid down for them by their masters.

The Founding Fathers were more terrified of majorities than they need have been. 'The press is indeed a great means of diminishing the evil; yet it is found to be unable to prevent it altogether', said Gouverneur Morris, who naturally could not foresee the infinitely greater scope of modern methods of indoctrination – movie, radio, tabloid, public school, etc. – and the power of modern political machines with their armies of precinct captains, ward-heelers and thugs. Any serious struggle of the masses can find at best only an extremely imperfect reflection in the parliamentary arena. Witness the fact that no workers' representative of any variety sits today in Congress.

The arena of constitutional government is, in fact, an arena in which only those whose differences are subordinate to their fundamentally common interests, can settle their differences with each other. Any serious outbreak of the class struggle will find the Constitution scrapped by both sides.

But even the sections of the bourgeoisie, in their struggle with each other, win advantages or lose them not in the realm of government but in the more important realm of production. The slaveholders controlled the national government, lock, stock and barrel, front 1848 to 1860, yet it was precisely in those years that industrial capitalism finally outstripped the South. Teddy Roosevelt 'busted' the trusts, Wilson brought the 'New Democracy' to Washington – to the end that it had finally to be admitted that trustification was here to stay. How much more true, therefore, must it be that the working class will win its battles outside the parliamentary arena!

This was once a commonplace of the Left-wing labor movement; only the degeneration of the Comintern makes it necessary to stress such an elementary fact. In every capitalist country, including America, the strike weapon was illegal until long after the workers, by struggle in the industrial arena, had actually won the right to strike by the simple method of persisting in its use. Only after this became an accomplished fact were the laws revised. To strike is now a right under bourgeois democracy: yet the specific content of the right varies from state to state and from year to year; for its actual content is based, not on the given law, but on the real relation of class forces in the given situation.

The electoral struggle has its functions in a well-rounded revolutionary movement; Liebknecht, Lenin and Trotsky have shown us how a tribune ascending the rostrum can call the masses to struggle. But the object of struggle will be secured, not in the parliamentary arena, but in the field and factory and street. Only that power welded by hands joined in field and factory and street can be relied on by the proletariat today.

Let the liberals and the Stalinists build their reformist edifices; they will crumble at the first blow. We, however, still stand with Marx in his answer to the reformists of his day: 'It is only in an order of things in which there will be no longer classes or class antagonism that *social evolutions* will cease to be *political revolutions*. Until then, on the eve of each general reconstruction of society, the last word of social science will ever be:

> "Combat or death: bloody struggle or extinction,
> It is thus that the question is irresistibly put"'.

2 Marx and Engels on the Civil War[6]
(*1938*)

George Novack

The Civil War in the United States, by Karl Marx and Frederick Engels. Edited with an introduction by Richard Enmale (New York: International Publishers, 1938).

Engels called the American Civil War 'the first grand war of contemporaneous history'. Marx later hailed it as 'the greatest event of the age'. Today when the nineteenth century has receded into the distance and the bourgeois power that issued out of the Civil War bestrides the world, we can realize the colossal magnitude of the conflict far better than they. The Second American Revolution stands out as the decisive turning point of Nineteenth century history.

All the more valuable therefore are the views of these two great working class leaders on the Civil War in the United States while it was still in progress, now made available as a whole for the first time in English. These writings consist of seven articles contributed to the *New York Tribune* and thirty-five to the *Vienna Presse* in 1861–1862 together with sixty-one excerpts from the correspondence between Marx and Engels during 1861–1866. The editor has also appended two addresses written by Marx for the First International, one to President Lincoln and the other to President Johnson.

In turning to these writings for the first time this reader received three immediate impressions. First, the evergreen quality of these articles written so many years ago. How little faded they are by the passage of time! Then the astonishingly intimate knowledge of American history possessed by Marx and Engels, which would go far to dispel the ignorant prejudice that these Europeans were unfamiliar with the peculiar conditions of the United States. Finally, the incisiveness of their most casual comments on personalities and events coupled with the remarkable insight of their observations. Again we see what inexhaustible vitality and prophetic power is lodged in the materialist interpretation of history discovered by these master minds, which enabled

6 Novack 1938.

them to plumb deep below the billowing surface of events and fathom the underlying formations and motive forces of history in the making.

These genial powers shine forth in the following quotation from the first article, which summarizes the sixty years of American politics before the Civil War in five succinct sentences.

The progressive abuse of the Union by the slave power, working through its alliance with the Northern Democratic Party, is, so to say, the general formula of United States history since the beginning of this century. The successive compromise measures mark the successive degrees of the encroachment by which the Union became more and more transformed into the slave of the slave-owner. Each of these compromises denotes a new encroachment of the South, a new concession of the North. At the same time none of the successive victories of the South was carried but after a hot contest with an antagonistic force in the North, appearing under different party names with different watchwords and under different colors. *If the positive and final result of each single contest told in favor of the South, the attentive observer of history could not but see that every new advance of the slave power was a step forward to its ultimate defeat.* (Marx, 'The American Question in England', *New York Daily Tribune*, October 11, 1861).

The rise and fall of the slave power is the grandest example of the dialectic in American history. The slaveholders had to be lifted to the heights before they were dashed to the ground and annihilated forever in the Civil War, an historical precedent it is good to keep in mind when the advancing world reaction seems to be carrying everything before it.

The first two articles of the series contributed to the *Vienna Presse* written in refutation of the arguments disseminated by the Southern sympathizers in England, are the meatiest portions of this collection. The pro-slavery advocates contended, first that the war between the North and South was nothing but a tariff war; second, that it was waged by the North against the South to maintain the Union by force; and, third, that the slave question had nothing to do with it.

Marx easily explodes the first argument with five well-placed facts to the contrary. In answer to the second, he points out that the war emanated, not from the North, but from the South. The Civil War originated as a rebellion of the slaveholding oligarchy against the Republican government. Just as the bombardment of Fort Sumter started the war, so Lincoln's election, gave the signal for secession. Lincoln's victory was made possible by the breach between the Northern and Southern wings of the Democratic Party, and the rise of the Republican Party in the new Northwest. The key to secession was therefore to be found in the upsurge of the Northwest. By splitting the Democratic ranks and supporting the Republican candidate, the Northwestern states upset the balance of power which had enabled the slave power to rule the Republic for six decades and thereby made secession necessary and inevitable.

With the principle that any further extension of slave territory was to be prohibited by law, the Republicans attacked the rule of the slaveholders at its root. A strict confinement of slavery within its old terrain was bound according to economic law to lead to its gradual effacement, in the political sphere to annihilate the hegemony that the slave states exercised through the Senate, and finally to expose the slaveholding oligarchy within its own states to threatening perils from the side of the 'poor whites'. The Republican election victory was accordingly bound to lead to the open struggle between North and South.

The assumption of state power placed a noose in the hands of the Republican bourgeoisie which they could draw as tight as they pleased around the neck of the slave power until they had succeeding in strangling it. Having lost control of the government to their adversary and faced with the prospect of slow death, the slaveholders determined to fight for their freedom – to enslave others!

The political contest which resulted in civil war was but the expression of profound economic antagonisms between the slave and free states. According to Marx, the most important of these was the struggle over the possession of the territories necessary for the expansion of their respective systems of production. In a striking phrase Marx states that 'the territorial contest which opened this dire epopee was to decide whether the virgin soil of immense tracts should be wedded to the labor of the immigrant or prostituted to the tramp of the slave-driver'. The Western lands were the rock on which the Union was shipwrecked.

To those who represent the slaveholder's rebellion as a defensive, and, therefore, a just war, Marx replied that it was the precise opposite. The dissolution of the Union and the formation of the Confederacy were only the first steps in the slaveholders' program. After consolidating their power, the slavocracy must inevitably strive to conquer the North and to extend its dominion over the tropics where cotton could be cultivated. 'The South was not a country ... but a battle cry'; the war of the Southern Confederacy 'a war of conquest for the extension and perpetuation of slavery'. The slave-owners aimed to reorganize the Union on the basis of slavery. This would entail the subjugation of North America, the nullification of the free institutions of the Northern states, the perpetuation of an obsolete and barbaric method of production at the expense of a higher economic order. The triumph of the backward South over the progressive North would deal an irreparable blow to human progress.

To those who argued that slavery had nothing to do with the Civil War because the Republicans feared to unfurl the banner of emancipation at the beginning of the conflict, Marx pointed out that the Confederacy itself proclaimed the foundation of a republic for the first time in modem history with slavery as its unquestionable principle. Not only the secession movement but the war itself was, in the last analysis, based upon the slave question.

Not in the sense of whether the slaves within the existing slave states would be emancipated or not (although this matter, too, must sooner or later be settled), but whether twenty million men of the North should subordinate themselves any longer to an oligarchy of three hundred thousand slaveholders; whether the vast territories of the republic should be planting-places for free states or for slavery; finally, whether the national policy of the Union should take armed propaganda of slavery in Mexico, Central and South America as its device.

Thus Marx proceeds from the political to the economic and finally to the social core of the Civil War. With surgical skill he probes deeper and deeper until he penetrates to the heart of the conflict. 'The present struggle between the North and South', he concludes, 'is nothing but a struggle between two social systems; between the system of slavery and the system of free labor. The struggle has broken out because the two systems can no longer live peacefully side by side on the North American continent. It can only be ended by the victory of one system or the other.' If this conclusion appears elementary to us today, it is only because history has absolutely confirmed it. But one has only to compare Marx's words at the opening of the Civil War with the writings of the other politicians of the period to appreciate their foresight.

In connection with this admirable account of the causes of the war, Marx underscores the crucial political, economic, and military importance of the border states. These states, which were neither slave nor free, were a thorn in the side of the South on the one hand, and the weakest part of the North on the other. The Republican government was inclined toward a weak, cowardly, and conciliatory policy of waging the war out of regard for the support of these ambiguous allies and did not throw off their constraining influence until the war was half over.

Marx and Engels followed the military aspects of the conflict with the closest attention. 'The General' in particular was absorbed by the tactics and strategy of the contending forces. He was justly impatient with the Fabian policies of McClellan and his 'anaconda plan' for surrounding, constricting, and crushing the South, advocating instead a bold and sharp stroke launched at the middle of the South. He thus anticipated in 1862 Sherman's decisive march through Georgia two years later. Exasperated by the manifold blunders and half-heartedness of the Union generals as well as the reluctance of the Republican bourgeoisie to use revolutionary methods in waging the war, he at one time despaired of a

Northern victory. But Marx, with his eye upon the immensely superior latent powers of the North and the inherent weaknesses of the South, chided him for being 'swayed a little too much by the military aspect of things'.

The majority of these articles deal with various international aspects of the Civil War, among them the diplomatic jockeying of the great European powers, so reminiscent of the present Spanish Civil War, as well as the intrigues of Napoleon the Little in the chancelleries of Europe and his adventures in Mexico. Marx and Engels were concerned with the international events as foreign correspondents, as residents of England, but above all as revolutionary proletarian internationalists. Marx kept close surveillance over the efforts to embroil England in a war against the Union and exposed the factors that kept the Palmerston government in check: the increasing dependence of England on American foodstuffs, the superior preparedness of the United States for war, the rivalry between the Whigs and Tories in the coalition cabinet and, last but not least, the fear of the people. Marx played a leading role in frustrating the plans of the war-hawks by mobilizing the English workers in huge public meetings of protest against the Southern sympathizers among the English upper crust.

These miscellaneous writings do not constitute either a comprehensive or definitive treatment of the Civil War and the revolution interlaced with it. Marx and Engels would undoubtedly have revised and elaborated not a few of the judgments they expressed at the moment in the light of subsequent developments. The last extracts from their correspondence show them in the act of changing their previous opinion of Johnson. Here are a few points that call for correction or amplification. In concentrating upon the more immediate causes of the Civil War, Marx and Engels do not delve into the general economic background of the conflict. Their survey needs to be supplemented by an account of the maturing crisis within the slave system and the impetuous rise of Northern capitalism which provided the economic premises of the Civil War.

Marx was mistaken in attributing the removal of Frémont solely to political intrigue. This Republican General was caught *in flagrante delicto*. His wife accepted expensive gifts from army contractors while the Department of the West under his command was a grafter's paradise. In one deal Frémont purchased 25,000 worthless Austrian muskets for $166,000; in another, financed by J.P. Morgan, he bought for $ 22 each condemned guns which the War Department itself had illegally sold a few months before for $ 3.50 each! And the House Committee of Investigation uncovered even worse cases of corruption. Possibly Marx became acquainted with these facts when he studied the official reports. That would account for his failure to return to the subject, as he promised.

The principal lack in these writings from our present standpoint is the absence of distinction between the separate and potentially antagonistic class forces allied on the side of the Union. In particular, insufficient stress is laid upon the special political position, program, aims, and interests of the Republican big bourgeoisie who headed the state and led the army. This was not accidental. Marx and Engels emphasized the broad outlines and major issues uppermost at the moment and more or less set to one side for future consideration the forces and problems which lurked in the background and came to the fore at a later stage of the struggle.

A few words must be said about the editor's introduction. It is liberally smeared with Stalinism. This substitute for Marxism is, like certain substitutes for mayonnaise, concocted by omitting or adulterating the principal ingredients. Mr. Enmale would have us believe that out of the Civil War a truly democratic government emerged in the United States.

'In its Civil War phase, the revolution abolished chattel slavery, and destroyed the old plantocracy', he remarks. 'At the same time it insured the continuance of democracy, freedom, and progress by putting an end to the rule of an oligarchy, by preventing further suppression of civil liberties in the interests of chattel slavery, and by paving the way for the forward movement of American labor'.

How Marx in his wrath would have hurled his Jovian thunderbolts at the head of the vulgar democrat who uttered such deceitful phrases – and in his name! The Civil War put an end to one oligarchy and marked the beginning of another, which Marx himself characterized, in a later letter to Engels, as 'the associated oligarchy of capital', which in its turn became the bulwark of reaction, suppressed civil liberties, and exerted every effort to check the advance of American labor. It is not impossible that Mr. Enmale is unacquainted with this letter, written on the occasion of the bloody suppression of the great railroad strikes of 1877 by the Federal troops, since it was omitted from the English edition of the *Correspondence* issued by the same house. But Enmale's ignorance of Marx's views does not excuse his crude falsification of American history since the Civil War. In fairness to the editor, it must be said that his notes and biographical index are accurate and very helpful.

The Civil War opened the road for the final triumph of the bourgeois-democratic revolution in the United States. During the fight to the death with the slavocracy, Marx and Engels in their capacity as revolutionary labor leaders correctly stressed the positive, democratic, progressive and revolutionary significance of the struggle waged by the bourgeois republic. They based their practical political policy on the fact that the struggle of the working class for its own emancipation would be promoted by the victory of the North and thrown back by the triumph of the Confederacy. At the same time they never proclaimed their political confidence in the Republican bourgeoisie, freely criticized their conduct of the war, and maintained their independence vis-à-vis their temporary allies.

In the years that have elapsed since its conquest of power, the capitalist regime has become the mainstay of reaction in the United States and throughout the world. While giving full credit to the achievements of the Second American Revolution, contemporary Marxists are first of all obliged to expose the negative bourgeois, reactionary sides of its character which historical development have thrust to the forefront. In this way they will remain true, not to the dead letter, but to the living spirit of Marxism embodied in these precious pages.

3 What is Socialism? (Lecture 2)[7]
(1938)

Albert Goldman

In the course of the first lecture I attempted to show that a very serious obstacle in the path of the working masses towards emancipation is the capitalist state, whether democratic or fascist. The mailed fist of the state cracks down upon the workers, even when they struggle against the bosses merely for a higher wage or better conditions. The mailed fist of the state says in effect: 'I am here to protect the property of my master. I do not care how much misery and suffering the people must undergo; capitalist property must be defended. Dare to touch that property and I will crush you'.

Deceit

If the capitalists were to depend upon force alone to guarantee their privileged position, their situation would be precarious indeed. After all they represent only a small minority of the people. In the United States there are probably no more than two to three million out of the forty-eight million gainfully occupied who could be considered as belonging to the capitalist class. As a matter of fact, the number of capitalist families in control of American industry and finance is a mere handful – sixty, according to a recent book that created so much excitement (Ferdinand Lundberg's *America's 60 Families*). The overwhelming majority of the population would benefit by a change from the present system to socialism. Against such a decisive majority the instruments of force at the disposal of the capitalist class could not prevail. If the working masses would be aroused and determined to abolish capitalism, the police and the army would be helpless, even if we assume that all of the soldiers would be loyal to the capitalist class.

What the capitalist class must depend upon, more than on force, is deceit. All the force in the world would not avail the capitalists if they could not

7 Goldman 1938.

deceive and confuse the masses. Even their police and their armies would not be reliable because the police and the army are composed of people who come from the working class and who permit themselves to be used against their class brothers simply because they do not know better. The rulers of our present social order see to it that the workers are subjected to a system of training which succeeds in making them believe that the present system is the best possible system, and that if there is anything wrong with it, it is only of a minor character and can be easily cured by changing the people who are in control of things. It is the deception of the masses, more than anything else, that assures the existence of a social order which brings so much misery and suffering to the vast majority of the people.

What institutions exist for the purpose of deceiving the masses? There are quite a few, the most important being the church, the press, the educational system and the radio. From early childhood every person is subjected to the influence of ideas which tend to make him respect authority, and to believe in things as they are. Obedience is the virtue stressed by religious teachers and by school teachers. Here and there, of course, there are teachers of more independent thought, who influence their students to question accepted doctrines and practices, but they are few and far between, and have no influence in the molding of general opinion.

Some of you may be religious and may possibly resent my statement that the church is one of the pillars of the capitalist system with its exploitation and war. I shall not deny that I am an atheist and that all advocates of revolutionary socialism look upon religion as contrary to science and reason, and as an effective method to make the masses reconciled to their fate on earth by promising them unbounded joys in heaven. I shall also not deny that some or all religious systems contain many noble teachings which are impossible of realization under the present system. One of the ten commandments, for example, imposes the duty not to kill, but look at the millions of men who are butchered in capitalist wars. There are many other precepts of a very idealistic nature which are conveniently forgotten by the churches.

If, because of your early training, you feel that religion is necessary for your peace of mind, well and good. But do not permit that to interfere with your participation in the struggle for the emancipation of the working class. At least distinguish very carefully between your religion which is a source of consolation to you and the church as an institution which functions on behalf of the ruling class. If any one doubts that the church is arrayed on the side of property, let him glance at the composition of the board of trustees of most of the churches. Almost invariably the same type of people are trustees of the churches as are directors of business corporations. Capitalists contribute heavily to the churches and they, who pay the piper, call the tune. There are, of course, exceptions to all general rules and at times one finds a minister of a church coming out in favor of the workers, but as an institution it is undeniable that the church is one of the most powerful guardians of the interests of the capitalist class.

In countries with a free and compulsory school system, the members of the ruling class depend upon the schools, more perhaps than upon the churches, to instill into the minds of the working-class youth a proper respect for all the institutions and ideas which ensure the continuance of the present system. Above all, the educational system attempts to imbue the young people with an intense patriotism. To be ready to fight and die for one's country (which, of course, means the country owned by the capitalists) is pictured as the highest of all virtues. The average boy or girl is graduated from school firmly convinced that the economic, political and social ideas and ideals that they have been taught are correct and necessary. They are prepared to fight, not in the interest of their class, but for things as they are, for the benefit of those who exploit them.

While the educational system, both religious and secular, molds the minds of the people in their earlier years, the press is the chief instrument in the work of confusing and deceiving them in later life. Day in and day out the capitalist press turns loose a veritable flood of lies and half-truths, the sum and substance of which is that capitalism is the best of all possible systems and that only people with vicious tendencies would want to change that system. And there is very little that those of us, who want to establish a new social order, can do in order to counter-act the propaganda of the capitalist press. To publish a paper or a magazine that can hope to acquire a large circulation requires tremendous capital. The large newspapers and magazines are owned by wealthy capitalists and depend for their advertisements on the big business people. They hire the best writers who are willing to sell their talents to those who can pay the highest price. On the other hand, the revolutionary press must depend upon the pennies of the comparatively few workers who have torn themselves away from the ideas supported by the ruling class. For every worker who has a chance to read a paper advocating the ideas of socialism, there are tens of thousands who read nothing except the capitalist press.

Besides the press there are the radio and the cinema subtly spreading the same poison that benumbs the thinking faculties of the workers. On all sides there stand the sentries of the rulers guarding the interests of the exploiting few. Force and deceit are the two watch dogs keeping the masses in subjection to a system which offers the vast majority of the people nothing but a low standard of living, insecurity and war.

Divisions in Ranks of Workers

Influenced by the false ideas propagated by the capitalist class, the workers not only fail to struggle against their real enemies but actually permit themselves to be arrayed against one another. They allow themselves to be divided on racial, national and religious grounds. Prejudices are fostered amongst the workers and thereby the struggle against the common enemy is weakened. The best example of a prejudice that causes untold harm to the labor movement is the prejudice of the white against the colored worker. Several centuries ago tens of thousands of Negroes were brought into this country (they were kidnapped in their native land) and sold into slavery. Through their toil the southern plantation owners grew wealthy. Because of the struggle between the northern industrialists and the southern plantation barons the Negroes were finally freed from chattel slavery only to find themselves members of the class of wage slaves. The white workers both of the South and the North were imbued with the prejudices of the ruling strata of society. Until very recently the colored workers were not permitted membership in the trade unions and even now most of the American Federation of Labor unions will not admit Negroes on the same basis as white workers.

It is essential that the white workers realize that this unreasoning prejudice against the colored workers can bring incalculable harm to the working class. There are millions of colored workers in this country, and it is inconceivable that the white workers can solve their problems without the willing and loyal co-operation of the Negro workers. The latter are the most exploited of all workers and they can be easily enlisted in the struggle against the capitalists. But the white worker must first recognize the colored worker as his equal in every respect. The white workers must fight on behalf of the social, political and economic equality of the Negro people and thus gain a mighty ally in the struggle for freedom.

In addition to the racial prejudice of the white workers against the Negroes, national prejudices exist amongst the white workers. In this country, because of the immigration of many different nationalities, we have a situation where Hungarians, Germans, Italians and workers of other nationalities toil side by side. The employers constantly try to create divisions and strife amongst the workers. False ideas of superior and inferior nations are cultivated in their minds, all for the purpose of destroying the solidarity of the working class.

Mighty forces stand in the path of the working class. The state consisting of the police, the army, the courts, the jails, the government; the institutions that exist for the purpose of subduing and deceiving the minds of the masses, such as the church, the press, the schools, etc.; the divisions in the ranks of the workers themselves, divisions that are fostered by the ruling class. Can these mighty forces ever be defeated? Will the workers ever unite and join in the struggle for true freedom and true equality? There are many who throw up their hands in despair, proclaiming the hopelessness of the struggle. Let us look into the matter a little further.

Difficulties Not Insurmountable

If we glance for a moment at history, we discover that there have been revolutions in the past and successful revolutions. Consider first, the French Revolution of 1789. Prior to that revolution France was under the domination of a class of noble landowners. They controlled the state in the same way that the capitalists control the present state; they were in charge of the church and, to a large extent, they moulded the ideas of the masses. At that time the merchants and industrialists, the predecessors of the present ruling class, were oppressed by the landowners. Industry and commerce had grown and developed but only to a limited extent because the feudal order, under which the landowners ruled, prevented their rapid evolution. The masses, consisting of the peasants in the rural areas and the artisans and workers in the cities, suffered want and privation. Revolutionists appeared on the scene demanding liberty and equality for the people, agitating for a change in the social system. Their demands were met by governmental repressions, by clubbings, jailings and shootings. But the feudal state could not solve the problems confronting the people. The productive forces, hemmed in by the feudal order, could not develop and function. The agitation continued, in spite of the repressive measures of the government. The class that took the lead in the struggle against the existing regime was the rising capitalist class; the masses, driven by suffering, followed that class, hoping that their condition would improve. Finally the Parisian workers and artisans revolted and in the course of a few years completely destroyed the feudal social system. Capitalism was victorious. The masses could go no further at that time for the reason that the ground was not yet prepared for socialism.

A social order which had at its command all the forces of the state and of the church was overturned by the masses who were kept in ignorance and subjection.

Another example of a successful revolution occurred in Russia. In 1917 the workers and peasants of that country overthrew the Tsar and eight months later they rid themselves of the capitalists and landlords and established their own government. Before the monarchy was overthrown, it appeared that the Russian people were destined to remain under the yoke of tsarism for ever and ever. The rulers had a tremendous army and a huge police force; the church kept the masses in ignorance. But misery and suffering compelled the masses to look for a way out. Neither the police nor the church nor the army could protect the monarchy. As a matter of fact, the army itself was infected with revolutionary sentiments, and the result was that the monarchy toppled over without offering any resistance. The same was true of the landlords and capitalists a short while later.

The lesson of these and other revolutions is clear. When the problems confronting a people cannot be solved by the ruling class, when the people are compelled to suffer without getting relief, when they behold an arrogant minority wallowing in luxury, indifferent to the fate of the masses, then they are in a mood to listen to those who propose a radical solution. The ideas which the ruling class pounded into the minds of the masses lose their hold and new ideas are accepted. The cover which blinded the workers is lifted from their eyes and they realize that they must take their fate into their own hands. No force on earth can stop them.

History teaches that when a system of society outlives its usefulness, when in the womb of the old society there has been prepared the possibility of a new social order, when the masses suffer needlessly, and when the ruling class is unable to solve the problems facing society – under such circumstances – the ideas representing the new social order are accepted by the masses, and instruments of force and deceit at the disposal of the ruling class are helpless to preserve the old order. A revolution occurs and a new social system comes into being.

Everything points to the fact that the capitalist system under which we live is subject to the same laws of historical development. It was born and grew to some extent under the system of feudalism. The capitalist class struggled with the feudal nobility for supremacy and, because capitalism was a social system superior to feudalism, the capitalist class was victorious. Capitalism then developed at a tremendous pace until it conquered the whole world. Although the masses did not gain the liberty and equality which they hoped for and which were promised them, the ground was prepared, through the development of the productive forces, for the establishment of socialism and the abolition of all inequalities. And now the capitalist system, after having reached the zenith of its development, is in a state of decline. In spite of the vast productive forces, the people are compelled to suffer for the need of food, clothing and shelter. Factories are idle when workers are looking for work; farmers are worried about selling their products at a time when people go hungry. The capitalist system has outlived its usefulness and must be replaced by a new system.

If it were a question solely of educating the masses through books, pamphlets and lectures, then indeed the difficulties in the way of changing the present system would be insurmountable. But the most effective teacher is life itself. The hardships which the workers are compelled to endure cause them to think and drive them to attempt some solution. They may be misled at first, by demagogues, or by the bureaucratic leaders of their own organizations, but ultimately they will see that there is no solution other than to take over the industries and operate them for the benefit of the people.

And once the wide masses rally around the ideas of socialism, nothing in the world can stop their progress. Neither the state, nor the church, nor the press, will save the present system.

Labor Must Lead in the Struggle for Socialism

Having considered the difficulties confronting those interested in changing our social order, and having shown that those difficulties are not insurmountable, it is incumbent upon us to proceed to an analysis of the general methods which, in our opinion, will succeed in bringing humanity to its ultimate goal. There are many persons who agree, or who claim to agree, with the socialist ideal but who differ amongst themselves as to the path which should be followed in achieving the goal. Are there many paths all equally good and all ultimately reaching the destination, or is there only one road with all other roads ending in a blind alley?

It is important, in the first instance, to answer the question: which group in society will be the spearhead in the struggle for a new society? From what I have said before, you can surmise that we socialists think in terms of classes. I pointed out that the capitalist class took the lead in destroying the feudal system with the masses of the people simply following the capitalist class. Of great significance is the fact that, not long after the capitalists achieved political power, they were confronted by the necessity of using that power to resist the encroachments of a new class. That new class consisted of the industrial wage workers who, even at that time, were herded together in factories and mines in fairly large numbers. Could there be anything more natural than for a large number of people working in one place to organize for the purpose of improving their conditions of labor? That is exactly what the workers did; they organized trade unions. In those early days the workers attributed their miserable plight to the machine and actually set about destroying machinery. But that period did not last long. Soon the workers realized that it was useless to fight against the machine which could be used for the benefit of labor as well as to oppress it; they saw that their struggle must be waged against the owners of the machine, the people who were reaping all the rich harvests as a result of the introduction of machinery.

In 1848 Karl Marx and Friedrich Engels published the *Communist Manifesto* and in that little book they analyzed the actual struggle that was going on in modern society, They pointed out that, just as the capitalist class struggled against the feudal landowners and finally conquered power, so now the industrial proletariat, or the wage-working class, is struggling against the capitalist class, and this struggle will go on until the working class will gain political power and reconstruct society on a socialist basis.

That the capitalist class and the industrial wage-working class are not the only classes in society is readily admitted by every socialist. All other sections of society, such as the farmers, the professionals, etc., may be grouped in the middle class. That class is an exceedingly important class, but in modern society those who control and operate the means of production play the decisive role. The capitalist class controls the means of production at present; the wage-working class is the only other class that can hope to control and operate the industries. Consequently the struggle for power is primarily a struggle between the capitalist class and the working class. The heterogeneous middle class cannot and does not play an independent role – it follows either the working class or the capitalist class.

Modern industry assembles the workers in large masses, making them susceptible to organization. Members of the middle class, especially the farmers, are scattered, and to organize them is far more difficult. Then again, and what is most important, the conditions under which the workers exist tend to make them appreciate the necessity for socialism. Within the factories, where thousands of workers are employed, there is perfect cooperation. Each worker does his own particular job and many of them working cooperatively turn out one product. A person working in a huge factory soon comes to realize that in the sphere of production, within the limits of one factory, there is socialism on a small scale. It is only outside the factory, in the sphere of distribution, that anarchy prevails. The idea of extending the order that exists within the factory to include all of economic activity seems most natural to the thinking worker.

On the other hand, members of the middle class like the farmer and the store-keeper work mainly as individuals and this tends to create an individualistic psychology in them. To the middle class, as a class, socialism appears contrary to 'natural law'. Radicalism amongst the farmers or small merchants is generally expressed in opposition to trusts and big business. The class-conscious worker has no reason to oppose big business because it is big; there is nothing to be gained and a lot to be lost by splitting up one big industry into a lot of small businesses. It is far easier to convince workers that what should be done is not to destroy the huge trusts but to take them over and operate them for the welfare of he people.

Modern industry, in addition to making the working class amenable to socialist ideas, has also placed it in a very strategic position. At any time the workers so desire, they can paralyze industry or breathe life into it, and this power enables them to control all of social life. The capitalist class controls industry at the present time because of its ownership, but it could not operate industry without the workers, while the latter have no need of the capitalists to keep the wheels of industry in motion. In an industrially developed country like the United States, the wage workers with their families constitute a majority of the population, but its actual strength is far greater than its numerical proportion. It is the only class that can challenge the right of the capitalist class to rule.

I am not suggesting that the working class should be arrayed against all other classes. While it is true that the middle class cannot see the advisability and necessity for socialism as clearly as the working class, it is also true that the middle class suffers under capitalism just as well as the working class. We revolutionary socialists are in favor of adopting policies which will gain the support of as many people as possible who are not members of the proletariat. Socialism will not only solve the problems of the workers but of all mankind. The working class at all times must attempt to show the farmers and other sections of the middle class that their welfare is bound up with the welfare of the workers. They are grievously mistaken who think that as soon as the workers gain governmental power they will immediately compel all the farmers and all the small business men to give up their farms and businesses to the government. A workers' government will show the farmers by example that they will be far better off by working together, with the latest machinery, on a cooperative farm than by tilling their own soil. Force against the farmers and other middle class elements to make them adopt socialist methods is absolutely excluded.

To gain the confidence and support of the middle class it is essential that labor should know what it wants and act decisively to get it. If it hesitates and flounders about, if it shows no ability to solve the problems that confront the middle class, then the middle class will turn to others for leadership. Fundamentally, the reason for the birth and growth of fascism is because of the failure of the working class to take over power and reconstruct society on a socialist basis. The World War of 1914–18 conclusively proved that capitalism had outlived its usefulness and had nothing more to offer mankind than self-destruction. It was the duty of the proletariat to take over social leadership and reorganize society. Its failure to do so (for reasons I shall mention later) enabled the fascists of Italy, Germany, and of other countries, to mobilize the middle class for the purposes of reaction.

History has placed upon the shoulders of the working class the task of solving humanity's problems. Failure to do so means to assure the victory of fascism the world over with the complete suppression of the workers' organizations, terrible imperialist wars, and the destruction of all civilization.

Workers Need Political Power

To achieve socialism labor must first gain political power. The capitalist class under feudalism had economic power; it required political power to consolidate and guarantee its economic power; it obtained political supremacy by a revolutionary overthrow of the feudal nobility. The workers under capitalism have no economic power (except in the sense that they can bring industry to a halt by withdrawing their labor power) and neither have they political power. Before they can take over the industries and proceed to construct a socialist society, they will have to take over the power of government.

What that means is that the workers must create their own state. Just as the feudal landowners had their state to protect their rule, and just as the capitalist class has its state to protect its dominant position, so must the workers organize their own state power for the purpose of establishing socialism. Whereas all previous forms of state served the purpose of guarding the property interests of a minority of the people against the majority, the workers' state will be the instrument of the vast majority of the population for the purpose of abolishing all forms of exploitation.

The workers' state will, in the first place, nationalize all the means of production now owned by the capitalists, and will operate them for the benefit of all the people. It will, in the second instance, guard its rule against any counter-revolutionary attempts by native or foreign capitalists. And, finally, it will proceed to organize production and to educate the people, so that socialism can actually function.

This is what is meant by the statement that the struggle of the working class is political in character. It is a struggle to wrest the political power away from the capitalists, and to establish the political power of the workers, a power which will build socialism.

What will be the form of the workers' state? At present there is the capitalist state with its police force and army completely separated from the people, with a bureaucracy, the top layer of which, is intimately connected with the big capitalists. The people are not permitted to bear arms except when they are drafted for war purposes. In democratic capitalist countries like ours the workers are allowed to vote for representatives in Congress and the voting takes place by geographical districts. The representatives are elected for a definite term and before there is another election that term must expire. In a workers' state the government will consist of a council or house of delegates composed of representatives elected by the workers at the place of their labor. These representatives will always be subject to recall and will receive no more than the average wage of any worker. With the exception of enemies of the working class, the whole population will be armed.

At present, in the countries where capitalist democracy prevails, there are provisions in the constitutions, or on the statute books, granting everyone the right of free press, free speech and free assembly. Leaving out of consideration the fact that the ruling class in actual practice limits those rights, and in critical moments abolishes them altogether, it is essential to understand that the poverty of the workers makes it exceedingly difficult for them to exercise those rights. Without the money to purchase printing presses, or rent assembly halls, the rights of free speech and free press are nothing but rights on paper. With the abolition of capitalism, the right of individual capitalists to own huge printing plants will be abolished, and the workers will then be in a position to take advantage of their privileges.

There will naturally be differences of opinion amongst the people as to policies to be pursued after the workers take over political power. Those differences will have to be decided in a democratic manner, just as at present in a democratic labor union differences of views exist and the majority prevails after discussion and voting, Any minority group will be furnished with the means, proportionate to its number, to enable it to present its viewpoint before the people.

Because there will be no small minority of capitalists monopolizing all the wealth, democracy in a workers' state will have real meaning. It will be limited only in the sense that no one person will be permitted to exploit any other person, I know that some of you are mentally comparing the picture I have painted of democracy in a workers' state with the terrible reality that exists now in the Soviet Union. I shall discuss the question of the Soviet Union before I am through. Here I want to point out that our program calls for just what I have indicated, and with the active participation of the workers that program can be realized.

Socialists, however, contend that the workers' state will not last for many generations. The necessity for any state exists only because there are classes in society, and one class requires the instrument of the state to rule over the other classes. Do away with classes and you do away with the necessity of any state. As soon as the workers in the most important capitalist countries take over political power and nationalize all of the industries; as soon as the industries are developed to a point where all the needs of the people will be satisfied; as soon as classes will disappear, and all of the people will be educated in the ideas of a new social order, then the state will lose its function and the various instruments of force will gradually disappear.

4 Lenin and Luxemburg[8]

(1938)

Max Shachtman

Two Legends have been created about the relationship between the views of Lenin and Rosa Luxemburg. Despite their antagonistic origins and aims, they supplement each other in effect. Neither one of the myth-makers approaches the extremely interesting and instructive subject from an objective historical standpoint. Consequently, the analysis made by each of them reduces itself to an instrument of factional politics which is, in both cases, the politics of reaction.

One school of thought, if such a term is permissible here, is headed by the faculty of Stalinist falsification. It covers up its reactionary objectives by posing as critics of Luxemburg and proponents of Lenin. A discussion of its arguments is rendered impossible by the very nature of its position, which formally prohibits both argument and discussion. Its scientific value is summarized in a few sentences from the papal bull issued by Stalin in 1932 in connection with the luckless Slutsky's study on Lenin's incorrect appraisal of Kautsky and Luxemburg: 'You wish to enter into discussion against this Trotskyist thesis of Slutsky's? But what is there to discuss in this? Is it not plain that Slutsky is simply slandering Lenin, slandering the Bolsheviks? Slander must be branded, not transformed into a subject for discussion'. The Stalinists have the Catholics' attitude toward their dogmas: they assume what is to be proved; their arbitrary conclusions are presented as their premises; their statement of the problem is at the same time their answer – and it brooks no discussion. *'Bolshevism' is absolutely and at all points and stages irreconcilable with 'Luxemburg-ism' because of the original sin of the latter in disputing the 'organizational principles' of the former.*

The other school of thought is less authoritarian in tone and form, but just as rigid in unhistorical dogma; and if, unlike the Stalinists, it is not wholly composed of turncoats from revolutionary Marxism, it has a substantial sprinkling of them. Their objectives are covered up by posing as critics of Lenin and

8 Shachtman 1938b.

defenders of Luxemburg. They include anachronistic philosophers of ultra-leftism and express-train travelers fleeing from the pestilence of Stalinism to the plague of social-democracy. Bolshevism, they argue, is definitely bankrupt. The horrors of Stalinism are the logical and inevitable outcome of Lenin's 'supercentralism', or – as it is put by a recent critic, Listen Oak, who seeks the 'inner flaws of Bolshevism' – of Lenin's 'totalitarianism'. Luxemburg, on the other hand, stressed the democratic side of the movement, the struggle, the goal. *Hence, 'Luxemburgism' is absolutely irreconcilable with 'Bolshevism' because of the original sin, of the former in imposing its Jacobin, or bourgeois, or super-centralist, or totalitarian 'organizational principles'.*

The use of quotation marks around the terms employed is justified and necessary, for at least in nine cases out of ten the airy analysts have only the vaguest and most twisted idea of what the disputes between Luxemburg and Lenin really were. In just as many cases they have revealed a cavalier indisposition to acquaint themselves with the historical documents and the actual writings of the two great thinkers.[9] A brief survey will disclose, I believe, the superficiality of the arguments which, especially since the obvious putrescence of Stalinism, have gained a certain currency in the radical movement.

Nothing but misunderstanding can result from a failure to bear in mind the fact that Lenin and Luxemburg worked, fought and developed their ideas in two distinctly different movements, operating within no less different countries, at radically different stages of development; consequently, in countries and movements where the problems of the working class were posed in quite different forms. It is the absence of this concrete and historical approach to the disputes between Lenin, of the Social-Democratic Labor Party of Russia, and Luxemburg, of the Social-Democratic Party of Germany, that so surely brings most critics to grief.

The 'organizational dispute' between Lenin and Luxemburg did not originate in the former's insistence on a break with Kautsky and the centrists before the war. When Stalin thunders against anyone 'who call doubt' that the Bolsheviks brought about 'a split with their own opportunists and centrist-conciliators long before the imperialist war (1904–1912) without at the same time pursuing

---

9 [Footnote by Shachtman]: So as not the clutter up the text with references, I am including all the works from which I quote in this article in a single footnote. They are: Lenin, *Collected Works* [in German]. Vols. IV, VI, VIII, X, XII. – Luxemburg, *Collected Works* [in German], Vols. III, IV. – Radek, *Rosa Luxemburg, Karl Liebknecht, Leo Jogiches*. – Martov and Dan, *Die Geschicte der russischen Sozialdemocratie*. – *Die Neue Zeit*, 1904, 1910. – *Lenin Anthology* [in Russian], Vol. II – Henriette Roland-Holst, Rosa Luxemburg: *Harr Leven en werken*. – Stalin, Kaganovich, Postyshev: *Questions Concerning the History of Bolshevism*.

a policy of rupture, a policy of split with the opportunists and centrists of the Second International' – he is simply substituting ukase for historical fact.

The truth is that Rosa Luxemburg reached a clear estimate of Kautsky and broke with his self-styled 'Marxian center', long before Lenin did. For many years after the turn of the century, Kautsky's prestige among all the factions of the Russian movement was unparalleled. The Menshevik Abramovich does not exaggerate when he writes that:

> A West-European can hardly imagine the enormous authority which the leaders of the German social-democracy, the Liebknechts, the Bebels, the Singers, enjoyed in Russia. Among these leaders, Karl Kautsky occupied quite a special place ... serving for all the Russian Marxists and social-democrats as the highest authority in all the theoretical and tactical questions of scientific socialism and the labor movement. In every disputed question, in every newly-arisen problem, the first thought always was: What would Kautsky say about this? How would Kautsky have decided this question?

Lenin's much-disputed *What to Do?* held up, as is known, the German social-democracy and its leader, Bebel, as models for the Russian movement. When Kautsky wrote his famous article, after the 1905 revolution in Russia, on the Slavs and the world revolution, in which, Zinoviev writes, under Luxemburg's influence, he advanced substantially the Bolshevik conception, Lenin was highly elated. 'Where and when', he wrote in July 1905, in a polemic against Parvus, 'have I characterized the revolutionism of Bebel and Kautsky as "opportunism"? Where and when have I presumed to call into existence in the international social-democracy a special tendency which was *not identical* with the tendency of Bebel and Kautsky?' A year and a half later, Lenin wrote that 'the vanguard of the Russian working class knows Karl Kautsky for some time now as *its* writer', and a month later, in January 1907, he described Kautsky as 'the leader of the German revolutionary social-democrats'. In August 1908, Lenin cited Kautsky as his authority on the question of war and militarism as against Gustave Hervé, and as late as February 1914, he invoked him again as a Marxian authority in his dispute with Rosa Luxemburg on the national question. Finally, in one of his last pre-war articles, in April 1914, *Wherein the German Labor Movement Should Not Be Imitated*, speaking of the 'undoubted sickness' of the German social-democracy, he referred exclusively to the trade union leaders (specifically to Karl Legien) and the parliamentary spokesmen, but did not even mention Kautsky and the centrists, much less raise the question of the left wing (also unmentioned) splitting with them.

It is this pre-war attitude of Lenin towards the German center – against which Luxemburg had been conducting a sharp frontal attack as early as 1910 – that explains the vehemence and the significant terminology of Lenin's strictures against Kautsky immediately after the war broke out, for example, his letter to Shliapnikov on October 27, 1914, in which he says: 'I now despise and hate Kautsky more than all the rest ... R. Luxemburg was right, she long ago understood that Kautsky had the highly-developed "servility of a theoretician" ...'.

In sum, the fact is that by the very nature of her milieu and her work before the war, Rosa Luxemburg had arrived at a clearer and more correct appreciation of the German social-democracy and the various currents within it than had Lenin. To a great extent, this determined and explained her polemic against Lenin on what appeared to be the 'organizational questions' of the Russian movement.

The beginning of the century marked the publication of two of Lenin's most audacious and stirring works, *One Step Forward, Two Steps Backward*, and its forerunner, *What to Do?*. The Russian movement was then in no way comparable to the West-European, especially the German. It was composed of isolated groups and sections in Russia, more or less autonomous, pursuing policies at odds with each other and only remotely influenced by its great revolutionary Marxists abroad – Plekhanov, Lenin, Martov, Potressov, Trotsky and others. Moreover, the so-called 'Economist' tendency was predominant; it laid the greatest stress on the element of spontaneity in the labor struggle and under-rated the element of conscious leadership.

Lenin's *What to Do?*[10] a merciless criticism of 'Economism', which he identified with 'pure-and-simple trade unionism', with *khovstism* (i.e. the policy of dragging at the tail of events, or of the masses), with opportunism. Social-democracy, he argued, is not a mere outgrowth of the spontaneous economic struggles of the proletariat, nor is it the passive servant of the workers; it is the union of the labor movement with revolutionary socialist theory which must be *brought into* the working class by the party, for the proletariat, by itself, can only attain a trade-union and not a socialist consciousness. In view of the dispersion of the movement in Russia, its primitive and localistic complexion, an all-Russian national party and newspaper had to be created immediately to infuse the labor movement with a socialist, political consciousness and unite it in a revolutionary struggle against Czarism. The artificers of the party, in

10 [This work by Lenin is most commonly translated into English as *What Is To Be Done?* – Eds.].

contrast with the desultory agitators of the time, would be the professional revolutionists, intellectuals and educated workers devoting all their time and energy to revolutionary activity and functioning within an extremely centralized party organization. The effective political leadership was to be the editorial board of the central organ, edited by the exiles abroad, and it would have the power to organize or reorganize party branches inside Russia, admit or reject members, and even appoint their local committees and other directing organs. I differ with the Mensheviks in this respect, wrote Lenin in 1904:

> The basic idea of comrade Martov … is precisely a false 'democratism', the idea of the construction of the party from the bottom to the top. My idea, on the contrary, is 'bureaucratic' in the sense that the party should be constructed from above down to the bottom, from the congress to the individual party organizations.

It should be borne in mind that, despite subsequent reconsideration, all the leaders of the *Iskra* tendency in the Russian movement warmly supported Lenin against the Economists. 'Twice in succession', wrote A.N. Potressov, later Lenin's furious enemy, 'have I read through the booklet from beginning to end and can only congratulate its author. The general impression is an excellent one – in spite of the obvious haste, noted by the author himself, in which the work was written'. At the famous London Congress in 1903, Plekhanov spoke up in Lenin's defense: 'Lenin did not write a treatise on the philosophy of history, but a polemical article against the economists, who said: We must wait until we see where the working class itself will come, without the help of the revolutionary bacillus'. And again: 'If you eliminate the bacillus, then there remains only an unconscious mass, into which consciousness must he brought from without. If you had wanted to be right against Lenin and if you had read through his whole book attentively, then you would have seen that this is just what he said'.

It was only after the deepening of the split between the Bolsheviks and the Mensheviks (Plekhanov included) that the latter launched their sharp attacks on Lenin's polemical exaggeration – that is what it was – of the dominant role of the intellectuals as professional revolutionists, organizers and leaders of the party, and of the relationship between spontaneity and the element of socialist consciousness which can only be introduced into the labor movement from without. Lenin's defense of the ideas he expressed in 1902 and 1904 on these questions and on centralism is highly significant for an understanding of the concrete conditions under which they were advanced and the concrete aims they pursued.

In 'The Fruits of Demagogy', an article written in March 1905 by the Bolshevik V. Vorovsky (read and praised by Lenin), the author quotes Plekhanov's above-cited praise of Lenin's *What to Do?* and adds:

> These words define perfectly correctly the sense and significance of the Lenin brochure and if Plekhanov now says that he was not in agreement, from the very beginning, with its theoretical principles, it only proves how correctly he was able to judge the real significance of the brochure at a time when there was no necessity of inventing 'differences of opinion in principle' with Lenin. In actuality, *What to Do?* was a polemical brochure (which was entirely dedicated to the criticism of the *khvostist* wing in the then social-democracy, to a characterization and a refutation of the specific errors of this wing). It would be ridiculous if Lenin, in a brochure which dealt with the 'burning questions of our movement', were to demonstrate that the evolution of ideas, especially of scientific socialism, has proceeded and proceeds in close historical connection with the evolution of the productive forces (in close connection with the growth of the labor movement in general). For him it was important to establish the fact that nowhere has the working class yet worked itself up independently to a socialist ideology, that this ideology (the doctrine of scientific socialism) was always brought in by the social-democracy …

In 1903, at the Second Congress itself, Lenin had pointed out that 'the Economists bent the staff towards the one side. In order to straighten it out again, it had to be bent towards the other side and that is what I did', and almost two years later, in the draft of a resolution written for the Third Congress, he emphasized the non-universality of his organizational views by writing that 'under free political conditions our party can and will be built up entirely upon the principle of electability. Under absolutism, this is unrealizable for all the thousands of workers who belong to the party'. Again, in the period of the 1905 revolution, he showed how changes in conditions determined a change in his views:

> At the Third Congress I expressed the wish that in the party committees there should be two intellectuals for every eight workers. How obsolete is this wish! Now it would be desirable that in the new party organizations, for every intellectual belonging to the social-democracy there should be a few hundred social-democratic workers.

Perhaps the best summary of the significance of the views he set forth at the beginning of the century is given by Lenin himself in the foreword to the collection, *Twelve Years*, which he wrote in September 1907:

> The basic mistake of those who polemize against *What to Do?* today, is that they tear this work completely out of the context of a definite historical milieu, a definite, now already long past period of development of our party … To speak at present about the fact that *Iskra* (in the years 1901 and 1902!) exaggerated the idea of the organization of professional revolutionists, is the same as if somebody had reproached the Japanese, after the Russo-Japanese war, for exaggerating the Russian military power before the war, for exaggerated concern over the struggle against this power. The Japanese had to exert all forces against a possible maximum of Russian forces in order to attain the victory. Unfortunately, many judge from the outside, without seeing that today the idea of the organization of professional revolutionists has already attained a complete victory. This victory, however, would have been impossible if, in its time, this idea had not been pushed into the foreground, if it hall not been preached in an 'exaggerated' manner to people who stood like obstacles in the way of its realization … *What to Do?* polemically corrected Economism, and it is false to consider the contents of the brochure outside of its connection with this task.

The ideas contained in *What to Do?*, which should still be read by revolutionists everywhere – and it can be read with the greatest profit – cannot, therefore, be understood without bearing in mind the specific conditions and problems of the Russian movement of the time. That is why Lenin, in answer to a proposal to translate his brochure for the non-Russian parties, told Max Levien in 1921: 'That is not desirable; the translation must at least be issued with good commentaries, which would have to be written by a Russian comrade very well acquainted with the history of the Communist Party of Russia, in order to avoid false application'.

Just as Lenin's views must be considered against the background of the situation in Russia, so must Luxemburg's polemic against them be viewed against the background of the situation in Germany. In her famous review in 1904 of Lenin's *One Step Forward, Two Steps Backward* (an extension of the views of *What to Do?*), Luxemburg's position was decisively colored by the realities of the German movement. Where Lenin stressed ultra-centralism, Luxemburg stressed democracy and organizational flexibility. Where Lenin emphasized the dominant role of the professional revolutionist, Luxemburg countered with emphasis on the mass movement and its elemental upsurge.

Why? Because these various forces played clearly different roles in Russia and in Germany. The 'professional revolutionists' whom Luxemburg encountered in Germany were not, as in Russia, the radical instruments for gathering together loose and scattered local organizations, uniting them into one national party imbued with a firm Marxian ideology and freed from the opportunistic conceptions of pure-and-simple trade unionism. Quite the contrary. In Germany, the 'professionals' were the careerists, the conservative trade union bureaucrats, the lords of the ossifying party machine, the reformist parliamentarians, the whole crew who finally succeeded in disemboweling the movement. An enormous conservative power, they weighed down like a mountain upon the militant-minded rank and file. They were the canal through which the poison of reformism seeped into the masses. They acted as a brake upon the class actions of the workers and not as a spur. In Russia the movement was loose and ineffectual, based on circles, as Lenin said, 'almost always resting upon the personal friendship of a small number of persons'. In Germany, the movement was tightly organized, conservatively disciplined, routinized, and dominated by a semi-reformist, centralist leadership. These concrete circumstances led Luxemburg to the view that only an appeal to the masses, only their elemental militant movement could break through the conservative wall of the party and trade union apparatus. The 'centralism' of Lenin forged a party that proved able to lead the Russian masses to a victorious revolution; the 'centralism' that Luxemburg saw growing in the German social-democracy became a conservative force and ended in a series of catastrophes for the proletariat. This is what she feared when she wrote against Lenin in 1904:

> … the role of the social-democratic leadership becomes one of an essentially conservative character, in that it leads to working out empirically to its ultimate conclusions the new experience acquired in the struggle and soon to converting it into a bulwark against a further innovation in the grand style. The present tactic of the German social-democracy, for example, is generally admired for its remarkable manifoldness, flexibility and at the same time certainty. Such qualities simply mean, however, that our party has adapted itself wonderfully in its daily struggle to the present parliamentary basis, down to the smallest detail, that it knows how to exploit the whole field of battle offered by parliamentarism and to master it in accordance with given principles. At the same time, this specific formulation of tactics already serves so much to conceal the further horizon that one notes a strong inclination to perpetuate that tactic and to regard the parliamentary tactic as the social-democratic tactic for all time.

But it is a far cry from the wisdom of these words, uttered in the specific conditions of Luxemburg's struggle in Germany, to the attempts made by syndicalists and ultra-leftists of all kinds to read into her views a universal formula of rejection of the idea of leadership and centralization. The fact of the matter is that the opportunistic enemies of Luxemburg, and her closest collaborator, Leo Jogisches (Tyzsko), especially in the Polish movement in which she actively participated, made virtually the same attacks upon her 'organizational principles' and 'regime of leadership' as were leveled against Lenin. During the war, for example, the Spartakusbund was highly centralized and held tightly in the hands of that peerless organizer, Jogisches. The Social-Democracy of Poland and Lithuania, which she led, was, if anything, far more highly centralized and far more merciless towards those in its ranks who deviated from the party's line, than was the Bolshevik party under Lenin. In his history of the Russian movement, the Menshevik Theodore Dan, who did not spare Lenin for his 'organizational regime', and sought to exploit Luxemburg's criticism of Lenin for his own ends, nevertheless wrote that the Polish social-democracy of the time shared in its essentials the organizational principles of Lenin, against which Rosa Luxemburg had polemicized at the birth of Bolshevism; it also applied these principles in the practice of its own party, in which a rigid, bureaucratic centralism prevailed and people like Radek, Zalevsky, Unschlicht and others, who later played a leading role in the Communist party, were expelled from the party because of their oppositional stand against the party executive.

'Bureaucratic centralism' was (and is) the term generally applied by Dan and Mensheviks of all stripes to Lenin and Luxemburg and all others who seriously sought to build up a purposeful party of Proletarian revolution, in contrast to that 'democratic' looseness prevalent in the Second International which only served as a cover behind which elements alien to the revolution could make their way to the leadership of the party and, at crucial moments, betray it to the class enemy. The irreconcilable antagonism which the reformists felt towards Lenin and Luxemburg is in sharp and significant contrast to the affinity they now feel towards the Stalinist International, in which full-blooded and genuine bureaucratic centralism has attained its most evil form. It is not difficult to imagine what Rosa Luxemburg would have written about the Stalin regime had she lived in our time; and by the same token it is not difficult to understand the poisonous campaign that the Stalinists have conducted against her for years.

The years of struggle that elapsed since the early polemics in the Russian movement, the experiences that enriched the arsenal of the great revolutionists of the time, and above all the Russian Revolution itself, undoubtedly served to draw the political tendency of Rosa Luxemburg closer to that represented with such genius by Lenin. Had she not been cut down so cruelly in the prime of her intellectual power, there is little doubt in my mind that she would have become one of the greatest figures and champions of the Communist International – not of the horribly twisted caricature that it is today, but as it was in the early years, It does not even occur to me, wrote Karl Kautsky, her bitter foe, in 1921, 'to deny that in the course of the war Rosa drew steadily closer to the communist world of thought, so that it is quite correct when Radek says that "with Rosa Luxemburg there died the greatest and most profound theoretical head of communism"'.

The judgment is a correct one and doubly valid because it comes from a political opponent who knew her views so well. It is worth a thousand times more than all the superficial harpings on the theme of the irreconcilability of Marxism's greatest teachers in our time.

5 Revolution and the Negro[11]
(*1939*)

J.R. Johnson (C.L.R. James)

The Negro's revolutionary history is rich, inspiring, and unknown. Negroes revolted against the slave raiders in Africa; they revolted against the slave traders on the Atlantic passage. They revolted on the plantations.

The docile Negro is a myth. Slaves on slave ships jumped overboard, went on vast hunger strikes, attacked the crews. There are records of slaves overcoming the crew and taking the ship into harbor, a feat of tremendous revolutionary daring. In British Guiana during the eighteenth century the Negro slaves revolted, seized the Dutch colony, and held it for years. They withdrew to the interior, forced the whites to sign a treaty of peace, and have remained free to this day. Every West Indian colony, particularly Jamaica and San Domingo and Cuba, the largest islands, had its settlements of maroons, bold Negroes who had fled into the wilds and organized themselves to defend their freedom. In Jamaica the British government, after vainly trying to suppress them, accepted their existence by treaties of peace, scrupulously observed by both sides over many years, and then broken by British treachery. In America the Negroes made nearly 150 distinct revolts against slavery. The only place where Negroes did not revolt is in the pages of capitalist historians. All this revolutionary history can come as a surprise only to those who, whatever International they belong to, whether Second, Third, or Fourth, have not yet ejected from their systems the pertinacious lies of Anglo-Saxon capitalism. It is not strange that the Negroes revolted. It would have been strange if they had not.

But the Fourth International, whose business is revolution, has not to prove that Negroes were or are as revolutionary as any group of oppressed people. That has its place in agitation. What we as Marxists have to see is the tremendous role played by Negroes in the transformation of Western civilization from feudalism to capitalism. It is only from this vantage-ground that we shall be able to appreciate (and prepare for) the still greater role they must of necessity play in the transition from capitalism to socialism.

11 Johnson 1939b.

What are the decisive dates in the modern history of Great Britain, France, and America? 1789, the beginning of the French Revolution; 1832, the passing of the Reform Bill in Britain; and 1865, the crushing of the slave-power in America by the Northern states. Each of these dates marks a definitive stage in the transition from feudal to capitalist society. The exploitation of millions of Negroes had been a basic factor in the economic development of each of these three nations. It was reasonable, therefore, to expect the Negro question to play no less an important role in the resolution of the problems that faced each society. No one in the pre-revolutionary days, however, even faintly foresaw the magnitude of the contributions the Negroes were to make. Today Marxists have far less excuse for falling into the same mistake.

The Negro and the French Revolution

The French Revolution was a bourgeois revolution, and the basis of bourgeois wealth was the slave trade and the slave plantations in the colonies. Let there be no mistake about this. 'Sad irony of human history', says Jaures, 'the fortunes created at Bordeaux, at Nantes by the slave-trade gave to the bourgeoisie that pride which needed liberty and contributed to human emancipation'. And Gaston-Martin the historian of the slave trade sums up thus: though the bourgeoisie traded in other things than slaves, upon the success or failure of the traffic everything else depended. Therefore when the bourgeoisie proclaimed the Rights of Man in general, with necessary reservations, one of these was that these rights should not extend to the French colonies. In 1789 the French colonial trade was eleven million pounds, two-thirds of the overseas trade of France. British colonial trade at that time was only five million pounds. What price French abolition? There was abolitionist society to which Brissot, Robespierre, Mirabeau, Lafayette, Condorcet, and many such famous men belonged even before 1789. But liberals are liberal. Face to face with the revolution, they were ready to compromise. They would leave the half million slaves in their slavery, but at least the Mulattoes, men of property (including slaves) and education, should be given equal rights with the white colonials. The white colonial magnates refused concessions and they were people to be reckoned with, aristocrats by birth or marriage, bourgeois their trade connections with the maritime bourgeoisie. They opposed all change in the colonies that would diminish their social and political domination. The maritime bourgeoisie, concerned about their millions of investments, supported the colonials, and against eleven million pounds of trade per year the radical politicians were helpless. It was the revolution that kicked them from behind and forced them forward.

First of all the revolution in France. The Gironde right wing of the Jacobin club, overthrew the pro-royalist Feuillants and came to power in March, 1792.

And secondly the revolution in the colonies. The Mulattoes in San Domingo revolted in 1790, followed a few months later by the slave revolt in August 1791. On April 4, 1792 the Girondins granted political and social rights to the Mulattoes. The big bourgeoisie agreed, for the colonial aristocrats, after vainly trying to win Mulatto support for independence, decided to hand the colony over to Britain rather than tolerate interference with their system. All these slave owners, French nobility and French bourgeoisie, colonial aristocrats and Mulattoes, were agreed that the slave revolt should be suppressed and the slaves remain in their slavery.

The slaves, however, refused to listen to threats, and no promises were made to them. Led from beginning to end by men who had themselves been slaves and were unable to read or write, they fought one of the greatest revolutionary battles in history. Before the revolution they had seemed subhuman. Many a slave had to be whipped before he could be got to move from where he sat. The revolution transformed them into heroes.

The island of San Domingo was divided into two colonies, one French, the other Spanish. The colonial government of the Spanish Bourbons supported the slaves in their revolt against the French republic, and many rebel bands took service with the Spaniards. The French colonials invited Pitt to take over the colony, and when war was declared between France and England in 1793, the English invaded the island.

The English expedition, welcomed by all the white colonials, captured town after town in the south and west of French San Domingo. The Spaniards, operating with the famous Toussaint Louverture, an ex-slave, at the head of four thousand black troops, invaded the colony from the east. British and Spaniards were gobbling up as much as they could before the time for sharing came. 'In these matters', wrote the British minister, Dundas, to the governor of Jamaica, 'the more we have, the better our pretensions'. On June 4, Port-au-Prince, the capital of San Domingo, fell. Meanwhile another British expedition had captured Martinique, Guadeloupe, and the other French islands. Barring a miracle, the colonial trade of France, the richest in the world, was in the hands of her enemies and would be used against the revolution. But here the French masses took a hand.

August 10, 1792 was the beginning of the revolution triumphant in France. The Paris masses and their supporters all over France, in 1789 indifferent to the colonial question, were now striking in revolutionary frenzy at every abuse of the old regime and none of the former tyrants were so hated as the 'aristocrats of the skin'. Revolutionary generosity, resentment at the betrayal of the colonies to the enemies of the revolution, impotence in the face of the British navy – these swept the Convention off its feet. On February 4, 1794, without a debate, it decreed the abolition of Negro slavery and at last gave its sanction to the black revolt.

The news trickled through somehow to the French West Indies. Victor Hugues, a Mulatto, one of the great personalities produced by the revolution, managed to break through the British blockade and carried the official notice of the manumission to the Mulattoes and blacks of the West Indian islands. Then occurred the miracle. The blacks and Mulattoes dressed themselves in the revolutionary colors and, singing revolutionary songs, they turned on the British and Spaniards, their allies of yesterday. With little more from revolutionary France than its moral support, they drove the British and Spaniards from their conquests and carried the war into enemy territory. The British, after five years of trying to reconquer the French colonies, were finally driven out in 1798.

Few know the magnitude and the importance of that defeat sustained at the hands of Victor Hugues in the smaller islands and of Toussaint Louverture and Rigaud in San Domingo. Fortescue, the Tory historian of the British army, estimates the total loss to Britain at 100,000 men. Yet in the whole of the Peninsular War Wellington lost from all causes – killed in battle, sickness, desertions – only 40,000 men. British blood and British treasure were poured out in profusion in the West Indian campaign. This was the reason for Britain's weakness in Europe during the critical years 1793–1798. Let Fortescue himself speak: 'The secret of England's impotence for the first six years of the war may be said to lie in the two fatal words St. Domingo'. British historians blame chiefly the fever, as if San Domingo was the only place in the world that European imperialism had met fever.

Whatever the neglect or distortions of later historians, the French revolutionaries themselves knew what the Negro question meant to the revolution. The Constituent, the Legislature, and the Convention were repeatedly thrown into disorder by the colonial debates. This had grave repercussions in the internal struggle as well as in the revolutionary defense of the Republic. Says Jaures, 'Undoubtedly but for the compromises of Barnave and all his party on the colonial question, the general attitude of the Assembly after the flight to Varennes would have been different'. Excluding the masses of Paris, no portion of the French empire played, in proportion to its size, so grandiose a role in the French Revolution as the half million blacks and Mulattoes in the remote West Indian islands.

The Black Revolution and World History

The black revolution in San Domingo choked at its source one of the most powerful economic streams of the eighteenth century. With the defeat of the British, the black proletarians defeated the Mulatto Third Estate in a bloody civil war. Immediately after, Bonaparte, representative of the most reactionary elements of the new French bourgeoisie, attempted to restore slavery in San Domingo. The blacks defeated an expedition of some 50,000 men, and with the assistance of the Mulattoes, carried the revolution to its logical conclusion. They changed the name of San Domingo to Haiti and declared the island independent. This black revolution had a profound effect on the struggle for the cessation of the slave trade.

We can trace this close connection best by following the development of abolition in the British Empire. The first great blow at the Tory domination of Britain (and at feudalism in France for that matter) was struck by the Declaration of Independence in 1776. When Jefferson wrote that all men are created equal, he was drawing up the death-warrant of feudal society, wherein men were by law divided into unequal classes. Crispus Attucks, the Negro, was the first man killed by the British in the war that followed. It was no isolated or chance phenomenon. The Negroes thought that in this war for freedom, they could win their own. It has been estimated that of the 30,000 men in Washington's army 4,000 were Negroes. The American bourgeoisie did not want them. They forced themselves in. But San Domingo Negroes fought in the war also.

The French monarchy came to the assistance of the American Revolution. And Negroes from the French colonies pushed themselves into the French expeditionary force. Of the 1,900 French troops who recaptured Savannah, 900 were volunteers from the French colony of San Domingo. Ten years later some of these men – André Rigaud, Lambert, Beauvais and others (some say Christophe also) – with their political and military experience will be foremost among the leaders in the San Domingo revolution. Long before Karl Marx wrote, 'Workers of the world, unite', the revolution was international.

The loss of the slave-holding American colonies took much cotton out of the ears of the British bourgeoisie. Adam Smith and Arthur Young, heralds of the industrial revolution and wage-slavery, were already preaching against the waste of chattel-slavery. Deaf up to 1783, the British bourgeois now heard, and looked again at the West Indies. Their own colonies were bankrupt. They were losing the slave trade to French and British rivals. And half the French slaves that they brought were going to San Domingo, the India of the eighteenth century. Why should they continue to do this? In three years, the first abolitionist society was formed and Pitt began to clamor for the abolition of slavery – 'for the sake of humanity, no doubt', says Gaston-Martin, 'but also, be it well understood, to ruin French commerce'. With the war of 1793, Pitt, cherishing a prospect of winning San Domingo, piped down on abolition. But the black revolution killed the aspirations of both France and Britain.

The Treaty of Vienna in 1814 gave to France the right to recapture San Domingo: the Haitians swore that they would rather destroy the island. With the abandonment of the hopes for regaining San Domingo, the British abolished the slave trade in 1807. America followed in 1808.

If the East Indian interest in Britain was one of the great financial arsenals of the new bourgeoisie (whence the diatribes of Burke, Whig spokesman, against Hastings and Clive), the West Indian interest, though never so powerful as in France, was a cornerstone of the feudal oligarchy. The loss of America was the beginning of their decline. But for the black revolution, San Domingo would have strengthened them enormously. The reformist British bourgeoisie belabored them, the weakest link in the oligarchic chain. A great slave revolt in Jamaica in 1831 helped to convince those who had doubts. In Britain 'Better emancipation from above than from below' anticipated the Tsar by thirty years. One of the first acts of the victorious reformers was to abolish slavery in the British colonies. But for the black revolution in San Domingo, abolition and emancipation might have been postponed another thirty years.

Abolition did not come to France until the revolution of 1848. The production of beet-sugar, introduced into France by Bonaparte, grew by leaps and bounds, and placed the cane sugar interests, based on slavery in Martinique and Guadeloupe, increasingly on the defensive. One of the first acts of the revolutionary government of 1848 was to abolish slavery. But as in 1794, the decree was merely the registration of an accomplished fact. So menacing was the attitude of the slaves that in more than one colony the local government, in order to head off the servile revolution, proclaimed abolition without waiting for authorization from France.

The Negro and the Civil War

1848, the year following the economic crisis of 1847, was the beginning of a new cycle of revolutions all over the Western world. The European revolutions, Chartism in England, were defeated. In America the irrepressible conflict between capitalism in the North and the slave system in the South was headed off for the last time by the Compromise of 1850. The political developments following the economic crisis of 1857 made further compromise impossible.

It was a decade of revolutionary struggle the world over in the colonial and semi-colonial countries. 1857 was the year of the first war of Indian independence, commonly miscalled the Indian Mutiny. In 1858 began the civil war in Mexico, which ended with the victory of Juarez three years later. It was the period of the Taiping revolution in China, the first great attempt to break the power of the Manchu dynasty. North and South in America moved to their predestined clash unwillingly, but the revolutionary Negroes helped to precipitate the issue. For two decades before the Civil War began, they were leaving the South in thousands. The revolutionary organization known as the Underground Railway, with daring, efficiency and dispatch, drained away the slave owners' human property. Fugitive slaves were the issue of the day. The Fugitive Slave Law of 1850 was a last desperate attempt by the Federal Government to stop this illegal abolition. Ten Northern states replied with personal liberty laws which nullified the heavy penalties of the 1850 law. Most famous perhaps of all the whites and Negroes who ran the Underground Railway is Harriet Tubman, a Negro who had herself escaped from slavery. She made nineteen journeys into the South and helped her brothers and their wives and three hundred other slaves to escape. She made her depredations in enemy territory with a price of $40,000 on her head. Josiah Henson, the original of Uncle Tom, helped nearly two hundred slaves to escape. Nothing so galled the slave owners as this twenty-year drain on their already bankrupt economic system.

It is unnecessary to detail here the causes of this, the greatest civil war in history. Every Negro schoolboy knows that the last thing Lincoln had in mind was the emancipation of Negroes. What is important is that, for reasons both internal and external, Lincoln had to draw them into the revolutionary struggle. He said that without emancipation the North might not have won, and he was in all probability right. Thousands of Negroes were fighting on the Southern side, hoping to win their freedom that way. The abolition decree broke down the social cohesion of the South. It was not only what the North gained but, as Lincoln pointed out, what the South lost. On the Northern side 220,000 Negroes fought with such bravery that it was impossible to do with white troops what could be done with them. They fought not only with revolutionary bravery but with coolness and exemplary discipline. The best of them were filled with revolutionary pride. They were fighting for equality. One company stacked arms before the tent of its commanding officer as a protest against discrimination.

Lincoln was also driven to abolition by the pressure of the British working class. Palmerston wanted to intervene on the side of the South but was opposed in the cabinet by Gladstone. Led by Marx, the British working class so vigorously opposed the war, that it was impossible to hold a pro-war meeting anywhere in England. The British Tories derided the claim that the war was for the abolition of slavery: hadn't Lincoln said so many times? The British workers, however, insisted on seeing the war as a war for abolition, and Lincoln, for whom British non-intervention was a life and death matter, decreed abolition with a suddenness which shows his fundamental unwillingness to take such a revolutionary step.

Abolition was declared in 1863. Two years before, the movement of the Russian peasants, so joyfully hailed by Marx, frightened the Tsar into the semi-emancipation of the serfs. The North won its victory in 1865. Two years later the British workers won the Second Reform Bill, which gave the franchise to the workers in the towns. The revolutionary cycle was concluded with the defeat of the Paris Commune in 1871. A victory there and the history of Reconstruction would have been far different.

The Negro and World Revolution

Between 1871 and 1905 the proletarian revolution was dormant. In Africa the Negroes fought vainly to maintain their independence against the imperialist invasions. But the Russian Revolution of 1905 was the forerunner of a new era that began with the October Revolution in 1917. While half a million Negroes fought with the French Revolution in 1789, today the socialist revolution in Europe has as its potential allies over 120 million Negroes in Africa. Where Lincoln had to seek an alliance with an isolated slave population, today millions of Negroes in America have penetrated deep into industry, have fought side by side with white workers on picket lines, have helped to barricade factories for sit-down strikes, have played their part in the struggles and clashes of trade unions and political parties. It is only through the spectacles of historical perspective that we can fully appreciate the enormous revolutionary potentialities of the Negro masses today.

Half a million slaves, hearing the words Liberty, Equality, and Fraternity shouted by millions of Frenchmen many thousands of miles away, awoke from their apathy. They occupied the attention of Britain for six years and, once again to quote Fortescue, 'practically destroyed the British army'. What of the Negroes in Africa today? This is a bare outline of the record.

French West Africa: 1926–1929, 10,000 men fled into the forest swamps to escape French slavery.

French Equatorial Africa: 1924, uprising. 1924–1925, uprising, 1000 Negroes killed. 1928, June to November, rising in Upper Sangha and Lai. 1929, a rising lasting four months; the Africans organized an army of 10,000.

British West Africa: 1929, a revolt of women in Nigeria, 30,000 in number; 83 killed, 87 wounded. 1937, general strike of the Gold Coast. Farmers, joined by dockers and truck drivers.

Belgian Congo: 1929, revolt in Ruanda Urundi; thousands killed. 1930–1931, revolt of the Bapendi, 800 massacred in one place, Kwango.

South Africa: 1929, strikes and riots in Durban; the Negro quarter was entirely surrounded by troops and bombarded by planes.

Since 1935 there have been general strikes, with shooting of Negroes, in Rhodesia, in Madagascar, in Zanzibar. In the West Indies there have been general strikes and mass action such as those islands have not seen since the emancipation from slavery a hundred years ago. Scores have been killed and wounded.

The above is only a random selection. The Negroes in Africa are caged and beat against the bars continually. It is the European proletariat that holds the key. Let the workers of Britain, France, and Germany say, 'Arise, ye children of starvation' as loudly as the French revolutionaries said Liberty, Equality, and Fraternity and what force on earth can hold these Negroes back? All who know anything about Africa know this.

Mr. Norman Leys, a government medical officer in Kenya for twenty years, a member of the British Labour Party, and about as revolutionary as the late Ramsay MacDonald, wrote a study of Kenya in 1924. Seven years later he wrote again. This time he entitled his book *A Last Chance in Kenya*. The alternative, he said, is revolution.

In *Caliban in Africa*, Leonard Barnes, another milk and water socialist, writes as follows: 'So he [the South African white] and the native he holds captive go spinning down the stream fatally, madly spinning together along the rapids above the great cataract, both yoked to one omnipotent hour'. That is the revolution, wrapped in silver paper.

The revolution haunts this conservative Englishman. He writes again of the Bantu, 'They crouch in their corner, nursing a sullen anger and desperately groping for a plan. They will not be many years making up their minds. Time and fate, even more prevailing than the portcullis of the Afrikaner, are driving them on from the rear. Something must give; it will not be fate or time. Some comprehensive social and economic reconstruction must take place. But how? By reason or by violence? …'.

He poses as alternatives what are in reality one. The change will take place, by violence and by reason combined.

'We Have a False Idea of the Negro'

Let us return again to the San Domingo revolution with its paltry half a million slaves. Writing in 1789, the very year of the revolution, a colonist said of them that they were 'unjust, cruel, barbarous, half-human, treacherous, deceitful, thieves, drunkards, proud, lazy, unclean, shameless, jealous to fury and cowards'.

Three years later Roume, the French Commissioner, noted that even though fighting with the royalist Spaniards, the black revolutionaries, organizing themselves into armed sections and popular bodies, rigidly observed all the forms of republican organization. They adopted slogans and rallying cries. They appointed chiefs of sections and divisions who, by means of these slogans, could call them out and send them back home again from one end of the province to the others. They threw up from out of their depths a soldier and a statesman of the first rank, Toussaint Louverture, and secondary leaders fully able to hold their own with the French in war, diplomacy, and administration. In ten years they organized an army that fought Bonaparte's army on level terms. 'But what men these blacks are! How they fight and how they die!' wrote a French officer looking back at the last campaign after forty years. From his dying bed, Leclerc, Bonaparte's brother-in-law and commander-in-chief of the French expedition, wrote home, 'We have ... a false idea of the Negro'. And again, 'We have in Europe a false idea of the country in which we fight and the men whom we fight against ...'. We need to know and reflect on these things today.

Menaced during its whole existence by imperialism, European and American, the Haitians have never been able to overcome the bitter heritage of their past. Yet that revolution of a half million not only helped to protect the French Revolution but initiated great revolutions in its own right. When the Latin American revolutionaries saw that half a million slaves could fight and win, they recognized the reality of their own desire for independence. Bolivar, broken and ill, went to Haiti. The Haitians nursed him back to health, gave him money and arms with which he sailed to the mainland. He was defeated, went back to Haiti, was once more welcomed and assisted. And it was from Haiti that he sailed to start on the final campaign, which ended in the independence of the five states.

Today 150 million Negroes, knit into world economy infinitely more tightly than their ancestors of a hundred years ago, will far surpass the work of that San Domingo half million in the work of social transformation. The continuous risings in Africa; the refusal of the Ethiopian warriors to submit to Mussolini; the American Negroes who volunteered to fight in Spain in the Abraham Lincoln Brigade, as Rigaud and Beauvais had volunteered to fight in America, tempering their swords against the enemy abroad for use against the enemy at home – these lightnings announce the thunder. The racial prejudice that now stands in the way will bow before the tremendous impact of the proletarian revolution.

In Flint during the sit-down strike of two years ago seven hundred Southern whites, soaked from infancy in racial prejudice, found themselves besieged in the General Motors building with one Negro among them. When the time came for the first meal, the Negro, knowing who and what his companions were, held himself in the background. Immediately it was proposed that there should be no racial discrimination among the strikers. Seven hundred hands went up together. In the face of the class enemy the men recognized that race prejudice was a subordinate thing which could not be allowed to disrupt their struggle. The Negro was invited to take his seat first, and after the victory was won, in the triumphant march out of the factory, he was given the first place. That is the prognosis of the future. In Africa, in America, in the West Indies, on a national and international scale, the millions of Negroes will raise their heads, rise up from their knees, and write some of the most massive and brilliant chapters in the history of revolutionary socialism.

6 The Right of Revolution[12]

(*1941*)

William F. Warde (George Novack)

The defendants in the Minnesota case have been indicted on the ground that the Socialist Workers Party seeks to persuade workers and farmers 'that the Government of the United States is imperialistic, capitalistic and organized and constituted for the purpose of subjecting workers and laborers to various and sundry deprivations and for the purpose of denying to them an alleged right to own, control and manage all property and industry in the United States', and that it is desirable and necessary that the workers and farmers bring about a revolutionary change in this system.

This is one point in the indictment that the Socialist Workers Party acknowledges as true. We are the Party of the Socialist Revolution in the United States. We maintain that the present capitalist government does not represent the interests of the American masses but acts on behalf of the few rich families who monopolize economic and political power. We propose that the organized workers and farmers of the United States replace this utterly reactionary regime with their own administrative power, which shall govern on behalf of the laboring majority instead of the exploiting minority of the plutocrats.

We further insist that the working people of this country have every right to take this revolutionary step and that our party has every legal and democratic right to advocate it. We advocate this openly in our publications and public meetings and not, as the FBI-Gestapo falsely alleges, by secret and conspiratorial methods. We have no reason to conceal our aims or camouflage our revolutionary position. We have nothing to hide from the American people, for our party has no interests separate and apart from their interests. Our program can be realized only through the action of the popular masses. They must first be convinced of its correctness and educated in its spirit. This requires that our program persistently and publicly confront the programs of all other parties and display its superiority over its competitors in the political arena.

12 Warde 1941.

There are conspirators at work today against the welfare of the American people. But they are not the Trotskyists. They are the Roosevelts, the Stimsons, the Knoxes – leaders of the imperialist plunderbund, who lie to the conscripts, who conclude secret diplomatic and military agreements, and are ready to drag the US into war against the will of 80 per cent of the people. Behind these stooges stand the Mellons, Rockefellers and Morgans, who dictate their actions and impose their private profiteering policies upon the nation. These are the real conspirators against the people!

The indictment charges us with being followers of Lenin and Trotsky and of holding up as an example to the American workers the Bolshevik revolution of 1917. We proudly plead guilty to this charge. The Socialist Workers Party consciously carries on the great traditions of revolutionary Marxism, exemplified in the teachings and actions of the Bolshevik movement led by Lenin and Trotsky. But we are not only international revolutionists; we are also American revolutionists – and we are equally proud of carrying on the traditions of revolutionary struggle that created the United States and made it in many respects paramount among the nations of the earth.

The American Revolutionary Tradition

It is no exaggeration to say that no other section of humanity has had a more revolutionary career than we Americans. No other people has displayed more revolutionary energy.

We Americans won our independence through a revolutionary uprising. We gained and preserved our democratic rights by militant measures. We eliminated chattel slavery from this continent by civil war. If ever any people had reason to trust in the effectiveness of revolutionary methods to attain their ends, it is the American people.

The history of the American people is a history of uninterrupted revolution. The original settlements on this continent were offshoots of that great social revolutionary movement of the 16th, 17th and 18th centuries which transformed Europe and was eventually to change the world. This was the struggle of the rising capitalist system against the dying feudal order. The breakup of the old Europe under the impact of the new capitalist forces gave the impetus to the discovery, exploration and exploitation of the New World and supplied the elements for building up its colonies. Early American history derives its world-historical significance from the part it played in this process of continuous world revolution that accompanied the expansion of capitalism.

That bourgeois-democratic revolution, which started out from western Europe in the 15th century, marched forward from city to city, from country to country, from continent to continent, until by the end of the 19th century it had conquered and joined together the whole globe from its most civilized centers to its most remote and barbarous regions. This social revolutionary movement was fundamentally responsible for the existence of American civilization as we know it today. Without that international revolution, the Indians might still be enjoying peaceful possession of North America, the Roosevelt family might never have left Holland nor Tobin's forebears Ireland.

In the further course of their historical development, the American people passed through two tremendous national revolutions: one at the end of the 18th and the other in the middle of the 19th century. These revolutions marked great steps forward in the lives of the American people.

The First American Revolution won independence for the oppressed colonists, eliminated many vestiges of feudalism, united thirteen colonies into one nation, and set up a democratic republic. It gave the United States of America the most advanced form of government, which became a model and inspiration for progressive forces throughout the world in the following century.

But that did not end the need for revolutionary action. In order to maintain the social gains and extend the political conquests acquired through the First Revolution, it became necessary to initiate another in 1861. This Second American Revolution preserved the unity of the United States against the attempts of the secessionist slaveholders to split it in two. It defended the plea of equality at the base of American democracy against the degenerate counter-revolutionary clique which made slavery the cornerstone of the Confederacy. It emancipated the slaves and destroyed the economic and political power of the slaveholders who had misruled the country for 60 years. The victory of the North helped safeguard not only this country's independence but the independence of the rest of the American peoples from the vultures of European imperialism.

The victorious revolution of the Union over the Confederacy paved the way for the prodigious achievements of that Golden Age of national progress and world prosperity which followed the Civil War. It encouraged the virile young European labor movement and the democratic forces in Latin America.

Such have been the accomplishments of the American people in their revolutionary vigor!

Whatever else they may be taken to signify, these mighty events testify that revolution is no less native to our soil than to Europe. They confirm the fact which lies at the basis of Marxist theory, that fundamental social problems involving antagonistic class interests cannot be settled fully and finally by mutual accommodation but must find their solution in life and death battles between opposing social forces.

The Written Heritage of American Revolution

In line with their bold and heroic struggles, the most cherished traditions of the American people are permeated with the spirit of revolutionary democracy. Take the text of that extremely subversive document, The Declaration of Independence, written by Thomas Jefferson, to whom Roosevelt's so-called 'Democratic' Party pays homage yearly. In its second paragraph there is this categorical justification for the right to revolution:

> We hold these truths to be self-evident, that all men are created equal, that they are endowed by their Creator with certain inalienable Rights, that among these are Life, Liberty and the pursuit of Happiness. That to secure these rights, Governments are instituted among Men, deriving their just powers from the consent of the governed. That whenever any Form of Government becomes destructive of these ends, it is the Right of the People to alter or abolish it, and to institute new Government, laying its foundation on such principles and organizing its powers in such form, as to them shall seem most likely to effect their Safety and Happiness.

Further, 'It is their right, it is their duty, to throw off such Government and to provide new Guards for their future security'. To our militant forefathers, revolution was not simply a right but, under certain circumstances, even a duty!

The history of the Republican Party is likewise tainted with revolutionary doctrine. In a speech before the first Republican state convention in Illinois in 1856, Abraham Lincoln, the idol of the Republican Party, declared: 'The government, with its institutions, belongs to the people who inhabit it. Whenever they shall grow weary of the existing government, they can exercise their constitutional right of amending it, or their revolutionary right to dismember or overthrow it'.

We Trotskyists take our stand beside Jefferson and Lincoln in defense of the right of revolution. This is the most precious and inalienable of democratic rights, the foundation and safeguard of all others. If the patriot leaders of 1776 had not acted upon this right against the cries of the conservatives and the Crown, the American people might today still belong to the British empire. If the Radical Republicans had relinquished their revolutionary rights during the Civil War, the slave-holders might not have been crushed.

In prosecuting us as revolutionists, Roosevelt ranges himself alongside of King George, the slaveholders and all the other tyrants in American history. The Smith Act which Congress passed in 1940 under White House pressure and under which the Socialist Workers Party members have been indicted, makes it a state crime to republish these words from the Declaration of Independence or these speeches of Lincoln. Will Roosevelt's Department of 'Justice' arraign Jefferson and Lincoln together with us for asserting the right to revolution?

Ruling Class Always Acts This Way

Throughout history, the ruling class has sought to set limits upon the action of the masses in defense of their legitimate rights and well-being. Thus today workers are told: 'You can beg the bosses for higher wages but you cannot strike to get them'. Or – 'You can strike in peace-time but not during war'. Or – 'You can strike against a private employer but not against the Federal Government'. Or – 'You can strike in non-essential plants but not in war industries'. The one purpose of all these admonitions is to restrain workers from exerting their full strength to improve their status.

Reactionaries have always been even more concerned with setting limits upon the political activities of the working class. 'We will permit you to vote for one of two capitalist parties, but you cannot have your own class Labor Party. You can ask us for reforms but you cannot remove us from power. We demand the privilege of dictating governmental policy, and if you attempt to take this supreme power away from us, we shall not abide by your majority decision'. Such are the haughty ultimatums ruling-class politicians always have issued to the people.

Fortunately, the progressive sections of the American people have never been intimidated by such dictatorial threats, nor have they heeded the prohibitions of would-be master classes for long. Whenever the entrenched powers of reaction have placed signs across the road to revolution, marked: 'No Thoroughfare', the masses have knocked aside both the obstructions and the obstructors and they have not done so in a polite and peaceful manner.

This is the main lesson to be drawn from American history – and it is one that the present capitalist rulers of the country wish above all to keep the people from learning. Just a few months before Roosevelt tried to remove the proletarian revolutionists of the Socialist Workers Party from the ranks of labor by means of trumped-up accusations, he endeavored to efface these revolutionary lessons from the course of American history. In a speech on January 6th of this year, Roosevelt set forth this falsified version of the permanent revolution in American history.

'Since the beginning of our American history, we have been engaged in change – in a peaceful perpetual revolution – a revolution which goes on steadily, quietly, adjusting itself to changing conditions ...'.

This official picture of American history, purged of all its mighty struggles and class conflicts, of all its progressive revolutionary content, no more resembles reality than does a Hollywood scenario. The American people have not moved forward in 'peaceful, perpetual revolution', as Roosevelt would have us believe, surmounting obstacles in their path as effortlessly as a millionaire's Cadillac climbs hills. Nor have they, 'steadily, quietly adjusted themselves to changing conditions'.

The Real Course of American History

On the contrary, at every stage of their progress, the American people have experienced other than peaceful struggles. The armed forces of half a dozen European powers fought against each other and against the aborigines throughout the Colonial period. The English colonists waged war against the Indians, the French, the Spanish, and finally against the mother country itself. As an independent nation, the United States warred against France, the Barbary Coast pirates, Canada, England, Mexico, Spain, Germany, Austria-Hungary, Turkey, China, the Soviet Union – and, as Roosevelt himself can best testify, its military adventures have only begun.

Side by side and interwoven with these external conflicts, there have unfolded profound and prolonged struggles between antagonistic sections of American society. Landless colonists against landed proprietors, indentured servants and slaves against their masters, small farmers against wealthy planters and capitalists, Patriots against Loyalists, plebeian revolutionists against reactionary patricians. In the first part of the 19th century American history revolved around the contest between the pro-slavery and anti-slavery forces, which culminated in civil war. Between the Civil and First World Wars, the exploited petty-bourgeois masses of city and country contended against the trusts and monopolies. In our own day, the strike struggles of organized labor against Big Business have involved greater numbers than the soldiers engaged in the Civil War. And, as the Memorial Day massacre at Chicago so recently reminded us, these battles exact many victims.

Those who condemn all use of force and violence thereby condemn the whole course of American history. For that history is the greatest of all advocates of force and violence. The present capitalist masters of the United States did not acquire state power by legal or peaceful means; they conquered and defended it arms in hand during the Second American Revolution. To establish their supremacy within the nation, they had to suppress the slave-holders on their right and the workers on their left. They have maintained power since against foreign rivals and against the working masses at home through force and violence. Only force and violence keep the Cubans, Filipinos and Porto-Ricans under American domination.

What We Teach the American Workers

The Federal indictment accuses the Socialist Workers Party of advocating the overthrow of the government by force and violence. This is a lie. We work to win the majority of the American people to our ideas by education and propaganda and we would prefer to have socialism established by peaceful means. This would undoubtedly be the most economical and desirable method of effecting the social changes which are needed to assure peace and security.

At the same time, we point out to the American people the lessons of their own history. The British Crown would not permit the Colonists to obtain their just rights and national independence without the most violent struggle. When the Republican Party was first elected to national power, the slaveholders would not abide by this democratic decision but sought, like Franco's regime, to find salvation in counterrevolution. In both these national crises, the progressive majority was obliged to resort to measures of revolutionary self-defense in order to repel and crush the counter-revolutionary minority.

Therefore, we say to the American people: Do not yield up your elementary right of self-defense. Strikers have the right to protect themselves against the attacks of employers' thugs and strike-breakers. Unions, like Local 544-CIO, have the right to defend themselves by union defense guards against fascist bands. The American workers and farmers have the right to safeguard themselves both from foreign and from domestic fascists.

Indeed, Roosevelt and the war makers invoke this very principle of national self-defense in justifying their impending participation in the imperialist conflict. Violence is permissible in their code when it serves plutocratic interests but it is forbidden in defense of the rights of the people.

Where are the real practitioners of violence to be found? Not amongst the Trotskyists but amongst their prosecutors. The Department of Justice uses the force of the FBI and the courts to persecute revolutionists for their opinions and to deprive them of their constitutional right of free speech. Daniel Tobin hurls 300 strong-arm men against the Minneapolis motor transport workers. Franklin Doublecross Roosevelt sends 3,000 troops against the North American strikers. And then they accuse the Socialist Workers Party of advocating force and violence!

The capitalist statesmen are extremely inconsistent in their attitude towards the right of revolution. Roosevelt himself approved Churchill's call to the German people to revolt against Hitler. His administration gives shelter and recognition to governments-in-exile, plotting revolutions in Poland, Czecho-Slovakia, Belgium and half a dozen other conquered countries. Recently Roosevelt appealed to the French people over the heads of their present rulers, asking them to repudiate Vichy's policies.

To the upholders of the present capitalist regime in the United States, therefore, revolution is not always and everywhere so reprehensible an affair. Some highly useful technical processes are excluded from this country because they endanger the vested interests of great corporations. They are, however, permitted to be used in other countries. So it is with revolution, as far as Roosevelt is concerned. A revolution would be bad for home consumption; it is good only as an article for export!

Revolution is Still the Motor of History

At this point some citizens may object: Revolutions were permissible and profitable here in the 18th and 19th centuries, but we Americans have no further need for a revolution. This aversion to revolution is scarcely original. The defenders of the status quo have never at any time admitted the need for revolutionary change desired by the masses. The Loyalists of 1776 condemned resistance against King George's men; the patriots answered these defenders of British oppression by reciting the ideas and recalling the deeds of the 17th century English revolutionists from Locke and Milton to Oliver Cromwell. The conservatives of John Brown's day were willing to have the American people remain slaves of the slave-holding oligarchy. But that did not prevent the revolutionists from fighting for their liberty and saving it for the nation.

Whatever repressive governments and short-sighted individuals may say or do, the revolutionary annals of the American people did not end with the 19th century. On the contrary, all signs point to the approach of another and greater revolutionary crisis here in the not too distant future. To those who have eyes to see and minds to think, the Third American Revolution is now being born.

This 20th Century revolution can only be proletarian in its leadership and socialist in its aims. It will complete the tasks of social reconstruction left unfinished by the great bourgeois-democratic revolutions of the two previous centuries. The Socialist Workers Party aspires to guide the workers and farmers of the United States through this inevitable revolutionary struggle and to lead them forward to victory and to a better world.

'If this be treason, make the most of it!'

Bibliography

Adamic, Louis 1934, *Dynamite: The Story of Class Violence in America*, revised edition, Gloucester, MA: Peter Smith.

Alexander, Robert J. 1991, *International Trotskyism, 1929–1985: A Documented Analysis of the Movement*, Chapel Hill, NC: Duke University Press.

Allen, Joe 2012, 'Confronting the Fascist Threat in the US in the Late 1930s, Part I: It can't happen here', *International Socialist Review*, 79.

Allen, Robert, with Pamela Allen 1974, *The Reluctant Reformers: The Impact of Racism on American Social Reform Movements*, Washington, DC: Howard University Press.

Anderson, Perry 1979, *Considerations on Western Marxism*, London: Verso.

Belknap, Michael 1977, *Cold War Political Injustice: The Smith Act, the Communist Party, and American Civil Liberties*, Westport, CT: Greenwood Press.

Bell, Daniel 1952, 'Marxian Socialism in the United States', in *Socialism in American Life*, Vol. I, edited by Donald Drew Egbert and Stow Persons, Princeton, NJ: Princeton University Press.

Bernstein, Irving 1969, *Turbulent Years 1933–1941*, Boston: Houghton Mifflin.

Bittelman, Alexander 1963, 'Things I Have Learned: An Autobiography', Boxes 1–2, Tamiment Institute, Elmer Holmes Bobst Library, New York University, New York, New York.

Blackburn, Robin 2011, *An Unfinished Revolution: Karl Marx and Abraham Lincoln*, London: Verso.

Boggs, James, Grace Lee, Freddy Paine and Lyman Paine 1978, *Conversations in Maine: Exploring Our Nation's Future*, Boston: South End Press.

Brecher, Jeremy, 1974, *Strike!* Greenwich, CT: Fawcett Premier.

Breitman, George (ed.) 1978, *Leon Trotsky on Black Nationalism and Self-Determination*, Second Edition, New York: Pathfinder Press.

Breitman, George 1982, 'Answers to Questions', in *The Founding of the Socialist Workers Party, Minutes and resolutions 1938–39*, New York: Monad Press/Pathfinder Press.

Breitman, George, Paul Le Blanc and Alan Wald 2016, *Trotskyism in the United States, Historical Essays and Reconsiderations*, Chicago: Haymarket Books.

Burnham, James 1940a, 'Science and Style: A Reply to Comrade Trotsky', mimeographed 1940; available as an appendix to Leon Trotsky, *In Defense of Marxism* (London: 1966); transcribed by Einde O'Callaghan for Encyclopedia of Trotskyism On-Line (ETOL), available at: https://www.marxists.org/history/etol/writers/burnham/1940/02/style.htm

Burnham, James 1940b, 'Letter of Resignation from the Workers Party, May 21'; Marxist Internet Archive, available at: https://www.marxists.org/history/etol/writers/burnham/1940/05/resignation.htm.

Cannon, James P. 1931a, 'Trifling With the Negro Question', *Militant*, 1 March.

Cannon, James P. 1931b, 'Silk Revolt Growing', *The Militant*, 1 August.

Cannon, James P. 1933a, 'Letter to Vincent Ray Dunne, 1 January', James P. Cannon Papers, State Historical Society of Wisconsin, Madison, Wisconsin.

Cannon, James P. 1933b, 'The Left Wing's Place is in A.F. of L. Unions', *The Militant*, 2 September.

Cannon, James P. 1933c, 'The Left Wing Needs a New Policy and a New Leadership', *The Militant*, 16 September.

Cannon, James P. 1934, 'Minneapolis and Its Meaning', *New International*, July.

Cannon, James P. 1936, 'Deeper into the Unions', *Labor Action*, 5 December.

Cannon, James P. 1938, 'The New Party Is Founded', *New International*, Vol. 4 No. 2, February.

Cannon, James P. 1939, 'Speech on the Russian Question', *SWP Internal Bulletin*, Vol. 2, No. 3, 14 November.

Cannon, James P. 1940, 'The Struggle for a Proletarian Party', *SWP Internal Bulletin*, Vol. 2, No. 13, February.

Cannon, James P. 1942a, *Socialism on Trial: The Official Court Record of James P. Cannon's Testimony in the famous Minneapolis 'Sedition' Trial*, New York: Pioneer Publishers.

Cannon, James P. 1942b, *Defense Policy in the Minneapolis Trial*, New York: Pioneer Publishers.

Cannon, James P. 1944a, 'The Dogs Days of the Left Opposition', *Fourth International*, March.

Cannon, James P. 1944b, *The History of American Trotskyism: Report of a Participant*, New York: Pioneer.

Cannon, James P. 1944c, *Why We Are in Prison: Farewell Speeches of the 18 SWP and 544-CIO Minneapolis Prisoners*, New York: Pioneer, pp. 10–15.

Cannon, James P. 1952, 'How We Won Grace Carlson and How We Lost Her', *Militant*, 7 July.

Cannon, James P. 1957, '1928: At the Sixth World Congress', *International Socialist Review*, Spring.

Cannon, James P. 1958, *Notebook of an Agitator*, New York: Pathfinder.

Cannon, James P. 1962, *The First Ten Years of American Communism: Report of a Participant*, New York: Lyle Stuart.

Cannon, James P. 1992, 'Letter to Ruth Querio', in *In Defense of American Trotskyism: Revolutionary Principles and Working-Class Democracy*, edited by Paul Le Blanc, New York: Fourth Internationalist Tendency.

Cannon, James P. 2008, *The Struggle for a Proletarian Party*, Chippendale, New South Wales, Australia: Resistance Books; transcribed by David Walters for Marxist Internet Archive, available at: https://www.marxists.org/archive/cannon/works/1940/party.

Cannon, James P. and Max Shachtman 1938, 'The Internal Situation and the Character of the Party', *Socialist Appeal*, 26 February.

Cannon, James P., Martin Abern and Max Shachtman 1928, 'For the Russian Opposition! Against Opportunism and Bureaucracy in the Workers (Communist) Party of America! A Statement to American Communists', *Militant*, 15 November.

Carr, E.H. 2004, *The Russian Revolution from Lenin to Stalin, 1917–1929*, Second Edition, New York: Palgrave Macmillan.

Carter, Joseph 1933, 'Unite to Smash Fascism! Forward to Communist Unity and Common Action of All Workingclass Organizations', *Young Spartacus*, March.

Cochran, Bert 1977, *Labor and Communism: The Conflict That Shaped American Unions*, Princeton, NJ: Princeton University Press.

Communist League of America, National Committee 1933, 'For a New Party and a New International', *Militant*, 30 September.

Countryman, Edward 2003, *The American Revolution*, Revised Edition, New York: Hill and Wang.

Danielson, Leilah 2014, *American Gandhi: A.J. Muste and the History of Radicalism in the Twentieth Century*, Philadelphia: University of Pennsylvania Press.

Deutscher Isaac 2015, *The Prophet: The Life of Leon Trotsky*, London: Verso.

Devinatz, Victor D. 2005, 'The Role of the Trotskyists in the United Auto Workers, 1939–1949', *Left History*, Vol. 10, No. 2 (Fall).

Devinatz, Victor D. 2007, 'A Reevaluation of the Trade Union Unity League, 1929–1934', *Science & Society*, 71 (November).

Dobbs, Farrell 1940, 'The Unions and Politics', *Fourth International*, July.

Dobbs, Farrell 1941, 'The FBI and the Unions', *Fourth International*, June.

Dobbs, Farrell 1972, *Teamster Rebellion*, New York: Monad.

Dobbs, Farrell 1973, *Teamster Power*, New York: Monad.

Dobbs, Farrell 1975, *Teamster Politics*, New York: Monad.

Dobbs, Farrell 1977, *Teamster Bureaucracy*, New York: Monad.

Dollinger Sol and Genora Johnson Dollinger 2000, *Not Automatic: Women and the Left in the Forging of the Auto Workers' Union*, New York: Monthly Review Press.

Draper, Hal (ed.) 1963, *Introduction to Independent Socialism: Selected Articles from Labor Action*, Berkeley, CA: Independent Socialist Press.

Draper, Theodore 1957, *The Roots of American Communism*, New York: Viking.

Drucker, Peter 1994, *Max Shachtman and His Left: A Socialist's Odyssey Through the 'American Century'*, Atlantic Highlands, NJ: Humanities Press.

Editorial 1938, 'The Dewey Commission', *New International*, January.

Editorial 1936, 'Workers Party Calls All Revolutionary Workers to Join Socialist Party', *New Militant*, 6 June.

Editorial 1937, 'The Crisis in the Party', *Socialist Appeal*, March.

Eley, Geoff 2002, *Forging Democracy: The History of the Left in Europe 1850–2000*, New York: Oxford University Press.

Evans, Les (ed.) 1976, *James P. Cannon As We Knew Him*, New York: Pathfinder.

Faue, Elizabeth 1991, *Community of Suffering and Struggle: Women, Men, and the Labor Movement in Minneapolis, 1915–1945*, Chapel Hill, NC: University of North Carolina Press.

Fleischman, Harry 1969, *Norman Thomas, A Biography: 1884–1968*, New York: W.W. Norton.

Foner, Philip S. 1977, *American Socialism and Black Americans, From the Age of Jackson to World War II*, Westport, CT: Greenwood Press.

Frank, Pierre 2010, *The Long March of the Trotskyists: Contributions to the History of the Fourth International*, London: Resistance Books.

Frölich, Paul 2010, *Rosa Luxemburg*, Chicago: Haymarket Books.

Gabriel, Mary 2011, *Love and Capital: Karl and Jenny Marx and the Birth of a Revolution*, New York: Little Brown and Co.

Geary, Rick 2009, *Trotsky, A Graphic Biography*, New York.

Ginger, Ray 2007, *The Bending Cross: A Biography of Eugene Victor Debs*, Chicago: Haymarket Books.

Gitlow, Benjamin 1940, *I Confess: The Truth About American Communism*, New York: E.P. Dutton.

Goldman, Albert 1936, 'Communists Play Follow the Leader', *Socialist Appeal*, August.

Goldman, Albert 1938, *What is Socialism?*, New York: Pioneer Publishers, 1938.

Goldman, Albert 1944, 'Farewell Statement', *Why We Are in Prison: Farewell Speeches of the 18 SWP and 544-CIO Minneapolis Prisoners*, New York: Pioneer Publishers.

Haverty-Stacke, Donna T. 2015, *Trotskyists on Trial: Free Speech and Political Persecution Since the Age of FDR*, New York: New York University Press.

Hofstadter, Richard 1970, *The Progressive Historians: Turner, Beard, Parrington*, New York: Vintage Books.

Hook, Sidney 1940, *Reason, Social Myths and Democracy*, New York: John Day Co.

Howe, Irving 1982, *A Margin of Hope: An Intellectual Autobiography*, New York: Harcourt Brace Jovanovich.

Hudis, Peter 2013, *Marx's Concept of the Alternative to Capitalism*, Chicago: Haymarket Books.

Independent Communist League of Boston [Antoinette Konikow et al.] 1928, 'What Is Wrong With The Communist Party?' *Bulletin No. 1*, December.

International Bolshevik Tendency (ed.) 1998, *The Transitional Program: The Death Agony of Capitalism and the Tasks of the Fourth International*, London and Toronto: Bolshevik Publications.

Jackson, Carlton 2008, *Child of the Sit-Downs: The Revolutionary Life of Genora Dollinger*, Kent, OH: Kent State University Press.

Jacobs, Paul 1965, *Is Curly Jewish?*, New York: Atheneum.

Jaffe, Philip J. 1975, *The Rise and Fall of American Communism*, New York: Horizon Press.

James, C.L.R. 1937, *World Revolution 1917–1936: The Rise and Fall of the Communist International*, New York: Pioneer Publishers, available at: https://www.marxists.org/archive/james-clr/works/world.

James, C.L.R. 1989, *Black Jacobins: Toussaint L'Ouverture and the San Domingo Revolution*, New York: Vintage Books.

Johnpoll, Bernard K. 1970, *Pacifist's Progress: Norman Thomas and the Decline of American Socialism*, Chicago: Quadrangle Books.

Johnson J.R. [C.L.R. James] 1939a, 'Preliminary Notes on the Negro Question', *Internal Bulletin* #9, June.

Johnson J.R. [C.L.R. James] 1939b, 'Revolution and the Negro', *New International*, December.

Johnson J.R. [C.L.R. James] 1939c, 'The Destiny of the Negro', *Socialist Appeal*, 21 November, 1 December, 9 December.

Keeran, Roger 1980, *The Communist Party and the Auto Workers' Union*, New York: International.

Kerry, Tom 1980, *Workers, Bosses, and Bureaucrats: A Socialist View of Labor Struggles Since the 1930s*, New York: Pathfinder Press.

Kornbluh, Joyce (ed.) 1998, *Rebel Voices: An IWW Anthology*, Chicago: Charles H. Kerr.

Korth, Philip A. 1995, *The Minneapolis Teamsters Strike of 1934*, East Lansing, MI: Michigan State University Press.

Lang, Frederick J. [Frank Lovell] 1943, *Maritime: A Historical Sketch and a Workers' Program*, New York: Pioneer Publishers.

Leab, Daniel J. 1967, '"United We Eat": The Creation and Organization of the Unemployed Councils in 1930', *Labor History*, 8 (Fall).

Le Blanc, Paul 1996, 'Trotskyism in the United States: The First Fifty Years', in *Trotskyism in the United States: Historical Essays and Reconsiderations*, edited by George Breitman, Paul Le Blanc and Alan Wald, Atlantic Highlands, NJ: Humanities Press, pp. 3–87.

Le Blanc, Paul 2015a, *Lenin and the Revolutionary Party*, Chicago: Haymarket Books.

Le Blanc, Paul 2015b, *Leon Trotsky*, London: Reaktion Books.

Le Blanc, Paul 2016, *From Marx to Gramsci: A Reader in Revolutionary Marxist Politics*, Chicago: Haymarket Books.

Le Blanc, Paul and Michael Yates 2013, *A Freedom Budget for All Americans: Recapturing the Promise of the Civil Rights Movement in the Struggle for Economic Justice Today*, New York: Monthly Review Press.

Lefebvre, Henri 2009, *Dialectical Materialism*, Minneapolis, MN: University of Minnesota Press.

Lens, Sidney 1980, *Unrepentant Radical: An American Activist's Account of Five Turbulent Decades*, New York: Beacon Press.

Levine, Bruce 2014, *The Fall of the House of Dixie: The Civil War and the Social Revolution that Transformed the South*, New York: Random House.

Marcuse, Herbert 1999, *Reason and Revolution: Hegel and the Rise of Social Theory*. Amherst, NY: Humanity Books

Matgamna, Sean (ed.) 1998, *The Fate of the Russian Revolution*, London: Phoenix Press.

Matgamna, Sean (ed.) 2015, *The Two Trotskyisms Confront Stalinism*, London: Workers' Liberty.

Militant 1929, 'Work Among Negroes', *Militant*, 15 February.

Militant 1934a, '10,000 Fill Mass Rally: Madison Square Gardens Jammed with Strikers', *Militant*, 31 January.

Militant 1934b, 'Big Crowd at Debate: Cannon and Lovestone Discuss Internationals', *Militant*, 10 March.

Militant 1934c, 'The End of the New York Hotel Strike', *Militant*, 10 March.

Millikan, William 2001, *A Union Against Unions: The Minneapolis Citizens Alliance and Its Fight Against Organized Labor, 1903–1947*, St. Paul: Minnesota Historical Society Press.

Mills, C. Wright 1962, *The Marxists*, New York: Dell.

Morrow, Felix 1936, 'The Spirit of the US Constitution', *New International*, February.

Munis, Grandzio 1942, 'A Criticism of the Minneapolis Trial', *International Bulletin*, 11/2 June.

Muste, A.J. 1934, 'The Workers Party is Founded', *New International*, December.

Muste, A.J. 1935, 'Labor Marshalls Forces for Banner May Day', *New Militant*, 20 April.

Nash, Gary B. 2006, *The Unknown Revolution: The Unruly Birth of Democracy and the Struggle to Create America*, New York: Penguin Books.

New Republic 1941, 'Civil Liberties in Minneapolis', *New Republic* (28 July), 103–4.

Nimtz, Jr., August H. 2000, *Marx and Engels: Their Contribution to the Democratic Breakthrough*, Albany: State University Press of New York.

Novack, George 1938, 'Marx and Engels on the Civil War', *New International*, February.

Novack, George 1941, *Witchhunt in Minnesota: The Federal Prosecution of the Socialist Workers Party and Local 544-CIO*, pamphlet, New York: Civil Rights Defense Committee.

Novack, George 1971, *An Introduction to the Logic of Marxism*, New York: Pathfinder Press.

Oehler, Hugo 1932, 'The Negro and the Class Struggle', *Militant*, 30 April and 7 May.

Palmer, Bryan D. 1994, *E.P. Thompson: Objections and Opposition*, London: Verso.

Palmer, Bryan D. 2007, *James P. Cannon and the Origins of the American Revolutionary Left, 1890–1928*, Urbana and Chicago: University of Illinois Press.

Palmer, Bryan D. 2013, *Revolutionary Teamsters: The Minneapolis Truckers' Strikes of 1934*, Boston and Leiden: Brill.

Preis, Art 1964, *Labor's Giant Step: Twenty Years of the CIO*, New York: Pioneer.

Prickett, James 1968, 'Communism and Factionalism in the United Automobile Workers, 1939–1947', *Science & Society*, 32 (Summer): 257–77.

Prometheus Research Library 2002, *Dog Days: James P. Cannon vs. Max Shachtman in the Communist League of America, 1931–1933*, New York: Spartacist Publishing Company.

Rees, John 1998, *The Algebra of Revolution: The Dialectic and the Classical Marxist Tradition*, London: Routledge.

Riazanov, David 1973, *Karl Marx and Friedrich Engels, An Introduction to Their Lives and Work*, New York: Monthly Review Press, available at: https://www.marxists.org/archive/riazanov/works/1927-ma/index.htm.

Rosengarten, Frank 2008, *Urbane Revolution: C.L.R. James and the Struggle for a New Society*, Jackson, MS: University of Mississippi Press.

Rosenzweig, Roy 1975, 'Radicals and the Jobless: Musteites and the Unemployed Leagues', *Labor History*, 16.

Rosenzweig, Roy 1976, 'Organizing the Unemployed: The Early Years of the Great Depression, 1929–1933', *Radical America*, 10.

Serge, Victor and Natalia Sedova 2015, *The Life and Death of Leon Trotsky*, Chicago: Haymarket Books.

Shachtman, Max 1933, 'Letter to Maurice Spector, 2 January', Max Shachtman Papers, Tamiment Institute, Bobst Library, New York University, New York.

Shachtman, Max 1936, 'Marxist Politics or Unprincipled Combinationism?', Workers Party, *Internal Bulletin*, No. 3, February.

Shachtman, Max 1938a, 'Revolution and Counter-Revolution in Russia', *New International*, Vol. 4, No. 1, January.

Shachtman, Max 1938b, 'Lenin and Rosa Luxemburg', *New International*, May.

Shachtman, Max 1938c, 'A Footnote for Historians', *New International*, December.

Shachtman, Max 1954, 'Twenty-Five Years of American Trotskyism, Part I: The Origins of American Trotskyism', *New International*, 20, January–February: 11–16.

Shachtman, Max 1963, 'The Reminiscences of Max Shachtman', Number 488, Oral History Research Office, Columbia University, New York.

Shachtman, Max 2003, *Race and Revolution*, edited and Introduced by Christopher Phelps, London: Verso.

Shachtman, Max and James Burnham 1939, 'The Intellectuals in Retreat', *New International*, January.

Shachtman, Max, James Burnham and Martin Abern 1940, 'The War and Bureaucratic Conservatism', SWP Internal Bulletin, Vol. 2, No. 6, January.

Shannon, David A. 1967, *The Socialist Party of America: A History*, Chicago: Quadrangle Books.

Socialist Workers Party 1938, *Declaration of Principles and Constitution of the Socialist Workers Party*, New York: Socialist Workers Party.

Socialist Workers Party 1939a, 'The Right of Self-Determination and the Negro in the United States of North America', adopted by Socialist Workers Party national convention, 7 July; transcribed by D. Walters, Marxist Internet Archive, available at: https://www.marxists.org/history/etol/document/swp-us/3rdconvention/swp02.htm.

Socialist Workers Party 1939b, 'The SWP and Negro Work', *Socialist Appeal*, 11 July.

Spector, Maurice 1929, 'The Cult of the "Third Period"', *Militant*, 15 September, 1 October.

Steward, Dwight 1974, *Mr. Socialism: Norman Thomas: His Life and Times*, Seacacus, NJ: Lyle Stuart.

Stone, I.F. 1941, 'The G-String Conspiracy', *Nation*, 26 July.

Swabeck, Arne 1931, 'United Front on Unemployment: An Open Letter to the Central Committee of the Communist Party of America', *Militant*, 15 February.

Swabeck, Arne 1934, 'The Decay of the Stalinist Party', *New International*, July.

Swabeck, Arne 1936, 'Roosevelt Steals Labor Party Thunder', *New Militant*, 16 May.

Swanberg, W.A. 1976, *Norman Thomas, The Last Idealist*, New York: Charles Scribner's Sons.

Trotsky, Leon 1929, 'Tasks of the American Opposition', *Militant*, 1 June.

Trotsky, Leon 1940a, 'An Open Letter to James Burnham', SWP Internal Bulletin, Vol. 2, No. 9, January.

Trotsky, Leon 1940b, 'From a Scratch – to the Danger of Gangrene', *SWP Internal Bulletin*, Vol. 2, No. 11, February.

Trotsky, Leon 1940c, 'Discussions with Lund', *National Committee Bulletin*, June.

Trotsky, Leon 1969, 'Discussions with Trotsky', in *Writings of Leon Trotsky [1939–40]*, New York: Pathfinder, pp. 251–89.

Trotsky, Leon 1975, *The Challenge of the Left Opposition, 1923–1925*, New York: Pathfinder Press.

Trotsky, Leon 1980, *The Challenge of the Left Opposition, 1926–1927*, New York: Pathfinder Press.

Trotsky, Leon 1981, *The Challenge of the Left Opposition, 1928–1929*, New York: Pathfinder Press.

Trotsky, Leon 1998, *The Transitional Program: The Death Agony of Capitalism and the Tasks of the Fourth International [1938]*, edited and introduced by the International Bolshevik Tendency, London and Toronto: Bolshevik Publications.

Trotsky, Leon 2012, *Writings in Exile, Selected Writings*, edited by Kunal Chattopadhyay and Paul Le Blanc, London: Pluto Press.

Trotsky, Leon, Arne Swabeck and Pierre Frank 1933, 'The Negro Question in America', *Internal Bulletin* #12, Communist League of America, 19 April.

Wald, Alan 1987, *The New York Intellectuals: The Rise and Decline of the Anti-Stalinist Left from the 1930s to the 1980s*, Chapel Hill, NC: University of North Carolina Press.

Warde, William F. 1941, 'The Right of Revolution', *Fourth International*, August.

Warde, William F. 1941, 'Capitalist Frame-Up: 1941 Model', *Fourth International*, December.

Widick, B.J. 1938, 'Labor Unity – A New Stage', *New International*, November.

Wolfe, Bertram 1928, 'Three Generals Without An Army', *Daily Worker*, 27 November.

Worchester, Kent 1995, *C.L.R. James, A Political Biography*, Albany: State University of New York Press.

Wright, John G. 1934, 'Shifts in the Negro Question', *New International*, Vol. 1, No. 4, November.

Zumoff, Jacob A. 2015, *The Communist International and US Communism, 1919–1929*, Chicago: Haymarket Books.

Index

CPSIA information can be obtained
at www.ICGtesting.com
Printed in the USA
JSHW020615301019
2125JS00001B/1